Opdycke's Tigers
in the Civil War

Opdycke's Tigers in the Civil War

A History of the 125th Ohio Volunteer Infantry

THOMAS CROWL

McFarland & Company, Inc., Publishers
Jefferson, North Carolina

LIBRARY OF CONGRESS CATALOGUING-IN-PUBLICATION DATA

Names: Crowl, Thomas, author.
Title: Opdycke's Tigers in the Civil War : a history of the 125th Ohio Volunteer Infantry / Thomas Crowl.
Other titles: History of the 125th Ohio Volunteer Infantry
Description: Jefferson, North Carolina : McFarland & Company, Inc., Publishers, 2019 | Includes bibliographical references and index.
Identifiers: LCCN 2019012052 | ISBN 9781476675923 (paperback : acid free paper) ∞
Subjects: LCSH: United States. Army. Ohio Infantry Regiment, 125th (1862–1865) | Opdycke, Emerson. | United States—History—Civil War, 1861–1865—Campaigns. | United States—History—Civil War, 1861–1865—Regimental histories.
Classification: LCC E525.5 125th .C76 2019 | DDC 973.7/3—dc23
LC record available at https://lccn.loc.gov/2019012052

BRITISH LIBRARY CATALOGUING DATA ARE AVAILABLE

ISBN (print) 978-1-4766-7592-3
ISBN (ebook) 978-1-4766-3645-0

© 2019 Thomas Crowl. All rights reserved

No part of this book may be reproduced or transmitted in any form or by any means, electronic or mechanical, including photocopying or recording, or by any information storage and retrieval system, without permission in writing from the publisher.

Front cover image *Battle of Chickamauga*, September 19 and 20, 1863, Kurz & Allison circa 1890 (Library of Congress)

Printed in the United States of America

*McFarland & Company, Inc., Publishers
Box 611, Jefferson, North Carolina 28640
www.mcfarlandpub.com*

Dedicated to the memory of all who served in Opdycke's Tigers.
"They can kill us, but whip us never!"

Cut from Maine granite and erected in 1894, the 125th's regimental monument stands on Snodgrass Hill on the Chickamauga battlefield. Photograph by the author.

Table of Contents

Preface — 1
Introduction — 5

1. Volunteers Wanted — 9
2. Central Tennessee — 19
3. The Road to the River of Death — 30
4. Chickamauga, Saturday, September 19 — 41
5. Chickamauga, Sunday Morning, September 20 — 48
6. Chickamauga, Sunday Afternoon, September 20 — 59
7. Bottled Up in Chattanooga — 70
8. Missionary Ridge — 80
9. Knoxville and East Tennessee — 97
10. Rocky Face Ridge — 113
11. Resaca — 125
12. New Hope Church — 133
13. The Battles for Kennesaw Mountain — 143
14. Peach Tree Creek — 166
15. The Fall of Atlanta — 180
16. From Atlanta to Pulaski — 197
17. Columbia and Spring Hill — 206
18. Franklin — 212
19. Nashville — 232
20. From Huntsville to Columbus — 248

Roster — 259
Chapter Notes — 274
Bibliography — 289
Index — 293

PREFACE

The soldiers who fought, and suffered, in the Civil War were overwhelmingly volunteers. In the summer of 1861, those Northern men who answered the call to suppress the rebellion were filled with what one veteran labeled "wild enthusiasm and extravagant self-confidence." Sprinkled among those who wanted to save the Union were idealists and ardent abolitionists fighting for a cause. Many expected a short war and fretted the excitement would be over before they got a chance to fight and give the slave-holding Southerners a sound thrashing on the battlefield.

By the summer of 1862, when Ohio was to provide 38 new infantry regiments for federal service, the potential volunteers were much less enthusiastic. Huge battles on a scale never seen in the New World had been fought in little-known places like Shiloh in Tennessee and the Peninsula in Virginia and produced casualty lists that numbered in the tens of thousands. No longer were men afraid the war would end before they got a chance to fight. The farmers, clerks, students, teachers, laborers, mechanics and merchants who would fill the ranks knew what they could expect. Few of these volunteers were radical abolitionists. They did not see black men, slave or free, as their equals. When those new recruits doffed their hats and raised their right hands to take the oath of allegiance and service, they firmly believed it was necessary to enlist "to settle forever the permanency of our form of government." They would be volunteering to save the Union.[1]

The 125th Ohio Volunteer Infantry was one of the last three-year federal regiments raised from Ohio in the Civil War. Command of the 125th Ohio was awarded by Ohio governor David Tod to a talented and ambitious captain in the 41st Ohio, Emerson Opdycke, a former merchant from Warren, Ohio, with good political connections and experience at Shiloh. Opdycke, in his early 30s, was one of those few volunteer officers who had a natural aptitude for war despite little formal education, no prior military training and no strong familial military tradition. Opdycke had enlisted as a private in the 41st in the summer of 1861, was elected first lieutenant the next day, and rose to captain. Considered by some a martinet, Opdycke was fearless and supremely self-confident, ambitious and intelligent, hard-working and argumentative. He knew what was needed to mold a disparate group of volunteers into soldiers in a fighting regiment.

The Battle of Chickamauga, September 19–20, 1863, was the largest battle fought west of the Allegheny Mountains in the Civil War. A Union defeat and a hollow Confederate victory, Chickamauga was labeled by one Union veteran turned historian "the hardest fought and bloodiest battle of the rebellion." Of 126,000 men involved, 28 percent became casualties. It was at Chickamauga that the 125th Ohio received its introduction to combat.[2]

During the epic battle, the 125th found itself alone, outnumbered and flanked by Confederate infantry in Dyer's cornfield on Sunday morning, September 20, 1863. With men falling right and left, Lieutenant Charles Clark, the youngest officer in the regiment, seized a fallen flag, waved it defiantly, looked to Colonel Opdycke, and shouted, "They can kill us, but whip us never!" A representation of the moment appears in bronze relief on the regiment's Quincy granite monument on the Chickamauga battlefield.[3]

Nine days after the battle, Brigadier General Thomas J. Wood, a West Pointer and Mexican War veteran who commanded the division that included the 125th Ohio, wrote in his official report of the engagement, "I desire to commend Colonel Opdycke, especially, to the favorable consideration of the commanding general. The record of his regiment (a comparatively new one and never before in general engagement) in the late battle will, I am sure, compare most favorably with that of the most veteran regiments engaged." Wood furthered his admiration for the 125th by labeling them "Opdycke's Tigers." The nickname stuck, and a tiger cut from Maine granite stands atop the monument.[4]

A little more than 14 months later, in late November 1864, the men of the 125th—veterans of battles at Missionary Ridge, Resaca, Kennesaw Mountain, Peach Tree Creek and Atlanta—found themselves in middle Tennessee as part of Major General David Stanley's Fourth Corps. With the Harpeth River at its back, a small, outnumbered Union army under the command of Major General John Schofield was ordered to delay the Confederate army of General John Bell Hood while a defense of Nashville could be organized by Major General George Thomas. Colonel Opdycke, now commanding a brigade, refused a direct order to place the 125th and the rest of his brigade in an exposed position, choosing instead to place it in reserve. When General Hood launched one of the largest assaults of the Civil War—17,000 men—at Franklin and broke the Union line, Opdycke's men were just yards away. The bluecoats spontaneously charged the break, blunted the Southern attack, re-established the line and snatched victory from the jaws of defeat. General Stanley wrote in his official report, "I saw Colonel Opdycke near the center of his line urging his men forward. I gave the colonel no order, as I saw him engaged in doing the very thing to save us." Union general George Thomas later shook Opdycke's hand and told him, "Colonel Opdycke, your brigade saved the army at Franklin."[5]

The 125th Ohio was not rewarded for helping save the Union army at Franklin by being mustered out when the war was over. Instead it was sent with the Fourth Corps to Texas in the summer of 1865 for four miserable months to discourage French adventurism—specifically their Foreign Legion—in Mexico from crossing the Texas border. Only when that threat had passed were Opdycke's Tigers sent home to Ohio. At the time of their discharge, most companies—originally 100 men strong—averaged only three dozen soldiers.

Unlike the regimental histories written by the veterans themselves after the Civil War, this is not a sanitized version of the 125th Ohio's history. The Ohioans were nearly captured at Dandridge, Tennessee, due to the ineptitude of army command. There were feuds among the officers, most notably one between Colonel Opdycke and Major Joseph Bruff that resulted in Bruff's arrest. There was difficulty recruiting soldiers in 1862 and 1863 to the extent that it was January 1864 before a full complement of 10 companies was in the field. The regiment's lieutenant colonel, David H. Moore, a Methodist cleric from Athens, Ohio, ably led the regiment during the Atlanta campaign only to resign in September 1864, when he decided that he was being punished by God for not remaining in the pulpit. There were deserters, drunkards and threats of insubordination. These less explored stories are likewise part of the history of the 125th Ohio and found in primary source material available only in the last 25 years.

More than 2,000 regiments fought under the stars and stripes in the Civil War. Of those, 900 suffered more than 50 combat deaths. One hundred thirteen of those battle-tested regiments came from Ohio. The 125th saw 111 officers and men die in battle out of the 1,030 men that appeared on its rolls. Civil War soldiers referred to experiencing combat as "seeing the elephant." Opdycke's Tigers saw the elephant, bravely stalked it, and, in the end, could claim a role in saving the Union.[6]

The author would like to acknowledge the assistance of the following individuals and organizations in the research for this book: the Warren-Trumbull County (Ohio) Public Library; Scott County (Kentucky) Public Library; United States Army Military History Institute; staff at the Carter House in Franklin, Tennessee; South Hill Gallery, Lexington, Kentucky; Ohio History Connection and John Haas, manuscripts curator; Dr. John and Sherry Koella, Roger Kelley and Robert Jarnagin, Dandridge, Tennessee; Barbara Bruff Hemmingsen; Hal Jespersen, maps and the kind and patient staff at McFarland. The author alone bears responsibility for any and all errors or omissions.

Introduction

There would not have been a 125th Ohio Volunteer Infantry but for the determination and ambition of one man: Samuel Emerson Opdycke. A born leader and a bit of a martinet, Opdycke had little formal education and no military training prior to 1861. Yet he was courageous and one of those rare volunteer officers who possessed a natural aptitude for war. And it didn't hurt that he knew the right people and had good political connections. Whatever the 125th Ohio would be—even its very existence—it would owe to Emerson Opdycke. This truth was acknowledged by the placement of a bronze medallion of Opdycke's likeness on the regiment's only monument on the Chickamauga battlefield. When Opdycke called the 125th *his* regiment, it was no exaggeration. It would be a reflection of him and fight the way he believed war should be waged. For the religious and highly patriotic Opdycke, the Civil War was purely "a battle for God, and the Right."[1]

Samuel Emerson Opdycke was born in Hubbard Township, Trumbull County, Ohio, on January 7, 1830. His paternal grandfather served in the Revolution. His father, Albert, had seen service in an Ohio militia regiment during the War of 1812. Opdycke's Dutch roots had provided him with a light complexion, gray eyes and brown hair. He was physically above average for a Civil War soldier at five feet, 11 inches, 160 pounds. Young Emerson's formal education was scanty, even for antebellum Ohio. At 16, he went to work for his brother-in-law Oliver Patch, a Warren, Ohio, dry goods merchant. Young Opdycke was a fast learner and his ambition was in full flower when, after five years behind Patch's counter, he opened a saddle and harness business in Warren. Three years later, the California gold fields beckoned. Young Emerson closed his business in 1854 and with a small party of like-minded young adventurers from Warren headed for California. The good mining claims were long since locked down, so the Warren merchants opened a book and stationery store in booming San Francisco. A little less than three years later, Opdycke returned to Ohio with money in his pockets.[2]

Colonel Emerson Opdycke, 1863. A prewar dry goods merchant, Opdycke rose from first lieutenant to colonel in eighteen months. Reproduced from Charles T. Clark, *Opdycke Tigers* (1895).

Back in Warren, Opdycke renewed his partnership with Patch. In March 1857, Emerson married Lucy Wells Stevens, his prime motivation for returning to Ohio. The Stevens family was one of Warren's most prosperous and his marriage gave Opdycke entrée into Warren's upper class. Emerson and Lucy's union would remain strong for the duration of Opdycke's life. In September 1858, Lucy gave birth to Leonard Eckstein Opdycke, a sickly, weak boy who would be their only child.[3]

One of those prominent Warren men who became Opdycke's friend was Jacob D. Cox. A bookish, introverted young lawyer, Cox had attended Ohio's liberal Oberlin College. The young lawyer and part-time newspaper editor led a public affairs discussion group that included Opdycke. Cox was elected to the Ohio Senate on the Republican party ticket in 1859 and became a follower of Ohio governor Salmon Chase, friend of James Garfield and decidedly anti-slavery, although he believed blacks should accept second class citizen status. Cox's ideas, analysis and writings influenced Opdycke and challenged him to think. As the secession crisis unfolded nationally in 1860, Opdycke and Cox—now a rising Republican star—were keenly interested. Opdycke was vigorously opposed to slavery, but was not a radical abolitionist. "I am heartily opposed to Slavery," he wrote, "but I do not think them among us would better their condition much."[4]

When war became a reality in April 1861, Seth Bushnell, a wealthy Trumbull County farmer, was encouraged by Ohio governor William Dennison to raise an infantry company in response to President Lincoln's call for 300,000 volunteer soldiers. With Opdycke as his assistant, Bushnell raised most of a 100-man company at a patriotic mass meeting held in Hartford, Ohio, on August 2. On the 26th, in Cleveland, the men were mustered into service as Company A, 41st Ohio Volunteer Infantry. Following militia protocol, the company elected its officers—Bushnell, captain, and Opdycke, first lieutenant.[5]

To turn the raw volunteers into soldiers, the army sent to Cleveland a West Point professional with Ohio roots, William B. Hazen. Once an Indian fighter and later an instructor of tactics at West Point, Hazen, 35, was now a colonel of volunteers and tasked with molding the 41st Ohio Infantry into a fighting regiment. The former professor confronted an untrained and undisciplined mass of recruits, most of whom had never even seen an American soldier in uniform prior to enlisting. Union army volunteer soldiers in 1861 were a cross-section of American society and were highly patriotic and motivated. The volunteers wanted, demanded, to see their officers work as hard as they were expected to work. Hazen understood this and drove himself as hard as his men. The rigorous training and conditioning for army life sent many unfit recruits home. Hazen was considerate of those physically unable to endure military life, but had no mercy for those unwilling to adapt.[6]

Hazen gave his elected and eager, neophyte officers special attention. He established an officers' school which was a condensed version of what was taught at West Point. The new officers were instructed in tactics, the Articles of War and military science. Of the 32 officers in the 41st, some with previous military experience, Lieutenant Opdycke informed his wife that he stood first in Hazen's school by November.[7]

In early November 1861, Colonel Hazen took the 931 officers and men of the 41st south. The regiment wintered in Louisville, Kentucky, where Major General Don Carlos Buell was assembling an army. The 41st became part of Brigadier General William "Bull" Nelson's division. Colonel Hazen, as a professional, was given command of the brigade and Lieutenant Colonel George Mygatt assumed command of the regiment. Three-fourths of volunteers over the age of 40 didn't last in field service, and Captain Seth Bushnell, the far side of 40, was one of them. Bushnell resigned and Opdycke became captain of Company A. General Nelson's division was sent to occupy Nashville on February 27, 1862.[8]

Marked as a rising officer, Opdycke served stints training a couple of raw Indiana regiments, which gave him confidence—not that he lacked it—and bolstered his considerable military ambition. That winter, Company A served as General Nelson's personal camp guard, and Opdycke boldly asked the crusty Nelson if he had what it took to command a regiment. "Yes," retorted Nelson, notorious for his dislike of volunteer officers, especially those with political connections. Opdycke got the endorsement in writing.[9]

In mid–March, General Buell's army began the march to join Major General U. S. Grant's army on the Tennessee River at Savanah, Tennessee. It was a journey of more than a hundred miles that would end at Shiloh in early April. The 41st Ohio saw its first combat on the second of two chaotic days of fighting on the bluffs just west of Pittsburg Landing on the Tennessee River. The green soldiers of the 41st handily repulsed a rebel attack and were then ordered by General Buell to make a forlorn bayonet charge on the questionable logic that if they were attacking, they couldn't run for the rear. Captain Opdycke seized a fallen flag, waved it defiantly and urged the 41st forward. Moments later, Opdycke reluctantly relinquished the flag, and its glory, to the acting lieutenant colonel, Aquila Wiley—a "mean trick" in Opdycke's mind. Wiley was shot within minutes. Opdycke applied a makeshift tourniquet to the man's severely wounded leg and then rejoined the charge—more a foot race by armed boys—as musket balls passed harmlessly through his frock coat. A hundred yards from a Southern artillery battery, Opdycke found his young tent mate, Lieutenant James McCleery, on the edge of consciousness after shrapnel had nearly severed his hand. McCleery refused assistance and Opdycke plunged forward. The 41st overran a Confederate artillery battery—and promptly lost it to a rebel counter charge. Now it was the federals turn to run for the safety of their lines, and in doing so, Opdycke was struck by two spent bullets that inflicted minor wounds. Once the bluecoats rallied back where they began their fruitless half-hour charge, a head count revealed that 142 of 373 men of the 41st were killed or wounded. The devastated regiment was sent to the rear, but Captain Emerson Opdycke was not ready to quit. He tried in vain to attach himself to two other Ohio regiments still fighting. Their rejections Opdycke dismissed as a refusal to share the glory.[10]

Having "seen the elephant," as Civil War soldiers called a man's first combat, Opdycke wrote Lucy that he was alert to the danger, but put his duty first. The experience Opdycke acquired during the largest battle of the Civil War to date gave him new insight as a military officer. In an April 29 letter home Opdycke tried to explain his reason for exposing himself in front of the regiment at Shiloh and in doing so enunciated what he believed about leading soldiers. He was emphatic that "if an officer leads, his men will be pretty sure to follow." In closing the letter, Opdycke let his ambition and confidence show: "How I would like to have a regiment of my own for the next great contest."[11]

After Shiloh, the combined armies of Grant and Buell spent the rest of the spring in a glacial advance toward the vital Confederate rail junction of Corinth, Mississippi. Corinth fell to the federals, eventually, but the prize—the Confederate army—retired to fight another day. Captain Opdycke hated the tedium of the dull campaign. As a senior captain in the 41st, he occasionally commanded the regiment. This taste of authority only whetted Opdycke's appetite for his own regiment. In July 1862, after the severe fighting at Shiloh and in Virginia, President Lincoln issued a call for an additional 300,000 volunteers. Emerson Opdycke thought the new soldiers should be drafted since "volunteering will be months too slow."[12]

During the spring of 1862, Opdycke began his personal campaign for praise, recognition and promotion. The captain became miffed when Colonel Hazen—his brigade commander—failed to mention him specifically in the brigade's official report—only alluding to "to the gallantry shown by the Forty-first Ohio Volunteers." Writing to Lucy, he huffed about not receiving "at least one handsome line in that document." Despite his pique, Opdycke supported Hazen's promotion to brigadier because Hazen deserved a star.[13]

Some men in high places did notice Emerson Opdycke during the summer of 1862. His name was bandied about for appointment to field grade rank in one of the new Ohio regiments. In July, Captain Opdycke requested duty as recruiting officer for the 41st Ohio. Late in the month a rumor circulated that he was considered for the lieutenant colonelcy of the 105th Ohio, a new regiment to be raised in primarily Mahoning and Trumbull counties, Opdycke's home district.[14]

On August 6, Opdycke returned home to recruit, but not before stopping briefly in Columbus to see Ohio governor David Tod, who had the authority to name regimental officers. Opdycke pressed his case for regimental command. Tod was a former Democrat state senator, party patriarch and prominent businessman in the Mahoning Valley who was unabashedly pro-Union and pro-Lincoln. When a coalition of pro-war Democrats and Republicans nominated David Tod for governor under the Union Party banner, he won election in a landslide. More important, for Opdycke, Tod had been postmaster in Warren and knew him well.[15]

Four days after Opdycke returned to Warren, it was announced that Ohio needed to raise 14 new regiments in just seven days. Incomplete regiments then forming and unattached independent companies being formed would be assigned to these new regiments. One of the last new regiments, designated the 125th Ohio, was to be recruited from the far northeast Ohio counties of Trumbull, Mahoning, Ashtabula, Geauga and Lake—the same area being canvassed by the veteran 19th Ohio, 41st Ohio and the new 105th. Opdycke's regimental command aspirations got a boost from his hometown newspaper, *The Warren Tribune*, when it called him "a man of unflinching courage." The *Tribune* editorialized, "We hope Governor Tod will issue orders for the formation of the 125th regiment which was assigned to this district, and place Capt. Opdycke at its head." The *Western Reserve Chronicle*, where former state senator and now brigadier general Jacob Cox had ties, added its endorsement: "By his conduct on the battle-field, he has shown himself to be a man of unflinching courage, and as by his actual services he has as fairly deserved promotion, as he is well qualified by nature and by study, to fill a higher position, and we hope he may get one." Governor Tod agreed. On September 15, Opdycke wrote with uncharacteristic succinctness in his field diary, "Given the 125th Regiment to raise and command." Emerson Opdycke, who, a little more than a year earlier had been selling harness in Warren, had his regiment.[16]

1

VOLUNTEERS WANTED

Getting Governor Tod to appoint him colonel of the new 125th Ohio may have been the easy part for Emerson Opdycke. Now, he had to recruit 1000 men in a region where two established regiments were scrounging for replacements and a new one was being raised. Those men who filled regiments in 1861—Ohio journalist Whitelaw Reid called them "the most ardent, the most willing, and the most patriotic"—were scarce by the fall of 1862. The $100 government bounty, in effect since May 1861, had proven a poor incentive. Enlistments were declining, especially in regions like southern Ohio, where abolitionist ideals were unpopular. Nevertheless, the Union army needed soldiers and a draft, first for the militia and later for the federal army, became increasingly more likely. Public opinion had also shifted to the belief that all eligible men of military age should be considered for service. There would be exemptions for the unfit and the rich could still hire a substitute to avoid service. But a draft would make it clear that eligible men should serve or face the scorn of their patriotic neighbors. The Militia Draft Act, passed July 17, 1862, established uniform recruitment procedures for states to follow and identified men 18 to 45 as draft eligible for service in state militias. Draft committees were created to establish recruitment quotas for local districts and if enough volunteers could not be enlisted, a draft would follow—a civic disgrace for any patriotic community. The government bounty could be supplemented by local bounties from money raised in bounty fund drives.[1]

Representatives from each Ohio county's draft committee met on August 17, 1862, to set quotas for each county by number of companies for the new regiments forming as a result of the July call for volunteers. Ohio's share of the 300,000 was calculated to be almost 37,000. Trumbull County, Opdycke's home, was to raise two full companies for the fledgling 125th after already sending almost 2000 men to the federal army. The county committees further reduced that to a set of quotas for villages, cities and townships where prominent men were recruited to form companies with the offer of officer's rank as inducement. According to army regulations, 10 companies of 100 men were required for a full strength regiment. Actual enlistment was generally accomplished by holding patriotic war meetings attended, it was hoped, by potential volunteers. Those enlisting for three years would receive a $100 bounty from the government—payable upon completion of two years' service. Privates would receive a regular pay of $13 a month, $17 for sergeants and $60 for captains—no other pecuniary inducements were offered. It was anticipated by the draft committees, in a fit of wild optimism, that these new soldiers could be mustered in by October 1. The new 105th Ohio would be at full strength by mid–August and any excess recruits would, by order of the Governor, go to the 125th.[2]

The 125th's first company came from the 105th. On September 16, 1862, Company A of the 125th was sworn—mustered—into service. The men were so new to soldiering that the order to remove their caps and raise their right hands produced confusion. Expecting to be part of the 105th, some disappointment was manifest when the company found itself assigned to the 125th—a slight to Colonel Opdycke who knew how to hold a grudge. The company was raised in Mahoning County by Joseph Bruff, a 35-year-old former Republican state legislator and farmer of Quaker extraction. When Bruff had been nominated for the legislature, the *Western Reserve Chronicle,* called him "an honest, solid, intelligent man." In the legislature, Bruff—nicknamed "Honest Joe"—supported school funding and giving women control equal to their husbands over property and children. Solidifying his "radical" views, Bruff opposed changing the Ohio Constitution to disenfranchise anyone with African blood. Bruff, who had no prior military experience, had been granted permission by allies in Columbus to raise a company in return for a captaincy. One of his men described Bruff as "well educated, a quiet but firm-appearing man, very much earnest in his work, insisting on promptness and good order." His men found him "kind hearted and fatherly" when off duty. Overall, Bruff was courageous, compassionate and stubborn, but sometimes slow to act. In an army that was a slave to seniority, Bruff would become the regiment's senior captain. First lieutenant was Robert Stewart, 26, who was generally "smiling and jolly" but "imperious in reproof at the slightest infraction."[3]

Lieutenant Colonel Joseph Bruff. A prewar Ohio state representative, Bruff was known as "Honest Joe" to many of his colleagues. Reproduced from Clark, *Opdycke Tigers.*

The 125th's recruits were posted to Camp Cleveland, located on what was later known as University Heights. It was a Spartan life. The new recruits drilled eight hours a day—work they found harder than harvesting on the farm. The barracks, which housed 40 men, were constructed of unplaned pine boards that oozed sap on warm days. A tier of shelves along the side served as bunks and bristled with splinters. A narrow shelf along the end served as a table for the men who ate standing. For bedding there was straw and gray wool blankets. Knapsacks served as pillows. Each recruit was issued a tin cup, knife, fork and spoon. At mealtime, bread was sliced on the shelves while meat, soup and vegetables were brought from the cook shack and ladled out. Coffee was dipped from a steaming kettle. One soldier likened the process to feeding a gang of "hobos" where it was every man for himself.[4]

It wasn't hard to get a furlough, however. In November, Private Edwin Woodworth of Company B wrote his family that he would "be home in 3 or 4 weeks if nothing happens." If something happened, the recruit instructed his parents to write just before Christmas that his father was sick or dying and he could obtain a furlough that would last through New Year's. That December, two men from Company B took "French furlough" and deserted. They weren't the only ones. Keeping men in Camp Cleveland was a challenge. The lax camp commander freely issued day passes to the city where families could visit and taverns beckoned. After dark, it wasn't hard slip by the camp guards.[5]

Standing in opposition to this lax discipline was Lieutenant Colonel Emerson Opdycke—he wouldn't be a full colonel until there was a full regiment—who supervised the training of his soldiers with a fervor that rivaled his military education under Bill Hazen. "Our Colonel could tolerate no delay; he was here, there and everywhere, urging us on," Sergeant Ralsa Rice wrote of the Opdycke as instructor. "Each one felt that himself was the special object of his attention." One of Rice's comrades left his impression of the colonel. "He looks like a hero, six feet in stature, a fine figure, graceful and quick in movement, blue eyes of the kind that seem to look through and see just what you are thinking; and how they

Private Edwin Woodworth. A reliable letter writer who never rose above private, Woodworth lost a finger while in the trenches around Atlanta. Reproduced from Clark, *Opdycke Tigers*.

do flash when an awkward fellow goes wrong on drill!" The recruit also recalled, "His voice is immense. A thousand men in line will readily hear his commands."[6]

Opdycke established his own officer's school based on Bill Hazen's curriculum. His new officers studied the usual texts, such as Silas Casey's *System of Infantry Tactics*, supplemented by Opdycke's own practical questions. For example, an officer had to know why the companies were arranged in the order B, G, K, E, H, C, I, D, F, A, left to right when viewed from the rear, when in line of battle. The answer was the two senior captains, A and B, were afforded the places of honor and responsibility on the flanks while C as the color company displayed its flags in the center. Of the colonel's teaching, one former student noted. "Such energetic teachings will long be remembered by most of us."[7]

Although Bruff's company was mustered in mid–September, it was obvious to Opdycke that raising a regiment would be a difficult task and take well beyond the October 1 deadline. Ohio had already put over 100,000 men in uniform. A month after mustering Bruff's company, there were just three companies ready to be sworn in and a three more that were close. Due to the demands of war, army regulations were relaxed to reduce the minimum number of companies needed for a regiment to be accepted into federal service from ten to eight.[8]

Ralsa Rice served in the 125th Ohio for three years. He recalled the fall of 1862 as a time when many men realized there was no alternative to service and they began to put their affairs in order. "All this required time," Rice wrote, "and not until early autumn did volunteering become general. The 125th Ohio was one of a large number of regiments from Ohio that was composed of the class mentioned.... There was not a drafted man in it." Many of the militia draftees went to fill the depleted ranks of regiments in the field where they were required to serve only 18 months.[9]

It wasn't until November 1 that the second company, designated Company C, was mustered. In federal regiments, Company C was the color company, charged with guarding the national and regimental flags, collectively a regiment's most important symbols. Opdycke shrewdly surmised that having a color company mustered would place the 125th in a better position to retain its independence in the event of consolidation of understrength regiments. Company C was raised in Trumbull County by 24-year-old Edward P. Bates, a former classics student and teacher who had served three months in the 19th Ohio. The first lieutenant was Ridgely Powers. Both men were seen as "bright men" by their comrades and would become trusted subordinates of Colonel Opdycke.[10]

A couple of weeks later, November 17, 89 men in Company B took the oath. The company was recruited in Trumbull County by Albert Yeomans, a 35-year-old lawyer from Kinsman. Yeomans brought 34 of his townsmen into the company. The first lieutenant was Elmer Moses, a former sergeant in Opdycke's old company in the 41st Ohio. Both men were described as "tall, fine looking gentlemen." One of the sergeants was the 24-year-old Rice, a former cavalryman discharged for disability in March 1862 after nearly dying from measles, mumps and bronchial constriction. A doctor told Rice that *if* he recovered, it would take a year. But Rice, married at 19 to a woman five years his senior and already the father of two, wanted to escape domesticity, despite his nasty, lingering cough. Rice would frankly chronicle the 125th's record. Five days later, Company D, was

Left: Captain Edward Bates, 1863. By the end of 1864, the reliable Ed Bates was the senior captain in the Army of the Cumberland. Reproduced from Clark, *Opdycke Tigers*. *Right:* Captain Ridgely Powers, 1864. A post-war cotton planter in Mississippi, Powers became governor in 1871. Reproduced from Clark, *Opdycke Tigers*.

mustered. Most of the principle organizers were from Portage County, Ohio. Freeman Collins from Ravenna, Ohio, would become regimental sergeant major.[11]

That fall, Emerson Opdycke divided his time between Warren and Cleveland. On one trip, he stopped in Portage County to purchase a seven-year-old gelding for $175. Officers were required to provide their own mounts, and a regimental colonel was entitled to have up to four horses, if he could afford them. The animal's name, "Major," wouldn't do in the heat of battle, so the colonel's horse became "Barney." A spirited animal requiring an experienced horseman, Opdycke described the gelding, as a "noble animal." Later Opdycke would acquire a second horse he called "Tempest."[12]

On December 5, four understrength companies of the 87th Ohio, and a few men from the 85th Ohio arrived in Cleveland. Both regiments had been three months of service units, serving from June to September 1862. The 85th never exceeded battalion size—four companies—and was never mustered into federal service. The 87th had reached regimental size and was sent to Harpers Ferry, Virginia. When Harpers Ferry was

Captain Ralsa Rice, 1864. After the war, Rice turned from farming to politics, serving as Trumbull County auditor in the early 1880s. Reproduced from Clark, *Opdycke Tigers*.

surrendered to Confederate Major General Stonewall Jackson in September 1862, the men of the 87th became prisoners without firing a shot in anger. A technicality saved the Ohioans when it was discovered that the surrender officially occurred after the 87th's three months of serviced had expired. Remarkably, the Confederates agreed to let the men go home without parole since they were technically no longer soldiers. When the 87th returned to Ohio, Governor Tod authorized its colonel, Henry Banning, to raise a three-year regiment. But by November, Banning had only 200 veterans and new recruits primarily from Knox and Richland Counties in north central Ohio. This contingent was sent to the 125th Ohio, where Opdycke's recruits recognized the military experience of the newcomers instantly. One scribe noted, "their clothes fit and their belts do not chafe. They were at home [in camp] quietly without confusion or excitement."[13]

Ezra B. Taylor, a politically connected Warren lawyer, had been lieutenant colonel designate of the 125th Ohio. Taylor declined and Henry Banning, a lawyer in his mid–20s from Mount Vernon, Ohio, accepted the lieutenant colonelcy making the 125th his third regiment in 18 months. George Wood, 25, and an early organizer of the 125th, was appointed major. Wood had been a captain in the 7th Ohio, severely wounded in Virginia, and discharged for disability. Incredibly, Wood—in constant pain from his wound—wanted back in the army. Only a month separated from the 7th, Wood enlisted in the 125th, bringing more combat experience than any other officer.[14]

Edward Whitesides, a native Kentuckian who resided in Pittsburgh, had been a first sergeant in the 87th. As a former express agent, Whitesides had the clerical skills to be adjutant of the 125th. The well-respected Dr. Henry McHenry, a 42-year-old physician from Napoleon, Ohio, was appointed regimental surgeon. A formal medical education was required of Ohio's regimental surgeons, along with 10 years of experience—assistant surgeons just five—and examination before a medical review board. Opdycke would come to value McHenry above all other medical men. When citing the low incidence of disease in the 125th compared to other new regiments, Opdycke credited Dr. McHenry, who Opdycke noted, "Dr. McHenry keeps almost every man in the regiment fit for a fight … I look upon McHenry as a treasure of a doctor." The assistant surgeons were John E. Darby, who had been in the same capacity in the old 85th, and Porter Yates.[15]

Opdycke had definitive opinions about what he wanted in an officer and didn't suffer ones he considered lacking. As these understrength regiments were absorbed, Opdycke tried to retain the best men. Inevitably, however, some good ones were passed over. One was David H. Moore, a young Methodist minister from Athens, Ohio, who was the senior captain in the old 87th and was slated to be lieutenant colonel in a new 87th. Instead, Opdycke offered Moore the chaplaincy. But Moore wanted to fight, declined and resigned. Sterling Manchester, from Ashtabula, Ohio, was the captain of one of the 87th's small companies and he, too, was shunted aside. A disappointed Manchester vowed to win a captaincy in another regiment. By mid–December, Banning's four small companies were combined to become companies E and F of the 125th. Captain Steen Parks commanded F, raised primarily in Knox County. The remaining unassigned men were combined to form companies G and H. Company H was commanded by steely-eyed Captain Anthony Vallendar, a Prussian army veteran with an amusing tendency to wild exaggeration.[16]

After six days of Christmas leave, Opdycke returned to Cleveland December 31 and found orders waiting. The 125th Ohio was ordered to Covington, Kentucky, as part of a general mobilization to confront the northward thrust of the Confederate Army of the Tennessee. In retrospect, the delay in filling the regiment had been fortuitous. The Mahoning Valley's 105th had filled its ranks quickly and had been sent into battle at Perryville, Kentucky, less than two months later, where inadequate training resulted in over 30 percent casualties. Opdycke, appointed a full colonel on January 1, was relieved to be leaving Cleveland. The city's taverns and brothels were distractions and frequent visits from families a nuisance. Opdycke admitted to his wife that he would be glad to leave Cleveland.[17]

Captain Edward Whitesides, 1862. Whitesides was a rare Pennsylvanian in the ranks of the 125th. Reproduced from Clark, *Opdycke Tigers*.

The rebel offensive was blunted by fighting at Stones River near Murfreesboro, Tennessee, over New Years. Nevertheless, Opdycke's orders were unchanged. The War Department needed regiments more than ever in the western theater and urged Ohio governor Tod to send every man he could to the field, including understrength regiments. All leaves and furloughs were canceled. On the 2nd, the 124th Ohio, composed mainly of Clevelanders, left camp in the city with less than 600 men in nine companies. Opdycke had only eight companies but carried 630 men on the rolls. Tod promised Opdycke the two companies to fill the 125th as soon as they could be recruited. It was a hollow promise.[18]

On January 3, Opdycke's men marched down muddy Cleveland streets to the rail depot. Displaying Opdycke's tutelage, the *Cleveland Herald* reported that the regiment "looked finely and marched well." The men had a martial appearance in their long blue overcoats, slouch hats, with knapsacks on their backs and haversacks over their shoulders. The real business of soldiering, however, their muskets, were as yet unavailable. The men boarded a train bound for Cincinnati as grumbling infantrymen were crowded into passenger cars, two to a seat. Opdycke insisted his officers ride in the cars with their men and place guards at the doors as a precaution against desertion. The next day in Cincinnati, the regiment marched straight to the stern-wheel packet *Diamond*. Before the steamer started downriver, the Ohioans received their muskets and camp equipage from depots in Newport, Kentucky. Captain Bates' Company C took charge of the national and regimental flags—the symbolic heart of any Civil War regiment. The regimental flag followed the pattern prescribed by the War Department—a federal eagle over a banner that read "125th O.V.I." on a navy blue field surrounded by gold fringe.[19]

The 125th's most important piece of equipment was the Model 1861 .58 caliber Springfield rifled musket. A year and a half into the war, good small arms were still in short supply and the recruits had only a few old surplus Belgium-made .69 caliber pieces with which to train. The Massachusetts manufactured Springfields cost the government $18 and were the best rifles the northern arsenals could produce. Opdycke called them "the very best in the world." Still in short supply, the 125th received Springfield muskets as consolation for going into the field undermanned. A muzzle-loading single shot weapon, the .58 caliber Springfield fired a conical, one ounce, soft lead Minie ball from a rifled barrel. Almost five feet in length, the Springfield weighed nine and three quarters pounds and had a range of over 800 yards.[20]

Civil War riflemen were supplied with paper cartridges that had the bullet fixed in one end of a paper tube filled with just under four grams of black powder. These cartridges, both loose and in 10-round packages, were carried in a cartridge box with a 40-round capacity that hung from a shoulder strap. The ignition caps were carried in a cap box worn on the belt. Loading the musket on the drill field was set to time. According to the regiment's historian, Charles Clark, the order "Load in nine times, Load!" sent hands in unison to the cartridge box followed by biting off the end of paper cartridge. The black powder was poured down the muzzle. The right thumb pressed the paper and lead ball into the muzzle to be rammed home by the iron ramrod. The percussion cap, in a separate box on the belt, was placed on the nipple below the cocked hammer. "Each movement is distinct," Clark explained, "the process in unison as perfect as the motions beating to time."[21]

Drill rarely included loaded weapons, perhaps because accidents were commonplace. Marksmanship was practiced sparingly by firing at empty cracker boxes at 200 yards.

Realistically, a well-trained soldier could fire 10 rounds in five minutes and put six shots in a two-foot square at 100 yards. The better marksmen could consistently hit a one-foot square at 300 yards. In actual combat, under enemy fire, kneeling behind a breastwork or lying in the mud, it was another matter. Scared and nervous soldiers were often guilty of firing too high, firing the ramrod or forgetting to pull the trigger at all, while rapidly reloading. In one Ohio regiment's first battle, a veteran noted, "The air seemed full of ramrods." So poor was Civil War marksmanship that one authority suggested that 900 pounds of lead was fired for every casualty. Noted historian William C. Davis concluded, "The marksmanship of the average Civil War soldier never proved to be exceptional."[22]

Lieutenant Charles T. Clark, 1863. Clark was the youngest officer in the 125th, a captain before his 21st birthday. Reproduced from Clark, *Opdycke Tigers*.

The rifle's bayonet was a foot-long triangular iron spike that locked by a ring to the rifle's muzzle with a twist of the wrist. More intimidating than effective, the men found bayonets more useful as cooking utensils, candle holders and tent pegs. Musket barrels and bayonets were rubbed, or burnished, until they were a metallic silver color. Marching in column, the sun glinting off the barrels and bayonets, a regiment resembled a shimmering snake that was visible for miles. The officers' weapons included a government issued sword for which $20 was deducted from their pay. They had to supply their own side arms, usually .36 or .44 caliber six-shot percussion revolvers, carried holstered on the hip. The pistols were close quarter weapons at best.[23]

The 125th steamed down the Ohio River toward Louisville. On the journey, an officer asked Colonel Opdycke his opinion of the ultimate destination of the 125th and learned Opdycke's choice was the Army of the Cumberland. Asked why Major General William S. Rosecrans' army instead of General Grant's Army of the Tennessee, Opdycke believed that Grant would have completed his campaign to open the Mississippi River by the spring of 1863. New regiments, like the 125th, that were sent to Grant would likely be destined for garrison duty, Opdycke thought. He abhorred that idea. Now that he had a regiment, Opdycke intended to fight it. The Army of the Cumberland, on the other hand, he thought was destined to advance to Chattanooga, then Atlanta and finally the Atlantic coast. There would be many opportunities for battle. Furthermore, Opdycke wanted to fight under Rosecrans instead of Grant, whom Opdycke had not forgiven for being caught unprepared at Shiloh. General Rosecrans was from Ohio, a West Pointer, 43 years old, and after his victory at Stones River, considered one of the best commanders in the Union army.[24]

Opdycke, who would be forever proud of his regiment, could not resist bragging to his wife that the 125th received great praise for its order and discipline on its journey south. Volunteer soldiers would accept punishment for an infraction and maintain respect for a commander only if the punishment was deemed fair and timely. Opdycke's favored punishment for minor infractions such as loud swearing, quarrelling or drunkenness was drenching with cold water, which was said to be both effective and amusing.[25]

The 125th, like all regiments, was plagued by desertions when it left Cleveland. Charles Clark noted that men were lost to desertion in Cleveland as well as to disease and transfer to the cavalry. Overall, Ohio regiments had a desertion rate of 44 per 1000 soldiers. Of Opdycke's 751 recruits mustered into service in Cleveland, there were just 600 available for duty when the regiment arrived in Cincinnati. The missing were either sick or deserters. Enlistees were paid part of their bounty at enlistment, and professional bounty jumpers, who took the money and deserted, were common on the streets of Cleveland. As recruiting ramped up, these men would enlist under fictitious names, desert at the first opportunity and repeat the process, sometimes with the aid of unscrupulous ward or township committeemen who paid them to fill their quotas. "It is just as well for the reputation of the regiment that they are gone," wrote one of Opdycke's men of the deserters. Many Ohio officers chose to believe that the bounty jumpers were not Ohioans but out-of-staters or Canadians. Of the 600 soldiers remaining in the regiment, Clark observed, "Those remaining are from good Ohio stock."[26]

The 125th arrived in Louisville shortly after midnight on January 5. Rain, snow and mud became their constant companions in camp. A schedule of six hours of drill a day resumed, followed by fatigue duty, guard duty and dress parade. The officer's school resumed. Many of the rank and file thought the schedule overly strenuous, and few regiments drilled as hard as Opdycke's men. But the colonel decreed that daily drill would only stop during active campaigning. The presence of Major Wood's wife in camp muted some of the more vocal and profane grumbling, but by the third week of January, Mrs. Wood was eager to return home. The Major's wife didn't care for the quality or preparation of the rations. The men were quartered in old Sibley army tents—teepee-like canvas tents 15 feet tall. The conditions in January in Louisville were unpleasant—a storm the 15th dropping 18 inches of snow. Two older fellows from Captain Yeoman's company, solid citizens and farmers back home in Ohio, deserted. According to Sergeant Rice, "If the earth had suddenly engulfed them, their disappearance would not have been more surprising." Opdycke reluctantly admitted the loss of five men to desertion in Louisville.[27]

At the end of January, the 125th was assigned to the Tenth Division of Don Carlos Buell's Army of Kentucky. Brigadier General C. C. Gilbert—a West Pointer breveted for gallantry at Shiloh—commanded the division. He was appointed a brigadier by President Lincoln, but was never confirmed by Congress. At Perryville in September 1862, his performance was substandard and his prospects in the army in the winter of 1863 were declining.[28]

The division was ordered to Nashville, Tennessee, on the Cumberland River by way of Fort Donelson. Opdycke approved. "I am utterly disgusted with Kentucky," he wrote of the slave-holding state whose citizens he believed disloyal to the Union. At the wharf, Opdycke objected to his men sharing the crowded deck of a riverboat with a hundred army mules, so the regiment transferred the next morning to the *Clara Poe* which cast off on February 1. The regiment arrived at Fort Donelson on the evening of February 3.[29]

Fort Donelson had been attacked by Confederate cavalry earlier in the day and repulsed by the garrison of Illinois troops who shot down over 200 of the attackers. On the 4th, some officers from the 125th commandeered a skiff to slip away and walk the battlefield. Lieutenant Ralsa Rice and Sergeant Henry Glenville, a former Cleveland newspaper printer, were both awed and horrified at the sight of the mangled remains of enemy soldiers and horses just yards from the muzzle of a federal cannon. If any testament to the effectiveness of cannon loaded with canister rounds was needed, this was it. Lieutenant Charles Clark, the youngest officer in the regiment, wrote of the battlefield visit. "It was a sickening sight. It is safe to predict that we will never again visit a battlefield just after the conflict from idle curiosity."[30]

On February 6, the regiment left a fog shrouded Fort Donelson and headed up the Cumberland River. The next afternoon, observant residents of Nashville could see a black smudge on the northern sky. At 5 p.m., the Union flotilla arrived at the city's wharfs. Five hundred seventy-two men formed around the regimental flag of the 125th. Camp diseases had plagued the regiment since arriving in Kentucky. Colds, measles, pneumonia and typhoid ravaged the susceptible population of young men. Officers and men alike were just learning good sanitation, hygiene and food handling. Two men had died, including one of the oldest, 44-year-old John Badenborrough. Major Wood was in poor health, and Opdycke sent him home to recover and recruit. Several men were discharged by the surgeon as unfit, and probably should not have been mustered in the first place. This natural process of sifting out those not fit for field service took place in all new regiments and overall the 125th had fared better than most, thanks to Dr. McHenry. Overall, western regiments in the Union army experienced rates of illness of 16 percent, and mortality of 4 percent in 1862.[31]

Despite the difficulties and hardships encountered thus far by the Ohio volunteers, Lieutenant Ridgely C. Powers, writing under his pen name "Ceylon" in the *Western Reserve Chronicle*, summed up the feelings of his comrades that winter in a February 10 letter. "The patriotic fire that burned so fervently two years ago has not abated.... Better that we should all perish than that a cause so nefarious, so unjust, so void of every principle of right as urged against us, should succeed."[32]

2

Central Tennessee

Opdycke's wish to be under Major General William S. Rosecrans' command was fulfilled in February. Gilbert's division became part of the Army of the Cumberland, which was still in Murfreesboro, licking its wounds from the Stones River battle. On February 12, Gilbert's division was ordered to cover a portion of Nashville's extensive outer defenses. The 125th went to Franklin, Tennessee, a dozen miles south of Nashville on the strategically important hard surface Columbia Turnpike. In a cold drizzle, the neophyte soldiers hoisted heavy packs and marched. One infantryman—who estimated his burden at 60 pounds—observed, "Carrying a heavy knapsack, box and gun is harder work than farming."[1]

When the brigade was three miles from Franklin, scouts reported a rebel cavalry company in town. Since Opdycke's men were familiar with skirmish drill, General Gilbert ordered the 125th to front of the column. Companies A and B were deployed as skirmishers, and the regiment advanced at double quick. Company B's Captain Albert Yeomans, lacking combat experience, yielded operational command of his company to First Lieutenant Elmer Moses, who had seen action at Shiloh with the 41st Ohio.[2]

A village of 1500 in Tennessee's cotton belt, Franklin lay on the south side of a sweeping bend in the Harpeth River. Southern cavalry had burned the bridge in town, so the only way in meant fording the cold river. The skirmishers plunged into the icy water. Like an apparition, a single Confederate cavalry officer appeared on the opposite bank when the bluecoats were mid-stream. When Corporal Rolin Barnes climbed the bank, the two adversaries exchanged brief glances. The rebel fired his pistol at Barnes, and missed. The corporal brought his musket to bear, but the piece was too waterlogged to fire. The Confederate galloped away.[3]

Gray cavalry charged the wet skirmishers as they struggled up the slippery, four-foot river bank. Colonel Opdycke rode to the river's edge, made a snap decision and ordered the entire regiment to wade the frigid, waist deep water to reinforce the skirmishers. A few stray shots from the butternuts pierced the cold air. Opdycke's skirmishers, including many sharpshooters, responded with a ragged fire aimed at the turnpike filled with rebel horseman. The Ohioans continued to fire until their sights were set for the highest elevation and the enemy was well out of range. The 40 men of Company B fired as many as 10 rounds apiece. Local residents reported seeing wounded among the retreating Confederates, including a horse shot in the tail.[4]

Opdycke deployed Company F to the right of the pike and Company B to the left as skirmishers. Led by those two companies, the 125th pushed through town, driving the cavalrymen out. The enemy halted briefly on a rise in the pike near the toll house and near the brick farmhouse of a prosperous local farmer, Fountain Branch Carter. The sight of blue infantry was enough to send the Southerners down the turnpike toward Columbia, Tennessee, firing ineffectively from horseback as the galloped away. There was no Union cavalry available to pursue.[5]

Companies B and F advanced down the pike past the Carter house and beyond before establishing a picket line. The men of the 125th Ohio, their shoes full of water from crossing the river and weighted down with their knapsacks, were exhausted and footsore after marching 18 miles. The action that afternoon could hardly even be labeled a skirmish. There were no Yankee casualties. Yet, as Charles Clark noted in his history, this was "the first time the 125th Ohio was under fire." That cold February day also marked the 125th's introduction to the rigors of campaigning. There were lessons to be learned about keeping their weapons dry and crossing rivers. According to Clark, "the extraordinary exertion and exposure, especially by new troops, is sure to entail sickness." The 125th had been fortunate to leave only a handful of men in hospitals in the rear, compared to the 124th Ohio which had left 40. The hard march and exposure to ice cold water, however, sent a number of soldiers to the hospital within a few days.[6]

The 125th was the only regiment on the south side of the Harpeth River, so General Gilbert—who seemed to prefer the river between him and the enemy—ordered it to occupy the town and placed Opdycke in charge of Franklin. The Colonel chose a building in the Harpeth Academy for his headquarters. The Colonel sent a company to guard each of the roads leading into the village. Companies B and F were pulled back at midnight to rejoin the regiment which bivouacked in Franklin's abandoned female seminary.[7]

Central Tennessee was new to the Ohioans, one of which thought the Franklin area of central Tennessee was "the richest country I ever saw." Another observer saw only secessionists and labeled it "rotten to the core." The military age men were mostly in the Confederate service. The old men in town were sullen toward the Yankees and the women constantly badgered Opdycke for passes through the lines to visit their husbands in the Confederate army at Columbia, which Opdycke refused. The ladies complained, but Opdycke felt complimented. Company B manned a picket post at the Carter farmstead on the Columbia Pike on the south edge of Franklin. The Carters were secessionists and slaveholders with sons in the Confederate army. Sergeant Rice found the family kind and the patriarch, Fountain Branch Carter, "of an honest, sterling nature." Two teenaged daughters that remained at home drew the attention of the company officers. The girls would entertain and simultaneously irritate by playing and singing Southern patriotic airs. When Colonel Opdycke heard a stirring rendition of "Dixie," he informed General Gilbert who issued an injunction against it. The incident prompted the historian of the 124th Ohio to call Opdycke "an excellent officer ... but a pronounced martinet" who "had not a particle of humor in his composition."[8]

The Carter place was more farm than plantation, and the main house was just a four room brick structure with a frame addition and stood west of the turnpike. A separate brick kitchen, a smoke house, an office and slave quarters completed the farmstead. A few hundred yards south down the road on the opposite side was Carter's cotton gin that processed locally grown cotton. The slaves had fled to Nashville and there was no one to operate Carter's cotton gin, so the boys of Company B pitched in and ran the gin.[9]

The few local Unionists had been scorned and abused by their secessionist neighbors and they viewed the Union occupation favorably. Opdycke became acquainted with the town's Unionist physician, Dr. Daniel Cliffe, a native of Wooster, Ohio. Dr. Cliffe had been drafted into duty as a Confederate surgeon, and had tended wounded at the battle of Mill Springs, Kentucky. His wife had been arrested for being a Unionist but was later released. Opdycke became a regular at the Cliffe's dinner table.[10]

Recruiting for the 125th was proceeding at a snail's pace. By mid–February, there were just 600 men in camp. From Warren, Major Wood wrote to Opdycke that he planned to see if he could raise two companies from Ohio state troops guarding prisoners on Johnson's Island near Sandusky. But Wood's festering wound hardly made him an energetic recruiter and nothing came of it. In mid–March, Wood informed Opdycke that he intended to resign. Wood would be dead before the decade closed.[11]

By the end of February, Opdycke was in operational command of three infantry and one cavalry regiment on the south side of the Harpeth River. The river in winter often rose so as to be unfordable and the bridges were frequently washed out. Opdycke's skirmishers regularly traded shots with enemy cavalry south of town. Re-enforcing Opdycke's command might not be possible if the rebels attacked in strength. On March 4, General Gilbert sent a brigade under Colonel John Coburn of the 33rd Indiana 12 miles down the Columbia Pike toward Spring Hill as a reconnaissance in force. A half mile from Thompson's Station, Coburn's outnumbered brigade walked into a trap and were caught in a crossfire. After a brief fight, over 1200 surrendered. Only Coburn's artillery, cavalry and rearguard—composed of the 124th Ohio—made a fighting withdrawal. The soldiers of the 124th later admitted their escape was achieved only by the "best of running." Back up the road in Franklin, Colonel Opdycke heard the heavy firing in the distance, and on his own initiative, ordered the 125th down the Columbia Pike. The regiment halted at the advanced federal picket line when it met the retreating remnants of Coburn's column. General Gilbert ordered Opdycke back into camp in Franklin over the Colonel's vigorous protests. Under orders to retreat across the Harpeth River if attacked, Opdycke declared to his wife that he would likely disobey the order. The blame for the dismal affair fell on General Gilbert.[12]

Emboldened by their successful attack on Coburn, Confederate Major General Earl Van Dorn's cavalry became more aggressive around Franklin. Federal authorities took the Coburn disaster seriously, and on March 7, Major General Gordon Granger, a West Pointer twice breveted during the Mexican War, arrived in Franklin with a full division of infantry to augment the 8000 bluecoats already in the vicinity. Granger assumed command and led a general advance toward Thompson's Station on March 9, where the outnumbered rebels made brief stand before retiring. The 125th didn't fire a shot. A cold and stormy day followed, but Granger continued south to Rutherford Creek. Since the bridges had been burned, and the creek was at flood stage, the Southerners were untouchable. The 125th bivouacked in the cold rain, without shelter, 16 miles south of Franklin. The temperature dropped, but with the enemy just across the creek, campfires were prohibited. Granger, in his report, noted, "The men and animals suffered greatly from the storm on the 10th." The Confederates retired south across the Duck River on the 11th, so Granger reversed course and returned to Franklin. The mounted officers of the 125th followed Opdycke's example and let some of the chilled and foot sore infantrymen take turns riding their horses while the officers carried the men's rifles. The gesture was not forgotten by the foot soldiers. Two days later Lieutenant Clark was ill with stomach pain and Private George French with fever and delirium. Both survived.[13]

During the movement on March 10, one of General Gilbert's staff accused some men from Company H of the 125th Ohio of stealing hams from a smokehouse along

Rutherford Creek. The officers of the company vigorously denied it. Gilbert was a fierce disciplinarian and late in March, he had First Lieutenant Riley Merrill of Company H arrested and threatened with court martial. Opdycke considered Merrill "worthless" as an officer and generally the colonel approved of Gilbert's discipline, yet he felt that Merrill was blameless. To save Merrill and his family disgrace, Opdycke persuaded Gilbert to allow Merrill to resign. Many officers saw Gilbert as a martinet with what historian Gerald Linderman called "qualities antithetical to courage." By April, Gilbert—whose promotion to brigadier was never approved by the Senate and was technically only a captain—was on his way out of division command.[14]

On the 15th of March, the infantrymen of the 125th Ohio were issued shelter tents and the officers, wall tents, which indicated active campaigning in the future. The shelter tents were two sheets of canvas five feet square with a row of buttons or holes around the perimeter. Two joined halves were stretched over a guy rope strung between two muskets stuck into the ground by their bayonets. The shelter halves created a low two-man tent, nicknamed a "pup tent" because no creature could enter except on all fours. Four sheets joined with a rubber blanket stretched across one end yielded a four-man tent. Each man carried one canvas sheet with his blanket roll which eliminated the need for wagons to transport shelter for the men. By time the soldiers of 125th were issued theirs, the Union army had distributed 300,000 of the versatile shelter tents. Much larger and taller wall tents were issued for the officers whose tents served as both shelter and office.[15]

From mid–March to mid–April, the 125th remained in Franklin, drilling, and working in shifts to complete an earthen fort on the north bluff of the Harpeth River near the railroad bridge. Army engineers had situated the fort so that one side faced the river, and artillery within its walls could shell the river crossings and the town of Franklin itself. The other sides of the future Fort Granger required a steep ascent across open ground to assault. The 12-foot-high ramparts were of packed earth, supported by timbers, and topped by a parapet. Fort Granger enclosed almost 12 acres, could mount 24 guns and hold nearly 8000 men. Situated near the strategic hard surface pike, Fort Granger was the largest earthen fort in the defensive line south of Nashville.[16]

Escaped slaves flocking to the federal armies in the south and were referred to as "contrabands" by the Yankees. The officers prepared food and ate in small groups known as messes, and they generally employed these ex-slaves to do the cooking. Opdycke, and the handful of officers who formed his mess and drew rations with him, employed a mulatto cook and "Philip" as a servant. Philip was paid $10 a month and five cents per piece for washing clothes. The same was true of the company messes when in camp, and the 125th employed 120 contrabands as cooks and laborers while in Franklin. The African assistant cooks of companies C, D, E and G—George Rummage, Henry Statler, Jordan Hardin, and Henry Richards—were honored for their service by being formally enlisted in the regiment, and carried on the rolls as undercooks with the rank of private.[17]

After the Thompson's Station debacle and Granger's brief pursuit of the rebels, the Yankees didn't venture far from Franklin. In late March, men of Confederate Major General Nathan Bedford Forrest's cavalry captured over 700 Union infantrymen guarding the railroad nine miles north of Franklin and in the Union rear. Lieutenant Powers—writing under his alias "Ceylon"—commented in the *Cleveland Herald* on the two rebel successes. "Our generals are too sleepy; they have not got the bold dash and wide-awake courage necessary to conduct an army successfully." Powers and many of his comrades believed that only Rosecrans, victor at Stones River, had "a just conception of the character of the war" and "has devised measures, which properly supported, would send the rebellion howling to its dark home."[18]

Rosecrans' spies learned that Van Dorn planned to attack Franklin on April 8, and he dispatched reinforcements to General Granger, who already had two small infantry divisions—Gilbert's mustered less than 2800. The Confederates were at Spring Hill, Tennessee, south of Franklin with an estimated 9000 mounted troopers. All Union soldiers, except pickets, were withdrawn to the north side of the Harpeth and the 125th bivouacked a mile from town near a limestone spring. The weather was fine, the peach trees in blossom and the roads dry. Two days later at mid-day, with a south wind at their backs, Van Dorn's cavalry came straight up the Columbia Pike at Franklin. Only the 40th Ohio was south of the river holding the skirmish line. The 40th held the Johnnies for two hours around the Carter place, depleted their ammunition and retreated through the village toward the pontoon bridge pursued by a Mississippi cavalry regiment. Van Dorn, meanwhile, prepared a plan to take his troopers upriver on a flank attack toward the federal left. Colonel Opdycke had sent Sergeant Henry Glenville, the former printer, into Franklin that morning to print blank recitation books for the officer's school at the newspaper office. Glenville—whose real name was Henry Glenville Shaw—was taken prisoner temporarily, but escaped when his captor was shot. Dr. Cliffe and his wife ran from their residence by one door as the Confederates were entering another. Opdycke had temporarily sent seriously ill Quartermaster Sergeant Mervin Hillis to recuperate with the Cliffes, and the enemy captured him. Hillis was later released.[19]

The Confederate cavalry reached the Harpeth River and made a run at the pontoon bridge. First Lieutenant William Cushing and some of his men from Company H were guarding the approach when five gray troopers charged the bridge and demanded Cushing surrender. Private Malcolm Thompson leveled his Springfield and shot the rebel captain. The other Ohioans in the squad shot two more Johnnies and captured two. Discovering Van Dorn's flanking movement, Granger devised a plan to send cavalry upriver, ford the river and strike Van Dorn's troopers in the rear. At 4:15, Granger sent the 125th and 113th Ohio, along with two cannon, four miles east to the river ford at Hughes Mill and assist the Union cavalry in striking the rebel rear. However, when the infantry arrived an hour later, the federal cavalry had already been driven back across the river and Van Dorn's men were retiring toward Spring Hill. In his report, Granger wrote glowingly of the potential of his plan, but stopped short of criticizing General David Stanley, commanding the cavalry, for not standing his ground. Southern artillery was neutralized by cannon fire from Fort Granger and Granger's cavalry quickly secured Franklin. Of the Mississippians who charged into town, Granger wrote, "few of this regiment who came into town returned." The Mississippi major in command died of a fractured skull when he collided with a federal horseman. About 30 rebels were reported killed in the raid, perhaps 300 were wounded or captured. A dozen Yankees were killed.[20]

Although the action in Franklin was little more than a skirmish, Sergeant Ralsa Rice wrote "there had been enough firing to constitute this a battle." The Union high command agreed and the engaged regiments stitched "Franklin" on their regimental flags. After this stinging repulse, the Confederates made no further moves on Franklin while the federal presence was so strong. This left the area too quiet in Colonel Opdycke's opinion.[21]

For the month of April, the anticipated seasoning of the new soldiers in the 125th resulted in 14 deaths from disease and 12 discharges for disability. A half dozen officers resigned or transferred—needed men lost before a significant combat action. In early May amid peaceful days, the 125th joined the rest of its division in cutting timber on the Carter farm for a new camp and clearing fields of fire for Fort Granger's artillery. Sergeant A. C. Dilley of Company C was still impressed with the Harpeth valley writing home that it was "the most beautiful country I have ever seen" and that his northern Ohio home could not match the central Tennessee weather.[22]

As Rosecrans stockpiled supplies for the coming campaign season, the soldiers in the field found themselves on short rations. Opdycke wrote on May 1 to Lucy that his men were suffering. The soldiers had not received a ration of potatoes since leaving Ohio, and fruits and vegetables were in short supply. This deficit brought a flurry of relief packages from home and the independent sanitary commissions that attended the army's welfare outside of government channels. So effective was this work that by mid–May, the men were recording daily rations of fresh wheat bread and vegetables. The soldiers got fitter. This largesse wasn't just affecting the men, Barney was sleek and fat as well.[23]

With Major Wood resigning, Opdycke's choice for major of the 125th was the former teacher and student of the classics, 24-year-old Captain Edward P. Bates, Company C, whom the colonel called "the best Captain in the regiment." Unfortunately, Bates was second in seniority to Captain Joseph Bruff of Company A, for whom Opdycke had a personal, but unexplained, dislike. So Bates could not be major. Lieutenant Colonel Henry Banning, "an energetic and efficient officer" resigned to accept command of the 121st Ohio. However, the understrength 125th Ohio didn't currently warrant a lieutenant colonel, and the position remained vacant. In addition, the 60 days originally granted Opdycke to raise the full regiment had passed, and the army paymaster refused to pay Opdycke as a full colonel, until Governor Tod personally intervened on Opdycke's behalf. Colonel Opdycke reasoned that if he selected a major from outside the regiment there might be a better chance of recruiting the last two desperately needed companies. The logical choice was the Methodist minister turned soldier from Athens—24-year-old David H. Moore. Opdycke offered Moore the position if he could raise the last two companies and the regimental officers signed a letter to Governor Tod endorsing Moore.[24]

In April 1863, Moore traveled to Columbus, and was formally offered the position of regimental major, which was officially dated May 22. His commission was dependent on recruiting those elusive final two companies for the 125th, whether volunteers or conscripts, it didn't matter. The

Lieutenant Colonel David H. Moore, 1864. A graduate of Ohio University, Moore was one of the best educated men in the regiment. Reproduced from Clark, *Opdycke Tigers*.

indefatigable Moore became the regiment's chief recruitment officer in the Buckeye state. With dark, curly hair, and boyish looks, Moore's recruiting style would be a mix of the evangelical and patriotic. He wrote Opdycke that if appeals to patriotism were inadequate, he would "preach them a sermon." Moore was optimistic he could recruit two companies. But, reality intervened. Morale in the Union army and the North was at a low point in the winter and spring of 1863. The December defeats of Ambrose Burnside at Fredericksburg, Virginia, together with W. T. Sherman's repulse at Chickasaw Bluffs, Mississippi, cost over 14,000 casualties. U. S. Grant was mired in the mud around Vicksburg. Former congressman Nathaniel Banks' army was stalled before Port Hudson. The Army of the Potomac, despite a succession of commanders, seemed incapable of cornering Robert E. Lee. The Lincoln administration had little to show for the unprecedented bloodshed.[25]

Politically, the Emancipation Proclamation changed the justification for the war from one of saving the Union to one of liberation, provoking new debates about the validity of the war from Congress to main street. Opdycke wrote his brother in June, "I am convinced that to have a permanent peace we must destroy slavery." In 1863, support for secession was at its peak in Ohio. Northern Ohio, home to most of the men in the 125th, was staunchly anti-slavery, but as a man rode south in Ohio, he could feel the abolitionist fervor cool, and along the Ohio River, support for secession was significant.[26]

In the Ohio fall election of 1862, gloom over military reversals and the initial unpopularity of the Emancipation Proclamation meant that 14 of 19 congressional seats went to Democrats. Anti-war Democrats, exemplified former Ohio congressman Clement Vallandigham, opposed every aspect of the war and were an emboldened force in Ohio. Considered traitors by the Unionists and unflatteringly labeled "Copperheads" after the venomous snake, the anti-war movement was vocal. Vallandigham scolded Republicans, "Money you have expended without limit and blood poured out like water. Defeat, debt, taxation, and sepulchers—these are your only trophies." The Copperhead rallying cry was "To maintain the Constitution as it is, and to restore the Union as it was."[27]

Soldiers' letters home grew increasingly critical of the national government and Union commanders. Keeping men already in the field there was a challenge. The Army of the Potomac, after being mauled at Fredericksburg in December 1862, experienced outright desertions that ran several hundred a day. It wasn't desertions that vexed Colonel Opdycke, but endless requests for furloughs from his men instigated by families back home. Exasperated, on May 13, he wrote an open letter to the *Western Reserve Chronicle* in reply to one woman's plea that she needed her husband at home. The colonel pointed out that the women of the Confederacy were supporting the rebellion and Northern women could put it down, not by wanting their men to come home but urging them to stay with the army.[28]

The Union army needed men and volunteering had declined, so to compensate, a federal draft law was grinding through Congress. The South had invoked a draft a year earlier. Under the Union draft law passed in March, all men aged 20 to 45 would be subject to conscription. There would be exemptions, of course, for the infirm and those in militia units. Most objectionable to soldiers was the commutation clause which favored the rich and permitted a man to pay a substitute $300 to avoid service. As one soldier wrote, "The blood of a poor man is as precious as that of the wealthy." Of the almost 170,000 Northerners drafted during the war, half paid a substitute to avoid service. In the 125th Ohio, there was one recorded substitute, Joel Carr, who replaced Appollos P.

Morse, and served the entire war honorably. The attitude toward military service in the North in 1862–1863 was summed up by one historian when he wrote that society "did not demand that civilians—even strong patriots—make any specific sacrifice as their duty to the nation. They only had to obey the laws and then look to their own consciences for guidance."[29]

Opposition to the draft was significant and occasionally violent. Enrollment officers were physically assaulted by anti-war agitators. Copperhead firebrands openly encouraged disobedience to the law in Ohio, even violence. In Canton, an anti-war editor was jailed. In Holmes County, Ohio, that June 400 soldiers were sent to suppress anti-draft violence that ended after two men were wounded—one a draft enrollment officer—and 12 jailed. Army recruiters, like Major Moore, faced real physical danger. In this volatile political landscape and with his personal safety not assured, David Moore had to find a couple hundred recruits to fill Colonel Opdycke's regiment.[30]

On June 2, the 125th Ohio marched to Triune, Tennessee, 14 miles east of Franklin, where all of General Granger's troops were converging. The weather was pleasant, wheat was turning in the fields, corn was knee high and peaches were ripe. Stopping at a fine secessionist home for lunch, Opdycke turned a blind eye when some of the men stripped a secessionist's garden of onions.[31]

William Rosecrans reorganized and consolidated his army on June 8, creating a "reserve corps" commanded by General Granger. The 125th was transferred to the Third Brigade, First Division, 21st Corps, Army of the Cumberland. This move was facilitated by Rosecrans' chief of staff and future U.S. president, Brigadier General James Garfield, a prewar Republican state senator from Northeast Ohio who was acquainted with both Jacob Cox and Emerson Opdycke. Garfield was in Opdycke's eyes "a big brained, able man," who was a smart, industrious, self-educated volunteer officer, much like Cox—now an army general—and Opdycke. The Colonel respected Garfield *and* saw him as a powerful friend.[32]

In a letter home on June 14, Opdycke admitted he couldn't recall the name of his brigade commander. Colonel Charles Harker would become one of the most influential officers in Opdycke's military career. Harker was a rising star in the army, and it was the 125th's good fortune to be joining Harker's Third Brigade which consisted of the 64th and 65th Ohio and the 3rd Kentucky—all seasoned, veteran regiments. Two weeks later, Opdycke wrote, "We like Colonel Harker very well." Born in New Jersey, Charles Garrison Harker had been orphaned as a child, and befriended by a local congressman who appointed him to West Point, Class of 1858. Short in stature, "Little Charlie" Harker was, at 28, five years Opdycke's junior. Harker's hairline was receding and he favored the popular sideburns over a full beard. Known to be a connoisseur of wine, he always seemed to have a bottle to share, but didn't tolerate drunkenness. After serving two years on the frontier, then Captain Harker was promoted to colonel, and given command of the 65th Ohio in November 1861. At Stones River at the end of 1862, Harker commanded a brigade—the "Sherman Brigade" named for Ohio senator John Sherman, brother of Major General William T. Sherman. His division commander, Brigadier General Thomas J. Wood, thought Harker's battlefield performance outstanding, and recommended him for promotion, which would come later. Harker's volunteer soldiers initially saw him as a rigid disciplinarian—a common complaint by volunteers of West Pointers—even perhaps a martinet. Within months his brigade saw the benefit of his approach.[33]

The Third Brigade was one of three in Brigadier General Thomas J. Wood's First

Brigadier General Charles G. Harker, 1864. Orphaned at a young age, the diminutive Harker was befriended by a congressman and appointed to West Point in 1854. Reproduced from Clark, *Opdycke Tigers*.

Brigadier General Thomas Wood. Wood received a brevet for gallantry in the Mexican War, and was a second cousin of Confederate General Ben Helm. Library of Congress.

Division. Wood, 39, was a Kentuckian, and an 1845 graduate of West Point, where his first roommate was U. S. Grant. Wood was brevetted during the Mexican War for gallantry. He spent two years in the cavalry in the West before going to Europe on leave of absence from 1859 to 1861. Wood—intelligent and urbane—was a small man sporting a Van Dyke beard and a permanently sunburned complexion from his time in the field. In 1861, Wood advanced quickly up the ranks replacing resigning Southerners. Within eight months Wood was a cavalry colonel. By fall, he was home in Kentucky as a brigadier general. As part of Buell's army, Wood turned in solid performances at Shiloh and Perryville. At Stones River in December 1862, his division held firm against rebel assaults. Wounded, Wood refused to leave the field until evening.[34]

Wood's division was part of Major General Thomas J. Crittenden's Corps. While Wood and Harker were excellent professional soldiers, the 44-year-old Crittenden merely looked like one. Another Kentuckian, the son of a U.S. senator and brother of a Confederate major general, Crittenden was a lawyer and politician. Dark of complexion and hair, ramrod straight of posture, Crittenden was an aide to General Zachery Taylor during the Mexican War, and had a diplomatic stint in the interwar years. The secessionist crisis of 1861, landed Crittenden command of the Unionist Kentucky state forces as brigadier general. Fond of both whiskey and profanity, Crittenden's performance at Shiloh was judged good enough to win him promotion to major general in July of 1862. At Stones River, where he led over 14,000 men, the Kentuckian's performance was lackluster. Whatever his deficiencies as a commander, he was loyal to General Rosecrans and often that was all Rosecrans required. The troops who served under Crittenden generally held him in high regard during the summer of 1863. Opdycke considered Crittenden's corps the army's best.[35]

After the victory at Stones River, William S. Rosecrans' Army of the Cumberland enjoyed a fine reputation as an efficient, effective force. Rosecrans cared about his men, seeing to it that they were well fed and outfitted. Both the troops under his command and people back home cheered the man they called "Old Rosy." Ohio journalist Whitelaw Reid, a Rosecrans devotee and former aide, agreed that "few officers have been more popular with their commands, or have inspired more confidence in the rank and file." An Ohioan with a stellar West Point record, Rosecrans was respected as a first-rate military mind. Within months of Fort Sumner, Rosecrans was a brigadier general. He was physically powerful, six feet tall, and had bow legs. His contemporaries remembered him for his florid, heavy, graying beard and aquiline nose. The general possessed a strong, almost obsessive work ethic. As a devout Catholic in an army of Protestants, he was ready to debate theology with anyone. Rosecrans' faith did not exclude profanity, so long as it wasn't blasphemous, which augmented his famous temper. Liquor was not excluded from his headquarters, but Rosecrans was no drunk.[36]

Despite his military brilliance and the loyalty of his men, Rosecrans had significant faults. Although he tended to underestimate his opponents while overestimating himself, Rosecrans could be chronically slow to take the offensive. In a fight, he had an unfortunate tendency to become excited and confused. And significantly, Rosecrans was blind to ineptitude in his loyal cadre of subordinates. Whitelaw Reid wrote after the war, "The man that could do this was hopelessly ignorant of human nature; hopelessly deficient in that foremost quality of a General which teaches how to select the right men for the right places." But perhaps Rosecrans greatest undoing was his inability, fueled by his considerable ego, to get along with his superiors. By the fall of 1862, Rosecrans had succeeded in alienating Secretary of War Edwin Stanton, Army Chief of Staff Henry Halleck and his one-time superior, Ulysses S. Grant. Nevertheless, with few alternatives, President Lincoln overlooked army politics, and in October 1862, Rosecrans was appointed a major general and ordered to replace the unpopular Don Carlos Buell in command of the Army of the Ohio, which became the Army of the Cumberland.[37]

At Stones River, Rosecrans men were forced to fight a desperate defensive battle when a surprise Confederate attack crushed Rosecrans' finely crafted offensive battle plan. After suffering 13,000 casualties, the Army of the Cumberland eked out a victory. This lucky result came at a time when Union fortunes were at low tide, and Lincoln wrote Rosecrans, "You gave us a hard-earned victory, which, had there been a defeat instead, the nation could scarcely have lived over." After Stones River, Rosecrans was widely considered as one of the war's best generals, North or South. In June 1863, Opdycke wrote his brother John that he had met General Rosecrans "I like him very much. He is a fine specimen of a soldier," Opdycke wrote. The opinion of the common soldier was expressed by the 125th's Sergeant Henry Glenville who informed readers of the *Cleveland Herald* that the soldiers in the field had "every confidence" in General Rosecrans. At 43, the general was at the peak of his career.[38]

Rosecrans popularity did nothing to make recruiting in Ohio any easier. Recruiting, even just two companies, was a difficult task Major Moore discovered. He sought out prominent local men across eastern Ohio with previous military experience and put them to work signing up recruits as his proxies. The prize for the recruiters was an officer's commission in the 125th Ohio. "If a good man is *instrumental* in securing 30 recruits," Moore asked Opdycke, "I will be at liberty to assure him a lieutenancy, will I not?" Good recruiters were essential if Moore was to reach his goal. One veteran Moore desperately wanted was Sterling Manchester of Ashtabula County who had served in the old three-month 87th Ohio as sergeant major. Of Manchester, Moore wrote Opdycke, "He is energetic and *persistent*." Manchester was approved for a commission. Compounding Moore's recruiting challenges, the State of Ohio was enlisting men for two six-month militia regiments. One of Moore's recruiting agents was chased away from Camp Cleveland for attempting to steal six month men not officially mustered. Moore came to realize that "great majority" of available men would take their chances with conscription.[39]

The second week of June, Confederate general John Hunt Morgan left his base in Tennessee with almost 3,000 cavalrymen. On July 8, the raiders crossed the Ohio River, and invaded Indiana. Moore wrote Opdycke, "John Morgan has invaded Indiana. If he gets out, somebody's to blame, *sure*." Five days later, Morgan's troopers entered Ohio, throwing all of southern Ohio was in an uproar. Morgan's raid assumed exaggerated proportions. Almost 55,000 Ohio militia were called to arms to augment the 7,000 federal cavalry pursuing Morgan. All recruiting was suspended, and federal officers on detached duty were ordered to report to the Ohio adjutant general. That included the eager and energetic Major Moore, who was sent to assist the militia in his home county of Athens.[40]

On July 18, in a foolish encounter near Rutland, Ohio, Moore and one of Morgan's men exchanged pistol shots. "I drew on him instantly," Moore later bragged to Opdycke. The rebel trooper "whirled his horse broadside and threw himself alongside Indian fashion." Moore fired and heard the cavalryman swear as both men rode away in opposite directions. Moore rode off unharmed and later learned that his shot only grazed the back of the Confederate's neck. Fifty or so gray clad troopers chased Moore a short distance before giving up. Moore wrote Opdycke of his first combat, "I enjoyed it. Twas refreshing."[41]

A day later, Moore rode after the Union cavalry chasing Morgan. After dark that evening, near Coolville, Ohio, Moore mistakenly rode into a rebel detachment and was captured within sight of the camp of a company of sleeping Ohio militia. During the night, as his captors slept, Moore managed a harrowing escape, walking and riding the 17 miles back home to Athens in time for breakfast on July 20. By early afternoon, remounted and armed with a shotgun—the rebels having confiscated his fine Colt pistols—Moore was again in pursuit. Four miles north of Cheshire, Ohio, a hundred of Moore's former captors surrendered. Moore and the Southern commander of the detachment, a Kentucky Lieutenant Colonel, Cicero Coleman, became lifelong friends as a result of Moore's brief captivity. As the pursuit of Morgan carried the federal cavalry away from Athens, Moore remained behind with the local militia. John Hunt Morgan was later captured in northeast Ohio's Columbiana County. Despite losing a horse, tack and two revolvers to Morgan's men, the Major of the 125th was pleased with himself, telling Opdycke, "Haven't I had quite an exciting campaign, with home as a base of supplies?" Opdycke found Moore's adventure amusing. Nine months later, Moore's second son was born.[42]

3

THE ROAD TO THE RIVER OF DEATH

By mid–June 1863, the Army of the Cumberland had been in camp at Murfreesboro, Tennessee, almost six months. During the Civil War, the campaigning season typically began in early May, and the War Department had been pressuring William S. Rosecrans to take his army into the field for weeks. Rosecrans' army occupied the center of a Union front line that extended across the country from Virginia to the Mississippi River. Rosecrans argued that his army should not move until Grant had captured Vicksburg. In reality, Old Rosy—a nickname bestowed by his soldiers—had no intention of moving until he was ready, his complex battle plan perfected, his men and animals fit, and supplies were present in abundance. The Ohio journalist Whitelaw Reid wrote five years later of Rosecrans' excuses, "on the whole they will hardly seem now to have afforded sufficient cause for the delay."[1]

Braxton Bragg's Confederate Army of the Tennessee was just 30-odd miles south of Murfreesboro below the Duck River where it had remained unmolested all winter. For his spring offensive, Rosecrans would have 67,000 men in four infantry corps and 40,000 draft animals for transport. Huge quantities of material had been accumulated in central Tennessee, including 40,000 crates of hardtack biscuits. Satisfied that all was as close to ready as he could make it, Rosecrans planned to move his army during the last week of June. However, Rosecrans had become so obsessed with secrecy, that even his corps commanders were unsure of the overall battle plan and his orders to them one historian called "unclear and imprecise."[2]

On June 21, the 125th Ohio marched the 17 miles to where Colonel Charles Harker's brigade was camped near Murfreesboro. The next day, General Garfield introduced Opdycke to Rosecrans. Opdycke reported to his wife that Rosecrans was smarter than he expected, but the free flow of spirits at Rosecrans' headquarters met with Opdycke's disapproval. The 23rd, the bluecoats were issued 12 days of rations and given marching orders. Opdycke wrote Lucy that he wanted a fight, but suspected the enemy would retreat south of the Tennessee River.[3]

After his defeat at the beginning of the year, General Bragg had taken his army south to Shelbyville, Tennessee. The railroad town of Tullahoma, southeast of Shelbyville, served as a supply depot. East of Shelbyville, the terrain turned rugged as the Cumberland Mountains rose 1800 feet featuring high hills broken occasionally by passes, called "gaps." The rebels had control of the resource-rich Duck River valley from which they had foraged the last six months. Bragg lobbied Richmond hard for reinforcements all winter but any available Confederate manpower was sent to defend Vicksburg. In June 1863, Bragg counted 55,000 men in two infantry corps. These troops were spread in a thin defensive arc from Shelbyville to Manchester, Tennessee, with very active cavalry ranging well beyond both flanks. The best hard surface road ran straight from Murfreesboro to Shelbyville, while only poor dirt tracks went through the gaps. Bragg, purely in a defensive mode, believed any federal offensive would come straight down the hard-surface road. Thus both Shelbyville and Tullahoma were well fortified, while the gaps to the east were only lightly defended. If forced to retreat, Bragg could use the Nashville and Chattanooga Railroad and fall back from Tullahoma all the way to Chattanooga.[4]

While forcing the Confederates out of central Tennessee was the immediate goal for Rosecrans, the ultimate prize was the rail junction city of Chattanooga, 100 air miles southeast of Murfreesboro. Capturing Chattanooga would open the way to Atlanta and beyond. However, in addition to a Confederate army between Murfreesboro and Chattanooga, the Duck and Elk Rivers formed natural barriers and to the east, the Cumberland Mountains. Beyond those obstacles were the 2000 foot main ridges of the Appalachian Mountains and the 1000-foot-wide Tennessee River. If Rosecrans couldn't bring Bragg to battle in middle Tennessee, then his next opportunity might lay south of Chattanooga.[5]

Rosecrans preferred not to squander his men's lives by directly assaulting the entrenched Confederates at Shelbyville. Instead, he chose military deception. He ordered a feint directly down the good road to Shelbyville by Major Generals Gordon Granger and Alexander McCook's army corps. Concurrently, the main thrust would be a flanking movement by the corps of major generals Thomas Crittenden and George Thomas, who were to pass around the Confederate right and concentrate at Manchester, Tennessee, 12 miles northeast of Tullahoma. After moving down the Shelbyville Road for a few miles, McCook would take his corps on Thomas and Crittenden's path. If successful, Bragg would be flanked and the railroad to Chattanooga threatened. Federal infantry occupying Manchester would compel Bragg to retreat south, ceding middle Tennessee to the Union without a fight.[6]

The Army of the Cumberland began moving from its Murfreesboro camps on June 24. The Yankees marched straight into eight consecutive days of rain. Crittenden sent two of his divisions, Tom Wood's followed Major General John Palmer's, slogging down the muddy road on a wide left hook toward Manchester. Brigadier General Horatio Van Cleve's division remained behind to guard Murfreesboro. The 125th marched at 7 a.m. on June 24 passing through Bradyville at noon, where the stone paved pike ended and the dirt roads began. From the start, the worst enemy the Yankees faced was mud. The 125th only made six miles on the 24th. Colonel Opdycke wasn't exaggerating when he wrote his wife, "I never saw such indescribable roads." Another Ohioan labeled the soil "a mixture of quicksand and glue when wet." Under ordinary conditions, the dirt tracks through the hills would have been as good for the army to move on as the hard turnpike. Rain soaked roads threw Rosecrans careful plan seriously off schedule, as the mule trains carrying the army's supplies became hopelessly bogged down in the thick mud. If left behind unguarded, enemy cavalry raiders would destroy them. To speed up the march, some commanders ordered the camp equipage and even officer's baggage abandoned and burned. Only provisions and ammunition were to be spared. New to campaigning, the men of the 125th had dutifully clung to their heavy overcoats, but now they left a trail of blue wool to mark their path.[7]

Slowed by the bad roads, the first of George Thomas' divisions didn't reach Manchester until the 27th. It was two more days before McCook and Crittenden's men arrived at the same destination. When the Union army occupied Manchester, Bragg immediately abandoned his entrenchments at Shelbyville as Rosecrans predicted. Gordon Granger's corps and Union cavalry replaced the Confederates. On the 30th, General Thomas' corps continued beyond Manchester to Crumpton's Creek.[8]

Opdycke's boys made only five miles in two days slogging over muddy hills. This tedium continued for Harker's brigade on Sunday, June 28 when it traveled only 10 miles in heavy rain. Two of the brigade's wagons were hopelessly stuck and burned, a move that cost Opdycke his best boots and tent, while other officers in the brigade lost uniforms and personal valises. The horses and mules were put on half rations as forage ran low. The 29th was spent in camp. On June 30, serving as guards for the remaining wagons, the 125th slogged the last four miles into Manchester. It had taken seven days for the regiment to advance just 32 miles. Opdycke endeared himself to his men on the march by carrying as many as five muskets to relieve his tired soldiers. Although the Confederates were still 11 miles away at Tullahoma, Rosecrans had unnerved Bragg. The Southerners fell back across the Elk River, and on July 2, they abandoned middle Tennessee completely by retreating across the Tennessee River and then east all the way to Chattanooga, destroying the railroad as they went. From July 1 to 4, Harker's brigade marched and countermarched in the vicinity of Manchester. The 4th was spent in a camp 15 miles from Manchester. The men celebrated July 4 while suffering hunger pangs after five days on half rations. Not surprisingly, the foraging across the local countryside was described as "vigorous." While there had been some fighting at the gaps, overall casualties had been minimal. Both armies lost about 600 men in combat, but Bragg lost 1600 as prisoners and many uncounted Tennesseans deserted the secessionist cause. The loss of central Tennessee, followed immediately by the Confederate defeats at Gettysburg and Vicksburg, was a severe blow to Southern morale.[9]

Historians would call the eviction of the Confederates from central Tennessee in just nine days, the Tullahoma Campaign. One chronicler labeled it "as brilliant as any in American military annals." But coming on the heels of hard-fought victories at Gettysburg and Vicksburg, Rosecrans' almost bloodless triumph went practically unnoticed. "Brilliant as were these operations," journalist Reid was to later suggest, "they lacked the element of bloodshed which goes so far toward fixing the popular standard of appreciation." Furthermore, Washington continued to press Rosecrans to pursue the Confederates, which left Rosecrans disgusted and resentful. While Rosecrans languished in his pique, and reveled in his personal superiority over Bragg, he failed to fully appreciate that "a campaign like that of Tullahoma always means a battle at some other point." The victory at Tullahoma failed to suppress questions about Rosecrans in Washington. Some gossips blamed alcohol. Opdycke doubted the general was a heavy drinker. Regarding the commander of the Army of the Cumberland's generalship, Opdycke had come to understand that many high ranking officers in the army didn't share the public's high esteem of Rosecran's ability.[10]

Wood's division went into camp one half mile northwest of Hillsboro, Tennessee, just a few miles from Manchester on July 8. The Army of the Cumberland would remain inactive for six weeks. The Wood's division was less than 50 air miles from Chattanooga. Southern cavalry had damaged the railroad and heavy rains made the roads almost impassable hindering the movement of supplies to the army. What had been a single day's ration of sugar, coffee and hardtack was now stretched to three days. Foraging became an obsession, and according to 125th's Lieutenant Ridgely Powers, "everything that men or horses could subsist upon have been appropriated." Authorized barter for foodstuffs and forage from local farmers went on daily with a pound of salt equal to a roasting chicken. Illiteracy among the Tennessee farmers was commonplace and some clever soldiers substituted clipped newspaper advertisements for paper money. Higher officers' pay enable them to purchase food. So much so that Colonel Harker had a dinner party on August 11 for the field grade officers in his brigade. According to Colonel Opdycke the table groaned under oysters, roast chicken, fresh and cooked tomatoes, pastry and round after round of Catawba wine which left some officers tipsy.[11]

Drill and officer's school resumed in Opdycke's regiment, and he introduced two new movements: "advance firing" and "retreat firing." In both maneuvers, the files were doubled to four men deep with intervals between the files through which rear rank men passed at a run to the front, firing and halting to reload with the next rank moving further forward and so on. In retreat, the process was reversed. One regimental diarist noted, "It looks like an effective maneuver." At drill, the 125th was second to no western regiment and "were often dubbed 'regulars' by men serving in regiments less thoroughly instructed," Lieutenant Clark proudly noted. Lieutenant Ridgley Powers told readers of the *Cleveland Herald*, "I have heard it remarked repeatedly by outsiders that our regiment is the best drilled and best disciplined of any in the Division."[12]

After Morgan's capture in July, Major David Moore returned to the much less exciting task of recruiting. The new draft law, Federal Enrollment Act of 1863, provided for state quotas to be filled "in a reasonable time." Failing that, a draft would be held, but the details were yet to be decided, leaving state authorities, recruiters and potential draftees wondering whether draftees would be allowed to choose the regiments they would be assigned to or be apportioned to existing regiments based on manpower needs. As a further complication, conscripts from the nine-month militia draft from in the fall of 1862 were being mustered out increasing manpower needs that much more.[13]

While the army was inactive, Colonel Opdycke sent several men, including Captains Steen Parks and Anthony Vallendar, Surgeon McHenry, Sergeant Major Seabury Smith and two other sergeants, and several enlisted men, to Ohio for recruiting with the encouragement and complicity of General Garfield. Parks had been a company commander in the old 85th Ohio, and the German-born Vallendar was a veteran of the Prussian army with ties to the German community. Lieutenant Ridgely Powers, still in Hillsboro, attempted to persuade potential recruits. "Come on boys, and let us close this war up strong," he wrote in a letter to the *Western Reserve Chronicle*.[14]

A bounty of $100 for a minimum two year's service was available for volunteers with few takers. Despite the $100 bounty, Moore and his assistants were reduced to picking up one or two recruits here and there across Ohio. A tip led Moore to a detachment of unassigned volunteers calling themselves sharpshooters and waiting at Camp Dennison in Columbus to enlist in the cavalry. In Moore's words, "I went for 'em." A man schooled in persuasion, Moore told the men how fine the 125th was, how they could be members of the finest regiment of their division, that they could be mustered next week and get their enlistment bounties. Even though Moore didn't know if the sharpshooters could actually shoot, he promised, over supper, the best shots the dubious honor of skirmishing as sharpshooters in their first fight. To his "utter surprise," 29 signed up. He sealed the deal by promising the group's captain, Aquila Coonrod, the captaincy of Company I. Coonrod was a Shiloh veteran with almost 18 months of service with two Ohio regiments, having resigned in the summer of 1862. Moore believed Coonrod to have a good military bearing and reputation, but of questionable intelligence and too fond of alcohol. Nevertheless, Moore went straight to Governor Tod, who pushed the paperwork through the adjutant general's office. There were now enough men to muster Company I into service on September 25, 1863. One hundred and four men boarded trains and headed for Tennessee. Moore told Opdycke his success was the fruit of Providence.[15]

Officer appointments were a minefield faced by Northern governors. The state governor had the authority to appoint regimental officers from the rank of colonel down. Only generals required congressional approval. The difficulties with the system were succinctly summarized by Whitelaw Reid in *Ohio in the War* when he wrote of the anomalous position of regimental officers "owing their commissions to the Governor of their State, but owing him no obedience, looking to him for promotions, but looking elsewhere for the orders under which promotions must be won." Ohio governor David Tod—a very political war Democrat elected on a Union Party ticket—chose no coherent policy at all. Tod made appointments at different times by seniority, ability, recommendation of the county military committee or regimental colonel, even mere personal acquaintance. Tod refused to grant colonels complete control to select their regimental officers. As a longtime acquaintance, Emerson Opdycke found Governor Tod approachable and sympathetic. Tod would be leaving office at year's end and how his successor might handle this thorny issue was unknown and a cause of some concern for the officers in Ohio regiments.[16]

Rosecrans' remained inactive as the railroad from Nashville was repaired as far as Bridgeport on the Tennessee River in northeast Alabama, a couple dozen miles west of Chattanooga, and supplies brought forward. Finally, on August 15, Rosecrans was ready. Lieutenant Clark of the 125th wrote in his diary, "Our sick men have been sent from regimental to general hospital. We anticipate orders to march." The campaign to seize Chattanooga was about to begin.[17]

Old Rosy's plan was to maneuver Bragg out of Chattanooga by threatening his supply line from Atlanta. That meant crossing the Cumberland Mountains and then the Tennessee River. To navigate these natural obstacles, Rosecrans divided his army into three widely separated columns. When the Army of the Cumberland lumbered into motion on the 16th, Crittenden's corps was on the left, north, flank. George Thomas in the center and Alexander McCook on the right. It began to rain. The 125th Ohio marched as rearguard for Tom Wood's division, trailing the division's 250 wagons as they wallowed through the mud laden down with 20 days of supplies. Opdycke had responsibility for the exhausted teams that fell behind leaving the 125th to wrestle the mules out of the mud. Well behind the main body of the corps, Opdycke drove his men hard the following day on just five hours' rest to close the distance to the main wagon train.[18]

Thirteen miles southeast from the Hillsboro campground, the men got their first glimpse of the Cumberland Mountains. Wood's division would have to ascend 1200 feet through a steep valley along muddy track. The wagons were reduced to half loads and details of 100 men used ropes to drag the mule teams up the mud slicked road. This hard labor had to be repeated to get the full load to the top leaving the poor mules' feet and legs bloody from the ordeal. Opdycke and his officers took their turns at the ropes, and the colonel, soaked perspiration, had to drop out when he became faint, later recalling that "everything looked blue." This backbreaking, exhausting work lasted all night by the light of torches and the sound of regimental bands playing patriotic music. By 10 a.m. on the 18th, the task was completed. General Wood congratulated his soldiers for completing 48 hours of "the severest labor." Colonel Harker told Opdycke, "You have done nobly, sir," and handed him a glass of Catawba wine.[19]

The objective for Wood's men on the 19th was 28 miles away—Therman, Tennessee. Opdycke walked 14 of those miles letting the footsore—including Captain Yeomans suffering a sore heel—take turns riding Barney, who was himself lame the next day. With Opdycke leading the way, the last five downhill miles into the Sequatchie River Valley were done at the double quick. Miraculously, the 125th made the march without any straggling. They camped, on the 20th, 25 miles from Chattanooga and feasted on peaches from a nearby orchard.[20]

On the 24th, a few miles from Chattanooga, some units of Rosecrans army traded artillery shells with the enemy posted along the Tennessee River. Opdycke accepted that Rosecrans strategy was to maneuver the Confederates out of the city, however, he said, "I would as soon they make a stand here, as to oblige us to follow them further south." Rosecrans' battle plan called for a feint north of the city. Crittenden's corps—the left column—was northwest of the city and spread from Pellam to Pikeville, Tennessee. Horatio Van Cleve's division was on the army's left flank at Pikeville. Wood's division was on the corps' right, deployed from Pelham to the Sequatchie Valley and 21 miles north of Jasper. Thomas' corps was on Wood's right, in the federal center. McCook's corps was at Bridgeport, Alabama, on Rosecrans' right flank.[21]

Two of Crittenden's brigades advanced toward Harrison's Landing—north of Chattanooga—to suggest an attack might come there. Meanwhile Rosecrans put the rest of his army in motion crossing the Tennessee River at Bridgeport, Battle Creek and Shell Mound, Alabama. By 9:30 p.m. on September 3, Harker's brigade had completed crossing at Shell Mound on flatboats before bivouacking just four miles from the Georgia state line. The 5th, each man received three days of rations, and transportation was reduced to one wagon per regiment. Harker's Third Brigade marched at 1 p.m., covering eight miles and halted near the rail station of Whitesides in the gorge of Raccoon Mountain.[22]

Leading Wood's division, Harker's men took to the road at 6 a.m. on September 6. Skirmishing with rebel cavalry began immediately and continued to intensify as the Yankees approached Wauhatchie, the critical rail junction of the Nashville and Chattanooga Railroad with the Trenton and Chattanooga Railroad. Wood's men were slightly southwest of Chattanooga, south of the Tennessee River and near the base of Lookout Mountain where rebel signalmen easily spotted them. Wood's division was badly exposed—14 miles from any other friendly troops—so Wood retired a mile and a half to a more defensible position.[23]

The morning of the 7th, Tom Wood repositioned his division on the wagon road from Trenton to Chattanooga. Rosecrans ordered Wood to make a reconnaissance in force toward the north end of Lookout Mountain, and Harker's brigade was directed to advance cautiously, don't cross Lookout Creek and return by nightfall. Harker moved out at 1 p.m. Three hundred yards east of Wauhatchie, rebel cavalry pickets materialized. Companies B, D, and E of the 125th joined companies from the 3rd Kentucky on the advance skirmish line. The enemy pickets fell back and the Southerners retreated firing as the bluecoat skirmishers advanced. With Lookout Creek on his right, Harker eased along the valley toward the Tennessee River and a spur of Lookout Mountain that was four and a half miles from the Chattanooga. After a brisk skirmish in dense woods, Company D charged a house sheltering enemy sharpshooters and dispersed them. Harker continued to feel his way forward. When the Union skirmishers reached Lookout Creek,

Confederate artillery opened on the Northerners from the Lookout Mountain at a range of 1100 yards. Despite poor artillery ammunition, the pre-sighted enemy fire was accurate enough to force Harker to withdrew with the loss of one man killed. Harker reported that the enemy controlled the wagon road that passed between the base of the mountain and the river. Wood was pleased with the work and with some exaggeration wrote in his official report, "I know no parallel in military history to this reconnaissance." Harker, in turn, congratulated Opdycke on the behavior of the 125th's skirmishers, under Captain Ed Bates' direction, noting, "they did not act like new troops."[24]

McCook's and Thomas' corps, penetrating deeper into north Georgia south of Chattanooga, now posed a threat to Bragg's line of retreat toward Atlanta. The Confederates withdrew from the city on September 9. By 11 a.m., led by Colonel George Buell's brigade of Wood's division, Crittenden's men raised the stars and stripes over Chattanooga. Harker's brigade marched into town through acres of deserted, trash-choked Confederate camps. The brigade halted in front of a house that had been a Confederate headquarters just hours before. There were smiles all around. With little fighting and few casualties, Rosecrans had driven Bragg's Confederates from middle Tennessee into north Georgia, effectively ceding the state to the Union. There had been no rebels around to surrender Chattanooga, but Harker's boys did find two battle Confederate flags. Harker kept one and the men tore the other apart for souvenirs.[25]

A week earlier, Ambrose Burnside with 15,000 men had taken Knoxville. It had taken two years for Union armies to rescue the beleaguered East Tennessee Unionists, but now in early September 1863, they held both principle cities, Chattanooga and Knoxville. It was one thing, brilliantly done, to seize east Tennessee. It would be another to keep it, at the end of a long tenuous supply line, in the face of a determined Confederate counter-attack.[26]

Many of Rosecrans' contemporaries and historians have suggested that he should have stopped at Chattanooga, fortified the place and consolidated his gains. Instead, an uncharacteristically aggressive Rosecrans plunged into the north Georgia hills, mountains and woods in pursuit of Braxton Bragg, whom he judged unwilling to fight. In U. S. Grant's post-war opinion, "Rosecrans had very skillfully maneuvered Bragg south of the Tennessee River, and through and beyond Chattanooga. If he had stopped and intrenched, and made himself strong there, all would have been right."[27]

Braxton Bragg was smart, didn't lack for personal courage, and showed occasional imagination and boldness. But he had a career-long reputation for not getting along with people he disliked, which was almost everyone, and not inspiring confidence in his men. Bragg—a strict disciplinarian—was contemptuous of volunteer soldiers and the conscripts flowing into the Confederate armies. He also was oblivious to changing military tactics that emphasized defense over assault. And that one intangible in battle, luck, had never dined in Bragg's headquarters. One biographer simply noted that Bragg "was not lucky" as a commander. By September 1863, the 46-year-old Bragg was in poor health and the fight had gone out of him. However, in the valley of West Chickamauga Creek in the north Georgia woods, Braxton Bragg's fortunes, in spite of his many faults, were about to change.[28]

A seemingly complacent and divided Union army occupied north Georgia. Something of the professional soldier stirred in Bragg and he saw an opportunity. In a major shift in Southern strategy, Confederate Lieutenant General James Longstreet Corps was being slowly transferred by rail from Virginia to re-enforce Bragg. This weeks' long transfer over rickety and inefficient rail lines would give Bragg numerical superiority over the federals, and perhaps some backbone. The original Confederate battle plan was to attack Rosecrans' dispersed corps piecemeal, beginning with Crittenden on the 13th, and defeat them individually before they could consolidate. Bragg's failure to win the loyalty of his subordinates, who worked almost as hard against him as for him, doomed that plan.[29]

On the same day Bragg's aborted assault on Crittenden was set to take place, Rosecrans realized Bragg's threat to his divided forces. He ordered a new concentration in McLemore's Cove located about 20 miles south of Chattanooga on the east bank of Chickamauga Creek behind Pigeon Mountain. McLemore's Cove was directly in front of George Thomas' corps. McCook's corps was ordered north to Steven's Gap and arrived on Thomas' right. Crittenden was sent south to Lee and Gordon's mill, on Thomas' left. Crittenden's men advanced, unsure of the Confederates' location or dispositions. According to the 41st Ohio's historian, "The irregular marches, and bivouacs in places chosen not because they were good camping ground, were proof enough that our forces were feeling their way, held in readiness for emergencies."[30]

Crittenden's corps didn't tarry long in Chattanooga after receiving orders to pursue the enemy down the Lafayette Road, toward Ringgold, Georgia. Brigadier General George Wagner's Second Brigade of Wood's division, remained behind to guard Chattanooga. Harker marched at 8 a.m. on the 10th for Ringgold, with three days of rations in each man's haversack. It was a dusty, dry march made worse by having to follow the clouds of dust from Crittenden's Second Division, Major General John Palmer's. Camp was made that night 10 miles from Chattanooga where the road crossed Chickamauga Creek. Local

Lee and Gordon's Mill. The 125th guarded the Chickamauga Creek ford there in September 1863.

contrabands offered questionable intelligence that the Confederates were closer than Rosecrans believed.[31]

To that end, Rosecrans had Wood send Harker's men on a reconnaissance down the La Fayette Road at dawn on the 11th. Harker's brigade reversed and marched back to Rossville at 5:30 a.m. East of Rossville on the road to Gordon's Mill, Harker left his wagons and two sections of the 6th Ohio Artillery to protect this possible route of retreat. The 125th Ohio and two companies of the 64th Ohio were delegated as infantry support under Opdycke's overall command. The remainder of the brigade warily continued south, proceeded by a heavy skirmish line. About three and a half miles south of Rossville, near Cloud Church, a mortally wounded rebel cavalryman told Harker that there were two brigades of General Nathan Bedford Forrest's horsemen in his front. Further down the La Fayette Road and 11 miles from Chattanooga, the local citizenry insisted that there wasn't any enemy infantry between Harker and Gordon's Mill. As the Third Brigade pressed on down the road, Southern cavalry resistance increased. About mid-afternoon, Crittenden arrived at Tom Wood's headquarters and directed him to push across country with his remaining brigade, Colonel George Buell's, and support Harker.[32]

The Third Brigade reached Gordon's Mill, a dozen miles from Chattanooga, at 4:30 p.m. and began digging fortifications. The grist mill was a prominent local landmark on the west bank West Chickamauga Creek where the La Fayette Road forded the creek. Harker sent a courier on a fast horse to General Wood, emphasizing his brigade's exposed position and his intention to withdraw at dark. However, a 6 p.m. dispatch from Wood directed Harker to hold his position, because Colonel Buell's brigade was coming to reinforce him. When Wood arrived at 10 p.m., it was dark and he could easily see the rebel campfires across the creek. The fires illuminated a sizable part of the eastern sky and indicated to Wood that "the foe was present in considerable force." Harker assumed his brigade had been pushing cavalry pickets, when in reality it had been Bragg's rearguard his men confronted. With the Confederates all around in strength, Harker was grateful to be reinforced. Opdycke was summoned and arrived just after 1 a.m. "My isolated condition was," Harker wrote, "a precarious one." Wood later praised Harker for displaying "great judgement, skill and gallantry combined." Harker had found the Confederate Army of the Tennessee.[33]

With a battle looming, water would be important. It had been hot and dry for three weeks. While on the La Fayette Road the afternoon of the 11th, Charlie Harker had noted in a dispatch to headquarters, "There is no good water for a camp between here and Rossville." To anyone commanding thousands of thirsty men, horses and mules this should have been important information.[34]

The next day, September 12, small groups of rebel cavalry pickets began a disconcerting sniping along the Third Brigade's front and flanks at Gordon's Mill. Harker decided to test their resolve by sending one company from each regiment across Chickamauga Creek and down the La Fayette Road. The companies were deployed on either side of the road and advanced rapidly. After passing the brigade picket line, enemy skirmishers were encountered and bullets whistled through the air. After driving the dismounted enemy horsemen a half mile, the blue skirmish line stumbled into a Confederate artillery battery. The men halted and dropped to the ground as enemy shells burst overhead.[35]

Hearing the artillery open, Colonel Harker rushed forward with three regiments and a section of the 6th Ohio Artillery. In an attempt to capture the enemy battery, Harker sent the 3rd Kentucky to the left of the road, the 125th Ohio to the right and the 64th Ohio straight ahead with the skirmishers. The enemy battery withdrew. Harker's men advanced about one and a half miles into the woods beyond Gordon's Mill where they met Bill Hazen's brigade—including the 41st Ohio—from Major General John Palmer's division on its own reconnaissance. Opdycke was pleasantly surprised. Their next meeting would be under more severe circumstances. The Third Brigade returned to the mill having suffered three or four wounded.[36]

On the 13th, Harker took the 125th Ohio to Crawfish Springs, a couple air miles southwest and one of the few good sources of water. Companies A, C and H manned the outposts with the 4th U.S. Cavalry. The Ohioans uneventful stay lasted until the next morning. When the regiment returned to Lee and Gordon's, Colonel Harker took the 125th and 64th Ohio across Chickamauga Creek again on a reconnaissance for about two miles, driving off a cavalry squadron. Three men in the 64th were wounded. Opdycke was invigorated by the action, writing, "This energy and activity suits me." Later in the day, a column of dust was observed five miles off to the left and Harker deduced that the Confederates were beyond Pigeon Mountain but still east of Chickamauga Creek. Rosecrans was informed. An impatient Opdycke wished the enemy would consolidate their forces and fight.[37]

The untested volunteer soldiers of the 125th sensed an impending fight. "We had premonitions of an approaching storm," Lieutenant Ralsa Rice wrote. The prospect of battle weighed heavily on everyone's mind. All was quiet on the 17th, but artillery firing was heard on the right. Twenty rounds of extra ammunition, in addition to the usual 40, was issued to each man in the brigade. A roll call of the 125th showed 16 officers and 298 men present for duty.[38]

About noon on the 18th, Harker was notified that an enemy column was advancing on Colonel Buell's men on the Third Brigade's right. Eventually, dust was seen rising from the La Fayette Road across the creek. Directly across the Chickamauga, the ground was level and clear within a 1000 yard square and beyond that was dense woods. When gray infantry broke cover, Harker was temporarily deceived by what he thought was a flag of truce until the enemy column deployed in a line of battle. When the Southerners were in range, Harker had the 6th Ohio battery open fire. The Johnnies retired to the woods. An enemy battery opened fire on Buell's brigade and again the 6th Ohio fired, silencing the rebels. The Third Brigade spent the afternoon at the barricades, ready to fight. Sharpshooting and skirmishing continued. Artillery fire was heard off to the left in the distance.[39]

The Chickamauga wilderness south of Chattanooga was no general's choice for a battle. West Chickamauga Creek was deep, the banks either rocky and tree lined, or steep and swampy. Even during the dry summer of 1863, the Chickamauga was deep enough to limit crossing to the fords present along its course. The valley along the west bank of the creek was level in spots, rolling in others. Much of the terrain was covered by a dense wooded thicket composed of low growth dogwood, oak, cedar and pine, clogged with berry briars, and honeysuckle, poison oak and trumpet vines. Occasionally the undergrowth gave way to mature forests of oak and pine. It was poor country for any kind of agriculture except subsistence farming. Trees were cut or girdled to produce haphazard fields of sparse corn laced with decaying stumps. The inhabitants, whose speech was almost unintelligible to Yankees, lived in one or two room log cabins, with perhaps a barn or outbuilding completing their farmsteads. The Rossville-LaFayette Road cut through the center of the valley west of the creek, almost acting as a boundary between the dense, low land along the Creek and the higher more open ground to the west. General Thomas described the ground between the LaFayette Road and Chickamauga Creek as "so dense it is difficult to see fifty paces ahead." Both armies were stumbling toward one of the war's largest battles in this nearly impossible terrain.[40]

4

CHICKAMAUGA, SATURDAY, SEPTEMBER 19

By the evening of September 17, all four corps of the Army of the Cumberland were in position to support each other in case of attack. McCook's Corps anchored the right flank from Bailey's Crossroads near Steven's Gap to Frick's Gap of Lookout Mountain. George Thomas' Corps was in the center in the vicinity of Pond Spring in the valley of the West Branch of Chickamauga Creek. Crittenden's Corps compromised the left flank of Rosecrans' army from the vicinity of Lee and Gordon's south to a point east of Crawfish Springs. General Wood's two brigades on the scene—Harker and Buell's—held the left flank of the Union army. Harker's brigade was entrenched astride the La Fayette Road where it crossed Chickamauga Creek. Gordon Granger's Reserve Corps was at Rossville, directly south of Chattanooga, holding the gaps in Missionary Ridge that served as Rosecrans' line of retreat for the 60,000 Union soldiers south of the Tennessee River.[1]

Braxton Bragg had let the opportunity to strike the dispersed Union army slip through his fingers. Undeterred, he revised his plan. The right flank of the Army of the Tennessee was near Lee and Gordon's Mill and the left at La Fayette. The rail head where Longstreet's men from the Army of Northern Virginia would arrive was at Ringgold, Georgia, directly east of Lee and Gordon's. Bragg ordered a shift of his army to his right, and an attack on Crittenden's left aimed at Chattanooga. Success would allow the rebels into Rosecrans' rear and put them squarely between the Union army and Chattanooga.[2]

Rosecrans' countered this risk to his left flank by shifting his army northeast beginning on the afternoon of the 17th. Crittenden extended his left flank north along the La Fayette Road by relocating the divisions of Major General John Palmer and Brigadier Horatio Van Cleve from the right of Wood's division to the left. Bragg's planned attack on Crittenden was set for the 18th, but poor roads and persistent resistance by Union cavalry delayed the Southern flanking movement.[3]

Companies A and H from the 125th joined other companies from Harker's brigade as part of a strong picket line east of Chickamauga Creek. Around noon on the 18th, heavy skirmishing erupted, but Harker's skirmishers sought cover in rifle pits and behind trees and held. Lieutenant Charlie Clark noted proudly in his regimental history, "125th men probably fired the first shot by our infantry in the battle." The first shot would have many claimants.[4]

After dark on the 18th, Thomas and McCook pulled their corps back and marched north by the left flank. Thomas reached the hardscrabble Kelly farmstead, and its little cornfield hacked out of the woods, about daybreak. McCook slowly followed Thomas.

The Union line now extended beyond Bragg's right flank. "Bragg's plan of fighting," Clark wrote in his history, "with his back to Chattanooga and driving Rosecrans up the valley, was no longer practicable."[5]

The sun rose on the 19th over the fog shrouded valley of Chickamauga Creek where thousands of men in blue, gray and butternut were only a few hundred yards apart. During most of the night Harker's men at Gordon's Mill could hear rebels on the move across the creek. The Third Brigade was roused at 3 a.m. to stand at arms. Nothing happened until daylight when Harker's pickets across the Creek once again became involved in brisk skirmishing with the enemy. The bluecoats around the Mill were expecting a battle, but nothing significant developed. Across the Creek, at 8 a.m., a mass of enemy troops was seen several hundred yards distant in the bottom land slipping through trees toward the Union left. General Wood ordered the 6th Ohio Artillery to harass them, another "first shot" of the battle. The Johnnies disappeared, intent on massing where they believed the Union left was, not on attacking at Gordon's Mill.[6]

Had Bragg wheeled to attack toward Gordon's Mill in strength, his superiority in numbers would have easily crushed Crittenden's corps. Instead, Brigadier John Bannon's infantry division, from Thomas' corps, probing east in the fog early on the 19th, bumped into enemy cavalry, and then infantry, two miles north of Bragg's right about the same time the 6th Ohio Artillery went into action. Within an hour, a confused battle began in earnest in the woods and thickets west of the Chickamauga. The roar of Bannon's musketry intensified and gun smoke rose high into the clearing sky to the north. The tactical situation had changed. "Bragg was fighting with his *face* towards Chattanooga," Clark explained, "and his opponent in full possession of the roads leading there." Thus far, Old Rosy had effectively checked Bragg's flank attack.[7]

Those bluecoats on Harker's skirmish line on the east bank of the creek engaged in increasingly heavy skirmishing with their foes. Harker's regiments nervously waited at the grist mill for over three hours, each infantryman weighed down with extra cartridges and the field officers waiting by their saddled horses for the order to move. Anticipation weighed heavily on all ranks. Random shots from Confederate sharpshooters were an unnerving aggravation. In the early afternoon, a contraband crossed the lines and told Wood that the Confederate troops moving across his front were Confederate Brigadier General Bushrod Johnson's division of Longstreet's corps.[8]

At 3 p.m., a staff officer brought Harker orders. The Colonel leapt on his horse bringing the entire command to attention. With the order to "Forward-Double Quick-March!" moving down the ranks, Wood's two brigades faced left and headed up the La Fayette Road toward the sound of the gunfire. One of McCook's brigades took their place. Dust from the road was thick and heavy, and brushfires started by artillery shells smoldered, poisoning the hot air and choking the soldiers North and South alike. Canteens were quickly drained of precious water. As Wood's division marched north, its progress was slowed by the wounded and not so wounded seeking the field hospitals at Crawfish Springs and its reliable water. Wood's column stretched to almost a mile as dehydrated men dropped out in the heat. After moving north three quarters of a mile a leaden hail of spent bullets began to fall among the men. To the front, the voices of thousands of combatants blended with musket and artillery fire to create a ceaseless buzz of battle.[9]

At about 3:30 p.m., Wood's men arrived at the Viniard farm, one and a half miles from Lee and Gordon's. Ordered to take a position on the right of Van Cleve's division, Wood wasn't certain where that was. No staff officer was present to provide directions.

The fight was in the woods to the east of the road and it was impossible to see dispositions of friend or foe. The mass of wounded men and ambulances searching for the rear was proof of the need for reinforcements. As Wood rode ahead of his division in search of directions, fellow division commander, Brigadier General Jefferson C. Davis from McCook's corps found him. Davis asked Wood to send a brigade to support Colonel Hans Heg's brigade, heavily engaged in the woods around a log school house just 50 yards east of the La Fayette Road.[10]

Crittenden was located and consented. His chief of staff, Colonel Lyne Starling, led Harker's brigade up the road to the log school house where it deployed in two lines facing east. The 125th was in the brigade's front battle line on the left flank by the school house. To the right, the 64th Ohio extended the line south. The 3rd Kentucky and 65th Ohio formed a second rank just west of the road. The ground in front of Harker was gently rising and covered with dense undergrowth, perfect for an ambush. Adding to the confusion, somewhere in the front were broken federal brigades retiring in disorder. Harker ordered the regimental commanders to hold fire until all the friendly troops were in their rear.[11]

His regiment about to experience serious combat for the first time, Colonel Opdycke gave brief instructions to the men he had groomed for a year for this moment. "Men of the 125th Ohio, if I or others fall, stand in the ranks till victory is ours.... If you love your country, aim low—aim well." No man should leave the ranks to care for a wounded comrade, Opdycke cautioned, since the best way to help them was to win and hold the battlefield.[12]

The battle Harker's men had marched into was very fluid, and before anyone took a step forward, news arrived that the enemy had broken through between Heg's brigade's left and Van Cleve's division's right. Wood directed Harker to change position again obliquing his line to face northeast. Harker had barely competed his realignment when new information indicated the enemy was on the La Fayette Road and moving south. Harker recognized this new development would "expose my left flank and rear." This time Wood had the Third Brigade refuse its left so it was at right angles to the road forming a line with an apex facing the enemy. In this formation, Harker sent his brigade up the road at a run. Wood remained at Harker's side for the first half mile until he was confident the young Colonel had command of the situation. In his report, Wood indicated that he had "perfect confidence" in Harker's ability to handle his brigade. Wood turned around and rode back down the road to bring Buell's brigade forward.[13]

The 125th and 64th made good progress as they labored in a northeasterly direction through the undergrowth and timber—"a perfect jungle" in Harker's estimation—north of the Viniard farm field. It was a terrible battle ground of dense woods clogged with heavy undergrowth and choked with thick powder smoke. "No one commander could see the flanks of his regiment," an officer in McCook's corps recalled. Harker's brigade was on its own now, groping north on the road. The mass of retreating and panicked Union soldiers heading for the rear was unnerving. "There was very great confusion among the troops which had been engaged," Harker later wrote, "and no one seemed to have any definite idea of our own lines or the position of the enemy. I was compelled, therefore, to resort to my own judgment alone and be guided by the general direction of the firing."[14]

The Third Brigade unknowingly marched straight into portions of three Confederate brigades crossing the La Fayette Road. Harker's men took fire from the front and flank.

Harker deployed the 65th Ohio and 3rd Kentucky to Opdycke's left on the west side of the road, creating a single brigade front to meet the threat. The 125th continued northeasterly into woods "so dense we could see but a few rods in any direction" in the thick smoke, that made the fog of battle tangible. The 64th Ohio drifted even further east while Harker took the 65th and 3rd Kentucky straight up the road.[15]

Harker's brigade had stumbled into the unprotected flank of Confederate Brigadier General Bushrod Johnson's Provisional Division, newly arrived from Virginia. The rebels had broken through the Union line between Van Cleve's division and Heg's brigade and penetrated as far west of the La Fayette Road as the Dyer farm. Van Cleve's division fell back. Two Confederate brigades, Colonel John Fulton and Brigadier Henry Clayton's were attacking in a northwest direction. Confederate Brigadier John Gregg's rebels were moving southwest on the east side of the LaFayette Road trying to turn Heg's flank, while attempting to maintain their organization in the timber and undergrowth.[16]

About 200 yards from the road, the 125th Ohio exited the heavy undergrowth into more open timber and surprised Gregg's Tennessee brigade. Opdycke sent word to Harker that there were Johnnies in his front. Due to the denseness of the woods and powder smoke, Harker could not visually direct his entire brigade. Showing his confidence in Opdycke, Harker ordered him to oversee both right hand regiments and clear any rebels in his front. The 125th's appearance startled two exhausted Tennessee regiments that had been struggling for nearly two hours to fight in the heat and dense brush. Seemingly simultaneous volleys were exchanged. "Our volley had been delivered an instant in advance of that of the enemy," Lieutenant Clark remembered, "and his loss in wounded and killed far exceeded that of the 125th." The Southerners broke, some running into the blue line to surrender, the rest retreating toward the creek. "Got in rear of Reb line and chased a number of regiments," Opdycke wrote of the action, "I took three prisoners, Adjutant [Capt. Edward G.] Whitesides, three and others three…. Firing severe. We were surrounded." In that initial volley, Ordnance Sergeant James Morris was killed and 11 wounded. Private William Meek was one of the wounded and left for dead. Nine rebels including one officer were captured.[17]

On the 125th's right, the 64th Ohio encountered the Confederates "somewhat detached from their main line." The 64th's Colonel Alexander McIlvain recalled, "I immediately engaged them, and, after a brisk fire of nearly half an hour, they fled in confusion." Twenty prisoners were taken while five Ohioans were wounded. General Gregg was shot from his horse by skirmishers from the 64th.[18]

While Opdycke's men were engaged, Harker continued north with the left two regiments in a line at right angle to the road. After only 100 yards, the Yankees collided with three Arkansas regiments that appeared on Harker's left flank. The Southerner's lashed out at the left of the 3rd Kentucky. With parade ground precision, the two federal regiments returned fire. "Soon found the foe on every front," Colonel Henry Dunlap of the 3rd wrote, "fought at every point of the compass; no confusion; changed front forward and to the rear in good order under fire." Harker responded by sending the 65th at the Confederates and the Johnnies fell back into the vegetation east of the La Fayette Road. The Kentuckians secured 118 prisoners. Dunlap lost one killed and nine wounded.[19]

Continuing to advance under the forest canopy west of the La Fayette Road, the 3rd Kentucky and 65th Ohio encountered a Tennessee regiment facing west in the open pine woods on a ridge on the Brotherton farm. Harker's boys emerged from the brush just 40 yards from the Tennessean's left flank and rear. "We discovered a line of troops moving by the left flank in the direction of the left wing of my regiment," wrote Confederate Lieutenant Colonel Watt Floyd of the 17th Tennessee. "Before we could determine who they were, the commands 'halt, front,' were given by the commander of the leading regiment, and they immediately discharged a volley at our men. A general stampede of our men ensued. So sudden and unexpected was the attack from our rear that every man seemed to act for himself, regardless of orders." The 17th Tennessee ran 200 yards to the La Fayette Road to the protection of their brigade front. The 65th Ohio took 11 officers and 60 enlisted Tennesseans prisoner, including its wounded major.[20]

The Third Brigade had gone a half a mile since their first contact with Confederates. At that very moment, Bushrod Johnson was personally attempting to rally his worn and surprised soldiers. A gap in the brigade line had opened between the 3rd Kentucky and the 125th Ohio. As Opdycke was deploying skirmishers, he received an order from Harker to rejoin the rest of the brigade, and close the gap.[21]

Two Tennessee regiments counter-attacked the 3rd Kentucky. Bullets zipped and ricocheted; clipping leaves, severing vines, breaking small branches, and plowing furrows in the dirt. All but one mounted officer in the 3rd was unhorsed while Charlie Harker lost two horses in short order. The 65th formed on the Kentuckians' left giving Harker's line a somewhat convex shape toward the enemy. Lieutenant Colonel Horatio Whitbeck commanding the 65th along with five line officers and at least 30 enlisted men fell quickly. It took courage and strict training for men to stand and take fire that could come from any direction. "In this position there was some of the most brilliant fighting that it has ever been my fortune to witness," a proud Colonel Harker wrote in his official report. The 65th Ohio held, and suffered more casualties than the rest of the brigade combined that afternoon and took over 200 prisoners. The Confederates withdrew. Colonel Opdycke disengaged and brought the 125th and 64th out of the timber efficiently. "This gallant officer brought up his regiment to me," Harker noted in his report, "closing the gap that necessarily existed, with but slight loss, while he did good service in punishing the enemy." The 125th tallied one killed and 11 wounded. "Being now completely detached from my division, and having cleared everything on my front and left," Harker wrote in his official report, "I resolved to rejoin my division." Only later would it become clear that Harker's brigade had been fighting within Bragg's lines. The Third Brigade retired to the Viniard farm.[22]

Among Harker's prisoners were Texans from James Longstreet's Corps. Many wore regular Confederate uniforms, which differentiated them from western Confederates who wore piecemeal combinations of civilian and military clothing. One of Harker's boys cockily asked a rebel, "How does Longstreet like the Western Yankees?" The unimpressed Texan retorted, "You'll get enough of Longstreet before tomorrow night!"[23]

Harker's tenacious drive up the La Fayette Road against Bushrod Johnson's unsupported left flank helped convince the Confederate to pull his division back across the La Fayette Road. "This advance of my division," Johnson—a rare Ohio-born officer turned secessionist—later recorded, "unsupported by any movement on my left [of Confederate troops] was pushed quite as far as was judicious." By sunset Johnson's men were 600 yards east of the La Fayette Road. Harker had pulled back to the southwest—a respectable distance between two wary adversaries.[24]

When Harker's brigade went up the La Fayette Road, Wood's other brigade, 29-year-old Colonel George Buell's, was left at the Viniard farm with no instructions. Buell had command of the brigade for just four months. He faced his men east toward the woods and waited. Not 10 minutes after Harker headed up the road, Yankees retreating in disorder poured out of the timber and undergrowth. The fugitives streamed through Buell's brigade carrying it back across the La Fayette Road, behind Harker's rear, closely pursued by Southerners. General Wood personally rallied Buell's brigade and led it forward. Wood's horse was killed and an aide was shot at Wood's side. Massed artillery from Wood's division west of the road, firing shells with short fuses, slowed the enemy and broke their formations, but not before they came within 50 yards of the big guns. The Johnnies launched a new assault 10 minutes later, but the concentrated fire of several batteries and infantry ended it. "The fire was most effective and deadly," one observer wrote. During this action, from 4 to 6:30 p.m., the 6th Ohio Artillery, from Harker's brigade, fired 209 shells, 20 of which were the shotgun-like canister.[25]

With the fighting in the local area sputtering out at sunset, Harker was able to take up a position to the left and rear of Colonel Buell's reformed brigade, west of the La Fayette Road. They went into the line on the forward slope of a low hill and threw up log barricades. To the front was a cleared field of the Brotherton farm, eight to 10 acres, which the enemy had previously advanced and then retired. So fierce and confused was the fighting on this end of the Union line that the trees were scarred from bullets and shrapnel from every point of the compass.[26]

The rebels were in the woods beyond the Brotherton field. Casualties from the fighting had remained where they fell, and after sunset soldiers, blue and gray, came out to search the field for wounded comrades. After this brief respite to aid the wounded, sporadic musket fire resumed. Although the night was marked by a chilly north wind as a cold front moved through north Georgia, no campfires were permitted. The men of the 125th Ohio, some without blankets, waited, cold and hungry with muskets at the ready and their weary muscles stiffening in the cold. Across most of the battlefield, wounded men groaned, cried for water, and if smoldering fires in the woods reached them, screamed. By 6 a.m. sunrise, frost would blanket the valley and the wounded left on the field would be freezing."[27]

Overall, Harker's brigade had been lucky that day. "Nearly every brigade in our army had been in action, most of them under fire much longer and suffered greater losses than our own," wrote Lieutenant Clark, "We were favored by fortune in not being sent in until late in the day, and also in the opportunity to do good effective work with comparatively light losses."[28]

That evening, Rosecrans telegraphed the War Department. "The army is in excellent condition and spirits and by the blessing of Providence the defeat of the enemy will be tomorrow." Rosecrans' optimism made President Lincoln, disappointed too often in the past by his generals, uneasy. Rosecrans had a captured Texas captain brought to headquarters. The stalwart Texan gave no information and had a blunt and prophetic warning for Rosecrans, "We are going to whip you most tremendously in this fight."[29]

Rosecrans called a council of war for his senior commanders at the widow Eliza Glenn's cabin, a half mile west of the La Fayette Road behind the center of the Union line. No general disputed the obvious—that the terrain made the valley a poor place to fight. The battle had been fought by feeding in brigades piecemeal. While the Union corps commanders lacked an accurate count of the day's casualties, all agreed the losses were heavy. On the positive side, the federals had managed to cobble together a compact, continuous battle line and they still held the La Fayette Road. At one point during the morning, a two mile gap had existed between Thomas on the left flank and Crittenden in the center, but Bragg failed to capitalize on it. The Union line had held, although most of the actual four square mile battlefield was occupied by the enemy.[30]

Charles Dana, the former journalist tasked with reporting Rosecrans' actions to the War Department, was at the conference and his presence dampened talk of a retreat. In reality, a withdrawal in the dark through McFarland's Gap could in itself be disastrous. An exhausted George Thomas, drifting between sleep and wakefulness, pressed for reinforcements for his corps on the left. The discussion alternated between a general hope Bragg would withdraw and the possibility that another day on the defensive might punish the attacking Confederates sufficiently to produce a victory. Rosecrans decided to stay on the defensive along the present line.[31]

A glaring omission at Rosecrans' council of war was the lack of input from colonels and generals on the front lines. Historian Glenn Tucker later called this "a surprising isolation from those who had been on the actual firing line." In addition, none of the generals in blue seemed concerned that some of the day's bag of prisoners included men from Longstreet's corps, most recently in Robert E. Lee's Army of Northern Virginia. Rosecrans issued orders, through his chief of staff, James Garfield, to adjust the lines and refuse the flanks. There were eight federal divisions in the line, and two of Crittenden's divisions, Wood's and Van Cleve's were placed in reserve. Three of Granger's Reserve Corps brigades were in camp at Rossville, Georgia, just four miles away if needed. Rosecrans, with the weight of command heavy on his shoulders, was too tense to sleep and paced in front of the Glenn cabin eating hard crackers and drinking what was said to be cold tea.[32]

In the rear of the army, surgeons and their assistants at the field hospitals worked by the light of blazing fires treating wounds and providing food, water and blankets. Medicinal whiskey circulated. All too frequently, a motionless form was added to the long line of dead. "A field hospital just after a battle is the most gruesome and harrowing picture presented by the changing panorama of war," recalled one member of Harker's brigade who experienced it that night. "Words have no meaning when one attempts to portray the awful scenes of suffering and death."[33]

That evening, Tom Wood and Charley Harker, both West Pointers, were overheard discussing the volunteer soldiers in their command. Wood had shared the professional soldier's disdain for volunteers, who were often judged undisciplined and unreliable. Wood's mind had changed. "If I were given my choice between regulars and volunteers, I would choose volunteers troops. They will 'stick'; you can fight them as long as you please ... they will fight as long as they can pull a trigger."[34]

5

CHICKAMAUGA, SUNDAY MORNING, SEPTEMBER 20

In the early morning hours of September 20, the battle lines of the Army of the Cumberland were adjusted in accordance to Rosecrans' orders. Shortly after midnight, Wood's two brigades—part of the army reserve—moved a mile west of Brotherton's farm, past the Dyer tanyard, to a ridge that was part of the eastern edge of Missionary Ridge. The 125th camped on the slope, ate a hasty meal and crowded around bonfires built to hold the evening chill at bay for a few hours' rest. Water was limited, but during the night some kindly Indiana cavalrymen filled 400 canteens for Harker's thirsty men.[1]

When General Thomas arrived back at his corps headquarters at 2 a.m., he learned that he lacked the manpower to extend the left flank of his corps—and therefore the entire army—to the La Fayette Road. Thomas asked Rosecrans for Major General James Negley's division, which had been detached from Thomas' corps earlier, and now held a position near the center of the army's front. While it would have been more logical to send Wood or Van Cleve instead of pulling Negley out of the battle line, Rosecrans agreed to Thomas' request. Rosecrans, preoccupied and worried, did not immediately send the orders.[2]

Lieutenant General James Longstreet had arrived at the Ringgold, Georgia, rail head Saturday afternoon. It wasn't until 11 p.m. the Longstreet located Bragg's headquarters. To accommodate the reinforcements from Virginia, Bragg reordered his army by dividing it into two wings of about 20,000 men each. The right wing would be commanded by Lieutenant General Leonidas Polk and the left by James Longstreet, whose arrival was accompanied by one of his battle-tested infantry divisions. Since Rosecrans was only thinking defensively, Bragg would have the offensive initiative. Orders were prepared for a daylight attack beginning on the extreme right with Polk's corps and rolling from right to left down the Confederate line. Considering that Bragg had just re-organized his command structure, it was a risky and ambitious plan for the thick woods and undergrowth along Chickamauga Creek. "On the most open parts of the Confederate side of the field, one's vision could not reach farther than the length of a brigade," Longstreet—who would have to fight this battle by instinct—later recalled.[3]

Rosecrans remained at his headquarters a half mile west of the La Fayette Road. Early Sunday morning, after Catholic mass, Old Rosy was ready to ride his lines. Although nattily attired in black pants, white vest and blue coat devoid of rank, there was an air of gloom about the general when he needed to project confidence. A Cincinnati newspaper correspondent, William Bickham, was present, and recalled: "Rosecrans is usually

Five. Chickamauga, Sunday Morning, September 20

brisk, nervous, powerful of presence, and to see him silent or absorbed in what looked like gloomy contemplation, filled me with indefinable dread." Rosecrans mounted a rawboned gray horse named Robey, and without a word of encouragement to his staff, cantered north to inspect his lines, beginning with Thomas' dispositions on the left flank. After confirming for himself Thomas' need for more men, Rosecrans at last ordered Negley's division from its position near the center of the Union line at the Brotherton farmstead to reinforce Thomas, although it would have made more sense to send one of the reserve divisions or one of McCook's.[4]

Leonidas Polk, the Episcopal bishop turned Confederate lieutenant general, commanding of the right wing of Bragg's army, saw no reason for haste on that Sabbath morning. His opening attack was to begin at dawn, before 6 a.m. local time. But procrastination was Polk's constant companion, and it was nearly 8:30 a.m. when his troops finally moved. Thomas had put the night to good use digging in around the Kelly farm. His men were exhausted, but had some protection behind a log and earth barricade. One of Negley's brigades, Brigadier John Beatty's, reached Thomas at daylight and was placed in a thin line on Thomas' left flank. When Polk's infantry finally attacked they pushed through Beatty's brigade within an hour. George Thomas had to rapidly shift brigades to block the Confederates from getting into his rear.[5]

Harker's and Buell's brigades along with one from Van Cleve's division, Colonel Sidney Barnes,' were directed to relieve the remainder Negley's division at the Brotherton farmstead. Wood brought his division forward to a ridge a quarter mile behind Negley's men and halted, unsure of where to deploy. He stubbornly refused entreaties by other commanders on the scene to advance further forward, insisting that Rosecrans' order, which came through General Crittenden, placed his division on the ridge. When Rosecrans arrived and found Wood had not replaced Negley in the line, he told Wood to "Hurry up and relieve General Negley on the line." An enduring controversy developed over whether Rosecrans lost his temper with Wood. "I certainly did not feel censured by Gen. Rosecrans." Wood wrote after the war. Either way, Wood was a professional and he followed orders. Negley, who was severely ill with diarrhea and shouldn't have been on the field, initiated a glacially slow movement toward the hard pressed Union left. For his part, Rosecrans now appeared outwardly cheerful and confident, however, some veterans of the Army of the Cumberland saw something else. "I did not like the way he looked," one soldier later wrote. Another recalled, "He was in a bad plight."[6]

Harker's brigade was deployed in two lines in the center of Wood's divisional line. The 125th was behind the 64th with the 65th on its right, behind the 3rd Kentucky. Colonel Barnes' Brigade was on Harker's left and Buell's on the right. Harker ordered Opdycke to take command of the second line, the 125th and 65th. Rebel pickets began sniping at Wood's skirmishers as soon as the Yankees reached the Brotherton field. On his own initiative one of Buell's regimental commanders, Colonel Frederick Bartleson, impetuously led his 100th Illinois in a charge on the annoying rebel skirmishers. Unknown to Bartleson, he had charged into the vanguard of Confederate Brigadier General Bushrod Johnson's massed infantry division. An unseen Southern artillery battery firing canister and enfilading rebel musket fire crushed the Illinoisans and left Bartleson severely wounded. In short order, this disastrous little fight degenerated into ragged skirmishing. During lulls in the local firing, the increasing roar of battle could be heard from Thomas' end of the line.[7]

By mid-morning at army headquarters, an increasingly nervous and befuddled Rosecrans was shifting multiple units around the battlefield like chess pieces to support the hard pressed left flank. "I have known him ... to grow so excited, vehement and incoherent as to utterly confound the messenger," reported William Shanks, a *New York Herald* correspondent and keen observer of Rosecrans. "In great danger, as in small things, this nervousness incapacitated him from the intelligible direction of his officers or effect execution of his plans." Between 10:15 and 10:30, the Union commander issued orders for no fewer than four divisions to change position, mostly to support Thomas' corps which bore the brunt of the current fighting. Between 10:30 and 11 a.m., Rosecrans ordered two brigades of Major General Phil Sheridan's infantry division of McCook's corps to Thomas. This left only one of McCook's divisions and a brigade on the federal line south of Tom Wood's men. At 10:45, recognizing the need to fill gaps in the line caused by these maneuvers, Rosecrans began issuing orders to correct the situation.[8]

An inexperienced, young aide from army headquarters, carrying orders to General Thomas, thought he detected a gap in the Union line between Wood's and Reynold's divisions. The aide made no further examination, and upon reaching army headquarters, diligently reported what he believed he saw. Rosecrans was attempting to reduce the length of his line by shifting units to the left. One division ordered to move was Brigadier General John Brannon's division on Wood's left. Had Brannon moved, a gap could exist between Wood and Reynolds. However, in the inevitable fog of war, Brannon had not moved. General Garfield, the chief of staff, was fully occupied furiously writing orders to fulfill Rosecrans rapid-fire instructions. Rosecrans turned to another less experienced aide to write the order for Wood to move and close the gap in the line. The urgent order for General Wood read, "The general commanding directs that you close up on [Major General Joseph] Reynolds as fast as possible, and support him." General Crittenden, who was loitering at headquarters, received the order and passed it to his chief of staff, Colonel Starling, without reading it. Starling dispatched an aide to Wood with the order.[9]

General Wood's brigades were comfortably secure behind a low, log breastworks in the woods west of the La Fayette Road overlooking the Brotherton farm. Wood's infantrymen and their officers focused their attention on the woods across the open field where they knew the Confederates were concealed. Their front was quiet. About 11 a.m., Crittenden's orderly found Wood and Twentieth Corps commander, Major General Alexander McCook, sitting under a tree behind Buell's brigade at the southern end of the division line. The orderly gave the order to a colonel on Wood's staff who signed for it. Wood read it and showed the order to McCook who told Wood he should immediately move out by the left flank. McCook would have Brigadier General Jefferson Davis fill the gap left by Wood's departure. Tom Wood set about implementing his orders. The actual order was kept by the staffer for preservation, tucked in the man's sword sash. Wood and McCook interpreted the order to mean that Wood should pull his men out of the line, march north behind Brigadier General John Brannon's division, which was on his immediate left and between Wood and Reynolds, and act in support of Reynolds men. Rosecrans' hasty order would become one of the most famous of the war.[10]

A major from McCook's staff was present and left this recollection. "As Brannon's whole division intervened between Wood and Reynolds, whom he had been ordered to support, no one present thought of any other meaning than that taken by Wood." After the battle, Wood would become one of the potential scapegoats for the outcome. Some argued that Wood should have questioned the order and waited for clarification since he knew no gap existed. Most of the soldiers in Wood's brigades defended him, contending that he did his best to obey the tenor of the order for haste in moving toward the sound of battle. Wilbur Hinman, veteran of the 65th Ohio, wrote, "Its language fully justified the wrong construction given to it by Wood." General Wood had his own opinion of the thought he should disobey Rosecrans' order: "The commander of an army in which such a view of insubordination should be dominant could scarcely be envied."[11]

First Colonel Barnes and then Harker obeyed orders to withdraw without question. The Third Brigade marched at the double quick by the left flank north into the woods on the wagon track known as the Glenn-Kelly Road. Sharp skirmishing erupted along the main battle line to the east as Harker's men jogged up the road. Colonel George Buell, the civilian engineer and a cousin of General Don Carlos Buell, balked at his orders because his skirmishers were engaged with rebels and some of the wounded from the 100th Illinois were still lying between the lines. Wood agreed to leave Buell's skirmishers in place until they were relieved by McCook's men.[12]

At that moment 11,000 Confederates in eight brigades under James Longstreet's direction were compressed into just 70 acres, 600 yards east of the Brotherton farm. This hammer blow was masked by timber and undergrowth. When Polk's attack on the Union left bogged down, a hastily revised Confederate battle plan called Longstreet's men to punch through the federal line on the Union right to the La Fayette Road. Once in possession of the road, the attackers were to turn north, rolling the federal line up and getting in the rear of George Thomas' strongly fortified position at the Kelly farm a mile north. Polk had gone from being the strike force to merely a diversion for Longstreet's attack on the Union center. With the arrival of Longstreet's reinforcements, Bragg had as many infantrymen as Rosecrans.[13]

Confederate skirmishers were already dueling with their Union counterparts at 11:10 when the gray onslaught began to move forward. Jefferson Davis' division of McCook's corps was still attempting to stretch itself to fill the gaps left by Wood and Sheridan, and was directly in the path of Bushrod Johnson's Confederate division which was leading the assault. The rebels scattered the Union pickets, and within minutes, Davis' division was routed. The Confederate attack caught George Buell's brigade in motion and fractured it, driving most of Buell's men toward Dyer's farm and the high ground west of it. Only the 58th Indiana, which Buell had personally organized, remained on the road. Courageously, Buell stood on the breastworks, shouting and trying unsuccessfully to rally his men. To the distraught Buell, it appeared that his poor brigade had been "swept from the field." Five brigades of bluecoats were routed by Longstreet's attack. General Brannon, whose division was on the northern edge of the gap in the Union line, refused his right regiments to try and protect his flank.[14]

McCook's corps fell back. Some of his troops, including Phil Sheridan's division, tried to rejoin the fight later in the day with no success, eventually they retiring to Rossville. The other reserve division from Crittenden's corps, Brigadier General Horatio Van Cleve's, was routed. Both organized and broken units fell back to a ridge west of Dyer's large cornfield. Some stood to fight while most fled over the ridge to the Dry Valley road that led to Rossville. Crittenden himself watched the disaster unfold from Dyer's field and ordered the Northern artillery batteries there to retreat to the ridge where he hoped the infantry would rally to protect it. Twenty-six cannon were unlimbered where they could sweep Dyer's field in their front and shell the woods to the east.[15]

Within 20 minutes the rebels had crossed the La Fayette Road, rolled over the Brotherton farm and pushed into the woods east of the Dyer farm field. The Confederate brigades commanded by Colonel Cyrus Sugg, Brigadier General Evander McNair, Colonel James Sheffield and Brigadier Jerome Robertson had swept aside all Yankee opposition and were poised to sweep out of the shadowy gloom of the woods and into the bright, open field beyond. For the former Ohio Quaker, Bushrod Johnson, that Sunday would be the peak of his military career. "Our lines now emerged from the forest into open ground on the border of long open fields, over which the enemy were retreating," Johnson recalled. "The scene now presented was unmistakably grand." The Union artillery on the ridge was formidable, but the rebels could see few blue infantry standing to protect them which made the batteries ripe for capture.[16]

Federal wagon trains, artillery and panicked infantry units created a massive logjam as they crowded the Dry Valley Road as the main artery of retreat. Rosecrans and his headquarters staff were trying to reach General Thomas on the army's left. On the Valley Road they ran into a shower of canister and musketry from Bushrod Johnson's Confederates on the high ground above them. To many of those who saw him, Rosecrans had the look of a defeated man. "We are in a desperate situation," the War Department's man, Charles Dana, concluded at that moment. "The whole right of the army had apparently been routed.... I have never seen anything so crushing to mind as that scene." As Rosecrans continued up the Dry Valley Road, he encountered routed bluecoats closer to McFarland's Gap than he had expected. He could hear the cheers and musketry of the advancing rebels. "I became doubtful," he recorded, "whether the left had held its ground" and continued riding north toward Rossville."[17]

Two privates from the 125th arrived with rations from Chattanooga at sunrise on Sunday. James Morrison, teamster, and James Ramsey, wagon guard, decided to rest their mules before returning. When Longstreet's attack came, the two were caught in a stampede to the rear. The intrepid soldiers loaded their wagon with wounded and headed west, demonstrating more courage than those teamsters who cut their wagons free and rode way. Morrison's wagon caught on a sapling in the woods and Ramsey had to crawl underneath to cut the sapling with a dull hatchet. Freed, the duo managed to navigate through the jam of wagons, artillery and fugitives on the Dry Valley Road and reach the safety of Chattanooga.[18]

Many of the Army of the Cumberland's wounded were being collected at field hospitals near Crawfish Springs. However, the Springs were now three miles beyond the Union right and east of Missionary Ridge. The single, crowded road hindered movement of wounded to Chattanooga. Nevertheless, by Sunday morning 4500 of Saturday's casualties had been sent. When the Confederates broke through, they mistook the hospital flags for battle flags and shelled the hospital. Empty supply wagons parked nearby were pressed into service as ambulances and the wounded were hastily evacuated to Chattanooga.[19]

About 20 walking wounded men from Harker's brigade set out for Chattanooga on foot just 30 minutes before the enemy captured Crawfish Springs. "It was an excessively painful and fatiguing journey," one participant recalled. "All were more or less weakened by loss of blood, and some were only able to keep along by the constant assistance of their comrades. But we pressed on, fourteen long weary miles, and toward evening we reached the town, in a condition of utter exhaustion." In Chattanooga, all was in panic and a constant stream of casualties turned every house into a hospital. On the eve of the battle, there had been only sufficient medical supplies and space prepared for 500 wounded. Unable to locate a surgeon, Harker's men dressed their own wounds and lay down to sleep on a hard wood floor.[20]

After starting Harker and Buell's brigades north moments before the Confederate breakthrough, Tom Wood rode ahead to find General Reynolds division. He met George Thomas riding south in search of promised re-enforcements. Wood showed Thomas the order from Rosecrans and Thomas confirmed that General Reynolds didn't need any help, but the army's left flank did. Thomas readily agreed to assume responsibility for sending Wood north. Wood turned his horse around and rode down the road into chaos.[21]

General Crittenden's attempts to piece together an infantry support for his massed artillery west of Dyer's field had failed. Most of the stampeded bluecoats kept going through the artillery batteries and out of the battle. The artillerists alone couldn't stop the charging Southerners. When the guns were flanked on their right and the Southerners began picking off the battery horses, General Crittenden realized the position was untenable. Fifteen of the Union cannon fell to the enemy. Believing that Rosecrans and McCook were likely casualties, Crittenden decided it was his duty to ride to Chattanooga and see to its defense.[22]

Once he was past the rear of General Brannon's division, Colonel Harker halted his brigade on the Glenn-Kelly Road north of a small blacksmith forge to await orders. Stray musket rounds rattled through the leaves. One hundred yards north was the south slope of a low ridge on the Snodgrass farm. An excited lieutenant from Brannon's staff intercepted Harker and pressed for help with Brannon's now imperiled right flank. General Wood appeared, recognized the danger and, on his own initiative, agreed to the request. Harker turned his men about and formed a line of battle that was almost perpendicular to the main Northern battle line, facing south. The Third Brigade had only gone a short distance when they were fired on from the right. Through field glasses looking south, Wood could see the Dyer farm cornfield "swarming with enemy." Wood deduced that the Confederates were "seeking the rear of our solid line of battle." Although obviously outnumbered, General Wood decided to send Harker's four regiments right at the enemy in Dyer's field. In his official report, Wood explained, "The enemy, at all hazards, must be checked." One the 65th's men later wrote, "Harker's brigade was thrown out to check the enemy as one throws a piece of meat to a savage dog to gain time." Colonel Harker adjusted his line to face Dyer's cornfield. One hundred fifty yards in front was a low worm rail fence on the north end of the cornfield. The fence wouldn't offer much protection, but it was better than nothing. To the west, the Confederates were closing on a wooded knoll on Harker's flank. The rebel battle line was 350 yards beyond the fence.[23]

Bushrod Johnson's Confederates had swept across the Dyer cornfield by now. Following Johnson were three brigades from John Bell Hood's division from Lee's army: James Sheffield's Alabamans, Jerome Robertson's Texans and Henry Benning's Georgians. Benning's brigade turned north in the woods toward Brannon's division, now the right flank of the truncated Union front. Sheffield followed Bushrod Johnson tacking slightly to the right across the Dyer cornfield in the direction of a prominent knoll on the northwest side. Robertson moved northwest through the corn between Sheffield and Benning. It was Robertson and Sheffield's men that had alarmed Tom Wood.[24]

Before Harker's line was set, Wood ordered the 125th and 64th Ohio forward to seize the fencerow. As the men of the 125th primed their Springfield muskets for the first time that Sunday morning, Opdycke reminded them to "aim low, aim well, waste no shots." With the command "Forward double quick!" Opdycke led his men through the thin woods that separated them from the fence. Ordnance Sergeant Henry Glenville was felled by a ball that passed through his right side and back. Color Corporal William McGittigan was killed and fell on his still cased colors. Without hesitation, the Ohioans pulled the fence rails into a low breastwork, dropped to the ground and delivered a spontaneous volley into Robertson's flank. The Texans turned to face Harker's men and reciprocated. Rapid volleys were exchanged. One of the Texans later wrote of the encounter with Harker's brigade, "That was the meanest, most unsatisfactory place I struck during the whole war." The stunned Texans fell back to the woods on the east side of the cornfield.[25]

Major General John Bell Hood, temporarily commanding Longstreet's corps, was on the field urging Bushrod Johnson forward when he witnessed the Texans rout. Hood told Johnson, "Go ahead and keep ahead of everything," sending him toward the Dry Valley Road. Hood rode into the woods to try and rally Robertson's Texans, a brigade he once commanded. Hood belittled Harker's bluecoats, telling his soldiers, "Those fellows are shooting in the tops of the trees." The Texans ignored Hood. Seeing Joseph Kershaw's brigade of South Carolinians approaching the cornfield, Hood started in that direction and within moments was engulfed in a shower of bullets from Harker's brigade. One ball smashed Hood's femur just below his right hip in a wound that would cost him his leg. Hood, whose left arm was still in a sling from a wound at Gettysburg, slid from his saddle and would be reported killed by both New York and Richmond newspapers. The two brigades that were stung by the Third Brigade's volleys later reformed, but did not fight again that Sunday. Benning's Georgians course took them within 200 yards of the right flank of Reynold's division where they were met by a bayonet charge by the 105th Ohio. Benning's brigade, caught unprepared, simply disappeared into the woods and out of the battle.[26]

Lieutenant Henry Glenville, 1864. Glenville was born in England and apprenticed a printer in Cleveland. His full name was Henry Glenville Shaw. Post-war, Shaw was a journalist, lieutenant colonel in the New Jersey National Guard, and, in 1871, became one of the founders of the National Rifle Association. Reproduced from Clark, *Opdycke Tigers*.

No one doubted Emerson Opdycke's willingness to fight especially General Wood, who, despite raging musketry, ordered Opdycke to lead the 125th and the 64th into the wavering rebel brigades ahead. Orders echoed through the regiments to double the files, making four ranks. Intervals were set to allow the rear rank to face forward a few paces, fire a volley, fall to the ground to reload and repeat the process. Fixing bayonets left no doubt these Yankee intended to close with their enemy. When the signal came to charge, the 125th momentarily hesitated. Inexperienced, but not foolhardy, the Ohioans could see they were two regiments pitching into two enemy brigades and looked anxiously to

Opdycke for reassurance. In 19th-century armies, according to one historian, "fear was not an anxiety to be shared but a weakness to be stifled." The Colonel spurred a prancing Barney through the ranks of the 125th to the front, raised his hat and ordered the Ohioans to advance, firing by rank as they went. Opdycke's men swallowed their fear, raised a yell and surged forward. A few were betrayed by their anxiety, like Sergeant Rollin Barnes, whose accidental discharge of his rifle sent a bullet into the gunstock of a man in his front. Barnes' second attempt to fire his musket launched his steel ramrod toward the enemy. Green soldiers facing combat for the first time could be a danger to their comrades as well as the enemy. "It was difficult to tell from which we suffered most, the fire of the enemy, or the bad marksmanship of the line in the rear," one Yankee wrote after his first charge.[27]

The 64th and the 125th charged for 400 yards, firing by ranks, to the remnants of a rail fence on a low rise in the copse of trees where General Hood had just been wounded. All except the officers dropped to the ground. Within moments, Captain Albert Yeomans suffered a severe wound in the thigh, but remained on the field. While on the ground, Private James Floody was struck in the back by a ricocheted bullet and temporarily paralyzed. Second Lieutenant Albert Barnes, acting Company E commander, was shot in the thigh, breaking his femur. He fell into Confederate hands. Wood directed Opdycke to send skirmishers to the south side of the trees to harass the enemy in what Wood eloquently termed "the now debatable ground of the contending bodies."[28]

The knoll on Harker's right was tenuously held by Sheffield's Confederates who were winded after their mile-long advance. Recognizing immediately the tactical significance of the knoll to the defense of Dyer field, Harker sent the 65th Ohio and 3rd Kentucky to seize it simultaneous with Opdycke's charge into Dyer's field. Those two regiments drove the rebels back into Dyer field. Harker positioned the 65th and 3rd to enfilade Sheffield's Confederate brigade. The 65th Ohio held the knoll with Colonel Buell's 58th Indiana in the woods to the right. The 3rd Kentucky formed a line to the left of the 65th and joining Opdycke's right. Sheffield Confederates limped eastward toward the safety of heavy timber bordering the corn stubble. The Third Brigade formed a continuous battle line across the cornfield from the knoll to the copse of trees.[29]

Harker's men in Dyer's field could see another battle line in the distance—longer and stronger than its predecessor. It was an impressive sight, and Opdycke admitted six days later that a description was "beyond the reach of my pen." According to Lieutenant Clark, just when Harker's men should have "poured the entire contents of our cartridge boxes into those battalions as rapidly as possible," the Yankees held their fire. To Tom Wood's experienced eye, the opposing troops, with their bayonets fixed and guns at right shoulder, were too well drilled for Bragg's men. Furthermore, they carried dark red flags and their "blurred and greasy and dusty uniforms so resembled our own when travel stained that they might have been Sheridan's division." Wood ordered a ceasefire since "the thought of firing on our comrades in arms being too horrible to contemplate." When the new battle line had closed to 400 yards, Opdycke called for volunteers—Sergeant Barnes stepped forward—to go move into the cornfield for a closer look. It was high noon.[30]

While everyone was transfixed by the unfolding spectacle, George Thomas quietly rode up behind Charlie Harker. Thomas had a report of unidentified infantry in Dyer's field and rode over because he was expecting two of Phil Sheridan's brigades to reinforce him. Thomas studied the distant line through field glasses and told Harker to have his color bearers stand and uncase their battle flags. Thomas gave first Colonel Harker, and then Opdycke, instructions they probably didn't need—if the unidentified troops fired on them, they were to return fire and resist their advance.[31]

"Most conspicuous of all for heroism were those charged with bearing and guarding the colors," historian Bell Irvin Wiley wrote of Civil War color-bearers. "In numerous instances the color-bearers continued defiantly to wave their cherished emblem in front of the enemy after the cloth had been shot into shreds by enemy fire." The flags were unfurled and Colonel Harker rode his horse beyond the battle line of the 65th to get a clearer view of the distant infantry. By now it was obvious that the opposing battle line would easily overlap the Third Brigade on both flanks. A second line was forming behind the first. When Harker and his color bearers were subjected to a spray of Minie balls, all doubt evaporated. Heavy volleys of musketry erupted.[32]

The enemy had made good use of the federal uncertainty. Confederate Brigadier General Joseph Kershaw was perplexed by the silence, but used it advantageously. As his men marched north toward Harker's men, Kershaw pulled one regiment out of line and sent it double quick across the Yankees front toward the rear of the knoll. These South Carolinians were to find and envelop the right flank of Harker's line. The rest of Kershaw's men were now advancing on the bluecoats at a jog with bayonets lowered periodically halting to fire volleys. Kershaw said of Harker's brigade, "His colors were ostentatiously displayed along the lines." Six color bearers from the 125th fell in a matter of minutes. Youthful Corporal William Thorn was one of the first to fall. The flags were perforated by bullets and the regimental flag staff was shot in two. Lieutenant M. V. B. King commanding the color guard was grazed by a round. Corporal James Dickson was holding a flag aloft when a bullet grazed his forehead and shattered his left hand.[33]

Corporal William S. Thorn. A color corporal, Thorn was wounded at Chickamauga and Missionary Ridge where he carried the colors two-thirds of the way to the top. Reproduced from Clark, *Opdycke Tigers*.

The 58th Indiana to the right rear of the 65th Ohio held the woods behind the knoll and once the South Carolinians got into a ravine in their rear, the Indianans fled. The 65th Ohio on the Indianans left received a blistering volley in its right flank from the South Carolinians. Threatened from the front and flank, Harker ordered his old regiment back, leaving the knoll to the enemy. The 65th left a third of their number on the field. Major Samuel Brown, less than a day in command, was mortally wounded. The 65th fell back to the high ground near the log buildings of George Snodgrass farmstead.[34]

The Confederates next focused their attention on the 3rd Kentucky in the open corn stubble at the base of the knoll. The

3rd's Colonel Henry Dunlap tried to meet the threat by refusing his flank, to no avail. Dunlop believed he lost 80 men in mere moments. Taking fire from the right flank and rattled by groups of Union stragglers still running through their lines, the 3rd Kentucky fell back in disorder. General Wood rode into them in an attempt to rally his fellow Kentuckians. When his horse was shot, Wood seized another and joined his soldiers streaming toward the high ground in the rear. Captain Joe Bruff's Company A of the 125th rose to follow the 3rd but froze under Colonel Opdycke's steely gaze. Gesturing with his sword, Opdycke's voice rose above the din of battle, "Back to your posts until I order you away!"[35]

The 64th and 125th fought a separate battle from the 65th and 3rd. The two Ohio regiments engaged the center and right of Kershaw's line—three South Carolina regiments—coming with fixed bayonets. Opdycke's men looked to him, questioning their chances. The volleys from the 64th and 125th staggered the enemy, whose lines lost perfection but doggedly forged ahead. The South Carolinians holding the knoll to the west were in a position to sweep across the rear of the 125th and 64th cutting off their escape route. At 12:50, Colonel Harker directed the brigade to retreat 500 yards north to the Snodgrass farm.[36]

The 64th Ohio retired. Colonel Opdycke's blood was up and he held the 125th firm. The approaching Confederate line was thinner, but no less resolute. Lieutenant Charles Clark was waving one of the flags when he was knocked down by a ball. He escaped severe injury when the bullet was stopped by his silver watch after plowing through the rubber poncho draped over his shoulder. With Kershaw's Gettysburg veterans just 100 yards away, Clark, his narrow face streaked with sweat, looked at his wrecked watch and shouted to Opdycke, "They may outflank us and kill us, but whip us, they can never." This moment in Dyer's field would be immortalized in bronze on the regiment's battlefield monument 30 years later. Finally, conceding the obvious. Opdycke pulled the 125th back toward Snodgrass hill in his rear, firing as it went to slow the enemy. Corporal John Warman, who would eventually become color sergeant of the regiment, carried the regimental flag back to Snodgrass Hill. Casualties were significant. At least, 18 men from the 125th were killed or mortally wounded in Dyer field. Countless others were wounded.[37]

Kershaw later claimed Harker's brigade "broke" in Dyer's field, while Harker insisted he "retired by battalions." Lieutenant Clark offered this observation on the retreat in his regimental history. "The man who has himself tried walking off with an enemy in pursuit firing as fast as our guns can be loaded, bullets whistling about him and spattering against trees, and comrades falling in every direction, will realize that the power of discipline prevailed where Opdycke commanded." Two men were recorded as being killed instantly in this retreat, Privates Thomas Hall and William Jennings.[38]

The 125th withdrew to the fence at the north end of Dyer's field. There Opdycke's men halted and unleashed three volleys at the pursuing Confederates. An unidentified Union regiment fled through the right wing of the 125th causing confusion, but order was quickly restored. Joined by some men of the 3rd Kentucky, the 125th retired to a fence below the Snodgrass homestead and fired three more volleys. On the slope of the hill, the Ohioans again turned and fired a volley. This was repeated at the crest of the hill. This withdrawal continued as Harker's brigade was directed toward the eastern end of the Snodgrass hill, about a half mile west of General Thomas' corps' fortified position on the Kelly farm.[39]

Private Charles Reed was shot through the hand and chest part way up Snodgrass Hill. Reed was believed dead, and his comrade, Private Peter Knapp was allowed to go out and retrieve Reed's watch and personal effects. A rebel sharpshooter's bullet grazed Knapp's head and he was rendered insensible for some time. Both recovered, but Knapp remained a prisoner until the war ended and he was released from Andersonville.[40]

Of the fight the Yankees made in Dyer's field, Chickamauga historian Peter Cozzens wrote: "The significance of Wood's and Harker's actions to the preservation of the Union left was incalculable. Not only did their counterattack neutralize two Confederate brigades, but … it bought time." That time was put to good use by other stalwart federals who rallied to create a patchwork defense of Snodgrass Hill.[41]

6

CHICKAMAUGA, SUNDAY AFTERNOON, SEPTEMBER 20

The Third Brigade's sacrifice in the Dyer field gave a few Union generals an hour to pull together a defensive line on high ground west of the La Fayette Road around the Snodgrass farm known as Horseshoe Ridge. A handful of short secondary ridge spurs—referred to as "hogbacks" by the locals—branched off the south and east sides. Shallow ravines separated the hogbacks. Horseshoe Ridge was mostly wooded, but the forest floor was more open where livestock grazed. The eastern end of the Ridge where the Snodgrass homestead was located and the valley beyond toward Chickamauga Creek, was cleared and planted in corn. The cultivated ground ran almost due north-south for a distance of 500 or 600 yards. To General Wood's experience eye, the cleared Snodgrass spur was a natural parapet because of the "abruptness of the declivity" of its slopes. Infantry holding the spur could advance to the crest, stagger the enemy with plunging musket fire and retire behind the safety of the crest to reload. If this tactic was employed by two alternating ranks, the position was very strong indeed. "In addition, there was a moral effect," Wood noted in his report, "in its command over the ground south of it which inspired the courage of troops holding it." Horseshoe ridge was classic high ground and very defensible.[1]

Earlier Sunday morning, General Thomas had ordered Major General James Negley to gather artillery and position it on the ridge to protect the right flank of his Kelly farm line. When Longstreet's men broke through, hundreds of fleeing Yankees from Generals Brannon and Van Cleve's divisions crossed Horseshoe Ridge in their flight to McFarland's Gap and Chattanooga. One of Negley's brigades had positioned itself immediately south of the Snodgrass cabin. Brigadier General John Brannon managed to rally some of the fugitives, including some of Buell's brigade. These bits and pieces were positioned to the west of the Snodgrass cabin on a short, steep and narrow hogback which paralleled the La Fayette Road. Negley had some units from his division along with the assembled artillery. However, using the excuse that the cannon could not be protected from capture, Negley sent most of them to McFarland's Gap, three miles northwest. General Negley's actions on September 20 were not typical of the man, but Opdycke still described Negley as a coward and an imbecile in a letter home. While a later inquiry cleared Negley, Chickamauga marked the end of his military career.[2]

The 125th was the last regiment to leave the Dyer field around 1 p.m. By 1:30, Harker's brigade had become the left flank of the Horseshoe Ridge line. The Third Brigade was on a spur facing southeast and the right flank was occupied by the 65th Ohio. The 3rd

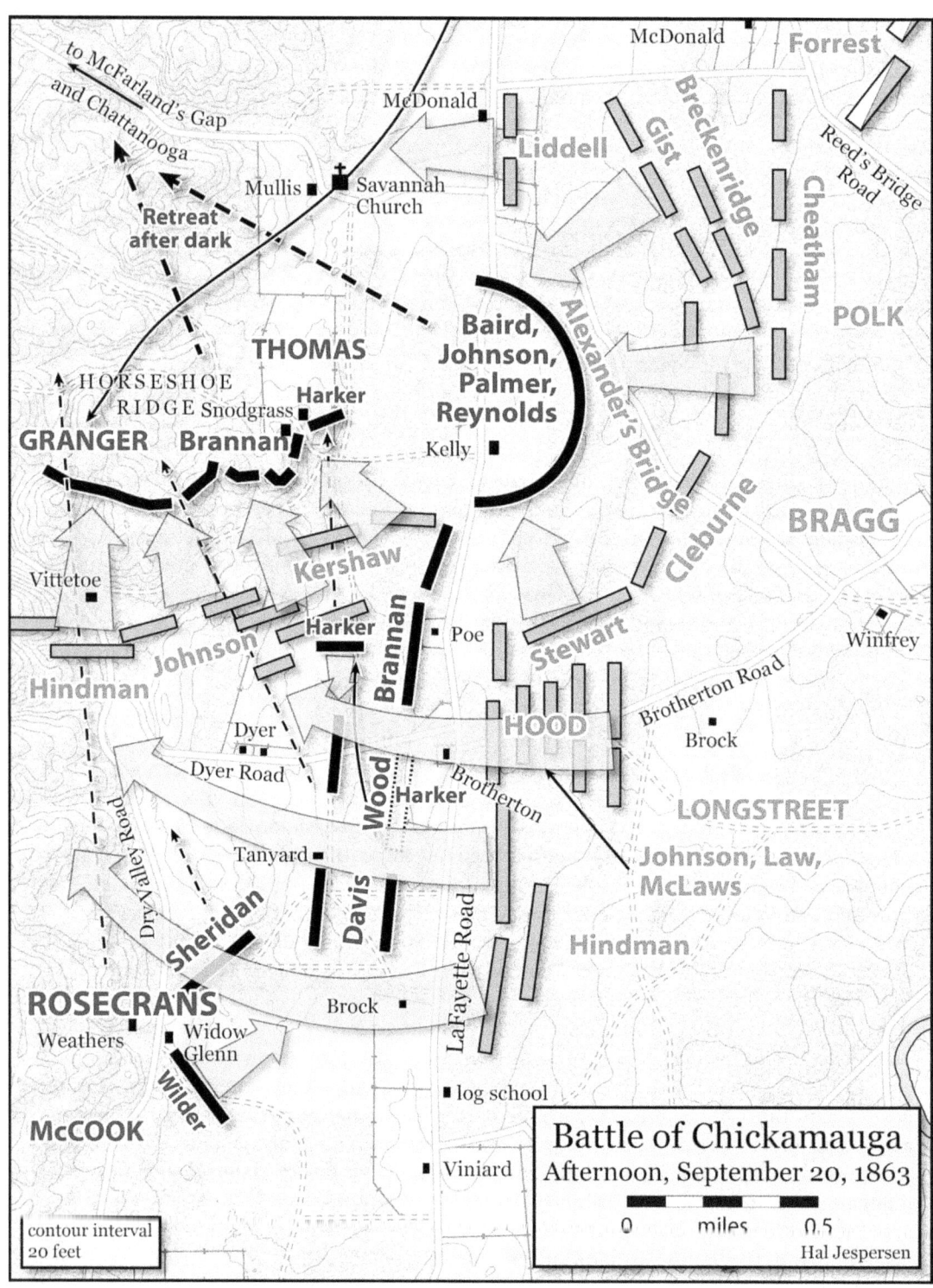

Battle of Chickamauga, September 20, 1863. Movements of Harker's Brigade from Brotherton's to Horseshoe Ridge. Map by Hal Jespersen.

Kentucky was behind the 65th. The 64th Ohio was posted on the 65th's left, with the 125th on the extreme left flank. General Thomas' divisions continued to hold their fortified position on the Kelly farm a half mile east of Horseshoe Ridge leaving a gap in the new truncated federal line between Harker's men and Thomas'. Shortly after Wood established what remained of his command on Snodgrass Hill, General Thomas arrived with his extended headquarters staff. Thomas established a headquarters in some trees beside the Snodgrass lane and in the rear of the 64th Ohio. From that location, trees blocked the General's view of his divisions on the Kelly farm, but he could see his line of retreat north to the McFarland's Gap road.[3]

George Thomas' presence had an electrifying effect on the Yankees from privates to generals. He was the highest ranking Northern officer on the battlefield. These western Yankees weren't ready to quit fighting and they recognized George Thomas as "the right kind of man to tie two," in 19th-century vernacular. Thomas admonished Colonel Harker, "This hill must be held, and I trust you to do it." Caught up in the moment, Harker responded, "We will hold it or die here!" The 125th Ohio—in their first real battle—held the critical the left flank, and Thomas told Opdycke, "Colonel, you must hold this position at all hazards." Opdycke, who had spent two years in the army preparing for this moment, replied, "We will hold this ground or go to Heaven from it!" A cheer rose. Thomas believed the best teacher for soldiers was actual combat. "It is not to touch elbows and fire a gun but how to do them under fire," he once said of making soldiers. The Ohioans had benefited from Opdycke's superb training and performed admirably in their first battle. In his official report, Tom Wood took credit for ordering Opdycke to charge in Dyer field. When Wood directed the Ohioans into position on Horseshoe Ridge, he told Opdycke, "Colonel, that charge was a grand thing, and if I live, it shall be made official and go into history." Wood, who would have few positive memories of the 20th, later declared that the Ohioans had fought like tigers. Forever after, the 125th would wear their new nickname with pride, "Opdycke's Tigers."[4]

Brigadier General Joseph B. Kershaw's Confederate brigades had pursued Harker from Dyer's field to the southern edge of Horseshoe Ridge. Kershaw halted south of the Ridge in a ravine near the Dry Valley Road. Toward 1:30, Kershaw's regiments spontaneously launched a disjointed attack on one of the hogbacks of Horseshoe Ridge southwest of Harker's spur. The Southerners—veterans of Gettysburg's wheat field—clawed their way to the crest under heavy fire before being repelled. Kershaw's 15th South Carolina marched into the woods below the Snodgrass cornfield. Harker's brigade was lying on the ground behind the crest of the hill. From their saddles Harker and Opdycke saw the Southerners and ordered the brigade to its feet. Opdycke had the 125th advance 10 paces to have a good look at the approaching rebels before ordering a volley seconds later. According to Lieutenant Clark, "Apparently, every man in the enemy's line fell." But he conceded some may have run away.[5]

The 125th immediately slipped back behind the crest without loss, setting the pattern of firing and retiring to reload in safety. In seconds the air overhead was filled by zipping minie balls as the Southerners returned fire. "Thereafter until night, the regiment seldom rose to fire a volley without sustaining loss," Clark wrote. Musketry raged along the hogbacks southwest of the Snodgrass cabin to the cornfield in Harker's front. The Confederates charged up the slopes of Horseshoe Ridge two or three times—an exhausting and bloody business. Confederate casualties covered the hillside among the cornstalks. Kershaw had expected little sustained opposition. "After one of the most gallant struggles I have ever witnessed," Kershaw reported, "I was compelled to fall back to a point about 250 yards back." A scratch force of broken federal regiments, amounting perhaps two brigades, and Harker's men had effectively checked the center of Longstreet's force.[6]

General Longstreet rode up to Confederate brigadier Benjamin Humphrey whose Mississippi brigade that was pushing the Yankees toward Horseshoe Ridge. "Drive them, General, these western men can't stand it any better than the Yankees we left in Virginia," Longstreet told Humphreys. Nevertheless, the Mississippians advanced cautiously past the blacksmith's forge and toward the Snodgrass cornfield. As Humphreys' Mississippians approached Horseshoe Ridge on Kershaw's right, the strength of the Union line became obvious. Humphreys' estimated he might lose half his brigade in an assault. Longstreet accepted Humphreys' assessment and the Mississippians withdrew without attacking.[7]

Those Union soldiers rallying around General Thomas were there to stay. On other battlefields, it was common to see uninjured soldiers helping their wounded comrades to field hospitals in the rear to escape the mayhem of the firing line. However, on Snodgrass Hill, Tom Wood recalled, "When the first assault was made, I noticed that men who fell were carried back by their comrades and laid down a few yards from the line, those who bore them hastening back to their places; then I knew their pluck was up, and they could not be driven from the position."[8]

After Kershaw's attack, the musketry slackened to random shots on the eastern end of Horseshoe Ridge. Confederate sharpshooters climbed the taller trees and, concealed by foliage, made the ridge a dangerous place for mounted Union officers. Most field officers either dismounted or stayed clear of the crest. Colonel Opdycke exhibited no fear of that danger zone remaining on his horse. Captains Ed Bates, and Ed Whitesides followed Opdycke's example and remained mounted. A week after the battle, the colonel informed his wife that "Longstreet's sharp shooters climbed into some trees, a little to my right oblique, and in addition to the terrific musketry, sent special compliments to Barney. One ball cut through my blouse, some grazed Barney.... By remaining on horse I constantly kept myself informed, of the enemy, and so was able to direct my fire, to the front, or right oblique as was most needed. When the powder-smoke shut out the view, I could readily tell the proper direction to fire by the point from which the balls came about me." At about 2 p.m., Whitesides' bay horse, "Billy"—previously Major Wood's horse—was shot from under him. The Adjutant was unhurt. Barney's bit was broken during the battle, but Opdycke never explained how. Opdycke claimed to be the only officer in the division *not* to have his horse shot. Why did Opdycke remain mounted when most officers abandoned their horses? He later explained to Lieutenant Ralsa Rice his reason. "There is no greater coward in the regiment than I. But my will predominates. If fear is master, then reason suffers. I keep my horse because I can reason my chances of being hit are no greater, or even as great. With my horse I am constantly on the move."[9]

Colonel Opdycke's courage on Snodgrass Hill made a lasting impression. "While the storm was beating with its fiercest fury upon Snodgrass hill," Wilbur Hinman of the 65th Ohio later wrote, "Colonel Opdycke sat upon his horse, at the summit, sweeping the field with his keen eye, and with his sword indicating to his men where to direct their fire most effectively. Unheeding the bursting shell and hissing bullets, he sat, calm and collected, a scene for a painter." In his study of the motivations of Civil War soldiers, *Embattled Courage*, Gerald Linderman recognized Opdycke's example on Snodgrass Hill as "the very incarnation of soldierly bearing and manly courage."[10]

Major General Gordon Granger—four miles north at McAfee Church—had been listening to increasing battle sounds to the south since around 10:30 a.m. As the fighting became more intense, Granger was increasingly uncertain what to do with his three brigades from his Reserve Corps. Rosecrans had earlier indicated that Granger should protect the army's line of retreat. As the terrible sounds of battle and accompanying smoke and dust clouds shifted, Granger got the sense that the battle might be moving toward Thomas' rear. On his own initiative, Granger decided to reinforce General Thomas' divisions. At noon, he started down the La Fayette Road toward the sound of the guns with two brigades—six of the eight regiments had never seen combat—under the command of Brigadier General James Steedman, a Mexican war veteran and Ohio newspaper editor.[11]

It wasn't long before Granger's men encountered wounded men, the inevitable skulkers with their demoralizing news, and neat rows of dead at a Northern field hospital. The road wasn't clear of Confederates or safe from their artillery, so Steedman's men went through the fields at a jog. At the Snodgrass house, Thomas was startled when clouds of dust rose from the dry cornfield to the north. It was a bit before 2 p.m. and Kershaw had just broken off his attack when Granger rode up to General Thomas. Steedman asked how the fighting was going. Reflecting on the seemingly disjoined rebel attacks, Thomas indignantly replied, "The damned scoundrels are fighting without any system."[12]

Between 2 and 3, the Confederate divisions of Bushrod Johnson and Thomas Hindman launched an attack on the federal right flank in the woods on the western end of Horseshoe Ridge where the enemy's line overlapped the thin Yankee battle line. The main assault was to the west of Snodgrass,' but Joseph Kershaw's brigade was instructed to engage those Yankees on the Snodgrass spur. Seeing the danger to the federal right, Thomas immediately sent Steedman's two brigades. The sudden appearance of the bluecoats with the colorful General Steedman in the lead, waving a battle flag, surprised Johnson's men. For his timely arrival and theatrics, Steedman—nicknamed "old Steady" afterward—would emerge from Chickamauga almost as famous as Thomas.[13]

The fighting was fierce and confused in the woods on the flank, lacking any resemblance to Harker's precision volley fire. Bitter fighting raged for a half an hour, between Yankees behind rude breastworks and the rebels taking cover wherever it could be found. According to Chaplain John Hight of the 58th Indiana, "The contest on that part of the field had become a kind of free fight, and there was no difficulty in a soldier, who was so inclined, finding a situation where he could get all the fighting he could attend to." Stalled, the Confederates launched a counterattack to cover their retreat. By 3 p.m., the Confederates were repelled and Steedman's line established to protect the right flank of the Horseshoe Ridge line. Thomas' scratch force on Horseshoe Ridge—representing parts of 20 brigades—were arrayed in a compact semi-circle less than a mile in radius and faced 39 Confederate brigades.[14]

Almost as important as the 3900 men Granger brought to the fight were the 95,000 rounds of ammunition in his wagons. All of the Army of the Cumberland's reserve ammunition was in wagons trapped in the exodus to Chattanooga. The ammunition boxes lying among the corn stalks on Snodgrass Hill were almost empty and the contents of the cartridge boxes of dead and wounded emptied. Steedman's men had consumed half of their 40-round basic issue. Harker's boys, down to just two or three rounds, were given just a handful of cartridges from Steedman's meager supply. Sniping and skirmishing continued unabated between periods of heavy musketry leading many bluecoats to fire 100 to 150 rounds that day. Gunpowder fowled many muskets rendering them useless.

The Army of the Cumberland consumed two and a half million rounds of small arms ammunition in the two day battle.[15]

Early in the afternoon, General Rosecrans and his chief of staff, Brigadier James Garfield, were on the Dry Valley Road. The two men had just ridden through a 300-yard gauntlet of enemy musket and artillery fire concentrated on retreating Yankees on the road. Rosecrans later wrote that he "found the routed troops far toward the left and hearing the enemy's advancing musketry and cheers, I became doubtful whether the left had held its ground, and started for Rossville." Once at Rossville, the two generals halted again and tried to decipher what they could hear in the distance. "On consultation and further reflection," Rosecrans wrote in his official report, "I determined to send General Garfield there [toward the sound of battle] while I went to Chattanooga." Rosecrans rode off to Chattanooga and accusations that he abandoned his army. Historian Glenn Tucker opined, "The great mistake of Rosecrans' career was in not going back to Thomas instead of sending Garfield." On the other hand, Garfield's ride down the La Fayette Road to the beleaguered Thomas would eventually land him in the White House.[16]

During his five mile ride to Thomas, Garfield claimed to have been fired on by a "rebel battalion," which killed one orderly, another aide's horse and wounded Garfield's mount. Reaching Thomas at 3:30 Garfield brought only bad news—no ammunition between Snodgrass Hill and Chattanooga and no reinforcements. At 3:45, Garfield sent a dispatch to Rosecrans describing Thomas' situation and the battle raging around the Snodgrass farm. "The hardest fighting I have seen today is now going on here," Garfield told Rosecrans. "I never saw better fighting than our men are now doing." He believed that if Thomas could hold on another hour, the day could be salvaged. Garfield advised Rosecrans, "I think you had better come to Rossville to-night and bring ammunition."[17]

General Rosecrans was in Chattanooga where there were only rumors of General Thomas' predicament. Those who saw Rosecrans described him as "broken in spirit" and he did nothing to inspire confidence in those he met. Assistant Secretary of War Charles Dana sent a frantic and overly pessimistic telegraph to the War Department in Washington at 4 p.m. exaggerating the scope of the Northern defeat. "It was wholesale panic," he told the War Department. "Chickamauga is as fatal a name in our history as Bull Run."[18]

While ammunition was in short supply on Horseshoe Ridge, water was almost nonexistent. The Southerners held Chickamauga Creek, and water had been a scarce commodity for the Yankees since the battle began. Nearly every canteen was empty and many soldiers had not a drop of water since the previous evening. "The intense suffering occasioned by this lack of water can hardly be imagined," wrote Robert Kimberly, historian of the 41st Ohio. It was standard procedure for the infantrymen to tear open their paper cartridges with their teeth. "Before night, men's tongues were swollen and their lips blackened and cracked until the power of speech was gone," Kimberly wrote. Remedying the situation meant sending volunteers loaded down with canteens on a perilous search for water. Many men sent in search of water in the woods filled with thirsty federal stragglers and rebel soldiers never returned. Late in the afternoon the Yankees were beginning to show signs of exhaustion. General Wood assumed the role of cheerleader by encouraging his weary boys to cheer with gusto despite their dry throats. Not only did this revive the federals' spirits as Wood intended, but it also gave the Southerners pause as they pondered whether or not Union reinforcements had reached the battlefield.[19]

Longstreet had allowed the battle to proceed under the direction of his subordinates during the early afternoon, but now Thomas' defense would get Longstreet's full attention. He asked Bragg for reinforcements, but was told none were available. Shortly after 4, Longstreet decided to commit his only fresh reserve on the battlefield, Brigadier General William Preston's untested 4000 man division. These Southerners were sent to attack the eastern most hogback of Horseshoe Ridge and Harker's spur. General Kershaw, a Confederate veteran of many eastern battles, said of planned assault, "This was one of the heaviest attacks of the war on a single point." Five Confederate infantry brigades prepared to go forward. Brigadier Archibald Gracie's brigade was the largest in Preston's division and it deployed in a single line of battle. With the brigade's battle flags unfurled for the first time, the enthusiastic Southerners started off at the double quick. When Gracie's line encountered the face of the first hogback, its linear alignment fractured. The right half of Gracie's brigade drifted into the Snodgrass cornfield and the deadly volleys of Harker's brigade. Caught in a crossfire from bluecoats on the left and Harker's men in front, the Gracie's men took whatever cover they could find as they tried to claw their way up the slope toward the Snodgrass cabin. The Yankees poured volley after volley into them. One Alabama veteran later wrote, "I shall attempt no recital of what followed—the heart grows sick at the memory."[20]

To help the hard pressed Harker, a two gun artillery section from the 18th Ohio Independent Battery—equipped with three inch iron rifles—was sent over from the right flank. Colonel Opdycke indicated to the battery captain where to position the guns in front of the regiment so the canister rounds would be most effective. The artillerymen were reluctant to take such an exposed position, but Opdycke prevailed. The artillery section was placed 200 yards east of the Snodgrass house. The other section of the 18th Battery eventually joined it.[21]

A half mile east in the Kelly field, the sound of musketry and artillery from Snodgrass Hill began to intensify about 3 p.m. Brigadier General William Hazen remembered it as a "fearful onslaught ... with apparently varying fortunes." Close to 4 p.m., two division commanders, Major General John Palmer and Brigadier General Richard Johnson, at the Kelly farm decided to send a brigade to Thomas' aid. Ammunition was equally scarce on that front and staff officers sent to locate much needed ammunition that afternoon had not returned. A quick check revealed that Hazen's brigade had the fullest cartridge boxes—40 rounds per man. Hazen's men had neither eaten nor had much water for a day, nevertheless, his four regiments plunged into the dense woods filled with Southerners that stood between them and Horseshoe Ridge at the double quick. Hazen's brigade formed a two regiment front and pushed through with sharp skirmishing and reached Snodgrass Hill about 4:30.[22]

A grateful George Thomas sent Hazen to support Harker' brigade on the spur. Hazen's regiments fell in on Opdycke's left extending Thomas' flank. Hazen found Opdycke's men rapidly firing by company, a tactic Opdycke had learned back in the 41st Ohio under Hazen's tutelage. The old 41st was still with Hazen and upon seeing Opdycke, it raised three cheers. Hazen offered to relieve the 125th Ohio with the 9th Indiana, but Opdycke declined. Instead it was arranged for the three regiments to alternate volleys. When three regiments of Gracie's Confederate brigade appeared, those volleys from the Ohio and Indiana infantry were devastating. According to Colonel Isaac Suman of the 9th Indiana, a Mexican War veteran, this rotating fire tactic "was very destructive to the enemy, speedily driving him from his position," and convincing the rebels to retire. In Bill Hazen's opinion, "The effect of firing volleys upon the enemy has invariably been to check and break him." One Tennessee regiment lost half its number among the corn stalks. Bullets that didn't find their mark rattled eerily through the dry cornstalks. After the war, Union veterans and illustrators saw themselves in perfectly aligned ranks delivering well timed and deliberate volleys at a hapless enemy. The reality of the fighting on Snodgrass Hill was more chaotic and deadly. When the bluecoats exposed themselves on the crest to fire a volley, return fire from the enemy was so severe the newly arrived 41st Ohio suffered a dozen wounded in a few minutes.[23]

Down amid the cornstalks, thick smoke and zipping musket balls, the brave Southerners repeatedly charged but were unable to dent the federal line. In the woods on the right flank, however, the Johnnies forced the Yankees back and swarmed onto one of the hogbacks, gaining a toe-hold on Horseshoe Ridge. Here the battle raged with "unabated fury" for an hour and a half until sunset. General Longstreet—a veteran of nearly all the major battles in Virginia—later observed that his soldiers were "not strong enough for the work" of completely dislodging Thomas' force, but the Southerners clung to the ground they held and localized outbursts of gunfire lasted until dark.[24]

Before Garfield's report from Snodgrass Hill reached Chattanooga and lacking any knowledge of the situation, General Rosecrans sent a dispatch to General Thomas to "assume command of all the forces ... and assume a threatening attitude at Rossville." Ammunition and rations would be sent there. Thomas received the order an hour before sunset at 5 p.m., and initially balked at withdrawing under fire, preferring to wait until dark. Garfield, as Rosecrans' man in the field, agreed with him. The ammunition shortage and subsequent Southern successes on the right flank meant that a Union retreat was just a question of time. Thomas sent orders for a withdrawal, and to distribute the last of the ammunition to the troops on the left of his line, including Harker's brigade. The fighting slackened toward sundown and finally sputtered out as darkness enveloped the battlefield.[25]

A withdrawal from contact with an active and dangerous foe was hazardous and needed to be done quietly and incrementally lest the enemy attack the retiring force. The federal withdrawal began at the Kelly farm. The abandoned breastworks were quickly discovered by the enemy, and Bill Hazen recalled the eerily disconcerting rebel cheers that rose from that part of the battlefield. The federals started to retire from Snodgrass Hill at 7 p.m. with Harker's brigade leading the column, and each brigade from left to right following in turn. Bill Hazen's brigade was the last to arrive at the Snodgrass field and the last to retire with the 18th Ohio battery. Now it was the soldiers of Harker and Hazen who cheered, hoping it would be interpreted by the Confederates as the arrival of reinforcements. Lacking ambulances and wagons, the Yankees took what wounded they could. Private John Strealy of the 125th, his ankle shattered, was carried by his comrades until they commandeered a gun carriage to transport him. Stready died the next day. A thin skirmish line was left to hold the Confederates in place. Portions of three unlucky Union regiments in the woods south of the Snodgrass cabin were captured before they could slip away.[26]

The last of the Union pickets to leave Snodgrass Hill heard a gentle rustling in the cornfield as they slipped away from the bloody ridge. This was followed by quiet footsteps. "A hundred yards away," recalled Lieutenant Colonel Robert Kimberly of the 41st Ohio, "there on the open crest, their figures standing out against the lighter sky, were the Confederate skirmishers who had followed up through the cornfield. On both sides it was a good-bye without words." According to Lieutenant Clark, not more than 5000 Yankees walked away from Snodgrass Hill. Thomas' disengagement and successful withdrawal of the 20,000 men remaining on the battlefield was a remarkable feat.[27]

In the pale moonlight as they hiked to the road to Rossville, the bluecoats heard the cries of the wounded who lay in the woods begging for water and help to the rear. "Listening to these poor fellows by the wayside was harder than facing another Confederate charge," remembered one Ohio officer. Otherwise, it was a quiet retreat, the tired men lost in their own thoughts. Historian Bruce Catton summed up the feelings of the Thomas' men: "They had prevented complete disaster, but still they had been licked and now they were in full retreat." It did not go down well.[28]

Lieutenant M.V.B. King of the color guard was wounded when the 125th stopped to fire a volley from the base of Snodgrass Hill. Shot through the chest, King was left for dead. Lying among the dry corn stalks, he survived three major enemy assaults on the hill that passed over him, plus small arms exchanges and canister rounds from Union cannon. King later admitted he was amazed the enemy continued to charge only to be driven back in confusion by heavy volleys. "This was continued until the ground was literally covered with their dead," King later told Opdycke, "and night closed the scene. Every volley you gave I saw the rebs tumble dead and wounded to the ground." King eventually crawled to the tree line, only to have rebel sharpshooters steal his boots and sword. That evening, King reached a cabin where he remained several days with little attention before making it to Crawfish Springs and Confederate captivity. King wrote Opdycke two months later from home that his right arm was paralyzed and that he was "doomed to a long siege of sickness and pain." King was eventually discharged for disability. General Rosecrans estimated his army left 2500 wounded on the field after the fighting ended.[29]

Lieutenant M.V.B. King, 1863. Although badly wounded at Chickamauga and believing he faced a life of misery, King lived to become a member of the regimental monument committee in 1893. Reproduced from Clark, *Opdycke Tigers*.

Thomas had been visible to all his men on Snodgrass Ridge that Sunday afternoon. According to author Shelby Foote, Thomas gave the "impression of doggedness and imperturbability" to all who saw him. George Thomas made his reputation and career that afternoon in north Georgia. Charles Dana, had spent the afternoon in Chattanooga, but what he heard allowed him to telegraph praise for Thomas, Harker and Hazen to the War Department, but the lion's share went to General Thomas. "Thomas seemed to have filled every soldier with his own unconquerable firmness," Dana wrote. "Our troops were as immovable as the rocks they stood on." The newspapers would pick up on the theme, and George Thomas would become "the Rock of Chickamauga."[30]

The 125th Ohio took 315 officers and enlisted men into the Chickamauga battle. One hundred and five men from the 125th had become casualties—a third of the regiment. In a testament to Opdycke's discipline, only five men were missing. Of the missing, three had been straggling. Two had just returned from the hospital and were weak and the third lacked shoes and suffered burned feet crossing burnt turf. A fourth man had remained with the wounded Lieutenant Barnes in Dyer field. One man from Company B, Private Perry Fitch, was captured and died in Richmond in December. Tom Wood was impressed and suggested no other unit in the army had so few missing. Sergeant Hezekiah Steadman summed up how the Ohio Tigers felt about their performance: "The 125th have met the enemy and stood the test most nobly."[31]

At roll call the morning of the 21st near Rossville, fully half of those Ohio Tigers present for duty had minor wounds or injuries. Sergeant Jacob Jewell, handsome and fair-haired, would bear a scar on his cheek from "the kiss of a minie." Sergeant John Williams was wounded in the leg and hand. Youthful Private Thomas Loutzenhisar had been knocked down and bruised by a bullet. Sergeant Henry Penfield was wounded in the left hand. Private William Porter, had been badly bruised by a bullet that passed through his knapsack. Private Alexander Vesey was severely bruised by a shell fragment. Private John Goetz, a German immigrant, suffered a finger injury and Private James Needs, an unspecified wound. The list continued into the dozens.[32]

Longstreet's biographer, H. J. Eckenrode, called Chickamauga "the hardest-fought, most desperate engagement of the American Civil War." This was a debatable assessment, but it was a terrible battle. Colonel Harker's brigade suffered almost 400 casualties over the two days of fighting. The Army of the Cumberland lost over 16,000 of the almost 58,000 that began the battle. Bragg's Army of the Tennessee, counted almost 18,500 casualties out of 68,000. The 35,000 combined casualties—roughly a third of the combatants—was greater than either of the two day battles of Stones River or Shiloh by 10,000. Of Longstreet's attackers, 8000 became casualties and a dozen regiments walked away with more casualties than survivors. For the Confederates, these were soldiers that would be difficult to replace.[33]

Chickamauga was perhaps the most surprising Confederate victory of the war, and possession of the battlefield was something new for the Army of the Tennessee. When the Confederates stopped cheering, reality set in. "The Confederate and Federal dead, wounded and dying were everywhere scattered over the battlefield," wrote Tennessee private Sam Watkins. "Men were

Sergeant Jacob Jewell. Jewell was slightly wounded at both Chickamauga and Nancy's Creek. Reproduced from Clark, *Opdycke Tigers*.

lying where they fell, shot in every conceivable part of the body.... And then to see all those dead, wounded and dying horses, their heads and tails drooping." The Snodgrass clan returned to their cabin shortly after the battle to find it a bloody shambles inhabited by wounded soldiers. They didn't return until war's end.[34]

The Southerners were unprepared for the overwhelming task at hand. Out in the fields and thickets west of Chickamauga Creek, nearly 4000 men lay dead. That Sunday night the battlefield was eerily illuminated by lanterns and torches held high by the ghostly figures of civilians and soldiers alike searching for relatives and comrades amid the carnage. Corpses wearing blue, gray and brown were everywhere. Groups of a dozen or more dead horses marked battery positions. Men were found frozen in death still aiming their muskets at their enemy. Whatever tragedy, lost in prehistory, moved the Indians who inhabited the region to name the creek Chickamauga—dead man's river—was overshadowed by the grim Civil War battle fought there. It was a place that would forever belong to the spirits of the dead.[35]

7

BOTTLED UP IN CHATTANOOGA

By the morning of the 21st, the Army of the Cumberland was drawn up south of Chattanooga blocking the mountain gap at Rossville in a hastily prepared defensive line that ran along Missionary Ridge with the right flank crossing the valley to Lookout Mountain. Harker's brigade was positioned near Rossville and some companies of the 125th Ohio were detailed as skirmishers. It was mid-morning before the Confederate army appeared on the road from Ringgold, and afternoon before the rebels attacked the skirmish line in front of Harker's brigade. The skirmishers from the 125th were flanked when the bluecoats on their right fell back. Sergeant Henry Russell was shot in the leg and one of his comrades, John North, carried him back to the stretcher bearers. With four men on the litter, Russell was started down the opposite slope of Missionary Ridge. Enemy artillery began shelling the Yankees on the Ridge, but most of the shells went over the mountain and landed in the rear. One shell exploded near Russell, killing one stretcher bearer and wounding two. Russell was dropped and knocked insensible before finally reaching an ambulance. The Confederate attack was repelled. Undercover of darkness, the federals withdrew to the Chattanooga defenses and the 125th entered Fort Wood. Union skirmishers served as rear guard on Missionary Ridge, including a company from the 125th, until midnight. Bragg's men didn't pursue the Northerners, content to let them retire to Chattanooga unmolested.[1]

Sergeant Russell's ambulance deposited him in the old Critchfield Hotel in Chattanooga now a 500 patient hospital. He lay unattended on the wood floor for two days without a blanket and only his shoes for a pillow. Finally, in intense pain, Russell persuaded a captured Confederate surgeon to examine his wound—there were only 40 surgeons available for 4000 wounded. The doctor found that Russell had been shot in the thigh with an old fashioned buck and ball load—one musket ball and three buckshot—of the type used in old smoothbore muskets still in Confederate service. The one-ounce lead ball passed through Russell's leg, but one buckshot lodged near the bone. The surgeon removed the buckshot, dressed the wound, and Russell was given a new cotton hospital uniform. Two days later, he was transferred to an army hospital. Russell survived, and was promoted to second lieutenant before the end of the war.[2]

By the military conventions of the 1860's, Chickamauga was a Southern victory. A dispatch from Bragg's army in a Richmond newspaper declared, "Our victory is complete." In Washington, President Lincoln knew Chickamauga was a serious defeat, and in the wee hours of the 21st, he told one of his secretaries, "Well, Rosecrans has been whipped, as I feared." But it was a hollow victory for the South. Thousands of men were lost to the Confederate army that could not be replaced, and the Yankees still held Chattanooga.

Seven. Bottled Up in Chattanooga

Charles Dana wrote three days after the battle, "The net result of the campaign thus far is that we hold Chattanooga and the line of the Tennessee River. It is true this result has been attended by a great battle with heavy losses, but it is certain that the enemy has suffered quite as severely as we have." Colonel Opdycke wrote his wife a week after the battle that despite the loss "the campaign is a success." For the Yankees, occupying Chattanooga was success enough.[3]

With the passage of time, the battle of Chickamauga was seen as a fight that should never have taken place. Rosecrans had misread Braxton Bragg. Albion Tourgee of the 105th Ohio concluded "that the battle of Chickamauga was a useless slaughter." Time altered Opdycke's opinion as well, and in an 1880's magazine article, he also suggested that Rosecrans should have consolidated his gains in southeast Tennessee before pursuing Bragg. "With so much to lose and so little to gain, it is clear that the battle of Chickamauga ought not to have been fought."[4]

Chattanooga's strategic importance far exceeded its size. A small town of barely 4000, it lay on the south side of the Tennessee River between Chattanooga Creek on the west and Chickamauga Creek on the east. South of Chattanooga to the west, the terrain was dominated by Lookout Mountain and to the east, Missionary Ridge. Between the mountains was the four-mile wide valley of Chattanooga Creek that ran south. Missionary Ridge—500 feet high—rose from the valley floor two miles east of Chattanooga, and ran slightly southwest from Chickamauga Creek for a distance of 15 miles. The western slope of Missionary Ridge opposite Chattanooga was marked by fallen timber, huge rock outcroppings and slashed by ravines. It was steepest on the west slope from Chickamauga Creek to the narrow gap at Rossville, Georgia.[5]

Southwest of Chattanooga, Lookout Mountain dominated the landscape as it ran southwest from the Tennessee River as a continuous ridge for 85 miles. Down river from the town, the Tennessee River looped south and followed the base of Lookout Mountain, which rose abruptly at a 45-degree angle to a height of 800 feet. Virgin timber, mountain laurel and rock outcroppings covered this slope. A third of the way to the summit there was a pronounced bench a couple hundred yards wide. From the bench, the mountain again rose steeply another 500 feet to a point where the forest ended in a massive rock outcropping—slick stone bare of even moss—that jutted out toward the river. An impressive sight to behold, locals referred to this point of Lookout as the "nose." Opposite the nose on the north river bank in a sweeping bend was a broad plain known as Moccasin Point. Militarily, Lookout Mountain commanded all the transportation routes into Chattanooga through the narrow Tennessee River valley west of town. Chattanooga's strategic value lay in its location. Wagon roads, river traffic and three railroads all converged at the town giving it the nickname "Gateway to the South." Any Northern plans for a thrust into Georgia would logistically require Chattanooga as a starting point. Once captured, it had to be held.[6]

The morning of the 22nd, Rosecrans' men could take heart from the news that they were staying east of the Tennessee River. The Army of the Cumberland immediately began construction a permanent defensive perimeter around Chattanooga. "It may be chivalrous to stand up in an open field and be shot at," explained Lieutenant Ralsa Rice, "but in our minds it was no indication of superior bravery.... A breastwork, however slight, has formidable look. All this came to our army intuitively and we were hardly encamped at Chattanooga before fortifying became a mania."[7]

Every house, barn and fence anywhere near the fortifications was devoured for construction materials. The civilian property owners were gone and the houses were plundered for the sheer novelty of it. Beyond the fortifications, every remaining structure was burned to clear fields of fire. This wanton destruction of private property was a new experience for the federal citizen-soldiers, but few officers bothered to get headquarters' permission. The day had begun "delightfully pleasant," but by sundown, columns of black smoke rose from burning buildings and then hung like a menacing cloud over the Tennessee Valley.[8]

Two days after the battle, Rosecrans had 35,000 men able to defend the city—more than enough for a well-fortified position. The Union defenses were anchored on the right at the base of Lookout Mountain downriver from Chattanooga and on the left on the Tennessee River above town. On an impromptu inspection of the Chattanooga line, General Garfield pointed out the 125th to Rosecrans and commented, "There general are the boys who stood to their posts, and the colonel who kept on his horse, all the time." Rosecrans delivered a short pep talk. Overall, the Army of the Cumberland was still enthusiastic about their commander and greeted him with shouts and cheers. But as one veteran noted, "The army did not even know the story of those two sulfurous days under the trees of Chickamauga. They thought their leader had simply been forced to fight at a disadvantage and that the army had escaped destruction through his skill."[9]

On September 28, Opdycke wrote a strongly worded letter to his wife regarding the debacle along Chickamauga Creek. He labeled Generals McCook and Negley cowards, Van Cleve, an imbecile and his corps commander, Crittenden, just merely incompetent. None in Opdycke's opinion should command troops in battle. The Colonel, who had a knack for meeting the right people, told Lucy Opdycke that he had already discussed this with James Garfield and Charles Dana. In fact, Opdycke had also pressed for Rosecrans removal. He told Lucy that his opinion of the generals was universal in the ranks and that Garfield and Dana "know it." Generals Wood and Hazen felt the same. Dana campaigned to have Crittenden and McCook removed. For McCook, the collapse of his corps came on the heels of a similar performance at Stones River.[10]

On September 29, a flag of truce allowed ambulances from the Army of the Cumberland to bring in the more gravely wounded held in Confederate hospitals. Overall at Chickamauga, where artillery had seen limited use, gunshot wounds—with their better prognosis—predominated. Those 1740 wounded repatriated were paroled by the Confederates—prohibited from fighting until exchanged for a Southern prisoner. One of those wounded was Opdycke's orderly, 19-year-old Ethan Briggs, who had been shot in the foot. The wound became gangrenous and his leg amputated above the knee. Opdycke sent his regards—visitation was restricted—and was told that Briggs didn't want his family to know his leg was amputated only that he was wounded in the foot. A month later the boy died. With obvious emotion, Opdycke wrote Lucy, that Briggs died happy and concluded, "I miss the boy very much." According to Surgeon Glover Perrin, Medical Director of the Army of the Cumberland, because the Union army abandoned the battlefield to the enemy, many amputations were not performed in a timely manner. The result, Perrin noted, was that "many cases of injuries of the knee and ankle joints subsequently proved fatal that might have been saved by timely amputation." Lieutenants King and Barnes were also paroled. King survived, Barnes did not. Forty-two-year-old Private Patrick Welch—confined for foot problems—was in a field hospital and likewise paroled. Sergeant Glenville's wound had been dressed by a Confederate surgeon the evening of the 20th, but he remained on the field until the 24th. He was paroled and survived after months of hospitalization. Documented wounds in Rosecrans' army numbered 9700 and as many as 7000 were packed into Chattanooga in the days following the battle waiting transfer to Nashville by train or wagon. At least one private from the 125th, Joseph Sperry, died during the journey to Nashville.[11]

Immediately after the battle, the Army of the Cumberland had rations for only 10 days and ammunition for just two days of full scale fighting. As soon as the outer line of fortifications and forts was complete work began on a second interior line. Harker's brigade completed and held the line around Fort Wood. The fort was located on a conical hill 200 feet in elevation southeast of town, and about two miles from the western slope of Missionary Ridge. Fort Wood was just 150 feet square, but was packed with artillery—six rifled cannon, two smoothbore howitzers and the 6th Ohio Artillery battery. The larger 30-pound rifled guns had a range of four miles but their accuracy was questionable at that distance.[12]

The Confederates advanced on Chattanooga cautiously. They first took possession of Missionary Ridge and parts of the valley of Chattanooga Creek. As the Southern skirmishers advanced, localized sharp musket exchanges erupted. Companies F and G of the 125th Ohio were engaged for a few hours in front of Fort Wood before the rebels halted at a respectful distance. Artillery exchanges that night were spectacular—"a magnificent sight," according to one Ohio officer. On September 24, the Confederates occupied Lookout Mountain after General Rosecrans foolishly pulled the Union defenders back—a move that disgusted Colonel Opdycke. The rebels then advanced west along the south bank of the Tennessee River to the rail head at Bridgeport, Alabama. For all intents and purposes and with minimal opposition, the Confederates had gained control of the land and water routes into Chattanooga from the east, south and southwest. October 1, the first rain since August 16 fell. On October 5, after wrestling their cannon through the mud, the Confederates began a generally ineffective shelling the federal lines from Lookout Mountain. Few federal casualties resulted—a wounded man here, a mule killed there. General Thomas considered the shelling to be trifling, and Colonel Opdycke believed the odds of being hit were very small. After a week, the rebels shifted from daily bombardments to sporadic ones. One afternoon, 230 shells were fired into the Union camps from Lookout Mountain with little to show for it. Return fire from Northern batteries was equally ineffective.[13]

President Lincoln was pessimistic about the chances of holding Chattanooga, especially with Rosecrans in command. Secretary of War William Stanton wasn't ready to cede Chattanooga and proposed reinforcing the Army of the Cumberland with men from the presently inactive Army of the Potomac. A skeptical Lincoln accepted Stanton's recommendation and approved sending 15,000 men and 3000 horses and mules in two infantry corps—Major General Oliver O. Howard's Eleventh Corps and Major General Henry W. Slocum's Twelfth Corps. "Fighting Joe" Hooker, who had been bested by Robert E. Lee at Chancellorsville in May, was resurrected from obscurity to command the expedition. The unpopular Hooker was known to be disagreeable, sharp tongued and possessed of a ruthless ambition. His only real supporter was Lincoln, who liked Hooker's fighting spirit. Leaving on September 25th, the federals made the unprecedented 1200 mile rail trip from Manassas, Virginia, to Bridgeport, Alabama, in less than a week, arriving on the 30th. Hooker's men were initially positioned to protect the rail lines from Bridgeport back to Nashville. In addition to unsoiled uniforms and excellent equipment, Hooker's men brought one innovation—the corps badge.[14]

In early October, the Medical Department finally granted Colonel Opdycke and Adjutant Whitesides permission to visit wounded members of the regiment recuperating in Chattanooga hospitals. One private, John Williams, had been shot in the base of the skull with the bullet exiting his left eye during the fight in Dyer's field. Williams' days were filled with hours of delirium interrupted by brief periods of lucidity. Opdycke knelt down beside the man's right eye and asked if Williams recognized him. The private correctly identified Opdycke and talked clearly of the charge in which he was wounded. Williams died the next day. Another soldier with an open chest wound also died the next day. In all, four wounded men from the 125th died on October 4. Opdycke wrote his wife that he feared more wounded would die "but <u>the nation</u> must be saved at any cost." Writing 30 years later, Lieutenant Clark was able to account for a dozen that died in the Chattanooga hospitals.[15]

On September 28, the War Department ordered the reorganization of the Army of the Cumberland. George Thomas' Fourteenth Corps remained untouched, while the diminished corps of McCook, Granger and Crittenden were consolidated into the new Fourth Corps. Major General Gordon Granger was assigned the command, in part because he was a friend of Charles Dana. McCook and Crittenden were relieved and sent before a court of inquiry. Both were exonerated eventually, but their military careers were over. In Emerson Opdycke's opinion, Crittenden was innocent of any pretensions, and not too smart. The general's success was due to his troops, Opdycke told his wife. General Van Cleve was relegated to garrison command in Murfreesboro, while General Negley never held field command again. Ten days later, and immediately after an interview with General Rosecrans, Opdycke used his acquaintance with Charles Dana to discuss army affairs and press for Rosecans' removal—a bit of political intrigue that was at best unprofessional.[16]

In the new Fourth Corps, Harker's four regiments were joined by those of a small brigade of Illinois troops and transferred to Major General Phillip Sheridan's division. "He is esteemed the best division commander in this army," Opdycke wrote of Sheridan in a letter home. "I hope I may find him to be all that I expect of him." The pugnacious little Irishman with Ohio roots languished as a second lieutenant in the regular army until 1861. Solid performances at Perryville and Stones River insured his promotion. Phil Sheridan drove his men hard and was a strict disciplinarian, a point he would drive home in mid–November when his men witnessed the public execution of two Illinois deserters from Colonel Frank Sherman's brigade. After actually meeting Sheridan, Opdycke commented, "I am much pleased with him." Lincoln left a colorful physical description of the short, muscular Sheridan as "a brown, chunky little chap, not enough neck to hang him, and such long arms that if his ankles itch he can scratch them without stooping." As a commander, Sheridan would become a giant.[17]

The five small Illinois regiments, the 22nd, 27th, 42nd, 51st, and 79th were judged to be "composed of excellent material, tempered in the fire of battle." A former Chicago bookkeeper, Colonel Luther Bradley, of the 51st Illinois had held command of the small brigade, but now returned to his regiment. The depleted regiments in Harker's brigade averaged about 250 men. There were over 150 regiments in Rosecrans army in the same condition. After the re-organization, most brigades were now composed of eight to 10 such regiments. Harker's new command became the Third Brigade, Second Division, Fourth Army Corps. The Third Brigade was relocated to Sheridan's sector on the line facing Rossville, which was south of their former position. One member of the brigade wrote after the war, that to have served under Sheridan "was a source of pride to every soldier that he led." Of his former division commander, Tom Wood, Opdycke wrote his wife that he still thought highly of Wood, but less so since the battle. Wood still held a divisional command.[18]

By the 10th of October, Longstreet's men had fanned out along the south bank of the Tennessee River from Lookout Mountain almost to Bridgeport, Alabama. Rebel sharpshooters surprised a federal wagon train on the north bank of the Tennessee, and proceeded to pick off a quarter of the draft animals while sowing confusion among the teamsters. One of Harker's men serving as a teamster was killed. Thereafter, enemy riflemen and artillery made the Tennessee River and the wagon road too perilous to travel. One supply route from Nashville to Chattanooga remained open. Now everything the army required had to come by rail from Nashville to Stephenson, Alabama, south of Bridgeport. From there, wagons hauled the supplies to Jasper, Tennessee, then up the Sequatchie Valley before turning directly south across Walden Ridge to Chattanooga, an overland distance 60 to 70 miles. The passage over Walden's Ridge was difficult during a drought because it offered no water and little forage for draft animals. When it rained, the road was described by one chronicler as "a greasy, washed out hell." Rebel cavalry raids were a constant threat. In early October, Confederate horsemen attacked a wagon train in the Sequatchie River valley, plundering and burning 400 wagons while capturing 2000 mules. The supplies for three Union divisions were lost along with ammunition for the entire army. Wilbur Hinman, of the 65th Ohio summed up the situation: "Chattanooga was under siege."[19]

Back in the relative safety of Ohio, David Moore's recruiting difficulties were compounded by the need to fill the new companies *and* replace the Chickamauga losses. According to Moore, bounties in the $300 to $400 range were being contemplated for volunteers to *new* regiments. That left established ones, in the field, at a competitive disadvantage. "It is so unfair," Moore wrote Opdycke in late September. Moore was again optimistic by early October. "I feel quite confident that I could have another maximum company by the first of November." Moore had at least 17 veterans of Opdycke's Tigers at work recruiting in Ohio from Cleveland and Warren to Mount Vernon, Athens and Marietta. In Marietta, Moore and three assistants, including future regimental chaplain John Lewis, secured a military band and stumped the county like electioneering politicians. They held a meeting every night appealing to the patriotism of any potential recruit who would listen. At one stop 13 miles from Marietta, Moore held a Saturday evening meeting, preached Sunday morning and concluded with another meeting Sunday evening. He wrote Opdycke, "I stir up the people to prepare the way for my officers—am acting as a *recruiting John the Baptist*." By mid–October Company K was just a handful of men short, and Moore sent one of his ablest recruiters, Sterling Manchester from Ashtabula County, to Cleveland to secure the last men needed to fill the roster. Manchester had been sergeant major of the old 87th Ohio, and had already recruited over 30 men for the company. Moore considered him "a live man and a successful recruiter." On December 5, 1863, Company K was mustered into service in Columbus, giving the regiment a full complement of companies for the first time in its year long history.[20]

On October 16, Charles Dana again wired Secretary of War Edwin Stanton and painted an even dimmer picture of the situation in Chattanooga: "because our dazed and hazy commander cannot perceive the catastrophe that is close upon us, nor fix his mind upon the means of preventing it. I never saw anything which seemed as lamentable and hopeless." Abraham Lincoln, based on what he was told, likened Rosecrans' actions to those of a "duck hit on the head."[21]

By mid–October rain had turned the only supply road into a quagmire. Wagons sunk into the mud axle deep, and mule teams floundered in the thick muck. Escort troops man-handled wagons out of ruts and pried exhausted mules from the mud. The flow of supplies was reduced to a trickle and Chattanooga's warehouses held just two days' worth. A full ration was three meals a day, and the Army of the Cumberland was on half rations. The full daily ration for a horse was 14 pounds of hay and 12 pounds of grain. This allotment was reduced by three quarters. By the 18th, the six mule teams were too weak to pull full wagon loads through the mud over the mountains, so the weight had to be reduced. The artillery horses couldn't survive on so little feed, and Lieutenant Clark noted, "a few days more and most of them will be dead." Ten thousand horses and mules died in six weeks.[22]

Commanding officers reduced the battle of Chickamauga to written reports in October and Tom Wood was generous to the 125th Ohio and its colonel. "I desire to commend Col. Opdycke ... and his regiment [a comparatively new one, and never before in a general engagement] in the late battle," Wood wrote. "The credit is mainly due to the colonel commanding.... I commend him to the Commanding General as an officer capable, and worthy of commanding a brigade." Opdycke was pleased, but told his wife that if he got a brigade, he would want a division. Wood's praise and recommendation was heart-felt, but in reality Emerson Opdycke was a relatively junior colonel and unlikely to advance in rank or responsibility anytime soon. In the same report, Wood recommended Colonel Harker for promotion to brigadier.[23]

Being hungry in Chattanooga did not prevent Ohio soldiers from voting in the Ohio governor's race on October 13. The Ohio Republican/Union party had selected John Brough for governor—an up by the bootstraps, self-made man and a Jacksonian Democrat who had been state auditor. Though anti–Republican, Brough broke from the strict anti-war Democrat line to get the Union Party nomination. Brough supported Lincoln and the prosecution of the war, while his opponent was the arch anti-war Democrat and Copperhead Clarence Vallandigham. A disgraced and deported former congressman, Vallandigham ran his campaign from exile in Canada. The election was never really in doubt. This was the first time Ohio soldiers could vote—although the law was unclear on whether those stationed outside the state could. Those who voted went overwhelmingly for John Brough who won the governorship by an unheard of margin of 100,000 votes, including a 20 to 1 landslide among Ohio soldiers. A grateful President Lincoln wired Columbus the next day, "Ohio has saved the Nation."[24]

No general's popularity was greater in the North than Ulysses S. Grant in the fall of 1863. When the secretary of war heard from Dana that Rosecrans was possibly contemplating a retreat from southeast Tennessee, Stanton frantically arranged a meeting with Grant. The third week of October, the two met in Indianapolis where Stanton gave Grant the choice of two sets of orders. Both gave Grant unprecedented command over virtually all the Union forces between the Mississippi and the Alleghenies. The only difference was that one set left Rosecrans in command of the Army of the Cumberland and the other replaced him with George Thomas. Grant, an aggressive fighter, was unenthusiastic about Thomas, a general he knew to be slow to take the offensive. Fortunately for the Union cause, Grant disliked Rosecrans' generalship more than Thomas' lethargy. Grant immediately relieved Rosecrans and ordered Thomas to "hold Chattanooga at all hazards."

Thomas—whose forte was defense—responded with unusual force, "We will hold the town till we starve." Grant would later comment in his memoirs. "I appreciated the force of this dispatch later when I witnessed the condition of affairs which prompted it. It looked, indeed, as if but two courses were open: one to starve, the other to surrender or be captured." Grant set his trusted lieutenant, Major General William T. Sherman, and some of the Army of the Tennessee in motion for Chattanooga from Vicksburg and Memphis. Emerson Opdycke's opinion of Grant had improved since talking with the Washington insider, Dana, and he suggested that success now would make Grant peerless in American history. Ulysses S. Grant, whose prewar career was marked by failure and scandal, now held the largest military command in American history—400,000 men in 12 army corps. Grant was, as one veteran described him, the man "who held in his hand the destiny of the Union."[25]

By the evening of October 19, the change in command of the Army of the Cumberland had become common knowledge. Colonel Opdycke wrote home, "Rosecrans has had a false reputation ... and the battle of Chickamauga was lost because of his inefficiency and incapacity." George Lewis, an officer in the 124th Ohio, later observed, "Never in the history of the Army of the Cumberland had the spirit of its officers and men been more depressed." Nevertheless, the opinion of many common soldiers was voiced by Wilbur Hinman of the 65th Ohio: "It was with deep regret that the army parted with 'Old Rosy.'"[26]

The Rock of Chickamauga enjoyed tremendous respect in Chattanooga. Opdycke expressed confidence in Thomas, not as a brilliant military leader, but rather as "firm, solid and industrious" with "an irreproachable character" and "a pure and unselfish love of country." From further down in the ranks, Hinman reported that the rank and file soldiers had "boundless admiration" for George Thomas. "Though sometimes slow," Hinman conceded, "he was always safe and sure." Colonel Frank Sherman commanding a brigade in Sheridan's division wrote that "our men will fight under him with the greatest confidence wherever and whenever he will."[27]

As October drew to a close, those Yankees in Chattanooga were reduced to the equivalent of one meal a day, and a little parched corn. Daily foraging parties returned nearly empty wagons. Hungry soldiers stole each other's rations, officers' rations, and animal feed, picking grains of corn dropped on the ground. To keep their scarce rations from being stolen, soldiers slept on their haversacks. One Ohio soldier admitted that "stealing whatever one could get his hands on to eat became not only prevalent, but popular." Coffee was used once and then dried for reuse. Shelter was likewise inadequate. One disgusted officer wrote, "There is not a hog sty in all Illinois that is not roomier and warmer than that which the enlisted man of the Army of the Cumberland has." A soldier from the 55th Ohio wrote afterward, "Possibly no set of men were more completely starved during the war of the rebellion ... save only the prisoners at Andersonville." Starving mules roamed the valleys north of Chattanooga, having been turned loose in the barren country where there was not enough wild bunch grass to feed even one mule. A black market flourished in Chattanooga for anything edible. Animal hides were boiled until chewable. Hardtack crackers sold for 50 cents, a cow's tail, $10. The quality of the food was questionable. Diarrhea became a significant problem and even Colonel Opdycke—normally a man of robust health—suffered from a rare bout of "bowel trouble." He recovered quickly with the gift of fresh food from his old comrades at the 41st Ohio.[28]

The picket line was usually the most dangerous place when two armies confronted each other behind static lines. But many individual soldiers felt the way Albion Tourgee of the 105th Ohio did when he wrote, "Killing men on picket is murder, not war." Informal truces were commonplace and a brisk trade in food, tobacco and newspapers developed, although officers were ordered to discourage it. A conscientious volunteer officer like Colonel Opdycke regularly prowled the skirmish line, but accepted the situation. By unwritten agreement, pickets generally did not fire on one another in course of regular picket duty unless one side was believed to be spying on the other—an officer with field glasses might draw fire. Newspapers were much sought after, but in early October, Union commanders stopped this exchange fearing the Southerners learned too much military information.[29]

In a chilly rain on the evening of October 23, Ulysses S. Grant rode into Chattanooga. Still lame and sore from a horse fall some weeks before, Grant had just endured a tortuous two-day ride through decaying horseflesh and thick mud along the road that served as Chattanooga's only supply line. When Grant arrived at the small, whitewashed clapboard house on Walnut Street that served as the headquarters of the Army of the Cumberland, George Thomas was waiting. No one doubted that the wet, mud-spattered, tired U. S. Grant had arrived to take personal charge. After dinner Grant willed his pain away, and consulted with the senior officers of the army, speaking little and listening well. One junior member of Thomas' staff observed that Grant's "mind was dwelling not only upon the prompt opening of a line of supplies, but upon taking the offensive against the enemy." After Vicksburg, the western soldiers considered Grant invincible. Still, the slim, slightly stooped little man with the slouching gait in the common soldier's uniform devoid of rank, hardly appeared up to the task of saving Chattanooga. Yet, up close, a firm, square jaw gave an indication of the force of his character and will-power. Grant sent a dispatch to the War Department that evening with a request that Sherman be given command of the Army of the Tennessee. A new day was dawning for the Union war effort in the West.[30]

On his way north and to obscurity, Rosecrans had met with Grant and outlined his plan to open a shorter supply route. Grant supplemented this information with a personal reconnaissance of the lines on October 24. Near Lookout Mountain, Confederate pickets of the Army of the Tennessee got their first look at Grant and failed to fire even a single shot at the Union officers. "But I suppose," Grant speculated in his memoirs, "they looked upon the garrison of Chattanooga as prisoners of war ... and thought it would be inhuman to kill any of them except in self-defense." Grant wasted no time. By the 28th, utilizing the plan Rosecrans' staff had prepared, the Yankees seized Brown's Ferry on the Tennessee River northwest of Chattanooga and Joe Hooker's men were in Lookout Valley west of the mountain. The Tennessee River was now open from Bridgeport to Kelly's Ferry for river traffic and a wagon road, out of range of rebel artillery on Lookout Mountain, ran the last eight miles across Brown's ferry into Chattanooga. Grant had the famous "cracker line" up and running in less than a week. A Confederate attempt to expel the Yankees from the south side of the river failed. Grant, the old quartermaster, ordered "a good supply of vegetables and small rations" be immediately sent from Nashville. The flow of supplies increased, but as Grant observed, "the capacity of the railroad and steamboats was not sufficient, however, to supply all the wants of the army, but actual suffering was prevented." Despite Grant's words, two weeks were required to get the soldier's rations up to two meals a day at which time one private in Company B wrote home, "We don't have as much to eat as we would like, but we don't grumble much."[31]

Confederate general Braxton Bragg lost his chance to starve the federals out of Chattanooga when the river road opened. Bragg's Army of the Tennessee sat in its lines on Lookout Mountain and Missionary Ridge and in between. There were plans to send east two rebel divisions—11,000 men—to hold the Tennessee Valley from Chattanooga to Knoxville. Yet the loss of Lookout Valley had some Confederates questioning the decision to hold the Chattanooga line at all. But Bragg was stubborn and uncompromising in his desire to stay, despite the fact that his army was almost as hungry as the federals, lacked horses and mules, and was spread very thin on terrain where rain swollen streams could block Bragg's ability to shift re-enforcements around.[32]

Grant believed, with no concrete evidence, that the defeat at Chickamauga and subsequent prolonged hunger had sapped the Army of the Cumberland's fighting spirit. Grant decided to await the arrival of his men from the Army of the Tennessee—W. T. Sherman and 20,000 men in five divisions—before taking the offensive. Sherman was presently marching east from Vicksburg and needed no urging, yet crossing the Cumberland Mountains in southern Tennessee, proved as difficult for Sherman as it had for Rosecrans earlier in the year. On November 13, in advance of his troops, Sherman reached Bridgeport, and a day later he was in Chattanooga.[33]

Concurrent with Sherman's arrival and after seven weeks in transit, the three officers and 80 enlisted men of the 125th's new Company I arrived in Chattanooga on November 16, where they were welcomed to "a full share of short rations and arduous duties." Company I included the sharpshooters Moore had snatched in Columbus and was commanded by their leader, Captain Aquila Coonrod. Opdycke's initial assessment of Coonrod was not flavorable, thinking the captain was pompous. Moore remained in Ohio organizing Company K. That same day, the paymaster arrived in Chattanooga for the first time in four months followed by regimental sutlers who prepared to reap a rich harvest from the newly paid soldiers.[34]

Over at General Bragg's headquarters on Missionary Ridge, the relationship between Braxton Bragg and James Longstreet was deteriorating rapidly to one of mutual distrust. Confederate President Jefferson Davis suggested that Longstreet take his infantry corps to Knoxville, dispose of Ambrose Burnside's small Union army and then return to Virginia. This move would require a major reshuffling of Confederate forces on the Chattanooga front. Bragg accepted Davis' suggestion, although he could ill afford to lose Longstreet's 15,000 soldiers. Longstreet departed on November 5, and was in Loudon, Tennessee, by the 13th, 20 miles from Knoxville. Burnside's Army of the Ohio was at the end of a tenuous 100-mile supply line, but well dug in around the city and equal to Longstreet in manpower. The War Department in Washington expected Grant to protect Knoxville and its Union loyalists. It would be up to Grant to determine how.[35]

8

MISSIONARY RIDGE

With the cracker line open, Grant could turn his attention to pushing the Confederates back into Georgia. The key to the Confederate line overlooking Chattanooga was Missionary Ridge. Force Bragg to abandon Missionary Ridge and the rebels would have to retreat into north Georgia. The enemy's right flank was anchored on Tunnel Hill south of Chickamauga Creek. Grant prepared a plan to send Sherman's divisions east from Brown's Ferry on the Tennessee River and through the hills north of Chattanooga where they would be invisible to the enemy. Bragg would have to guess Sherman's destination after leaving Brown's Ferry: Missionary Ridge or Knoxville. Sherman would reappear at a point on the Tennessee upriver from Chattanooga and just below the mouth of the Chickamauga Creek where he would force a crossing of the river, advance and take Tunnel Hill. If successful, this maneuver would turn Bragg's right flank and threaten his railroad supply base at Chickamauga Station on the Western and Atlantic Railroad.[1]

On the federal right flank, General Hooker was given the ambitious task of advancing from the northwest side of Lookout Mountain to Chattanooga Valley on the mountain's east side. If successful, Hooker was to push on to Rossville and establish his line across Missionary Ridge and into Chickamauga Valley to the east. Such a maneuver would turn Bragg's left flank and threaten his rear. The difficulty for Hooker, as Grant saw it, was "to get from Lookout Valley to Chattanooga Valley in the most expeditious way possible." Grant didn't expect Hooker to succeed, only divert attention from Sherman's effort.[2]

The Army of the Cumberland, still short of horses and rations, was to hold the center of the Union line opposite Missionary Ridge. Privately, Grant told Sherman that the men of Thomas' army had been so demoralized by the battle of Chickamauga that he feared they could not be got out of their trenches to assume the offensive. Grant trusted Sherman to take the lead in the offensive "after which, he had no doubt the Cumberland army would fight well." Grant apparently believed that the most he could expect of Thomas' men was to pin Bragg's troops in place on Missionary Ridge to prevent any re-enforcement of the flanks while Sherman and Hooker did the heavy lifting. No one expected Thomas' troops, or any troops, to take the steep, fortified Missionary Ridge by direct assault. This supporting role was an affront to the pride of those soldiers who held out on Horseshoe Ridge and endured the two months of privation that followed.[3]

Major General Ambrose Burnside's small Union army isolated 100 miles away in Knoxville had been a source of anxiety in Washington since Rosecrans' defeat at Chickamauga. The fear in the War Department only deepened when military intelligence indicated Longstreet's Corps moving in that direction. Burnside's supplies were dwindling and he was contemplating withdrawing from the region unless he was resupplied and

Eight. Missionary Ridge

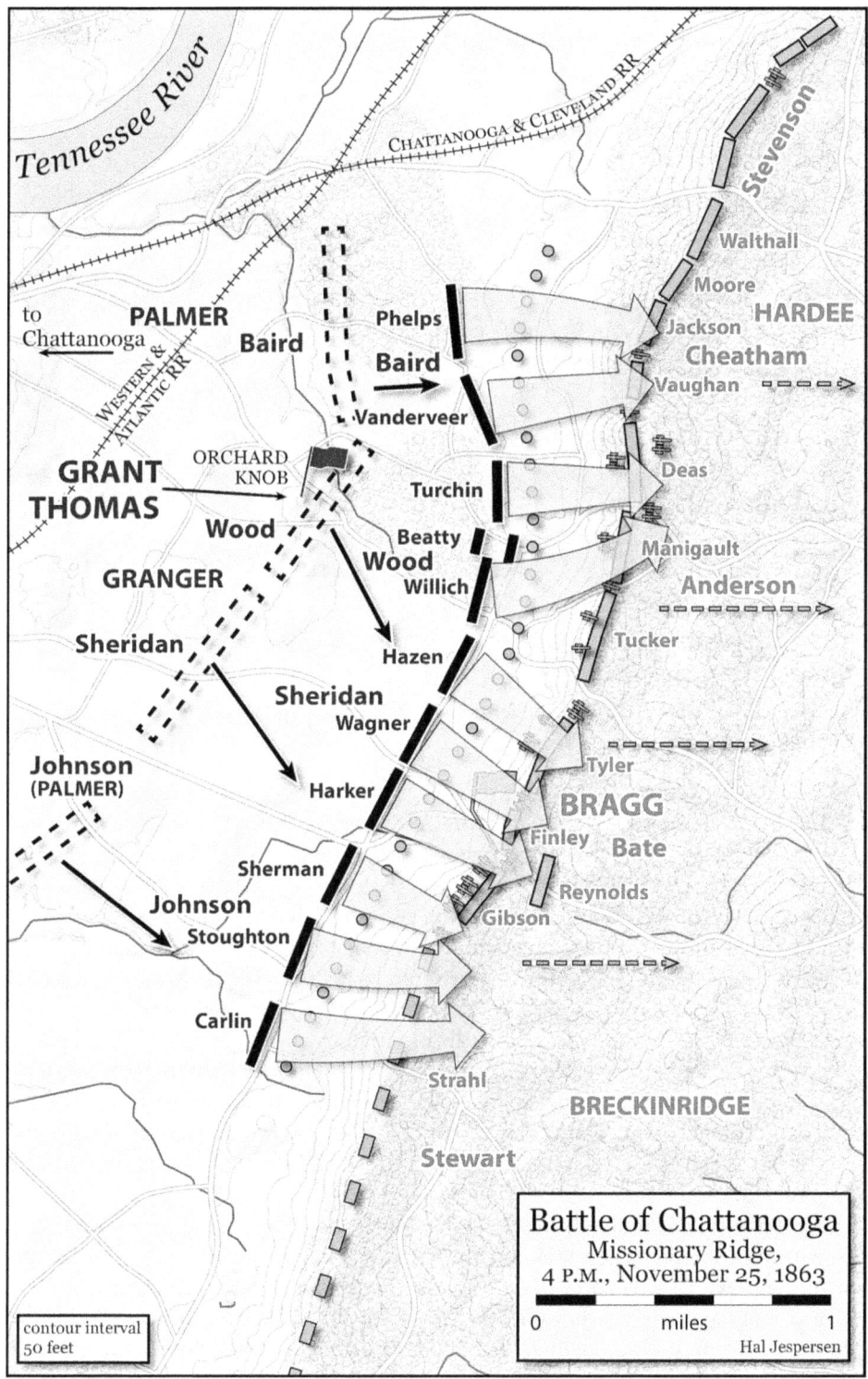

Missionary Ridge. Assault by Sheridan's Division on Missionary Ridge, November 25, 1863. Map by Hal Jespersen.

A ramshackle town of a few thousand residents in 1863, Chattanooga was an important rail junction. Library of Congress.

reinforced. Grant, preferring attack to retreat, told Burnside that Longstreet "should not be allowed to escape with an army capable of doing anything this winter. I can hardly conceive of the necessity of retreating from East Tennessee. If I did so at all, it would be after losing most of the army." Grant's pending Chattanooga offensive now had the added dimension of preventing Bragg from sending reinforcements to Longstreet.[4]

Sherman had four divisions within striking distance of Chattanooga by November 20. Union soldiers in Chattanooga were told to keep their haversacks and cartridge boxes full. Rain, and the inevitable mud, delayed Sherman's Brown's Ferry river crossing. But once Sherman disappeared into the hills north of town, Bragg concluded that he was headed for Knoxville, since in Bragg's mind the north end of Missionary Ridge was too rugged to be assaulted. Bragg and his generals prepared reinforce Longstreet by rail so he could defeat Burnside before Sherman could arrive. Two small Confederate divisions were withdrawn from Missionary Ridge on the 22nd and started toward the rail head at Chickamauga Station.[5]

Federal pickets immediately detected the Southern movement. To confirm this intelligence, Grant ordered a reconnaissance in force of the Southern picket lines in front of Missionary Ridge. Tom Wood's division was chosen to advance straight ahead while Sheridan's division would protect Wood's right flank from counter-attack. Wood's objective would be Orchard Knob, which rose 100 feet from the valley floor, and stood about a mile from the rebel lines at the base of Missionary Ridge and the same distance from the federal line at Fort Wood. The west slope of Orchard Knob was steep. A rocky ridge covered thin timber trailed off the Knob southwesterly for over a half a mile. General

Wood called Orchard Knob "the citadel of this line of entrenchments." There were Southern rifle pits and low fortifications on the higher ground and along the western base of Orchard Knob. Immediately east of Orchard Knob, a belt of timber about a half mile wide masked rebel movements at the base of Missionary Ridge. The valley floor from Fort Wood to Orchard Knob was clear and the railroad crossed the north end.[6]

On the morning of the 23rd, Wood and Sheridan's divisions were camped in the outer line of fortifications. Wood's division held the line east of Fort Wood to the Tennessee River, and Sheridan's division held the right to the Rossville Road. The Fourteenth Corps was on Sheridan's right. Major General Oliver O. Howard's Eleventh Corps was sent to fill the space between Wood's left and the river. Every man in Granger's corps had 100 rounds of ammunition in his cartridge box. Two months of inactivity and boredom, along with the bitter taste of defeat, were about to come to an end.[7]

At noon on the 23rd, Wood and Sheridan were ordered to prepare to advance to Orchard Knob. Should Bragg contest the movement, his infantry would likely either come down the Moore farm road—which ran almost arrow straight from the base of Missionary Ridge below Bragg's headquarters to the Union Fort Negley—or up the Rossville Road which ran to Fort Negley from the southeast. Buglers signaled Wood's 8000 men and Sheridan's 6500 to form and move onto the plain between the opposing picket lines. The Eleventh Corps joined them on Wood's left. "The troops fell in as if for parade," remembered Charles Clark, "without blankets or knapsacks, flags unfurled, drums beating." Harker's men could look right from their assembly point across the open plain and see curious Confederate pickets watching from the edge of their rifle pits—like groundhogs on their holes, according to one veteran.[8]

During the Civil War west of the Alleghenies, large bodies of troops were rarely seen. Yet, here outside Chattanooga, 25,000 Federal soldiers stood at attention in perfect order under a crisp, blue autumn sky, their bayonets sparkling in the sun. Even for professionals like Grant and Thomas, this was the largest assembly of troops in one field they had seen. "It scarcely ever falls to the lot of man to witness so grand a military display," Wood wrote in awe. "My division seemed to drink in the inspiration of the scene." Across the way, on Missionary Ridge, Braxton Bragg and his officers tried to divine the meaning of the show unfolding in the valley. Was it a review in Grant's honor or, more ominously, the prelude to an attack? Bragg dismissed it as a review.[9]

At 2 o'clock, a signal gun in Fort Wood fired and Wood's division advanced, its skirmishers jogging ahead. Federal artillery from two forts open fire. Wood's two lead brigades were aimed toward Orchard Knob and the fortifications to its right. Rebel pickets retired as the Yankees advanced, finally falling back on the grand picket reserve near Orchard Knob. Wood's left brigade charged the fortified picket line in its front and pushed the rebels off the Orchard Knob. The right brigade was Bill Hazen's and it faced stubborn opposition. A sharp fight ensued, the brunt of which was endured by just two regiments, one of which was the 41st Ohio which lost a quarter of its number in just 30 yards. Colonel Aquila Wiley led a final, successful bayonet charge. Most of the rebel skirmishers fled toward Missionary Ridge. General Wood was following his division, and galloped to the top of Orchard Knob, where he had his men extend their lines to protect their flanks and dig in. Orchard Knob had been secured in 20 minutes. At about 3 p.m., Wood sent a courier to General Thomas for further instructions.[10]

Phil Sheridan's division was ready for a fight. Harker's brigade was in the center of the division battle line. George Wagner's brigade was on its left, and Frank Sherman's brigade was on Harker's right. To better control his nine regiment brigade, Harker divided it into two demi-brigades. Emerson Opdycke was given command of a demi-brigade composed of the 125th, 64th and 65th Ohio, 3rd Kentucky and 79th Illinois. Colonel Nathan Walworth of the 42nd Illinois commanded the other demi-brigade and four regiments. Captain Bates commanded the Ohio Tigers in Opdycke's absence.[11]

At 1 p.m., Harker's brigade was directed to occupy a low hill known as Brushy Knob, which was a key point on the Union picket line about a half mile in front of the main federal line. Wagner's brigade was directed toward the north end of Brushy Knob. Harker's brigade angled toward the southern end. Harker's men formed across Brushy Knob and in the rear of the Union picket line. Harker deployed his brigade in two lines, with the 65th Ohio as skirmishers. A battery of artillery was sent out to Brushy Knob. Three regiments stood in a line of battle—the 261 man 125th Ohio, the 65th Ohio and 79th Illinois—while the rest of the brigade was deployed in a double column to the rear of the hill for protection from enemy artillery fire. Colonel Francis Sherman's brigade was placed in reserve. When Wood's division passed Harker's left, it was Sheridan's cue to advance. The brigades of Wagner and Harker went forward, shooing rebel pickets away after a brief, but sharp exchange of musket fire. After moving only a little over 200 yards, Sheridan's division halted on a low ridge in a former cotton field about 3 p.m. The 65th Ohio and 79th Illinois moved forward as skirmishers. Work on a low line of rifle pits started immediately. Harker's men dug their holes from Wagner's right to the Moore farm road. Harker's right was slightly refused. The 125th didn't fire a shot.[12]

Wood had somewhat exceeded his orders for a simple reconnaissance by pushing the enemy off Orchard Knob and digging in. Back in Fort Wood, there was thought of recalling Wood. Thomas wanted to stay, and Grant acquiesced, and Wood was told to "hold and strengthen your position." A formidable breastwork was in place before dark. Even at that, Wood fretted in his new advanced position, so shortly after dark, Sheridan's division slid to the left 300 yards. Detachments were sent back for the haversacks and extra ammunition. Some companies of the 125th spent the night on the picket line where Southern pickets were so close that conversations in ordinary speech could be heard. Newly arrived Company I—Captain Coonrod's men—got an up close look at the enemy that night.[13]

As dusk approached, Grant and Thomas rode out to congratulate Wood. Grant was pleasantly surprised by the Army of the Cumberland's actions. "The troops moved under fire with all precision of veterans on parade," he wired the War Department. "Thomas's troops will entrench themselves, and hold their position until daylight, when Sherman will join the attack from the mouth of the Chickamauga, and a decisive battle will be fought." A mile away on Missionary Ridge, Bragg wasn't contemplating a counter-attack. The Southerners simply didn't have enough manpower—they were outnumbered two to one—and chose not to risk what they had to restore a distant picket line. So they sat on Missionary Ridge and waited.[14]

The morning of Tuesday, November 24, Charlie Harker reported "all was quiet on my immediate front." From their valley location, the 125th, like all the Army of the Cumberland, had a panoramic view of Lookout Mountain and Missionary Ridge and whatever action a new day might bring. When the sky was clear, the bluecoats could see their foes up on the heights looking down on them, literally as well as figuratively, as they had for the last two months. Straight ahead of Harker's men, up the Moore farm road, were Bragg headquarters where the Confederate general had spent the last two months peering down on General Thomas and his hungry army in Chattanooga.[15]

Eight. Missionary Ridge

General Wood's success on Orchard Knob was at odds with Grant's larger aims. Bragg had believed, right up until the shooting began on Orchard Knob, that his left flank on Lookout Mountain was Grant's main objective. Now he realized the need to protect his center and right, and he began adjusting and re-enforcing his army accordingly. Bragg removed troops from Lookout Mountain and recalled those units headed for Knoxville. He ordered the men on the Ridge to dig in—something not considered in the previous two months. Confederate artillery was recalled from the valley in front of Missionary Ridge. The rebel generals were unsure how best to defend Missionary Ridge—from the crest or the line of rifle pits at its base. Indecisively, they chose both options.[16]

Grant was led to believe by General Burnside's pessimistic dispatches, and Washington's fears, that Knoxville was in serious danger. Burnside's tenuous supply line ran all the way from Lexington, Kentucky. However, not being truly besieged, Burnside was in a better position to supply his army by foraging. And his men were well entrenched. "Dispatches were constantly coming, urging me to do something for Burnside's relief," Grant remembered. "There was no relief possible for him, except by expelling the enemy from Missionary Ridge and about Chattanooga."[17]

On the 23rd, Grant had ordered divisions along the Tennessee River to congregate in Lookout Valley under General Hooker's command. Hooker had grander plans that went beyond Grant's intended feint. He ordered his men to take Lookout Mountain on November 24. Once in control of the summit, Hooker intended to go over the Mountain, down into Chattanooga Valley and thence into Bragg's extreme left near Rossville, Georgia.[18]

Sherman was at last ready to attack on November 24, having moved his men into position for a river crossing. Tuesday, November 24 dawned overcast with a drizzling rain, still, by 6:30 a.m. Sherman had two divisions, 8000 men, across the river less than two miles from Missionary Ridge with not a rebel in sight. Uncharacteristically, Sherman hesitated, opting to wait until one more division was across. Despite prodding from Grant, it was 1:30 before Sherman cautiously advanced. When Sherman's bluecoats finally encountered the enemy he realized he had made a grave error, the result of inadequate reconnaissance, compromised visibility and poor maps. Missionary Ridge didn't run straight to the Tennessee River as assumed, but instead it terminated in a series of steep, but separate hills which included Tunnel Hill. Faced with this unexpected development and less than an hour of daylight, Sherman chose to halt and dig in, unaware that he could easily have pushed through the few Confederates in his front.[19]

On the right flank, Hooker, unlike Sherman, didn't lack confidence. His command outnumbered the depleted enemy on Lookout Mountain by as much as five or six to one. He planned to attack up a road on the Chattanooga side of the mountain. Once his men secured the bench part way up the mountain, Hooker believed the rebel position at the summit would collapse. To back up his assault, Grant had given Hooker a quarter of the available artillery. Hooker's opening cannonade was grand, rolling up the valley "filling it as an organ does a little church."[20]

At 10:30 a.m., the sound of musketry cutting through the mist announced that Hooker's men had made contact with the rebels. Fighting in the fog and drizzle, but with the help of Confederate bungling, Hooker's soldiers fought their way up Lookout Mountain. The Army of the Cumberland found itself in the unusual position of spectator to the grand drama in the natural amphitheater formed by the Tennessee River valley. A foggy haze rolled in and out adding an air of mystery to the action. Cheers of the victorious federals on Lookout drifted down faintly from the mountain. Just after 2 p.m., Confederates standing at the base of Missionary Ridge two miles away watched in astonishment as the clouds cleared revealing Yankees waving the stars and stripes over nearly a half mile of Southern breastworks on Lookout. On the opposite side of the line, George Thomas threw his hat in the air and Colonel Opdycke remembered "the whole army rent the sky with thundering cheers." By sunset the Yankees were on the summit. Hooker was ready, he reported, to descend into Chattanooga Valley. "In all probability the enemy will evacuate tonight. His line of retreat is seriously threatened by my troops." In fact, Bragg had already issued a withdrawal order leaving only a token rearguard. Major General Joe Hooker was always good copy, and newspaper reporters with the Union army wired stories to their editors about his fantastic success in what became the legendary "battle above the clouds." Basking in his success, Hooker allowed himself to be delayed by the anemic Confederate rearguard long enough for them to withdraw their artillery. Colonel Opdycke thought Hooker should have seized the artillery and was disappointed in a man he thought a good corps commander.[21]

Bragg faced a crisis. Sherman was threatening his right flank and Lookout was lost on the left. In the rear, Chickamauga Creek was rising from the recent rains possibly cutting off retreat. Should the rebels stay and fight or retreat? Bragg decided to stay and attack Sherman after reinforcing his right flank. The argumentative and authoritarian Bragg was not the kind of general who enjoyed the confidence of his troops or who could rally them to fight against poor odds. Infantrymen in both armies shivered through the cold early morning hours of November 25. Even colonels, like Emerson Opdycke, found it necessary to leave their tents to stand by the fire during the night.[22]

In his headquarters in Fort Wood, U. S. Grant was vexed by Sherman's failure to secure Tunnel Hill—the key to Grant's battle plan. Grant told Sherman to attack "at early dawn" on the 25th. Thomas' men would make a demonstration in the valley in support of Sherman about 8 a.m. "Your command," Grant instructed Thomas, "will either carry the rifle pits and ridge directly in front of them or move to the left [toward Sherman], as the presence of the enemy may require." Hooker had even less to do being directed to merely divert Bragg's attention with a threatening display on Lookout Mountain. Thomas amended Grant's order and told Hooker to send scouts forward and find out if the enemy had evacuated Lookout. If affirmative, Hooker should proceed into Chattanooga Valley to menace the Confederate left on Missionary Ridge.[23]

November 25, dawned a beautiful, crisp, clear day, and by 9 a.m., Grant, Thomas, Granger and their staffs on Orchard Knob, had a clear view of Bragg's headquarters on the summit of Missionary Ridge. Sherman should have launched his attack at "the dawn of the day," about 6:30 a.m., yet rebels were still clearly visible on Tunnel Hill. Sherman had over 16,000 men opposing just 4000 rebels on Tunnel Hill. Yet he dithered. His men had spent the night entrenching for an improbable counterattack and they were spent. Sherman recalled "the sun had barely risen," at 8 a.m. when his attack began. Sherman had become uncharacteristically cautious, sending just two of his nine brigades—just 1100 infantrymen—forward in a direct assault on Tunnel Hill. A frustrated and impatient Grant reluctantly endorsed Hooker's proposed descent from Lookout Mountain and attack the Southern left flank.[24]

By 10 a.m., despite desperate fighting, Sherman had advanced little. Mid-afternoon, the Confederates counterattacked through the railroad tunnel, up the ravines, and down the slope of Tunnel Hill. The surprised Yankees were driven to the foot of the hill. Sherman admitted that two of the brigades "fell back in some disorder." Their counterattack a success, the triumphant Southerners retired back up Tunnel Hill. Over on the right, the once confidant General Hooker was now stalled at Chattanooga Creek, a mile short of the Rossville gap. If anything was going happen on November 25, it would be up to Thomas' veterans to do it.[25]

Grant and Sherman agreed that Southern troop movements visible in the distance were designed to re-enforce Bragg's right flank in front of Sherman. Grant guessed that this would weaken the rebel center. At about 2:30, he asked his old West Point roommate who stood nearby, Tom Wood, if his division together with Sheridan's could take the rifle pits at the base of the mountain. The proposed line of attack would traverse a belt of cottonwoods in the immediate front, followed by open cotton fields and cleared forest to the enemy's rifle pits at the base of the ridge, a distance of about a mile. There was a second broken line of rebel fortifications half way up the slope and finally the main line on the crest bristling with artillery. An advance in force directly on Missionary Ridge might convince Bragg to reinforce his center and reduce the pressure on Sherman. Wood replied, "I think we can carry the entrenchments at the base of the ridge." General Thomas was characteristically hesitant to commit his remaining four divisions—two from the Fourteenth Corps and two from the Fourth Corps, about 19,000 men—to even a demonstration against the 14,000 rebels on Missionary Ridge. By 3 p.m., Grant—ever more anxious about Sherman's situation—ordered Thomas' infantry to charge the rifle pits. When General Granger was slow passing on the order, Grant went straight to Wood and told him to make the charge at once. "You and Sheridan are to advance your divisions, carry the entrenchments at the base of the ridge, if you can, and if you succeed, to halt there."[26]

The Fourth Corps was impatient to do something. There was, men later remembered, a collective, if irrational, desire to attack. Responding to Grant's order, men rose, retrieved stacked muskets, unfurled their flags and fell into line. One officer poetically wrote afterward, "Death ... seemed to wait in grim satisfaction for the banquet which man was preparing to glut his insatiable appetite with." Harker's brigade was facing diagonally in the direction of Rossville and to align with Missionary Ridge had to advance several hundred yards in a left wheel. As each regiment reached its designated starting point in the open timber, the men were ordered to lie down, except for flank guides to mark their position. The bare trees extended half way across the plain, offering some meager shelter from exploding artillery shells but no camouflage. The enemy began a slow artillery fire, but their ranging was poor and the shells did little damage. However, one veteran noted of the artillery "there was the harassing uncertainty as to where the next shell might explode." Beyond the timber, the ground descended slightly to a small stream before rising to the open plain with the Southern earthworks about a half mile distant. On the far side of the rebel works, the ground was clear for 200 to 300 yards to the base of the mountain where the rugged ascent began. The west face of Missionary Ridge was steep and mostly covered with a moderately heavy growth of timber. A few clusters of crude huts had been constructed behind the works for shelter for the pickets.[27]

Colonel Harker sent the 65th Ohio out to the rebel picket line, 400 paces to the front, on reconnaissance. It was deserted. Two companies were sent even farther forward to probe for Confederates. They went as far as the edge of the belt of timber at which point they saw no enemy from there to the base of the mountain.[28]

By Granger's direction, each brigade was to deploy in two battle lines 200 to 300 paces apart with skirmishers in front, and with one or two regiments in reserve. Sheridan arranged his division with Wagner's brigade on the left flank, Harker's in the center and Sherman's, the right. Harker again divided his nine regiments into two unofficial demi-brigades—Emerson Opdycke commanded the demi-brigade on the left; Colonel Walworth, the right. The 42nd Illinois was deployed as skirmishers. Walworth's front line was composed of the 27th Illinois; 22nd and 51st Illinois formed the second battle. Opdycke's had the 3rd Kentucky, and 64th Ohio in the front rank, with the 65th and 125th Ohio in the second line and the 79th Illinois in reserve in a double column 200 yards further back. Harker instructed Opdycke and Walworth to advance on the signal from Orchard Knob. Opdycke's regiments were to guide on Wagner's brigade on their left, and, according to Opdycke, "were to carry the rifle pits at the foot of Missionary Ridge with the bayonet."[29]

In reality, the Confederate defenses looked more imposing from a distance. Despite its importance, there had been no effort to fortify Missionary Ridge. The main line of Southern earthworks at the foot of Missionary Ridge consisted of a trench behind a dirt parapet that lacked a head log or firing ports. There was hardly enough Southern infantry available on this portion of Missionary Ridge to man one defensive line well, much less three, and in some places the rebels were eight feet apart. The men in the trenches at the base of the mountain were particularly vulnerable. On the morning of November 25, it was decided that should the Yankees come, the men in the trenches would fire a single volley at 200 yards and then retire up the face of the mountain, skirmishing as they went. At the crest, the enlisted men could see that their trenches were poorly sited to defend the steep undulating western slope and its ravines. Confederate artillery on the summit was positioned such that the muzzles of their cannon could not be depressed sufficiently to cover the slope. Instead, artillerymen would have to rely on plunging fire—cannon functioning more like mortars—which could realistically cover a zone just 200 yards out onto the plain. Jogging bluecoats could pass through this killing zone in minutes. Additionally, the nine Southern batteries present were dispersed so widely as to not be able to support each other if threatened. There were no infantry reserves and no coherent withdrawal instructions. The entire plan for the defense of Missionary Ridge was best described by one historian as "chaotic improvisation."[30]

Waiting for the six signal cannon on Orchard Knob to fire, the Union infantry lying in the thin woods could only wait and wonder what was in store for them. A captain Wood's division echoed the feelings of many bluecoats when he wrote, "It is the dreadful waiting that is more terrible than the shock of battle." Among the officers there was some confusion about the objective. Not everyone received orders as crisp as those General Grant gave Tom Wood. Many, like Phil Sheridan, were left guessing what they were to do: stop at the rifle pits where they would be most vulnerable or keep going? To Sheridan, the rebel earthworks at the base of the Ridge looked like an indefensible death trap and he sent a staff officer back to Granger for clarification.[31]

While he waited, Sheridan told his officers, "as soon as the signal is given, the whole line will advance, and you will take what is before you." Wagner' brigade, on the left, was to guide on General Wood's division which believed it was to go to the top of Missionary Ridge. Harker's men would guide on Wagner, even if that meant advancing up the mountain. On Harker's right, Colonel Frank Sherman's brigade was to "make an assault on the first line of works at the base of the hill." The 79th Illinois Colonel Allen Buckner recalled, "I knew nothing of an order to halt at the rifle pits, neither do I believe any colonel on the line did." The signal cannon fired before Sheridan received Granger's clarification.[32]

Captain Ed Bates had responsibility for the 125th while Opdycke commanded the demi-brigade. Bates was not the senior captain, Captain Bruff was, but Opdycke wanted Bates experience and quick thinking. There were 11 officers and 250 men present for duty. Company I was the newest and largest company, twice the size of any other. On the 25th, the 125th was relieved of picket duty at 4 a.m. At 3 p.m., the regiment took its place in the second line of battle behind the 64th Ohio. The 65th Ohio was on the left and the 51st and 22nd Illinois were on the right. When the order to advance to came, Opdycke told Bates to maintain his connection to the left, follow the 64th and support it, if needed.[33]

A half mile in Harker's front in the rifle pits at the base of Missionary Ridge were three regiments of Floridians. A second irregular line of rebel breastworks could be seen about halfway up the slope in front of Colonel Sherman's brigade. The small farmhouse that served as General Bragg's headquarters was directly in front of Harker on the summit behind a continuous line of breastworks. Tennessee and Georgia regiments held the line to the right of Bragg's headquarters and Louisianans were posted to the left. The west slope of Missionary Ridge was marked by ravines, and felled trees. A rough farm road ran from the base of the mountain to Bragg's headquarters. Cobb's Kentucky artillery battery, six bronze 12-pounder cannon, was aimed straight down the road from the farmhouse.[34]

From the summit of Missionary Ridge, the Confederates could watch as Thomas' men maneuvered on the vast plain below. According to Emerson Opdycke's watch, the assault began shortly before 4 p.m. after a total of six cannon shots, two at a time two seconds apart. Thousands of soldiers in faded blue uniforms rose to their feet and dressed ranks automatically. While the sound of the fifth and sixth cannon shots still echoed around the Tennessee River valley, hundreds of shiny brass bugles sounded the advance. "As far as I could see," Lieutenant John Shellenberger of the 64th Ohio wrote years later, "stood two lines of bluecoats with beautiful flags waving and bright arms gleaming in the pleasant afternoon sunshine." The Northern battle line stretched for two miles, an intimidating sight. "The moral effect which it produced upon the enemy must have contributed greatly to our success," Shellenberger speculated. The Confederates "would naturally get the impression that they were being attacked by overwhelming numbers." Caught up in the moment, the 125th's Hospital Steward, James Scott, found a musket and joined the ranks. Four federal divisions stepped off as crisply as the dry twigs snapping under their feet. Charley Harker called the start "handsome." The rebels did indeed overestimate the number of Yankees by a factor of two or three. After passing through the trees, the unobstructed plain stretched before bluecoats who began to jog as the rebel artillery quickened the pace of their shelling. The approaching blue lines alone were enough to send a trickle of Southerners, with the inclination and opportunity, toward their rear.[35]

The Southern artillery barrage echoing around the valley was initially stunning. Opdycke had the impression that "the whole mountain seemed to vomit forth grape, canister and musket balls." Two cannon on the Ridge seemed aimed directly at the 64th and 125th, although in reality they were alternating fire right and left with spherical case shells—fused hollow iron cannonballs filled with black powder and musket balls. But the shells were exploding 20 or 30 feet in the air—too high to cause serious injury—mere "round balls of smoke," according to Lieutenant Shellenberger. Thomas' artillery responded, and the combined effect of 100 cannon shook the ground and temporarily deafened soldiers blue and gray as the echo bounced around the valley. The fire from the Yankee guns produced what one witness described as "a roof of smoke and iron hail." While the rebel cannonade was initially impressive, it was mostly ineffective which led Lieutenant Colonel Robert Kimberly of the 41st Ohio to observe that "a feeling of new confidence came upon the men as they moved on, always too fast for the Confederates depressing of their pieces." General Grant observed "the damage done was in small proportion to the ammunition used." Chickamauga veteran Ambrose Bierce noted of artillery in general, "The infantry soldier feels a confidence in this cumbrous arm quite unwarranted by its actual achievements in thinning out the opposition."[36]

Emerging from the timber, the men of Harker's brigade could see the rebel earthwork at the base of Missionary Ridge as a slash of yellow clay. Those few forward Southern pickets posted on the plain retreated, and a spontaneous cheer arose from the bluecoats as they hastened across the open ground. The occasional Yankee fell, and Wood's division went from quick step to double quick—a change Harker called "imprudent." To maintain alignment, Wagner's brigade moved to double quick march and Harker's men were forced to run to catch up while struggling across a marshy patch of ground. Bill Hazen's brigade of Wood's division—with less distance to travel—reached the Southern breastworks at the base of Missionary Ridge first. The empty fortifications were immediately occupied by both of Hazen's battle lines. Enemy sharpshooters made Hazen's position unhealthy. When the 41st Ohio's Colonel Wiley swung off his horse, he was shot in the knee—a wound that cost him his lower leg. Lieutenant Colonel Robert Kimberly assumed command of the 41st, and, in his words, "it was destruction to remain" where they were. Colonel Hazen was lying just a rod from Kimberly but the noise of battle was so intense commands were impossible to hear. Hazen looked at Kimberly and signaled him to go up the slope.[37]

When Harker's brigade emerged from the timber, its officers instantly realized that the battle line was not parallel to the Confederate front. The farther to the right a unit was, the farther it had to travel to reach the enemy position. Realignments to correct this while moving under fire opened a gap between the 3rd Kentucky and the 64th Ohio which unmasked the 65th Ohio in the second line. Harker ordered the 65th forward to fill the gap. The 79th Illinois in columns in the rear spread out into a line of battle to lessen the danger from artillery fire. The Floridians in the trenches on Harker's front fired a volley at the charging Yankees at 300 yards. A few skirmishers from the 42nd Illinois went down before they crossed the earthworks where only surrendering Johnnies crouched. Harker's front line was right behind and both continued on to the timber at the base of the ridge without stopping. Once the bluecoats were over the trench, the enemy artillery began to fire canister rounds and musketry began by volley. According to Lieutenant Shellenberger "men went down before the canister like ten pins." Wagner and Harker's front line ran as far as the timber at the base of the Ridge before throwing themselves to the ground and returning fire. Lieutenant Shellenberger noted, as he caught his breath, "I could see by the way the bullets were striking the ground behind us and barking the trees above us, that while lying close, the enemy could not reach us with their fire." Except for a few of the Illinois skirmishers, Harker's brigade had yet to fire a shot.[38]

All three of Sheridan's brigades reached the breastworks within moments of each other and just 10 minutes after starting out. Wood's division started into the timber on the west slope, and Wagner's brigade struggled to follow. A few of the Floridians fired a second ragged volley before retiring up the mountain like "a flock of sheep with dogs at their heels." After charging a mile with blankets, rations, knapsacks and 80 rounds of ammunition, Harker admitted, his soldiers were winded and somewhat disorganized. "I regretted," Harker wrote, "to see the troops to my left move up the ridge before they had time to rest a few minutes." The 3rd Kentucky's Colonel Dunlop, on the left of the brigade's front, thought fatigue proved the most difficult obstacle his men faced. Rebel riflemen were forced to aim over their fortifications making them clear targets. Wagner's brigade to Harker's left had less cover and suffered in a nasty crossfire.[39]

Harker's second line, including the 125th, likewise passed over the Confederate trench, then a swell of ground where Lieutenant Clark recalled the "fire was very hot," before joining the front line regiments at the edge of the timber. The trailing 79th Illinois halted at the first trench where, according to their colonel, Allen Buckner, "the fire from the rebel artillery and small arms was terrific."[40]

Lacking specific orders, many federal officers saw no reason to halt at the base of Missionary Ridge. General Wood had given his brigade commanders little guidance beyond taking the first line of works, and now he watched in surprise as Hazen's boys began the ascent. As Wood sat his horse among the second line of his division, he was implored by his men to be allowed to go forward. "General, we can carry the ridge!" they yelled, itching to erase the stain of Chickamauga. Wood made an instantaneous decision. "Men, go ahead," he shouted above the rising roar of rebel fire. The general knew he was exceeding Grant's orders—for the second time in two days—and he knew his career was on the line. Wood later conceded, "Nothing but success could excuse this palpable disobedience of orders."[41]

Watching through field glasses, Grant was incredulous when he saw Thomas' men heading up the ridge. Thomas denied ordering an attack and Gordon Granger told Grant, "They started without orders." And then he added with true emotion, "When those fellows get started all hell can't stop them." Seeing Wood's men amid the timber and rock, Grant growled, "If Wood fails, by God he'll pay for it." Granger sent an aide to Wood and Sheridan to ask if they had ordered their men up, and, if they were confident of success, to forge ahead. When the staff officer found Wood, the general denied giving the order—he had only acquiesced to the inevitable. He then asked "who in hell was going to stop them." If General Granger would support him, Wood said he would take the crest. At the same time, Sheridan's aide was rushing back to Phil Sheridan with a clarification of Grant's original order to stop at the base of Missionary Ridge.[42]

Sheridan's man reached Wagner's brigade first and Wagner ordered his men to fall back. Retreat exposed Wagner's brigade to a vicious fire from the Southerners above, so some soldiers ignored the order and clung to their positions. Colonel Harker was compelled to fall back when Wagner did and he told Opdycke to return to the first line of captured rifle pits and reform. Colonel Dunlap of the 3rd Kentucky regarded the retreat as foolhardy and three or four dozen of his Kentuckians stubbornly refused. The 64th's Lieutenant Shellenberger told his colonel the order was "manifestly a blunder," but pulled back while some of the 64th decided to stay. The 125th had just arrived at the timber line when the recall ordered arrived. As Opdycke saw it, those men on the slope with decent cover elected to stay put, while those caught in the open retreated to the crowded trench. From the 125th, Captain Parks and Lieutenant Stinger and 40 of Opdycke's Tigers ignored the order and took shelter under a rock outcrop. Colonel Frank Sherman's brigade on the Division's right had the farthest to travel and had just reached the Confederate breastwork where his men stopped to recover their breath. According to Colonel Sherman—the son of a Chicago mayor—"We had done all that we had orders to do." However, Sherman's brigade faced a second line of Southern breastworks 400 feet up the slope where the enemy had rallied and were now pouring rifle fire into his men that sounded to Sherman like swarming bees. Colonel Sherman finally concluded, "To stay where we were was destruction … there was no choice for us but to advance."[43]

Colonel Sherman's brigade started up even as the left of Harker's brigade came back down. Many of Sherman's men balked at the idea of charging uphill at rebel earthworks. Frank Sherman was sympathetic. "It was therefore not strange that men required much urging to induce them to brave the danger." A less sympathetic Sheridan charged into Sherman's men on his black charger cursing and swearing, and, if need be, applying the flat of his sword to cowering soldiers. Once they were moving, Sheridan rode over to Harker and Opdycke. Along the way, he told the 125th as he passed, "It's all right boys; when you catch your breath you can go on again." Sheridan's division was going up. Instantly, Captain Bates gave the order, "One Hundred and Twenty Fifth, forward!" The regiment had gotten all of five minutes' rest. Bates' men started up the 600 yards to the summit, moving right to avoid steeper ground and in minutes were even with Sherman's brigade which had just taken the second trench line in their front. Opdycke later informed his wife he had a problem with shirkers in two regiments of his demi-brigade. The 125th wasn't one. Opdycke zigzagged back and forth behind the line herding the stragglers up the slope. Some of them claimed to be wounded, but offered no proof. Opdycke used the point of his sword to keep the men he referred to as "cowards" moving.[44]

During the charge, Captain Joe Bruff was struck in the right side by a musket ball. Bruff escaped with a flesh wound and bad bruise, saved from more serious injury by the wallet in his breast pocket that contained over $200 he was keeping for his company. The minie ball passed completely through the money, but stopped short of entering Bruff's chest. The Captain later joked that enemy bullet had placed "the Rebel stamp on his money." Sergeant Freeman Thomas took Bruff's place.[45]

Despite the sharp angle of the slope, many of the field officers rode to the summit, picking their way along trails and foot paths made by the retreating rebels. Colonel Dunlap of the 3rd Kentucky rode and carried the Stars and Stripes all the way. Harker and Sheridan stayed on their horses despite the obvious danger. Opdycke started the ascent on Barney. A rebel bullet passed through the blanket roll behind his saddle. Opdycke told his wife that as he was urging Barney up the slope when a bullet passed through the animal's mouth and broke the bit. Opdycke calmly dismounted from the bleeding horse and removed a revolver from a saddle holster. One of Opdycke's aides, Quartermaster Abner Carter gave the colonel his mount, and Opdycke once again started up. Barney would recover. Three quarters of the way up, the quartermaster's horse was shot in the shoulder. Opdycke finished the ascent on foot.[46]

As the federals struggled up Missionary Ridge their once perfect formations dissolved amid the rocky and broken terrain. The enlisted men attached themselves to any officer who seemed to be going up and took advantage of every bit over to rest a moment or reload. Bill Hazen later wrote, "The strong men, commanders and color-bearers, took the lead in each case, forming the apex of a triangular column of men." The Yankees were winded but determined. Colonel Sherman later recalled that the eyes of his men staring out of smoke and powder begrimed faces were "wild with the light of battle." Opdycke was among his men, his blood up, laughing at the danger, revolver in hand, encouraging some while threatening to shoot any who tried to slip away. Corporal William Thorn carried the 125th's flag two thirds of the way up the slope until wounded when Corporal John Warman of Company F took over and went to the summit. A Union colonel later said of the common soldiers, "This was their fight; their officers had nothing to do with the advance."[47]

Shortly before 5 p.m., amid the lengthening shadows of sunset, the bluecoats neared the summit of Missionary Ridge. The last 30 yards in front of the Southern defenses had been cleared leaving little protection for the attackers. The Yankee onslaught paused. The rebel cannon could not be depressed sufficiently to be effective and Confederate riflemen had to expose themselves to shoot. The two foes traded rifle fire, and rebel artillerymen used their explosive shells like hand grenades. Jeers of "Chickamauga" from the Johnnies above that drifted down the mountainside. On Orchard Knob, Grant and Thomas, eyes glued to field glasses, waited. After picking off some artillerymen to silence a battery, some of Hazen's infantrymen fixed bayonets and jumped over the breastworks into the midst of the defending Southerners who fled. To the right, a Southern artillery battery fired into Wood's men at 30 yards stunning them before galloping to the rear. Then, spontaneously, the entire blue line surged forward again. Bragg's men began to scatter. "The Federals [ran] over us like a herd of wild cattle," admitted one Johnny.[48]

In Charlie Harker's official report, he stated the right of his brigade was the first to reach the crest. The left of the brigade, Dunlop's Third Kentucky regiment, arrived moments later at the stable to the left of Bragg's headquarters. Most of the 125th Ohio came over the crest to the right of Bragg's headquarters, while the 40 or so detached men with Captain Parks completed the ascent with other regiments to the left. Harker's brigade leapt over the earthworks and into the enemy. A solitary Confederate stood and aimed at Colonel Harker, who slashed at the man with his sword before a lieutenant shot the assailant at close range. Like most of the Third Brigade pouring over Bragg's defenses, the Ohio Tigers had lost any semblance of organization. Colonel Opdycke reached the summit of Missionary Ridge on foot. On the crest, a sharp-eyed private from the 64th Ohio unceremoniously shot a mounted Confederate in the back and gave the captured horse to the colonel.[49]

As Harker's boys clamored over the enemy defenses, Cobb's Kentucky battery became visible through the smoke on the narrow crest near Bragg's headquarters. Two guns were to the left of the house, and four to the right. The rebels had been firing grapeshot and canister at Harker's men as they climbed. This was the first experience for most of the 125th with "marching up to the cannon's mouth" and Colonel Opdycke likened the sensation of grapeshot going through the air to a flock of pigeons darting past. The 64th Ohio, 79th Illinois and 125th Ohio all surged toward the guns. Confederate infantry rallied in support of their artillery. It was hard fighting as the enemy tried, and failed, to get their bronze 12-pounder Napoleons away. Two of the pieces stood out, bright new cannon fresh from the Atlanta foundry—bronze tubes shining in the fading sunlight. Painted on their tails were the names "Lady Breckenridge" and "Lady Buckner" in honor of the wives of the two famous Confederate generals from Kentucky. Just a minute or two later Wagner's brigade clambered onto the crest after having suffered 700 casualties—twice those of Harker or Sherman—in the battle. All Wagner's men could do was watch as Southern infantry and wagons raced toward the rear.[50]

Opdycke was convinced the 125th had been one of the first regiments to plant its flags on the enemy earthworks. Five days later, the *Cleveland Morning Leader* reported, "The Illinois regiments and the 41st, 93rd, and 125th Ohio were among the first on the ridge." Which Union regiment was the first to the summit of Missionary Ridge would be hotly debated in veteran's halls for decades to come. Grant wrote in his memoirs of the charge up Missionary Ridge, "The crest was reached, and soon our men were seen climbing over the Confederate barrier at different points in front of both Sheridan's and Wood's divisions." The 125th's Lieutenant Clark concluded, "All circumstances justify the conclusion that each regiment did its best."[51]

A few Yankees were pursing the enemy down the opposite side of Missionary Ridge when the buglers recalled them. The men of Opdycke's demi-brigade went wild over their success, as did every Yankee on the summit. "The huzzas long and loud, the throwing up of hats, the shaking of hands, the embracing, and the tears which were shed," Frank Sherman wrote his brother, "told of hearts full to overflowing." Phil Sheridan was mobbed by his men. A letter to the *Western Reserve Chronicle* noted that for days afterward, "even the wounded soldier forgets for the moment his sufferings while he contemplates the great work he has accomplished." Never one to stop fighting, Opdycke was in the process of having a captured cannon turned to fire on the enemy when Colonel Harker rode up and embraced him. Under Opdycke's critical eye, a Kentucky cannon was fired as a parting salute to the enemy by men of the 125th and 65th Ohio. The youthful Charlie Harker leapt from his horse, ran up the tail of Lady Breckenridge and jumped on the bronze barrel only to discover it was still too hot touch. In all, Opdycke claimed the capture of six artillery pieces for his demi-brigade. He personally sent a caisson and six mule team, which had been seized by two privates from the 79th Illinois, back to Chattanooga.[52]

As the Southerners hurried for their rear, a private from the 125th—John Simpson serving as a personal guard for Colonel Harker—noticed three Johnnies attempting to escape with a wagon load of arms and ammunition. After a chase in which Simpson killed one rebel, he captured the wagon. For his quick action, Simpson was allowed to drive his prize to Sheridan' headquarters. A surrendering Confederate on Missionary Ridge summed up the feelings of many butternuts that afternoon. "The men who could make such a charge could storm Hell and take the Devil by surprise."[53]

Braxton Bragg was shocked by the sudden collapse of his defenses on Missionary Ridge. Only minutes before, he had been heartened to see Phil Sheridan's brigades—directly in front of his headquarters—retreat downhill in what looked like victory. Now, with no reserve troops to plug the gap in his defenses, he could do little about the federal lodgment. The Army of the Cumberland was on Missionary Ridge, and a hole had been punched in the center of the Bragg's line. The unthinkable—collapse of the impenetrable center of the Missionary Ridge—had occurred in just an hour and a half. A forlorn Bragg sat astride his mount, large battle flag in one hand, trying to rally his retreating men. He failed, and his soldiers streamed past the general, what little confidence they had in him gone. Finally, Bragg could see nothing but lines of blue clamoring over his fortifications and turned his horse east to follow his army to safety. Those Northerners who crossed the narrow summit to peer down the eastern slope were treated to a new sight for the Army of the Cumberland, whole brigades of butternuts and batteries of artillery running downhill in an inglorious rout. Only one Confederate division retained its organization and spirit, that of Major General Patrick Cleburne. To him, Braxton Bragg left the unenviable task of slowing any Union pursuit long enough for the defeated army and its trains to escape across Chickamauga Creek.[54]

When Grant and Thomas arrived on the summit, they were engulfed by jubilant Yankees who credited their generalship for the victory. Lieutenant Shellenberger thought General Wood deserved some credit since his division had drawn the rest up Missionary Ridge. As time passed, the veterans, like the 125th's Charles Clark, began to see the taking of Missionary Ridge as "the special work of the rank and file, because it was begun without orders and carried on finally without much organization." An Indiana captain remarked, "I thought I detected in the management [of the battle] what I had never discovered before on the battlefield—a little common sense." Captain G. W. Lewis of the 124th Ohio concluded that "the great battle of Missionary Ridge was won by the *individual moral force of the volunteer Union soldier*."[55]

On the summit of Missionary Ridge, three of the four federal division commanders were content to let their disorganized and exhausted soldiers rest and the Southern army withdraw at its leisure. But not Phil Sheridan. Moments after taking the enemy line on the crest, Captain Bates had begun to reform the 125th under its regimental flag. Sheridan ordered the 125th Ohio to retain its position, and directed Harker and Wagner to reform their brigades for a pursuit down the road toward the Confederate supply depot at Chickamauga Station. Wagner, as senior, was placed in command.[56]

George Wagner sent what remained of his brigade down the east slope of Missionary Ridge. Colonel Harker told Opdycke to take his demi-brigade down the Chickamauga Station road on Wagner's right. Captain Parks and his 40 men were closest to the road, and Opdycke sent them ahead as skirmishers with the rest of the Opdycke's Tigers and his demi-brigade in support. Colonel Walworth's demi-brigade was on Opdycke's right. As soon as Harker and Wagner cleared the crest, Sheridan moved Colonel Sherman's brigade down the road behind them in reserve. The advancing Yankees captured straggling rebels by the dozen along with abandoned cannon and limbers. A short distance from the summit of Missionary Ridge, the road to Chickamauga Station split. In twilight, Colonel Harker sent Opdycke and his demi-brigade with Wagner's brigade down the left fork that went directly to Chickamauga Creek. Colonel Walworth's demi-brigade was directed down the right fork.[57]

A steep, high ridge on the road a mile east of Missionary Ridge slowed the rebels as they tried to get their loaded wagons and cannon over. In growing darkness, Captain Park's skirmishers found Cleburne's rearguard ascending the ridge and a hot fight ensued. Wagner, Opdycke and the regimental commanders quickly established a battle line—Wagner to the left of the road and Opdycke to the right—and sent it forward. The advance was blocked by Cleburne's musketry and two well-placed cannon. For the next hour, muzzle flashes illuminated increasing darkness. Charlie Harker called it "a very stubborn fight."[58]

Phil Sheridan decided to break the deadlock by sending Wagner's men on a flanking movement to the left. But by then Cleburne had decided to withdraw after delaying his pursuers for an hour. On the vacated hill, Southern supplies and two abandoned rebel field pieces were seized, one credited to Captain Park's men, the other to Wagner's brigade. "To Colonel Opdycke," Harker wrote in his official report concerning his fight with Bragg's rearguard, "is due whatever praise my brigade may have received for the battle on the second ridge." Sheridan's exhausted division dropped to the ground the moment the order to halt was given. Harker's brigade bivouacked and ate supper—a meager meal of hardtack and coffee—about 8 p.m. under a clear, moonlit sky. The food was overshadowed by the arrival of Captains Powers and Moses, their fellow recruitment officers and some convalescents. Having left Ohio on the 16th, they finally caught up with the 125th that evening just hours after the momentous victory on Missionary Ridge.[59]

Phil Sheridan sat on his horse in the dark contemplating the military opportunity he knew was slipping away. "Having previously studied the topography of the country thoroughly, I knew that if I pressed on my line of march would carry me back to Chickamauga Station, where we would be in the rear of the Confederates that had been fighting General Sherman, and that there was a possibility of capturing them by such action." Sheridan's division was on this pursuit alone and the general knew better than to continue without reinforcements. He turned his horse back toward Missionary Ridge for orders. There was no Northern pursuit because no one in the Union high command ordered one. While General Grant had been pleased to discover that Sheridan—whose division had suffered the most casualties of any Union division engaged—was chasing the retreating Confederates, he issued no orders. Sheridan found General Granger in Bragg's old headquarters, and passionately argued his case for an immediate pursuit. Granger had already requested permission from Thomas for just such a move. With no response as yet, Granger gave Sheridan permission to go as far Chickamauga Creek, five miles down the road, but not to cross it.[60]

At midnight, more ammunition was issued, and at 1 a.m. Sheridan's entire division advanced down the road on Opdycke's demi-brigade, led by the 65th Ohio deployed as skirmishers. Two hundred more prisoners fell into Opdycke's hands. At 3 a.m., the bluecoats reached Chickamauga Creek at Bird's Mill where the enemy had burned the bridge. When daylight came, Opdycke was ordered to prepare a means of crossing the creek. General Bragg assumed Grant would pursue, and moved rapidly first to Ringgold, Georgia, 10 miles southeast, and ultimately, to Dalton, Georgia, another 15 miles south and east. With the Confederate lead growing, the planned crossing of Chickamauga Creek by Sheridan's division was canceled. At 2 p.m. on the 26th, Harker's brigade was sent to their camps in Chattanooga. After the war, Sheridan wrote, "I was much disappointed that my pursuit had not been supported, for I felt that great results were in store for us should the enemy be vigorously pursued."[61]

Opdycke wrote Lucky Opdycke on November 27 that Captain Bates "did finely" commanding the 125th. Harker's brigade accepted the surrender of 503 Southerners—300 by Opdycke's demi-brigade—on the 25th. The chaos at the summit made it difficult to tell who seized what cannon. "In regard to the number of pieces of artillery," Harker reported, "it will probably be difficult to reconcile the reports of my regimental commanders with the reports of other regiments and brigades." However, Harker emphatically stated, "from my personal observation, I can claim a battery of six guns." The colonel concluded, "Missionary Ridge will forever stand an enduring monument to the noble and brave officers and men who fell so gloriously while scaling its summit." The 125th took 261 men into battle and lost two killed and 30 wounded. Privates Rueben Bunnel and William Miller were killed immediately. Four men eventually succumbed of wounds. Sheridan's 6500 man division lost 20 percent.[62]

Grant's losses in the Chattanooga battles amounted to 5900 men. Bragg's, over 6500, most of which were prisoners, including many drafted Tennesseans who readily surrendered. The rebels lost 40 cannon. The Confederacy lost Chattanooga forever, opening the way to Atlanta and the heart of the South. One clear-eyed young Confederate officer remarked of the loss of Chattanooga, "this is the death knell of the Confederacy."[63]

9

Knoxville and East Tennessee

Major General Ambrose Burnside—the Union general responsible for the disaster at Fredericksburg—had led 15,000 soldiers into Knoxville on September 2. A week later he took control of the Cumberland Gap, 50 miles north and chased the Confederates into Virginia. Despite Tennessee's secession from the Union, most of East Tennessee's independent, non-slave holding mountaineers had remained loyal to the United States. President Lincoln had taken a special interest in these folks, who rebelled against the Confederate draft and suffered under secessionist occupation. Knoxville was located on the north bank of the Holston River about 100 miles northeast of Chattanooga and a short distance east of where the French Broad River joined the Holston River. Strategically, the Knoxville vicinity was traversed by vital railroads—especially the East Tennessee and Virginia Railroad—that moved men and military stores east-west across the Confederacy. To hold this vast, mountainous area, Burnside had just shy of 23,000 men by mid-November. Expanding upon old Southern earthworks, Burnside's engineers constructed good defensive earthworks around much of Knoxville.[1]

Lieutenant General James Longstreet's force arrived in the Knoxville vicinity in mid-November. Burnside and Longstreet were about equal in strength, yet Longstreet lacked sufficient forces to completely encircle Knoxville. Burnside's supply lines were blocked, but loyal Tennesseans were able to sneak some food into the city. Longstreet had been concerned about provisioning his army in East Tennessee from the beginning and now he was on end of a tenuous supply line in pro-Union country where foraging was difficult. Hunger would be a constant companion for men of both armies in the weeks to come.[2]

General Grant in Chattanooga was constantly reminded of Burnside's plight by the War Department. In his last telegram on November 23, Burnside warned that he had 10 to 12 days of supplies and beyond that time frame, he might have to surrender or attempt retreat. As soon as Missionary Ridge been taken on the 25th, Grant directed that the Fourth Corps be readied to march to Burnside's relief on the 27th after being resupplied and re-enforced to a strength of 20,000. Sherman and Hooker would tend to Bragg.[3]

Granger's men were hardly fit for active campaigning. They had only recently begun receiving full rations, were still clad in the same threadbare uniforms they had worn through the siege and their shoes were so badly worn that some men were barefoot. They had little winter clothing. And these Fourth Corps soldiers were about to embark on what one veteran labeled "the most disagreeable, comfortless and altogether wretched campaign of its entire army service."[4]

After a personal reconnaissance to reassure himself that Bragg was really retreating to Dalton, Georgia, Grant gave final approval for Granger to move on the 27th. The

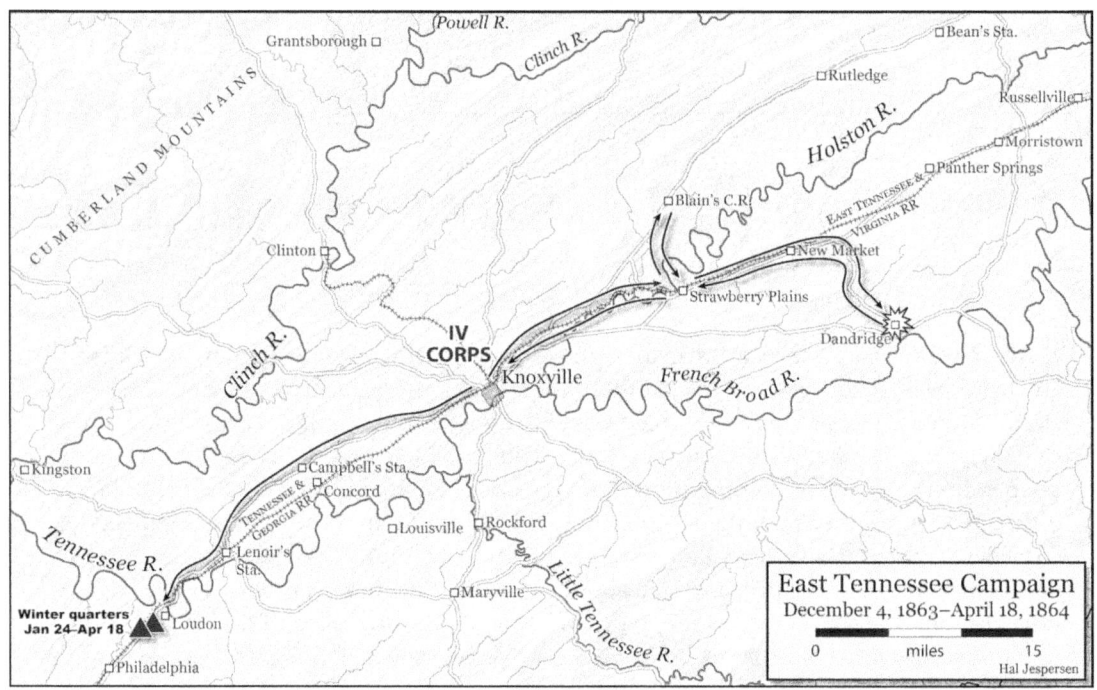

East Tennessee Campaign. Fourth Corps movements from December 1863 to April 1864. Map by Hal Jespersen.

Knoxville expedition would mean abandoning the opportunity to further inflict damage on the wounded Confederate Army of the Tennessee. "Had it not been for the imperative necessity of relieving Burnside, I would have pursued the broken and demoralized retreating enemy," Grant conceded. Sheridan's division returned from Bird's Mill to Chattanooga on the evening of the 26th and prepared to march. Because of a lingering shortage of mules, just one wagon per regiment was permitted. Each soldier was expected to carry his own blankets and rations. For field officers like Opdycke this meant leaving his personal effects and all but one colored servant in Chattanooga. The sick, and wounded were left with Dr. McHenry in the city's hospitals. The steamer *Chattanooga* was loaded with supplies and was to keep pace with the corps as it marched along the south side of the Tennessee River. Despite his instructions from Grant, Granger didn't move his corps on the 27th, confirming Grant's belief that Granger wasn't up to the task. On the 28th, Grant wrote that Granger "was very reluctant to go, he having decided for himself that it was a very bad move to make." The next day, Grant told Sherman, "I am inclined to think, therefore, I shall have to send you." Sherman saw the military necessity of relieving Burnside, but he didn't see the point of occupying East Tennessee. Sherman made it clear to Grant that when Burnside's relief was accomplished "I want to get out." Sherman did not intend to let either himself or his troops languish in what he saw as an unimportant backwater of the war. Grant told Sherman to take to Knoxville three of his own divisions, two from the Fourth Corps and one from the Fourteenth Corps.[5]

At daylight, Saturday, November 28, Sheridan's division began the journey to Knoxville by crossing South Chickamauga Creek in the rain and ever-present mud. Colonel Opdycke expected to be gone two weeks—plenty of time, he reasoned, to send

Longstreet back to Virginia. Sheridan's men marched seven miles. There were no tents to ward off the November cold and large fires were kept going all night. The 29th's advance took Sheridan's men to the shelter of an oak grove within a mile of the Unionist village of Harrison's Landing, 12 miles from Chattanooga. Under a clear night sky, the 125th was issued a two thirds ration of beef from a herd being driven along with the Union column.[6]

A sense of urgency to relieve Knoxville was building in the Union ranks. Aggressive and supremely confident, Opdycke wrote home that he feared that the Confederates would retreat before the federals could destroy them. The march resumed in wee hours before dawn on December 1. Opdycke's demi-brigade was given the lead—the Colonel again on his favorite mount, Barney—and 20 miles later arrived at the Hiwassee River about 2 p.m. These marches in mud and over frozen dirt destroyed many soldier's rotten shoes, which were replaced by rude footwear fashioned from sheep pelts. Opdycke's five regiments were unopposed in crossing the Hiwassee on barges. All of Sheridan's division was over by morning followed by General Wood's division.[7]

Sheridan's men arrived at Fork Creek, six miles from Philadelphia, Tennessee, on December 3, where it joined General Sherman's men. Opdycke saw the region as good farm country that was unfortunately populated by feuding secessionists and Union loyalists. The secessionists were generally wealthier than the unionists, which, according to Opdycke, made foraging their farms—primarily for local corn, bacon and ham—morally acceptable. On December 4, the Division expected to meet the resupply boats at Loudon, but the riverboats were unable to pass the shoals below Kingston on the Tennessee River. When they abandoned Loudon, the Confederates had destroyed the rail bridge, and no ford being available, a bridge had to be constructed across the Little Tennessee River at Morgantown, Tennessee.[8]

Longstreet decided to attack Knoxville on November 29 before Sherman arrived. The Confederates were repulsed—Longstreet's admitted losing over 800 soldiers—yet the rebels remained before the city until the night of December 4. The morning of the 5th the Fourth Corps followed the Sherman's Fifteenth Corps across the bridge at Morgantown. Early that afternoon, 15 miles from Knoxville, Sherman learned that Longstreet had retreated east abandoning his Knoxville siege. With a new spring in their step and a small ration of cornmeal in their haversacks, Harker's men passed through Marysville, 15 miles south of Knoxville, on December 5.[9]

Generals Sherman and Granger rode into Knoxville on December 6. On the road in, Sherman noticed a herd of cattle "which did not look much like starvation." Sherman found Burnside quartered in a large, fine mansion "looking very comfortable." Sherman offered to help Burnside pursue Longstreet "though in fact my men were worn out, and suffering in that cold season and climate." Burnside told Sherman that he just needed Granger's two divisions—10,000 men—who, with his own, would push Longstreet out of Tennessee. Granger objected and complained bitterly about the hard treatment of the Fourth Corps, which Sherman ignored. Sherman dined at Burnside's headquarters that evening. "I had seen nothing of this kind in my field experience," Sherman recalled of the abundant food and elegant table service. Burnside explained that he had never really been completely surrounded and received supplies locally which was a revelation to Sherman. "Had I known of this, I should not have hurried my men so fast," a disgusted Sherman wrote 20 years later. As per his understanding with Grant, Sherman and four divisions left Knoxville and arrived back in Chattanooga on December 16. According to

Wilbur Hinman of the 65th Ohio, it was left to the Fourth Corps "to drag out a wretched existence for more than two months in the East Tennessee wilderness." For many in the 125th that winter would be remembered as the worst experience they had in the army. As Corporal Chester Tuttle later explained, "We were without shelter nearly all winter and had but little clothing during the same and not much to eat."[10]

On the morning of December 9, Harker's brigade crossed the Holston River and went into camp a mile from Knoxville with details sent to guard the Holston River crossings. Knoxville met with Opdycke's approval because "there are so many real union people." Ridgely Powers described the condition of the Brigade in a letter to the *Western Reserve Chronicle*: "Our men were much fatigued, and many of them nearly shoeless. We had all the time been on half or two thirds rations...." The men mostly lived off the country, foraging up to 20 miles and offering vouchers for needed supplies—butter at $1.50 a pound and chickens at $1 each. As of the 12th, Opdycke felt the army adequately provisioned, but hungry for news and mail. That evening he acquired a copy of a Cincinnati newspaper and read its handful of pages to all the assembled officers.[11]

Ambrose Burnside had been requesting replacement since October, claiming ill health. He was relieved by General Grant as of the 12th and replaced in departmental command by his chief of staff, Major General John G. Foster. Command of Burnside's Ninth Corps was held by Major General John G. Parke. Both generals had been Burnside men and, like many from the Army of the Potomac, were intimidated James Longstreet and his infantry.[12]

The day Burnside rode out of Knoxville, General Granger appealed to Grant and Sherman to transfer the Fourth Corps to Chattanooga because of its lack of equipment, poor physical condition of the men, worn clothing and shoes, few animals and lack of cold weather gear. Granger was convinced that Longstreet was returning to Virginia. On the 15th of December, General Grant told Foster to send Granger's men to Chattanooga when possible. The next day General Halleck in Washington alerted Grant to rumors that Longstreet was reversing himself and preparing to move again on Knoxville. Halleck believed that no Union forces should leave East Tennessee until Longstreet was no longer a threat. Grant ordered Foster to advance immediately in Longstreet's direction, but Foster declined, citing bad roads and inadequate supplies. Meanwhile, the Fourth Corps began constructing huts for protection from the winter weather.[13]

Marching orders reached Sheridan's division on the evening of the 15th, to prepare to move with three days of rations and 60 cartridges. Wood and Sheridan were being sent to Blaine's Crossroads—seven miles north of where the Virginia railroad crossed the Holston River at Strawberry Plains. Sheridan's men—Wagner's brigade of seven regiments and Harker's of nine in two demi-brigades—would take the train while Wood's men would march. Departing on the East Tennessee and Virginia Railroad at 2 a.m., Opdycke's demi-brigade moved slowly northeast on a train pulled by a small engine fired with green wood supplemented by lard to make the boiler fire hotter. The little locomotive's engineer was pessimistic about the chances of the overloaded train completing the journey on tracks slippery with frost. Opdycke insisted and the train chugged away from the station. The little locomotive eventually did grind to a halt, but a determined Opdycke detailed 60 men to push. The train groaned into Strawberry Plains—16 miles northeast of Knoxville—about dawn. Late morning, Harker and Wagner's brigades began the trek to Blaine's Crossroads where they would be in the center of a defensive line that included elements of the Ninth and Twenty-Third Corps and stretched from Clinch Mountain

Nine. Knoxville and East Tennessee

More than one veteran noted the absence of strawberries at Strawberry Plains. Library of Congress.

south to the Holston River. This show of force was meant to dissuade Longstreet from attacking Knoxville from the northeast.[14]

Without adequate protection from the bone chilling cold, the bluecoats improvised shelters from scavenged materials and pine boughs. Heaping log fires were built in front of rock outcroppings to radiate heat. The loyal Tennesseans were victimized by foragers wearing blue and gray. "The destitution and consequent hardship and suffering of the troops, and citizens living within the theater of operations," wrote Lieutenant Clark, "is almost without parallel in the history of warfare." General Granger complained to George Thomas on December 19 that "the suffering and privations now being undergone by our troops are most cruel." When General Foster had clothing and supplies earmarked for the Fourth Corps diverted to his Ninth Corps, Sheridan had the next shipment concealed in forage wagons and slipped it past Foster's inspectors.[15]

Longstreet's main camp was at Russellville, Tennessee, on the Virginia Railroad about 30 miles northeast of Strawberry Plains in an area previously untouched by predatory foraging. Rebel cavalry held a picket line from Rutledge south to Mossy Creek—10 miles east of Strawberry Plains—and then south to Dandridge. That Christmas 46,000 cold, hungry and armed men—what one resident called "the ebony plumed vulture of despair"—descended on the region between Holston and French Broad Rivers. Harker's brigade at Blaine's Crossroads was 20 miles from Knoxville. It was cold, the men had no tents and according to one soldier it took 25 acres of the best woods to keep the men warm just one week.[16]

The long, slow grind of recruiting finally ended for Major Moore on December 5 when Ashtabula's Captain Sterling Manchester and his Company K were sworn into United States service. Company K, accompanied by Moore, left Ohio December 3 and, gathering some convalescents along the route, arrived in Chattanooga on December 10. Lack of transportation to East Tennessee stranded all soldiers destined for Granger's corps in that city. On Christmas eve an expedition bound for Knoxville composed of 150 wagon loads of supplies and 2500 men pulled out of Chattanooga. The expedition was commanded by Colonel Bernard Laiboldt of the 2nd Missouri Infantry. Moore was given charge of the 530 federal soldiers bound for Harker's brigade.[17]

The brigade sized force covered six miles of the hundred or so to Knoxville on the 24th. It was assumed that rebel cavalry would harass Laiboldt's wagon train and that evening, a few Southerners, under a flag of truce, arrived to spy on the expedition. On December 26, Laiboldt's caravan rolled into Cleveland. A cold rain accompanied it on December 27 when the bluecoats marched into Charlestown, Tennessee, 10 miles northeast of Cleveland. Crossing the Hiwassee River the next morning the detachment was attacked by a marauding Confederate cavalry unit from Bragg's army. Colonel Laibolt formed a defensive perimeter—Moore commanded the left flank—to forestall the cavalrymen while the remaining wagons crossed. Once the wagons were safe, Laibolt "charged with the infantry in double quick on the astonished rebels and routed them completely." The enemy cavalrymen—numbering 1600—were no match for infantry and their repulse cost them over 170 casualties. Two Yankees were killed and 10 wounded. Moore's men were given charge of over 100 enemy prisoners.[18]

In the contested valley between the Holston and French Broad Rivers there were frequent and sharp skirmishes between the Union and Confederate armies. There were significant skirmishes on December 24 at Hay's Ferry and December 29 at Mossy Creek. General Grant arrived in Knoxville on December 31 for a week to inspect the troops, confer with their commanders and plan strategy. Grant's arrival was accompanied by a period of intensely cold weather. In Knoxville, the thermometer fell to zero, while further east in New Market—where six Confederate pickets froze to death—it reached 20 below. Grant took note of his soldiers worn clothing and estimated 40 percent of them were shoeless. He ordered General Thomas to send forward all available supplies in Chattanooga, but Thomas had little to send. Nevertheless, Grant expected General Foster to attack and drive Longstreet's Confederates east beyond Bull's Gap and Red Bridge, over 50 miles northeast of Knoxville. Preparatory to that attack, Grant ordered the Ninth and Twenty-Third Corps to Mossy Creek, and the Fourth Corps to Strawberry Plains.[19]

For those Union troops whose three year enlistments were expiring, re-enlistment came with the offer of a 30-day furlough, to be granted only when they could be spared. Most men in the northeast Ohio regiments—the 19th, 41st, 64th and 65th—re-enlisted. Gripped with patriotic fever, a majority of the 125th signed the rolls on January 4 to re-enlist for three more years also. But there would be no leave for Opdycke's men, because the War Department decreed that regiments with less than two years' service were not eligible for a furlough. According to Charles Clark, "That decision did not prevent us from serving to the end of the war, but it did deprive us of a visit to home and loved ones."[20]

On January 4, Moore's detachment and Laiboldt's wagon train crossed the Tennessee River and entered into country one Tiger thought "was the very best I have seen in the south." The wagon train was at Loudon, 52 miles from Harker's brigade at Blaine's Crossroads. Even guarding a supply train, Laiboldt's detachment was placed on reduced rations—the coffee ration in particular was cut by 75 percent. Foraging had become standard practice and on a cold but clear January 9, one of Laiboldt's foraging parties, brought in 33 sheep and one cow.[21]

In an early January letter from Blaine's Crossroads, Opdycke cheerfully informed his wife that the 125th was well situated and healthy, enjoying the fresh air. In reality, Harker's brigade was out of rations and animal fodder by January 10. The discomfort of his poorly clothed and fed Ohioans began to weigh heavily on the colonel who felt for his soldiers. The Ohioans were issued one-half pound of ground corn—cob included—and either a half pound of beef or a quarter pound of pork a day. Sometimes they went 48 hours with no rations. Some men slept so close to their campfires that clothing and blankets were occasionally scorched. "The hardships and exposure told severely upon the men," remembered Lieutenant R. K. Hulse of January 1864.[22]

Harker's men were sent 19 miles up the Holston River to forage. The men marched hungry, having only meat to eat the day before, and that evening they slept in the snow. Longstreet's pickets shadowed them on the opposite bank of the river. When the brigade turned away from the river to begin foraging the country, three Confederates deserted and reported that the country was well picked over by Longstreet's men in recent weeks. At dawn of the 12th, Colonel Harker left Opdycke in command of the brigade on the Holston and rode back to Blaine's Crossroads to report the futility of foraging. General Sheridan, in turn, complained to General Granger about the lack of sufficient food. "Colonel Harker," Sheridan reported, "started for Bean's Station or vicinity yesterday to try and get some [rations], and without anything to eat for his officers and men." Sheridan requested "that my division be removed to some other locality where I can better help my troops." Opdycke continued to dispatch foraging parties and managed to partially fill 30 wagons in a region where Longstreet's men had appropriated even the farmer's seed grain. Back at 3:30 p.m., the entire command, including the usually tireless Opdycke, was exhausted. The army needed to relocate a more favorable foraging area. "We feel the uselessness of remaining here and are all desperately anxious to leave," the colonel wrote his wife.[23]

By mid–January 1864 there was snow on the ground and the rivers were high with floating ice further interrupting the flow of supplies from Knoxville. General Foster informed U. S. Grant on January 15 "I am forced to abandon all idea of active operations" because the soldiers "were suffering for want of tents, food, clothing and medicine." He blamed an outbreak of diarrhea on a diet that was predominantly meat, and less than a full ration of that. Not far away, Longstreet and his 26,000 men faced the same hardships.[24]

On January 14, Lieutenant Colonel Moore, Captain Sterling Manchester, and Company K arrived at Blaine's Cross Roads to share the regiment's discomfort. David Moore was at last united with Colonel Emerson Opdycke, the man he called his "brother/father." Colonel Opdycke wrote in his field diary on the 15th, "Colonel Moore does finely. <u>He will do!</u>" Moore had no time to become acquainted with his new comrades. The next day Colonel Harker's brigade was ordered to begin a "never-to-be-forgotten" march to Dandridge, Tennessee.[25]

The countryside within 20 miles of Knoxville had been very efficiently "plundered and robbed" by the rebels, according one Ohio observer. It was rumored that the bottom land along the French Broad River, east/southeast of Knoxville, offered good foraging, with estimates of over 60,000 bushels of corn below Dandridge, Tennessee, alone. On January 14, General Foster ordered the two divisions of the Fourth Corps and one of the Twenty-Third Corps to advance from Blaine's Crossroads to Dandridge, 34 miles east of Knoxville and on the north bank of the French Broad River. These three divisions were to cross the Holston River, proceed to Dandridge, bridge the French Broad, take a strong defensible position and forage south of the river. Granger's men would be making this movement in cold rain and snow while subsisting on reduced rations, and living without tents.[26]

The afternoon of the 14th, a Union force of 22 cavalry regiments and a brigade of infantry all commanded by Brigadier General Samuel Sturgis, seized Dandridge. The next morning, Sturgis established a defensive line northeast of town. Behind Sturgis, 59 federal regiments were moving east from Strawberry Plains toward Dandridge and Mossy Creek. Twenty-five miles east, Longstreet set 79 regiments in motion toward Mossy Creek and Dandridge. The divisions of Micah Jenkins and Bushrod Johnson were specifically send down the Morristown Road toward Dandridge to protect that important foraging area. Longstreet himself would accompany the leading cavalry to Dandridge. To forestall the rebel advance until the Union infantry could arrive, Sturgis planned an attempt to flank the gray cavalry in his front on the morning of the 16th. However, the appearance of Confederate infantry thwarted Sturgis' plan and drove his cavalry back to the outskirts of Dandridge.[27]

The bulk of the fast-moving Northern force arrived at Dandridge on the evening of Saturday, January 16, filling the village with soldiers and empty wagons. Sheridan's division guarded the wagons while Sturgis' cavalry formed a screen on the roads two miles east of town. For his part, Longstreet planned to attack the cavalry line in the morning. By daylight on the 17th, a Confederate infantry division was just three miles out the Morristown Road north of Dandridge, if needed.[28]

Early Sunday morning, Sturgis' cavalry was ordered to screen operations in the Dandridge area by picketing two miles northeast of the town from the French Broad River to the Morristown Road. Colonel Israel Garrard's blue cavalry division occupied the center of the picket line and covered the road to Chucky Bend. On Garrard's left was Colonel Oscar LaGrange's brigade of Colonel E. M. McCook's cavalry division and to Garrard's right was Colonel Frank Wolford's brigade. The terrain was hilly with a mixture of open fields, forest and creeks. The Yankee infantry divisions would deploy around Dandridge while men from Sheridan's division, mainly Harker's brigade, assembled a wagon bridge across the French Broad River downriver from the town.[29]

Shortly after first light, General Sheridan scouted along the fog-shrouded French Broad below town for a suitable site for a temporary bridge. Locating a narrow place in the river, he ordered Harker's brigade to begin construction using some wagons as piers. The 125th, with just under 400 men, was detailed for picket duty with the cavalry east of town. Due to Lieutenant Colonel Moore's inexperience in command, Captain Ed Bates was appointed acting major to assist. The Tigers were sent out the Chucky Bend Road east of Dandridge. Ahead of them would be cavalry pickets watching the approaches to Dandridge from the north and east.[30]

Lieutenant Colonel Moore—riding a fine mule after his small Tennessee mare gave out—took the regiment out the Chucky Road. The regiment went down into the valley of a small creek and back up the next hill before halting on a ridge near the Neff farmhouse, about two miles from town. Moore sent companies A, C, F and I forward as skirmishers under Captain Bates' command. The forward picket posts were located on a ridge about a quarter mile further east in open fields—companies A and C to the right of the road and F and I to the left. The picket reserves from each company were back in woods bordering the open fields. The remaining six companies of the 125th would constitute a grand reserve on the Chucky Road. The right of Moore's picket line connected with that of the 93rd Ohio Infantry—just 200 men—from Hazen's brigade, which had the same duty as the 125th and picketed down to the river on their right. To the left of the 125th's was the 1st Wisconsin Cavalry of Colonel LaGrange's brigade. To the left of the 125th's position were open fields, and to the right, a field bordered on three sides by open timber. A quarter mile back and on the brow of the hill in the regiment's rear was the main body of Colonel Israel Garrard's cavalry division. On Garrard's right, Colonel Frank Wolford's cavalry division covered the Hay's Ferry Road and picketed down to the river. The 93rd Ohio was in front of Wolford's horsemen. Moore asked headquarters to send another infantry regiment to support the Wisconsin cavalry on his left, but it never came. Nevertheless, it was assumed by officers of the 125th that the rest of their brigade would come to their assistance in a fight.[31]

About midday the bridge was completed and Colonel Harker rode across to test it. After riding a short distance into the woods on the opposite bank, Harker discovered more water ahead. After a few minutes scouting, Harker realized the bridge ended on an island. Sheridan was furious over this error, the result of poor maps and fog.[32]

Out the Chucky Road east of Dandridge, the morning had been quiet, interrupted only by a stray hog that ventured into the picket line and was butchered. David Moore had time to consider that it was his wife's birthday. At noon, blue and gray cavalry pickets began to exchange shots out east of town. As the pressure increased, the cavalrymen were instructed to fall back through the infantry pickets. Some stopped to alert Moore that there was considerable Confederate infantry out in front. In fact, Garrard's horsemen in front of the 125th had bumped into dismounted cavalry, while McCook's horsemen on the left had encountered a battalion of South Carolina infantry. Sharp small arms fire erupted a half mile east of the 125th's left flank from the direction of the Morristown Road.[33]

When General Parke—in direct command of the Dandridge expedition—learned that Confederate infantry were headed his way, he was overcome by concern that he might face a reinforced James Longstreet and ordered that a full engagement be avoided. Sheridan, Wood and Granger all preferred the entire Fourth Corps attack, but instead, Parke would spend the afternoon pondering a full retreat.[34]

Enemy horsemen were now in plain sight of Moore's pickets. According to the lieutenant colonel, his picket outposts were attacked at 3 p.m. and their reserves went to their aid. The federal cavalry on the 125th's left was driven back and in Moore's words, the fight became "general and severe." Moore's advanced infantry pickets were dislodged. A second charge by dismounted cavalry, forced companies F and I to retreat. Moore sent Company H forward at the double quick to a split rail fence midway to the ridge to support the skirmishers. The company was able to drive the dismounted rebel cavalry back off the crest of the ridge, but South Carolina sharpshooters on their left flank made the position untenable for long. Acting regimental adjutant Lieutenant Seabury Smith—only recently promoted from sergeant major—was shot dead at Moore's side by a sniper, and the lieutenant colonel miraculously avoided injury when a bullet ripped through his overcoat sleeve. Sergeant John Simpson of Company G volunteered to take Smith's place.[35]

Lieutenant Seabury Smith, 1863. After he was killed at Dandridge, Smith was wrapped in a blanket and buried by his comrades in the town cemetery. Reproduced from Clark, *Opdycke Tigers*.

As the firing intensified along the rail fence, Corporal Noah Wiley was struck in the center of the forehead by a spent ball that passed through a fence rail. Dazed, he said, "Lieutenant, let us retreat." This was met with peals of laughter by his fellows, but retreat was inevitable. Seeing Company H come forward, companies F and I had retired from the base of the ridge back toward the regiment on the road. Some of the men of Company F coming back down the road, stopped at a farmhouse, took cover in a shed and began sniping at the enemy. Too late the men realized that it would be impossible to retreat from their position in daylight. In Company F, Mexican War veteran, Private Conrad Wing, was shot in the head, and two other Ohioans were wounded and two captured. A corporal and a private from Company H were captured hiding behind a stump they used for cover. Two of men escaped the shed under the cover of darkness. Companies A and C, on the right and under the direction of Captain Bates, twice faced charges by dismounted enemy cavalry, but with the help of one company from the 93rd Ohio, repulsed the enemy. When a third attack came, Bates' men—outnumbered 3 to 1—fell back, but remained as skirmishers, halting at the edge of the woods to the right rear of the regiment. Other skirmishers retreated in the face of the Confederate onslaught. Some men of Company F returned along the road—where Southern bullets struck the Neff farmhouse—while the remainder of Company I took to the fields. A sergeant and a private failed to retire with their company and were captured.[36]

With the Wisconsin cavalry forced back and the enemy was in position to flank Moore on the left. The entire regiment came under vigorous musketry, and Southern artillery "played upon us furiously," according to Moore. Garrard's artillery responded with some success, but the cavalry division retreated to the next ridge in the rear of the 125th. Moore ordered eight companies of regiment along the road into a large, semicircular depression in the field to the left of the road and 200 yards in front of the creek. This "natural rifle pit" as Moore called it, afforded some protection if the men laid down. To the more distant rebel artillerymen, the Yankees seemed to simply disappear. Around 4 p.m., a line of dismounted Southern cavalry and infantry from General Bushrod Johnson's division crested the distant ridge a mile out the road. The enemy foot soldiers filled

Bowl-like depression or natural rifle pit on the Dandridge skirmish site that shielded the 125th late in the afternoon on January 17, 1864. Small trees are growing from the bottom. Photograph by the author.

the ridge "as far as we could see to the right and left," according to Lieutenant Clark. When these infantrymen came into range on the regiment's left, Private George Murdock, a 37-year-old Scotsman in Company B, rose up and fired without orders, touching off a ragged volley. Moore settled the men and ordered them to fire volleys by rank which drove the rebels back on his front and left, only to repeat the process when the enemy came on yet again. "For so few in numbers our fire was terrific," Sergeant Ralsa Rice remembered. "The fields were full of objects for our aim."[37]

Rather than another frontal assault across an open field, the enemy chose to advance on the flanks where there was more cover. One gray line came through a cornfield on the regiment's left flank. Moore refused his left company and ordered firing by rank to the left oblique which drove the Southerners back. These volleys coming from a concealed enemy temporarily confused the Confederates, who were uncertain of what they faced. Still, whenever the Tigers stopped firing, the Johnnies advanced again. Confederate artillery fire was steady, but too high to be a danger to the men in the depression.[38]

Almost simultaneously, another line of Southern battle flags was seen advancing to the edge of the timber on the right of the road, and according to Lieutenant Clark "gave us a hot fire." The 125th was caught in a crossfire. To the right of the road, Captain Bates made a bold decision and ordered companies A and C to charge straight at the enemy, supported by some of Colonel Garrard's dismounted cavalry. Emerging from their concealment, yelling with bayonets lowered, the 125th's two most veteran companies drove the battle line of Johnnies back almost a half mile into their second battle line at the base of the ridge. Two men from Company C were wounded—including Walter Cheney who, at 15, was the youngest soldier in the regiment—and one captured. Bates men were too winded to pursue the enemy. Moore later wrote his wife, "Nothing but the nature of the ground saved my men from slaughter. God directed me to the position I took up. The volleys from the concealed force dismayed the enemy."[39]

To the right of Captain Bates skirmishers, the 93rd Ohio was driven back toward the river in the same attack and pursued by overwhelming numbers of enemy accompanied by artillery fire. Opposing batteries dueled briefly before the Southern artillery retired. Colonel Wolford dismounted the 12th Kentucky Cavalry and sent it in to reenforce the beleaguered 93rd. The Kentuckians and Ohioans were able to stop the Confederates and regain some of the lost ground, but in doing so the 93rd lost contact with the 125th. The two infantry regiments were separated and isolated as low hanging clouds settled in and darkness approached.[40]

Generals Sheridan and Harker visited Moore during the afternoon to witness the fighting, but left no new orders. Opdycke's demi-brigade was on the island in the French Broad and upon hearing the distant musketry, Colonel Opdycke "felt uneasy." He would have personally gone to his men, but Colonel Harker mistakenly told him the 125th had been ordered back. After sunset, with the 93rd having left the field, the 125th was alone on the line with only cavalry as support.[41]

Opdycke's Tigers were down to 10 rounds of ammunition each. Colonel Garrard's two cannon supporting the 125th were unable to halt the Confederate infantry. Under the cover of darkness, the enemy moved a strong line of pickets up close to the Union line. Moore described his situation to his wife: "No instructions, no orders, no reinforcements; the enemy still augmenting force closing upon us, stretching away beyond both my flanks." The Tigers needed to get out of what Sergeant Ralsa Rice called "this death trap." Moore decided to retire to the hill in his rear hoping darkness would hide his move. It didn't entirely, and the Confederates detected the 125th as it left the safety of the depression. Unable to aim in the dimming light, the Southerners nonetheless sent volleys in the direction of the retreating Yankees. One man from the 125th was killed and several wounded crossing the creek and climbing the hill in their rear. Sergeant Simpson—the volunteer adjutant—was at Moore's side and was shot in the arm at the creek and when he reached the crest of the hill was shot again in the side and his horse killed. Another private was mortally wounded—dying shortly after his comrades carried him from the field. Moore reformed the regiment on the crest of a hill behind the creek where the cavalry had been earlier in the day. Responding to the sound of gunfire, Colonel Garrard and some dismounted troopers came up behind the 125th. Moore approached Garrard and pointed out the precarious position in which his regiment found itself without orders to retire. Garrard—who just months ago had seen half of the 7th Ohio Cavalry trapped and captured—understood and told Moore to take the 125th back to the second ridge in the rear while two regiments of his troopers would assume picket duty. It had begun to rain.[42]

Moore took his men a half mile back toward Dandridge and posted them on the wooded hill over which the Chucky Road passed. Garrard's cavalrymen and Moore's infantrymen began quickly building bonfires to suggest they had been reinforced and were staying. Moore was disconcerted to discover that no one seemed to know where the Fourth Corps was. He sent Captain Bates to Dandridge to find someone in authority to give him instructions. At last the 125th was ordered back to town. The Ohioans rejoined Harker's brigade in Dandridge around 10 p.m. It was then that the officers of the 125th learned that a retreat had been under consideration all afternoon. General Parke had decided that evening to retreat to Strawberry Plains before the rain made the roads impassable. The bluecoats began forming ranks to withdraw from the Dandridge area about 11 p.m. From the enlisted man's point of view, Private Edwin Woodworth summed up the day succinctly. "About one o'clock the pickets commenced firing and we stood our ground until dark." David Moore expressed his frustration with the Union high command in a letter to his wife: *"We were left unprotected for fear of bringing on a general engagement, as Longstreet was regarded as too strong for us."* For his part, James Longstreet, upon seeing those bond fires, assumed the Yankees were staying to fight. He moved forward some infantry and artillery, and his men settled in for the night expecting the worst tomorrow and planning to cover his own retreat. The entire line of General Sturgis' cavalry advanced later that evening and the enemy fell back to the protection of the heavy timber with little incident. About 9 o'clock, the Union cavalry was likewise ordered to retire.[43]

The Tigers marched through the night to Strawberry Plains. At 3:30 a.m. Harker's brigade stopped briefly and a tired Colonel Opdycke slept leaning against a tree. The march resumed at 8:30 a.m. in a rain that had turned the roads to mud. The brigade arrived at Strawberry Plains and crossed the Holston River that afternoon and the bridge was burned shortly thereafter. Five more miles toward Knoxville and they bivouacked, exhausted, hungry and thoroughly chilled, even though it was the first night in two weeks above freezing.[44]

Wilbur Hinman of the 65th Ohio recalled the action at Dandridge as a "spirited attack by a considerable rebel force." But like thousands of similar fights in the Civil War, it drew little attention. Phil Sheridan, Tom Wood, and Gordon Granger were all disgusted with Parke's leadership which ceded all the territory east of Strawberry Plains to Longstreet without a fight. Harker and Sheridan both complimented the 125th's conduct, and in Colonel Opdycke's eyes, his boys "fought like Tigers." Only luck and good leadership prevented the regiment from being destroyed or captured. Of what became known as the Battle of Dandridge, Colonel Opdycke recorded in his field notebook, "125th fought like Tigers." And of his new lieutenant colonel, he said, "Col. Moore is splendid, everyone likes him and he handled the Ohio Tigers finely." Sergeant Rice judged Lieutenant Colonel David Moore "well worthy of our confidence, a strategist of no mean order." Of Captain Bates' assistance Moore wrote, "I am greatly indebted." Nevertheless, in sum, the battle had been a very minor affair in a campaign the Union command wished to forget.[45]

Officially, the Ohio Tigers lost five men killed, 15 wounded and seven captured, five of whom died in the notorious Southern prison camp at Andersonville, Georgia, the following summer. Lieutenant Smith's comrades reluctantly buried him in the Dandridge cemetery without benefit of a coffin. Private Mathias C. Callahan was believed mortally wounded by both Union and Confederate surgeons who examined him and listed as such on the rolls. He was left in the care of a Unionist family and two months later he reappeared in New Market, weak but alive. The fighting cost the 93rd Ohio 12 killed and wounded, LaGrange's cavalry lost 46, but captured 19 rebels. Total Union losses were 107—for the Confederates it was estimated at 150.[46]

Eventually, it became evident that General Longstreet's attack at Dandridge was made to cover *his* desire to avoid bringing on a general engagement. The casualties the

125th suffered on January 17 seemed unnecessary. Referring to General Parke, Lieutenant Colonel P. C. Hayes commanding the 103rd Ohio wrote that the Dandridge expedition was "the product of a brain terribly befogged and shamefully timorous, and from beginning to end, indicated the utmost incompetency." Opdycke expressed the feeling of the entire Fourth Corps when he wrote his wife, "This Department is a tragedy of errors and I am sick of it."[47]

On January 21, the Third Brigade left Strawberry Plains for Knoxville. Harker's and Wagner's brigades arrived at Loudon on the 24th. The two brigades crossed the Tennessee River on flat boats and went into winter camp two miles from town—30 miles southwest of Knoxville. Loudon's reputation for moral debauchery was such that Opdycke forbade any of his command from entering it. Log huts were erected, food and supplies became more abundant and camp equipage was sent from Chattanooga. Opdycke departed for Warren—where friends, admirers and an expensive gold watch awaited him—on January 27 on a 60-day furlough. Lieutenant Colonel Moore was left in charge and began a regular correspondence with Opdycke. It was a quiet mid-winter with only one uneventful four-day sortie when Longstreet sent some infantry across the Holston at Strawberry Plains. Longstreet finally returned to Virginia for good in April.[48]

David Moore was officially mustered as a lieutenant colonel on January 30, 1864. Who would replace him as major? In a purely seniority based promotion system, it would go automatically to the senior captain, Joseph Bruff of Company A—the 36-year-old farmer, Republican partisan, and former state representative. Emerson Opdycke personally disliked Bruff, but by most accounts, Bruff was a competent, but not gifted, officer. Colonel Opdycke's choice for major was Captain Bates, the second ranking captain and a clearly a superior officer. Bates had begun his career as a 22-year-old private in 19th Ohio, enlisting in April 1861, and was elected captain of the 125th Company C in September 1862. Bates was taller and bigger than most soldiers at six feet, 160 pounds and better educated having briefly studied classics in college.[49]

Commissions and promotions in the volunteer regiments were the governor's to make. Governor David Tod had no specific policy regarding promotions. Some he based on seniority, some on recommendation of the regimental colonel and some were completely political and arbitrary. As early as August 24, 1863, while Moore was still officially a major, Opdycke was promoting Bates to succeed Moore. Governor Tod, who probably knew Bruff, verbally approved Opdycke's recommendation of Bates. However, Bates was then the only commissioned officer in his company, so no official action was forthcoming. Nevertheless, as long as Tod was governor, Opdycke was confident could keep Bruff from becoming regimental major.[50]

However, Tod was not re-nominated and John Brough was elected to replace him in 1864. Brough was known to be a friend of enlisted soldiers everywhere. If a complaint of mistreatment arose from the ranks, Brough was known to personally intervene, antagonizing Ohio colonels. Brough differed greatly Tod in his belief that seniority should be the *only* consideration in promotion. Nevertheless, Colonel Opdycke paid a visit to Brough on February 4 on his way home to Warren, and recorded in his diary that he had persuaded the governor to block Bruff's promotion. However, the next day, Brough issued General Order No. 5. The opening sentence read: "Herewith, all vacancies in established regiments, battalions or independent companies will be filled by promotion according to seniority in the regiment." With this single order Brough gained the lasting animosity of many Ohio officers in the field. In Brough's somewhat unrealistic view and faulty logic, incompetent soldiers should never become officers in the first place. Governor Brough's new policy supported Captain Bruff's claim to the majority. David Moore's opinion of Brough's policy was unpastor-like: "Oh, that policy of Brough's is damnable! Merit is ignored! Aspiration is crushed out! It is damnable!"[51]

The Bruff vs. Bates for major controversy divided the regiment. On February 14, Moore wrote Opdycke that both Bruff and Bates were anxious to hear from Opdycke, who had promised to resolve the controversy. Moore wrote, "I am anxious. I think the officers are nearly equally divided between B. & B., fear so, at least. Am still full of hope that you may bring it out all right." Bruff presented his commission as major to Lieutenant Colonel Moore on February 27. "Now I wish you were here," Moore wrote Opdycke. Although Bruff had the commission, he had to be sworn in as major by a mustering officer. Moore told Opdycke, "While he has that in his pocket, if I put Capt. Bates in command over him, it won't seem right at any rate. It leaves me in a very unpleasant situation.... All of Bruff's clique are in rapture over Gov. Brough's policy of promoting solely by rank." It would take all of Moore's pastoral diplomacy to keep the lid on the divided regimental officer's corps. Eventually, the petty feuding between the Bates and Bruff partisans reached Colonel Harker who didn't want any part of it. He followed the book, directing that Bruff should be regarded as a captain when Moore was absent, not a major, but command of the regiment was to be left with Bruff as senior captain. Harker specified this arrangement was only until Colonel Opdycke returned. On March 8, Capt. Joseph Bruff was mustered as major, and a bitter Ed Bates resigned his commission as a captain. Just days later, Bates reversed his decision and asked Colonel Harker to allow him to resume his command. Harker readily agreed. Captain Bates could easily have won promotion to major or higher rank if he switched regiments, but he was devoted to the Ohio Tigers and his men.[52]

Opdycke returned to the 125th determined to marginalize Major Bruff. In a late April response to his wife's query regarding Bruff, Opdycke informed her that the new Major was modest and obedient. However, Bruff was given no duties and bunked with the surgeons. Opdycke labeled him "quite useless." Emerson Opdycke hated to lose, and wasn't done with Major Bruff.[53]

General Grant's assistant inspector general conducted an inspection of the Fourth Corps in late February, and pronounced Harker's brigade as deserving of "especial notice." The 125th was cited in particular for its drill and cleanliness of arms, the only regiment in the three army corps mentioned by name. The inspector general also noted in his report, "Clothing is not good ... some regiments being badly deficient." New uniforms were in short supply, but Harker himself intervened to correct the deficiencies. By April, the health of the 662 officers and men was good. Drinking was a perennial problem and Moore arrested the former sharpshooter, Captain Coonrod, for being drunk on duty as regimental officer of the day. By late February, gambling had become endemic and single sweep by the provost netted 42 soldiers accused of betting. According to Moore, "Three from 125th, only two whom, Company D, were guilty."[54]

Colonel Opdycke was returning to the regiment on April 2 when he learned of Phil Sheridan's departure to take command of the Union cavalry in Virginia. Opdycke hated to see Sheridan transferred, unless he was replaced by General Cox, which was unlikely. The Colonel reached camp in Loudon on April 4 where a newly constructed headquarters awaited him. Moore now assumed many of the duties that Opdycke had performed himself. Refreshed from his furlough, Opdycke was ready to have the country "purified from slavery" even if more men were lost. For himself, Opdycke was ready to accept whatever God willed for him.[55]

On April 10, 1864, Charlie Harker was promoted to brigadier to rank from the Battle of Chickamauga. The 17th brought orders to march the next day for Cleveland, Tennessee, 30 miles east of Chattanooga and near the Georgia state line. With the fine weather of spring, the Tigers broke winter camp on April 18 and marched to Sweetwater, leading the division with their band playing and flags unfurled. They arrived at Cleveland on the 21st where the next two weeks would be spent preparing for the 125th's greatest test thus far: the campaign for Atlanta.[56]

10

Rocky Face Ridge

Ulysses S. Grant ascended to command of all Union forces on March 2, 1864. Politics as much as military necessity dictated that Grant would have to stay near Washington. William T. Sherman was given overall command of the western armies. Across the line in Georgia, Braxton Bragg—scapegoat for the loss of Chattanooga—was replaced by Lieutenant General Joe Johnston. As Grant and Sherman rode the train from Nashville to Cincinnati in March, Grant outlined his plan for war west of the Alleghenies, and issued written orders on April 4. According to Sherman, "Neither Atlanta, nor Augusta, nor Savannah, was the objective, but the 'army of Jos. Johnston' go where it might." So the Confederate Army of the Tennessee was to be the quarry, and it would be Sherman's task to destroy it. Of his task in Georgia, Sherman famously wrote his wife, "All that has gone before is mere skirmishing. The war now begins."[1]

As of April 10, Sherman had at his disposal west of the Alleghany Mountains approximately 178,000 men in three armies. From this total he had to maintain garrisons throughout his four military departments and protect his supply and communication lines as he advanced into Georgia. Logistics would be the controlling factor in any offensive action Sherman planned. Nashville—150 miles from Chattanooga—would be the primary Union supply base during the Atlanta campaign. Chattanooga—120 miles from Atlanta—would be the forward base for any move into Georgia. Sherman would have to rely on wagon roads and a single track railroad—the Western and Atlantic—between Chattanooga and Atlanta to move supplies. The primary rivers of the region flowed at right angles to his planned advance rendering them useless for transportation. Taking Atlanta would be a battle for control of the railroad.[2]

Sherman would take three armies into Georgia: the Army of the Cumberland, 61,000 men and commanded by Major General George Thomas; the Army of the Tennessee, commanded by Major General James B. McPherson, 24,500 men; and the Army of the Ohio—an army in name only with a single corps—Major General John M. Schofield commanding, 13,500. The infantry would be accompanied by 254 cannon. The Army of the Cumberland would generally serve as a blunt force instrument in the center of most formations while the two smaller more mobile armies would generally maneuver on the flanks. The Army of the Cumberland was divided into three corps, the Fourth, the Fourteenth, and the Twentieth. The Fourth Corps—now wearing a triangular corps badge—with three divisions, would be commanded by Major General Oliver O. Howard. Sheridan's Second Division was now commanded by Brigadier General John Newton. Howard had commanded the Eleventh Corps, which was merged with the Twelfth to create the new Twentieth Corps, under Major General Joe Hooker's command. Gordon

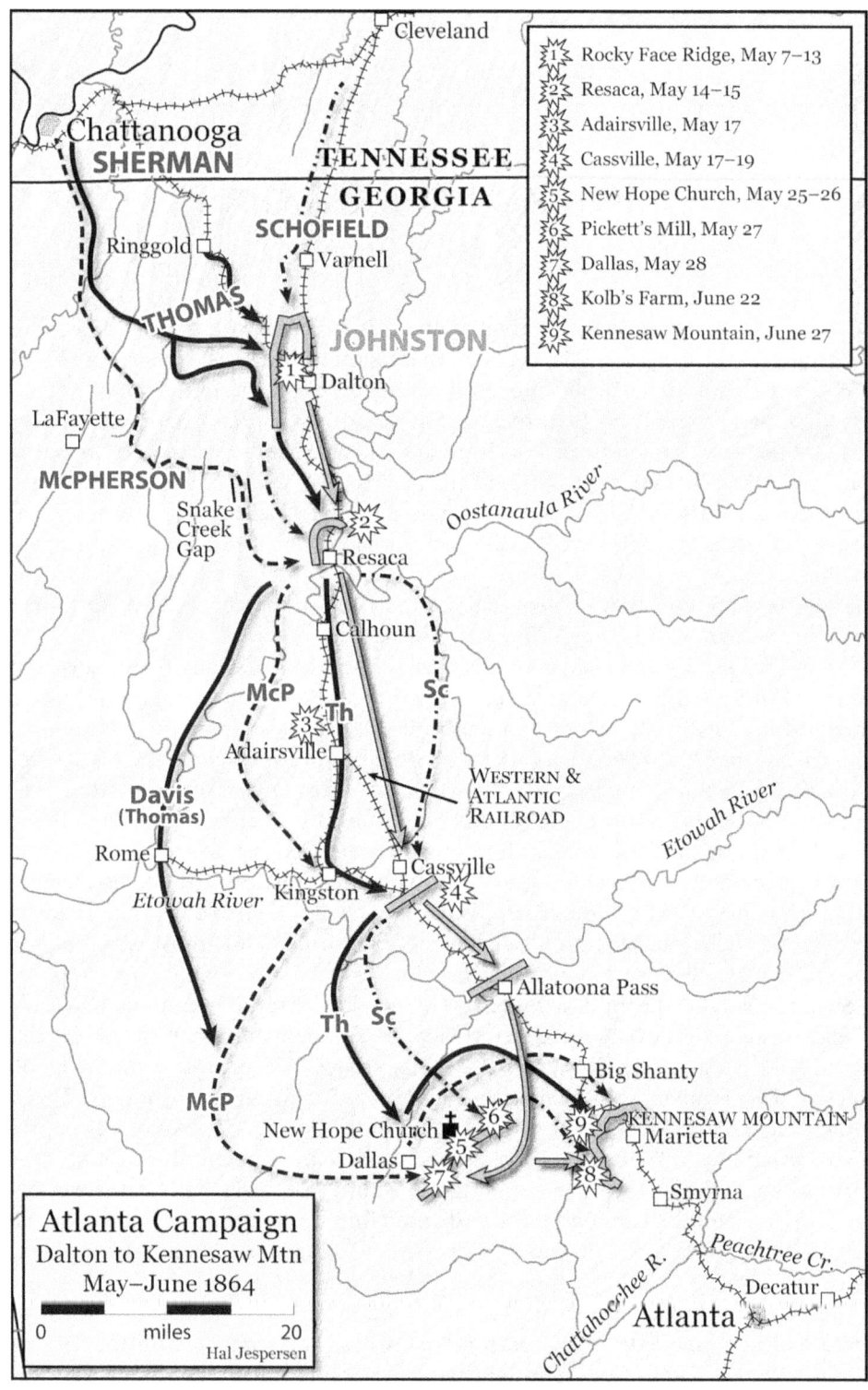

Atlanta Campaign. Army movements from Dalton to Kennesaw Mountain, May to June 1864. Map by Hal Jespersen.

Granger, who failed to impress either Grant or Sherman, was shunted to a noncombat command.³

Howard—the holder of two college degrees and a devout Christian—had commanded a corps in the Army of the Potomac before coming west with General Hooker in October. Personally brave—Howard left an arm in Virginia—his performances at Chancellorsville and Gettysburg were lackluster. One historian wrote of Howard that no general had survived so many tactical errors of judgment and disregard of orders and yet been repeatedly promoted. Howard reviewed the Fourth Corps on April 11 and met the regimental commanders afterward. Opdycke found him strictly temperate and a Christian gentleman. "We are all much pleased," Opdycke wrote his wife.⁴

Major General Oliver O. Howard. After the war, Howard became a champion of Negro rights, a founder of both Howard and Lincoln Memorial universities, and superintendent of West Point. In 1893, he received the Congressional Medal of Honor for bravery at Seven Pines in 1862. Library of Congress.

John Newton was the son of a Virginia congressman and a West Point classmate of William Rosecrans and James Longstreet. The handsome 41-year-old Newton was a brigadier general when he assumed command in April of the Second Division. Newton had been denied permanent rank as a major general for criticizing Burnside after the defeat at Fredericksburg, Virginia. Most recently Newton had briefly commanded a corps in the Army of the Potomac, only to be ousted in a reorganization in March. Sent west, Newton had a solid, but not stellar, record. Opdycke compared Newton to James Garfield physically and opined, "I think we shall like him." Then hedged, "At least such are my first impressions."⁵

Newton's Second Division had three brigades, Colonel Frank Sherman's First—once commanded by Phil Sheridan—Brigadier George Wagner's Second and General Harker's Third. The Third Brigade was composed of nine small infantry regiments: the 22nd, 27th, 42nd, 51st, and 79th Illinois; the 64th, 65th, 125th; Ohio, and the 3rd Kentucky. There were two artillery batteries attached, Battery M, 1st Illinois and Battery A, 1st Ohio Light Artillery. The 125th was considered "extraordinary" in size with 517 officers and men, its ranks bolstered by returning convalescents and new recruits. The 64th and 65th Ohio had had little success recruiting in Ohio during the winter, and were just half as large as the 125th. Harker needed a new brigade adjutant, and he commandeered Captain Ed Whitesides—a fellow with the serious look of a career clerk—who had been the 125th's adjutant. Ridgely Powers took Whitesides place as regimental adjutant. Opdycke extracted a promise from Whitesides not to drink anything intoxicating while at Harker's headquarters. Whitesides, accompanied by a colored man servant, began duty April 26.⁶

"The problem of the supplies is the most difficult," Sherman confided to Grant as he planned his campaign. Sherman intended to leave Chattanooga with 100,000 men and 35,000 animals, and by the end of April he planned to have stockpiled at Decatur, Alabama, and Chattanooga 70 days of provisions and forage. Sherman's quartermasters estimated that 130 rail cars carrying 10 tons each had to reach Chattanooga *every day* from Nashville to supply Sherman's three armies. A shortage of railroad rolling stock would necessitate trains running round the clock with rail traffic limited to military supplies—soldiers would march, horses and cattle would be driven from Nashville. Express companies would be allotted only one car per day to carry small parcels for the soldiers. If the supply chain was interrupted—and it likely would be by accidents and marauding enemy cavalry—Sherman reasoned his soldiers could live off the land. After learning from the 1860 census that Georgia had a million residents, Sherman wrote, "If they can live, we should not starve." In fact, fresh meat for the men and fodder for the animals would likely have to be procured locally. Sherman was not Rosecrans, and wouldn't be a slave to logistics, however. The chief quartermaster at Chattanooga understood that Sherman would advance in early May "if he has to eat his mules."[7]

Sherman decreed that each regiment was restricted to one wagon and one ambulance. Each officer and enlisted soldier was required to carry enough food and clothing for five days. Officers would eat the same fare as their men. Any noncombatants—"useless mouths"—were shipped to Nashville. Division and brigade supply trains were to transport food—bread, flour, salt, sugar, coffee, salt pork or bacon—ammunition and clothing only. No tents, chests or trunks were permitted, and officers' baggage was reduced by half to one small valise. Tents were limited to medical needs except one tent was allowed to each headquarters for use as an office. Lieutenant Wilbur Hinman of the 65th later wrote, "During this campaign the men were to have absolutely nothing except what they carried on their backs—company officers, ditto."[8]

Sherman would lead by example employing one wagon for his headquarters. "I think that is as low down as we can get until we get flat broke," he colorfully explained, "and thenceforward things will mend. Soldiering as we have been doing it for the past two years, with such trains and impediments, has been a farce, and nothing but absolute poverty will cure it." Sherman's headquarters made do with canvas wall tent flies which they improvised over whatever poles they could scrounge. General Thomas, on the other hand, refused to abandon his headquarters, something he blamed on his officers. Not only did Thomas have a headquarters tent, but he also had a large wagon that could be converted into an office if necessary. Sherman and his staff referred to this as "Thomas's circus." Sherman commented on Thomas' violation of orders, "Being good natured and slow to act, he never enforced my orders perfectly." On the other hand, one of Thomas' staff officers noted Sherman's preference for commandeering a private home each evening and described Sherman's entourage on the march as "a motley throng of mules and darkies, loaded down with mess-pans, camp-kettles, and all sorts of noisy implements" trailing Sherman's staff and orderlies.[9]

The supplies needed to keep those 100,000 men and their animals in the field dictated that Sherman not stray too far from the Western and Atlantic Railroad. North Georgia was mostly inhospitable to military operations being a rough, mountainous country of piney woods and brush with a few farms and the occasional plantation. There were few good roads and the region was bisected by three major rivers, the Oostanaula, Etowah and Chattahoochee. The Allegheny Mountains oriented northeast to southwest immediately below Chattanooga forming a number of narrow parallel valleys which were drained by tributaries of Chickamauga Creek flowing north. After crossing the Tennessee line near Graysville, Georgia, the Western and Atlantic ran southeast to Dalton. Blocking the way to Dalton was Rocky Face Ridge, a 500-foot "mountain" with a craggy, rocky summit. The railroad passed through a gap in Rocky Face—Mill Creek Gap—which because of its towering, rocky cliffs, was also known as Buzzard's Roost Gap. Rocky Face continued north from Mill Creek Gap for three miles until it broke into a series of small hills. The east slope of Rocky Face descended into Crow Valley, and Dalton lay a mile or so southeast of Mill Creek Gap. The Gap was flooded by the rebels in May 1864 by damming the creek which blocked the wagon road and railroad. Any army following the railroad south would need to go over or around the natural obstacle that was Rocky Face Ridge.[10]

It was General Bragg who chose to defend Dalton and, his successor, Joe Johnston, had stayed and spent the winter constructing defenses around it. The rebel breastworks protected approaches into Dalton from the west and north by looping from below Mill Creek Gap north along the crest of Rocky Face for a mile and a half before angling east above town and terminating southeast of Dalton below where the East Tennessee and Georgia Railroad from Knoxville merged with the Western and Atlantic. These well prepared defenses were manned by veteran infantry which numbered just under 43,000 on May 1 but would grow to 65,000. The Achilles heel of the position was that the Yankees could flank it. A fact that was true of nearly every possible Confederate position between Chattanooga and Atlanta. Nevertheless, Joe Johnston believed that any flanking maneuver would be lengthy, arduous and time consuming. He determined to employ a defensive strategy of trading ground for time while luring the Yankees south away from their base of supplies and hoping an impatient Sherman could be induced to decimate his army attacking impregnable rebel defenses.[11]

Grant had decided that the Union spring campaign would step off the first week of May 1864. For his opening movement, Sherman planned to use his superior numbers to advantage and send Thomas and Schofield's men directly down the railroad. The Army of the Cumberland would march south down the railroad from Chattanooga toward Dalton, Georgia. Not only was Thomas' the largest army, but it had in Sherman's eyes, the best army engineers, railroad men, spies and provost marshals. Schofield's small force would operate on Thomas' left. Following a tactical plan Thomas had once advocated to Sherman for his army, General McPherson's Army of the Tennessee would embark on a flanking maneuver around the Union right in hopes of getting through Snake Creek Gap southwest of Rocky Face and into the rebel rear unchallenged allowing the railroad to be cut at Resaca, 12 miles south of Dalton.[12]

Long anticipated orders to begin the decisive campaign for Atlanta arrived at divisional, brigade and regimental headquarters on May 1. The order sending all surplus baggage to the rear confirmed the reality for the common soldier. The Fourth Corps was consolidated around Cleveland, Tennessee. At noon on May 3 the long walk to Atlanta began for the 125th as it trekked down familiar roads from Cleveland toward Dalton covering 13 miles and camping near Red Clay Springs on the Georgia line. Magnolia blossoms and a warm south wind greeted the blue columns. General Cox, tanned and fit, found Opdycke on the march and the two old friends had a "very pleasant chat." Cox had a letter from General James Garfield, now in Virginia, who wrote that the Army of the Potomac was excellent, but it accepted defeat too easily. Garfield further believed that the fate of the Republic rested on the upcoming campaigns, especially in the West. In a letter to Lucy Opdycke that contained a Georgia wildflower, Colonel Opdycke forcefully expressed the view that every individual should do his patriotic duty to the best of his ability. That would be how Opdycke would conduct himself, and he would expect nothing less from his men in the historic summer and fall of 1864.[13]

Brigadier General Jacob Cox. Cox became governor of Ohio in 1866, served as secretary of the interior in Grant's administration, was elected to Congress in 1876 and served as president of the University of Cincinnati. Cox was a prolific writer on the history of the war. Reproduced from Clark, *Opdycke Tigers*.

Thomas' army roughly followed the railroad south from Ringgold, Georgia, converging on the railroad tunnel west of Rocky Face Ridge by May 6. The rebels were expected to fight for yet another aptly-named Tunnel Hill. The Fourth Corps divisions of Generals David Stanley and Tom Wood were sent around the north end of the hill, while Newton's men were to cover the corps' right flank to the south. At 4 a.m. on the 7th, the Fourth Corps advanced. The 125th marched at 5:30 as Harker's brigade moved with the division on a flank march toward the tunnel. The rough road was blocked at intervals by trees felled by Confederate skirmishers who retreated stubbornly. After four miles, in the face of more determined resistance, Newton—primed to expect an all-out engagement—deployed his men in a battle line before pushing ahead. However, when Harker's men reached the tunnel, they found it already in the possession of other federal troops who had easily flanked Southerners off the hill. "I do not see much fighting here," Opdycke wrote home, "it is to be regretted that the enemy will not fight us here, for could we meet him now we would put a period to the end of the war in this section."[14]

Southeast of the railroad tunnel, the next natural barrier was Rocky Face Ridge and its crest was three miles of rocks and boulders from its northern end to Mill Creek Gap, nicknamed the "Buzzard's Roost." Its summit bristled with almost 1700 feet of jagged stone fortifications. The western face was covered with vegetation and was too steep for a man on horseback to climb. An assault on Rocky Face would be twice as difficult as Missionary Ridge, in Opdycke's opinion. The east side sloped gently into Crow Valley. Dalton—the important junction of the Western and Atlantic and East Tennessee and Georgia railroads—lay behind Rocky Face. By late Saturday afternoon, May 7, Harker's brigade had advanced into the valley at the base of the western slope of Rocky Face.[15]

Sherman's plan was for the Army of the Cumberland to "press strongly at all points in front" of Rocky Face and pin the Confederates in their stone defenses. Sherman suggested that Howard should try to take the annoying enemy signal station overlooking the Buzzard's Roost. Late in the afternoon, Harker and Howard sat on their horses in the valley west of Rocky Face intently scanning its abrupt, boulder strewn western slope with field glasses. Howard asked Harker if his men could take the northern end from the rebel skirmishers entrenched there and reconnoiter the crest. Harker's reply was lacking in conviction. "We can try," he told Howard.[16]

The 125th was the largest regiment in his brigade and at 5 a.m. on the 8th, Harker summoned Opdycke to headquarters. He gave Opdycke a local guide, told him to deploy his men as skirmishers and make a reconnaissance of the north end of Rocky Face where the slope was the least steep. Harker would directly support Opdycke's effort with the 64th and 65th Ohio while all the Fourth Corps unleashed a fusillade of musketry at the crest. Harker told Opdycke, who needed no encouragement, to seize a foot hold on the summit, if possible. Harker warned Opdycke that the enemy could easily reinforce any enemy skirmishers encountered.[17]

At 6 a.m. on Sunday, May 8, Harker's brigade marched a mile around the north end of Rocky Face and occupied a small gap that led into Crow Valley. The day was hot, and the steepness of the north face would force all ranks to claw their way toward the summit on foot. Opdycke selected companies E and F as skirmishers under Major Bruff's command, supported by Company D. Opdycke sent some of the regiment on a feint to the left while sending the bulk of the 125th straight up the west slope under the cover of trees. Opdycke, not trusting Bruff, accompanied his skirmishers and was one of the first to the narrow, rocky summit at 8:30. The Ohioans ascent was unmolested and the bluecoats appeared unexpectedly on the left of a ragged line of unsuspecting rebel skirmishers near the crest. Lieutenant Wilbur Hinman of the 65th remembered Opdycke during that attack as "conspicuous for his courage." The Alabama pickets made the expected brief, bold show on the summit, and then abandoned their fighting holes to retreat sullenly down the eastern slope. "A volley or two, which went high" was how Lieutenant Colonel Moore recalled the initial reception from the enemy pickets.[18]

The Southerner's feeble resistance encouraged Opdycke. At 8:50 a.m., he exuberantly sent Harker his compliments, writing, "The crest is ours and we are driving the enemy south toward Dalton." He pushed the 125th southward along the narrow crest until he met a Confederate force advancing along the same track. The exchange of musket fire was severe and the Tigers took cover behind rocks as bullets ricocheted in all directions. Opdycke succeeded in deploying Captain Bates' Company C into a battle line and they unleashed a volley or two. His men charged diagonally south down the crest and drove the enemy back a third of a mile before encountering a stone breastwork. A natural rock palisade towered over the crest at that point and the enemy had augmented it with a four foot wall of stone that Opdycke saw as "musket proof." The addition of Southern artillery to the crest made the stone fort as impregnable as any European king's castle. Bruff's skirmishers clawed to within 75 yards of the Southern line before being halted by gusts of grapeshot and musketry. Two privates from Company C were killed in the attack.[19]

Harker's orders to halt finally caught up with the aggressive Opdycke. The less rugged eastern slope of Rocky Face offered the opportunity for the rebels to easily organize a counterattack on the 125th's left. By 10:30, the 15th Wisconsin from Wood's division had also scaled the north end of Rocky Face and was in the 125th's rear. Opdycke prevailed upon the 15th's commander to position his men to protect the 125th's exposed left rear flank. To discourage a rebel counterattack, the rest of Harker's brigade streamed onto the crest, and planted their flags while giving a rousing cheer. At 11:30, the 65th Ohio replaced the 15th Wisconsin and a Union signal station—which could communicate by flags with headquarters on the tunnel hill—was established. The reward for taking this part of the crest was a panoramic view, in the bright morning sun, of Johnston's fortifications and the huge Southern supply depot in Dalton. The rebels, having overcome their surprise, rallied and opened a ragged musketry on Harker's men from the breastworks on the crest and the east slope. Harker's brigade had gained a foothold on the summit of Rocky Face, but failed to capture the Confederate signal station, or the Buzzard's Roost. Still, it was better than General Howard had expected against a place General Sherman had called "the terrible door of death that Johnston had prepared for them in the Buzzard's Roost." Taking the hill cost the 125th four killed—Privates Cornelius Infildt, Marion Murphy, Eli Swinehart and Simeon Carlton—and 21 wounded, two mortally, almost all after the summit was reached. Private Carlton had previously served with the 23rd Ohio, a regiment raised by William Rosecrans that included Rutherford Hays. Captain Steen Parks of Company F was shot through the wrist, but remained on the field until the fight was over. A little over a month later, Parks resigned his commission.[20]

The fighting done by Harker's brigade was only a small part of the battle action that Sunday. There was a general advance by three Union corps. The most serious fighting occurred in front of Major General Joseph Hooker's 20th Corps at the south end of Rocky Face where a federal attempt to storm the Ridge, which included hand to hand combat, was repulsed at Dug Gap. The Yankees did secure a foothold at Mill Creek Gap by gaining a spur at the entrance. Colonel Henry Banning, former lieutenant colonel of the 125th now commanding the 121st Ohio, commanded the skirmish line.[21]

Even during lulls in the fighting, minie balls zipped overhead and clipped tree branches, one spent round falling on Opdycke's hat. The 125th was relieved by the 3rd Kentucky at 6 p.m. after a hard day of skirmishing. Through sheer manpower, for no horses could climb the west or north slopes of Rocky Face, the 3rd Kentucky managed to muscle two cannon up to the crest that night. The limbers were left in the valley and every round of ammunition had to be hand carried up the steep slope. Worse still, the nearest water was two miles in the rear, forcing men with mouths dry and gritty from black powder, to make the long, arduous journey to fill canteens. That evening the campfires of the entire Confederate Army of the Tennessee could be seen twinkling in the darkness that settled over Crow Valley.[22]

Sherman ordered Thomas to continue to demonstrate and distract the enemy while McPherson's army tried to slip past Johnston's left flank. The skirmishing began at 4 a.m. Monday, May 9, and continued all day. About 2 p.m., McPherson had his army in position northwest of Resaca, Georgia, at Snake Creek Gap. However, by dusk, McPherson had mistakenly decided Resaca was too strong for him and pulled back. Sherman was critical of McPherson's timidity. "He [McPherson] had in hand twenty-three thousand of the best men of the army, and could have walked in to Resaca." This would have forced Johnston's army into retreat. Sherman let McPherson off by acknowledging he was following discretionary orders. His disappointment evident, however, when Sherman wrote, "Such an opportunity does not occur twice in a single life." However, after the war, both Union General Jacob Cox and Confederate General Joe Johnston wrote that McPherson's decision was the correct one at the time. General Sherman's first flanking maneuver in the Atlanta campaign failed not in strategy, but in execution by a general new to army command.[23]

George Wagner's brigade moved to the left of Harker's at the north end of Rocky Face. The crackle of musket fire was heard all day on the 9th as heavy skirmishing continued. Late in the day, Newton was ordered to send Wagner from his position on the

Crow Valley side of the Ridge, to attack the rebel rifle pits which were a part of the defenses of the stone fort. If Wagner gained any advantage, Harker was to attack the enemy defensive works on the summit which had stopped the 125th the day before. The 79th Illinois was to advance as skirmishers. The 64th was to spearhead Harker's attack, followed by the 3rd Kentucky and then the 125th Ohio. The terrain dictated a flank attack.[24]

Wagner's Second Brigade made a tentative effort that eventually ground to a halt, and Wood's division was likewise repulsed on the right. Harker misread the increasing gunfire of failure as success. At 5:45 p.m., he ordered an assault, sending Captain Whitesides, his new adjutant, to give the order to the 64th Ohio. The life of a brigade staff officer, as chronicled by Ambrose Bierce, was "not a happy one." Dispatched from the safety of the rear to deliver an order to a front line field officer, who was often not easy to find, exposed the young staffer to sharpshooters, general musketry and artillery shells that even soldiers flat on the ground or behind breastworks avoided. And once the recipient was located, the young officer was subject to unnerving alterations of emotion when he saw the potential consequences of his message.[25]

Colonel Alexander McIlvaine, the 64th's commanding officer, was 44 and the regiment's fourth colonel. McIlvaine was a good soldier, but Harker and Opdycke considered him only competent at best as a field officer and a poor disciplinarian. After delivering Harker's orders, Whitesides noted the strength of the enemy breastworks and realized the gravity of the order. "Well, I must get out of this, I am getting demoralized," Whitesides recalled thinking, realizing that there would be no scaling ladders and only the two cannon the Kentuckians had manhandled to the summit for support. The narrowness of the crest limited the attack to only a six- to 12-man front, charging diagonally from the flank. The rocky ground insured that even that narrow front would be difficult to sustain. The courageous 64th Ohio erroneously charged through the 79th Illinois skirmishers before the rest of the brigade was ready, and lost 88 men before they were stopped cold, and dropped into the safety of a ravine. Colonel McIlvaine heard a wounded man crying out beyond the ravine. Unwilling to wait until darkness to rescue the man, the Colonel asked a captain to send someone to the man's relief. When the captain refused, calling the order "certain death," McIlvaine —a father figure to his men—impetuously decided to go himself. McIlvaine went only a few yards before receiving a mortal abdominal wound.[26]

Colonel Allen Buckner of the 79th Illinois was shot through the body and his skirmishers halted and took cover. The 3rd Kentucky, followed by the 125th, jogged ahead in support of the 64th. Major Bruff led companies B, D and G as skirmishers. The rebel fire was relentless. The Kentuckians were repulsed less than 100 yards from the rebel works. Lieutenant Colonel William Bullitt was shot through the thigh as his Kentuckians planted their colors behind a hastily thrown up breastwork 200 yards from the enemy. A few of the bluecoats jumped over the six- to 10-foot bluff and ran down the west slope to escape. The 125th was likewise repulsed. Some of the Tigers were forced off the crest following the Kentuckians, but most of the men hung on, taking cover among the rocks on the crest from which they sniped at the enemy and exchanged insults. Confederate sharpshooters returned the favor, and added to the Yankees discomfort by rolling rocks down on them.[27]

Lieutenant Colonel Moore led 30 men in a brave but foolhardy charge on the enemy's stone bastion. They were pinned down less than 100 yards from their objective—close enough to see the Southerners' coat buttons. Over 50 years later, Moore recalled the charge: "I must have been dazed, for I suddenly became aware that there was no one charging between me and [the Rebel] works ... and found that I was going it alone." Moore followed those men who slid down the bluff to take cover among the rocks where they joined other Yankees harassing the enemy with steady rifle fire. With the 64th's Colonel McIlvane mortally wounded, Moore was the ranking officer within shouting distance. Corporal Luther Calvin was at Moore's side and as he was raising his musket to fire, he was shot in the face. The soft, lead musket ball entered Calvin's left temple moved diagonally down and shattered his right lower jaw before exiting and striking Moore a stinging blow on his hip. The lieutenant colonel turned in time to catch the unconscious Calvin as he fell. Calvin's rifle was found to have been fired, indicating he and the Confederate who shot him had fired simultaneously. A bullet clipped a lock of hair from the temple of a corporal from the 65th Ohio crouched beside Moore. This little squad remained pinned down, clinging to rocks for protection, and ducking sharpshooters until Harker's men were relieved by Wagner's at about 10 p.m. Corporal Calvin was left for dead. Privates Francis Gorlock, George McCollum and William Sleinel were killed on the 9th, and four mortally wounded: Privates William Dana, Jesse Sample, Anthony Porter and Thomas Cassady—shot by a sharpshooter while going for water. The 125th bivouacked on a spur of Rocky Face on the eastern slope.[28]

In a letter to his wife the next day, Moore matter-of-factly related his experience on Rocky Face. "I was hit four times, once by a ball which passed through a corporal's head, struck me in the back of the hip and lodged in the lining of my blouse; that only *stung*. Another stripped my right coat sleeve below the elbow, a fragment of another hit me in the left breast; still another struck my right lower bowels. These last two hurt, but are only *slight*; they do not lay me up." Opdycke admired Moore's pluck, writing, "He suits me." The two day fight on Rocky Face Ridge cost the 125th 55 killed and wounded. Captain Anthony Vallendar of Company I was wounded, secured detached duty and did not return to the regiment for a year. In Harker's brigade, 31 were killed and 113 wounded on the afternoon of May 9. The next day Northern litter bearers found Corporal Calvin alive and sitting against a rock. He lived to be mustered out in June 1865. Moore kept the bullet, which purportedly bore the marks of Calvin's teeth.[29]

Sherman's general orders to his army commanders were to avoid serious casualties. Nevertheless, Confederate reports mentioned five separate assaults on Rocky Face. "The zeal of the troops and subordinate commanders turned the intended skirmish into something very like a ranged battle," General Cox wrote. General Newton's official report praised the Third Brigade. "General Harker and the officers and men of his brigade highly distinguished themselves for gallantry and good conduct."[30]

There was no movement on Rocky Face Ridge for the next two days. It was an uncomfortable camp made worse because water had to be hauled from a spring at the base of Rocky Face by details of men struggling with a half dozen canteens each. On the 10th the 125th was on picket, but there was only scattered firing. The enemy threw three artillery shells into the 125th's camp to no effect, and received three in return. At 10 p.m. on the 10th a severe rainstorm swept the area lasting all night, drenching the men and cleansing the battlefield. On May 11, the rain turned to drizzle and the temperature dropped. The brigade remained hunkered down on Rocky Face as musketry crackled on the skirmish line. The rebels tried to shell Harker's line, but were silenced by Union cannon.[31]

On the 12th, Harker's brigade descended to a new position on a rise which extended the north end of Rocky Face northeast into Crow Valley. The 125th's right flank joined Colonel Sherman's brigade of their division while the left flank was covered by the 64th Ohio which was facing east. Strong defensive works were thrown up. When it was the 125th's turn to go on picket on the 12th, Colonel Opdycke wanted to know the disposition of the enemy in his front. He sent regimental adjutant Lieutenant Powers, Sergeant Sharon French and Private Zalmon Morris to scout. Beyond the tree line on the 125th's front the men found an open field extending a quarter mile down the valley. On the edge of the field, near the brush at the eastern base of Rocky Face the three men found a small frame cabin. Leaving Morris and French concealed in the brush, Powers skirted the open field until he was able to enter the cabin. From this vantage point, he located the Southern pickets on the lower end of the field. While observing the pickets, Powers saw two unarmed Confederates enter the field out of sight of the picket posts. The two Johnnies walked leisurely up the valley, absorbed in conversation, to within a couple hundred yards of the cabin. French and Morris saw them also, and with leveled muskets emerged from the brush and ordered the men to surrender. The prisoners proved to be a lieutenant and quartermaster sergeant from the 36th Georgia, who had been captured and paroled at Vicksburg by Grant's army. The Lieutenant asked to be allowed to leave a note explaining his capture for his company, but Powers refused, not wishing to delay his return any longer. That evening a rebel skirmish line advanced setting off a heavy round of musketry, but little else.[32]

Sherman decided to send nearly his entire army around Johnston's left toward Resaca on May 10. Only the Fourth Corps and some cavalry remained on Rocky Face as a diversion. Concealed in the valleys and deep pine woods, Sherman's army began concentrating west of Resaca on the 12th. When Johnston realized that Sherman had made Rocky Face untenable, he abandoned his Dalton trenches on the night of the 12th. Sherman's strategy to follow the railroad while using his superior numbers to both hold the Confederates in place and simultaneously flank them out of their defenses was at last successful. General Cox observed, "The first important step in the campaign had been successfully taken, and the enemy had been compelled to evacuate the impregnable lines about Dalton, with but trifling loss on Sherman's part."[33]

Friday the 13th proved fortunate for the Fourth Corps—the Confederates in their front had vanished. Immediately, the Yankees began a happy pursuit with the regimental bands playing "Hail Columbia" and "Yankee Doodle." Details of soldiers from each of Harker's regiments remained to bury the brigade's 27 dead. Newton's division occupied the middle of the column moving south on the Rome-Dalton road that paralleled the railroad. Harker's brigade marched passed empty Confederate fortifications and camps, where they found bullet ridden, blood stained posts where it appeared Confederate deserters had been shot. Lieutenant Ralsa Rice saw irony in the treasonous Southerners executing traitors. "Thus, the Confederate government under Jeff Davis was making treason odious."[34]

The 125th entered Dalton at 11 a.m. There was some looting in the town, which had been a Confederate supply depot, and Harker's brigade liberated 30 or 40 pounds of peanuts and some tobacco. The tenacious rebel rearguard forced the Fourth Corps to fight for all of the eight miles made that day. With Dalton under federal control, Sherman was able to push his supply trains right up to the very rear of his army, yet, in a nod to the tenuous nature of the single track railroad, prudently instructed all his army commanders to keep 10 days of meat and bread on hand and forage the countryside when possible.[35]

Having flanked Johnston out of Dalton, Sherman had the bulk of his army moving around the Johnston's left flank, while the Fourth Corps was following the Southern rearguard down the rails toward Resaca, Georgia, where the Western and Atlantic crossed the Oostanaula River. As generals in blue studied their maps, it was clear that Resaca was the next logical place for Johnston to defend the railroad. A ramshackle little village named for a battle in the Mexican War, Resaca might well become the site of the next contest in the Sherman's drive for Atlanta.[36]

11

Resaca

Resaca was located on the north bank of a looping bend of the meandering Oostanaula River which flowed southwest. A mile east of town, the smaller Connasauga River paralleled the railroad from Tilton, Georgia, south. To the west, Camp Creek, a tributary of the Oostanaula, also flowed parallel to the railroad and merged into the Oostanaula a mile or so west of town. Johnston's earthworks were strung across the high ground above the east bank of Camp Creek from the Oostanaula northward a couple miles before hooking east as across the Western and Atlantic rail line before finally terminating on a westward sweeping bend of the Connasauga River. A half mile below town, a wagon and a rail bridge crossed the Oostanaula River.[1]

All of Sherman's army, except the Fourth Corps, arrived at the west bank of Camp Creek opposite Johnston's defenses on the 13th. McPherson's army was the right flank resting on the Oostanaula River. The bulk of the Army of the Cumberland held the center on McPherson's left. Schofield's single corps was on Thomas' left and constituted the federal left flank. By the evening of the 13th, the Fourth Corps—last to leave Rocky Face—was within two miles of Schofield's right on Camp Creek, and about five miles north of Resaca. Harker's brigade camped at 10 p.m., and spent the night in a line of battle—the 125th in the second battle line behind the 3rd Kentucky.[2]

Mid-morning on the 14th under a hot, bright sun, Newton's division on the Fourth Corps' right flank, approached Schofield's left. The Fourth Corps had not completely closed up on Schofield when Sherman ordered an immediate attack by the two Twenty-Third Corps divisions—Brigadier Generals Jacob Cox's and Henry Judah's—and two from the Army of the Cumberland's Fourteenth Corps on Schofield's right. An impatient Sherman was throwing four divisions at Southern defenses no Yankee had scouted. Schofield's bluecoats forced their way across a succession of steep, narrow ridges and gullies covered with dense second growth forest and brush that marked the head waters of Camp Creek. After about a half mile, the Yankees arrived at the narrow valley of Camp Creek from which they could make out the enemy's fortifications a quarter mile away. The Southern skirmishers west of Camp Creek withdrew back across the creek as musketry and artillery fire erupted along the line—the opening salvo of the first full scale engagement of the Atlanta campaign.[3]

General Judah launched an impetuous attack that was not coordinated with the divisions on his flanks. Judah's sudden move left both Cox on his left and the Fourteenth Corps on his right, behind. Judah's men struggled across Camp Creek, but tremendous fire from the enemy stopped them on the muddy east bank of the creek. When the musketry slackened, the bluecoats scrambled back to the ridge in their rear and began digging in.[4]

Jacob Cox's division advanced into the fray across rough terrain from a more northerly direction than Judah's men. At 1:30 p.m., Cox's division launched the first of four attempts to cross Camp Creek, the last of which drove the advanced Confederate picket line back 300 yards to a strong line of Confederate entrenchments on east bank of the west branch of Camp Creek. This placed Cox's men under fire from the front and right, with enemy infantry massing on Cox's open left flank. In one of Cox's Ohio regiments—the 103rd—the entire color guard resolutely refused to lie down for safety and all nine were shot—their action later immortalized on the Soldier's Monument in Cleveland. The captain commanding the regiment and a second captain killed by a cannonball were part of the over 70 casualties of the 103rd that afternoon. After an hour in this precarious position, Cox's ammunition was depleted and difficult to resupply across the creek. Schofield's corps quit the field after losing about 1200 men and failing to reach the main rebel earthworks. Finally, Newton's division arrived on Cox's left.[5]

Charlie Harker's brigade and Brigadier General August Willich's brigade from Wood's division were ordered to replace two of Cox's brigades on the front line. Preparatory to assuming a position on the line, General Harker sought guidance from Cox whom he found seated on a log with one of his brigade commanders. The moment Harker arrived, a rebel shell exploded between the men. Harker was thrown from his horse, stunned and badly bruised, forcing him to temporarily turn brigade command over to the ranking colonel, Luther Bradley of the 51st Illinois. Cox was only dazed. The 125th was passing nearby, and Lieutenant Ralsa Rice called out to Cox, "General, this is a warm place!" to which Cox responded, "Yes, you are right about that."[6]

To reach Cox's advanced position across the creek, Harker's brigade had to cross the creek valley where enemy artillery on the right and was able sweep the ground with a fire Opdycke characterized as "severe." An artillery shell landed in the 27th Illinois from Harker's brigade killing and wounding two dozen men. Cox later wrote that while crossing the open ground enemy artillery shells were knocking federals over like bowling balls. On the east side of the valley a series of low hills offered some cover.[7]

Old logs hastily gathered and thrown along the far bank of the creek constituted the first line of rebel breastworks captured by Cox's men. Colonel Opdycke found this breastwork "tolerable." Harker's brigade moved quickly ahead to the low undulating hills east of the creek. Cresting one, the bluecoats could make out the main Confederate line 300 yards ahead. The order "Lie down!" came seconds ahead of a volley of musketry. A few bluecoats were observed among the bushes on the west slope of a hill between the opposing lines. Believing the stranded Yankees were one of Cox's regiments, Colonel Bradley ordered the 125th forward to relieve it. Colonel Opdycke spurred Barney and shouted, "Forward! Come on, boys!" What the 125th found was only a score of Cox's boldest skirmishers who chose to stay hunkered down behind a few logs for cover instead of running a gauntlet musket and artillery fire to reach their retiring brigade. Opdycke got his regiment down in a ravine behind the crest of a small hill and ordered the men to prepare to fire a volley. Then the colonel, who could be vain of his courage, rode out in front of the line to "look ahead to see where to direct the regiment to fire."[8]

Within moments, Opdycke was wounded in the left arm by a musket ball that ricocheted off a tree. The partially flattened, jagged bullet entered an inch above the elbow, missed the bone and main artery, but partially severed the tendon before exiting. The wound bled profusely, and Opdycke fainted from the shock, slipping off Barney into the hands of his men. He quickly recovered, however, and once assured his men were properly aligned, went to the rear to have his wound treated to staunch the bleeding. General Cox, recalled seeing Opdycke, his uniform stained with blood, leave the field, still on his horse but supported by two of his men. Lieutenant Colonel Moore was now in command.[9]

The Tigers remained in their advanced position where the only protection was the contour of the ground. Men were hit as incoming rounds skimmed across the crest of the small hill. Most, but not all of the regiment, was firing prone. However, Company B had to stand and move a few steps forward to fire effectively. Company A was on higher ground and had even less cover. They suffered severely with six killed and six wounded. Company C, holding the colors, had five wounded, and Company I, six. Regimental Sergeant Major Henry Bell was one of the wounded. A freak accident cost Sergeant Reubin Steele an eye when a rifle he picked up exploded when fired, possibly from multiple unfired loads. A minie ball shattered the bones of Sergeant Alexander Postlewait's, left leg, but he avoided amputation.[10]

Private Caleb French, 1863. French was Colonel Opdycke's favorite orderly. Reproduced from Clark, *Opdycke Tigers*.

Revived after having his wound treated, Colonel Opdycke returned to the rear of the 125th to sit on Barney and observe. About 5 p.m., after fighting three hours and with their cartridge boxes nearly empty, Harker's brigade was replaced by Colonel Sherman's. The 125th took a position in a woods in the rear of the front line, about 400 yards from the base of the hill where Opdycke was wounded. The exhausted men hastily threw up breastworks of logs and dirt, and found some safety in their new position.[11]

Opdycke later admitted that the surgeons urged him to go to the division field hospital. Instead, stubborn Dutchman he was, Opdycke stoically lingered in the rear until the 125th was relieved before going to the brigade hospital. The surgeon of the 65th Ohio, Dr. John M. Todd, examined Opdycke's wound and found the spent bullet in his coat sleeve, bits of his uniform coat and shirt still clinging to it. Opdycke saved the bullet for his son. The medical staff agreed Opdycke's wound would be painful, but wasn't considered life threatening. Opdycke acquiesced to spending the night in the hospital tent. Colonel Dunlap of the 3rd Kentucky assumed command of Opdycke's demi-brigade.[12]

Generals Thomas and Schofield wisely decided to launch an artillery barrage instead of another assault at the enemy. Batteries were deployed west of Camp Creek subjecting three Confederate divisions to intense artillery fire from less than a mile away. In one sector, a shell fell every five seconds. There was little Confederate return fire as rebels abandoned their fortifications for the safety of the rear.[13]

The Fourth Corps left flank was unsupported as it straddled the Dalton wagon road

Post-battle view of Resaca battlefield. Library of Congress.

straight north of Resaca. General Johnston saw an opportunity for a flank attack and ordered Major General John Bell Hood's corps to crush Howard's flank. The rebel attack failed—halted by a single Indiana artillery battery. Thomas moved a division from Hooker's corps from the center of the Union line west of Camp Creek to Howard's left. Hooker, theatrically leading his men, arrived near dark, but in time to stop Hood on the far northern end of the line between the Dalton road and the railroad.[14]

The battle at Resaca was the result of General McPherson's previous failure to seize Snake Creek Gap. Perhaps it was fitting then that his men along the Oostanaula River should seize a bridge across Camp Creek and a hill on the other side that overlooked both the wagon and railroad bridges. A Confederate counterattack failed. With Sherman's men within striking distance of the bridges and the river at his back, Johnston ordered a pontoon bridge placed across the river a mile upstream of Resaca to keep his retreat options open.[15]

Early Sunday morning, May 15, after a cold spring night, the 125th Ohio joined their comrades in constructing breastworks along a high ridge a half mile from the enemy. David Moore, with the incessant sound of musketry and artillery in his ears, sent Opdycke a note. Moore was apprehensive about the responsibilities of regimental command, but concluded, "My trust is in God." Of Moore's ascent to regimental command, one private wrote, "the boys do not think as much of him as they do the colonel."[16]

Colonel Opdycke left the field hospital and the afternoon of the 15th, a badly bruised General Harker, and Colonel Opdycke—his arm wound still seeping—bravely rode the brigade lines to encourage the men. Opdycke told his men that "he was going to be with his boys until this campaign was over and see them safe." To his wife, Opdycke downplayed the severity of his hurt, but did admit it was "an ugly wound." Considering the primitive state of Civil War medicine, it was an injury that could easily cost him his arm, or even his life. Infection was expected and a purulent discharge of malodorous pus was "laudable" in the surgeons' eyes. The wisdom of Opdycke's decision to stay with the Tigers was yet to be determined.[17]

Sherman expected Johnston to retreat, but to keep the pressure on, he decided to continue Hooker and Howard's fight on the north end of the line on the morning of May 15. Musketry crackled and artillery boomed along the entire length of the Union line beginning early on the 15th. One veteran recalled, "We were rapidly becoming accustomed to being under fire all the time. The 'bing' of the minie seemed to be losing many of its terrors, and the boys took narrow escapes as a matter of course." McPherson's artillery shelled the railroad bridge below Resaca to deter the enemy from crossing the Oostanaula River. It was early afternoon before Hooker and Howard, maneuvering in difficult terrain, felt ready to move forward. Bloody, but indecisive, fighting followed for rest of the day on that front. As the afternoon faded, some of McPherson's soldiers crossed the Oostanaula. Joe Johnston's initial optimism turned to pessimism, and all Confederate offensive operations ceased as the Johnnies prepared to retreat across the river under the cover of darkness. Those soldiers, blue and gray, not fighting spent the day digging. By sundown, strong earthworks on opposing high ground menaced each other across a deadly no man's land. On the 16th, Sherman proposed a general advance so he could contract his lines freeing manpower for another flanking movement.[18]

About 10 p.m., the Yankees were subjected to a fusillade of musketry and artillery. Newton's skirmish line advanced and met an advancing Confederate line that had sallied out of their breastworks. The Southerners retired. The attack had been a diversion—a parting shot—to cover Johnston's withdrawal south across the Oostanaula River to Calhoun, Georgia. The retreating rebels burned the bridges behind them.[19]

The fighting along Camp Creek cost the 125th 11 men killed, 45 wounded. In his report on the battle, Colonel Luther Bradley admitted that the brigade "suffered severely" in the Resaca action. Touring that portion of the battlefield occupied by the 125th on the 14th, an army surgeon noted trees the diameter of a man's arm cut off by musket balls. "How it is possible that a single man escaped with his life is more than I can understand," the doctor remarked. Across Sherman's three armies there had been about 3000 killed or wounded. "In one week the 125th had lost over one hundred men," recalled Lieutenant Clark of the opening week of the Atlanta campaign. "At that rate only the lucky few could hope to see Atlanta at the end of the campaign."[20]

Lieutenant General Leonidas Polk's small corps joined Johnston's army and Georgia militia was assigned to protect the rebel rear. The Southern army now numbered about 70,000 men. General Cox observed, "From the 15th of May for a month the forces of the two armies were more nearly equal than at any other time in the campaign." Resaca had been a sanguinary and barren Union victory. Johnston had escaped with few casualties. Now the Yankees would have to push deeper into Georgia pursuing a foe proven clever and resourceful on the defensive. Nonetheless, one Ohio colonel saw the battle for what it was: "It was a victory, and we thanked God for that." In Sherman's calculation, the successes at Rocky Face and Resaca "gave us the initiative and the usual impulse of a conquering army."[21]

The Western and Atlantic Railroad, ran straight south for 30 miles from Resaca to Calhoun, Adairsville and finally Kingston a couple miles north of the Etowah River. From Kingston, the rails turned southeasterly past Cassville and on to Etowah Station on the river. A spur line followed the river west from Kingston to Rome—a manufacturing center of some strategic import. The terrain between the Oostanaula and Etowah rivers was more open and arable than any other part of north Georgia. The two rivers merged near Rome, Georgia to form the Coosa River. South of the Etowah was a range of rugged hills, traversed by a deep gap—the Allatoona Pass. If Johnston was searching for the right geography to strike an offensive blow against his foe, the region between Oostanaula and Etowah rivers was favorable.[22]

The federal pursuit of Johnston's retreating army began at daylight on Monday, the 16th. Harker's brigade led the division and the 125th entered Resaca at 9:30 in good spirits. The dusty little town had suffered severely from Union artillery fire. The Confederates had abandoned some supplies in Resaca including flour, four old artillery pieces, tents and the real prize—a thousand sacks of corn for the horses. The railroad trestle had been burned, but the fire on the wagon bridge was extinguished by the Fourth Corps. Before repairs were begun, Harker's brigade crossed single file, balancing on timbers, and continued leading Newton's division toward Calhoun. Leaving town, Harker's men found the road strewn with dead men and animals, killed by federal rifled cannon sighted by moonlight and fired from a mile and a half distant. Sherman's entire army crossed the Oostanaula and Connasauga rivers at three different points and swarmed south in pursuit of the enemy. The 16th was warm, bright and dusty, and water was once more a precious commodity in the rolling, forested hills. The rebel rearguard, composed of Major General Joe Wheeler's cavalry, contested every ridge before melting away to repeat the process on the next hill. Harker's brigade marched with the 42nd Illinois, 3rd Kentucky and the 64th Ohio as skirmishers. The men of the 125th were deployed as flankers. Harker's brigade finally camped at 6:30 p.m. near Calhoun after trading musketry with the gray cavalry for the better part of seven miles. Emerson Opdycke wouldn't stay with the walking wounded two miles in the rear. Instead he endured a rough ambulance ride back to the 125th.[23]

By May 17, Joe Johnston had decided to make a stand at Cassville, Georgia. There were two routes into the Cassville area—a 10-mile wagon road that ran straight from Adairsville to Cassville, or along the railroad that ran from Adairsville through Kingston and east to Cassville. The Cassville defensive line—Johnston's personal design—was constructed on a series of low hills running roughly north to south a mile south of Cassville, and blocked both the railroad and wagon road. The Etowah River was 10 miles southeast. Johnston positioned Major General William Hardee's corps at Kingston and the corps of Polk and Hood at Cassville. Johnston hoped to lure Sherman into dividing his army to attack both locations so the Southerners could defeat it piecemeal.[24]

As Sherman's army followed the Confederates south on the 17th, General Hooker's corps and the Army of the Ohio were directed down the road to Cassville; Thomas and McPherson along the railroad to Kingston. When McPherson swung west to avoid crowding Thomas' divisions, the Union army was more dispersed than they had been since May 5, just as Johnston hoped. Despite being uncertain of the rebel's position, Sherman was confident and willing to take a risk. "If we can bring Johnston to battle this side of the Etowah," he told John Schofield, "we must do it even at the hazard of beginning battle with but part of our forces." Ohioan Jacob Cox later diplomatically labeled Sherman's seeming carelessness strategy of inviting a rebel attack "calculated audacity."[25]

Newton's division headed south on the direct road from Calhoun to Adairsville. Colonel Frank Sherman's First Brigade had the point position and endured a costly running battle with Wheeler's gray cavalry. Two miles from Adairsville, the Southern earthworks grew stronger and were backed by artillery. General Howard deployed the Fourth Corps to attack, but with darkness approaching, General Thomas called a halt, although heavy musketry and artillery fire continued until 9 p.m. For Sherman's First Brigade it was the worst day of the campaign with 167 men lost.[26]

At daylight on May 18 the enemy rifle pits at Adairsville were found to be empty. Union railroad gangs had the Western and Atlantic running supplies into Resaca and would replace the bridge over the Oostanaula River in three days. Newton's men marched three miles beyond Adairsville that morning before halting until 2 in the afternoon. The day concluded with the Fourth Corps just three miles from Kingston. Demoralized and exhausted Johnnies were commonplace all along the line of march and the 125th took four prisoners—the entire army 4000. Opdycke, who had gotten some much needed bed rest in Adairsville, felt well enough to have a dinner of oysters, fresh milk and butter with Harker at brigade headquarters. He reassured his wife that his wound was healing, in the words of the doctors, "upon first intention"—terminology indicating no infection.[27]

"Our advance has been a constant skirmish," the 125th's Second Lieutenant Alson Dilley told readers of the *Western Reserve Chronicle*. "Every stream has fortifications on its banks.... Every hill they hold until we crowd them off. They post themselves within the border of woods, and rake us [with rifle fire] from safe concealment.... Every evening we come upon them too late for a general engagement." The countryside between Resaca and Kingston was the best the Ohioans had encountered in north Georgia, and the passing of two enemy armies left it devastated. The Southerners fought for every plantation house, which was invariably burned as a result. One Ohio soldier wrote that "at all times of day and night the heavens were lurid with the flames of rebel homes."[28]

May 19 dawned hot and humid. The Fourth Corps marched at 5 a.m. with General Stanley's division in front, followed by Wood and then Newton. By 8 a.m. the bluecoats occupied Kingston, and Harker's brigade paused to rest in a shady grove of trees. Four miles down the road just outside Cassville, Stanley's men found the Southerners comfortable behind substantial earthworks. Just that morning, Johnston had told his men that the marching was over and it was time to turn and fight. "I will lead you to battle," Johnston confidently told his troops. And there was reason for confidence—the Confederate army now numbered close to 75,000, the largest Southern army ever assembled in the West.[29]

The Fourth Corps deployed for battle with General Stanley's division in the center, Wood on the right and Newton on the left. As General Hood prepared strike a blow on federal left, Union cavalry passing around the Confederate right flank were mistaken for a strong Union infantry force. Fearful of being flanked, Johnston reluctantly ordered a retreat to the new line a half mile east and south of Cassville. When the facts were known, Hood was blamed for missing a golden opportunity to strike Sherman and a rebuke came from President Jefferson Davis himself. A chagrined Hood would never again allow himself to be accused of over-caution.[30]

As the Yankees swarmed around Cassville, they could not see the town for the forest, but they could see freshly dug earthworks on the hills beyond. Although they continued to believe that Johnston would not attack, Thomas and Sherman thought that he might choose to defend his new line. Sherman directed General Howard to put 30 or 40 artillery pieces in position and shell the rebel trenches at a range too great for the enemy to return fire. An hour and a half of shelling later, the Yankees advanced toward Cassville in the face of very heavy skirmishing. As daylight faded, the bluecoats stopped just west of Cassville. The bombardment had been effective in demonstrating key vulnerabilities in the Confederate defenses, and during a late evening council of war, Generals Hood and Polk declared their inability to hold their respective positions. Furthermore, Johnston discovered that Sherman had cavalry across the Etowah River just west of Kingston. Chagrined at his failure to bring on the promised engagement, Johnston decided his best recourse was to retreat south of the Etowah. With axmen mimicking the sounds of earthwork construction, the Southern retreat began after midnight.[31]

Learning of Johnston's departure early the next morning, May 20, Sherman decided that Thomas and McPherson should encamp around Kingston and Cassville to rest their men. Schofield's small army was sent after the retiring Confederates. Just before 9 p.m., Schofield arrived at the Etowah River 10 miles from Cassville, but the enemy had escaped across the Etowah, burning the bridges behind them. General Sherman established his headquarters in Kingston and allotted three days for rest and resupply. Harker's brigade camped three miles southeast of Kingston in an oak grove. Despite having supposedly full rations the brigade had not eaten for a day and, happily, four days of rations were issued. During the 21st and 22nd, the men rested, bathed, cleaned equipment, and battled noxious insects. For having endured 17 days for hard campaigning, the men of Harker's brigade were in remarkably good condition, save a few cases of diarrhea. Sherman's quartermasters turned Kingston into a supply depot. Baggage wagons arrived with a change of clothes—the first in two weeks—and shelter tents. Opdycke's wound continued to heal under cold water bandages, although he had limited use of the arm. He hoped to resume command of the 125th in 10 days.[32]

The Union army was 50 miles from Atlanta. Between the federals and the city the next natural obstacle was the Allatoona Hills where the railroad slipped through a pass on its way south. One officer in the 125th described the Hills as "not the thing to run squarely against." Sherman had seen this part of Georgia as a young pre-war army officer. "I therefore knew that Allatoona Pass was very strong, would be hard to force, and resolved not to attempt it," Sherman later wrote, "but to turn the position, by moving from Kingston to Marietta via Dallas." It was 25 miles to Dallas and another 20 east to Marietta, Georgia. Marietta was on the Western and Atlantic, immediately below the imposing Kennesaw Mountain and roughly 10 miles from the Chattahoochee River, which was the last major geographical barrier before Atlanta. The Army of the Cumberland would be the main column to Dallas. Schofield would stay on Thomas' left and McPherson, the right. Dallas itself was west of Marietta across a tributary of the Etowah referred to as Pumpkin Vine Creek. Sherman was confident there would be a major battle between Kingston and the Chattahoochee River. "I have no doubt we must have a terrible battle at some point near the Chattahoochee," he wrote, confident that he had the best army. The only question for Sherman was where would Johnston choose to fight.[33]

12

New Hope Church

Colonel Opdycke wrote his wife on May 23 from the camp near Kingston that the army was issued 20 days of rations in preparation for a move. Opdycke was confident of winning a battle in open country, and if the rebels chose to fight behind breastworks, they could be flanked from them. Opdycke's optimism reflected the feelings of everyone from W. T. Sherman down to the lowliest private. The federal army had crossed the Etowah River—Sherman's "Rubicon of Georgia"—and were eager to push on for Atlanta. Although this would be another flanking movement, it would be difficult for Sherman to move 100,000 men with speed and stealth. The roads were poor, the maps bad, the country full of enemy spies and every night campfires marked the Yankees' location. Nevertheless, Sherman intended to drive his army hard and question every delay.[1]

Before the movement began, Colonel Frank Sherman was replaced in command of Newton's First Brigade—for the fourth and last time—by the more senior Brigadier General Nathan Kimball, a fierce-looking former doctor and soldier from Indiana who had fought at Antietam. Brigadiers George Wagner led the Second brigade and Charles Harker the Third.[2]

The Yankees started south on a warm, dusty Monday, May 23. The supply trains were loaded with 20 days of necessities which Sherman was prepared to stretch to 30, if necessary, by foraging the countryside. The company officers' equipage was carried by mule, one per company, often driven by a colored servant. Each private soldier carried a tent fly or rubber blanket, his haversack with rations, a canteen, and a small coffee pot or mess pail. There were no new, well packed knapsacks for the men or fresh white collars for the officers. Where this army was going, these trimmings wouldn't be needed.[3]

The Army of the Cumberland took aim for Dallas, Georgia, 25 miles south of Kingston, 20 miles west of Marietta and just east of Pumpkin Vine Creek. The Fourth Corps crossed the Etowah at Gillem's Bridge at noon. As usual, the river crossings were bottlenecks, and Newton's division was the last in the Fourth Corps' column which translated into Harker's brigade not crossing the Etowah until 9 p.m. Harker's boys continued on five miles to Euharlee Creek, a tributary of the Etowah, which they crossed about 11 p.m. before camping.[4]

The rugged Allatoona Hills south of the Etowah still had to be negotiated. On Tuesday, May 24—marching on too little sleep—the Fourth Corps made a hard march through the pine covered hills to Burnt Hickory. "No words can express the severity of that march across the Allatoona hills, through heat and dust, now halting to form in line of battle as the enemy made a more stubborn resistance," Company E's Second Lieutenant Henry Steadman informed *The Jeffersonian Democrat*. "Halting when night came on, too weary to cook our supper, we would sink down upon the damp ground to rest." A sleepy-eyed chap who had been commissary sergeant, Steadman had stuck to his horse while assisting Opdycke at Chickamauga, earning his lieutenant's bars. The Hills were known for small gold deposits, and occasionally men found pieces of gold bearing quartz. But there was little time for prospecting, the march to Dallas would resume in the morning.[5]

The Confederate army was not complacent. When Johnston learned that Sherman's whole army was across the Etowah on the afternoon of the 23rd, he set his army in motion. By the 25th, the Southerners occupied a fortified line along the Dallas-Acworth road, east of and roughly parallel to Pumpkin Vine Creek. Hardee's Corps was on the left south of Dallas, Polk occupied the center and Hood's corps was on the right, centered on the New Hope Church crossroads. The rebel fortifications skillfully followed a series of high wooded hills and were concealed in the dense pines and heavy undergrowth. The ground in their front was open and easily swept with musketry and cannon. The banks of Pumpkin Vine Creek were steep and as much as 50 feet high. This formidable defensive position covered the roads from Dallas to Atlanta, Marietta and Acworth. Likewise, for those from New Hope Church going in the same direction. "The whole of Johnston's line was admirably chosen for defense," General Cox conceded.[6]

Mid-morning on the 25th, the Army of the Cumberland began tramping and creaking south from Burnt Hickory, west of Pumpkin Vine Creek, toward Dallas. The forest around the bluecoats was dark and still, a thick riot of green spring foliage. It was a pretty May day, one participant recalled, coming on the heels of a full moon. Hooker's Twentieth Corps had the privilege of the main road that day. Its 16,000 men, veterans of hard battles east and west, made it the largest corps in the Union army. Hooker—"Fighting Joe" to his admirers—was vain and profane, imperious and a braggart, but not reckless. As Hooker's men crossed Pumpkin Vine Creek, their skirmishers exchanged shots with rebel cavalry pickets. Across the Creek, Hooker mistakenly sent one of his divisions down the road to New Hope Church, and after two miles it bumped into Confederate General John Bell Hood's pickets in front of New Hope, five miles northeast of Dallas and 30 miles from Atlanta. The gray skirmishers, on a patrol up the road, fought hard before retreating, bluecoats on their heels. At 2 p.m., Hooker halted to consolidate his corps.[7]

Hooker notified George Thomas, who, comparing reports arriving at his headquarters, suspected there was a significant number of enemy in his front. The Fourth Corps was ordered to advance and support Hooker. In reality only a single 4000-man division from Hood's Corps was in front of the Twentieth Corps. Since losing his leg at Chickamauga and the use of an arm at Gettysburg, Hood had healed sufficiently to lead men in battle, albeit strapped awkwardly and uncomfortably to his horse. While he didn't look the part, with his sleepy eyes, sad face and battered body, the 33-year-old Hood was aggression personified. The rest of his military career could be summed up with one sentence: "Death is far preferable to defeat."[8]

On Sherman's order, Hooker arranged two fresh divisions in two brigade fronts for the attack—a massive, tightly packed punch aimed at an unknown number of Confederates somewhere ahead. Advancing with parade ground precision through a cathedral-like forest, Hooker's divisions dropped into a valley within artillery range of the concealed rebel line. Suddenly the air was filled with musket balls, canister shot and shrapnel. The fighting between the experienced blue and gray veterans was severe, and could be heard halfway to Burnt Hickory, five miles removed. Hooker's three divisions were unable break the rebel lines. With late afternoon came a tremendous thunderstorm—torrential rain, cracks of lightening and booms of thunder—that made this battle deep in the forest seem surreal. The muzzle flashes diminished but never ceased. Finally, with cartridge boxes empty and a clearing sky at twilight, drenched men mutually agreed to stop shooting. Hooker's men reluctantly fell back, minus almost 1700 casualties. Cheers of victorious Southerners echoed in the woods. In history books, this would be identified as the Battle of New Hope Church. Hooker's men simply nicknamed the place "Hell Hole." An ordeal in the Georgia woods had begun that would last for more or less 11 days.[9]

Howard's divisions were seven miles from Dallas when General Thomas ordered them to support Hooker. Newton's division, forced to pick its way around Hooker's stalled supply trains, led Howard's corps. Newton's men crossed Pumpkin Vine Creek about 6 p.m. coming up on Hooker's lines at dark, 7:30 p.m., following the heavy storm. Captain John Tuttle from the 3rd Kentucky in Harker's Brigade was a reliable diarist with an uncanny knack for becoming separated from his regiment. That evening, Tuttle found himself wandering through the rear of the Twentieth Corps as it desperately fought the Southerners. "The rain came down in torrents and…. It was so dark one could not see his hand before him," Tuttle wrote of the chaos. "Thousands were crowding forward to relieve those who had been fighting … without the slightest regard to organization for that was impossible. Those relieved came back in swarms, some carrying their wounded comrades." Although some of Newton's brigades managed to form a line of battle on Hooker's left by 8:30, it was too late make any impact. The 125th was not engaged, but camped in battle formation at 9:30.[10]

With morning's first light, Harker's brigade discovered itself within 300 or 400 yards of the Confederate trenches, unseen in the blackness of the previous evening. When the Yankees began to stir, Louisiana sharpshooters began to ply their deadly trade. In the light of day, the Fourth Corps wheeled forward aligning them with Hooker's left flank. Tom Wood's division filled the gap on Newton's left. The Corps was now east of Pumpkin Vine Creek on a series of hills with a narrow open valley in front. Opposite them was the Confederate right wing which formed an angle in front of New Hope Church as it was refused to protect the flank.[11]

Schofield's Twenty-Third Corps came up on Wood's left, and became the left flank of the Union army. While maneuvering, John Schofield was unhorsed by an unseen branch and bruised so General Cox assumed temporary command. McPherson's two corps centered on Dallas to Hooker's right. Between Hooker and McPherson, a division from the Army of the Cumberland's Fourteenth Corps was deployed, but gaps existed that were fortunately undetected by the Johnnies in the thick woods. Sherman's eight mile line—constructed under fire—covered the road from Dallas almost to Allatoona. Howard's men entrenched as quickly as possible under annoying rebel musketry until two lines of works were completed. After dark, on the 26th, artillery was brought into position. The combatants were only 100 yards apart in a few places and brisk skirmishing ensued. Northern skirmishers were confined to the relative safety of their shooting holes and could only be relieved after dark. Officers riding between the crests of the hills were subjected to deadly sharpshooter fire.[12]

Building breastworks consumed a part of almost every day during the push for Atlanta as soldiers on both sides came to appreciate the safety mounds of earth offered. By the time they reached New Hope Church, common soldiers had become expert in the construction of breastworks. As one veteran remarked, "Every man is to some extent his own engineer." Each company was responsible for their position. Once the officers selected the location, a skirmish line was established and the rest of the men, with muskets close at hand, began cutting and dragging trees, rocks, rails or anything that would stop a bullet, into a rude barricade chest high. Circumstances permitting, a ditch was dug inside the barricade, perhaps three feet deep, with the dirt thrown over the barricade. When the digging was done, the earthworks were taller than a man. A step was placed in the ditch so a soldier could see over the parapet to shoot and step down to reload. Head logs, 18 inches or more in diameter, were oft times placed on the parapet with a narrow opening or loophole for the riflemen underneath. To prevent injury to men in the ditch, skids reaching from the parapet to the back of the ditch were placed at intervals in case a log was dislodged by a cannon shot. Sometimes all the brush and saplings in front for 50 yards were cut to create a field of fire. If cut to fall away from the earthwork, trimmed and sharpened, the vegetation could become a formidable abatis to slow attackers. According to General Cox, all this was accomplished in an hour from the time the men stacked their arms.[13]

On the 26th, Colonel Opdycke returned to duty a week earlier than originally intended. He told Charlie Harker that he preferred to remain with his regiment. But Harker needed Opdycke to command a demi-brigade, and Emerson Opdycke's last stint in regimental command lasted less than a day.[14]

While much of the 125th built earthworks that afternoon, Major Bruff took Company B and two companies of the 65th Ohio to the forward picket line. The skirmishing was serious and Lieutenant Ralsa Rice, now commanding a company, asked Major Bruff if he could change tactics and fight Indian style instead of the traditional Napoleonic method. "Take your own way, so long as you get there," Bruff told Rice. The major's small detachment fought brush and brambles initially, before entering 300 yards of open woods. When the forward blue skirmishers were at last sighted, they could be seen trading shots with their rebel counterparts in earnest. Rice told his company, "Every man for himself. Take advantage of everything offering protection. We have not a man to spare." At that moment, brigade adjutant captain Ed Whitesides appeared and began upbraiding Rice for his non-regulation skirmishing tactics. "Don't you know the tactics better than that?" Immediately, two bullets zipped past Whitesides and he instinctively ducked behind his horse. "I believe they are shooting at me!" he exclaimed mounting quickly, and galloping toward the rear, coattails flapping.[15]

The Confederate fortifications were somewhere in front of Bruff's men concealed in the forest and underbrush, and Bruff's task was to pinpoint them. When a bugle sounded, Company B raced forward, plunged into thick undergrowth and collided with Southern skirmishers. Private Nathan Hatch, a Trumbull County lad, ran straight into the Johnnies, but withdrew unmolested. Rice's men pushed the gray pickets aside and encountered a ravine in front of a high bluff. Rice retired a few yards for a better view, taking cover behind an oak tree and instantly became a target. Utilizing his hat as a decoy to draw fire, Rice escaped when Sergeant William Fitch, a rare Pennsylvanian in the 125th, drew down on a Southern marksman. Company B clawed its way forward from tree to tree until Lieutenant Rice saw a slash of red earth amid the thick vegetation indicating a part of the miles of Confederate trench lines that angled across the landscape. The Lieutenant gathered his small company behind the safety of large deadfall. Rice estimated his company was ahead of even the divisional skirmish line. Sergeant Fitch crept out to where he had aimed his earlier shot and recovered a rebel haversack with a bullet hole and an officer's sword and belt. Rice claimed the scabbard. With no orders to retreat,

Company B held the position until relieved at dark by Company H. Major Bruff had managed to get his men 150 yards closer to the Confederate fortifications without loss.[16]

A steady skirmish fire between the lines—sometimes less than 200 yards separated them—continued day and night. Every day the fortifications grew until Sherman believed them "as formidable as first class works of defense." Sherman rode the lines daily, close to the front, and yet never saw more than a dozen enemy soldiers at one time, an indication of how much these 19th-century soldiers had embraced trench warfare. Lieutenant Steadman wrote in *The Jeffersonian Democrat*: "For eleven days we were engaged in a constant and almost uninterrupted skirmish with the foe, whose position was too well chosen and too securely protected by heavy works to allow any hope of success by direct assault." The rare breaks in the shooting were marked by taunts shouted and rocks thrown across the void. Heavy firing of musketry or artillery throughout the night made sleep difficult, and the men were often roused two or three times a night to face some unseen, fictional threat. Rebel sharpshooters made it imprudent to even raise a head above the breastworks. The best imported English Enfield rifles in the hands of veteran Confederate soldiers were easily capable of hitting a man's head at 300 yards. The Southern sharpshooters armed with Whitworth rifles mounting telescopic sights were deadly from twice that range. Miles removed from the railroad, Sherman's supplies began to dwindle, and even the monotonous daily issue of hard tack, pork, coffee and sugar was halved.[17]

Still unwilling to admit that he was facing most Johnston's army, Sherman decided, yet again, to test the flanks of the Confederate line before him. His orders outlined two actions for the 27th. James McPherson's army before Dallas was to push straight at the enemy in hopes of closing up on General Hooker's right. Meanwhile, Howard's Fourth Corps was to pass around the Twenty-Third Corps on the Union left and attack the Confederate right somewhere northeast of New Hope Church in the direction of the Western and Atlantic Railroad. That nobody in blue knew exactly the location of the gray right flank posed a potential problem. This dilemma worsened when General Hood correctly divined that Sherman would strike for the railroad. Hood persuaded Johnston to reenforce the right with the best division in the Southern army—Major General Patrick Cleburne's. Tom Wood's division was tapped to lead the "arduous and dangerous task." Wood objected—his men had spent the night building new breastworks—to no avail. The attack again would be by a heavy fist on a narrow front—columns of brigades. Bill Hazen's brigade was chosen to spearhead the assault. Hazen's regiments were small—an average of 200 men each—and fought out after three years' service. Attacking in columns, successive supporting brigades were usually only minutes apart to maintain the momentum. For reasons that were not clear, there would be 40 minutes between brigades, negating the sledgehammer effect. Tom Wood told Oliver Howard, "We will put in Hazen, and see what success he has." No one told Hazen of the time delays.[18]

Johnston's veterans were awakened with an artillery barrage on the 27th along the fronts of the Army of the Ohio and Army of the Cumberland. McPherson got underway early and by noon he had concluded he could not turn the Southern left, leaving his men to skirmish and posture the rest of the day. The Fourth Corps didn't move until almost noon. Most of the terrain around what was known as Pickett's Mill—a gristmill on Pumpkin Vine Creek two miles northeast of New Hope Church—proved to be forest laced with winding unmapped wagon tracks and choked with undergrowth growing on steep hills and in deep ravines. Worse, when Wood's men arrived at the position where the Confederate flank was supposed to be, they found new breastworks. In vain, the bluecoats probed for Johnston's flank which Hood continued to push farther east. Finally, just after 4:30 with his corps strung out across the landscape, Howard decided to attack south where he *guessed* the Southern right should be.[19]

Hazen's 1500 man brigade—including the 41st and 124th Ohio—stepped off in two lines, on a front of just 200 yards. It was hard going as the Yankees battled the thick undergrowth initially before stumbling into concealed enemy earthworks and vicious volleys of musketry provided by Cleburne's infantry. The enemy's works were only waist high, but that was still better than what Hazen' men had. Hazen claimed his men followed their colors to within 10 yards of the enemy before they were stopped. Here developed what Hazen's topographer, Lieutenant Ambrose Bierce, labeled a "dead line"—a mythical line established by the gods of war which assaulting troops were unable to cross. The line became reality as the bodies of the fallen piled up. The bluecoats slugged it out with the rebels for about 50 minutes, but when new troops failed to arrive and their ammunition was depleted, most Hazen's brigade withdrew. The 124th's Captain George Lewis later claimed, "Our brigade was the worst cut up of all the battles in which we were engaged."[20]

Wood shoveled other brigades into the battle, but they endured a furious cross fire, and were repulsed in succession when their ammunition was exhausted. Hazen's brigade lost 560 men. Hazen, visibly moved as he watched his depleted brigade stagger back, later claimed the battle was "the most fierce, bloody and persistent assault of the Atlanta campaign." Opdycke's old 41st Ohio lost nearly half its number. General Wood's division suffered over 1400 casualties, and General Howard himself received a minor wound from a shell fragment. Many wounded were left on the field. This unsuccessful flanking attempt would be known as the Battle of Pickett's Mill. Lieutenant Ambrose Bierce, writing after the war, would label this blundering attack ordered by the generals in blue as "the Crime at Pickett's Mill."[21]

During the fighting on Friday, May 27, Harker's brigade performed the mundane, yet risky work of strengthening breastworks. No gentlemen's truce here, enemy sharpshooters randomly shot men carelessly exposed. The 125th's Private William Miller was killed and Private Warren Fishel was wounded. The picket line was even worse—the 64th Ohio lost eight men before the 125th replaced them at dark. Digging rifle pits in the dark attracted a rebel volley that forced the Ohioans to take cover. Returning to their work, a few dug while most were deployed in the front with cocked muskets.[22]

Although Pickett's Mill was possibly Sherman's worst defeat of the Atlanta Campaign and it cost him a week's delay, it did put the Union army that much closer to the rail line at Acworth. By the morning of the 28th, Sherman had decided to swing further east and gain the railroad at Acworth, just south of Allatoona Gap. McPherson's army was to withdraw from the Dallas area and move left, deploying on Thomas' left flank. Confederate attacks that afternoon temporarily delayed McPherson's maneuver. The rest of Sherman's army engaged in heavy skirmishing to hold the enemy in place. Opdycke's demi-brigade moved into the frontline of breastworks where he could see the rebel entrenchments through the trees and the Southern skirmishers were in easy musket range. Twice the enemy sallied forth from their line to test Opdycke's men, and twice they were beaten back. Opdycke's demi-brigade had four casualties in a day and a half. The 125th had one man slightly wounded.[23]

That evening, the rebel skirmishers and the 125th's pickets agreed to a temporary ceasefire, to which Opdycke acquiesced. The Southerners claimed to have been on Rocky

Face Ridge when the 125th seized part of it. Asked by the Northerners how soon they were going to "light out," the Confederates replied, "Lighting out is played out; we've got our place now." Sunday, the 29th, the 125th enjoyed a day in the rear. Lieutenant Colonel Moore read aloud from a May 28 copy of the *Atlanta Constitution* obtained in a trade across the line. The paper was brave and hopeful in tone, especially since only 400 Southerners were lost at New Hope Church. The fighting by McPherson's men, some under the stars, inspired Opdycke to write his wife that "the roll of musketry and the deep thunder of the artillery seemed to fill the Heavens with sound." McPherson's men repulsed the Johnnies each time leading a confident Opdycke to tell his wife, "The rebs are better at defense, than an attack."[24]

On the morning of the 30th it was back to the front for Opdycke's demi-brigade. By now the leaves and branches of the trees and brush were closely cropped by musketry and artillery, and the two lines could clearly see each other. The incessant skirmishing continued all day. Opdycke's boys requested another newspaper trade but were answered by gunfire. Southern officers had burned their soldiers' letters and newspapers to discourage exchanges of information. After another brief explosion of musketry around 10 p.m., the 125th had a comparatively quiet night. The next day Private Edwin Woodworth wrote his parents from the hellish trenches, "I hope that the God of Abraham may see me safe through this war."[25]

Probing and posturing by both armies resulted in continued heavy skirmishing all along the trench lines. On June 1, Harker's brigade took part in an extension of the Union line to the left. Thursday, June 2, seven companies the 125th were detached to protect an artillery battery that was receiving regular sniper fire. The battery pulled out at noon when rain began to fall—rain that was a daily curse, soaking generals and privates alike. Five men in the 125th were wounded during the duty. Lieutenant Clark wrote, "Balls fly in all directions." Opdycke, in a rare display of pessimism, admitted to his wife that the battle centered on New Hope Church had become tiresome and monotonous. His log-suffering soldiers were dirty and verminous. He had the 3rd Kentucky on the skirmish line, and it lost four men. Opdycke—his wounded arm useless—casually reported that a bullet had passed through his tent and another landed at his feet.[26]

Sherman's army needed a rest. A Michigan sergeant wrote home that "the boys are very much tired out, and several have gone to the rear.... There is not half the levity and profanity that I have usually seen in camp." There had been little opportunity for foraging the last month of hard marching and ceaseless skirmishing. The men were living on hard tack and bacon washed down with coffee—brewing sanitized the polluted surface water. The diet was unbalanced, and scurvy appeared—in some divisions it would affect 20 percent—sending men with bleeding gums and loose teeth to the rear. Lice, the ever-present plague of all armies, thrived on dirty men stationary in damp entrenchments. Conditions were just as bad in the rebel army. Someone was going to have to move. In 1897, Colonel Robert Kimberly of the 41st Ohio recalled those trying days: "Far down in the heart of the enemy's country, with the base of supplies so distant as to be practically cut off as to anything but ammunition and crackers and coffee and bacon; with only the dog-tent for a shelter, and for cooking utensils tin cups and frying pans—the whole outfit for shelter and living carried on the soldier's back.... A campaign in Africa would hardly be farther from home."[27]

On the 3rd, Harker's brigade fought off a Southern charge on the forward rifle pits, losing several men. The men of the 125th kept their heads down and suffered no casualties.

When he was wounded, Colonel Opdycke had forsaken the rear hospitals, and he finally admitted to Lucy that it was his fear that if Lieutenant Colonel Moore were to become a casualty, Major Bruff would assume command. The Colonel's enmity toward Bruff had not faded. It appeared, instead, to have grown with every step farther into Georgia.[28]

Before dawn on the 4th, Harker's brigade moved about a half mile to the left to a position of less danger. During the day on the 4th, amid a day long rain, Union cavalry entered Acworth uncontested and achieved a junction with the rail line. Sherman slid his entire army east behind the Army of the Ohio so that by nightfall, Schofield was the right of the line covering the evacuation of the hospitals and wagon trains. That night, while the 125th was on the skirmish line, the Confederates abandoned their lines and fell back toward Marietta. Slogging through foot-deep mud that swallowed shoes and wagons on equal terms, the rebels fell back to a line that ran from the railroad to Lost Mountain, some six miles southeast. Confederate general William Hardee, writing the next day, said, "We had last night, the hardest marching I have known troops to encounter." Once again the fear of being flanked persuaded Joe Johnston to retreat.[29]

On the morning of the 5th, after what was called "the darkest night of all the dark nights," federals on picket duty were greeted with silence. Despite the opposing fortifications being less than 100 yards apart in some places, the enemy had slipped away. The weary Yankees cheered the discovery. The ordeal of the "Hell Hole" had come to an end. To the Northerners, who occupied the battlefield, it was a technical victory. However, Johnston had blocked the Union advance for almost two weeks and inflicted about 4500 casualties on the bluecoats at a loss of perhaps 3000 of his own men. Despite the abysmal conditions the Johnnies had endured, the stand at New Hope had preserved, if not improved, Southern morale.[30]

This time when Johnston and his men retreated, Opdycke was not sorry to see them go. Life in the trenches was becoming unbearable. Enemy bullets whizzed overhead regularly. Opdycke himself had not washed his face in 10 days except behind the protective cover of a tree. General Howard called the time spent in the trenches around New Hope Church "the hardest times which the army experienced."[31]

The Southerners gone, David Moore, suffered an attack of "bilious colic"—severe pain in the upper abdomen. Major Joseph Bruff assumed temporary command, and sent companies D, F, H, and K through the abandoned works and drove off a few Southern cavalry pickets. Harker ordered Bruff to advance the skirmishers another half mile, but the Johnnies had decamped. The muddy roads were in such bad condition after the enemy's retreat that Sherman's men were forced into the fields to advance. The 125th captured four sleeping rebel soldiers on their scout. The Tigers returned to the abandoned works that evening to sleep.[32]

June 6 promised to be a very warm day. Harker's brigade marched at 6 a.m. through the mud and covered just eight miles by 3:30. They encamped in a pleasant wood with good water four miles west of Acworth, Georgia, the newly designated supply depot for Thomas' army. Colonel Opdycke's wound did finally suppurate—the happy appearance of ugly pus the surgeon's expected. Afterward, the wound healed more rapidly. A week later, and a month from his wounding, Opdycke put his arm in his coat sleeve for the first time. The arm was still useless, and would be for three months according to Dr. McHenry—only a slight inconvenience in Opdycke's mind. The colonel later admitted to his worried wife that if he had to do it again, he would have gone to the rear. "The example has been of some value I hope," Opdycke told her referring to those men who went to the rear needlessly. Like every other soldier who had suffered through muddy trenches, moldy blankets and half rations consumed under almost constant gunfire fire, Emerson Opdycke was glad to move on. An officer of the 125th wrote, "Although no general engagement, the duty has been very fatiguing for ten days under dropping fire continually." One member of the brigade summed up the experience: "The days and nights were about equally full of wretchedness." To add to the good feeling, the next day, Charles Harker officially became a brigadier general.[33]

Although Sherman had forced Johnston out of the formidable Allatoona Hills, which was a partial victory, he failed to reach Marietta. Nevertheless, despite the mud, constant skirmishing and shortage of bread, morale among the bluecoats remained high. As General Cox later recalled, "The certainty of ultimate success was undoubted." One Ohio artilleryman wrote: "I cannot think there are sufficient rebels in the state to defeat us. The General [Sherman] is a man of bravery and is well experienced in the art of war, and he battles in earnest." The Yankees understood that the road home ran through Atlanta.[34]

General Sherman, put a good face on New Hope Church and Picket's Mill, telling his wife, Ellen, that his flanking movement had been a "perfect success." In a June 12 letter, Sherman re-iterated his role in Grant's grand spring offensive, as much for his morale as his wife's. "As long as I press him [Johnston] close and prevent his sending anything to Lee I fulfill my part of the Grand Plan." Perhaps feeling he could speak candidly to his wife, Sherman, his blood up regarding the Union offensive in 1864 told her, "Every man in America should now be aroused, and all who will not help should be put in petticoats and deprived of the right to vote in the affairs of the after nation."[35]

With the Confederate army gathered in front of Marietta, the railroad was open to Big Shanty, Georgia, within sight of Kennesaw Mountain. As Sherman wrote of Johnston's withdrawal south and his gaining the railroad "we effected the change without further battle." Both armies were tired. Sherman called the country from Chattanooga to Big Shanty "nearly a hundred miles of as difficult country as was ever fought over by civilized armies." That 100 miles cost Sherman over 9000 casualties, 2000 killed. Its failed defense cost Johnston a like number. The 125th had seen 107 men killed and wounded during May 1864. In Sherman's estimation—and his opinion mattered most—the first stage of his campaign to take Atlanta was completed.[36]

The Confederate government was tiring of Joe Johnston's campaign of retreat. Braxton Bragg, sent to access the situation in Georgia, wrote President Jefferson Davis on June 4 that either Robert E. Lee in Virginia or Johnston in Georgia must defeat their adversaries before the Union juggernaut gained unstoppable momentum. Bragg interpreted Sherman's brief pause after New Hope Church as one to acquire re-enforcements. Indeed, that occurred. Sherman received re-enforcements on the 8th when Major General Francis Blair's Seventeenth Corps reached him with 9000 effectives, almost equal to his losses.[37]

For the next phase of the march toward Atlanta, W. T. Sherman had determined to maintain a closer proximity to the railroad. As historian Albert Castel explained: "Having failed in his attempt at a wide, bold sweep around the enemy flank, he [Sherman] now intends to push straight ahead, at all times keeping his army in contact with the railroad. He hopes and sometimes even believes that Johnston will fall back across the Chattahoochee rather than risk battle with that river at his back. Sherman also realizes that it is very possible that Johnston will make a stand north of Marietta, where the mountainous terrain offers strong defensive positions."[38]

The Confederates had abandoned New Hope for a newly constructed line between Lost and Brush Mountains, two to three miles north of Kennesaw Mountain with Pine Mountain sitting as a salient at its center, all northwest of Marietta. General Leonidas Polk's corps was in the center, John Bell Hood's on the right and William Hardees' on the left. This new line covered the approach to Marietta to the north and west. Here the mountains were not a continuous chain, but rather a scattering of high elevations that rose above the Georgia pine forests like geologic monuments. They provided yet another strong defensive position for the Southerners.[39]

Opdycke's Tigers endured life in the trenches and on the skirmish line, but avoided those few terrible hours of bloodletting endured by Hooker's divisions at New Hope and Hazen's brigade at Picket's Mill. There would be other costly mistakes by the generals. And the next time Sherman would impatiently send men into a hellish killing field, the 125th would not be exempted. In a letter to his sister, Brigadier General Charles Harker noted that many gallant officers and brave men had fallen in battle thus far in the campaign. "Before this reaches you thousands of others must fall," Harker continued. "Who they will be, God in his infinite wisdom alone knoweth."[40]

13

The Battles for Kennesaw Mountain

Sunrise on June 10 brought a bright and beautiful morning that changed over to rain in the afternoon—the seventh straight day of rain. Regardless, with their haversacks full of rations, Harker's Third Brigade started down the road to Atlanta at 11. The terrain was still marked by hills, but growing more subdued. The geography east the Western and Atlantic and Marietta, was more favorable for offensive military operations, but for the Union army, the risk of being flanked and losing connection with the railroad outweighed the advantages. The only realistic option was straight ahead. To reach the Chattahoochee, Sherman sent McPherson's army toward Marietta on the left of the Union column. Thomas' men went straight ahead to Kennesaw and Pine Mountains, while Schofield marched down the Sandtown Road to Lost Mountain on the federal right. The Army of the Cumberland marched in three columns: Howard's Fourth Corps in the center, flanked by Palmer's Fourteenth on the left and Hooker's Twentieth on the right. Each column was preceded by skirmishers supported by a battery of rifled cannon. For the Fourth Corps General Stanley's division led, followed by Newton's and finally, Wood's. Due to long halts caused by traffic congestion on the muddy roads and determined enemy skirmishers, Newton's entire division marched only three miles before camping and entrenching.[1]

The rain continued on the 11th accompanied by chilling easterly winds. Streams were swollen, the red Georgia clay was so soggy that any movement quickly churned it to something akin to glue, and the 11th became another three mile day. The 125th spent the day bobbing around fruitlessly through rain and sticky red mud from one position to another until 10 p.m. Major General Francis Blair's Seventeenth Corps arrived and joined McPherson's army as it began yet another flanking maneuver.[2]

Digging replaced marching on the 12th or 13th as rain continued to fall. One Fourth Corps officer observed that the rebels had "a strong position about a mile to the front and right on a considerable hill." This was part of a fortified Southern line that ran southwest from Pine Mountain through Gilgal Church to Lost Mountain. The bluecoats endured a week in wool uniforms that were never dry, and slept in the brush to avoid the wet ground. "The principal characteristic of our present position are rain, smoke, mud, and stray balls flying around our heads," observed John Tuttle of the 3rd Kentucky. A bit of sunshine the evening of the 13th offered the promise of better weather. The 125th went on picket at 4 p.m., 200 yards in front of their fortifications. To the east, in front of Brush Mountain, a federal supply train pulled into Big Shanty, Georgia, just five miles in Sherman's rear, and 28 miles by rail from Atlanta. For the first time in three weeks, Sherman's army could be supplied directly from the railroad.[3]

Tuesday, June 14, the skies cleared and Sherman ordered that a strong skirmish line press the Confederates hard without bringing on a general engagement. General Thomas advanced the right of Palmer's corps and the left of Howard's east of the Pine Mountain toward Kennesaw Mountain. The 125th—three companies on the line and one in reserve—participated in brisk skirmishing and gained some ground on the east side of Pine Mountain. Three men were wounded. Opdycke's entire demi-brigade advanced after dark to consolidate and fortify the position. Those three casualties were hardly noticed in an army where a couple hundred every day was the norm. The morning of June 14, however, would be remembered as the day a very lucky artillery shot, ordered by Sherman personally, killed Confederate General Leonidas Polk on Pine Mountain. More importantly tactically, the rebels disappeared from Pine Mountain that night.[4]

The clear predawn darkness suggested a fair day on the 15th. Colonel Opdycke was up at 4 to check his picket line and his men informed him that the Southerners were gone. Harker's brigade advanced a half mile and occupied the empty Confederate line. The Northerners were impressed by complex Southern trenches that were almost fort-like. When Sherman was satisfied the butternuts were gone, he ordered Thomas to conduct a reconnaissance in force between Pine Mountain and Kennesaw Mountain that afternoon. The task was assigned to the Fourth Corps and Newton's division was given the lead with three of Harker's regiments at the point. The country was rolling and covered with dense woods and undergrowth. Advancing cautiously at 3 p.m., with a heavy skirmish line in the front, the Yankees discovered another line of Confederate fortifications a mile away. This new line of trenches ran almost east to west along the divide between the Etowah and Chattahoochee River watersheds. Union officers with binoculars could easily see the new defenses south of Pine Mountain with a line of inferior fortifications connecting to the mountain. As it had been for weeks, the skirmishing was serious. Two Confederate skirmish lines were driven back before the federals reached the main rebel line. Harker lost 45 men in the advance. Instead of attacking so late in the day, General Thomas ordered the entire Fourth Corps artillery forward to shell the enemy line. The 125th was in reserve and not engaged.[5]

Sherman felt Thomas' reconnaissance had been conducted too cautiously, and continued to entertain the idea of having the Army of the Cumberland mass and punch through the center of the Confederate line. "It may cost us dear," Sherman confessed to the War Department. Still, with the Chattahoochee River only 15 miles in Johnston's rear, should the Yankees break through, it would be nearly impossible for Confederates to escape whole across the river. On the 16th, Schofield and Thomas maneuvered to put part of Johnston's line at Gilgal Church in an artillery crossfire. That night, the Southerners evacuated the Gilgal Church line for a new one four miles west of Kennesaw Mountain behind Mud Creek, their fourth strong position since crossing the Etowah River. This new fortified line ran southwest from Brush Mountain to Mud Creek effectively blocking the railroad and wagon roads that ran into Marietta and crossed the Chattahoochee River beyond. The Confederate Army of the Tennessee now occupied a semicircular position eight miles long. This latest position wasn't intended to be held long, however, for Johnston immediately began work on a new line in front of Kennesaw Mountain.[6]

Sherman was increasingly frustrated by what he perceived to be the Army of the

Cumberland's over-caution. Thomas' troops seemed "timid in these dense forests of stumbling on a hidden breastwork," Sherman complained, primarily to Grant. "A fresh furrow in a ploughed field will stop the whole column," he fumed, "and all begin to entrench. I have again and again tried to impress on Thomas that we must assail, not defend; we are on the offensive, and yet it seems the whole Army of the Cumberland is so habituated to be on the defensive that, from its commander on down to the lowest private, I cannot get it out of their heads." This was an exaggeration, of course, because the Army of the Cumberland had done the bulk of the fighting thus far. The real injustice lay in Sherman's belief that Thomas' men "cannot keep up with my thoughts and wishes."[7]

A joint operation involving Schofield, Hooker and Howard's men closed on Mud Creek the morning of June 17. Tom Wood's division led the Fourth Corps which, after three miles, reached the banks of Mud Creek. Heavy rains—destined to last several more days—arrived late on the 17th drenching everything, filling the trenches with muddy water and hampering all movement. Wet pant cuffs tucked into water-logged shoes would eventually become moldy. Cold winds and lice would increase the misery and lengthen the sick rolls. At 5 p.m., the 125th moved forward to support the skirmish line and spent the night in the rain.[8]

At 8 a.m. on the 18th, three regiments of skirmishers from George Wagner's brigade splashed across Mud Creek—"a deep swift stream"—under fire. The Southern pickets were evicted and Harker sent the 3rd Kentucky into the fray to hold the gains. To conceal themselves amidst the thick undergrowth in the dim mist, rebel skirmishers were discovered with stuck brush in their belts for camouflage. General Newton followed Wagner's gains with the entire division and closed the gap between the adversaries to less than 250 yards. To hold the position, the best marksmen in each company directed their aim under the rebel's head logs and into the loopholes beneath as well as into the artillery embrasures. Heavy exchanges of musket fire—supplemented by six artillery batteries—continued for five hours despite heavy rain. Caught in a vicious crossfire, the Southerners took a beating. By evening, not a bush remained standing between the lines. The 65th Ohio claimed to have expended 100 rounds per man. Opdycke's demi-brigade suffered 50 casualties; the 3rd Kentucky, 24; the 125th, two killed, eight wounded, one fatally. Private Mark Shields, shot in the face lost several teeth, but survived. Sergeant James Wetzel, slightly wounded at Resaca, was killed. Private John Vanhoof was killed by a sharpshooter when he briefly sat near a fire in the rear warming himself. Private Henry Green died a month later. Opdycke matter-of-factly informed his wife that he was in the saddle until 1 a.m. and that a minie ball came within an inch of his spine. General Thomas was pleased with Howard's effort telling him that Sherman was "at last very much pleased." The men of the 3rd Kentucky received a half ration of whiskey for their effort.[9]

With two Union divisions poised to break the center of his line and Schofield's army threatening to turn his left, Johnston's army withdrew two miles that night to his ninth position since May 8—the Kennesaw Mountain line. Kennesaw Mountain—actually two peaks, Big and Little Kennesaw—dominated the landscape northwest of Marietta and west of the Western and Atlantic Railroad. Big Kennesaw rose to 700 feet above the surrounding country. To the northwest, confronting the Yankees, it was steep, rocky and intimidating. Little Kennesaw rose slightly southwest of Big Kennesaw, was 400 feet tall and free of timber. South of Little Kennesaw was Pigeon Hill, just a hillock of 100 plus feet. The two mountains were connected by a low saddle resulting in two miles of high ground that commanded the vicinity and offered the last best defensive position before the Chattahoochee River. Johnston's 10 miles of defenses began north of Marietta and east of the railroad. From Kennesaw south, the Confederate line blocked the wagon roads to Marietta from the west. The fortifications were a marvel of military engineering complete with cleared fields of fire and abatis in front. But Johnston barely had enough soldiers to cover the 10 miles and they were spread thin in the trenches.[10]

The 125th Ohio shoveled mud and cut trees for the new breastworks until 2 a.m. on the 19th. Based on reports from forward scouts that the rebels in front were gone, Major Bruff took three companies forward to investigate at 3:30 a.m. He found what all the Fourth Corps skirmishers did—the rebels were gone. Opdycke's demi-brigade led Newton's division in pursuit. After two or three difficult miles marked by heavy skirmishing, the Kennesaw Mountain line of Confederate entrenchments came into view. After examining the line through field glasses, General Howard pronounced the Confederate line "almost impregnable." Opdycke's men dug new trenches until sundown. The day's only casualty in the 125th was Lieutenant Freeman Collins—promoted from acting Sergeant Major for gallantry at Chickamauga—killed instantly just yards from Opdycke by a piece of shrapnel that passed through his body during an artillery exchange. General Harker narrowly escaped wounding when a live shell passed close enough to singe his mount's mane. "Never mind, boys," Harker joked about the close call to those around him, "a miss is as good as a mile. Besides, here is plenty of timber for more generals." The Fourth Corps lost about hundred men the 19th.[11]

By the night of the 19th, Howard's Corps was drawn up on Noses (or Noyes) Creek. David Stanley's division was astride the direct road from Gilgal Church to Marietta. Newton's division was on the left of Stanley and one brigade of General Wood's division on Stanley's right. The Fourteenth Corps was on left of Howard's and Hooker's Twentieth was on the right across Noses Creek. Opdycke wrote home that evening by the light of a candle fixed to a tree by a knife. He admitted not having slept but four hours in the last 48. "This is rough soldiering," Opdycke told Lucy. Captain Wilbur Hindman of the 65th Ohio acknowledged the hard days. "They were one incessant round of lying in the trenches, marching, fortifying and skirmishing. It was not an uncommon thing to pitch and strike tents three or four times within twenty-four hours. Scarcely a day but one or more places in our ranks were made vacant by death, wounds or disease."[12]

James McPherson's army held the extreme left flank of Sherman's line and on Monday, June 20, his men were able to advance to the very foot of Big Kennesaw. Palmer's Fourteenth Corps closed on the southern spurs of Kennesaw. The Twentieth Corps extended its line to the right and closed to within 100 yards of the enemy line in desperate hand to hand combat. The aggressive Yankees were now "inconveniently near to our main line," according Confederate corps commander William Hardee. The 125th started another rainy day improving breastworks with clay, log and stone in plain view of the enemy, resulting in two privates and a negro servant being wounded. A rebel shell burst among Company B when it hit a head log held in place by bayonets, stunning several of the Tigers, slicing the shoulder of Ralsa Rice's coat and wounding Private Wesley Fishel, the man next to Rice, in the head.[13]

Colonel Opdycke was division officer of the day on the 20th, and he commanded the entire divisional skirmish line. Acknowledging the danger, Opdycke rode his secondary mount, Tempest. At 4 p.m., Opdycke was ordered to make a demonstration, accompanied by all the Fourth Corps' artillery, to detract from a thrust being made by Hooker and Schofield's men in their sectors. Opdycke sent a regiment running and yelling

Thirteen. The Battles for Kennesaw Mountain

toward the Southern skirmish line before pulling up short and unleashing several volleys. The startled enemy skirmishers broke and ran back to the relative safety their main fortifications. Opdycke, in a move reminiscent of his wounding at Resaca, fearlessly rode forward 200 yards, and found no rebel pickets, where there had been dozens minutes before. So zealous had been Opdycke's demonstration that General Newton sent a courier to ask Opdycke if he was being attacked. There was no immediate response from the Confederate artillery to the Union barrage. Then, in Opdycke's words, the Confederates replied with "deafening salvos" sending shells into the Union batteries and lines. The artillery duel continued until after dark. The 125th was detailed to protect one of the artillery batteries initially and after dark retired a half mile to the rear.[14]

By Sherman's personal count, June 21 was the 19th straight day of rain. The roads were impassable and where men and wagons went into the fields, those likewise became quagmires. Supply wagons could barely reach the front even though the depot at Big Shanty was just six miles behind the army's left flank. Sherman was impatient to move "the moment weather and roads will permit." Anticipating a federal move around his left toward Marietta, Johnston relocated Major General John Bell Hood's corps from his right flank to his left, during the night of the 21st. Both Hood and Hardee realized that Sherman would soon force Johnston south of the Chattahoochee River. However, they wanted to fight before retiring to Atlanta. "We would prefer to go there whipped rather than not to fight at all," Hardee wrote his wife on June 19.[15]

As part of a movement to lengthen the Union line so Schofield could pass Johnston's left, Newton's division moved from the center of the Fourth Corps line to the right, replacing a division from Hooker's corps. About noon, units from Wood and Stanley's divisions reclaimed a small hill in their front that had changed hands on the 20th. Both Wood and Newton then pushed their full divisions 400 yards closer to the Southern works—Opdycke's men were the point—expelling enemy pickets, and by 7 p.m. were firmly entrenched there. The firing—Opdycke labeled it "mad music"—continued all night. Harker's Third Brigade was eventually relieved by the Second. The Corps had 250 casualties, while the 125th Ohio lost six to wounds, two severely. Corporal William Lee was shot through leg and disabled. Writing Lucy of the day's work, Opdycke praised Lieutenant Colonel Moore's performance as acting commander of the 125th, calling him "good as gold."[16]

The sun rose June 23 on a rare dry day. Sherman planned to continue strengthening his right flank by pushing Schofield and Hooker's men east toward Marietta. Hooker's line ran from Howard's corps to the Powder Springs-Marietta Road. To the south, Schofield's men were feeling their way east. The two Union thrusts were to meet about four miles west of Marietta in cleared fields along the Powder Springs Road known as the Kolb Farm. Hooker—who once commanded the Army of the Potomac—had developed a low opinion of Sherman's generalship. Furthermore, by late June, Hooker was in a pique because his corps had led more assaults and suffered more casualties than any other, while Sherman continued to clearly favor McPherson's army—a common lament in the Army of the Cumberland.[17]

Standing in Hooker's way on the 22nd were elements of Hood's corps which had arrived the night before. They were deployed on Hardee's left flank and blocked the Powder Springs Road. Hooker's men captured some of Hood's men in the afternoon, and Hooker came to mistakenly, and adamantly, believe he faced all of Johnston's army. He dug in and sent word of his impending doom to headquarters. Hooker sent two regiments forward along the Powder Springs Road to see what Confederates lay ahead and they bumped into Hood's men. Hooker assumed he would be attacked. Although unfamiliar with the terrain and the federal dispositions, Hood decided to do just that on his own responsibility—Johnston was neither notified or consulted. General Cox agreed with the most logical explanation, that "he evidently hoped that he could outflank the National army on that side."[18]

The result was predictable. Hood's men at first chased Hooker's boys and then charged their breastworks with disastrous results. The battle was over in 90 minutes. The rebels suffered about 1000 casualties while Hooker lost about a third of that number. Hood withdrew after dark. Despite his victory, Hooker, illogically, continued to assert to Thomas and Sherman that he faced three Southern infantry corps. Sherman scoffed. "There cannot be three corps in your front," the commanding general wrote, "Johnston has but three corps, and I know from personal inspection that a full proportion is now and has been all day on his right and center." The following day Sherman had a personal conference with Fighting Joe, and chastised him for his overestimation of the enemy in his front, and his tendency to act independently of the rest of the Army of the Cumberland. As Sherman recalled the incident, "I told him that such a thing must not occur again; in other words, I reproved him more gently than the occasion demanded." Sherman had kept his temper in check. This reproach by Sherman, no matter how mild, would further poison the deteriorating relationship between the two generals. The same could be said for the deteriorating relationship between Johnston and the aggressive, independent Hood. Despite the casualties and acrimony among the generals, the truth was that Hood's rash attack had blunted Sherman's advance on that flank.[19]

The morning of the 22nd, Harker's boys were relieved on the front line by George Wagner's brigade. Like most days, heavy skirmishing and artillery exchanges raged up and down the opposing lines. The movement of Hooker's corps forward necessitated Newton's entire division to swing forward to maintain its connection with Hooker's left flank. The 125th was called up from reserve when the division moved, and worked building new breastworks under fire until 9 p.m. Confederate artillery accounted for three enlisted Ohioans wounded, two fatally. One private, William Sheets, lingered three weeks before passing. The Fourth Corps casualties numbered about 250 that afternoon. After dark, Stanley's division shifted to Newton's right.[20]

Lieutenant Ambrose Bierce was a topographer and often on the Kennesaw picket lines. "The men on duty there were lying in groups of two to four behind little banks of earth scooped out of the slight depression in which they lay, their rifles protruding from green boughs with which they had masked their small defenses," he recalled. "The forest extended without a break toward the front—a forest formidable with possibilities of battle." Bierce was wounded in the head on June 23.[21]

No federal officer knew for certain if the slash of fresh earth on a low hill in front of Newton and Stanley's divisions constituted the main rebel works or a skirmish line. Thomas told Howard to press forward with a reconnaissance on the afternoon of the 23rd—"demonstrations with skirmish line and strong supports," in military terminology. After spending the night on the front line, the 125th was in camp on the 23rd when it was again sent forward. The picket line of Newton's division was held by soldiers from Wagner's brigade, the 57th Indiana on the left and the 26th Ohio on the right. Colonel Frederick Bartleson of the 100th Illinois—a casualty at Chickamauga—was division officer of the day and overseeing the skirmish line. It was his task to probe what lay in front.

Lieutenant Colonel Moore advanced the 125th to a position in the immediate rear of trenches occupied by the 100th Illinois. The 125th was to reinforce the 57th Indiana if needed. Private Robert Rice of Company B had a premonition of impending doom and confided in his lieutenant, Ralsa Rice (no relation), that there would be a fight, and he would be killed. "I want you to notice that I go as far as anyone in our company," he resolutely told Lieutenant Rice.[22]

At about 4 in the afternoon, all the army's artillery that could be brought to bear—130 cannon—unleashed a brisk fire on the enemy line for 15 minutes. For the infantrymen nervously awaiting the order to advance, it seemed like an hour. One rebel officer in a Tennessee regiment described the shelling in his diary: "Kept up the heaviest cannonading I think I ever heard." An officer on General Hardee's staff claimed, with some exaggeration, that over 500 artillery shells fell around the house and garden where Hardee had his headquarters.[23]

Private Robert Rice. Rice had a premonition of his death on the Kennesaw Mountain line. Reproduced from Clark, *Opdycke Tigers*.

When the artillery fell silent, half of the 57th Indiana rose up and surged forward from their rifle pits at the double quick. Once those men cleared the picket line, the other half of the regiment charged. The Indianans met heavy resistance, but, on the right, successfully drove the Confederate skirmishers back to their main line and took some prisoners. The main rebel line was, as always, formidable, and protected by abatis. It was far too strong a defensive works to be anything other than the main defenses. To the federal left, the Southern skirmishers held their ground. An angle in the Confederate line enabled the Southerners to lock the left of the 57th Indiana in a crossfire. The Hoosiers, their losses heavy, abandoned their position and retreated. Colonel Bartleson attempted to rally the skirmishers at the front and was shot dead.[24]

Having tested the strength of the earthworks in their front, the bluecoats should have been withdrawn, but weren't. Bartleson was dead and in the heavy vegetation and clouds of powder smoke, a vacuum in command developed. The Yankees became "hotly engaged," according to one Ohio officer. There was no safety in the captured picket holes for the Northerners, so the men sought cover behind trees and began firing. Unfortunately, the small trees provided minimal protection, and more bluecoats fell. As the skirmishers began drifting back, the enemy followed. Sensing the 57th Indiana was in trouble, Lieutenant Colonel Moore ordered companies B, E and K of the 125th forward under Major Joe Bruff's command. Captain Sterling Manchester, commanding Company K, led the way, sword in hand. The three companies disappeared into an increasing cloud of gray-white battle smoke that was enveloping the battlefield. They pushed the enemy pickets back but received a galling fire from the main Southern line. Private Nathan Hatch of Company B was the first to be killed. Moments later Manchester emerged from the smoky cloud stumbling and pale. A minie ball had shattered the captain's left arm, severed the artery and entered his chest leaving a gaping wound. Through sheer will, Manchester walked back to safety before collapsing. Moore helped put Manchester on a stretcher, removed his sword, field glasses and haversack, moistened the captain's lips with water and loosened his coat. Moore offered a prayer before sending the captain to the surgeon. It was obvious to all who saw the wound that Manchester could not survive.[25]

Captain Sterling Manchester. Lieutenant Colonel Moore had attended Manchester's wedding in the summer of 1863 and the men were close friends when Manchester was killed near Kennesaw Mountain. Reproduced from Clark, *Opdycke Tigers*.

At the very front of the Union assault, as he promised he would be, Private Robert Rice fell mortally wounded as Lieutenant Ralsa Rice looked on. Lieutenant Henry Donaldson, commanding E, was wounded. Private Emory Gilmore of Company B, was shot through both legs. After half an hour, the 125th, the 26th Ohio and the 57th Indiana fell back to the safety of their rifle pits leaving some dead on the field. Dark brought an end to the firing and the Southerners crept back to their forward rifle pits. This fruitless attack cost the 125th dearly—three were killed and 14 wounded, two mortally. The rebels reported heavy charges on their skirmish line and 15 prisoners. There was no report of Confederate losses except the 12th Tennessee on the Southern skirmish line that afternoon "suffered heavy" with three men killed—just another day on the skirmish line for headquarters. But not to Lieutenant Ralsa Rice. Considering the futility of the whole affair, he wrote, "It was a sorry day." That same afternoon the enemy attacked Stanley's division on Newton's right, but were handily repelled. The Fourth Corps lost 279 men on the 23rd of June for no measureable gain.[26]

The following day Regimental Chaplain J. W. Lewis wrote Manchester's young wife from the field hospital where the captain lay dying telling her that her husband would die. Manchester remained lucid to the end. "Tell my wife that I did my duty to my country," he gasped, a true Victorian era soldier to the end, "and died in a good cause." Opdycke considered Manchester a brave soldier and both he and Moore were much affected by the captain's death. Manchester was Moore's comrade in the old 87th and fellow recruiter for the 125th. Moore had attended Manchester's wedding and wrote his widow. Moore and Opdycke arranged to send Manchester's body home to Ohio for interment, accompanied by a last unfinished letter stained with blood.[27]

Sherman had three difficult options open to him. One was to try to flank Johnston's army on the left with McPherson's men. This would require thinning the line to free up manpower and waiting for better weather and more supplies, maybe a week or two. The second option—favored by General Thomas—was a continuation of trench warfare to pry Johnston out of his lines. An impatient Sherman rejected both. The last option was a frontal attack. Sherman believed the move of Hood's corps meant a strengthening of Johnston's left while weakening the center where Hardee's corps now faced at least two federal army corps. A direct assault on an enemy grown complacent behind his strong fortifications might succeed. Here, after complaining of Thomas' lethargy for weeks, Sherman an opportunity to "inspire motion into a large, ponderous and slow, by habit, army." The morning of the 24th, at the suggestion of an attack, Thomas told Sherman that the Confederates his front were "very strong," and argued that his men were tired and his lines too thin to concentrate enough men for a frontal assault. However, in Sherman's mind "there was no alternative but to attack 'fortified lines.'" Should the attack fail, it could be "justified on sound military principles." The dye was cast.[28]

When Thomas read Sherman's attack order, his reaction was, "This is too bad." John Palmer of the Fourteenth Corps told Sherman "this whole army could not carry the position." Thomas admitted, "I fear it will be so." However, Thomas made no formal protest, realizing it would do no good considering his strained relationship with Sherman. McPherson decided to express no opinion and remain optimistic. Schofield was spared voicing his misgivings when Sherman reduced his role to demonstration status after inspecting the fortifications in front of the Twenty-Third Corps.[29]

Post-battle photograph of the fortifications on Kennesaw Mountain. Library of Congress.

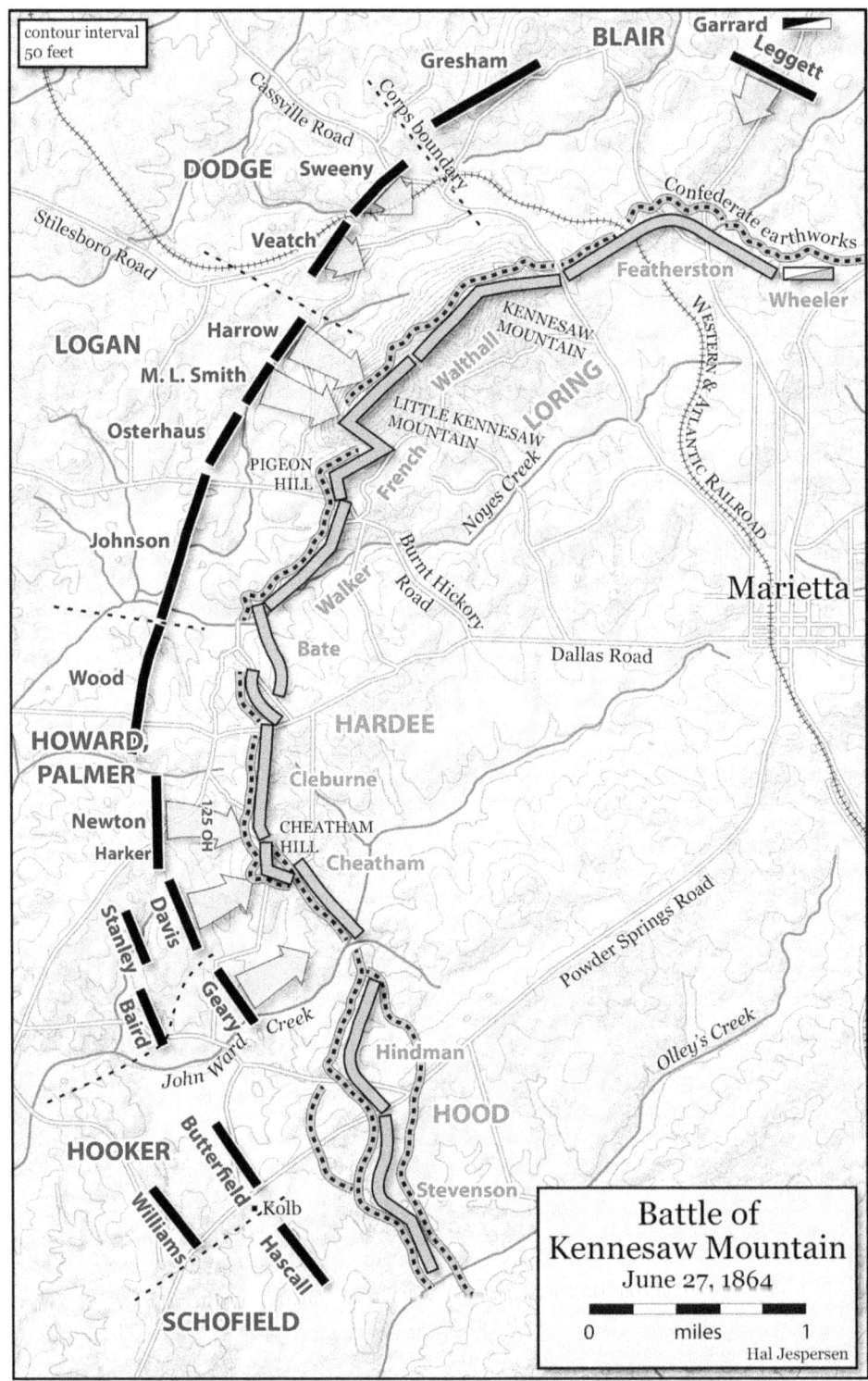

Assault on Kennesaw Mountain, June 27, 1864. Attack of Newton and Davis's divisions. Map by Hal Jespersen.

Thirteen. The Battles for Kennesaw Mountain

Sherman ordered the assault for June 27. "Each attacking column will endeavor to break a single point of the enemy's line, and make a secure lodgment beyond." Sufficient reserves would be allotted to exploit any breakthroughs. Preparatory to those attacks, Schofield's soldiers would demonstrate along the Powder Springs Road on June 26. The next morning, McPherson would both demonstrate and attack Johnston's north flank just south of Kennesaw Mountain and Pigeon Hill along the Burnt Hickory Road. Lastly, heavy skirmishing and artillery fire was ordered along the entire front. It was assumed that these actions would distract the enemy while Thomas' army, as usual, made the main assault in the center. Sherman stressed secrecy—the rank and file were not to be told.[30]

June 24 was and oppressively hot and there was mercifully little fighting for the Fourth Corps or the 125th which was relegated to picket reserve duty. On Saturday the 25th, the Tigers were far enough removed from the action to bathe and clean equipment. There was an ominous feel in the air as the field hospitals were hastily emptied. Opdycke's demi-brigade was reduced to four regiments when the understrength 79th Illinois was transferred to Bradley's demi-brigade replacing the 22nd Illinois which had gone home. The 125th, by Colonel Opdycke's count, had lost 148 men since the campaign began. General Harker reported his brigade's casualties for May 3 to June 25 at 676 killed, wounded and missing.[31]

General Thomas had the critical task of selecting the points of attack along the four miles of front lines from Little Kennesaw south along an undulating ridgeline. Much of the rebel trench work was obscured by dense brush and trees until a man was within 100 yards. The earthworks themselves were well designed by 19th-century military standards, including cleared fields of fire and abatis extending as much as 50 yards from the trenches. After as close a look as he dared make and finding no obvious soft spot, Thomas chose to attack a salient in the rebel line and to the north of it toward the Dallas Road. This sector of the Union line was occupied by the divisions of Generals David Stanley and Jefferson C. Davis. This sector included the low ridge where Captain Manchester was mortally wounded on the 23rd and was 400 yards from the enemy—far enough removed that the attacking columns could form out of sight behind the ridge. The assault was to be made by one division from Howard's corps, to be selected by General Howard, and one from Palmer's corps, chosen by General Thomas. Thomas chose Davis' division, but Howard illogically chose Newton's division instead of Stanley's. Howard's reasoning isn't clear, and while Newton's division had performed well to date, being chosen for this assault was no honor. "General, I am sorry this assault has been decided on," Stanley told Thomas, "and I know it will fail." Thomas responded, "I fear it will be so."[32]

The Confederates worked daily to strengthen their already formidable eight-mile line that was manned by 45,000 seasoned infantry, while cavalry guarded the flanks. The Johnnies in the trenches could not be prudently stretched much thinner, and Richmond had no reinforcements to send to Georgia. The Confederate generals knew the Kennesaw line would ultimately be abandoned but not before a fight, lest the morale of the men—behind very well constructed earthworks—would suffer. Lastly, any withdrawal without a fight could trigger Johnston's removal as army commander by President Jefferson Davis. Taking these into account, Johnston decided to wait for Sherman's next move and hope the impatient Ohioan would make a mistake.[33]

The salient in the Confederate line chosen as the center of Thomas's attack was the junction between two of Hardee's divisions—Pat Cleburne on the right, and Benjamin Cheatham on the left—and had minimal abatis in its front. Newton's division would be attacking just north of the angle at Cleburne's division, while Jefferson Davis' division would strike south of the angle at Cheatham's division. Less than 100 yards in front of the most advanced federal picket posts was a ravine after which the ground rose with varying degrees of steepness toward the Confederate defenses. Eighty yards or so in front of the works, the wooded hillside rose steeply to the main breastworks held by veteran Tennesseans, Arkansans, Texans and Mississippians. All the immediate countryside not part of the Southern fortifications was covered by small oaks, pine forests and dense undergrowth.[34]

Sherman set the attack for 8 a.m. Monday, June 27. Howard chose a "column of division" attack formation that placed regiments in a column one after another. Prevailing military doctrine considered this formation best for attacking fortified positions—many men assaulting a narrow front. The manual proscribed a front 50 to 75 yards wide, with 10 yards between regiments and 100 yards between brigades. For Harker's brigade this translated in to a formation just 75 by 150 yards. Howard chose this formation because it was mobile, compact and more easily concealed by the vegetation and terrain for the first hundred yards or so. After the columns broke cover, Howard was counting on a wholesale charge at the double quick to the enemy fortifications.[35]

The formation dictated by Howard was not without problems. Soldiers tended to bunch up if the head of the column slowed. One of Newton's soldiers expressed this concern: "Damn these assaults in column. They make a man more afraid of being trampled to death by the rear line than he is of the enemy." The columns were bound to slow because soldiers, blue and gray, by 1864 "had become reluctant to press home their attacks, since they understood only too clearly what dangers they would have to run." A delay or unsuccessful attack could turn the column formation into a disorganized mob—a definite liability.[36]

To reach their starting points, Newton's three brigades would pull out of their present position and slide south and form in the rear of Stanley's breastworks. Stanley's division would slide to the left to fill the gap left by Newton's movement and support that division's attack. Troops were shuffled behind the lines, primarily at night, in preparation for the attack. Sherman had a hill behind Thomas' attack cleared for a temporary headquarters and telegraph lines laid to Schofield and McPherson's headquarters.[37]

June 26, Pentecostal Sunday, was pleasant and quiet, as even the artillerymen decided to cease their futile shelling, except for perhaps a brief exchange lasting only half an hour. The sounds of regimental bands drifted on the air and chaplains offered sermons. Across the line, Southern ladies from Atlanta celebrated the Sabbath by riding to the lofty crest of Big Kennesaw, from which they could view the Yankee hordes four miles away. On Newton's front, the Sunday the calm was broken by a rare rebel sharpshooter who slipped forward to fire a shot or two before vanishing deeper back into the pine forest. The evening was clear and the sunset crimson, so colorful that one Yankee wrote, "The trees and woods seemed touched and set on fire." The brilliant sunset suggested fair weather tomorrow. As the day ended, Newton's 5000 men were supplied with 60 rounds of ammunition—as clear a sign of a fight as any—and told to be ready to march tomorrow morning at sunrise. Tuttle of the 3rd Kentucky wrote succinctly in his diary, "Hell expected." Lieutenant Rice of the 125th, whose company had participated in the ill-fated skirmish attack of the 23rd, considered the chances of success "one out of a hundred."[38]

Early Monday morning a dense fog enveloped the battle lines. Up and down the Union line, noncommissioned officers roused their men at 3 a.m. Just before daylight,

Newton's division relocated several hundred yards to the right and was positioned between the federal breastworks and forward picket line of Stanley's division. As the sun rose, the much anticipated attack order was read to the rank and file. The men were to go forward in light marching order, which meant dropping knapsacks and haversacks, and keeping only full cartridge boxes, canteens and muskets. Each company was to detail one man to guard its equipment in the safety of the rear. In Company B, Captain Elmer Moses, who had been with Opdycke at Shiloh, couldn't face the possible life or death choice, and passed the decision to Lieutenant Ralsa Rice. After looking each man in the eye—men the Lieutenant had lived with and fought with for over a year and a half—Rice selected the oldest.[39]

Captain Elmer Moses, 1863. Moses was shot twice in the left leg during the Kennesaw Mountain charge and never returned to duty. He survived the war. Reproduced from Clark, *Opdycke Tigers*.

General Harker's usual personality was described by an acquaintance as "all sunshine." Therefore, Private Lyman Root of the 125th, doing duty as brigade postmaster, was surprised to find an uncommonly melancholy Charlie Harker in his tent finishing his correspondence that fateful morning. When the general finished his last letter, he told Root that he had been ordered to charge the enemy breastworks. Root had heard rumors about how strong the enemy trenches were, and said that he feared that half the brigade and Harker might be killed. The General responded, "I hope not." After Root's departed, Harker gave his adjutant, Captain Ed Whitesides, his carefully arranged private papers, money and instructions in the event he was killed. "I shall not come out of the charge alive today," the general told Whitesides.[40]

As the temperature climbed toward 90, the Confederates on the line pulled blankets over their trenches for shade. The irrepressible Private Sam Watkins of the 1st Tennessee in Cheatham's division wrote, "As the sun began to mount toward its zenith, everything became quiet. We all knew it was the dead calm that precedes the storm." Not far from Watkins, two Southern cannon at the salient were loaded with canister rounds and concealed with brush.[41]

Harker's briefing of his regimental commanders promised to be a solemn affair. Four of the senior officers were colonels, the other four, lieutenant colonels—all experienced citizen-soldiers and almost all were older than their general. Harker disapproved of the attack formation, but, in accordance with orders, directed that the men should charge with their muskets loaded and bayonets fixed, but unprimed so they couldn't be fired. Harker wanted no one tempted to stop and shoot until the brigade closed to within a few yards of the rebel breastworks. Nineteenth-century commanders often ordered this, but in doing so were asking their soldiers to respond unnaturally to their fear. After perfunctory reminder by Harker that Colonel Bradley was his successor, the colonels mounted their horses and rode back to their regiments leaving Harker's white charger alone on the picket line.[42]

As ordered, Newton's division was aligned in two columns for the attack, with Harker's brigade deployed on the right while Wagner's brigade was on the left. The terrain dictated that Kimball's brigade be placed in Wagner's left rear to support Wagner's attack. Harker placed the 51st Illinois and 3rd Kentucky in the forefront, the 27th Illinois, 65th Ohio, 64th Ohio, 79th Illinois were in the middle and 42nd Illinois brought up the rear, followed by the pioneers. Field officers were given the option of going in mounted or on foot, since a man on a horse was an obvious target. General Harker, who would be conspicuous on his white horse, instructed Captain Whitesides, whose duties required a horse, to remain at the forward federal rifle pits until the last regiment, 42nd Illinois, had passed—a place of relative safety for his aide.[43]

Fifteen minutes before the attack was scheduled to begin, Opdycke, as division officer of the day, was directed by General Newton, to organize a strong skirmish line to precede the assault columns composed of two regiments from Harker and Wagner's brigades. Newton's instructions to Opdycke were to clear the gray skirmishers in front of the attacking column, "smack up to the Rebel works." If possible, the skirmishers should go over the breastworks; if not, wait and go over with the columns. Finally, if the attacking columns were "knocked to pieces" Opdycke's skirmishers were to cover their retreat. From Harker's brigade the Colonel chose his own 125th Ohio. From Wagner's brigade, Opdycke wanted the 57th Indiana, alongside whom the 125th had fought on June 23. Wagner gave the 57th's commander, Lieutenant Colonel Willis Blanch, a choice of the skirmish line or a place in the column. Blanch chose to go with Opdycke. Lieutenant Charles Clark called the task before the skirmishers "the highest possible test of heroism and discipline."[44]

Newton's men were unfamiliar with the terrain in front of Stanley's division, and Stanley's men were adamant that no soldier could cross the no man's land and survive. Lieutenant Rice, on the regimental left, was informed by an officer that it would be foolhardy to even hold up a hand on the picket line. Captain Moses of Company B summed up their mission as meaning death or captivity to all those lucky enough to *actually* get as far as the Southern breastworks. The 125th would advance with Major Bruff commanding the regimental right wing and Lieutenant Colonel Moore the left.[45]

The Confederates on the skirmish line and around the salient heard the federal movements before they could see Union soldiers in the fog shrouded landscape. As soon as the fog was gone, rebel skirmishers and sharpshooters opened a deadly musket fire while the officers of the 125th were finishing their final instructions. Colonel Opdycke directed his men to disperse into a skirmish line—the men four feet apart—advance to the forward federal rifle pits and lie down. Scheduled to begin at 8 a.m., it was almost 9 before the seven artillery batteries of the Fourth Corps—cued by a single shot from Thomas' headquarters—began firing explosive shells, shattering the calm of the morning, raining pine needles and iron shrapnel on all below and putting forest birds to flight. Despite the impressive pyrotechnics, the Johnnies were safe in their trenches.[46]

Fifty to a hundred yards beyond the last rifle pits, a 20-foot-deep ravine held a branch of the John Ward Creek—the last safe haven in no man's land. Beyond the ravine, the ground rose to the crest of Cheatham Hill. The first Confederate picket line was in a shallow trench behind a few fence rails. In front of Harker's men, the rebel rifle pits were at the edge of a woods—notable for its heavy undergrowth—located half way up the gradual slope of the hill a hundred yards beyond the ravine. To the rear of the enemy's pickets, the ground rose more sharply to the main breastworks which cut across the military crest of the ridge on ground cleared of underbrush and small trees. Before the main breastworks was a belt of obstructions consisting of felled trees, sharpened branches and stakes, interlaced brush, all bound together with wire. Occasional well concealed paths were left for pickets to come and go. From the ravine to the abattis, the ground was covered by underbrush identified by the Kentuckian John Tuttle as "black jack bushes." The main Confederate fortifications would not be visible to the Opdycke's skirmishers until they were within 100 yards of them. There was a ditch in front of the packed clay earthworks which were topped with the usual head log over a firing loophole. Attacking infantry would have to charge up the slope through brush and small trees to reach the abattis and then struggle through it to reach the actual fortification. One proud Johnny in Cleburne's division noted that "it would have been an uphill business for a rabbit to creep through" his part of the line. For some soldiers of the Confederate Army of the Tennessee, still armed with smooth bore muskets firing shotgun-style "buck and ball" loads with limited range, this close in work was ideal. Except in rare instances, all the attacking Yankees would see of their foe would be the flashes of their muskets under the head logs. Eight or 10 artillery pieces, loaded with canister rounds, had been placed along Cleburne's breastworks. Because Harker's brigade would be attacking into the angle formed by the salient with the main line, it would be taking fire from the front and right.[47]

Lieutenant Ephraim Evans, 1862. Evans died of his Kennesaw Mountain wounds on July 8, 1864. Reproduced from Clark, *Opdycke Tigers*.

Newton's men spent a long hour contemplating their fate while waiting for Davis' division to get into position. The corps artillery's first salvo was also Opdycke's signal and he had his bugler sound "forward." His skirmishers plunged into the brush with a yell and fixed bayonets, and were greeted with heavy skirmish fire followed by musketry from the main Southern works. The Confederates didn't waste artillery on the dispersed skirmishers. Within moments, Lieutenant Ephraim P. Evans, Company D of the 125th, was mortally wounded, a bullet striking his hip and ranging down to lodge in his leg. The skirmish line dropped into the ravine for a momentary reprieve from the gunfire. Commands were whispered along the line. On Opdycke's verbal order, the Tigers and Hoosiers came boiling out of the ravine, swept up the slope, and received another volley from the rebel skirmishers. With the 125th taking the lead, the Yankees refused to be slowed by the black-jack bushes and tangled vines that clawed at their uniforms and caught their feet. In moments, they were over the barricade of fence rails at the edge of the timber and among the enemy skirmishers before the Southerners could break for the rear. A Confederate lieutenant brandishing a sword emerged from the brush and demanded the surrender of Lieutenant Colonel Moore and Captain Moses. Moore drew what Opdycke labeled "a dangerous looking pistol" and the Lieutenant surrendered. Private Isaac Brown of Company B jumped into a rebel rifle pit and took five prisoners. Thirty more of the Southern pickets surrendered, including three officers, and Moore sent them back with walking wounded or just pointed them toward the rear. Lieutenant Rice thought they took more prisoners than the regiment had men in the skirmish line. Captain Moses—wounded at Shiloh—was struck twice in the left leg, breaking the bone. Two of Moses' men dragged him to safety as command of Company B fell to Lieutenant Rice. Opdycke's skirmish line had punched holes in the enemy picket line across a 200 yard front.[48]

The main line of Southern fortifications was just 100 yards ahead. The federals caught their breath, barely protected by the reverse side of the shallow picket holes and fence rails, as they sized up the obstacles in their path. Then, in a rush, the 57th Indiana and 125th Ohio charged from the captured rifle pits. The contour of the ground on Harker's brigade's front would keep the attackers out of sight for part of that distance. As soon as the bluecoats were visible coming up the slope in the Southerner's front, a sheet of orange flame erupted from the breastworks which were seconds later enveloped in blue-gray gun smoke. That volley staggered the Yankees. Some of the Tigers reached the abatis, just 30 or 40 yards shy of the Confederate battle line, but the thin strand of Union skirmishers could go no further. Moore ordered his men to the ground where they sought protection behind rocks, stumps or in depressions in the earth. "As the line advanced beyond the enemy's rifle-pits," Lieutenant Colonel Moore wrote in his official report, "it was exposed to a more withering fire, but it moved forward in splendid style till it encountered the abatis in front of his main works, when I halted and lay down to await the charging column." The abatis, Lieutenant Rice remembered, was so thick that the bluecoats could never breech it "in any reasonable length of time." As bullets ripped air, the Ohioans remained prone, rising only to aim and fire. Their effort was enough to keep their opponents' heads down and behind their barricades, but not sufficient to alter the enemy's volume of gunfire.[49]

Harker and Wagner's columns started forward within minutes of 9 a.m. As Wagner's men were coming out of the ravine, Cleburne's men shifted their aim from Opdycke's thin line of skirmishers to the more tempting massed columns of bluecoats. A fortified four gun rebel artillery battery, slightly to the right, opened with canister and case-shot. Wagner's men held their formation, and were propelled by their own momentum into the blizzard of lead and iron. The 57th Indiana, stalled between the captured rifle pits and the abatis, joined the main column as it went forward. Wagner's leading regiment, the 40th Indiana, suffered badly from the artillery—106 fell—and the column instinctively veered away from the muzzles of big guns losing its cohesion. Exhausted by the heat and tension, their column beginning to dissolve, Wagner's men began dropping to the ground and crawling for any cover. Some of Wagner's stronger men claimed to have gotten within 15 or 20 yards of the enemy fortifications, where the abatis began, before being repulsed. The 100th Illinois did plant its flag on the parapet, but by then the momentum of the attack was gone. George Wagner pulled his men back to the safety of the ravine. Most retired in good order, a few, in confusion. From the ravine, Wagner's regiments dueled with the Southerners.[50]

Harker's men had to scale Stanley's division's works before beginning their charge. The 51st Illinois was the first up the soft earthen parapet and over the pine head log. Once beyond the line, the Illinoisans were vulnerable to Confederate bullets and shells. Instead of waiting for the next regiment to close up behind it so the column would remain compact, the 51st charged ahead, through the thorny, woody vegetation, toward the safety of the ravine. Each successive regiment did likewise, and the column lost its order. The 51st Illinois reached the old enemy skirmish line while the 42nd Illinois, in the rear, was still behind Stanley's works.[51]

At the old rebel skirmish line, Harker's regiments halted briefly to catch their breath before beginning a final sprint forward. Then, in succession, Kentuckians, Ohioans and Illinoisans broke for the enemy breastworks at a run. To their good fortune, the steep slope of the hill beyond the ravine kept them from the enemy's view until they crested a ridge in front of the abatis. The meticulously planned attack column had dissolved into clusters of men loyally following their regimental flags forward. Musketry torn into them from the front and shoulder of the salient to the right. As the federals came on, Cleburne's artillery on the slope of the hill were compelled to depress the muzzles of their guns until they reached the level where their charges of canister and grapeshot were splintering the wood stakes and tree trunks in the abatis in front. Cannon blasts cleared the brush and small blackjack oaks for 100 yards out. Burning fragments of cloth and wadding from each cannon blast fell on the slope touching off small fires in the dry leaves. "The concussion from the enemy's cannon," Lieutenant Tuttle recorded in his diary, "nearly unjointed my neck and the heat from them burnt my face."[52]

The attack ground to a halt as the artillery tore holes in the masses of charging men. Urged by their officers, Harker's men went forward as their courage dictated before falling to the ground to shoot back. The bravest, or most foolhardy, chose to stand just paces from the enemy and try to place their shots into the loophole, each miss marked by a shower of splinters. Some of Harker's strongest men pushed through the obstacles and briefly threw themselves on the dirt of the reverse side of the parapet, close enough to almost touch the muzzles of the rebel muskets. That was as far as they got. Harker's men kept up a determined fire, in part to keep the Southerners from coming out of their defenses after them. Grass fires and gun smoke had reduced visibility to the point that some men referred to it as "the terrible night of battle." Through the swirling smoke, Lieutenant Colonel Moore could see only piecemeal attacks on the breastworks as the men chose to go no further and some began drifting back to the ravine. Hugging the earth between leaf fires, choking on smoke in the sweltering heat and listening to the cries of the wounded while minie balls ripped the air, Harker's men found themselves as close to the Hell the Kentuckian Tuttle had predicted as living men could get. Lieutenant Colonel Moore estimated they actual attack lasted just 15 minutes.[53]

To re-enforce their line, fresh Confederate infantry had to briefly expose themselves by climbing over a traverse in the rear of the trench to get into the breastworks. Here rare targets presented themselves to the better Union marksmen when eddies of air opened holes in the smoke. Lieutenant Ralsa Rice, on the far left of Harker's front, took the role of marksman while three of his men passed loaded muskets to him. One piece misfired, forcing Rice to change to a kneeling position where he was struck on the top of the head by a spent bullet. Stunned, he fell, and was down long enough to be thought lost. But the irrepressible Rice revived, thanks to a stiff new hat and a deflected the bullet.

Many of the Tigers owed their lives that day to being downhill from the Southern breastworks causing the enemy to overshoot.[54]

Astride his white horse in front of Stanley's picket line, Charlie Harker sensed that his initial assault had stalled. He notified Howard and Newton at half past 9 that the works in his front were very strong, and artillery was decimating his front ranks. Harker also erroneously reported that part of General Davis' division on his right was falling back. Believing his men needed the personal urging of a trusted officer, Harker impulsively chose to lead a second charge. The General, followed by Captain Whitesides, spurred his horse forward around the right side of the brigade column. Down the ravine and up the other side they rode to the exposed crest. "Come on, boys!" Harker urged as he came on, reins in one hand and swinging his hat in the other. "Forward and take those works!" The roar of battle was so intense, however, that his commands could only be heard a few feet. Scant few of Harker's men saw their general's valiant charge—fewer still responded. Harker reached the 125th at the front where Company I was deployed and some of those boys rose up.[55]

Harker's charge fared no better than the first. The color sergeant of the 27th Illinois placed his battle flag on the enemy breastworks briefly marking the high water mark of the attack. In moments, the brave sergeant was shot, bayonetted and the flag taken by the 29th Tennessee. Lieutenant Alson Dilley, commanding Company I—just four months in that position—was shot in the head and killed just paces from the enemy works. Lieutenant Thomas Burnham, Company B, was seriously wounded in the thigh and helpless. Rebel sharpshooters continued to target him until he could drag himself to safety, but not before he was shot a total of four to six times and mortally wounded. The flagstaff of the 64th Ohio was shattered by gunfire. The color bearer of the 3rd Kentucky was killed instantly, the flag rescued by Private Benjamin Porter of Company I of the 125th. Captain Nahum Williams, acting major of the 65th, rallied to Harker only to be shot from his horse. Lieutenant Colonel Horatio Whitbeck, commanding the 65th Ohio, fell also, shot in the chest. It was Whitbeck's third wound. Captain Hinman of the 65th Ohio, a veteran of Stones River and Chickamauga, later wrote of the fight, "We never found a hotter place during all four years of army service."[56]

It was at this critical moment that a random bullet passed through Harker's left arm and into his chest, possibly lodging in his spine and lifting the general, not the biggest of men, completely off his mount. A simultaneous shot killed his white charger,

Lieutenant Alson C. Dilley, 1864. Dilley was killed while charging with General Harker. His body remained on the field for three days. Reproduced from Clark, *Opdycke Tigers*.

crimson blood staining its white coat. Some of the men caught Harker as he fell. A half dozen of his men, including Private James Willemin of Company F, carried the young brigadier to the rear. Opdycke offered a few words of encouragement as the general went by him. However, any veteran who saw Harker's chest wound knew it was mortal. Some of the junior officers and enlisted men, including Lieutenant Clark, believed Harker's charge was rash at best, reckless at worse. Opdycke, himself no stranger to recklessness, called Harker's brave effort "useless." Private Edwin Woodworth summed up Harker's charge best writing that Harker was "a brave man, too much so for his own good."[57]

While in the midst of the 3rd Kentucky, near the head of the column, Captain Whitesides was shot also—a severe flesh wound in his thigh. A tumbling bullet struck reverse end first at his trousers' pocket twisting his keys, smashing his ivory handled knife and ranging into his thigh carrying the knife with it. Whitesides was knocked from his horse and when he attempted to remount, another round killed the horse. Some men from the 3rd Kentucky carried Whitesides to the rear. When the captain arrived at the field hospital, he was placed next to Harker, whose chest wound left the young general struggling to breathe. Nevertheless, Harker managed to inquire, "Is that you, my dear boy?"[58]

Brigade command passed to Colonel Luther Bradley of the 51st Illinois. Opdycke would have dearly loved to have had the command, but he lacked the seniority. Bradley, 42, was a former Chicago militiaman and bookkeeper who had held brigade command previously. He had been shot twice at Chickamauga, and breveted colonel in the regular army for his bravery. Bradley was well respected. "I knew of no man in the army possessing more stirling soldierly qualities," wrote the 3rd Kentucky's Tuttle, "not even excepting 'Old Pap Thomas.'" Bradley knew a failed effort when he saw it. He notified General Newton of Harker's loss, and that the attack had stalled.[59]

Colonel Opdycke tried to rally the troops, but the opportunity, if there ever had been one, to break the enemy line had passed. Opdycke wasn't yet ready to concede defeat, however. Wagner's brigade lay close enough to the Confederate line that Opdycke believed that if Nathan Kimball's brigade was sent forward through Wagner's, it might succeed. An orderly arrived at division headquarters about 9:45 with Opdycke's suggestion. A little after 10 a.m., Thomas agreed to send Kimball's 1000 men forward. Wagner was to join Kimball's column when it reached the ravine. In their charge, Kimball's bluecoats faced the same murderous fire that Harker and Wagner's brigade endured, and got no further. Wagner's brigade made a half-hearted attack and was likewise repulsed a second time. The two brigades of Yankees struggled to stay alive and shoot back at an almost invisible foe. Nevertheless, one rebel officer recalled that "our troops literally mowed them down."[60]

Newton wasn't going to waste his men, and ordered them back 90 minutes after they had stepped off. When the order reached the front, Opdycke's skirmishers were told to fall back to the captured rifle pits by companies while the rest of the brigade scrambled back to Stanley's line. The men closest to the Confederate breastworks feared getting either captured or shot when they stood up. Bradley and Opdycke, the two most experienced officers, were no match for the fear that was infecting the brigade. Many of Harker's men broke for the rear. The Confederates rose up to shoot above the head log and poured volleys into their backs causing more casualties than the actual charge according to one veteran. The 3rd Kentucky's Colonel Henry Dunlap and John Tuttle, now acting regimental major, tried vainly to stem the tide. But the men fled "like an immense heard of infuriated buffaloes." Tuttle recalled. "I was run over and badly bruised but very glad to get off so well." Many of those soldiers didn't stop until they reached the safety of Stanley's line. The 3rd Kentucky lost 39 men including its major, two captains and a lieutenant.[61]

Left behind when much of the brigade broke, the 125th had no choice but to make a run for the captured rebel rifle pits in their rear—"the race of our lives," Rice called it. Some of Third Brigade rallied behind the meager cover of the rifle pits with the purpose of keeping the Johnnies behind their fortifications. Three dozen men of the 65th gathered about their colors, and some of the 64th did likewise, as did groups of cool-headed veterans from other regiments. Colonel Bradley remained near the front directing recovery of the wounded and reorganizing the shattered brigade. Wagner's brigade realized that Harker's men were retiring when they began receiving flanking gunfire from the right. Once Wagner's men began to fall back, they didn't stop until they reached the safety of Stanley's main line. Kimball's men did likewise, albeit in better order. His withdrawal, Kimball wrote, "was accomplished without confusion, under the most terrific fire from the enemy."[62]

Those smoldering fires in the underbrush threatened many of the wounded men. Confederate colonel Will H. Martin mounted the parapet with a white handkerchief. "Cease firing," Colonel Martin shouted at the Yankees, "and help get those men." A temporary ceasefire ensued while men from both sides hasten to drag the wounded to safety. "The rebels were generally very kind in allowing us to help off our wounded," recalled John Tuttle. Most of the wounded were brought off the field. The dead, however, remained. Taking advantage of the truce, staff officers from General Cleburne's division scoured the field and recovered 90 Union muskets.[63]

At 10:45, George Thomas wired Sherman that "General Harker's brigade advanced to within twenty paces of the enemy's breastworks and was repulsed with canister at that range, General Harker losing an arm. General Wagner's brigade, of Newton's division, supporting General Harker, was so severely handled that it is compelled to reorganize."[64]

The 125th held that captured skirmish line until relieved around 11 a.m. when it retired to the original federal skirmish line. The 125th Ohio was the first of Harker's brigade to reach the enemy breastworks, and the last unit to leave. At dark, Opdycke sent the 125th and 57th Indiana back to their brigades. Almost one out of every four of Moore's Tigers wouldn't be retrieving their knapsacks. The 125th went into the fight with 260 men of all ranks and 58 fell, 17 of whom died—more casualties than any other regiment in the Newton's division. The left wing of the regiment, commanded by Lieutenant Colonel Moore, suffered the most, having more open terrain to traverse. Moore escaped injury; Major Bruff received a slight wound. In contrast, the other skirmishing regiment, the 57th Indiana, reported a loss of 22 men. A Tennessean who fought Newton's men that morning wrote in his diary, "The enemy came within five feet of our breastworks and the slaughter was terrific as our troops literally mowed them down. We lost only 12 killed and wounded in our brigade."[65]

To the right of Harker's column, two brigades of Jefferson Davis' division attacked into the south side enemy's salient. They came closest to success of any Union assault on the 27th. As Davis' two brigades advanced, they unavoidably drifted to their right following the easiest terrain with the best cover and broke contact with the Third Brigade's right which led Harker to believe they had been repulsed. They weren't. Davis' men were badly fatigued after a third of a mile charge, and reduced to a loosely organized mob, yet they succeeded in planting several flags in the dirt at the base of the Southern parapet.

High tide here came when brigade commander Colonel Dan McCook placed his hand on the parapet moments before he was shot. The tenacious bluecoats hastily dug a breastwork with their bare hands just yards from the Confederate line. Davis' other brigade, Colonel John Mitchell's, likewise dug in after a 20-minute fight. This lodgment came at a severe price. Colonel Henry Banning's 121st Ohio was second in the attacking column and was caught in a crossfire of small arms and canister rounds. Banning lost 164 killed and wounded—half his men. Generals Thomas and Davis, receiving no reliable reports to the contrary, believed that McCook's brigade has been compelled to fall back also and didn't send re-enforcements forward. By the time, McCook and Mitchell's toehold became known to Thomas, the Confederates had re-enforced the salient and any chance for success evaporated. Jefferson Davis's men stayed put and strengthened their line through the afternoon and evening. His division lost 824 men in the assault on Kennesaw Mountain.[66]

A Confederate private who stood inside the salient—later known as the Dead Angle—left these thoughts of June 27. "I have heard men say that if they ever killed a Yankee during the war they were not aware of it. I am satisfied that on this memorable day, every man in our regiment killed from one score to four score." The loss in Cheatham's and Cleburne's divisions was reportedly just 260.[67]

Brigadier General Charles Garrison Harker died early that afternoon attended by chaplains from the 64th and 65th Ohio. Harker's courage—he had four horses shot from under him during the war—and professionalism was unquestioned. "In every place where the corps has been engaged this noble young man earnestly and heartily performed his part," General Howard wrote of Harker. "God grant that we may live like him, and if called to die have as good an earnest and enduring peace in heaven as our lamented General Harker." Opdycke felt the loss of a superior whose confidence he enjoyed calling Harker "brave and pure-hearted." Wilbur Hinman of the 64th Ohio called Harker "a soldier and a man 'without fear and without reproach.'" Harker's body was sent home to his native New Jersey for burial.[68]

Harker was just one of 231 casualties his brigade suffered, compared to Wagner's 215 and Kimball's 194. Overall, roughly 3000 Union soldiers fell on the 27th. Seven regimental commanders were killed or wounded and General Howard stated the obvious: "We realized now as never before, the futility of direct assaults upon entrenched lines already well prepared and well manned." Captain Ridgely C. Powers, serving as the 125th's adjutant and correspondent to the *Western Reserve Chronicle*, reported after the Union defeat at Kennesaw, "We do not shoulder as many muskets, nor is the step of our brave boys as elastic as formerly. But our courage is no way impaired. Love of country burns as bright in every heart, and our cause is none the less scared because it is costing us dearly."[69]

At a quarter to 11 that morning, George Thomas telegraphed Sherman that the assaults by the Army of the Cumberland had been repulsed. McPherson, on Thomas' left, had sent three brigades, 5500 strong, at Pigeon Hill south of Little Kennesaw Mountain. Those men faced more difficult terrain than the Cumberlands to the south, and still managed to get as close to the Southern breastworks. However, they were ultimately repulsed as well with a loss of 600 men.[70]

At half past one, Sherman asked Thomas if there is any chance of success if the attacks were renewed. "The division commanders report the enemy's works exceedingly strong; in fact, so strong that they cannot be carried by assault except by immense sacrifice, even if they can be carried at all," Thomas told Sherman. Despite his doubts about

Thomas, Sherman accepted his judgment. At 4:10, Sherman directed that any significant gains be secured. Later that day, Sherman wrote Thomas that he regretted the loss of young officers like Harker and McCook but defended the assault. "Had we broken the line to-day it would have been most decisive," Sherman argued, "but as it is our loss is small, compared with some of those East. It should not in the least discourage us. At times assaults are necessary and inevitable." General Cox believed the attack a worthy effort, but blamed failure on the antiquated nature of the attack in columns. "So hard it is to free ourselves from the trammels of old customs and mistaken practice!" After visiting the field hospital, Colonel Opdycke declared to his wife that "miserable blunders were made" in the battle. "The whole affair was useless and a mistake," wrote an officer in the 113th Ohio of Mitchell's brigade, "and Sherman's reason is not creditable to him or any good general."[71]

While the attacks by Thomas and McPherson were failures the day was not a complete loss. While Johnston was distracted by the attacks on his line, General Cox skillfully moved his division forward two miles and occupied a ridge between Nickajack and Olley's Creeks just a mile from the Chattahoochee. Schofield's small army was in position to effectively block the Confederates from extending their line south to the river and Cox had opened a path to the railroad near Smyrna, Georgia, five miles south of Marietta.[72]

Late in the evening, Sherman asked Thomas if he was willing to abandon the railroad in his rear make a flank march around Johnston's left in the direction of the Western and Atlantic below Marietta. As usual, supplying the army once it cut loose from the railroad was the main problem. "If with the greater part of the army," Thomas replied a bit testily, "I think it decidedly better than butting against breastworks twelve feet thick and strongly abatised." Sherman replied with a jab at Thomas' innate caution. "Go where we may," Sherman responded, "we will find the breastworks and the abatis, unless we move more rapidly than we have heretofore."[73]

After sunset on that bloody Monday, the Union army's brass bands struck up patriotic tunes, only to be interrupted by gunfire as the two nervous foes, now just yards apart in some places, exchanged musketry. The Yankees continued to cling to their meager gains while trying to recover any remaining wounded. By the time Monday became Tuesday, the 28th, Sherman had decided to flank Johnston thanks to Schofield and Cox's modest success on the right. Thomas and McPherson's men were ordered to accumulate 10 days of supplies and prepare to move quickly. That same day, Sherman received a wire from General Grant that offered further latitude in the march to Atlanta. "The necessity of holding Johnston with such a grip that he could not detach aid to Lee in Virginia," General Jacob Cox explained, "was one of the motives for active operations in front and continuously; but on the 28th Grant dispatched Sherman that this consideration might now be dropped out of the calculations." Grant was confident that Robert E. Lee, who was having problems supplying his Army of Northern Virginia, couldn't feed any re-enforcements even if they were available.[74]

The warm weather was hard on the wounded, but Opdycke's confidence in regimental surgeon, Dr. Henry McHenry and Private William Rawdon serving as nurse—was unwavering. One Fourth Corps surgeon, Kentuckian Clairborne J. Walton, writing two days after the battle, admitted, "I have amputated limbs until it almost makes my heart ache to see a poor fellow coming in the ambulance." The wounded were shipped to Nashville as quickly as possible. In Captain Whitesides' case that translated into a painful six mile ambulance ride the morning of the 28th to the railhead at Big Shanty.

From there he went by train to Chattanooga, arriving on the 29. The trip to Nashville was marked by a train accident that sent his car rolling down an embankment. Whitesides finally reached Nashville at 5 p.m. on the 30th.[75]

Emerson Opdycke lamented the loss of Ohio Tigers, whose unofficial motto was "a glorious victory or an honorable grave." Opdycke wrote his wife that his regiment was leaving "a bloody trail" across Tennessee and Georgia. Colonel Opdycke received the recognition he deserved from General Newton. "It is no injustice to the claims of others," General Newton wrote in his official report, "to state that General Kimball commanding 1st Brigade; Colonel Bradley commanding 51st Illinois; Colonel Opdycke commanding 125th Ohio Volunteer Infantry distinguished themselves by their conduct on this occasion." The praise stoked Opdycke's ambition, and he complained to his wife that he, not Bradley, should replace Harker. Opdycke genuinely believed that he deserved to command the brigade, no matter what Bradley's experience or qualifications.[76]

Joe Johnston was well aware that if Cox's division advanced his left flank would be turned. He immediately set engineers, Georgia militia and impressed negroes to work on two new lines just north of the Chattahoochee River. The northern most was a short distance above Smyrna and covered the railroad bridge which was in a deep bend of the river. The second line was about two miles from the river. In addition, the fortifications around Atlanta were being enhanced in a nod to what would be inevitable.[77]

The 125th spent a hot and humid Tuesday the 28th in reserve. At dusk the regiment relieved the 3rd Kentucky on the front line. Dark brought an end to random firing, and the bodies of some of the Union soldiers killed during the advance on the 23rd were recovered. One sergeant in the 125th was wounded by a spent bullet. Private Woodworth noted in a letter home that his Company B had left Tennessee with 40 men. On the 28th, just 25 men answered the roll call, the rest lost to illness, wounds or, in the case of four men, killed. Anguish evident in his letter, he concluded, "This is horrible."[78]

After two days, the bodies of the Union dead between the lines were blackened, bloated and infested with insects. A sickening smell enveloped the battleground and it was in the interest of all the living to bury those corpses. A truce along the line where Newton's men fought began about noon on the 29th. Northerners and Southerners, protected by white flags, left their trenches and began removing and burying the dead in shallow trenches, dragging the bodies with hooked bayonets. Lieutenant Dilley's body was identified and the grave marked. Not wishing to upset his wife with details, Colonel Opdycke merely wrote "the havoc of war is truly awful." Any good feelings created by the truce evaporated that night when a fierce firefight erupted around Cheatham Hill.[79]

On the 30th, a light shower cleansed the battlefield. General Thomas' official report simply stated "all remained comparatively quiet along the line." Down on the far right flank, General Cox's men could hear Confederate military trains arriving and departing Marietta and guessed they were removing military stores to warehouses in Atlanta—a sure sign the Confederates were preparing to move yet again.[80]

14

PEACH TREE CREEK

"It would not do to rest long under the influence of a mistake or failure," Sherman suggested in correspondence to the War Department after Kennesaw. It was obvious to Sherman that the path to Atlanta ran through the opening created by Schofield's advance on the 27th. Exploiting this opportunity meant Sherman would have to cut loose from his railroad supply line yet again and move around Johnston's left—no easy decision with bread, fruits and vegetables already in short supply. The terrain and roads in Schofield's sector were determined to be favorable for operations. Fulton, Georgia, on the railroad 10 miles south of Marietta, would become Sherman's new objective. Thomas and Schofield appeared to have doubts about the plan, but Sherman was confident, assuring Schofield, "I think I have contemplated every move on the chess board of war." James McPherson's army would lead which meant evacuating its position on the Union left flank and moving to the right. Thomas' men would have to stretch out to cover almost the entire Kennesaw line for a few days. The Army of the Cumberland was ordered to accumulate 10 days of rations and forage. Newton was told to put his battered division, now just 3500 effectives, into condition to move.[1]

For June, Sherman listed his losses at 7500 men. Of that total, 5500 came from the Army of the Cumberland. Johnston's losses, never exact, were pegged at 6000. On a percentage basis, the Sherman's loss was smaller, which allowed him to justify it by asserting that he was "maintaining our relative superiority, which the desperate game of war justified."[2]

Trench warfare continued while the generals studied their maps. The impregnable nature of the opposing earthworks reduced both opponents along the Kennesaw line to sharpshooting and artillery exchanges. On July 2, Union artillery fired 700 shells into Kennesaw Mountain. Clever snipers resorted to mirrors to aim their pieces without exposing themselves, and riflemen practiced ricocheting bullets off the head logs into the trenches. Those deadly English Whitworth rifles with telescopic sights in the hands of expert rebel marksmen—the Whitworth's were awarded winners of shooting matches—extended the danger zone to hundreds of yards. One soldier wrote that it was "really dangerous to walk about the lines at all" during daylight. During the day, many pickets had a gentleman's agreement against useless picket firing, however, after dark, significant firefights were initiated by jittery pickets responding to unexplained noise and even fireflies. These false alarms deprived men on both sides of sleep. Brief, informal truces—some lasted as long as 24 hours—occurred intermittently to trade coffee and tobacco.[3]

Sherman set his new flank march in motion on July 1—a hot, muggy day of misery for soldiers in wool uniforms. By July 2, Schofield was firmly established at a road junction

Fourteen. Peach Tree Creek 167

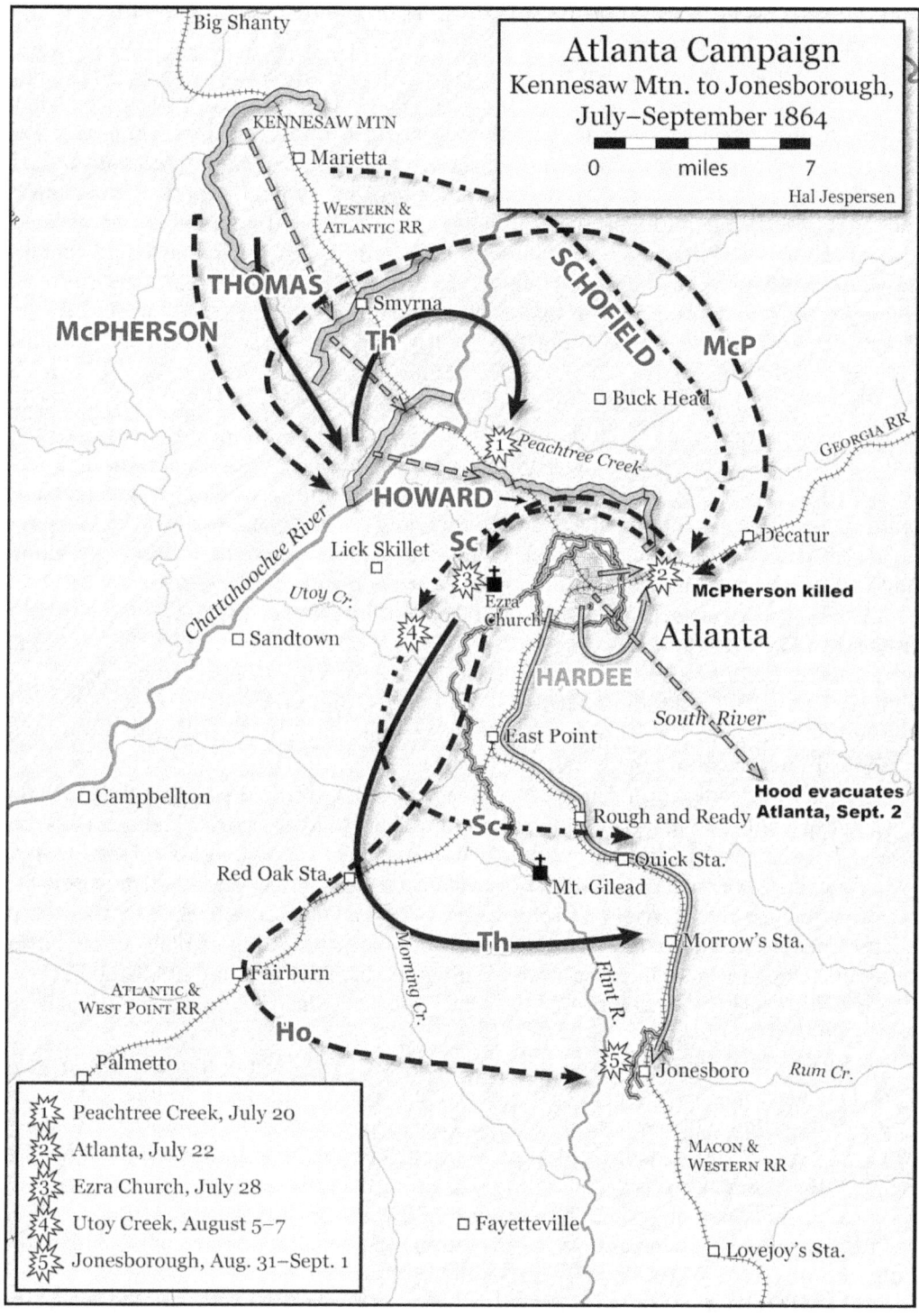

Atlanta Campaign. Army movements from Kennesaw Mountain to Jonesboro, July to September 1864. Map by Hal Jespersen.

four miles below the Confederate left and six miles from the Chattahoochee River. While the Yankees on the right were moving, the Army of the Cumberland fired iron and lead at the Southerners up and down the Kennesaw Line. Newton's division's artillery, over three dozen cannon, opened a barrage at 6 a.m. followed at 7 by 10 minutes of musketry on the skirmish line. In accordance with the informal prohibition against senseless picket firing, the rebels were forewarned and returned a sharp fire that was intentionally aimed over the heads of the bluecoats. McPherson's men began their poorly masked move south the night of the 2nd. With Sherman's infantry south of his left flank, Johnston decided to fall back to a new line at Smyrna Station on the railroad six miles south of Marietta.[4]

The Confederate withdrawal from the Kennesaw line was carried out with "consummate skill" according to one historian. The sporadic nighttime picket fire in the Fourth Corps front petered out about 2 a.m. July 3 as Cheatham and Cleburne's divisions disappeared into the night. Federal pickets knew almost immediately the rebels were gone. By 3 a.m. Sunday, July 3, Thomas informed Sherman, who feared a surprise attack. At sunrise, infantrymen on McPherson's front scouted Kennesaw Mountain as Sherman watched with a borrowed telescope, and found it abandoned. Within an hour, McPherson's infantry was in Marietta. The Army of the Cumberland rose before dawn and General Howard sent pickets to investigate the enemy's abandoned earthworks. General Stanley's division began the pursuit at 9 a.m., followed by Newton and Wood, trekking first to Marietta and then south along the Western and Atlantic's tracks.[5]

Leading elements of Stanley's division reached the grounds of the Georgia Military Institute in Marietta about 8:30, just as "Uncle Billy" rode into town. Marietta's residents were gone as was a mile railroad track. Although the march was less than five miles, the Yankees—trench bound for several days—were out of condition and the weather was hot and humid. Straggling and heat exhaustion was rampant. The Fourth Corps took 170 prisoners/deserters along the route.[6]

Bradley's brigade column started south about 8 a.m., proceeded down the Marietta road and passed the Georgia Military Institute about mid-morning. Lieutenant Ralsa Rice called Marietta "the most beautiful place we had met in the whole Southland." Opdycke climbed to the roof of the military academy where, in the clear morning sun, he could see the mountains of the Carolinas and Georgia. He later remarked to his wife in a letter that after 60 days under fire there was a profound feeling of relief to be out in the open. Along the march, a black man, William Hull, fell in with the 125th and became Major Bruff's servant for the rest of the war. Hull was valued enough to be carried on the regimental roster.[7]

The Fourth Corps continued along the railroad that afternoon, skirmishing with the enemy rearguard as they went. Stanley's men encountered the main Southern skirmish line four miles south of Marietta at Smyrna. The Corps deployed with Stanley's division's right resting on the railroad, Newton on Stanley's left and Wood on Newton's left. The Army of the Tennessee was deployed to the right of the railroad. Sherman continued to push, urging Thomas to "press the enemy to the wall" on July 4. "We will never have such a chance again," Sherman wrote, "press with vehemence at any cost of life and material."[8]

At daybreak on Independence Day, bands played patriotic tunes and there was a small celebration at Bradley's brigade headquarters that featured a milk punch. Although the timetable called for the march to begin at 8 a.m., it was early afternoon before Bradley's men moved and then only a half mile to construct new entrenchments. The work was done in sight of the enemy pickets who took occasional potshots at the Yankees, wounding some. McPherson's army was now on the Union right and marched along the Sandtown Road. The Army of the Cumberland edged closer to the Smyrna line pushing the skirmishers forward and taking nearly 100 Southern prisoners. Johnston's Smyrna line was well positioned to block the railroad and wagon roads to the Chattahoochee. Nevertheless, McPherson's approach made the position vulnerable, and the night of July 4, the Confederates retired to another position just north of the Chattahoochee that guarded the bridges over the river.[9]

Once again caught off guard by a Confederate retreat, Sherman's men took up the chase. The Fourth Corps, spearheading the Army of the Cumberland's pursuit, pushed down the east side of the railroad constituting the left flank of the Union army while encountering stiff resistance from the Southern rear guard. Blue infantry entered Vining Station on the Western and Atlantic Railroad a few miles south of Marietta by mid-afternoon. Wood's division assumed the front and forced a stubborn rebel rearguard from behind a barricade of rails and over the Chattahoochee River. With the secessionists occupying the opposite river bank, the Fourth Corps went into camp a half mile from the river. Bradley's brigade reached Vining's Station about 4 p.m. Skirmishers had earlier cleared a high hill that offered a panoramic view of the Chattahoochee River valley in front and Atlanta just nine miles away. By evening, Sherman's entire army was drawn up along the Chattahoochee line from Pace's Ferry on the left flank—occupied by Howard's corps—to Turner's Ferry on the right. Between those two ferry crossings could be seen multiple lines of fortifications, Confederate army camps and long trains of canvas-covered supply wagons.[10]

Opdycke, Lieutenant Colonel Moore and Major Bruff climbed the hill at Vining Station for their first look at what an Illinois major called "the promised land." Opdycke described the city of Atlanta as looking inviting and believed the army would take the city soon. The 125th Ohio marched two miles to the north, upriver, and went into camp in open timber. A rumor circulated that the Corps might remain there for a few days to rest, refit and be paid.[11]

The usual method of crossing the Chattahoochee—swollen by spring rain—in that part of Georgia was by flatboat ferry. All potential crossing points for a dozen miles along the river were covered by Southerners behind fortifications on the opposite bank. The nearest road bridge was 20 miles away at Roswell, Georgia—a textile manufacturing center on the west side of the river. Union cavalry secured Roswell on the 6th and destroyed the mills, but found the bridge was burned by the retiring rebels.[12]

The latest line of Confederate fortifications west of the Chattahoochee were about five miles long. In his usual fashion, Sherman had the Army of the Cumberland confront these works. Howard's corps was on the left at Pace's Ferry where the road from Marietta to Atlanta crossed the river, the other two corps covered the center near the rail bridge and joined McPherson on the right flank. Schofield's army was held in reserve near Smyrna to attack at any favorable point. In General Cox's opinion, the month of campaigning since the Etowah River was crossed had been an accelerated education in soldiering for the men, and that the army was confident and unified in purpose.[13]

With Roswell in federal hands, General Schofield was sent on Thursday the 7th to scout the river for potential crossings from Pace's Ferry north to Roswell. Schofield decided that the mouth of Soap Creek, six miles from Pace's Ferry offered the best chance of success. Sherman decided to feign an attack on Johnston's left below the Western and

Atlantic while he sent Schofield's army in the opposite direction toward Soap Creek. While the 125th Ohio rested and bathed on the 8th, Schofield's men slipped quietly through the forest in the rear of Howard's corps with canteens secured and flags furled. That afternoon, the 103rd Ohio of General Cox's division crossed Soap Creek with little opposition. Surprised rebel pickets abandoned half cooked meals in their haste to get away. Cox's entire 8000 man division was across the river and entrenched by midnight.[14]

Union cavalry crossed the river at Roswell and achieved a tenuous toehold on the east bank of the Chattahoochee on the 9th. Sherman ordered McPherson's men from the right flank of the Union army to the left. To temporarily secure the cavalry bridgehead until McPherson's men arrived, Newton's division was sent upriver 16 miles to Roswell. Bradley's brigade started for Roswell at dawn with 60 rounds of ammunition. Colonel Opdycke, Lieutenant Ralsa Rice and Orderly Sergeant Rufus Woods led the march along a road lined with shrubby, spiny chinquapin trees. The brigade moved up river in a rapid, dusty march, without wagons or baggage, in oppressive heat—"very warm for a Northern man in winter clothing"—resulting in two or three fatalities due to heat stroke. Roswell was reached by 3 or 4 p.m. and Bradley's men reached their destination by mid-afternoon and settled in the shade, brewed coffee and ate. Much of the town had been razed by blue cavalry, nevertheless, many of the men in the 125th agreed with Opdycke who thought Roswell was a lovely town. The Colonel described the countryside as productive but the local citizenry was generally afraid of the Yankees, thanks to rebel propaganda reports of Union atrocities.[15]

Late afternoon, Bradley's brigade marched two miles upriver. The Chattahoochee—said to be three feet deep and a couple hundred yards wide—had a rough and rocky riverbed which made even the shallow ford tricky, especially for horses shod with iron shoes and belly deep in swift water. That evening, Bradley's men forded the river and relieved some federal cavalry on picket. Once across, the right wing of the 125th went forward on picket duty—Company B was sent out a lonely road through the woods—while the left was situated behind small breastworks constructed by the cavalry. General Sherman appeared at the camp of the 125th's picket reserve, examined the terrain, saluted and rode away without fanfare. The 125th was 20 miles from Atlanta.[16]

Sherman had utilized his manpower advantage to out maneuver Joe Johnston, who lacked the men to adequately guard all possible river crossings. With Yankees on the east side of the Chattahoochee, the Confederate army withdrew completely from the west bank during the night of July 9, removing or destroying the six bridges they used to cross the river. The Southerners continued their withdrawal July 10 to a new position south of Peach Tree Creek—five miles from Atlanta. One Southerner wrote of the mood in Atlanta with Yankees at the doorstep, "The excitement beats anything I ever saw."[17]

On Sunday, July 10, Newton's division dug trenches on the south bank of the Chattahoochee until it was relieved by McPherson's Sixteenth Corps near nightfall. The brigade camped on a hill near the river. The following day, Newton's division re-crossed the river at 11:30 p.m. on a reconstructed foot bridge and on the 12th marched back to the camp near Pace's Ferry. Opdycke selected a pleasant wooded ridge parallel to the river for the 125th to camp. While encamped near Roswell, the officers foraged the countryside netting blackberries, butter, chickens, new potatoes, apples and flour. The chaplain acquired a milk cow, which became a permanent fixture in camp.[18]

Wood and Stanley's divisions marched to Power's Ferry—four miles southeast of Roswell—on the 12th where a pontoon bridge was erected across the river. McPherson united his army at Roswell on the 13th and Newton's division rejoined the Fourth Corps by crossing the river on the Power's Ferry bridge. With most of the Union infantry north of Atlanta, Sherman decided to rest and refit for five days while awaiting the outcome of a cavalry raid west of Atlanta sent to break the Atlanta and Montgomery, Alabama, railroad connection. The Yankees needed a rest. Diarrhea, scurvy, and malaria were swelling the sick lists and the soldier's ragged and dirty uniforms were infested by vermin.[19]

July 14 was the hottest, sultriest day many Northerners recalled experiencing. With time on his hands, Opdycke prepared a letter for his wife in which he expressed the sentiments of most Union soldiers regarding the fall elections that would pit Abraham Lincoln against a peace Democrat. "We must go on with the war, until the final triumph of our cause is secure." Failure to do so would result in years of anarchy and feuding, Opdycke believed. Lincoln must be re-elected.[20]

On July 17, Lieutenant General John Bell Hood replaced Joe Johnston as commander of the Confederate Army of the Tennessee. "The ostensible reason was his failure to defeat Sherman," General Cox wrote in his history of the battle for Atlanta, "and his unwillingness to give assurance that he could even answer for the permanent safety of Atlanta and its important railway connections." A Union spy in Atlanta delivered a local newspaper to Sherman reporting the change in Confederate army commanders. Sherman asked Schofield, who had been a West Point classmate and tutor of Hood's, about the man who now commanded the rebel army. Sherman learned from Schofield that Hood "was bold even to rashness, and courageous in the extreme; I inferred that the change of commanders meant 'fight.'" General Cox wrote of Hood's appointment, "If aggression was to be tried, it would be hard to find any commander better fitted than Hood to test it." While Hood's personal courage was never doubted, his wisdom and judgment were. In the opinion of Wilbur Hinman of the 65th Ohio, John Bell Hood "was a brave man, but rash and improperly equipped to handle a large army and conduct a great campaign." Hood's physical condition was precarious—one arm useless, the opposite leg amputated—two serious wounds in one year. Yet, Hood was given direction of the Confederacy's second most powerful army. A. P. Stewart was assigned to command Polk's old corps. General Cheatham assumed command of Hood's corps while Hardee, grumbling and displeased that he had not succeeded Johnston, retained his corps.[21]

The Union cavalry's raid proved a failure, so Sherman prepared to move south on July 18. McPherson's infantry began sweeping southeast with its objective the destruction of the Georgia Railroad—one of the Confederacy's vital transportation links—from Decatur east to Stone Mountain. Schofield's Army of the Ohio was aimed at Decatur. Thomas' Army of the Cumberland moved toward Atlanta with Palmer's corps on the right; Hooker's held the center and Howard's Fourth Corps was following the road to Buckhead, northwest of Decatur. Bradley's brigade started down the road at first light as it led Newton's division. Opdycke's demi-brigade was deployed as skirmishers with the 125th and 3rd Kentucky taking the front supported by the 64th and 65th Ohio.[22]

In the Fourth Corps path was a southeast flowing tributary of Peach Tree Creek known as Nancy Creek. A muddy stream at the bottom of a deep ravine—estimated as much as 20 feet deep—Nancy Creek was a formidable barrier to an army on the move. Infantrymen had to slide down the north bank, jump the creek and claw their way up the opposite bank. The crossing was complicated by a brigade of dismounted rebel cavalry deployed across the road where it ran uphill from the creek. These were some of Wheeler's men—to Opdycke they were "a set of cowards"—comfortable behind a log barricade and joined by a section of artillery. The 125th Ohio became heavily engaged. Opdycke ordered up the rest of his demi-brigade and a couple of cannon to disperse the enemy. In the middle of the hour-long firefight, Opdycke rode forward and attracted a volley from the rebels. The Colonel escaped, but a bullet struck his beloved Barney in the right shoulder and pierced his heart. Instantly killed, the animal folded silently under his rider, who dismounted as Barney was going down. Opdycke said of Barney, "I was much attached to him."[23]

Opdycke mounted his other horse, Tempest, and ordered the 125th forward with the 3rd Kentucky on the left. In positioning the 3rd Kentucky, Opdycke grew impatient with Captain John Tuttle—now commanding the regiment—for being unable to get his horse across the Nancy Creek ravine. Tuttle, who broke his leg in a riding accident a year ago, was understandably cautious. Opdycke attempted to demonstrate how to ride a horse over the deep ravine and succeeded in miring Tempest in the mud up to his girth. The colonel struggled from the ravine on foot and left Tempest for the orderlies and Captain Powers to extricate. Tuttle crossed the creek on foot after his mount spooked and ran away. The Colonel commandeered an orderly's horse and later acquired a captured rebel captain's mount. In his diary, Tuttle—no fan of Opdycke generally—referred to the Colonel's manner toward him that afternoon as "petulant."[24]

Wheeler's men retired down the road to another hill and deployed in front of a church. This time Opdycke sent the 65th Ohio forward also on the right of the 125th Ohio. The Northerners charged through underbrush and briars only to be rewarded by the sight of the Southerners galloping away. Opdycke's men paused to extinguish a fire in the church ignited by an artillery shell. Wheeler's cavalry made a third stand on the crest of another hill, but the bluecoats were so close in pursuit there was no time for a barricade. The cavalry unleashed a single volley which went high, and retired down the road to Buckhead where the bluecoats were on them before they could form for a fight. The Union skirmishers went a half mile further to General Wheeler's recently abandoned headquarters before halting just after noon and ending a six mile running fight. Bradley's brigade was now six miles from Atlanta. The federal skirmishers, by now experts at finding and using cover as they advanced, had nevertheless taken some casualties. The 125th lost one killed, Private Samuel Rogers, and five wounded, including Private Jesse Luse, who lost an arm and Sergeant Jacob Jewel, who was slightly wounded in the side. The body of a dead Confederate colonel was found and Corporal James Willemin captured a rebel captain who mistakenly rode into the Yankee's skirmish line. The Fourth Corps was just two miles from Peach Tree Creek. General Howard complimented Opdycke on his leadership: "You are doing first rate, Colonel, first rate."[25]

Tuesday the 19th, the 125th Ohio remained near Buckhead which was five miles south of Nancy Creek. Emerson Opdycke suffered from a rare headache and fever—treatment was cold compresses and fasting—but was fit by evening. Some of members of the 125th returned to Nancy Creek and buried Barney under a tree. A crude wooden marker, "My Horse Barney, Killed July 18th, 1864," marked the spot. The animal had been a general favorite among the Ohioans. Lieutenant Rice commented, "He had been with us a long time and shared our dangers as did few other horses in the army." Since Barney was privately owned, Opdycke would eventually file a claim to be reimbursed for the loss.[26]

The Bradley's 64th Ohio and 27th Illinois were sent on a reconnaissance down the road from Buckhead to Atlanta. Three miles down the Peach Tree (or Buckhead) Road, the two regiments reached Peach Tree Creek and found the secessionists in strong rifle pits on the opposite bank. The meandering Creek flowed west into the Chattahoochee River and was about 30 feet wide and five feet deep where the road crossed it at Collier's Bridge. Strategically, it was important as a natural barrier just four miles from Atlanta. The retreating Confederates had attempted to burn the Collier's Bridge, but enough remained to be repairable. When notified of this, General Howard withdrew Bradley's two small regiments and replaced them with General Wood's division. Bradley's men bivouacked on the north side of the creek close enough to hear the rebel bugle calls.[27]

Wood's bluecoats forced a crossing at dusk, advanced and drove the enemy pickets from a small earthen fort that guarded the bridge. The Confederates were known to be in force 1000 yards ahead, so a strong battle line was formed to protect the crossing while pioneers from the division repaired the bridge and work was begun to strengthen the breastworks. Nathan Kimball's First Brigade of Newton's division was sent across the creek to support Wood's men. Sherman urged Thomas to get across the creek in force quickly and to shift the Fourth Corps to the left to fill an unintentional gap between Schofield and Thomas' flanks. Sherman's army was now positioned in a crescent north and northeast of Atlanta from Howell's Mill on Peach Tree Creek on the right to Stone Mountain east of Decatur on the left. McPherson's men occupied Decatur and were dismantling the Georgia Railroad east to Stone Mountain. Schofield's corps was in the center and Thomas' three corps were on the right along Peach Tree Creek. Howard's corps was east of the Peach Tree/Buckhead Road and Hooker and Palmer's Corps were west of the road.[28]

With the bulk of the Army of the Cumberland's 50,000 soldiers separated from the rest of Sherman's men to the east, the Confederate high command saw an opportunity. The present Southern defensive line ran from the Atlantic and Western Railroad a couple miles south of the Chattahoochee in a semi-circle to the Georgia Railroad between Decatur and Atlanta, thus covering the northern approaches to Atlanta. The largest part of General Hood's 55,000 soldiers occupied a line of entrenchments south of Peach Tree Creek from the Chattahoochee near the railroad bridge to just east of the Peach Tree Road. General Stewart's Corps was on the left, Hardee in the center and Cheatham on the right. Cavalry units held the extreme right of the line. It had been General Johnston's plan to launch an attack into the gap on Thomas' left before the Yankees had ample time to erect fortifications, and General Hood embraced the strategy. Cheatham's corps would shift right to hold the Southern right flank opposite Schofield and McPherson. Hardee and Stewart were to swing forward into the gap and attack Thomas by division *en echelon* in rapid succession from right to left rolling up Thomas' line. Hood intended to make this an all-out attack, at the point of the bayonet if necessary. Once Thomas was defeated, the secessionists would turn on Schofield and McPherson. The attack was scheduled for 1 p.m. July 20.[29]

The 20th, a Wednesday, dawned cloudy. The gap between Thomas and Schofield had opened to nearly two miles. Wood's division was ordered to re-cross to the north side of the Creek and to join Stanley's division in moving east to connect with Schofield's right. All of Newton's division was ordered south across the Peach Tree Creek to join Kimball's brigade, and take up positions in the entrenchments Wood had occupied. This move left Newton's division alone on the Peach Tree Road. Less than a mile west of Collier's bridge, Early's (or Tanyard) Creek flowed north into Peach Tree. Some distance to the east, Pea Vine Creek did likewise. Because General Howard would be with the bulk of the Fourth Corps, he informed General Newton that he would receive orders directly from General Thomas for the day.[30]

George Wagner was ill and his Second Brigade was temporarily commanded by Colonel John Blake of the 40th Indiana. Blake's men crossed Peach Tree Creek in the morning and took up positions in earthworks that Hazen's brigade had completed on a low hill near the creek bank. Bottomland, some of it cleared, ran along the creek. Further south, the terrain devolved into low ridges and ravines separated by elevated spurs. Peach Tree Road traversed one of these spurs from the bridge to the closest ridge. Everything except the sparse farm fields was either covered by pine forests or thick, spiny undergrowth. A few hundred yards south of Collier's Bridge, astride the Peach Tree Road, was a wooded ridge. A few rebel pickets were posted there at the edge of the woods behind a rail fence, and their sniping had been accurate enough to seriously wound one of Wood's staff officers. Bradley's brigade followed Blake's. Two of Bradley's regiments relieved the last of Hazen's brigade, but the rest were delayed in crossing the Bridge by Wood's men going in the opposite direction until early afternoon. After advancing a few hundred yards down the road toward Atlanta, Bradley's men filed off the road to the right into a field in the rear of Kimball's brigade. After deploying into a formation of regiments massed in column, they stacked arms and assumed the role Newton's division's reserve. The 79th Illinois was sent to the left of the road to picket the left flank. The Yankees could not see their foe, but they knew the enemy was out there, somewhere.[31]

George Thomas arrived on the north side of the Peach Tree Creek in Newton's rear in the early afternoon and established his army headquarters. Sherman was pushing Thomas toward Atlanta, but Thomas didn't plan to advance until all of the Twentieth Corps was across Peach Tree. A division of Hooker's corps, General William T. Ward's, crossed the creek and formed in the valley of Early's Creek to the right of Newton's men, with only a skirmish line in front. In front of Ward's division were open fields, quite different from the heavy timber in Newton's front. Hooker's other two divisions crossed Peach Tree farther west and were positioned west of Early's Creek. Each division faced south with two brigades in front and one in the reserve. Beyond Hooker's right was the Fourteenth Corps. By early afternoon, the Army of the Cumberland was south of Peach Tree Creek and awaiting Thomas' order to move. Hooker and his staff relaxed under a shade tree. Expecting to move south shortly, Hooker's infantry made little effort to fortify their positions.[32]

Between 1 and 2 p.m., Thomas instructed Newton to send a strong skirmish line forward to drive the enemy pickets back. Newton sent the 44th Illinois of Kimball's brigade down the Peach Tree Road toward Atlanta. The Union skirmishers drove the Southern pickets from the ridge about a half mile ahead. Blake and Kimball's brigades were sent forward and deployed on the narrow ridge that ran at right angles to the road. Kimball's brigade aligned itself along the ridge to the right of the road, and Blake's brigade, to the left. Four guns from Captain Wilbur Goodspeed's Battery A of the 1st Ohio Artillery were placed on the road between the brigades. Luther Bradley's Third Brigade was repositioned along the road in the rear where the road traversed an elevated spur with the resulting formation resembling a "T." Kimball and Blake's brigades traded shovels and axes for muskets and began immediately to fortify the top of the "T" with a barricade of logs and fence rails. The 57th Indiana and 100th Illinois of Blake's brigade were sent to scout east along the ridge and creek bottom toward Pea Vine Creek. They found no rebels until they reached Pea Vine Creek and exchanged shots with enemy pickets on the east bank.[33]

Schofield and McPherson were pushing south from Decatur with four corps of Union infantry. Their line of march would take them past the Confederate right flank and into Atlanta from the east virtually unopposed, except for a couple thousand dismounted cavalry troopers. Informed of this danger around 10 a.m., General Hood directed General Cheatham to slide his corps a mile to the right to cover the Decatur road. Hardee and Stewart were directed to sidle their corps to the right also to prevent a mile long gap from forming between Hardee's corps and Cheatham's. About 1, after receiving 60 rounds of ammunition, Cheatham's infantry set off. Perhaps because he was new to corps command, or just didn't understand the order, Cheatham's movement was slow, cautious, and eventually, too far to the right. Hardee followed, trying remain in contact with Cheatham's flank, and failed to notify Hood of the extent of his move. This marching to the right consumed much of the early afternoon, and Hood's designated attack time of 1 p.m. passed in silence. Finally, about mid-afternoon, Hardee was in position, his right division, Brigadier General William Bate's was now well beyond the Peach Tree Road and, more significantly, the left flank of the Army of the Cumberland.[34]

Along Peach Tree Creek, some Yankees remarked on the ominously quiet afternoon, frequently a sign of unseen activity. Satisfied his men were ready to move south Newton ordered a skirmish line composed of the 15th Missouri and 73rd Illinois of Kimball's brigade forward about 3:30. Four hundred yards down the road they encountered rebel pickets in a hollow. These Southerners were prodded out of their rifle pits and pushed back. Advancing up a high ridge in their front, the Union skirmishers halted near the crest and sent scouts forward. Returning faster than they went forward, the scouts reported heavy columns of enemy infantry advancing to the left and front. The Confederates charged Union skirmishers and lapped around both flanks, demanding they surrender. Instead, Colonel Joseph Conrad of the 15th Missouri and Major Thomas Motherspaw of the 73rd Illinois ordered a retreat, their men retiring from tree to tree, firing as they went, until they reached the main line. Newton sent a courier to Thomas reporting a strong Confederate force is in his front. The ever cautious Thomas ordered Newton to halt—no fast march to Atlanta this afternoon—and entrench for the day.[35]

About 4 p.m., Hardee's attack began. The good part of 15,000 veteran Southern infantry were aimed at John Newton's three small brigades of 3200 men. To the east, Major General William Bate's Confederate division led the attack as Hood envisioned it. However, because of the morning's shift east, Bate's men were now so far to the right that they were not in contact with Newton's left flank, nor did they know where it was because Hardee had not ordered a reconnaissance. The rebels floundered forward through the thick woods and brush and found themselves fighting briars instead of Yankees in the creek bottom. Eventually, the famed Kentucky Orphan Brigade, bumped into the flank of 100th Illinois and 57th Indiana's skirmishers as they faced east. These two regiments were 600 yards from the rest of Newton's division and obviously outgunned. They fell back toward the creek firing two volleys. Lieutenant Colonel Willis Branch was forced to divide the 57th Indiana, sending half across the creek and keeping half on the south side in some old Southern rifle pits on the bank. The Indianans, joined by the 100th Illinois, dissuaded the enemy from crossing the creek by firing volleys into the flank of Bates' men, thus protecting the wagon and ammunition trains parked on the north bank. Years later, one Kentuckian labeled the Peach Tree fight "a slight engagement" for the Orphan brigade, but admitted they had "suffered some loss, mainly in skirmishers."[36]

The sound of musketry from Kimball's skirmishers reached Opdycke's ears, followed by a few panicked pickets running to the rear. These men failed to rally on Bradley and Opdycke who tried to stop them. Opdycke directed Lieutenant Colonel Moore to double quick the 125th across the road diagonally and into the woods. Finding no Johnnies there, the 125th returned to the Brigade's defensive line—facing east—on the Peach Tree Road with the regiment on the right of the line, a quarter mile from the bridge. Bradley's line solidified along the road behind a rail fence and had just settled in when Bate's Confederates charged out of the woods and brush and into the open bottomland of stunted corn and weeds east of the road. All the rebels could see were two cannon of Goodspeed's 1st Ohio Artillery ripe for capture and came on cheering. The momentum of the Confederate assault carried it forward some distance into the field. Goodspeed's big guns swept the field with blasts grape and canister. Bradley's men opened fire instinctively from behind the fence and poured a devastating volley into the enemy. The Southerners returned with a volley that mainly went high before retreating in some disorder.[37]

Almost simultaneously with Bate's charge on the road, the Confederates of Major General William Walker's division, next on Hardee's line, drove in Blake's skirmishers and came charging through the woods at his front and left flank. Caught in the act of entrenching, the startled Yankees barely had time to drop picks and shovels and grab their muskets. Blake and Kimball's brigades, protected by a log and fence rail barricade, fired a volley at the Southerners at 50 yards that staggered them. With rebels rounding Kimball's right flank, Colonel John Quincy Lane of the 97th Ohio reacted quickly by ordering the only reserves, the brigade's pioneers, to take a position on the brigade's flank. When the enemy got too close, Lane ordered them to fire a volley, fix bayonets and charge. Seeing the Confederates on Colonel Blake's flank, Colonel Bradley responded by sending three Illinois regiments to support Blake and Kimball.[38]

What remained on the road were the four regiments of Opdycke's demi-brigade. Opdycke formed his command on the road facing east, his men in a single line of two ranks parallel to the road. The 64th, 65th, 125th Ohio and 3rd Kentucky then advanced from the road into the bottom and up a low hill. The 64th Ohio took 18 rebel skirmishers as prisoners. When Opdycke's skirmishers, companies H and K of the 64th Ohio, approached the crest of the hill, they met enemy skirmishers from Walker's division charging and screaming at just 30 yards. Both foes fired almost simultaneously. Both sides wavered, steadied by their officers. Some of Opdycke's infantrymen lay down to fire. Behind the Southern skirmishers was a heavy column of infantry about to charge passed Opdycke's left flank toward the bridge. Southern success here could trap Newton's entire division south of the creek. Newton ordered Opdycke back to the more defensible position on the Peach Tree Road, facing east, where his men could help protect the bridge. "Our position was not advantageous for defense," Captain Hinman of the 65th recalled, "and our single brigade was evidently greatly inferior in strength to the force we must encounter." Opdycke suspected some of his regiments might break for the rear when ordered back. According to Hinman, "Our officers were cautioned not to permit their men to keep on running after regaining the road." When the bugles sounded, much of Opdycke's demi-brigade did break for the road. Opdycke admitted it "withdrew in not very good order, except the 125th Ohio." The 125th maneuvered into position while taking fire and the rest of the demi-brigade aligned on it.[39]

By now, in addition to Bradley's brigade, there were six Yankee cannon at the bridge—a battery of the 1st Illinois Artillery along with Goodspeed's two-gun section. Furthermore, General Thomas personally brought up a four gun battery of the 1st Michigan Artillery from Ward's division using the point of his saber to urge the battery horses forward. Those guns went into action on the north side of the creek to sweep the thickets and fields of the bottomlands and ravines with grapeshot and canister.[40]

When the Southerners cleared the timber, the Union artillery opened on their flank from across the creek and Opdycke's demi-brigade fired by volley at less than 100 yards, shocking the oncoming Southerners. The 125th fired five volleys while the artillery fired a dozen blasts of grape shot and canister that took the charging enemy in the flank. In General Thomas' own words, the artillery "relieved the hitch." The lead rebel units broke in disorder for the protection of a ravine, off Blake's left flank. The rout became infectious as the Confederates made for the protection of the timber taking fire from Blake's brigade which turned to fire into the enemy flank. Writing years later, the 125th's Charles Clark described the action. "The 125th Ohio fired five rounds per man, and probably hit more men than any upon any other occasion in the same length of time." What little return fire the Confederates managed was described as "light and wild," as only Southerners on the flank of the attacking column returned the Yankees' fire.[41]

Desultory firing on Bradley's front continued for an hour, primarily with Southern skirmishers who had re-occupied some of their old rifle pits in the woods. Bradley's brigade had 30 men down while estimates of rebel casualties ran to 10 times that. One Ohio officer summed it up succinctly: "Punished the Rebs severely." There was a tremendous firefight along the breastworks that protected Kimball and Blake's brigades to the front. General Ward's division from Hooker's Corps pitched into the Southerners on Kimball's right as the battle rolled along Thomas' front. The last of Hardee's divisions to attack was Cheatham's old Tennessee division, now Brigadier General George Maney's. Two of Maney's brigades cautiously attacked west of the Peach Tree Road where they encountered Kimball's brigade and the skirmishers from Ward's division of Hooker's corps. The bulk of Ward's men were several hundred yards back in the valley of Early's Creek. One Confederate brigade pressed forward through what one participant called "awful" small arms and artillery fire to within 100 yards of Kimball's line. Here they halted in a location where the crest of a hill and trees provided some cover exchanging musket fire until 10 p.m. The Tennesseans were later criticized for a lack of aggressiveness. Captain Alfred Fielder of the 12th Tennessee Infantry summed up the fighting on that part of the battlefield: "my opinion is we did not make it pay as the enemy fought mostly behind fortifications."[42]

"After the first attack until sundown the enemy made frequent attacks on my line," Newton wrote of the fighting along Peach Tree Creek, "though none so severe as the first, and a constant fire had to be kept up along my lines until dark." Newton's division had spoiled Hood's attack. Their part in the Battle of Peach Tree Creek was over. However, to the west, the battle raged on, marked by the incessant musketry and clouds of gun smoke billowing above the tree tops. By the time the next successive Southern division launched its assault, three brigades from Ward's division were charging up the hill to Kimball's exposed right flank. They met the rebels on the crest in an old-fashioned open field fight. Hooker's reserve brigades furiously dug and stacked fence rails to create fortifications. Having bought time, the front ranks fell back behind the new breastworks. For three hours, the Southerners repeatedly charged Hooker's line. With the creek at their backs, Hooker's veterans stood their ground and poured volleys of musketry and artillery fire into the attackers. A cheer arose when Hooker himself appeared on horseback, hat in hand, shouting that he had whipped the secessionists. Hooker's corps in the federal center received the brunt of the attack at Peach Tree Creek and, due to their failure to prepare fortifications, suffered most of the casualties.[43]

While the battle raged south of Peach Tree Creek, Schofield, McPherson and the two Fourth Corps divisions were advancing on Atlanta from the east-northeast— McPherson's men from the east along the Georgia Railroad and Schofield's men were on a parallel wagon road a mile and a half north while Howard's two divisions were a mile off Schofield's right. McPherson and Sherman believed that any attack by Hood would fall on McPherson. By early afternoon, the lead units of McPherson's 25,000 infantry south of the railroad were two and a half miles from Atlanta and opposed only by General Wheeler's 3500 dismounted troopers. Units on McPherson's left flank pushed forward south of the railroad. To signal his arrival, McPherson had one of the 1st Illinois Light Artillery's big 20 pounder Parrott rifles fire three explosive shells into the city, killing a small child. The war had come to Atlanta.[44]

There was little to prevent the Yankees from pushing into the city, except Wheeler. Cheatham's earthworks didn't reach to the railroad and his line could not be extended further east. Wheeler was ordered to hold his position on the flank at all hazards yet it was clear his dismounted cavalrymen were outnumbered. At 6 p.m., Hood ordered Hardee's reserve division, Pat Cleburne's, to move right and support Wheeler's cavalry. When the order came, Hardee was preparing to substitute Cleburne for Walker's division, and renew the assault on Newton along Peach Tree Creek. With darkness approaching and Cleburne sent east, Hardee canceled the attack. McPherson was again infected with caution and allowed Wheeler's determined troopers to delay his advance until darkness overtook the battlefield. By morning Cleburne's division would be in position. McPherson had wasted a rare opportunity to flank the Confederate army. It would be the second time—Resaca was the first—the young general would miss an opportunity with the potential to decide the Atlanta campaign. Sherman offered only an uncharacteristically mild rebuke of McPherson, perhaps enough for a man who was Sherman's friend and protégé.[45]

As the battle wound down, Company B of the 125th Ohio was ordered to picket east of Peach Tree Road. Lieutenant Rice followed a trail of blood through the weeds to the creek where he found a dying Johnny, disemboweled by grapeshot lying in the cool water of the creek. Rice later recalled, "Poor fellow, I could do nothing for him." Not far away in a ravine, Rice's men discovered a 17-year-old butternut, his femur shattered by a musket ball. The Yankees brought the boy in and laid him on a blanket under a tree with food and water. In great pain and with tears staining his face, the lad told his captors, "They told us that you-all would kill us if you took us prisoners. I didn't think you'd be so kind to me!" The Yankees sent him to a Union field hospital after learning his identity. The lad later died, and Rice wrote his family with the details of their son's wounding and death.[46]

Shortly after the battle, Captain Tuttle of the 3rd Kentucky wrote of seeing "the ground thickly strewn with their dead and wounded" in front of Bradley's brigade's position. Details of Yankees brought in some five dozen rebel wounded. Eventually 200 enemy dead were buried by Newton's men, a dozen by the 125th alone. Hood's estimated losses at Peach Tree Creek were between 2500 and 3000. The Army of the Cumberland lost 1700, almost all from Hooker's corps which bore the brunt of a standup, open field fight. Newton's division, which fought mostly behind barricades, lost only 100 men and in Bradley's brigade, three killed and 21 wounded. Just two of Opdycke's Tigers were wounded. Colonel Opdycke rode along the entire line of battle the next day and said he hadn't seen dead rebels so thick on a battlefield since Shiloh. Of Hood's first attack as army commander, Opdycke wrote his wife that he hoped Hood would "never do better."[47]

The cornerstone of the Union victory at Peach Tree Creek had been the successful defense of the Thomas' left flank by Newton's division. General Thomas, in his official report, praised the division "which gallantly stood its ground, repelling charge after charge, although his left was very much exposed." Newton, the West Pointer and Virginian, was breveted a brigadier general in the regular army in March 1865, in large part for his actions in the battle fought along the banks of Peach Tree Creek.[48]

General Sherman spent the day with Schofield and Howard northeast of the city and was unaware that Thomas' men were fighting a desperate battle. Sherman heard heavy firing in the area of Thomas' right for an hour or so that afternoon, but the rest of the battle, just two or three miles away, was masked from him by terrain and weather. Dispatches bearing a complete picture of the Peach Tree Creek battle did not reach Sherman until late that evening. "We had met successfully a bold sally," Sherman wrote of Peach Tree Creek, "and were also put on our guard ... the event illustrated the future tactics of our enemy."[49]

The 21st was a day of entrenching as close to the Southern skirmish lines as possible for Thomas and Schofield's men. The Army of the Cumberland was less than three miles from Atlanta, but General Thomas had no intention of advancing as long as Hood was still in his front. Wood's division moved to fill much of the gap in the Union line. McPherson's men captured Bald Hill south of the Georgia Railroad—just a mile and a half from Atlanta—after a stiff fight and entrenched. Both flanks of the Confederate army were unsupported and Hood knew he must relocate from Atlanta's outer defenses to an inner ring of fortifications, only a mile and a half from the city center. This he ordered for the night of the 21st.[50]

But General Hood wasn't going to sit in his fortifications—he was going to attack. Because of the strength of the inner ring of Atlanta's defenses, Hood designated a single corps—Stewart's—to guard the western and northern approaches to the city and hold the Army of the Cumberland in position. Hardee's corps was to march east through Atlanta and loop north to Decatur and strike into McPherson's rear at daybreak and roll up Sherman's line. Wheeler's cavalry was to seize Decatur where McPherson's supply trains were parked in the town square. Cheatham's corps, guarding the eastern entrances to Atlanta, was to advance northeast into shrinking gap in the Fourth Corps line once he believed Hardee's attack was successful. Lastly, if Cheatham succeeded, Stewart was to attack Thomas. It was a bold plan for an outnumbered and outgunned army fatigued from a desperate fight less than 48 hours earlier.[51]

McPherson became increasingly concerned throughout the 21st about his left flank since in military parlance it was "in the air," not protected by even so much as a squadron of cavalry. McPherson's alarm grew after bodies of Southern infantry were seen moving south of Bald Hill. After the fighting along Peach Tree Creek, Sherman was focused on closing the gap in the Fourth Corps and pushing the Army of the Cumberland closer to Atlanta. By dark Oliver Howard's artillery was within rifled cannon range of Atlanta, and the Army of the Cumberland's line was solidifying. As the evening wore on, McPherson became convinced that Hood was planning to strike his flank. At 3 a.m. on the 22nd, he sent Sherman an ominous dispatch: "I will simply remark ... that the whole Rebel army is not in front of the Army of the Cumberland."[52]

15

THE FALL OF ATLANTA

It was impossible to move thousands of soldiers quietly, even behind their own lines. Rumors spread among ever-alert Union skirmishers that something was afoot. Cautious Yankees began to edge forward and shortly before daylight it became general knowledge that the rebels had decamped. At dawn on the 22nd, Lieutenant Ralsa Rice and First Sergeant Rufus Woods, of Company B crept from the picket line into the woods in their front. Unable to tell in the dim light if the enemy's earthworks were occupied, the practical Rice fired a musket round into the trenches. Receiving no response, Rice and Woods eased closer and found the rebel line abandoned. Giving his report at headquarters, Rice was arrested by a staff officer for unauthorized firing at the front. Sergeant Woods hastened to Colonel Opdycke's tent, reported the enemy gone and informed Opdycke of Rice's arrest. The Colonel told Woods he would take care of Rice, concluding, "There must be more shooting before we are through."[1]

Sherman, for a while, at least, chose to believe that Hood was evacuating Atlanta. He ordered a general advance toward the city and rode with the lead elements of the Army of the Ohio marching west. When the blue column reached the home of a whisky distiller Thomas Howard, Atlanta came into view. The inner circle of Atlanta's fortifications was plainly visible as lines of fresh red earth on the hills just across the deep valley of Clear Creek. Also visible were thousands of Southerners furiously digging the new trenches. Sherman rode down into the valley until his party drew artillery fire. Hood was not giving up the city without a fight. Sherman ordered up artillery to harass the rebels. "A few batteries were soon in position," General Cox remembered, "and as they opened, the enemy vanished behind the works and the siege began." Federal skirmishers pressed up to the enemy line and fresh federal earthworks sprouted on every knoll. Sherman commandeered the Howard house for his headquarters.[2]

Along Sherman's Peach Tree Creek line, the Fourth Corps was on the left of the Army of the Cumberland, deployed from the Peach Tree Road east to Schofield's right flank. Newton's division was where it had been during the battle—Bradley's brigade was to the west of the road on Hooker's flank, while Kimball and Wagner's brigades were east of the road. Stanley and Wood's divisions were east of Newton's. Mid-morning, Newton's men shouldered their muskets and marched through the abandoned Confederate works. As the Cumberlands closed on Hood's inner line of Atlanta's defenses skirmishing intensified and the Yankees finally halted a half mile from the new rebel trenches. In Bradley's brigade, a 21-year-old musician in the 65th Ohio was killed by a solid shot and several men wounded. Once again, Thomas' men picked up their axes and shovels.[3]

During the morning of the 22nd, McPherson continued his advance west toward

Confederate earthworks north of Atlanta. Note the palisades. Library of Congress.

Atlanta along the Georgia Railroad from Decatur, eventually coming into contact with the Army of the Ohio on his right. Unknown to McPherson, Hardee's veterans were already past his left flank, but difficult terrain and fatigue had delayed Hood's planned daylight attack on McPherson's rear. Some of Hardee's men had marched 15 miles through the night to get into position. When they finally moved to press their attack, shortly after noon, they faced swampy, briar infested, forested terrain. When Hardee's men at last emerged from the vines, they bumped into two of Major General Glenville Dodge's divisions moving toward the federal left flank about a mile behind McPherson's front. Dodge's experienced infantrymen promptly changed front into a line of battle to meet the Confederates.[4]

Just as General McPherson was leaving Sherman's headquarters, the crackle of musketry intensified in his left rear and McPherson knew that a Confederate attack was underway. Shortly after giving Dodge orders, General McPherson and two orderlies blundered into a Confederate skirmish line in heavy timber and the General—resplendent in full uniform and riding a black horse—was killed. Major General John Logan of the Fifteenth Corps assumed temporary command of the Army of the Tennessee. The former

Illinois congressman was a staunch Unionist and a born leader. One historian labeled John Logan "the Union's premier civilian combat general." Lieutenant Clark of the 125th simply said that General Logan "was equal to the emergency."[5]

Logan rode his lines extolling his men to hold their embattled position. Sherman sent a single brigade from the Army of the Ohio toward Decatur in support of Logan and ordered the Army of the Cumberland to adopt a threatening posture along their sector of the front. Generals Schofield and Howard were with Sherman during the battle and suggested that their men counterattack. Sherman refused, saying, "I purposely allowed the Army of the Tennessee to fight this battle almost unaided ... if any assistance were rendered by either of the other armies, the Army of the Tennessee would be jealous." It was a missed opportunity as just 10,000 Southerners held four miles of trenches in Thomas' front. Logan's fight was confused, and the Army of the Tennessee was at times flanked and assaulted from the rear, its infantry fighting from opposite sides of the same breastworks. A key position was Bald Hill and it was held, but at the cost of 10 cannon, 15 stands of regimental colors and 1000 prisoners. About 4 p.m. Cheatham's corps succeeded in breaking through on Logan's right flank just north of the Georgia Railroad. Sherman turned the Army of the Ohio's artillery on the rupture. The Confederates had broken the Union line and come close to rolling it up, but after hard fighting, were repulsed. By dark, Hardee's men were in retreat.[6]

Charles Clark, writing 30 years later of what came to be known as the Battle of Atlanta, summarized the day's action. "The situation of the Army of the Tennessee was certainly critical; its commander dead, its several corps separated and furiously assailed in front and rear ... but like their comrades of the Army of the Cumberland on the 20th, officers and men stood by their colors and held their ground."[7]

The fighting on the 22nd would prove to be the most severe day of fighting around the city. Hood's loss was estimated at 8000. A thousand rebel dead were buried in front of one of Logan's divisions alone and 1500 prisoners taken. Federal losses were 3600 men and 10 pieces of artillery. General Howard said of the victory, "Our gain was in morale." Colonel Opdycke called it "inspiriting." The loss of the 35-year-old James McPherson, a rising star in the Union army, was incalculable. Later that evening Sherman said of McPherson, "I expected something to happen to Grant and me; either the rebels or the newspapers would kill us both, and I looked to McPherson as the man to follow us and finish the war." Despite the missed opportunities and surprises of the last three days, Opdycke wrote his wife that Sherman's leadership now commanded "universal admiration."[8]

While McPherson's men fought for their lives east of Atlanta, the Army of the Cumberland skirmished and dug. The terrain sloped gently and Bradley's brigade was pushed forward to ground that gradually descended toward the enemy trenches. In their front were two rebel redoubts—one left and one right—holding artillery. The 125th Ohio threw up a temporary log barricade for immediate protection as they were bombarded by the enemy's siege mortars—100-pound projectiles, nicknamed "camp kettles." Most fired in the direction of Bradley's brigade flew 50 feet overhead before landing half a mile in the rear in "cook's hollow," terrifying the black cooks working there.[9]

Beginning work at dark, an earthen breastwork 15 feet thick at the base and topped with a large head log was completed before dawn on the 23rd, despite significant enemy shelling. Lieutenant Rice oversaw the construction of that part in Company B's front. When Colonel Opdycke inspected the night's labors, he told Rice the slope was not steep enough because the bottom of the ditch in front was not visible. Lieutenant Rice determined to make the adjustment himself. At daylight, a hostile bullet buried itself in the fresh earth near Rice. Another round make a sickening thud Rice knew meant someone was hit. Rice's friend, Sergeant Fred Knight, who was setting a post for shade, was shot along the spine near the back of his neck, a simple wound that nevertheless troubled Knight for the rest of his life. Knight stayed with the regiment.[10]

One of Sherman's most immediate problems on July 23 was replacing McPherson and he sought George Thomas' opinion. Granting that Logan was personally brave and a good officer, Thomas expressed the West Pointers' classic objection to high ranking civilian officers—too politically ambitious and not adhering closely to orders. Sherman understood. General Cox, himself a citizen/soldier, wrote that Logan's most frequently criticized trait was "his querulousness and disposition to find fault with commands given him." Thomas recommended Howard—10 years out of West Point and an intelligent, professional officer. His record in Georgia was solid, but lackluster. But Oliver O. Howard was loyal, more experienced in command than Logan, executed orders promptly and without question and came with an excellent staff. Sherman knew Logan would be upset, but he wanted a professional in the position. "I wanted to succeed in taking Atlanta," Sherman said, "and needed commanders who were purely and technically soldiers, men who obey orders and execute them promptly and on time." In Colonel Opdycke's opinion the temperate, Christian Howard was "just the man" to replace McPherson. On July 27, Howard assumed command of the Army of the Tennessee.[11]

General Hooker was enraged that Howard was promoted and not him. Technically, Major General Joseph Hooker out ranked Howard, in fact he outranked Thomas and Sherman. Hooker had performed well thus far in the Atlanta campaign, but Sherman had a low opinion of him since June 22 and never considered him. Hooker in a pique, immediately asked to be relieved. Thomas endorsed Hooker's request—"approved and heartily recommended"—and sent it to Sherman who readily accepted it. Colonel Opdycke thought Hooker, despite his faults, an able corps commander and was appreciated by his soldiers. Hooker was transferred to an inactive command in the Midwest.[12]

Howard's promotion thrust Major General David S. Stanley, a West Pointer and the senior division commander, into the top spot in the Fourth Corps. Opdycke believed that Stanley "will do well with it." General Newton was losing Opdycke's respect because

Major General David S. Stanley. Stanley returned to Indian fighting after the war. He and Opdycke engaged in a lifelong battle over Opdycke's role in the battle of Franklin. Stanley was awarded the Congressional Medal of Honor in 1893 for his actions at Franklin. Library of Congress.

of his hard drinking and the Colonel told his wife that the division succeeded "in spite of him," the colonel wrote his wife. Another Ohio officer in the division described Newton as "sometimes a little querulous." No one could fill Harker's shoes—Opdycke had even sent a picture of Harker to his wife—but Opdycke had come to appreciate, even like, Bradley. Before the end of the month, Sherman had nominated Bradley for an honestly earned promotion to brigadier. On July 18, President Lincoln had called for 500,000 additional volunteers. Opdycke recommended Captains Bates, Powers and Moses as field officers in the new regiments, but he doubted Governor Brough would act on it. Gone were the days when Opdycke had the Ohio governor's ear.[13]

The citizens of the village of Kinsman in Trumbull County supplied a new regimental flag to the 125th after the Kennesaw Mountain battle. "The old one was shot to shreds," according to Lieutenant Ralsa Rice. The old flag, at Lieutenant Colonel Moore's suggestion, was given to Colonel Opdycke by the regiment as a token of appreciation.[14]

Poor food handling was a major contributor to the sick lists of any 19th-century army in the field. Officers were not immune. Opdycke complained of a fever which nearly sent him to bed on the 23rd. His cure was to consume a diet of milk and cornstarch. He admitted to his wife that both he and Lieutenant Colonel Moore, his mess mate, had been imprudent in their diet and that Moore was also experiencing digestive problems. David Moore, like most men, lacked Opdycke's recuperative powers, and would continue to be plagued by stomach problems.[15]

Riding his lines on Sunday, July 24, General Sherman arrived unannounced on Bradley's front. He questioned Lieutenant Tuttle of the 3rd Kentucky extensively about the enemy's dispositions on his part of the line. After Sherman departed, the enemy's artillery opened on the Division's front and the Yankees dug deeper and threw up traverses in their trenches. Late in the afternoon, Colonel Opdycke was seated under a poplar tree near headquarters and was briefly stunned when an artillery shell exploded feet from him. By evening, the rebels were sending 64 pounder shells at the federals. The 6th Ohio battery replied, occasionally firing "hot shot" into Atlanta—solid 12-pound cannonballs heated to act as crude incendiaries. After dark, Major Bruff took a crew of 300 men from the division forward 150 yards and worked them through the night to construct 400 yards of works. It was dangerous work, but there was only one man from the 125th wounded, Sergeant William Thompson.[16]

The military railroad was now running uninterrupted from Chattanooga to the rear of the Army of the Cumberland delivering vital supplies and removing wounded. With the destruction of the Georgia Railroad complete, Sherman decided to move Howard's men from the extreme left of the Union army to the right flank to sever the last remaining rail lines into Atlanta: the Atlanta and West Point and the Macon and Western Railroads. Those two roads shared track leaving the city for five miles to East Point, Georgia, where they branched going southwest to Mobile and southeast to Savannah. Sherman's goal was to extend his army southward to East Point and cut the rails which would sever Hood's remaining communication and supply routes. General Hood foresaw the danger and extended his fortifications southwest following Joe Johnston's tactic that General Cox labeled "the warfare of flanking lines."[17]

In front of the Fourth Corps line, Bradley's brigade constructed abatis and palisades all day on the 26th and at least one man was wounded in picket firing described as "very angry." By the morning of the 28th, two corps from the Army of the Tennessee had extended Sherman's right south to Ezra Church, three miles west of Atlanta, and were supported by a third infantry corps. General Hood thought he saw another opportunity to attack a Union force unprotected by fortifications at Ezra Church and gambled on another flank assault. Hood's old corps, now commanded by Lieutenant General Stephen D. Lee instead of the lackluster Cheatham marched out of the Atlanta trenches early July 28, and positioned itself to block Howard's advance. That evening, according to Hood's plan, General Stewart's Corps would slip in behind Lee and be in position to fall on Howard's unprotected right flank from the southeast. This time Hardee's corps alone would be holding the Atlanta line against Thomas and Schofield. General Cox referred to Hood's latest plan as "the repetition of the tactics of the 22nd, but with less brilliancy." As Howard's army pushed south, small arms fire increased along the skirmish line. Sherman was riding at Howard's elbow and Howard expressed the opinion that Hood was planning to attack. Sherman disagreed, but Howard was steadfast in his belief. "I said I had known Hood at West Point," Howard later wrote, "and that he was indomitable."[18]

General Logan's corps halted, just a mile and a half from their railroad objective, and his veterans hastily threw up barricades of logs, fence rails and whatever they could find for a little protection. Howard himself described what happened next. "With a terrifying yell, Hood's men charged through the forest. They were met steadily and repulsed.... The battle was prolonged for hours.... Hood, having again lost three times as many as we, withdrew within fortified lines. Our skirmishers cleared the field, and the battle of Ezra Church was won." The Southern dead were thickly strewn across the gruesome battlefield, most the result of small arms fire. One Ohio veteran recalled that he "never saw the [Rebel] dead lying so thick in my life." Sherman simply called the afternoon's work by Howard's men "a common slaughter of the enemy."[19]

Confederate losses were estimated at 3000 to 4000 compared to 700 for Howard's army. Perhaps even worse was the blow to morale. Unconfirmed reports from Union skirmishers told of Confederate infantry refusing to attack at the end of the day. Confederate prisoners interrogated by federal officers expressed the opinion that Hood's three assaults in less than 10 days were "useless and hopeless." General Hardee wrote later of Ezra Church, "No action of the campaign probably did so much to demoralize and dishearten the troops engaged in it." The old fighting spirit seen under Joe Johnston's tenure had evaporated in the 11 days of Hood's command. The losses Hood suffered in three assaults prompted Confederate President Jefferson Davis to write Hood a week later, "The loss consequent upon attacking [Sherman] in his intrenchments requires you to avoid that, if practicable." In Sherman's army, morale was high after three lopsided defensive victories, especially in the Army of the Tennessee. One Union officer wrote in his diary after Ezra Church, "We are in excellent spirits and propose to take Atlanta whenever Sherman wants it."[20]

As the battle near Ezra Church raged, the Fourth Corps drove back the rebel picket line in its front. Fifty-seven men of the 125th were engaged as skirmishers. One man was killed, Private Samuel Sailor, and one mortally wounded, Private George Shenefield. Sherman asked Generals Schofield and Stanley to explore the possibility of launching an attack on Atlanta from the northeast. Those generals reported facing strong fortifications laced with artillery that only a strong, well-coordinated attack stood a chance of breeching. Furthermore, like their opposites in gray, the bluecoat infantry had no stomach for such an assault. The intrepid skirmishers, as usual, continued their deadly game. During the 29th and 30th, the heat and humidity did not deter heavy artillery dueling along the Fourth Corps line. Colonel Luther Bradley received notification of a presidential appointment to brigadier general. Sunday the 31st was quiet enough for some incautious Yankees to climb the few remaining trees for a look into Atlanta. The view was "fine" according to one Ohioan, but he added, tongue-in-cheek, "got no invitation to come in so did not go." Hood's cumulative losses of 13,000 or so since the Yankees crossed the Chattahoochee represented a victory for the Union. However, author Shelby Foote noted that despite Sherman's lopsided victories, Hood's willingness to fight served notice to the Northerners that reaching the railroad in the Southern rear, and ultimately taking Atlanta, might be very costly.[21]

Hood's aggressiveness had made Sherman more cautious as his army moved through the countryside west of Atlanta. Artillery, North and South, was in action on August 1, and according to the 3rd Kentucky's Lieutenant Tuttle, the rebel shelling "was remarkably well directed and their shells were huge." Bradley's brigade remained in the position on the Peach Tree Road that it had occupied during the battle. John Schofield's Army of the Ohio withdrew from the extreme left flank and marched behind the lines to the extreme right the night of August 1. The following day, the Fourth Corps stretched to the left to fill those empty trenches. Newton's division was now the left flank of Sherman's army.[22]

"Up to the 25th of August there was no material change in the lines north of Atlanta," Lieutenant Clark wrote 30 years later of August 1864. "It was a month of hard work. The picket line was a skirmish line. There were demonstrations daily on some part of the line by one side or the other, the casualties in the Fourth Corps averaging about twenty-five per day for that period. There was also continuous artillery firing, our guns firing at the enemy's forts and those of the enemy generally aiming at our batteries, but occasionally varying the program by shelling our camps. The 125th Ohio took its regular turn on the skirmish line and on fatigue duty, working on entrenchments, and was fortunate in having very few casualties."[23]

With only a cavalry screen beyond the corps' left, General Stanley ordered a redoubt for artillery be constructed on a knoll 250 yards in front of the Union line and a half mile to the east of the 125th's camp. This military engineering work—an exposed and risky undertaking—would consume two weeks in August for the 125th Ohio. Colonel Opdycke objected to a project he saw no tactical value in the fort. General Newton agreed, but had his orders. Practically under the muzzles of rebel muskets and cannon, the 125th and 65th Ohio started excavating an elliptical enclosure 100 by 40 yards with heavy earth and log walls to resist artillery shells. A two-gun section of Union artillery was sent along as partial protection. Working in rotating detachments morning and evening from August 1 to 13, the 125th—exempt from all other duties—labored to complete the redoubt unofficially named Fort Opdycke. Harassment by enemy pickets required a foray by the 3rd Kentucky to seize the Southern picket posts. So perilous had the work become, Emerson Opdycke wrote his wife that he would have been happy never to return to the fort.[24]

Sherman continued to push his right flank—Howard and Schofield's troops—south from August 5 to 7. Artillery shells were fired into the city every five to 15 minutes, and the Army of the Cumberland skirmished and postured in support of this movement. As a distraction, part of Bradley's brigade was ordered at 3 p.m. on the 5th to advance the picket line and drive the enemy. The brigade advanced 300 yards, captured enemy rifle pits and kept up heavy musketry—perhaps 80 to 100 rounds per man—until dark. Three men in the brigade were wounded. Return fire by Confederate artillery was heavy and directed at the skirmish lines. The redoubt work spared the 125th any part in the action.[25]

Schofield got his corps as far as Utoy Creek, south of Lick Skillet Road and Ezra

Church, when he was repulsed by yet another Confederate defensive line on the 5th. The 7th, General Cox's division advanced south of the Sandtown Road west of Atlanta but was stopped by new rebel earthworks just two miles from the Atlanta and West Point Railroad. The federals probed for weakness—General Cox described it as "crowding their skirmish lines"—and found the Southern fortifications extended even farther south. After two days of testing Hood's defenses, and taking casualties, Sherman accepted that there were no soft spots in the Confederate line protecting the railroad and that he could not safely stretch his lines any further.[26]

That evening, General Newton promoted Colonel Opdycke to temporary command of the First Brigade, replacing Brigadier General Nathan Kimball, who was assigned command of the First Division—previously Stanley's—of the Corps. The First Brigade held the left flank of Sherman's army, and General Newton told Opdycke that he was the only officer he had he could trust in that critical position. The First Brigade was comprised of seven regiments: the 44th, 36th, 73rd, 74th, and 88th Illinois, 24th Wisconsin and 15th Missouri. "It is a good reliable body of troops," Opdycke wrote his wife, that he preferred it to the Third Brigade. Because of Newton's division's heavy losses, there was speculation that its three small brigades would be consolidated to two, and Opdycke expected his tenure to be brief.[27]

Holding the left flank was a tremendous responsibility, but Opdycke was supremely confident, telling his wife the new assignment did "not embarrass me one bit." The First Brigade's skirmish line crossed the Georgia Railroad and extended to site of fighting on the 22nd of July east of Atlanta. Beyond Opdycke's left was ground screened by Union cavalry. General Stanley knew the importance of Opdycke's position and offered to transfer the 125th to him. The Colonel was grateful, because he was concerned how Major Bruff and Lieutenant Colonel Moore would interact. Opdycke admitted to his wife that the two officers did not enjoy a good working relationship when the Colonel was away. Opdycke's new position included orderlies, two of whom came from Company B of the 125th, Privates John Gartner and James Pollock. The Colonel also coveted Captain Whitesides—still recovering from his Kennesaw wound—and Powers—adjutant of the 125th—for his staff.[28]

By the evening of Sunday August 7th, Sherman had decided to send his entire army on a flanking maneuver around his right to cut the railroad to Macon, Georgia, south of Atlanta. This meant cutting loose from his railroad supply line again. But first, Sherman decided to give his infantry a much needed respite. In the interim, Atlanta would be heavily shelled until it became "a used up community." To achieve this, Union artillery sent 5000 shells—a hundred per gun—into Atlanta on Monday, August 9. Three 32-pounder siege cannon with a range of two miles were unlimbered 200 yards to the right of the 125th's position. Unhindered by a steady rain, the big guns began firing every 20 minutes into Atlanta on the 10th. Both explosive shells with their fuses bright in the overcast sky and solid shot with their distinctive "whoosh-whoosh" sound, were fired. Lieutenant Rice wrote that "it was an interesting spectacle to watch these fiery messengers sailing over the tops of the trees with their long, curved flight, terminating in a crash over Atlanta." Despite the intense shelling, Sherman admitted that he lacked the patience for a siege. Nevertheless, because of the bombardment, Sherman informed Washington, "One thing is certain. Whether we get inside of Atlanta or not, it will be a used-up community when we are done with it." Miraculously, fewer than two dozen civilians were killed during the bombardment.[29]

Everyone in Sherman's headquarters knew that sooner or later Confederate cavalry would try to interrupt cut the Union army's supply line, and on August 10, the much anticipated Southern raid began. Confederate General Joe Wheeler with 4000 to 5000 troopers rode off determined to destroy as much of the Western and Atlantic Railroad from Marietta to Chattanooga as possible and then cross the Tennessee River and do the same from Nashville to Chattanooga. By disrupting the flow of Sherman's supplies, Hood hoped he could force the Yankees to retreat, chase Wheeler or launch a rash attack on the heavily fortified Southern defenses. The risk for Hood was that only three cavalry brigades would remain around Atlanta to scout and protect flanks. Wheeler would be gone a month, during which time the raiders burned the bridge over the Etowah, destroyed over 30 miles of track and bagged over 3000 horses and beeves. The rebel horsemen ranged as far as Knoxville before circling north of Chattanooga and as far west as Alabama. It was a daring raid, but the damage was temporary. Sherman had not been induced to leave Atlanta. Hood realized the obvious, "that no sufficiently effective number or cavalry could be assembled in the Confederacy to interrupt the enemy's line of supplies to an extent to compel him to retreat."[30]

Sherman was under pressure to take Atlanta. The longer he delayed, the more precarious militarily his position became. Veteran soldiers were going home as their three year enlistments expired. The huge stockpiles of supplies which filled warehouses in Nashville and Chattanooga in May were almost depleted. Union quartermasters estimated food supplies would be exhausted by September 15 and grain for horses and mules by the 1st. Politically, a success in Georgia was urgently needed to boost sagging Northern morale since Grant's campaign in Virginia had become a stalemate at the gates of Richmond after staggering losses in manpower. Lincoln had issued a call for another 500,000 men that summer and the threat of conscription hung heavily over the North. Republican party fortunes followed the decline in morale. Democrat newspapers in the north proclaimed the south on the verge of victory because of the "blundering, incompetent, and fanatical" administration of Abraham Lincoln. And then there was emancipation, which was proving unpopular in many states, especially in the Midwest. "You think I don't know I am going to beaten," Lincoln asked an acquaintance in August, "but I do." Desperate Republicans increasingly saw Sherman as their best hope for a victory that might turn around their slumping hopes, and the first crucial vote in the national election came in October in Indiana. Thus William T. Sherman, well-known for his distaste for politics, found himself obliged to consider the political implications of his military strategy.[31]

Sherman's dealt with the political problem by simply changing his stated objective in Georgia from being Hood's Confederate Army of the Tennessee, to the city of Atlanta itself. Sherman notified the War Department on the morning of August 13, that he planned yet another flanking movement to capture Atlanta's last remaining rail links to the Confederacy which would force Hood to abandon the city. Sherman proposed to leave the Twentieth Corps to guard the Chattahoochee River crossings in his rear. The remaining six infantry corps—over 60,000 men—would move in a counterclockwise arc from northwest of Atlanta to south of the city where Jonesboro on the Macon and Western would be the objective.[32]

Hood's army in early August counted 56,000 men present, but subtracting cavalry and Georgia militia—teenage boys and their grandfathers—only 33,000 were veteran infantry and artillery. Low morale reflected a pessimism expected of men eating poor rations and defeated in battle three times in a matter of days. Scurvy, dysentery and night blindness rendered perhaps half of Hood's army unfit for service by 20th-century standards. Some nights, whole skirmish lines surrendered in mass. Yet, the thin gray line held earthworks 15 miles long. Committed secessionists remained optimistic in the belief that Southern salvation lay in stymieing Sherman in Georgia as part of an overall military stalemate that would lead to the election defeat of Abraham Lincoln.[33]

The last shovel full of dirt was turned by the 125th in the unappreciated redoubt on Saturday, August 13. Since work there meant exemption from other even more hazardous duties, the 125th's Lieutenant Ralsa Rice admitted, "We may have nursed that job a little." The next evening after Sunday services, the 125th returned to the picket line. In the morning, Colonel Emerson Opdycke was given permanent command of the First Brigade. The regiments of two colonels in the brigade who ranked Opdycke were transferred. In return, Opdycke got the 125th Ohio, which in terms of manpower was equal to the two departing regiments. In terms of quality, Opdycke explained to his wife, the ones he was losing were inferior to the 125th. The colonel still wanted a brigadier's star, but during the last three months some of the luster had faded. Opdycke confided to his wife that he preferred a reputation as a good colonel to a poor one as a major general.[34]

The 125th got its transfer orders the same day, but a rumor of an impending Confederate attack kept the Ohio Tigers in the Third Brigade. The Third Brigade's pioneer corps—commanded by the 125th's Lieutenant Waldern Williams—prepared new rifle pits in front of the old line and the regiment advanced to them for picket duty. On the 17th, five federal pickets from the Fourth Corps were captured on a clear moonlit night without firing a shot. Opdycke told his men to shoot if attacked, regardless of the personal risk. An attempt on one of Opdycke's picket posts was met with musket fire days later. Opdycke's Tigers remained in Bradley's brigade. Unfortunately, as Opdycke had foreseen, the future of Harker's proud old brigade dimmed when, on the 17th, the enlistments of the veterans of the 3rd Kentucky expired, and they petitioned to be removed to the rear and mustered out.[35]

Preparations for Sherman's great flanking move began on the 17th but were suspended when Sherman decided to test the undermanned rebel cavalry screen with Wheeler absent. A raid by five brigades of blue cavalry commanded by Major General Judson Kilpatrick set off for Jonesboro to cut the Macon railroad. However, Kilpatrick's raid produced no permanent damage—the railroad was repaired in three days. Sherman reached the same conclusion as Hood on the chances of a quick and cheap victory by raiding cavalry. "I now became satisfied," Sherman wrote in his *Memoirs*, "that cavalry could not, or would not, make a sufficient lodgment on the railroad below Atlanta, and that nothing would suffice but for us to reach it with the main army."[36]

The evening of Sunday, August 21, Colonel Opdycke sat down with Lieutenant Colonel David Moore who was suffering from bowel problems and struggling in regimental command. The Colonel believed that Moore was not firm enough to control some of the strong personalities in the regiment. More importantly, Moore had come to the realization that his calling was to save men's souls, not send them to die. "He feels now that the Lord is displeased with him for not preaching." Opdycke wrote his wife. Also, according to Opdycke, Moore regretted not taking the regimental chaplaincy when it was offered. Moore wanted to resign, but Opdycke argued that crushing the rebellion was paramount. The Colonel departed unsure what his Lieutenant Colonel would decide to do.[37]

Sherman's soldiers in general were ready for the campaign to end. "Most of them," wrote historian Albert Castel, "have spent the last month engaged in the same sort of tedious, vicious and essentially useless type of warfare that was rehearsed at Dalton and Resaca, and perfected at New Hope Church and Kennesaw: digging, skirmishing, sniping, and more digging—all punctuated with bombardments and counter-bombardments, sporadic firefights and occasional local assaults, delivered or resisted." Snipers even shot the pet dog of the 2nd Illinois Light Artillery. The hot, humid Georgia weather and life in the stationary trenches primed both armies for disease. An unbalanced diet of hardtack, bacon and coffee was monotonous and there was little opportunity to supplement them by foraging. Occasionally, slabs of unsavory desiccated mixed vegetables were issued as were onions to be consumed raw—one bushel to a regiment—to prevent scurvy. Rarely herds of beeves were driven from Chattanooga arriving very thin from lack of decent grass along the way. Only the hindquarters cuts retained enough muscle to call beef and three quarters of the soldiers only got lean soup shanks. One surgeon in Thomas' army expressed the sentiments of many when he wrote, "I am sick, yes sick and tired of bloodshed." One officer in the 125th tersely recorded, "Been here for thirty-two days. Nothing accomplished toward the capture of Atlanta." Flanking had been Sherman's most effective strategy and his soldiers accepted the tactic as the most likely means to achieve victory.[38]

The cavalry raid a failure, Sherman "resolved at once to proceed to the execution of my original plan" of a grand flanking movement from northwest of Atlanta to south of it. Thomas was asked when he could be ready to move, and the Virginian indicated the evening of Thursday August 25th. Sherman accepted that. The three Union armies loaded their supply wagons the equivalent of 100 rounds of ammunition per man, 15 days of rations and 15 days of half rations of forage—the deficit to made up from the ripening Georgia corn crop. The big siege guns and all unfit and unnecessary men, wagons and animals would be sent back north across the Chattahoochee. This would be a very lean army that Sherman would take around the Confederate left flank. By the 24th, rumors of the impending movement had infected the entire Union army. Northern skirmishers were strictly forbidden from fraternizing with their opposites. Orders went out to the army the morning of Thursday, August 25, to prepare to move at dusk. "We have not the slightest clue to where we are going," Captain John Tuttle wrote. "From the preparation we have been making for the last two or three days the movement will evidently be one of considerable importance."[39]

The Army of the Ohio held the Union right from Utoy to Camp Creek west of the rail junction at East Point and would be the pivot for Sherman's move south. Bugles ended the day as usual the evening of the 25th and as soon as the last notes faded away the withdrawal from the Northern trenches began. From left to right in succession the Fourth Corps brigades crept away from their fortifications northwest of Atlanta. Pickets remained behind for a time to mask the withdrawal, while cavalry continued to screen the Union left flank. Opdycke's brigade led the withdrawal at 6:45 p.m. Bradley's brigade marched at midnight. Bradley's men, halted about daybreak on Proctor's Creek near the Western and Atlantic Railroad where the pickets rejoined them. The shelling of the city had stopped abruptly—a sure sign to the secessionists that something was afoot. When at dawn the Southern skirmishers discovered the Yankees gone, they pushed ahead in cautious pursuit. At sunrise Bradley's soldiers could see the Johnnies milling around in the empty breastworks scavenging abandoned rations. Confederate artillery shelled the rear of Bradley's brigade for an hour. At 8 a.m., Wood and Newton's divisions, having marched just four miles, about faced to the rear and hastily constructed a small fortification. In the distance, artillery could be heard from direction of Chattahoochee bridge which the Twentieth Corps guarded. A gray skirmish line advanced on the Fourth Corps, and despite heavy musketry, the Southerners were few in number and easily repulsed. Sherman's men resumed their march at 10 a.m. The Confederates forced the federals to halt and form a battle line two or three more times before the bluecoats finally turned south. The 3rd Kentucky's Captain Tuttle wrote in his diary, "Rebs could have damaged us considerably had they struck our left flank while we were in such rapid motion but they missed us entirely." Opdycke agreed, calling the withdrawal a "bold" movement.[40]

With Opdycke's First Brigade in the lead, Newton's division crossed Proctor's Creek and headed south. It was a hard and quick march for the Yankees in the heat and out of condition from weeks in the trenches. Just 31 members of 125th Ohio were present when the regiment halted to rest at 1 p.m. Sergeant Hudson Fitch of Company D fell back and was captured during the march. Newton's division encamped at Utoy Creek, to right of the Atlanta and West Point Railroad. This was just 10 to 12 actual miles from their start, but the men felt they had marched much farther due to the constant delays and winding roads. That evening all of Sherman's flanking force aligned along the road west from Atlanta to Sandtown. The Fourth Corps deployed for the night facing the rear in case of enemy attack.[41]

Based on no solid evidence, General Hood became convinced that Sherman was short of supplies and retreating back across the Chattahoochee River at Sandtown. This self-deception ignited celebrations in Atlanta and persuaded Hood to leave his three infantry corps in the Atlanta trenches, which by now extended south of East Point. Hood's inertia provided Sherman with a couple of days to move unopposed. General Newton's division brought up the rear of Thomas' army, covering the wagon and artillery trains, and did not start until early afternoon on the 27th. Bradley's brigade didn't move until 2 p.m., covered five miles, crossed Camp Creek and went into position to the right of Wood's division, near Mount Gilead Church four miles south of Utoy Creek. At that point Bradley's men occupied two hills in advance of the main line which they hastily fortified. Foraging was particularly good for green corn and vegetables. The day had been the first of three leisurely days on the road, covering just a few miles at a session, during which the 125th built six different lines of fortifications and skirmished with hovering rebel cavalry.[42]

The Union army continued a determined flank march from 27th to the 31st. Sherman's three armies swung in an ark from the Sandtown Road southeast toward the Atlantic and West Point Railroad and then east toward the Macon and Western Railroad. Schofield's men had the shorter, but most dangerous route, around the Confederate's at East Point with Rough and Ready the objective four miles southeast of East Point, on the Macon railroad. Thomas, as was customary, took the center route on Schofield's right through Red Oak—11 miles southwest of Atlanta—aiming to strike the Macon road between Jonesboro and Rough and Ready. Lastly, Howard's Army of the Tennessee made the widest arc on the right flank crossing the Atlantic and West Point near Fairburn and heading for Jonesboro—10 miles southeast of Rough and Ready—on the Macon line.[43]

Sunday morning August 28, Thomas' Fourth and Fourteenth Corps started early for Red Oak, seven miles from East Point and where the Confederate fortifications ended. Bradley's brigade didn't step off until 4 p.m., made just four miles and halted near the railroad. The Army of the Tennessee was five miles further south at Fairburn. Thomas and Howard's men were facing east where Hood—now fully awake to reality—was now shadowing them. The next day and a half were spent disassembling the West Point railroad by lifting entire sections, burning the ties and heating the rails before bending them around trees or telegraph poles. Sherman told Thomas to "be so thorough that not a rail or tie can be used again." The work was vigorous that night, with 12 miles of track destroyed and the rail cuts through the hills filled with earth, logs, rocks and booby trapped with loaded artillery shells. Only one third of the men did the actual work while the rest dug fortifications. Bradley's men moved half mile and started digging.[44]

Sherman ordered the Army of the Tennessee to move on Jonesboro on the 30th, but halt four miles west at a crossroads called Renfroe Place. Thomas' two corps were to march to a point three miles north of Howard's army. Schofield's men fell in behind Thomas and faced toward East Point—still held by one of Hood's corps—to protect the Union left. By the 30th, all of Sherman's army, except Schofield, was between the Atlantic and West Point and Macon and Western railroads and south of the crucial rail junction at East Point. When during the afternoon of the 30th, Thomas' infantry neared the Flint River that ran between the two railroads and was only two miles from the Macon and Western, Sherman boasted to Thomas, "I have Atlanta as certainly as if it were in my hand!"[45]

Newton's division began their trek on August 30 by crossing the Atlanta and West Point Railroad about 14 miles southwest of Atlanta and marching four miles east before halting and entrenching. Howard's men pushed forward in the face determined Southern resistance, and by midafternoon they reached Renfroe's, just west of the Flint River and the Macon and Western which roughly paralleled the river. The country lacked sufficient water for a thirsty army and Howard received Sherman's verbal approval to proceed to the Flint River, which was just a mile west of Jonesboro. Howard's men seized a half burned bridge over the narrow river as they drove the Confederates east. By dark, Howard had one infantry corps within a quarter mile of Jonesboro and the railroad. Unbeknownst to Howard, Jonesboro was lightly defended and could easily have been taken. Instead, Howard halted and fortified his position.[46]

General Hood believed that only the Army of the Tennessee was south of Atlanta until late in the day on the 29th. However, by daylight Hood realized the truth and immediately he ordered Hardee and Lee's army corps to Jonesboro. An attack was ordered on the Union right flank for the morning of the 31st with the goal of driving the federals back across the Flint River. If successful, on September 1, Stewart's corps was to throw its weight into the attack and drive all federal forces threatening Jonesboro back to the Chattahoochee. However, should the August 31 attack fail to dislodge the Yankees, Hood understood that Atlanta would be lost and his army would retreat to Lovejoy Station, south of Jonesboro. Hood alerted his supply officers in Atlanta to prepare to evacuate the city.[47]

Thomas and Schofield's men advanced toward the railroad north of Jonesboro on the 30th. Newton's division crossed Crooked Creek and halted in the rear to guard the Fourth Corps supply trains. Schofield reached the Macon and Western Railroad a mile south of Rough and Ready. General Cox's division took a position astride the railroad by mid-afternoon and preceded to dig in and destroy the track. When Sherman was notified, he was ecstatic. At long last he had cut the Macon and Western Railroad. The Fourth Corps struck the railroad midway between Rough and Ready and Jonesboro. He ordered Generals Schofield and Stanley to turn south, destroying the rails as they went. Sherman was explicit: "break the road good as you move south." Newton's division came up that evening and joined the rest of the corps to the left of Kimball's First Division. Work to destroy the railroad continued through the night.[48]

That evening, Bradley's pickets detected a large body of Confederates moving south on a road just a half mile to their front. Sherman was alerted. By the morning of the 31st, all three of Howard's corps were entrenched and prepared for an attack. "I had really expected an attack all day on account of the saucy position we occupied," Howard wrote. Sherman questioned Howard's assumption. "We must have that road," Sherman declared, "and it is worth to us a heavy battle." By early afternoon on the 31st approximately 20,000 Southerners occupied a semi-circular mile and a half line west of Jonesboro with the flanks anchored on the railroad. Hardee's corps was on the southern end, Lee's, the northern. As the attack orders were read to the rank and file, one Southern general could see that his soldiers had "not much fight in them." Howard had a similar number of men, but they were entrenched and backed by artillery. About 3 p.m., Hardee attacked from left to right. According to General Cox, "The attack was fierce, but neither in weight nor persistency did it seem to equal former efforts of Confederate infantry." After two hours of bumbling, half-hearted assaults, the fight at Jonesboro, and with it for Atlanta, was over. One Confederate colonel could see the stark reality: "the men seemed possessed of some great horror of charging breastworks, which no power, persuasion, or example could dispel." The rebels suffered over 2000 casualties. Howard's Army of the Tennessee suffered exactly 179. The Confederates withdrew to their entrenchments on the Jonesboro line.[49]

Unaware of what was transpiring on the battlefield south of Atlanta, the Democrat convention in Chicago reached its climax with the nomination of former Major General George B. McClellan for president on the first ballot. The party's goal was simple: a cessation of hostilities and negotiated peace leading to a restoration of the Union. The so called "peace before union" platform. The Democrats were confident their man would win.[50]

On the 1st of September after an early start, Bradley's brigade reached the railroad three miles below Rough and Ready, 21 miles south of Atlanta. Nathan Kimball's First Division led Stanley's corps down the tracks, and Bradley's men took a turn deconstructing the railroad until 4 p.m. "We had suffered a good many times from cutting our cracker line," Captain Hinman of the 65th Ohio wrote of destroying the last railroad into Atlanta, "and this was the first time our boys had found an opportunity to administer to the rebels a dose of their own medicine. It was a novel experience, and officers and men sprang to the work with the greatest zeal and vigor, not forgetting to give vent to their satisfaction in loud and repeated yells." Altogether, 12 miles of track were destroyed.[51]

General Hood ordered Lee's corps back to Atlanta and left Hardee's men to hold Jonesboro. Upon learning of this, Sherman improvised a plan to strike Hardee's right flank with Thomas' two corps. Thomas' men would advance down the railroad—destroying it as they went—and reach Jonesboro about noon. The two corps would deploy on Hardee's right flank and attack. The fog of war intervened and the Fourteenth Corps was not in position until 4 p.m. while the Fourth was still out demolishing track. George Thomas personally rode off to hurry Stanley's corps prompting Sherman to remark that this was "the only time during the campaign I can recall seeing General Thomas urge his horse to a gallop."[52]

Late in the day, the Fourteenth corps attacked alone and captured some Confederate trenches. Stanley's men didn't arrive until dark and formed a battle line. General Kimball's division, on the Fourteenth Corps left, encountered the enemy about dark. Newton's division arrived about 6 p.m. and was aligned on Kimball's left—Wood was in reserve—

with George Wagner's brigade in contact with Kimball, then Opdycke's brigade and lastly Bradley on the far left flank deployed in three lines. They advanced and connected with Opdycke's First Brigade's flank. At dark, they were ordered forward keeping the connection with Opdycke. Newton saw the terrain as "very unfavorable for attack…" marked by hills and ravines. The gray skirmishers were pushed back by the Fourth Corps after a short, but intense, fire fight. Newton's entire division faced minimal opposition—the 125th only saw dismounted cavalry—and advanced a third of a mile farther than the rest of the corps into the rebel rear. Kimball stumbled into the Southern earthworks about dark, as Newton passed around the enemy's flank. The Confederates retreated, melting into the darkness.[53]

Caught in deepening darkness, the 125th halted at the edge of a wood and deployed pickets. Captain Powers was checking the picket line—part of an adjutant's duty—when he was shown a Confederate field hospital discovered by a sentry getting water. After carefully adjusting the picket line to encompass the hospital, Powers and four men approached the main tent. It was so dark that Lieutenant Ralsa Rice blundered into a pile of amputated limbs which he described as "a gruesome tumble." Unaware his hospital was behind Union lines, the Confederate surgeon in charge demanded Powers' surrender. More armed rebels appeared until Captain Powers summoned his squad, and Sergeant James M. Murdock's bayonet settled the controversy. The hospital Power's captured included two or three surgeons, some male nurses and 150 wounded. In the darkness all along the skirmish line, soldiers blue and gray, fell into their foes hands, including 13 of Newton's pickets. The September 1 battle for Jonesboro resulted in 1275 casualties for the attacking federals and about 1000 for the rebels. Aside from Colonel Opdycke's horse being shot in the tail, there were no casualties of importance to the 125th.[54]

About midnight, explosions rocking Atlanta were audible in Jonesboro. Those pyrotechnics made for a sleepless night for Sherman desperate to know their meaning. Had Hood turned and crushed the Twentieth Corps guarding the Chattahoochee or, instead, destroyed his ammunition stores in Atlanta? No one in Jonesboro knew for sure. An impatient Sherman went so far as to ask a local farmer, pulled from his bed, for his opinion. The sound of explosions faded, only to return at 4 a.m. and rising to a grand finale before ceasing. With no telegraph to bring news, Sherman was left to worry.[55]

September 2 was the 120th day of the Atlanta campaign. At dawn, with Schofield now on the left of Stanley, the federal advance resumed only to discover that Hardee's men had slipped away. The federals followed the trail down the Macon and Western Railroad. Howard's men moved on roads to the right of the rails, while the Fourth Corps took the left. It was slow going with enemy skirmishers in front and late afternoon before the Yankees found Hardee's three divisions behind stout earthworks at Lovejoy Station, six miles south. A single brigade of General Wood's division attacked and was repulsed and Wood was wounded in the foot. Another probe of the rebel line at 4 o'clock was repulsed leading Sherman to order no further attacks until he was certain of what was happening in Atlanta. "I do not wish to waste lives by an assault," he told both Howard and Thomas.[56]

Unbeknownst to Sherman, that same morning, scouts from Henry Slocum's Twentieth Corps cautiously approached Atlanta from the northwest and found a delegation of city officials carrying a flag of truce in the abandoned rebel trenches. The surrender ended "a day of terror and a night of dread" that marked the Confederate army's evacuation of Atlanta. The War Department in Washington was notified immediately but it would be a day before Sherman received the news and learned the explosions represented 81 carloads of ammunition. Two corps of Hood's army and the Georgia militia had slipped past Sherman to the east and reached Lovejoy Station while the Yankees were preoccupied with chasing Hardee.[57]

Union cavalry, sent by Sherman, entered Atlanta on the 2nd and returned with news of the surrender that evening. On September 3, Sherman himself wired Washington the immortal words "Atlanta is ours, and fairly won." The political implications in a war weary North were obvious. As Sherman himself wrote in his memoirs, "Success to our arms at that instant was therefore a political necessity; and it was all important that something starling in our interest should occur before the election in November. The brilliant success at Atlanta filled that requirement, and made the election of Mr. Lincoln certain." The president personally thanked General Sherman and his army noting their "distinguished ability and perseverance." General Grant celebrated Sherman's "skill and ability" and ordered every cannon in the Army of the Potomac fired in the direction of the enemy.[58]

By sundown on the 3rd, every one of Sherman's men knew of the fall of Atlanta, although skirmishing continued. Immediately, the sick and wounded were ordered to Jonesboro. Lieutenant Colonel Moore, Captains Bates and Dickson were seriously ill and required transport by ambulance. Major Bruff was also ill, but stayed with the regiment. Opdycke, as usual, enjoyed fine health, but he observed that the Union army as a whole needed a rest. The 4th, the Confederates opened fire on the 125th's camp near Lovejoy as the regiment was preparing to take a turn in the Union breastworks. Private Thomas Stahl was killed, and one of the two wounded, Corporal Chester Tuttle, was shot in the chest. Tuttle carried the bullet, lodged near his heart, for the rest of his life.[59]

Sherman decided not to fight at Lovejoy and withdraw to Atlanta. Bradley's brigade started up the railroad during the evening of the 5th. The last of the Fourth Corps pickets departed undetected at midnight. The 7th found Bradley's men near Rough and Ready and on the 8th, they arrived in Atlanta camping two miles northeast of the Augusta railroad. Opdycke's First Brigade brought up the corps' rear as it marched into Atlanta, but the feeling of final success was not diminished. Opdycke enjoyed the sight of the Union army marching through Atlanta's streets as conquerors. "Sherman's strategy was brilliant and complete," he proclaimed. Atlanta, Opdycke decided, was the pleasantest place he had seen since leaving Louisville, Kentucky. Overall the bombardment had done little damage, although many a wall could be seen perforated by a shell. Sherman promised his long suffering men "a full month's rest, with every chance to organize, receive pay, replenish clothing and prepare for a fine winter's campaign."[60]

On the morning of the 9th, the 125th was finally transferred to Opdycke's brigade. The four month Atlanta campaign cost the Tigers 39 killed and 213 wounded and nearly all those who remained were ground down, except the irrepressible Opdycke. Now they would bid farewell to their comrades in the old Third Brigade and begin a new chapter as part of Opdycke's First. To accommodate this move, the 15th Missouri went to Bradley's Third Brigade when the 125th departed. The Ohioans joined the 24th Wisconsin, and five small Illinois regiments: the 36th, 44th, 73rd, 74th and 88th. Newton told Opdycke he got the better deal and the Colonel agreed. He felt the regiments of the First Brigade were better than the depleted ones in the Third Brigade. Overall, Opdycke was "much pleased" with his new brigade. Emerson Opdycke had ended the summer of 1862 with his own regiment, and now, with the summer of 1864 drawing to a close, his own brigade.[61]

The four month Atlanta campaign was a success for the Union on many levels. Manufacturing centers and railroads in north Georgia were captured or destroyed. An important rail and supply hub for the Confederacy had been taken. The federal army learned a great deal about the art and practice of warfare. Northern morale was lifted and with it the election hopes of the Republicans. Lastly, the South lost manpower which it could not replace, perhaps 35,000 men. While the North suffered 32,000 casualties, they came from a much larger manpower pool. The Union began the campaign with the Southern Army of the Tennessee as the objective, but ended it with Atlanta itself as the goal. The result was that John Bell Hood and his army—albeit much smaller—were now free to regroup and fight another day. The venerable Fourth Corps, Emerson Opdycke and his Tigers would face the Confederates in battle again before 1864 closed. And when they did the results would be more conclusive than those achieved in the Atlanta campaign.[62]

16

From Atlanta to Pulaski

William T. Sherman had no intention of resting on his laurels after the fall of Atlanta. This feeling was reinforced by U. S. Grant. "So soon as your men are sufficiently rested, and preparations can be made," Grant wrote, "it is desirable that another campaign should be commenced. We want to keep the enemy constantly pressed to the end of the war." Sherman evicted the few remaining civilians in Atlanta and began to fortify the city. Of his decision to depopulate Atlanta, Sherman famously said, "If the people howl against my barbarity and cruelty, I will answer that war is war and not popularity seeking." John Bell Hood's actions would influence whatever the next phase of the Georgia campaign would be and Grant and Sherman debated the possibilities. Would Hood invade central Tennessee, concentrate on interrupting Sherman's supply line or, if Sherman marched for the sea, follow him? On September 10, the Georgia governor dealt Hood an unexpected blow when he withdrew the Georgia militia and sent them home to harvest crops.[1]

As Opdycke settled in as commander of the First Brigade, he brought the 125th's Captain Ridgely Powers and Lieutenant Hezekiah Steadman in as part of his staff which included eight officers, a brigade surgeon, five mounted orderlies and assorted clerks. Lieutenant Colonel Moore's contraband, "William," would serve the colonel. He proudly wrote his wife that no unpleasantness or reticence had marked the command change in the First Brigade. Opdycke felt this was due to his reputation as a commander. Time alone would tell how successful Emerson Opdycke would be as a brigade commander.[2]

On a visit to Lieutenant Colonel Moore—recuperating in an Atlanta residence from his intestinal problems—Opdycke found his friend immersed in his Bible. Moore had come to believe that his physical illness was God's punishment for abandoning the pulpit and Moore wished to return to the ministry immediately. The Colonel questioned whether General Thomas would accept Moore's resignation, but Surgeon McHenry decreed that Moore could no longer withstand the rigors of military service. David Moore's September 10 letter of resignation expressed his desire to "resume preaching the Gospel." Colonel Opdycke sent Moore's request up the chain of command without comment. Emerson Opdycke's real concern was that Major Bruff would become commander of the 125th, and this opinion was freely expressed to army headquarters in a note Opdycke attached to Moore's resignation. Bruff, Opdycke informed headquarters, should not be allowed to command the 125th because he was "entirely incapable of so an important a trust." Opdycke urged that Bruff be pressured to resign, and failing that involuntarily muster him out "for the good of the service."[3]

On September 11, on the advice of the assistant regimental surgeon, Dr. James Buchanan—his friend and messmate—Major Bruff applied for medical leave, having suffered from both typhoid fever and erysipelas. The next evening Opdycke summoned Bruff to brigade headquarters and asked him to resign. Opdycke told Bruff he believed him incompetent to command a regiment. Blind-sided, Bruff asked to be allowed to consider resigning overnight. The next day Bruff told Opdycke that to resign "would be doing myself a grave injustice." Opdycke took his pen to Bruff's medical leave request and marked it "Disapproved."[4]

Emerson Opdycke next saw David Moore—weak, but purportedly cured—on September 17 at brigade headquarters. The Lieutenant Colonel had been unable to hold his feelings in check, Opdycke wrote his wife, and tearfully thanked him for his comradeship and told Opdycke that he was a better man, even a better pastor, because of their association. Moore's resignation was accepted by army headquarters. Moore had ably led Opdycke's Tigers through the brutal Atlanta campaign. Now his service was over and Opdycke summarized the sentiments of most in the regiment when he wrote, "I deeply regret to lose him."[5]

On September 23, Major Bruff's leave application was denied. Angry, Bruff took the highly unusual step of summoning all the regimental officers and explaining what had transpired between he and the Colonel. He concluded by asking them to vote on his reputation and integrity. While some officers declined to participate, those who did gave only a lukewarm endorsement. Lieutenant Colonel David Moore left the 125th early on September 24, to begin his journey home. Moore was barely out of sight when Opdycke had Major Bruff arrested. To his wife, Opdycke cited "numerous irregularities" as his reason for arresting Bruff, who was not given a list of charges when he turned in his sword at brigade headquarters. Instead of a court martial, Bruff would face a board of officers who would judge his competence for command. Army headquarters appointed a board and it was scheduled to meet in less than a week. Opdycke wanted Bruff out of the 125th and out of his brigade. At least temporarily, he had succeeded.[6]

Active campaigning suspended, George Thomas asked Sherman for permission to send his wagon trains back to Chattanooga to reduce the amount of forage—14 pounds for every horse and mule—shipped to Atlanta each day. Thomas speculated that General Hood would not attack Atlanta, but would be tempted to disrupt the 300-mile Union supply line from Nashville. For his part Sherman didn't want his army to lose its fighting edge garrisoning Atlanta. In denying Thomas' request, Sherman indicated he wanted the Army of the Cumberland to be ready to march with little preparation.[7]

The Confederates were not idle. Federal scouts found Hood's army on September 21, 24 miles south of Atlanta encamped between Palmetto and the Chattahoochee River. Sherman now agreed with Thomas that Hood intended to disrupt the railroad from Chattanooga. Hood did as expected and sent General Joe Wheeler's gray cavalry to harass the railroad south of Chattanooga, while Confederate General Nathan Bedford Forrest's horsemen were to cut the railroad in middle Tennessee between Nashville and Chattanooga. On the 24th, Forrest's troopers raided Athens, Georgia, capturing trains and Union soldiers—including Private Henry Adams of the 125th—who were traveling from Nashville to Thomas' army. Confederate cavalry in the theater numbered almost 20,000 veteran horsemen—including mounted Kentucky infantry—and were superior to the Union cavalry. Sherman wired the War Department, "I can whip his infantry, but his cavalry is to be feared."[8]

Sherman responded to Hood's moves by sending a division from each of the Fourth and Seventeenth Corps north to Chattanooga and Rome, Georgia. Sunday, the 25th, Newton's Second Division was ordered to Chattanooga at 11 a.m. for "temporary" duty. Opdycke's brigade broke camp and marched two miles to Atlanta where the men boarded cars for Chattanooga, all in less than two hours—a source of pride for Opdycke. However, due to typical army delays, the bluecoats sat packed into 25 rail cars until 5 p.m. The division did not arrive in Chattanooga until 1 p.m. the next day, September 26. General Thomas joined them on the 29th.[9]

Because of the sudden move to Chattanooga, Major Bruff's hearing was postponed indefinitely. Bruff had not received a list of the charges against him in the prescribed time and had returned to the regiment while still under arrest. He was re-arrested, given the list of charges and banished from the brigade, quartering with a colonel from Chattanooga's garrison. Regimental command fell to the reliable Captain Ed Bates.[10]

On the 27th Opdycke's brigade went into camp near the old Fort Wood. Bradley's brigade was directed to Bridgeport, Alabama, a vital rail hub on the Tennessee River. In Chattanooga, Opdycke commanded four forts and three and a half miles of picket line, including 50 cannon. An anonymous petition was circulated that requested Opdycke be transferred to command of the city replacing a less energetic 54-year-old colonel. The petition was not an affirmation of Opdycke's leadership. It was probably instigated by veteran soldiers in the First Brigade who did not share the Colonel's fondness for drill and saw him as a martinet. Opdycke squashed the petition, explaining to his wife that petitions of that sort were usually "mischievous" in nature.[11]

John Newton was reassigned to a backwater post in Florida, in part because of a reputed fondness for drink. Brigadier General George Wagner of the Second Brigade was Newton's likely successor. The 35-year-old Ohio-born Wagner was a former Republican Indiana state senator with no military experience when he was appointed colonel of the 15th Indiana in 1861. A year later Wagner was a brigade commander at Shiloh and in another year a brigadier general. To date Wagner had a solid military record. A September 1864 article in the *Atlantic Monthly*, which compared volunteer officers to regular ones, prompted Colonel Opdycke to suggest to his wife that he felt regular officers were more careful of their men and had better discipline which made for better soldiers. This was contrary to the view of most volunteer soldiers, and reflected Opdycke's own philosophy of leadership. The Colonel's opinion of Wagner was lukewarm. "W. is a queer

Brigadier General George D. Wagner. After the war, Wagner returned to the law and farming in Indiana. He died unexpectedly in 1869. Reproduced from Clark, *Opdycke Tigers*.

fellow, but I shall get on somehow." When Captain Ed Whitesides returned to duty, there was no position open for him as an assistant adjutant general, so instead, the Captain accepted the position of provost marshal for Wagner's division.[12]

Hood crossed the Chattahoochee River on September 29, and took aim for Marietta. October 3, Sherman put his army in motion. With the Twentieth Corps holding Atlanta, Sherman's remaining infantry corps advanced to Kennesaw Mountain, Smyrna and Pace's Ferry. A single rebel infantry corps reached the railroad north of Kennesaw and captured two small federal garrisons. From atop Kennesaw Mountain, on October 5, Sherman could see enemy campfires and bonfires along eight miles of railroad destroyed from Big Shanty to Acworth—the rails heated and bent in Sherman's fashion. A Confederate division attacked the Union garrison at Allatoona early on October 5. After fierce fighting and 700 federal casualties, the rebels were repulsed.[13]

As the fighting raged at Allatoona, Opdycke took six regiments south from Chattanooga by rail toward Dalton, Georgia, to protect the railroad. The expedition proved unnecessary, and Opdycke's force first halted at Resaca, and then backtracked to Chattanooga via Cleveland, Tennessee. The 125th and two other regiments were sent in pursuit of a phantom rebel cavalry raid on the 7th. On the return trip, a derailment near Resaca killed an Illinois surgeon and injured Captain Bates, whose wrist was dislocated. A second accident near Rocky Face Ridge resulted in the death of two soldiers. The accidents were blamed on the poor condition of the hard-used railroad. On the 8th, the brigade returned to Chattanooga via Cleveland.[14]

Completely seduced by the idea of a march through Georgia to the sea, Sherman telegraphed General Thomas on the 9th of his decision to wreck the railroad from Chattanooga to Atlanta and then "to make for the sea coast." Sherman informed Grant, "By attempting to hold the [railroads], we will lose a thousand men each month, and will gain no result. I can make this march and make Georgia howl!"[15]

The 10th of October, Hood crossed the Coosa River 15 miles below Rome, and Sherman ordered his army to concentrate at Rome. On the 12th, the Yankees halted within three miles of the place, but Hood was gone, decamping first to Resaca and then Dalton. When Sherman heard Hood was at Resaca on October 13th, he set his army in motion to close on the enemy. The Fourth Corps, without Wagner's division, marched from Rome to Calhoun to the old Resaca battlefield. This was a trek of 35 miles in 24 hours only to find the smaller, but more nimble Confederate army had vanished. With Major General John Schofield in command at Chattanooga, George Thomas traveled back to Nashville to prepare for its defense. The entire division, including Opdycke's brigade, were left to garrison Chattanooga. The Yankees marked time by repairing the fortifications. Hood's continued raids on the railroad set the division in motion, mostly riding the rails. They went to Ringgold and back on the 15th and 16th, then to Bridgeport, Alabama, on the 17th, arriving at noon. Starting at 6 a.m., the division returned to Chattanooga on the 18th, arriving at noon. That afternoon the First Brigade led the march out to the old battlefield at Chickamauga camping at Lee and Gordon's Mill after dark, 13 miles from Chattanooga. Opdycke found that he was in the exact spot of his headquarters a year ago. Captain Clark noted that the 125th had the "novel experience of eating breakfast in Alabama, dinner at Chattanooga, Tenn., and supper in Georgia." Finally, to escape being trapped as Sherman slowly closed in, Hood retreated southwesterly into Alabama, arriving at Gadsden on the Coosa River on October 20. Tired of the game, Sherman concentrated his forces near Resaca on October 20 to await the Confederates next move. By

October 26, the Confederates were at Decatur, Alabama, on the Tennessee River. After another 40-mile move downriver to Florence, Hood's hungry army—surrendering rebels requested for food before all else—went into camp. A lack of supplies, which had to come from the deep South, kept the Southern army there for two weeks.[16]

Emerson Opdycke, once a critic of Abraham Lincoln, was a full supporter now that the Atlanta campaign had successfully concluded. He wanted to see an overwhelming majority for Lincoln, and thought that a change of administrations "would be dangerous" for the nation. This would be the first election that empowered Ohio soldiers in the field to vote. General elections were held in Pennsylvania, Ohio and Indiana on October 11, and the Republicans prevailed with a solid majority. Eighty-nine percent of Ohio soldiers voted for a Republican congressional candidate. "Everything has gone Union," Opdycke rejoiced. Since the fall of Atlanta, there was never any doubt.[17]

From the 19th to the 21st, Opdycke's brigade drove 1000 cattle from Chattanooga to Alpine, Georgia, near the Alabama state line. The cattle were handed off to another Fourth Corps unit, except for 75 retained by Opdycke's men. The brigade remained at Alpine on the 22nd and 23rd foraging the fertile countryside for food—honey, chickens, sweet potatoes, molasses, wheat and ripe persimmons—to supplement the beef. To make life more pleasant, Opdycke's brigade headquarters acquired a contraband—Julia—to cook and wash. As the rebels retreated in a southwesterly direction, every private in Sherman's army could see that General Hood had no intention of fighting in Georgia. The cat and mouse game ended on October 20 when Sherman concentrated his army in the Resaca-Villanow area.[18]

Once Sherman confirmed Hood's move west into Alabama, he ordered General Stanley to take the Fourth Corps to Bridgeport, Alabama, and to expect all future orders to come from General Thomas' headquarters in Nashville. All three of the Corps divisions united for the first time in 31 days at Alpine on October 27. Opdycke was directed to call in all his foragers, and, early on the 28th, his brigade led the Corps on a 21-mile march to La Fayette, Georgia. Opdycke found new servant in John, a sad-looking contraband sitting by the road who was happy to be emancipated and given new clothes. The 29th was another 25-mile march to Rossville. On the 30th, Stanley's men camped near Lookout Mountain.[19]

Sherman was eager to depart Atlanta. On the 1st, Grant asked Sherman, "Do you not think it advisable, now that Hood has gone so far north, to entirely ruin him before starting on your proposed campaign?" No, Sherman replied, that was to be George Thomas' task. On November 2, Grant approved Sherman's plan. Grant wrote in his *Memoirs*, "Sherman thought Hood would follow him, though he proposed to prepare for the contingency of the latter moving the other way while he was moving south, by making Thomas strong enough to hold Tennessee and Kentucky. I, myself, was thoroughly satisfied that Hood would go north."[20]

Hood's supply problems gave General Thomas time to consolidate his army. At the conclusion of October, Thomas was still marshaling his forces which included Nashville garrison troops, the Fourth and Twenty-Third Corps, two infantry divisions from Missouri, poorly mounted cavalry and miscellaneous detachments in central Tennessee, about 55,000 men. General Thomas directed Stanley to move the Fourth Corps to Athens, Alabama. General Wood's division was the first to board trains in Chattanooga for Athens and then Pulaski, Tennessee, on the Elk River, 73 miles south of Nashville. Wagner's Second division was the last to leave Chattanooga.[21]

November 1, the First Brigade boarded rail cars at 11 a.m., and departed for Athens, Alabama, on rickety rails and packed into 36 rail cars. Due to overcrowding, some of the infantrymen were forced to ride on the roofs of the cars in occasional cold rain. The brigade arrived at Athens at 1 a.m. on the 2nd during a rain storm. Wet and chilled, the men were given time to dry out before slogging along muddy roads to a campground four miles from Athens, having traveled 123 miles by rail.[22]

Opdycke's brigade was ordered to march to Pulaski, Tennessee—a distance of 40 miles—but the brigade had only one horse for each regiment and no wagons for the entire brigade! Opdycke ordered one of his aides, the resourceful Lieutenant Steadman, to find some transport and the Lieutenant scrounged a handful of teams—a few mules, old horses, oxen, carriages and old wagons. On October 30, the army paymaster caught up with the brigade—Opdycke sent $350 home and Captain Whitesides, $1000—but not everyone was paid before the order to move arrived so Colonel Opdycke detained the paymaster and his all-important little green safe and took him to Athens. In case the brigade was attacked by rebel cavalry or bushwackers, Opdycke concealed the paymaster in a corner of one of the wagons. The Colonel considered the brigade's appearance somewhat ridiculous, describing the "motley thong" he commanded as composed of old carts, unruly pack mules, blind horses and half-starved oxen. The caravan moved out at 2 p.m. on November 3 in the rain on muddy roads—seen as "wretched beyond description" by one veteran—and made 11 miles before making a wet camp at dark.[23]

The next morning, November 4, a three hour march brought the brigade to the Elk River. The division's other two brigades crossed first, and when it was their turn at noon, Opdycke's men removed their pants before plunging into the cold, fast river 100 yards wide. Of the frigid, waist deep river crossing, Opdycke jokingly wrote his wife, "they went in with white legs but came out with very red ones!" An eight mile trek followed before encamping five miles from Pulaski. Opdycke's brigade finally arrived the next morning, the 5th, and set up camp on a ridge two miles west of town. The First Brigade, and the rest of Wagner's division, deployed in the Pulaski vicinity while awaiting the campaign to assume some definite form. Construction of fortifications and organized foraging began immediately. When a rebel housewife objected to having her yard and picket fence torn up for fortifications, she was told, "We are going to put up a better one of earth, it will last longer." Opdycke's pioneers spent two days working on three small dams intended to raise the Elk River and impede the enemy, and by the evening of the 12th, these were completed and the water was 10 feet deep. A part of the defenses built by Opdycke's brigade was named Lunette Opdycke on the order of General Stanley. Colonel Opdycke had a fine headquarters in the home of a Union sympathizer and Wagner's division remained at Pulaski, Tennessee, 80 miles south of Nashville, until November 22.[24]

The Northern infantry regiments sent to defend central Tennessee where universally understrength and well worn—Sherman selected the healthiest and strongest units to accompany him. U. S. Grant ordered all new recruits sent to Nashville. When the First Brigade passed through Athens, Georgia, Lieutenant Ralsa Rice and another officer were dispatched to scour Nashville for able bodied soldiers from First Brigade regiments and bring them south. Since Nashville had fallen to the Union in 1862, it had become a huge commissary depot and hospital. Northern soldiers moving to and from the Tennessee and Georgia campaigns invariably passed through Nashville which teemed with camp followers, contrabands, convalescents, and unscrupulous supply sergeants. Nominally, there were 4000 soldiers stationed in the city—garrison, medical and commissary troops. Troops in transit swelled that number, and many found excuses to linger, making Nashville a haven for skulkers, deserters and cowards. Lieutenant Rice called Nashville "a place for those brave enough to leave home but whose courage failed when called upon to face bullets. Of such as these there was a small army here." In a visit to a prewar hotel nicknamed "Zollicoffer barracks," Rice found the place filled with soldiers drawing rations and performing no obvious duty. Rice was further disgusted by the numerous fit men he found on bloated hospital staffs, including recovered sick and wounded who some army doctors retained as attendants.[25]

In two days, the two officers corralled 250 men. The soldiers were packed into the mail train heading south. The locomotive was derailed by bushwackers seeking to rob it, near Thompson Station, Tennessee. The heavily armed federals easily repelled the shotgun-toting ex–Confederates. Unable to right to locomotive, word was sent back to Nashville for a repair crew, and the men appropriated a barn for the night and foraged for food. Rice and his companion were served a decidedly unappetizing baked opossum for dinner at a farm house. The men arrived in Pulaski the next day.[26]

Tuesday, November 8, was national election day. Abraham Lincoln's challenger, Democrat George McClellan, was saddled with a platform that labeled the war a failure, something that didn't sit well with soldiers. Ohio soldiers in the field voted in overwhelming numbers for Lincoln. Over 80 percent voted for Lincoln compared to 53 percent of Ohio voters at home. McClellan proved popular only with draftees eager to go home. Two days later, thanks to the telegraph, the results of the election reached the army in the field. Lincoln won easily; McClellan carried only Delaware, Kentucky and New Jersey. Colonel Opdycke found the Republican victory "grand."[27]

Major Bruff—under arrest since September—was released on October 26, but banned from any command duties in the 125th. He got his day in court on November 10 in Pulaski. The charges leveled against Bruff were intended to demonstrate that he was a disruptive force among the regiment's officer corps and that he lacked the military competence to command a regiment. In addition, Opdycke added a more serious charge under the 77th Article of War which stated that any officer under arrest could not leave confinement unless released by a superior office. Bruff was clearly guilty of this and risked being "cashiered" for the violation. None of the charges were a "smoking gun" of incompetence, but Bruff's discussions with junior officers, while egalitarian, were a violation of military etiquette.[28]

The examining board was to assess Bruff's "capacity, qualifications, propriety of conduct and efficiency" as a commander which would be a subjective enterprise. The board was composed of three experienced officers from the Second Division of the Fourth Corps. Brigadier General Luther Bradley, Third Brigade commander; Colonel Joseph Conrad of the 15th Missouri—transferred from the First Brigade to the Third—and Lieutenant Colonel George Smith commanding the 88th Illinois in Opdycke's First Brigade. In addition to Bruff and Opdycke, 10 witnesses testified over four days from November 10 to 14. All the witnesses were officers from the 125th.[29]

Friday morning, November 11, the first witness—Captain Ed Bates—took the stand. Bates had spent more time commanding the 125th than Bruff and enjoyed Opdycke's confidence. Asked about the working relationship between Bruff and Moore, Bates—not an impartial observer—replied that there was "not a hearty cooperation in the management of the affairs of the regiment." Bates chalked this up to "jealousy or revenge on the part of Major Bruff." Moore in a fit of disgust, once told Opdycke that Bruff was "the very devil himself in deceit." Asked about the Major's handling of the skirmish line—one of Opdycke's criticisms of Bruff—Bates said that "his management does not beget confidence in his ability." How did Bates evaluate Major Bruff's combat command capabilities? "I know," Bates responded, "that he is slow to appreciate or perceive the place and importance of prompt action." When Bruff rose to cross-examine Bates, he asked if Bates meant to insinuate that a majority of the 125th's officers distrusted him and lacked confidence in him. Bates replied, "I mean to be understood as saying so."[30]

On the afternoon of November 11, it was Opdycke's turn. Opdycke described Bruff as a "fair captain." What had been Bruff's conduct in action? "His personal conduct," Opdycke replied, "has been satisfactory, so far as bravery is concerned." As a field grade officer, the Colonel was highly critical of Bruff. "His greatest incompetency," Opdycke said, "lies I think in the slowness and uncertainty of his mental operations. He seldom if ever gets the views of his superiors correctly when given a separate command and seldom if ever executes a command correctly." Opdycke offered as example, Bruff's handling of skirmish lines in various fights.[31]

Cross-examined by Bruff, Opdycke reminded the Major of difficulties he had with his company during instruction in Cleveland. The company wanted Bruff removed as captain, but Opdycke supported him. "I have always believed," Opdycke suggested, "that because I sustained you then you retained the place." Bruff was a supporter of current Ohio Governor John Brough's policy of promoting based on seniority alone, and constantly advocated for its employment. "All of Bruff's clique are in rapture over Gov. Brough's policy," David Moore wrote Opdycke in February 1864. Opdycke and Moore favored former Governor Tod's merit promotions. This was a constant source of friction in the 125th as Bruff agitated for seniority based promotions. David Moore wrote of Brough's policy, "Aspiration is crushed out!" Bruff's seniority had made him major, and bequeathed him Opdycke's everlasting animosity. "I think this," a blunt Opdycke told Bruff, "through the influence of friends [your] commission was issued." When Opdycke was asked his opinion of what would happen to the 125th if Major Bruff was placed in command, he replied harshly, "I am most absolutely convinced from my knowledge of him as an officer, and as a man, that the regiment would be so demoralized as to destroy its usefulness and throw it into disgrace."[32]

Nine more officers appeared before the Board on November 12 and 14. Some had served in Bruff's company. None exhibited the animosity of Opdycke and Bates and all seemed to believe Bruff was a solid officer and maintained discipline. The examining board questioned Bruff in depth regarding skirmish line tactics and then adjourned on November 14. Bruff was allowed to enter a written statement and it was read and attached to the record. The Board's deliberations were held in closed session and the results sent to department headquarters in Nashville. On the 19th, Opdycke wrote his wife, that the trial was over. In Opdycke's biased eyes, the case against Bruff was strong. However, the final decision on Major Joseph Bruff rested with George Thomas.[33]

At 7 a.m., November 16, Sherman mounted his horse—a blazed-faced fast paced little gelding named Sam—and departed Atlanta with 62,000 men. Atlanta he left in devastation—400 homes and a few churches were all that remained—a fitting punishment Sherman felt for city whose name had been stenciled on every wagon and cannon his soldiers had captured in three years of war. Ahead, there would be little opposition. Behind, he left Hood to the two commanders in whom he had the greatest confidence—

Thomas and Schofield. The same day Bruff's hearing concluded, John Schofield assumed command of those forces in the field that opposed the Confederate army in south central Tennessee. As Sherman rode out of Atlanta he reflected on the military situation. "It surely was a strange event—two hostile armies marching in opposite directions, each in the full belief that it was achieving a final conclusive result in a great war ... and that for better or worse, it would end the war."[34]

17

COLUMBIA AND SPRING HILL

On November 20, Confederate president Jefferson Davis—desperate to compel Sherman to abandon Georgia even if it meant sending Hood's army to the Ohio River—ordered the combative Hood to take the offensive. The Confederates left Florence, Alabama, on the 21st with 50,000 to 55,000 infantry, cavalry and artillery. Standing between the rebels and Columbia, Tennessee, was Hood's West Point classmate, John Schofield, and about 25,000 bluecoats. Delay Hood at Pulaski—70 miles south of Nashville—until November 25th, Thomas had instructed Schofield while he pulled together his army in Nashville and remounted the Union cavalry.[1]

General Hood was well aware of federal dispositions along the Elk River in south-central Tennessee. With rapid marching and some luck, Hood believed he could place his army between Schofield's force and Columbia, Tennessee, on the Duck River—30 miles north—cutting Schofield off from Nashville and pinning him south of the natural barrier formed by the river. Major General Nathan Bedford Forrest's gray horsemen headed north and reached Lawrenceburg, Tennessee, on the 21st—20 miles west of Pulaski—just as the weather turned. The temperature dropped and cold rain changed to snow in squalls. Hood's planned rapid march slowed.[2]

Alert to the threat Forrest posed to his right flank, Schofield immediately made preparations for a retreat north. General Cox's division was sent to Lynnville—10 miles north of Pulaski where a road from Lawrenceburg intersected the railroad—on the 22nd. Wagner's Second Division of the Fourth Corps joined Cox in the evening. The First and Third Divisions of the Fourth Corps didn't arrive in Lynnville until late on the 23rd. When it was learned that federal cavalry had been driven out of Mount Pleasant—just 10 miles southwest of Columbia—by a force of Southern infantry, Cox's division was immediately ordered to march 18 miles north to Columbia. By rapid marching on the turnpike, Cox's men arrived at Columbia early on the 24th and were able to intercept Forrest's cavalry just two miles west of town. Cox's division took a position one mile west of town with his right resting on the Duck River. General Stanley corps arrived about 10 p.m. and Wagner's division took a position on Cox's left that extended to the Pulaski Pike. General Wood's division fell in on Wagner's left facing south, and Kimball was on Wood's left extending the Union line to the Duck River above the town. The 125th found its place at 11 a.m., and constructed fortifications until dark. General Thomas ordered Schofield to hold the railroad and pontoon bridges over the Duck River in Columbia as long as possible while he weighed his strategic options.[3]

On November 25, the opposing pickets on the Columbia line skirmished all day. Mid-afternoon, Opdycke sent four regiments, including the 125th, down the pike toward

Pulaski on a scout. With companies A and F of the 125th acting as flankers, the Ohioans drove the enemy pickets down the pike a mile before meeting a large body of Forrest's dismounted cavalry unwilling to yield. Opdycke backtracked to Columbia. A new defensive line was begun north of the Duck River on low poorly defensible ground. A determined Confederate attack on the line south of the river on the 26th was repulsed. After dark on the 27th, all federal troops began withdrawing to the north bank. Wagner's division was the last to cross, and the 125th Ohio remained on picket duty out on the Pulaski pike 3 a.m. on the 28th when it crossed the railroad bridge just before it was burned. Second Lieutenant Henry Glenville and 30 men from the First Brigade were the last to leave after destroying military stores in town. The diminutive Glenville led a perilous crossing of the burning bridge while rebel pickets cheered them on. During the forenoon, the 125th moved two miles upriver, hastily built fortifications and then were permitted their first sleep in two days.[4]

Forrest's cavalry forced a crossing of the Duck River at Davis Ford and Huey's Mill— five to 10 miles upstream from Columbia—on the 28th, and cut the retreating federal cavalry off from Columbia. With no cavalry available on the 29th, Schofield sent a brigade up the Duck River on a reconnaissance and they discovered Confederate infantry—two infantry corps without artillery—crossing the river and moving north. Schofield realized that Hood—leaving his artillery and two divisions on the turnpike at Columbia—had stolen a march on him. It would be a 10-mile race up the turnpike for Spring Hill. Still, it was essential for Schofield to hold out in Columbia a bit longer to get all the Union wagon trains headed north, and to deny the rebel artillery the use of the turnpike. The Twenty-Third Corps two divisions and Tom Wood's Fourth Corps division were chosen to remain in Columbia, while General Stanley was ordered to Spring Hill with his two remaining divisions. The wagon train with 700 four-mule army wagons started immediately with a single Indiana infantry regiment as escort. A Union cavalryman described the wagon train as a "conglomeration of army wagons, ambulances, negroes and white refugees and the whole riffraff of a retreating army." Wagner's division led the infantry march for Spring Hill and Opdycke's brigade led the division. Four companies of the 73rd Illinois had the point as skirmishers. Schofield would stall for time at Columbia as long as he dared. But had he taken too big a risk?[5]

The wagons arrived in Spring Hill around noon and began parking west of town. The Indiana infantrymen marched through the village and past the female seminary where they were jeered by "she-rebels." When the infantry reached the north side of town, they discovered Forrest's horsemen—2000 to 3000 of them, some dismounted— preparing to attack. Only 300 Indianans stood between the enemy and the wagon train.[6]

Opdycke's brigade led the division' march, and a mile from Spring Hill, they encountered civilians fleeing the marauding gray cavalry. General Wagner ordered Opdycke to double-quick his brigade and then personally rode ahead to the village. What Wagner found in Spring Hill was federal cavalry retreating through the streets in the face of determined Southern horsemen. "Get out of the way, you sore-backed cavalry!" Wagner yelled at the blue troopers. The Indiana wagon escort and the four companies of Opdycke's 73rd Illinois that had been deployed as skirmishers, all were rallying behind a makeshift barricade. Opdycke's brigade, having just marched over 10 miles, was almost running as they followed in Wagner's wake. What was left of the 74th and 88th Illinois after the Atlanta campaign and expired enlistments had been consolidated into a battalion under one command and were pressed into service as skirmishers. The rest of the First Brigade formed a line facing northeast and advanced, shooing the rebel horsemen before them. The 125th Ohio was the fifth regiment in the column on the march and went straight through the town on the macadamized pike. On the north side of Spring Hill, the Tigers formed on the brigade left flank.[7]

"Just in the nick of time," wrote an Indiana sergeant of the First Brigade's charge through town, "in our very last extremity, a battery and brigade of the Fourth Corps arrived upon the field; a counter-charge was made. Forrest driven from the field in disorder, and the train saved." General Stanley told Wagner to seize control of enough ground to safely park the wagon trains in Spring Hill. The rebel troopers had vanished. An Illinois lieutenant recalled, "Outside of our line not a living thing could be seen."[8]

Opdycke's brigade continued north along the turnpike until about 2 p.m. when it met more Confederate cavalry moving south along the pike toward Spring Hill from Thompson's Station, a railroad depot four miles to the north. When they saw Opdycke's bluecoats, they rolled off to their left. Colonel Opdycke roared at his men, "On the right, into line! Begin firing!" The brigade unwound like a whiplash and rolled into line facing east. As every soldier came to the front, he brought his gun to his shoulder and began firing. The enemy troopers once again disappeared. The 125th marched to a dry creek where the banks formed a natural barricade. A ridge to the front blocked the view and with it the knowledge that General Cheatham's gray infantry corps was forming less than a mile away.[9]

Captain Bates was once again commanding the 125th—Major Bruff was now in Nashville—and Opdycke ordered him to deploy into a heavy skirmish line across the pike and facing north. The determined Confederate horsemen reappeared—these were Forrest's men—and they made repeated attempts at the wagons by flank attacks. Opdycke sent the 44th Illinois to the left of Bates' men, and the 24th Wisconsin to the Illinoisan's left until his thin line stretched to the railroad station one half mile northwest of Spring Hill.[10]

Colonel Lane's brigade had been following Opdycke's men and was roughly formed on the First Brigade's right. Lane drove the enemy from a hill half a mile east of the village after a sharp fight before retiring back halfway to the village where his veterans began to dig in. The Confederate cavalry kept Opdycke and Lane's brigades occupied with attempts to reach the wagons parked by the pike and the railroad station. Late in the afternoon, a squadron of hard charging rebel troopers came thundering down one of the many country lanes that crisscrossed area, and rode through the skirmish line. They were only dissuaded by a volley of musketry from a full regiment.[11]

At the same time Wagner had ordered Opdycke forward, General Stanley ordered General Bradley to halt his brigade—the last to arrive at Spring Hill—two miles from the village so that the artillery could pass before he resumed his march. The Fourth Corps six batteries were positioned on a ridge west of the Columbia Pike. General Stanley then sent Bradley to a wooded knoll half of a mile from town and to the right of Lane's brigade's position. Bradley's brigade contained 1500 men in six small regiments of which one third were untested recruits and draftees. Bradley formed with the 64th Ohio—five companies deployed as skirmishers—and four other regiments into a battle line and drove the enemy cavalry back almost a mile. The Yankees halted when they encountered steadfast Confederate infantry from the re-instated Frank Cheatham's corps which was three times the strength of Wagner's entire division. General Stanley had Opdycke and Lane take a semi-circular position eastward around the town so as to present the longest front possible in hopes of the deceiving the rebels into thinking their numbers were greater.[12]

After the encounter with enemy infantry, Bradley was ordered back to a wooded knoll—a dangerously exposed position—a half mile south of town that covered the southeastern approaches to Spring Hill. The bulk of Hood's infantry didn't arrive at Spring Hill until 3 p.m., but when it did, a leading regiment of Major General Patrick Cleburne's division attacked the left flank of the 64th Ohio's skirmish line. Well protected behind fence rails, the 64th offered a determined resistance. The Ohioans fell back to the wooded knoll occupied by the rest of the brigade after delaying for an hour of so a half-hearted Confederate push toward Spring Hill.[13]

Late in the afternoon—an hour before sunset—two Southern attacks on Bradley's exposed position by Pat Cleburne's division were repulsed. A third got around Bradley's right. The 64th Ohio and 42nd Illinois retreated as the enemy reached their rear and the brigade's situation had become so dire that it was one veteran judged "a question of legs to escape capture." From right to left the retreat became disorderly as each successive regiment broke for the rear. Opdycke expressed sympathy for Bradley but considered the retreat a shameful rout. Bradley's men finally reformed on the line of Opdycke's and Lane's brigades. General Bradley was shot in the arm—a wound similar to the one Opdycke had sustained at Resaca—and left the field. General Wagner took personal command of the brigade. Opdycke sent the 36th Illinois to stiffen the Third Brigade. The firepower of massed Corps' artillery was instrumental in stopping the enemy advance—the hail of shrapnel and canister created the illusion that more than a single federal division held the line. The Third Brigade lost about 200 men, including Bradley, who was replaced by the 15th Missouri's Colonel Joseph Conrad. Bradley's bravery at Spring Hill was eventually rewarded with a regular army commission as lieutenant colonel. The 125th had just one man wounded at Spring Hill, Private Quincy Latin, previously wounded at Resaca.[14]

As the day drew to a close, Wagner's division was spread in a semicircular line facing east stretching from the Columbia Pike south of the village around Spring Hill to the Nashville and Decatur Railroad station on the northwest. Opdycke estimated his brigade covered almost three miles and was stretched so thin as to be little more than a strong skirmish line. At nightfall, the 125th's Company B was posted at the turnpike tollgate north of town. They hastily barricaded the road. The campfires of the enemy could be seen—Ralsa Rice called them "so many blazing furnaces"—just over the hills a half mile to the east. Their light illuminated the turnpike running north to Thompson's Station.[15]

When the sound of heavy artillery firing during Bradley's engagement reached General Hood, he immediately suspected that Thomas had re-enforced Schofield from Nashville. With newfound caution, Hood sent General Stewart to position his corps on Cheatham's right east of Spring Hill behind Rutherford Creek. Stewart's corps would be in position to swing across the turnpike and block it. Stewart's soldiers bivouacked along a dry creek about 11 p.m. a mile north of Spring Hill—likely the same one used by the 125th earlier. Cox, Wood and Kimball were to withdraw from Columbia after dark. Each division was to be prepared to face east on a moment's notice if attacked. Stewart's men approached to within just 600 yards of the Columbia pike north Spring Hill, but made no effort to block the road. Instead they waited as Cheatham's corps—infected with caution—moved toward Bradley and Lane's brigades southeast of Spring Hill. General Cheatham later said of his reluctance to attack the bluecoats that the federal line "looked a little too long." Excess caution by Stewart and Cheatham allowed the Union army to avoid encirclement. Nightfall brought an end to the fighting.[16]

During the day, some of Forrest's cavalrymen had occupied Thompson's Station on the turnpike three miles north of town, well in Schofield's rear. When Schofield learned this about 9 p.m., he hurried north with two brigades from his old corps. At the northern edge of Spring Hill, Schofield encountered Lieutenant Ralsa Rice's Company B picket post at the tollgate. Schofield asked Rice about the campfires visible along the turnpike. Rice replied, "The enemy was there at dark." Schofield ordered a staff officer to bring forward a section of the first artillery battery he encountered and one company from the first infantry regiment. When these troops arrived, Schofield sent them up the road. No enemy was found, and the still of the night remained unbroken. Schofield led his two brigades to Thompson's Station unmolested, and dispatched aides to Franklin to telegraph a report to General Thomas.[17]

Schofield retraced his ride to Spring Hill, arriving at midnight. Cox's division was just reaching the southern outskirts of town where they could see the eastern hills illuminated with Hood's campfires, hear muffled camp conversations and watch Southern pickets walking post past their campfires. Cleburne's men heard the Yankee's and Cleburne informed Hood, who never replied. With the road clear to Thompson's Station, Schofield sent Cox up the turnpike. Stanley's corps was to follow. Schofield and Stanley debated the fate of the wagon train—Schofield wanted to burn it—and Stanley's argument to save it prevailed. The wagons followed Wood's division and eventually Kimball's division fell in with them. His army in motion, Schofield turned his horse toward Franklin, 12 miles up the pike.[18]

The fence corners near the pike were occupied by exhausted, sleeping rebels who barely stirred. Stealth was critical as Cox's troops passed Stewart's right flank. But there was no hiding the repetitive tread, clattering accouterments and rumble of wagons as the bluecoats eased past Hood's army. Cox's division marched into Thompson's Station and on to Franklin safely. Wood and Kimball followed. Tom Wood told Colonel Kimberly of the 41st Ohio, "Let your men keep well closed, and move in silence." Wagner's Second Division would bring up the rear. One of Bradley's officers remembered the night march as "the most trying in more than 3 years of soldiering." Rice and his comrades spent the rest of the night watching a line of soldiers, wagons and artillery perhaps 10 miles long march north to Franklin. Of the situation facing the Union army on November 29, Opdycke called it "an almost desperate situation." The 6th Ohio artillery was ordered by General Stanley himself to leave Spring Hill and head up the pike just after midnight. Stanley reportedly told the artillerymen: "I desire to say to you that you have not one chance in a hundred of reaching that place. There are more than thirty thousand rebels between you and Franklin, and you will undoubtedly be attacked or cut off before you get through." If attacked Stanley continued, the artillerymen should spike the guns, burn the carriages and caissons and ride the battery horses to Franklin. The artillerymen decided to fire a couple of rounds before doing anything so drastic.[19]

Around midnight General Hood was informed that Yankees, identified as stranglers, were marching north on the Franklin Pike past his right flank near Thompson's Station. An investigation at 2 a.m. found no activity on the pike south of town. An infantry division of butternuts was ordered to block the road, but the moon had set and the rebels—some Tennesseans—failed to locate the pike. By good fortune and Confederate bungling, two Northern infantry corps quietly slipped past the enemy to reach Thompson's Station. General David Stanley suggested the high risk march past the Confederates was akin to "treading on thin ice over a smoldering volcano." The only hitch had been an attack by Forrest's cavalry on the road north of Spring Hill that destroyed 10 wagons. At 3 a.m.,

Cox's vanguard reached the Winstead Hills, a prominent landmark just south of Franklin on the turnpike. Cox himself rode ahead to the first house on the south edge of village, the Carter homestead—a "little brick cottage," Cox called it—and established his headquarters.[20]

Two Kentucky regiments that served as rearguard at Columbia reached Spring Hill at 4 a.m. just as George Wagner's division was departing for Franklin. The division's Second and Third brigades were marched in parallel columns along the pike as they headed north. About 5 a.m., rail cars remaining at the station west of town were set alight. Opdycke's brigade had been the first into Spring Hill on November 29 and now was the last to leave. The Colonel later boasted that he was prepared to fight his brigade to the last man to save Schofield's army.[21]

Opdycke wanted to be as far north of Spring Hill as possible when the sun rose at 6:30. He arranged his seven regiments with three on the pike, two as rearguard and one each as flankers. Stanley gave Opdycke a two gun section from Battery M of the 4th U.S. Artillery as extra firepower. As rearguard, the First Brigade was to collect stragglers that were clogging the turnpike, lingering in fence corners and sleeping woodlots along the pike. Draftees and new recruits filled the depleted ranks of old regiments and completely new ones. Nearly a third of the men in Conrad's (Bradley's) brigade were recent replacements. These green soldiers were not physically fit and weighted down with overcoats and "immense" knapsacks. Opdycke ordered his men to cut the knapsacks free and use their bayonets to move the stragglers. Lieutenant Rice recalled, "When one was overtaken our boys would run up behind, cut the man's straps and, with threatening bayonets, compel a faster gait." Rice estimated the First Brigade herded 300 stragglers north. Opdycke called the task of herding hundreds of tired, inexperienced soldiers up the turnpike "almost indescribable." Southerners pursuing Schofield's men found a bounty of abandoned equipment.[22]

Skirmishing with cavalry began in the small valley at Thompson's Station. Forrest's troopers harassed the brigade and the combined 74th and 88th Illinois—the rearguard—suffered a few casualties while mortally wounding a Confederate officer. An officer in the 73rd Illinois described the fighting on the march to Franklin. "Small squads of Hood's men would ride up on the hills behind us or on either side, and amuse themselves by firing at us at long distance…. With more or less skirmishing, we arrived on the high hills south of Franklin about noon."[23]

"The failure of the Confederate high command at Spring Hill has endured to this day as one of the greatest missed opportunities of the entire war," historian Wiley Sword wrote of Hood's failure to trap Schofield in Spring Hill. The fiasco was a compounding of errors in judgment and will that left General Hood understandably irate. Typically, Hood cast blame on another, Cheatham in this case. The Corps commander's performance had been "absolutely woeful." But Hood's generalship was also to blame especially his tendency to not be certain his orders were executed. General Cox suggested that John Bell Hood was lacking the judgment and flexibility "to act with vigor in the presence of circumstances which throw doubt upon his plan." Hood did ask that Cheatham be relieved, but later dropped the demand. Both foes could agree with Luther Bradley's assessment when he wrote, "If only the enemy had shown his usual boldness, I think he would have beaten us disastrously."[24]

18

FRANKLIN

The village of Franklin was no stranger to war. The 125th Ohio had spent the spring of 1863 constructing fortifications and fending off Confederate cavalry in the town that sent its sons into Confederate service. Franklin lay within a deep, northeast curve of the Harpeth River south of Nashville. The Columbia Turnpike—the strategically crucial, hard surface, toll road—ran arrow straight into Franklin from the south. Located on the toll road on the south edge of town was the Carter family homestead. "We became well acquainted with the Carter household," Lieutenant Ralsa Rice recalled of their spring 1863 posting, "and were indebted to this family for many acts of kindness." One hundred seventy-five yards southeast of the farmhouse was the Carter cotton gin. Jacob Cox and his staff commandeered the Carter parlor as a temporary headquarters when they reached Franklin shortly before dawn on November 30. After an exhausting and stressful 20-mile march past Hood's army, Cox and his officers dropped their pistol and sword belts and fell asleep on the hard floor.[1]

Major General John Schofield intended to push across the Harpeth River and on to the safety of Nashville's defenses. When Cox's division arrived at Franklin before dawn, Schofield discovered that no pontoon wagons had arrived from Nashville to replace the damaged bridges over the Harpeth. Getting the wagon train, artillery and soldiers of his army across the river became Schofield's priority. The muddy banks of the old wagon ford were graded by federal pioneers to render it more useful. Planks were to be laid over the damaged deck of the narrow railroad bridge while pioneers rebuilt the wrecked wagon bridge from the water up. Until the Harpeth was bridged, the Yankees pouring into Franklin would be trapped with their backs to the river—a military condition no army commander wanted. Schofield wired Thomas, "A worse position than this for an inferior force could hardly be found."[2]

At dawn, Schofield found Cox at Carter farmhouse. "I never saw him so manifestly disturbed." Cox recalled of Schofield's visit. Schofield relinquished operational command of the two Twenty-Third Corps divisions to Cox and instructed him to construct a defensive earthworks centered on the Carter farmstead knoll to protect the army and its wagon trains in town.

Fort Granger—built partially by the 125th Ohio in 1863 on the high ground north of the river—had artillery that could send shells almost two miles south onto the level river plain east of town. Cox put his men to work improving the 1863 trenches which offered a mile long, semi-circular fortified line anchored on the river south of town and extending to the Carter Creek Pike north of Carter's farm. The key to Franklin's defense was the knoll where the Carter house stood on the Columbia Pike, a fact recognized by

The 125th charged through the back yard and desperate fighting swirled around the Carter House. Men from the 125th took up sharpshooting positions on the second floor, far right of photograph, either side of the chimney, not visible from this view. The turnpike is on the far side of the house. Library of Congress.

Opdycke in 1863, and now by General Cox who added artillery batteries to the defenses around the Carters' farmhouse.[3]

"They worked like beavers, using houses, fences, timber and dirt in their works," a local resident recalled, "By 2 o'clock of that day they had completed their breastworks." However, Union columns continuing to march up the Columbia Pike necessitated that an opening—referred to as a wagon gap—wide enough to accommodate double lines of wagons or artillery be provided on the Carter knoll. A few rods to the rear, this opening was guarded by a hundred yards of shallow breastworks, or retrenchment, that cut across the Pike from just east of the road to the far side of the Carter garden on the west. Confederate general Stephen Lee later conceded that the Franklin line was "one of the best I have ever seen." One Yankee remarked, "Our men were experts at building breastworks, but were novices at fighting behind them."[4]

For his Franklin headquarters the morning of the 30th, General Schofield chose the home of Emerson Opdycke's Unionist friend, Dr. Daniel Cliffe. For his part, Cliffe—who was also a boyhood friend of General Stanley—and his wife wanted a place on the wagon caravan heading to Nashville. Schofield arrived at the doctor's house about 9 a.m. after giving instructions for the bridging the river, ate breakfast and slept until noon. General Stanley was unwell, and when he reached Franklin later that morning, he joined Schofield at Cliffe's. Perhaps not by coincidence, by noon all 700 Union army wagons were drawn up in Franklin in a field called Cliffe's meadow.[5]

Two miles south of the Carter knoll on the Columbia Pike a row of hills marked the

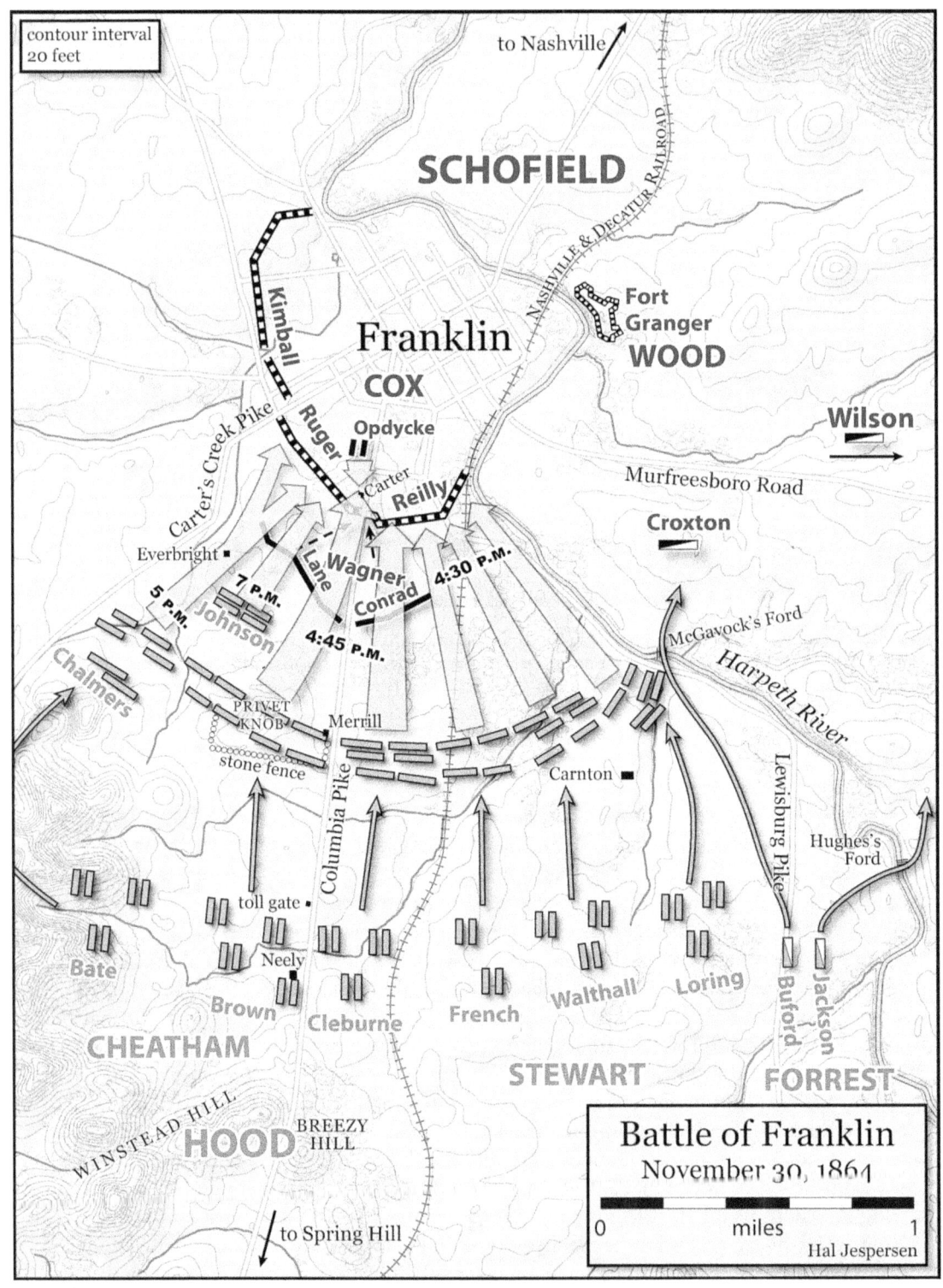

Battle of Franklin, November 30, 1864. Confederate assault and position of Wagner's Brigades. Map by Hal Jespersen.

south edge of the Harpeth River valley. The Turnpike crossed the hills through a gap between Winstead Hill on the west and Breezy Hill on the east. General Nathan Kimball's First Division of Stanley's corps reached Winstead Hill from Spring Hill about 10 a.m. Kimballs' men halted and Wood's division passed through them and continued straight up the Pike to Franklin. Schofield sent Wood's men across the Harpeth to protect the army's rear and the turnpike to Nashville. The Union right flank was lightly defended and Cox directed Kimball's division to occupy and fortify a line from the Carter Creek Pike to the Harpeth River below Franklin.[6]

Shortly before 11 a.m., George Wagner's division reached Winstead and Breezy Hills. General Stanley sent instructions to halt the division on the heights so the men could get breakfast. To the consternation of Opdycke's men, Wagner ordered the First Brigade to remain vigilant and keep the Confederate cavalry at bay by occupying the pass between the hills as well as the crest of Breezy Hill. General Stanley sent a two gun section of Battery G, 1st Ohio Light Artillery, to Opdycke, to relieve the 4th U.S. Artillery that had accompanied the brigade from Spring Hill. Colonels Lane and Conrad's brigades were sent to Opdycke's left and started their cooking fires. Although most of Kimball's division had departed for the right flank of Cox's defenses, one brigade still occupied Winstead Hill west of the turnpike. Forrest's cavalry probed the Union rearguard, found no soft spot and prudently withdrew to await infantry support. The brigade from Kimball's division departed for Franklin, and when more of the enemy appeared, Wagner placed his entire division in battle formation.[7]

Shortly after noon, and without orders from Stanley, Wagner got his men on the turnpike to Franklin with Colonel Lane in the lead. Opdycke's brigade remained the rearguard. The weather was exceptional for the last day of November in Tennessee—60 degrees and dry—a pleasant Indian summer day. Lane and Conrad's men adopted a leisurely pace. "When within half a mile of town," Wagner noted in his official report, "I met a staff officer from General Stanley, with written orders directing me to re-occupy the heights and hold them unless too severely pressed." Stanley also instructed Wagner to relieve Opdycke's brigade as rearguard, assigning either Lane or Conrad those duties. Opdycke's rearguard was just clearing the hills when they got the order to return.[8]

Wagner had spent the ride from Spring Hill feeding his rising anger. Like many of the soldiers in the Fourth Corps, he felt that Schofield was unfairly favoring his Twenty-Third Corps at their expense. Furthermore, Wagner felt his division was getting the worst of it. Had not almost all of the casualties at Spring Hill been from his division? Adding injury to insult, Wagner's horse had fallen leaving him with a badly bruised leg. The usually reliable Wagner was about to let anger, frustration and fatigue get the best of him.[9]

Opdycke's men had barely completed repositioning themselves on Breezy Hill when real trouble appeared. Through field glasses, Colonel Opdycke could clearly see two approaching Southern infantry corps—two parallel lines of infantry with flags unfurled—marching toward the hills. "Our last halt," Lieutenant Rice later wrote, "was made at the hills about two miles from Franklin. From the summit of one of these we had a view of the entire rebel army following us. They were forming for some purpose.... In their butternut, clay-colored clothing they looked like sands of the seashore—and fully as numerous."[10]

The Ohio artillery battery unlimbered its two three-inch rifled cannon in the road between the hills. Opdycke had the artillerymen fire a few rounds of explosive shells and solid shot at the advancing enemy. This gave the rebels temporary pause only, any holes in their lines closing quickly. A few hundred yards away, Southern sharpshooters crouched behind a stone wall and their English-made sniper rifles proved dangerous for mounted officers and artillerymen. A keen eyed sharpshooter put a bullet into Opdycke's horse, "Ben," about a half inch from the Colonel's thigh. Ben staggered, but kept his feet and Opdycke quickly found a new mount. Opdycke ordered the artillery to destroy the stone fence that sheltered enemy sharpshooters. The Colonel was told that Ben would die, but the horse was still alive two days later.[11]

The Confederates knew by now that only a brigade held the heights. Rather than fight the federals for the high ground, General Hood decided to simply flank the Union rearguard by sending Stewart corps to the right on a country lane that pointed toward the Lewisburg Pike near the Harpeth River. Cheatham's corps was behind Stewart and those rebels continued straight up the pike toward Opdycke. If Stewart got around Breezy Hill and Wagner's flank, the Johnnies could cut the Second Division off from Franklin. "Colonel Opdycke sent a messenger to report to me," Wagner noted in his report, "that the enemy was moving two heavy columns of infantry against our line … one column turning my left flank. I there upon withdrew my command and retired toward the main line." Wagner had decided that two enemy infantry corps was reason enough to retire and notified General Stanley. By 1:30 p.m., Wagner and his men—including Opdycke—were headed up the Pike toward Franklin's defenses.[12]

From the high ground on the north bank of the Harpeth, General Schofield could see General Cheatham's column marching over the crest of the Winstead Hill before splitting right and left when it reached the valley floor. The many Tennesseans in Cheatham's ranks raised a cheer at the sight of the Harpeth Valley stretched out before them. For those Yankee officers watching, the sight went from fascinating to ominous. What was Hood going to do? Schofield's tactical plan depended on Hood employing another flanking movement as he had at Columbia and Spring Hill.[13]

Half way between Franklin and Winstead Hill, just west of the Columbia Pike, stood a 70 foot limestone outcropping—identified as Privet Knob or Merrill Hill. As George Wagner rode along the Columbia Pike, he decided to reconsider Stanley's orders and make another attempt to delay the Confederates. As Colonel Lane's brigade drew abreast of Privet Knob around 1 p.m., Wagner ordered it and the Ohio artillery to Privet Knob. Lane's soldiers now became the rearguard—relieving Opdycke as per Stanley's order. The General continued Conrad and Opdycke's brigades toward Franklin as Lane's men, isolated in front of a growing Confederate presence, forlornly watched their comrades march toward the safety of Franklin.[14]

The ground between Privet Knob and Carter's knoll was slightly undulating, but offered no place for a suitable defensive stand. Nevertheless, in a seemingly arbitrary decision, George Wagner again halted, this time 600 yards south of the Carter knoll. Conrad was instructed to deploy his brigade in a fallow cotton field east of the Columbia Pike in a line roughly parallel to Cox's main line in the rear. Conrad utilized a slight rise, placing his own 15th Missouri west of the pike. The east flank of the brigade was held by the venerable 64th and 65th Ohio. Skirmishers were sent forward a full half mile. A small woodlot blocked the direct view down the Columbia Pike beyond the skirmishers. The ground to the left and in the rear, however, was "bare as a floor of any obstruction," and offered a clear view to the river. Conrad's position could not be seen by a man standing on the Carter knoll.[15]

When Opdycke's First Brigade arrived at Conrad's position. Wagner gestured for

Opdycke to put his men into the line on Conrad's right, west of the Columbia Turnpike. Emerson Opdycke was weary from hours in the saddle with no sleep or food, protecting the army's rear and shepherding stragglers. Opdycke took one look at the position Wagner had selected, saw its vulnerabilities and refused the order. Wagner repeated it. Opdycke had a reputation for a fiery and quick temper. He admitted as much in a letter of apology to the patient Luther Bradley after a quarrel. An even tempered man like Bradley, Opdycke wrote, "may not readily sympathize with one whose temper is less fortunately governed."[16]

Opdycke tried to "govern" his temper and pointed out that his men hadn't slept in two days, had been on rearguard duty since before sunrise deploying and redeploying in line of battle when not marching off the road through fields, brush and trees. The First Brigade had not eaten or even made coffee that day. Opdycke felt confident enough in his position to criticize Wagner's decision to fight in the middle of an open field, suggesting that those brigades in front of the earthworks were "in good position to aid the enemy and nobody else." Then Opdycke turned his back to Wagner and pointed his horse toward Franklin. Wagner kept pace as the two men argued and the Brigade dutifully followed. Finally, Wagner relented in the face of Opdycke's insubordination and decided the situation met Stanley's directive to place Opdycke's brigade in a supporting role. An exasperated General Wagner purportedly told Opdycke, "Well, Opdycke, fight when and where you damn please. We all know you'll fight." Opdycke, according to Lieutenant Rice, replied, "I think we can be of more use in rear of the main line."[17]

The argument concluded in the turnpike near the Carter house, so Wagner stopped to inform Cox of his troop dispositions. General Cox directed that Opdycke's men be placed on the west side of the pike a couple hundred yards north—toward the river—of the Carters' brick farmhouse. Cox also told Wagner to follow Stanley's previous orders "to hold the enemy back until they developed a heavy force manifestly superior to his own, and then slowly retire within the lines to fend off any attack." Furthermore, Cox indicated that when he withdrew, Wagner should place his brigades with Opdycke. By 2:30 p.m. the First Brigade's six regiments were massed on the reverse slope of the Carter knoll. "By some strange theory of combat," Captain Hinman of the 65th Ohio later wrote of his position, "these brigades were placed in this advanced position ... to receive the first impact of the expected charge and deaden its initial violence.... A single regiment deployed as skirmishers would have been far better." This last tactic was employed by most federal divisions on the line.[18]

The First Brigade had stacked arms in the yards and gardens north of the Carter house. Cox told Opdycke to keep his brigade in readiness, and Opdycke arranged it in a two regiment front formation with three regiments on either side of the turnpike facing the vulnerable wagon gap at the Carter homestead. The 125th Ohio was west of the pike, 150 yards north of the Carter House. A picket fence was knocked apart for firewood, and soon the aroma of coffee and frying bacon filled the air—their first food of the day. Captain Bates ordered each man's musket loaded and the bayonet fixed. Colonel Opdycke rode into town to visit the Cliffes. When Wagner's advanced skirmish line became engaged about 3:30, Opdycke's Tigers debated the possibility of a fight.[19]

While Opdycke and Wagner argued, John Bell Hood studied the Union defenses from Winstead Hill. The Civil War had taken much from Hood physically, yet he was absolutely devoted to his cause. Standing in the warm sun, a crutch supporting him, Hood would have to make a decision that would determine the fate of his proud army, his campaign into Tennessee and possibly the Confederacy. Schofield in Franklin was 12 miles from Nashville and its stout defenses, years in the making. The Yankees had given up the hills without a serious fight and now they were behind distant breastworks that were, to Hood's eye, less than formidable. The Yankees had their backs to the river. Schofield didn't want a fight, Hood reasoned, he was running, as he had been since Pulaski. For a fighter like Hood, it was not a difficult decision. He closed his binocular's case and rode to the top of the hill where he met corps commander A. P. Stewart. "General, I am going to make a fight right here," Hood declared.[20]

None of Hood's senior officers saw what Hood saw. The pugnacious little Irishman, Pat Cleburne, the best division commander in Hood's army, said that any attack would be "a terrible and useless waste of life." Cleburne's corps commander, Frank Cheatham, told Hood he didn't "like the looks of this fight," in which the federals were well fortified. Bedford Forrest urged another flanking movement. Hood ignored the advice. The Civil War in 1864 was not that of 1861. "The individual foot soldier was not the gallant hero of antebellum myth; he had become ammunition," wrote Pulitzer Prize–winning historian T. J. Stiles. "More than just expendable, he *had* to be expended to secure victory." Schofield had to be defeated before he could join Thomas. It was time, Hood announced, to drive Schofield "into the river at all hazards." Better to fight here where the defenses were hastily constructed than at Nashville "where they have been strengthening themselves for three years." Hood later told Cleburne, "Franklin is the key to Nashville, and Nashville is the key to independence." Hood's objective from the start of the campaign was Nashville. He knew he needed to defeat Schofield and Thomas piecemeal as he lacked the resources to defeat them combined. "I hereupon decided," Hood wrote a decade and a half later, "before the enemy would be able to reach his stronghold at Nashville, to make that same afternoon [November 30], another and final effort to overtake and rout him, and drive him into the Big Harpeth River at Franklin, since I could no longer hope to get between him and Nashville."[21]

Inside the Nashville defenses, just a half day's march north, General Thomas was anxiously awaiting the arrival of a veteran division from Major General A. J Smith's corps that was in transit from Arkansas. Thomas wired Schofield in the early afternoon, "Do you think you can hold Hood at Franklin for three days longer?" In a 3 p.m. telegram Schofield shot back, "I do not believe I can." A day maybe, but by then Forrest would undoubtedly be in his rear. Schofield proposed retiring to Brentwood, Tennessee, just below Nashville where well engineered fortifications waited. With one of Smith's Arkansas divisions and garrison troops summoned from Murfreesboro, the federals would be in a strong position. At Brentwood, Schofield assured Thomas, "I ought to be able to hold Hood in check for some time."[22]

Since early afternoon, the Yankees in Franklin had been watching the Confederates deploy from marching order to battle array on the plain two miles away. Cheatham's and Stewart's endless columns of infantry, rifle barrels and bayonets glimmering in the afternoon sun, gave "the appearance of a huge monster closed in folds of flashing steel," according one of Wagner's skirmishers who was hundreds of yards closer. As the Southerners maneuvered into position, their bands offered a spirited rendition of "Dixie" followed by rousing cheer. Near the Carter cotton gin, a federal band responded with "Hail Columbia" followed by a hearty cheer. The magnificent spectacle that presented itself on the plain south of Franklin had sparked a brief, festive moment. The musicians, however, would soon be trading their instruments for stretchers. There was serious work ahead.[23]

Out on Privet's Knob, Colonel Lane's brigade skirmished with the rebel line slowly edging toward his right flank. At 2:30 Lane sent a courier to Wagner detailing the threat. Wagner sent Captain Ed Whitesides from the division staff to Privet's Knob. Whitesides told Lane to temporarily leave a heavy skirmish line to hold the hill as long as possible, and withdraw the bulk of his brigade to a position to the right of Conrad and west of the Columbia Pike. When this withdrawal was complete, the two brigades would be deployed roughly parallel to the main line a half mile behind them and centered on the Columbia Pike. The two Ohio artillery pieces were placed between the two brigades on the Pike at what would be the position's apex.[24]

Conrad had only replaced Bradley the day before, so Wagner rode out to steady the man he referred to as a "curly-haired Dutchman." Wagner told the Colonel "to hold the line as long as possible." Lane appeared and got the same order. While Lane understood his instructions were to fight as long as possible before retiring, Conrad—trained by Prussians—appears to have believed his instructions were to hold his position to the last man. Conrad's sergeants were to hold their new recruits and draftees in line at bayonet point if need be. "Captain," Colonel Allen Buckner of the 79th Illinois confided to one of his officers, "my orders are to hold this position at all hazards. It is a mistake, and it means the wiping out of this command, but I have no discretion in the matter." General Wagner then rode back to the Carter house where he grandly told Cox that his two forward brigades had constructed defensive works "to meet any serious attack."[25]

General Cox rode to the Union left were a prominent knoll offered a panoramic view of the Harpeth valley. "Very few battlefields of the war were so free from obstruction to view," he remarked. What Cox saw was both awe-inspiring and ominous—Confederate infantry formed in double and triple lines of brigades, with artillery in the intervals between columns. Cheatham's corps was on the Columbia Turnpike with Pat Cleburne's division east of the road, John Brown's west of it, and William Bate's in echelon on Brown's flank. Stewart's corps was on the right of Cheatham—veterans all, and well led.[26]

Along Cox's line, his soldiers busied themselves by putting finishing touches on their breastworks. The retrenchment less than 100 yards behind the wagon gap at the Carter house was strengthened. The Carters' wood frame farm office and brick smokehouse were incorporated in the line. The left half of the retrenchment was held by the 44th Missouri and the right by several companies of the 183rd Ohio—two untested regiments that hadn't existed two months ago. On the far right sat four guns of the 20th Ohio Artillery. The far left was held by two cannon of Battery A, 1st Ohio Light Artillery that was still unlimbering. All six guns were under the temporary command of a colorful first lieutenant with a bull whip—Charley Scoville.[27]

At 3:30, Thomas telegraphed Schofield approving the withdrawal from Franklin. It was too late—Hood's men were already beginning a two mile journey that would determine the destiny of so many. The Southern bands played "The Bonnie Blue Flag" and "Dixie" to stoke Southern patriotism. The sight of the over 17,000 Confederates advancing in perfect order was impressive and unforgettable. "It was a grand sight!" Captain Levi Scofield wrote decades later. "Such as would make a lifelong impression on the mind of any man who could see such a resistless, well-conducted charge.... As forerunners well in advance could be seen a line of wild rabbits ... and quails by the thousands in coveys here and there would rise and settle.... On they came," Scofield continued, "and in the center their lines seemed to be many deep and unbroken, their red and white tattered flags, with the emblem of St. Andrews cross as numerous as though every company bore them, flaring brilliantly in the sun's rays." Just 15 minutes of marching separated Wagner's advanced brigades from the first line of rebels.[28]

Confederate intentions now clear, the Yankees dropped their shovels and grabbed their muskets. Once in position behind their breastworks, the sun on the burnished barrels of their Springfield and Enfield muskets led one civilian viewing the sight from a roof top to remember the Union line as "gleaming like a silver thread in the evening sun."[29]

The Ohio cannoneers between Lane and Conrad's brigades opened fire on the advancing Southern lines with explosive shells. A Missouri battery—it remains unclear how many Southern artillery batteries were on the field—fired from between the oncoming battle lines in response to the Ohio battery. An explosive shell grazed the Carter house and landed in the yard followed by a solid shot that hit the turnpike in front of the Carter house, spraying gravel and killing a pack mule on the bounce. Couriers leapt into their saddles and Yankees everywhere were suddenly in motion. An excited staff officer from Colonel Conrad found General Wagner and asked for direction. Wagner was blunt. "Stand there and fight them.... Tell Colonel Conrad," Wagner exclaimed, "that the Second Division can whip all hell." The officer protested that Hood's entire army bearing down on them. Wagner smashed his makeshift crutch into the dirt. "Never mind; fight them." Distant gunfire interrupted Colonel Opdycke's visit with the Cliffe's and sent him running for his horse.[30]

Oncoming rebel infantry and harassing fire from enemy sharpshooters forced the Ohio artillery to retire. The cannon were hitched to caissons by heavy rope so they could withdraw firing. When they reached the gap in the line at Carter's, one of the smoke blackened artillerymen warned the nearby infantrymen, "Old hell is let loose, and coming out there!"[31]

General Schofield was at his second headquarters of the day at the Alpheus Truett house—he had departed Cliffe's so distracted he forgot his gloves and dispatches—a half mile north of the Harpeth River on the Nashville road. Reports of Hood's army deploying for battle across the valley to the south arrived by breathless courier. Schofield ascended to a second story porch to see for himself. The increasing gunfire forced Schofield to admit that his belief that Hood would try another flanking movement was a miscalculation. The Confederates were marching across the plain straight at Cox's defensive line. It was a fortification, Schofield realized to his chagrin, that he had not even bothered to inspect.[32]

David Stanley—asleep at the Truett house—awoke at 4 p.m. to the sound of ragged musketry. Stanley shook off his malaise and headed for his horse. "Every preparation was made to repel an attack, although I believed the rebel commander would not dare one," Stanley wrote in his memoirs. "The Federal position was formidable. Why try this desperate assault?" For the official army record, Stanley admitted, "I felt so confident in this belief that I did not leave General Schofield's headquarters until the firing commenced."[33]

As the Confederates bore down on Conrad's forward skirmish line, the blue skirmishers unleashed a weak volley and fled. In the thin blue line that was Wagner's division there were veterans whose enlistments had expired and were due to be mustered out in Nashville. In Lieutenant John Shellenberger's 64th Ohio indignation over their predicament grew almost to mutiny. Even men described as "the best type of volunteer soldier" could hardly be held to the line. In his official report, Conrad acknowledged that any retreat might become a rout. Aside from surrender, only one other option remained. Conrad ordered his men to commence firing.[34]

When Cleburne's tough veterans emerged from the woodlot in Conrad's front, they halted, and calmly realigned themselves into two or three battle lines. Hood's order to "press them and shoot them in their backs as they run to their main line; then charge the enemy's works" echoed in their ears. Cleburne's ragged soldiers raised their famous rebel yell—a high pitched half animal, half man cry that a Union chaplain described as "something between the shriek of a woman and the scream of a panther." And then the Southerners broke into a run. Captain John Scofield remembered, "Their shouting seemed to show such confidence as men would have who had been led to believe that the line they were assaulting was a weak one."[35]

Captain Hinman was with Conrad's men. "In obedience to orders, the three thousand men of those ill-fated brigades firmly grasped their muskets and braced themselves to meet the shock." Badly outnumbered and flanked right and left, what Wagner's men did next was in that gray zone between brave and foolhardy. General Cox, with his panoramic view of the battlefield, could hardly believe it when "to the amazement of the thousands who were watching them, Wagner's infantry opened fire."[36]

Those two regiments at the apex of Wagner's line met the enemy head on in hand to hand combat. The remaining 10 regiments simply ran. Shellenberger estimated his men managed five or six shots each before running. Some of Lane's regiments didn't fire a shot, bringing loaded muskets with them as they fled. "It was every man for himself and the devil take the last man over the works," according to Captain Scofield. General Cox described the resistance of Wagner's two brigades as "a rattling fusillade for a few moments" that "checked for an instant" Cleburne and Brown's divisions. A few of the Confederates stopped to load and fire into the backs of the fleeing bluecoats. Most of the Johnnies—some barefoot—held their fire and ran over the Yankees shot by their comrades. The fugitives and their pursuers headed for the wagon gap and the breastworks on either side. The Southerners sensed an opportunity while the Yankees in the fortifications gritted their teeth and withheld their fire to avoid killing their comrades. The bluecoats could hear the rebels yelling, "Let's go into the works with them!" and "Right into the works with them!" The closer the rebels got, the more of them took up the chant. Eight hundred of Wagner's men never made it to Franklin.[37]

Realizing a battle was in the offing, Colonel Opdycke hastened from Cliffe's to confer with General Cox at his Carter house headquarters, but Cox was elsewhere. When the Confederate artillery targeted the Carter house, Opdycke took the initiative. Exiting the Carter house, he leapt into the saddle and rode onto the stone turnpike just yards from Company B which was on the left of the 125th Ohio's regimental front. Sergeant Thomas Sharp of Company E—once reduced in rank for unmilitary conduct—instantly had his men up and moving. Lieutenant Rice was feet from Opdycke, close enough to see the Colonel's eyes flash, and knew he was "alive to the situation." In his official report Opdycke recalled, "I commenced moving the command to the left of the pike for greater security to the men and for easier maneuvering in case of need." The consolidated 74/88th Illinois was just 200 yards from the wagon gap on the turnpike. Opdycke and his brigade were on the reverse slope of the Carter knoll and unable to see what was happening along Cox's forward earthworks. Although blind to what was beyond their horizon, what they could hear was chilling. "I heard the Rebel yell," Lieutenant Rice recalled, recounting what happened next, "and knew they were coming." It was nearing 4:30.[38]

Just paces ahead of the rebels and with Cox's men holding their fire, the first fugitives from Wagner's brigades reached the federal line at the Carter farmstead. When most of those men had reached safety, a few single shots rang out from the defenders and then the entire line from the cotton gin to beyond the Carters' garden erupted with a devastating musket volley at a distance measured in feet. The roar was deafening and the shock wave knocked even the uninjured down. West of the Carter garden, Private Ira Conley of the 111th Ohio remembered seeing the rebels close their ranks "only to be cut down as soon as we could load our guns again." Over a mile and a half back down the turnpike toward Spring Hill, General Hood heard the federal musketry erupt. "At this moment resounded a concentrated roar of musketry," Hood later wrote, "which recalled to me some of the deadliest struggles in Virginia."[39]

Three Confederate brigades plowed into the heart of Cox's defenses supported by two more—over 30 veteran regiments. In moments, the Confederates rebounded from the federal volley and reappeared from the cloud of gun smoke. Just west of the Pike, the 50th Ohio formed the left flank of Brigadier General Thomas Ruger's Twenty-Third Corps Second Division. Southerners began pouring through the wagon gap, quickly filling the Columbia Pike behind the breastworks and spreading into the rear. The 50th Ohio, just west of the turnpike, broke, one of its officer's shouting, "Every man for himself!" Sixty became prisoners while the faster afoot ran for the retrenchment line 60 yards away. The next regiment on the right, the 72nd Illinois, partially collapsed, but those who remained fought furiously with bayonets, clubbed muskets and axes. The untested 44th Missouri and the 183rd Ohio crouching behind the low retrenchment were first faced with Wagner's men running through them, and then the panicked 50th Ohio and 72nd Illinois intermingled with the howling rebels. In this confusion and terror, some of the Missourians fired into the Illinoisans. The 183rd's commander, Merwin Clark, was last seen alive standing atop the low earthwork waving a flag to rally his men. The regiment, with several key officers shot down, froze in the retrenched line refusing to move either forward or run away.[40]

The 100th Ohio was across the wagon gap from the 50th Ohio. Men from Wagner's brigades threw themselves over the parapet and into the defenders making it difficult for the 100th to fire on the enemy. "They [Wagner's men] filled our trenches so that we were unable to use our guns," the 100th's colonel wrote, "and creating considerable confusion, the enemy reaching the works almost simultaneously with them." Officers from both armies were shouting conflicting and confusing orders. The 100th Ohio and three companies of the 104th Ohio to their left fled—a break in the line that reached almost to the cotton gin. The Confederate onslaught rolled over the abandoned breastworks and rebel battle flags appeared along the parapet. From horseback, Colonel Opdycke witnessed the disorderly retreat of Lane and Conrad's men and the collapse of the Union line for rods right and left of the Carter house—some men running before Wagner's men reached the earthworks.[41]

Lieutenant Shellenberger, was both a fugitive and an eyewitness. "This break in our line was identical in extent with the front covered by the great body of Wagner's men in falling back. It was occasioned by the panic and confusion created by Wagner's men in crossing the breastworks. They [Cox's men] could not fire a single shot while Wagner's men were between themselves and the Rebels and the first Rebels crossed the breastworks side by side with the last of Wagner's men." Hundreds of enemy soldiers were pouring through the breech. However, the parade precision that marked the beginning of the charge had dissolved into clusters of individuals—exhausted but euphoric—gathered around their battle flags. Blinded by clouds of sulfurous gun smoke and confused by conflicting commands shouted over the din of battle—rebel officers consolidating their gains and Union officers trying to rally their men in the rear—the Confederate charge lost momentum.[42]

Battery A of the 1st Kentucky Light Artillery was positioned in the breastworks immediately to the left of the Columbia Pike. Unable to fire their loads of canister at the fast closing enemy for fear of hitting fellow Yankees, many of the artillerymen simply ran. The Johnnies seized four loaded three-inch rifled cannon without a fight, but the frightened battery horses had carried away the caissons and friction primers. Sixty yards back at the retrenchment, artillery Lieutenant Charley Scoville dryly noted that "there was some confusion" among his artillerymen when the rebels struck. Scoville and his bull whip, however, held his gunners to their pieces.[43]

George Wagner, back on his horse, was cursing and threatening with his broken stick, as he rode into the mass of Yankees surging toward the Harpeth River. Captain Scofield tried to help Wagner stem the tide when, in front of the Carter House, he was slightly wounded and his mount killed. The mob of panicked bluecoats—Lane and Conrad's men intermingled with Twenty-Third Corps soldiers—was so dense its current pulled the General and his horse with them into Franklin where Wagner began the arduous task of reforming his division.[44]

Of all the decisions Jacob Cox—that Oberlin College educated lawyer and politician—made November 30, the most crucial was his placement of reserves. In total, he positioned 10 regiments within 300 yards of the wagon gap. Cox placed not just Opdycke's brigade, but four regiments of James Reilly's brigade in reserve just east of the Columbia Pike. Lieutenant Colonel John White's 16th Kentucky was behind the east end of the retrenchment, a mere 70 yards behind the main federal line. Lieutenant Colonel Lawrence Rousseau's 12th Kentucky was on White's left flank. A hundred yards or so behind the Kentucky regiments was the Unionist 8th Tennessee, and behind the 8th was the untested 175th Ohio.[45]

After the first volley, gun smoke obscured Colonel White's view of what was happening those 70 yards to his front. But he could hear the confused shouts and increasing gunfire. When one of his men yelled in White's ear that the Southerners were coming over the works in his front, White didn't hesitate. He ordered the 16th Kentucky to charge. Unable to make himself heard above the din of battle, Colonel White clamored to the top of the low breastworks of the retrenchment, and waving his sword, signaled his men to charge. White was shot in the face, but stayed with his men. With a mighty Yankee huzzah, the Kentuckians surged into the maelstrom only to be almost run down by the 1st Kentucky's frightened battery horses charging driverless to the rear. The regiment lost three color bearers in rapid succession. To the left, in front of the 12th Kentucky, the federal fortifications—abandoned by the 100th Ohio and parts of the 104th Ohio—angled sharply to the southeast to encompass the old cotton gin. The Kentuckians leapt out of their low rifle pits and threw themselves at the enemy. Before the two Kentucky regiments reached the breastworks, they exchanged deadly volleys with the rebels, and then pitched into the Texans in their front who fired down into the Kentuckians or beat them with their muskets from the parapet. The Unionist 8th Tennessee—veterans of the Atlanta campaign—joined the rush forward as Reilly's reserves filled the break in the line between the cotton gin and the Columbia pike. One hundred fifty yards from the enemy, the 175th

Ohio—an untested mix of veterans and boys—leveled their bayonets marched into the fight. Lieutenant Colonel Daniel McCoy, who fought at Shiloh and Chickamauga, was wounded before the Ohioans reached the line. Reilly's four reserve regiments, Scofield recorded, "went pell-mell into the mass of Confederates that had taken our line and did not know what to do with it."[46]

Opdycke was in the act of repositioning his First Brigade when the Union regiments in front of him gave way. "While thus moving," he continued, "a most horrible stampede of our front troops came surging and rushing back past Carter's house, extending to the right and left of the pike. I first thought them only the Second and Third brigades of our division ... but soon I saw that the troops at the main works had left them." In seconds, the 125th faced "a mass of frightened recruits and panic-stricken men that came surging back, and the clash of arms, the whizzing of bullets, and the demonic yell of an elated foe was all that could be heard," remembered one veteran.[47]

"Neither Colonel White, nor Colonel Opdycke waited for the word to charge, but were in motion before the order could reach them," Cox later wrote. "White was the nearest the parapet and reached it soonest, but his line did not reach quite to the turnpike. The Carter house and out-buildings on the right of the road obstructed the movement to the front, and Opdycke made part of his brigade oblique to the left till clear of the obstacles, and they then charged headlong upon the enemy."[48]

On the Tiger's left, from atop his fidgeting horse, Major Thomas Motherspaw of the 73rd Illinois could see over the smoke and into the disaster unfolding. Those Illinois veterans knew instantly the federal line had been breached, and "our men perceiving and knowing the necessity of immediate action became clamorous to be led to the works." The brigade was moving, and Motherspaw assumed Opdycke had ordered a charge. "Forward, 73rd, to the works!" the major shouted. The 73rd raised a hearty yell, leveled their bayonets and charged. But, Opdycke hadn't ordered a charge and tried to recall the 73rd. It was an impossible demand—the 73rd was already on its way. Like Missionary Ridge, officers had become superfluous. Lieutenant Colonel George Smith's consolidated 74th/88th Illinois in front and to the right of the 73rd, joined the rush—one eager officer armed with just a hatchet and Sharps pepperbox pistol. Motherspaw was shot from his saddle, mortally wounded.[49]

Opdycke was closest to the 125th Ohio, and the Tigers instinctively looked to him for orders before plunging forward. After witnessing the Illinois regiments' spontaneous charge, Colonel Opdycke bellowed above the increasing din of battle, "First Brigade, forward to the works!" Captain Ed Bates—releasing the spooked horse he was unable to mount—faced the 125th and yelled, "Forward, double quick, march!" The men started at a run. Opdycke told his wife that the brigade lowered bayonets, gave long huzzas and rushed forward "in one of the grandest charges I ever saw."[50]

Immediately behind the 125th, 400 yards from the main fortifications, was the 24th Wisconsin which moments earlier had been gnawing on hardtack. Its teenaged major, 19-year-old Arthur MacArthur, leapt onto his horse and shouted, "Up Wisconsin!" sending his regiment on its way. MacArthur was moments later severely wounded in hand to hand combat in which he killed a rebel officer. MacArthur's replacement, Captain Alvah Philbrook, was shot through the head behind the retrenchment less than an hour later.[51]

The 36th Illinois—which would suffer the most casualties in Opdycke's brigade—was behind the 24th Wisconsin, in the First Brigade's rear. At Opdycke's command, Lieutenant Colonel Porter Olson shouted, "Forward to the trenches!" sending the Illinoisans into the breech. Olson roamed the rear of his regiment urging them as they pushed into the crowded, bloody yard west of the Carter house. Just behind the shallow retrenchment line, Olson—a former teacher—was mortally wounded and his body was carried away on a shutter torn from the Carter house.[52]

As Colonel Smith's consolidated Illinois regiments surged forward, his men were forced into the Columbia Pike by retreating troops who parted to the right and left the moment they saw the gleam of the First Brigade's leveled bayonets. The effect was to funnel those Confederates—a disorganized mass from Cleburne and Brown's divisions—charging down the Columbia Pike toward the Carter house and buildings. At the retrenchment, hand to hand fighting raged for its possession.[53]

Captain Bates, dashed to the front of the charging 125th and yelled above the din, "Come on, boys! We have always whipped them and we will whip them now!" Two runaway Kentucky caissons formed the first obstacles encountered by the 125th Ohio. The Ohioans scrambled to avoid the galloping horses as the caissons thundered by, finally stopped when an officer shot one of the lead horses dead. The 125th reformed without breaking stride. Next to confront the regiment was a staked, cedar fence on the north side of the Carter house which was too tall to climb over and fastened with large cut, iron nails. With musket balls rattling against the opposite side of the fence which refused to yield to blows from rifle butts, a few of Bates' men crowded through a narrow gate while the rest streamed around the ends. Companies B, G and K went left, while the rest of the regiment went right into the Carters' rear yard. One man, Sergeant Albert Matthews, went so far left that he fought with the Illinois regiments east of the Columbia Pike.[54]

When the fleeing bluecoats cleared the turnpike, what appeared was a mass of Southerners pouring over the main breastworks, through the wagon gap and running along the Columbia Pike toward the Carter house, pressed forward by the weight of Hood's second and third battle lines in their rear. Opdycke got his brigade into a ragged battle line along the left half of the retrenched line. The Colonel's favorite tactic in battle was volley fire, and according to Captain Bates with the enemy just 100 feet away, "here it was not only practical but essential, and was so delivered." Lieutenant Rice vividly recalled that the volley "wrought such destruction as I never before saw—dead men and wounded lay in actual heaps." When fired into the tight mob of rebels, Bates noted, "The chances of any ball missing were reduced to the minimum." The massed volley briefly stunned the disorganized mass of rebels, checking their momentum. An anonymous Southerner outside the breastworks witnessed the event and reported "in an instant the remnants of the victorious Confederates swarmed out of the captured works and ran for cover." The musket volley was followed by desultory firing combined with intense hand-to-hand fighting.[55]

The intensity of the close quarter fight defied description. "There was an indescribable melee at the conclusion of which the 125th and all the rest of Opdycke's regiments were at the barricades," wrote Charlie Clark, the regimental historian. A captain in the 24th Wisconsin simply said, "The fighting at this point was for a time, hand to hand." Even the term "indescribable melee" didn't do the intensity of the hand-to-hand combat justice. Fierce fights swirled around regimental flags. Private William C. Roberts, I, and Theophile Ducquet, D, each captured an enemy battle flag. Other were less lucky. Captain Robert Stewart of Company D, one of the 125th's senior captains, was killed near the Carter house as was Sergeant James Murdock. Lieutenant Darius Payne was likewise wounded and survived. Corporal Joseph Wilson was captured in the Carter yard and later escaped with two dozen other prisoners.[56]

General Stanley had shaken off his earlier malaise and charged up the Columbia Pike with his staff. Panicked bluecoats and stampeded horses impeded Stanley's movement until he entered the wake of the First Brigade which had cleared the pike. Stanley spurred his mount to a gallop as bullets whistled through the air. Lieutenant Rice expected the orderly bearing the Fourth Corps conspicuous square red ensign to be shot any moment. He wasn't. Cresting Carter knoll, Stanley saw rebel flags flying from the breastworks. "It was at this moment I arrived at the scene of disorder," recalled Stanley, who knew a rout when he saw one, "the moment critical beyond any I have known in any battle—could the enemy hold that part of the line? He was nearer to our two bridges than the extremities of our line." Stanley had intended to order Opdycke's brigade into the break, but he was too late. All the corps commander could do was urge the First Brigade forward, indicating to those around him they should charge. Stanley praised Opdycke for his initiative. "I gave the colonel no order," Stanley wrote in his official report, "as I saw him engaged in doing the very thing to save us ... to get possession of our line again."[57]

Opdycke had his eye on the abandoned federal artillery. A two gun section of Battery A of the 1st Ohio Light Artillery behind the retrenchment and west of Carter's house had been all but abandoned by their crews—only a corporal remained. Opdycke claimed his brigade retook an artillery battery and a section of another in the vicinity of the Carter house and his men worked the pieces. In a letter home, the Colonel noted specifically that the 125th retook a two-gun section and turned the cannon on the enemy just as he had instructed in Franklin a year and a half ago. According to Captain Bates, "Two guns at the right of the regiment that had been deserted by all but a single corporal, were quickly brought into action again." According to the battery commander, however, the two guns fired less than 10 rounds total in the battle.[58]

On the left flank of Opdycke's brigade, east of the turnpike, the 44th Illinois, commanded by Lieutenant Colonel John Russell, fought their way forward to the main breastworks with bayonets, clubbed muskets and fists. Some of the braver men of the 100th Ohio returned to help. Colonel Edwin Hayes of the 100th credited Opdycke's brigade with assisting in restoring his part of the line. Russell's infantrymen helped work the guns of the 1st Kentucky Artillery, a wounded gunner offering instruction.[59]

For all its ferocity, the severest fighting—the point blank volleys, the thrusting bayonets, the clubbed muskets, the angry fists—that swirled around the Carter farmstead lasted only about 15 minutes. Gun smoke hung heavy in the still air as evening approached. General Cox remembered that "after the first half hour's fighting it became almost impossible to discern any object along the line at a few yards' distance." In his memoir, Lieutenant Rice recalled the experience from ground level "from the first shots the smoke settled down in a peculiar manner—a little higher than one's head. Underneath this canopy the light was a pale, sickly yellow." In this true fog of war, Opdycke initially mistook the second retrenchment line for the front line and halted his brigade there. General Cox understood, "the outbuildings of Carter's house prevented the line from being distinctly seen from the turnpike even if the smoke had not formed so dark a covering." The Confederates were likewise blinded by the smoke and believed they held the center of the Union line. This error led their officers to continue to feed troops into what became a killing zone. "This resulted in greater destruction to the Confederate troops, by repeated assaults after all real chance of success was gone," Cox wrote. "Prisoners captured continually expressed utmost surprise, declaring they had supposed and had been informed that our lines were occupied by their troops."[60]

Once his brigade held the line, Colonel Opdycke turned his attention to strengthening it and bringing forward stragglers. Opdycke had no sympathy for unwounded men trying to escape the fighting. "I never worked as hard since I was born," he informed his wife, as he did attempting to drive fleeing bluecoats back to the breastworks. Levi Scofield affirmed Opdycke's actions. "He urged his men forward, placing himself where he could prevent stragglers from dropping out. He broke his revolver over men's heads, and then seized a gun, and whoever looked back within his reach was jobbed under the blouse. So he rushed them on," evicting rebels from the Carter yard and buildings. Opdycke glimpsed his old Warren friend, Jacob Cox, pursuing stampeded Yankees, hatless and amidst terrible gunfire.[61]

The cartridge boxes of Cox and Wagner's men were nearly empty. The ordnance wagons had been parked across the river, and were just now bulling their way through the demoralized mob that clogged Franklin's streets. On the right of the 125th, First Lieutenant David K. Blystone began a search for cartridges, while on the left, Sergeant Sharon French volunteered to find an ordnance wagon. In the heat of the battle, Colonel Opdycke mistook French, whose face was blackened by gunpowder, for a shirker and was about to strike him with his empty revolver when Lieutenant Rice intervened shouting, "This is Sergeant French; he is going for cartridges!" French returned quickly having met the ammunition wagons coming forward. Fourth Corps ordnance officers positioned wagons at convenient points behind the lines, and the men smashed open the pine boxes of 1000 paper cartridges—color coded by type of ammunition for easy identification. Lieutenant Blystone was shot in the left lung distributing cartridges near the Carter smokehouse.[62]

Stanley wasn't as charmed as Cox or Opdycke that afternoon. Just as the Northern line was being restored, Stanley received a grazing neck wound and his horse was hit opposite the Carters' front door. Some of the men in the 125th labeled Stanley's actions "heroism uncalled for." Stanley borrowed a horse and stayed on the field encouraging his men. Once the Union line was stable again, Stanley went in search of medical treatment. Most of the field hospitals were positioned far across the river and the ambulances were delayed crossing the crowded bridges. Most of the wounded that could walk were forced to make a slow, painful trek for treatment.[63]

After the struggle to expel the enemy from their breakthrough, the First Brigade was aligned across the breech. Behind the retrenched line from the Columbia Pike west it was the 74th/88th Illinois, the 24th Wisconsin, the 125th Ohio and the 36th Illinois. The 44th and 73rd Illinois were east across the pike on the main breastworks. Behind the retrenched line Opdycke's brigade and remnants of the 50th Ohio and 44th Missouri made for ranks three and four soldiers deep with rear ranks reloading and passing muskets to the front for firing. Opdycke established his brigade headquarters—as simple as planting his flag—in front of Carter's.[64]

In that intense quarter hour the tide turned. Reserves from the Twenty-Third Corps restored most of the main line from the cotton gin west almost to the Columbia Pike. Opdycke's First Brigade retook the front line just east of the turnpike and the second retrenchment line, effectively sealing the wagon gap. However, the main breastworks were not totally under Union control. "We had retaken the works, but that part of our line from the right of the garden to the pike, a distance of about 100 feet, was not yet restored," recalled the 125th's Lieutenant Ralsa Rice. Tenacious veterans from John C. Brown's Confederate division held the outside of the main breastworks on the edge of the Carters' garden, and firing over the parapet—often without aiming and too high—prevented the Northerners from retaking those works. Colonel Opdycke saw an officer and several private soldiers shot within feet of him. Three bullets tore through his brigade flag. A rebel sharpshooter later taken prisoner claimed to have taken deliberate aim at Colonel Opdycke six times, each a miss. "Captain Bates," according to Rice, "thought to construct a temporary barricade across the break and build a straight line across the lower end of the garden." Under the cover of the thick smoke, Opdycke's men scavenged material to strengthen an old barricade just 25 yards from the enemy. In General Cox's estimate "across the narrow interval the battle raged with most persistent fierceness."[65]

Waves of Southerners continued to come. Captain Scofield labeled the attacks "foolhardy and reckless." Yet Scofield could see the Southerners saw the futility of their mission. "They came forward in silence, their heads bent forward with their black or gray slouch hats pulled down and their arms up vainly attempting to shield them from almost certain death." A soldier from the 175th Ohio described his regiment holding fire until an assaulting enemy battle line was within a few paces of the works and then unleashing "a deafening volley [that] fairly mowed down everything in front." Twice, during lulls in the fighting, Colonel Opdycke stepped in front of the works on the Columbia Pike in the dim starlight to see the gruesome result of those volleys. "I never saw," Opdycke wrote, "the dead lay near so thick."[66]

The short November day ended soon after the heavy fighting began. The opponents were reduced to firing at each other's muzzle flashes. Rebels clinging to the outside of the earthen breastworks would claw their way to the parapet, peer over the top and draw fire from the front and flanks. Especially galling was fire from Yankees sharpshooters in nearby structures, like that from Sergeant French and a squad from the 125th in the Carter house. One member of the 41st Tennessee recalled that the sniping from buildings was "especially severe from Mr. Carter's immediately in my front." The shooting continued "until not an efficient man was left between us and the Columbia Pike, about fifty yards to our right." Sergeant Henry Ross entered the enemy lines three times under the cover of darkness and came away with half of the 125th's 80 prisoners.[67]

Away from the Carter knoll, on the Yankee left and right, there were no retreating Northerners to prevent the federals from firing into the advancing Confederate battle lines. The cannon in Fort Granger and about a dozen pieces in Cox's fortifications opened on Stewart's Confederate Corps when they came in range and began a systematic shredding of the advancing Confederates east of the Columbia Pike. From the cotton gin east to the Harpeth River, the federal breastworks were the strongest on the field replete with head logs and thorny osage orange abatis in front. When Southerners crossing the open almost unbroken plain closed to within 300 yards, the cannon began firing double canister rounds augmented by a "dummy"—an old sock filled with damaged musket ammunition. One Ohio officer recalled, "The enemy seemed to be swept out of existence with every discharge and yet they re-formed their lines and repeatedly charged to the muzzles of our guns, only to be swept away by the terrible storm of canister." One Confederate division commander believed his men faced "the most deadly fire that I have ever seen troops subjected to." Each time the firing slackened, Southerners clinging to the outside of the breastworks surrendered and were pulled over and into the trenches by the Yankees.[68]

Well after dark, 8 or 9 o'clock, Hood played his last card and sent his reserve division,

Major General Edward Johnson's, forward on the Union right where the locust grove—the remaining trees cut and shredded by bullets—stood. Johnson's men stumbled through the dark guided by torch bearers—conspicuous targets when they came in range. Nevertheless, aided by darkness, a few rebels penetrated the Union defenses setting off another flurry of hand-to-hand combat. The Southerners were expelled and the survivors huddled on the outer face of the breastworks where Yankee bullets and bayonets could not reach them. Recognizing failure, Johnson withdrew his men. This final night attack accomplished nothing except to add casualties.[69]

Out on the flat, open cotton field turned killing ground, any movement, real or imagined, brought a fusillade of gunfire. Corpses were riddled with bullets, wounded hit repeatedly and those trying to flee were pursued by minie balls. Fatigue began to overtake the foes as the day's adrenalin dissipated. Between 9 and 10, the firing slacked and eventually ceased. Out across the valley, John Bell Hood, having approved a withdrawal back to the ill-fated advanced position once occupied by Wagner's division, contemplated how he might resume the battle tomorrow. Under cover of darkness, those Southern soldiers huddled at the base of the breastworks or in the abatis either tried to sneak away or settled in for the night.[70]

By 10, the federals had only about an hour's worth of ammunition remaining. Lieutenant Rice estimated—probably over-estimated—his company fired an astounding 300 musket rounds *each*. If true, that quantity was "an amount in excess of any other battle we fought in." During the battle, General Stanley claimed the federals expended 90 wagon loads of musket and artillery ammunition from the Fourth Corps supply. Just before the battle opened, Schofield had asked Thomas to send one million rounds of infantry ammunition to Brentwood, 12 miles up the pike on the edge of the Nashville defenses.[71]

Shortly after 7, General Schofield, who never went to Carter's knoll, telegraphed Thomas that the enemy had been repulsed all along the line and that he would withdraw if Thomas approved it. Thomas, breathing easier with Smith's 9000 men in Nashville, congratulated Schofield on the victory and approved an immediate retreat. General Stanley agreed, but expressed concern about disengaging in the dark. But General Cox, actually present on the battlefield, dissented and tried to convince Schofield to remain, even offering to take personal responsibility for the outcome. Schofield thanked Cox for the day's work, but never seriously considered staying. Schofield had bought Thomas the time he needed and inflicted a heavy loss on Hood in doing so. U. S. Grant, with the benefit of hindsight, was critical. "Thomas made no effort to reinforce Schofield at Franklin," Grant suggested, "as it seemed to me at the time he should have done, and fight out the battle there." All wounded that could be moved were evacuated, but inevitably some were left behind. The Union dead remained where they fell.[72]

Tom Wood's division, on the north side of the Harpeth, was never engaged and thus was assigned to guard the bridges during the withdrawal. After being careful to leave a strong skirmish line behind in the breastworks, Cox's division began the Northern exodus about 10 p.m. There was no talking; no bands celebrating victory. Anything that might jingle on harness, saddle or belt was tied fast. The artillery and supply wagons headed for the bridges with wheels wrapped in blankets. The only sound was the tread of thousands of feet. A stable fire broke out in town, and threatened to illuminate the federal retreat, so the Yankees extinguished the blaze. The resulting black smoke hung over the village providing a smoke screen for the retreating Union army snaking through town in silence.[73]

At 11 p.m., the 125th Ohio fell back a few rods from their place in the retrenchment and formed in front of the Carter house. The Fourth Corps began to depart just after midnight led by Kimball's division followed by Opdycke's First Brigade of the Second Division. Opdycke left the 88th Illinois as rearguard pickets. The 125th crossed over the Harpeth River on the wagon bridge at 1 a.m. and an hour later was on the way to Nashville. At 2 a.m. the pickets rejoined the rest of the army on the north bank of the Harpeth without incident. Wood's men took up the wooden planking on the bridges and burned it. Seeing the flames, the suspicious Confederates lobbed a few artillery rounds toward the river, but ceased after a few minutes. Charlie Clark accurately read the mood of Hood's men when he wrote, "Doubtless the enemy's troops were too much exhausted to make an effective pursuit."[74]

As the 125th marched through the town, Captain Bates sent Lieutenant Rice and another man to look for his runaway horse. It was an impossible request, even on a moonlit night, to find a single horse in a village filled with stray animals. After going a short distance, the two war weary veterans decided to tell the captain his horse was dead so he could claim compensation for it. Rice explained, "While our lives were worth but little, this old horse was worth even less."[75]

Wagons of rations were sent down the turnpike from Nashville, and as the hungry men marched, crackers were distributed and bacon slabs consumed raw. Despite the food, Schofield's men were near the point of collapse. They had just fought an exhausting battle sandwiched between two night marches. Some men dozed as they walked. At halts, soldiers collapsed where they stood. A few endured ghastly nightmares of the battle whenever they closed their eyes. The 125th finally reached the safety of Nashville's outer defenses at 10 a.m. and halted near Fort Negley on the southeast side—20 miles from Franklin. There the men were issued fish and potatoes from the city's massive warehouses. Clark described the rations as "something new ... but acceptable." The Union infantry was granted an uninterrupted day of rest.[76]

By nightfall of December 1, all of Schofield's infantry was within the Nashville defenses, Wood's division bringing up the rear of the column. Hood's pursuit was limited—as was so often the case—to Forrest's cavalry. General Stanley, his neck wound covered by a bloody bandage, stopped in Brentwood, south of Nashville, for breakfast on the 1st with his boys. "Our men," Stanley recalled, "were more exhausted physically than I have ever seen them on any other occasion." Opdycke and many veterans considered the battle at Franklin the most strenuous they fought. He wrote Lucy, "the fact is I never made as much physical exertion in one day."[77]

Around the Carter house in the faint pre-dawn light only dead and seriously wounded Yankees remained. A lone federal corpse eerily propped up against a locust tree by his musket's ramrod kept watch at the Carter house. Fifty-seven dead bluecoats lay around the Carter smokehouse, its brick exterior pockmarked by bullets. In the rear yard, between the garden and the farmhouse a lone Southerner lay dead—the high water mark of Hood's attempt at Franklin and Confederate chances west of the Alleghenies.[78]

Toward dawn, here and there, Confederates crept forward to find empty breastworks. Word spread quickly of a victory. Almost immediately, the initial euphoria turned to horror. "It was a grand holocaust of death," recalled Confederate private Sam Watkins when he got his first view of the battlefield. "The dead were piled the one on the other all over the ground. I never was so horrified and appalled in my life." At daylight, Frank Cheatham rode out across the field where his corps fought. "The dead were piled up like stacks of wheat or scattered about like sheaves of grain. You could have walked all over the field upon dead bodies without stepping upon the ground.... In front of the Carter House the bodies lay in heaps.... I never saw anything like that field, and never want to again."[79]

General Hood was said to have wept when he rode into Franklin. He fooled no one when he congratulated his army on its "victory" which had bled his army white. It was easier to conceal the truth from the authorities in distant Richmond. In a carefully worded statement, Hood accentuated the positive when he stressed driving the federals into their inner lines, Schofield's night retreat and the possession of the field by his army. The "loss of many gallant officers and brave men" was Hood's only concession to the truth.[80]

A couple weeks after the battle, 1,750 Confederate graves were found in Franklin and 3800 wounded were still in hospitals around town. More than 700 rebels were marched to Nashville as prisoners after the battle. Any walking wounded were not included in this total. If 7000 was a rough estimate, then Hood lost a third of his infantry engaged, a steep price. "For the attackers it would be the worst five hours in Civil War history," Authors James Lee McDonough and Thomas L. Connelly wrote noting that number of Hood's men killed in action exceeded George McClellan's during the entire Seven Days campaign around Richmond, or Joe Hooker's at Chancellorsville. The officer corps of the Army of the Tennessee was decimated. Five generals were killed—including the irreplaceable Cleburne—seven wounded—among them future Tennessee governor John Brown—and one captured. Furthermore, 55 regimental commanders were casualties. According to one historian, "The inner workings of the army from top to bottom was an utter mess."[81]

Northern losses totaled 2300 of which 1000 were from Conrad and Lane's ill-fated brigades. The heaviest Union losses occurred around the breached center of the line. Between 20 and 30 Confederate battle flags were claimed by Union soldiers at a time when capturing 10 was considered a major victory. The loss of a regimental flag—the ultimate battlefield prize—meant not just defeat in battle, but the loss of the symbol of the regiment's very existence. In truth, many flags were simple picked up from the ground, so badly were many Confederate regiments decimated. The 125th Ohio got official credit for capturing two. Nine lucky Union soldiers were selected to take their trophies to the War Department and collect a Medal of Honor.[82]

Opdycke's First Brigade counted 13 officers and 217 enlisted men killed, wounded or missing. The 125th lost 32. Opdycke praised two of his longtime subordinates: Captain Bates—commanding the 125th—and Captain Powers—on Wagner's staff. The First Brigade captured 394 Confederates, including one Southern colonel, and nine battle flags. Opdycke commended his brigade telling them it was an honor to be in the First Brigade. In an army with only one medal to award, honorary brevet rank was given for meritorious service. On Opdycke's recommendation, Captain Ed Bates of the 125th was brevetted major in March 1865.[83]

The outcome of the battle at Franklin would have a profound impact on the rest of the war in the West. Some writers went so far as to call it "the Gettysburg of the West." Sam Watkins, the 1st Tennessee veteran of three and a half years of war, saw Franklin as "the finishing stroke to the independence of the Southern Confederacy." General David Stanley was succinct: "The ruin of the Confederacy was assured by this battle."[84]

19

NASHVILLE

Safe within the defenses of Nashville on December 1, Schofield's weary army could finally relax. In three harrowing days and two sleepless nights, they had marched 40 miles, fought two battles and slipped past a sleeping Southern army twice their numbers. "None but those who have experienced it can realize the unspeakable physical and mental prostration that followed such extreme and protracted test of endurance," wrote Captain Wilbur Hinman of the 65th Ohio. Major General John Schofield, his successful arrival at Nashville more a matter of good fortune than skill, collapsed into a deep sleep that lasted 24 hours. The intrepid Lieutenant Rice and much of the 125th slept soundly for a day or more. Of his exhausted comrades, Rice wrote, "We were giving to our country the best we had."[1]

On December 2 General Thomas inspected the Fourth Corps, and gave a short speech to Opdycke's brigade praising their actions at Franklin and telling the men that in a hundred years their descendants would be as proud of them as were the descendants of the men who fought under Napoleon and Frederick the Great. Emerson wrote Lucy that General Thomas shook his hand and complimented him. Thomas praised Opdycke—an officer he had known since Chickamauga—for his "skilled dispositions ... promptness and readiness ... and single personal gallantry" that saved the day at Franklin. After Thomas' inspiring words, Wagner's division marched to a new position between the Hillsboro and Hardin turnpikes and went to work improving the earthworks.[2]

Opdycke's personal post-battle press was likewise favorable. The *Cleveland Morning Leader* reported, "Colonel Opdycke greatly distinguished himself. Five hundred prisoners were taken by his brigade, and seven battle flags, two of which were taken by his old regiment, the 125th. Colonel Opdycke's charge saved the day." The *New York Daily Tribune* told its readers that "Colonel Opdycke of the 125th Ohio, commanding a brigade, especially distinguished himself." This heady praise easily convinced the Colonel that he was entitled to promotion to brigadier as the man who saved the Union army at Franklin. In letters the second week of December, he wrote Lucy, that if he wasn't promoted to brigadier for his actions at Franklin, he never would be promoted. Generals Cox and Stanley both endorsed Opdycke's promotion as did Schofield. "Col. Emerson Opdycke, commanding First Brigade," Schofield wrote, "which recaptured the lost portion of our line is spoken of by Generals Stanley and Cox as having displayed on that occasion the highest qualities of a commander. I cordially indorse their recommendation." Thomas agreed, and the promotion to brigadier that Opdycke had coveted for so long began to work its way through the army bureaucracy.[3]

George Wagner, however, was roundly condemned for his actions on November 30, privately if not publically. Opdycke privately suggested to his wife that Wagner deserved to be hung for ordering Conrad and Lane to stand and fight. Before the week was out, Wagner was relieved of division command and returned to brigade command. Rather than accept the humiliation of demotion, Wagner took indefinite leave. Opdycke commented, "I <u>almost</u> pity him." Wagner was among the first group of volunteer general officers released by the army in August 1865, ending his military career.[4]

Victory on the battlefield didn't translate into victory in Opdycke's feud with Major Bruff. The examining board's findings were released after review by General Thomas. The three Second Division examining officers decided that Bruff's capacity to command was "good." His qualifications were "sufficient." His efficiency to command was "fair." Lastly, the Board concluded that Bruff's conduct had been "injudicious in discussing the actions of superior in the presence of junior officers." The results were a mild scolding and a lukewarm endorsement. Approving the Board's findings and returning Bruff to duty was an easy decision for Thomas' headquarters. Volunteer officers were eagerly departing and robbing the service of experienced commanders. Here was an experienced officer who wanted to *stay* in the army. Released from arrest, Major Bruff assumed command of the 125th on December 3—the third man to officially command the Ohioans. History records little comment by members of the regiment and Clark's 1895 history was silent on the Opdycke-Bruff feud. Opdycke barely mentioned the Board's findings to his wife. By December 22, Captain Ed Bates, the reliable acting commander had left the regiment to become Opdycke's brigade quartermaster.[5]

George Wagner was replaced as division commander by Brigadier General Washington L. Elliott. A West Point dropout who enlisted during the Mexican War, Elliott served as General Thomas' chief of cavalry during the Atlanta campaign. Opdycke felt Elliott made a favorable initial impression on the division. General Stanley departed on medical leave, and Tom Wood—largely cleansed of the stain of Chickamauga—assumed Fourth Corps command. Brigadier General Samuel Beatty took over Wood's division. The 125th's Captain Ed Whitesides became Elliott's assistant adjutant general.[6]

On December 2, Hood's depleted army of 44,000—of which just half were infantry—approached Nashville, now the most heavily fortified city west of the Alleghenies. As General Hood took up residence in the fine Overton mansion on the Franklin Pike, his tattered army began digging earthworks about six miles from the city. Skirmishing and artillery fire reminiscent of the Atlanta campaign began with the worst to the left of the Elliott's Second Division and the 125th.[7]

In the week and a half since John Bell Hood's army had started north from Alabama, it had lost 7500 men and many of its best officers. Morale was low, and confidence in Hood, even lower. Confederate general P. G. T. Beauregard, Jefferson Davis' man and Hood's nominal superior, reported to Richmond, "It is clear to my mind that after the great loss of life at Franklin, the army was no longer in a condition to make a successful attack on Nashville." However, retreat was not in Hood's nature. He also rejected the sound options of fortifying south of the Harpeth River where Thomas would have to attack him, or crossing the Cumberland above or below Nashville to get into Thomas' rear. Instead, Hood chose a strategy too ambitious for his depleted army. "I therefore determined to move upon Nashville, to entrench," Hood later explained, and "to await his [Thomas'] attack." Charlie Clark noted in his regimental history of the 125th that Hood "wanted the moral effect of threatening Nashville." In military parlance, Hood's strategy was called passive defense. Fifty years earlier, Napoleon had called it "deferred suicide."[8]

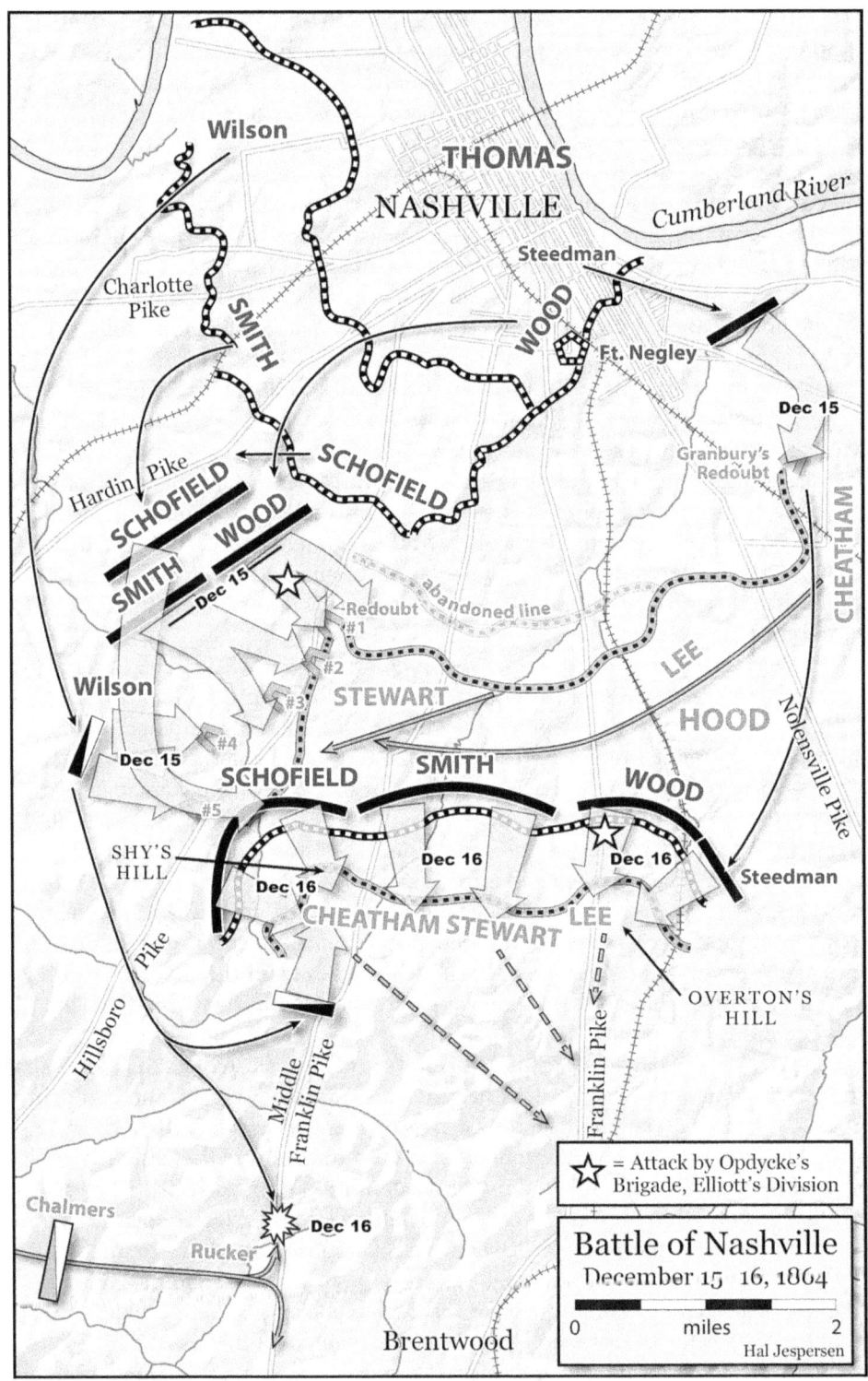

Battle of Nashville. Composite Map of the Movements of Wood's Fourth Corps, December 15–16, 1864. Map by Hal Jespersen.

On Monday, December 5, General Wood sent Colonel Opdycke on a reconnaissance of the Second Division front. Opdycke and his brigade's color bearer, the 125th's Clay Searight, rode for six hours covering ground as much as a quarter mile in front of the picket line. At one point the two men surprised an enemy picket post which wildly fired on them from a few yards. After returning safely, Opdycke produced a sketch of the terrain and Confederate dispositions. Wood and Opdycke spent an hour closeted with General Thomas discussing future operations and prompting Opdycke to believe his promotion to brigadier general was assured. Because of this scout, a detail from the 125th was sent between the lines to burn a house that could have sheltered rebel sharpshooters. Several men from the 125th returned to the regiment from the hospital or home about this same time. Henry Adams of Company G, captured in September, was exchanged and arrived in camp. Some of the 125th's baggage, in storage since April, arrived on December 6.[9]

On December 5, Hood sent General Forrest's cavalry, reinforced by infantry, on an expedition to attack Murfreesboro—20-odd miles southeast of Nashville and the site of the 1862 battle—and break the railroad between that place and Nashville. The attack failed, but it did keep the 9000 Yankees in the Murfreesboro garrison from joining the Nashville defenses.[10]

From the 2nd to the 6th, the weather remained mild, but from the 7th to the 12th, it deteriorated. A cold north wind on the 7th led to rain, sleet and snow on the 9th—a day so miserable that Opdycke's clothes and hat acquired a glaze of ice as he rode his picket line. An ice storm followed on the 10th leaving the roads slick and treacherous. Opdycke wrote his wife that Sunday was the coldest day he had known in the South and his men were suffering. The Northerners were uncomfortable, but the Southern soldiers—few tents, threadbare clothes, rotten shoes—were freezing in their trenches. The next morning, the 12th, was cold but sunny. December 13th, a southeast wind brought warming temperatures, turning ice into mud, and making camp life and picket duty very disagreeable. The 14th was wet and roads turned to axil deep mud. Neither side worked on their fortifications for five days.[11]

George Thomas had over 50,000 soldiers in Nashville's rings of trenches. Despite the numbers, it was a patchwork army composed of reserve and provisional troops alongside hard veterans, most of whom had never fought together. The Nashville garrison numbered 6000 infantry and artillery. Major General A. J. Smith—a 25-year regular army officer known for his profanity and as one of the best, if unsung, corps commanders in the Union army—brought 12,000 men from Arkansas in three divisions. Major General James Steedman—he of Chickamauga fame—brought 5200, including two brigades of colored troops, from Chattanooga. The battle depleted Fourth Corps and Twenty-Third Corps added 25,000. "The army was new to its organization, and though it did all that an army could do, Thomas could hardly have full faith in it till it had been proven," observed Jacob Cox.[12]

General Thomas, a former cavalryman, wanted a strong mounted force to confront the wily Nathan Bedford Forrest during any future pursuit of Hood's army. Major General James Wilson, commanding the cavalry, had 12,000 horse soldiers, some armed with potent Spencer repeating rifles. But horses were a problem. "There was a great scarcity of animals for the cavalry," General Cox wrote, "for the artillery, for the pontoons, and for the wagon trains, while the season was such as to use up the animals with double the rapidity." Impressed civilian horses—the government paid up to $160 for the best—filled the shortfall. By the 15th, Wilson would have 10,000 horse soldiers, twice those of Nathan Bedford Forrest.[13]

The city of Nashville was located in a bend in the Cumberland River with several turnpikes leading into Tennessee's capitol from the south and west. Nine miles south of city down the Franklin Pike were the Brentwood Hills whose average elevation was 350 feet. The turnpike passed through a gap where the village of Brentwood was located. Five miles from Nashville, the Franklin Pike passed over the base of a hillock known locally as Overton's Hill. The formidable Nashville fortifications were impeccably arranged for the most militarily advantageous use of the terrain in a 10-mile arc sweeping, on average, three miles from the state capital and stretching from the river above the city to the river below it. Thomas had positioned A. J. Smith's corps on the right flank of the defenses anchored on the Cumberland River three miles downstream from Nashville. Smith's left was near the Hillsboro pike, covering a front of three miles, two and a half miles from the city center. Wood's Fourth Corps was in the center, joining Smith on its right and Schofield's Twenty-Third Corps on its left, a few hundred yards east of the Granny White Pike. Schofield's corps extended almost to the Nolensville Pike. General Steedman's brigades were on Schofield's left, and cavalry covered the rest of the distance to the Cumberland, upriver from Nashville. To insure his army was ready for anything, Thomas ordered reveille for 4:30 a.m. each morning with the infantry under arms by daylight.[14]

General Hood lacked sufficient manpower to completely cover the 10-mile Union front. In fact, he had only enough infantry to cover four or five miles of it. He placed Lee's Corps in the center squarely across the Franklin Pike—the obvious line of retreat. Cheatham's Corps was on the right of Lee and Stewart's Corps was on the left. Cheatham's line extended to the rail line from Chattanooga, two miles west of the river and east of the city. Stewart's line ended at the Hillsboro Pike and was refused south along the road. A mile to the north, was Wood's corps. A half mile in front of Wood was a Confederate skirmish line anchored in a strong outpost on Montgomery Hill which was opposite a salient in Wood's line. To protect his vulnerable left, Hood also had begun construction of series of forts, or redoubts, on hills immediately west of the Hillsboro Pike where only rebel cavalry held a weak line to the Cumberland River. The truncated Confederate line sat astride four of the eight main roads into the city, the Nolensville, Franklin, Granny Smith and Hillsboro Pikes. While both armies were behind formidable breastworks, both of Hood's flanks were open to turning movements. Short on ammunition, Southerners were prohibited from firing their weapons unless attacked.[15]

Hood's vulnerabilities were obvious, and George Thomas' battle plan called for a grand left wheel maneuver with Wilson's cavalry, Smith's Sixteenth Corps and Wood's Fourth Corps. Swinging like a gate, the federal right hook, if successful, would land a vicious blow on Hood's left flank. Smith would first pivot on Wood's right four miles from the Brentwood Hills. Once Smith reached the Hillsboro Pike, Wood was to leave a heavy skirmish line on his extreme right, and form the rest of the corps on the Hillsboro Pike to support Smith's men and seize Montgomery Hill. On the Union right, General Steedman was to launch a diversion along the Nashville and Chattanooga Railway to deter Hood from moving troops to re-enforce the right. When the veterans in the trenches moved to attack, garrison troops and armed civilian employees would take their place in the trenches freeing nearly 50,000 veteran Union infantry and cavalry to strike Hood. All of Thomas' primary subordinates—five of six were West Pointers—approved of the plan which stood an excellent chance of not just evicting Hood from his lines, but destroy-

Period view of Union line at Nashville. Photograph taken at the time of the battle in mid–December. Library of Congress.

ing him. Spies had alerted Hood that a Union movement was afoot and on the 14th, he sent all of his supply wagons back five miles to Brentwood.[16]

Hundreds of miles east in Virginia, General Grant chaffed at what he saw as George Thomas' inaction in Tennessee. Grant bombarded Thomas with telegraphic threats and admonishments urging him to take the offensive against Hood. "Now is one of the finest opportunities ever presented of destroying one of the three armies of the enemy," Grant suggested to Thomas on December 8. The Union war effort was producing few gains in late 1864 and Grant was feeling the pressure to accomplish something meaningful. There was real fear in Washington that the longer the Confederates were unmolested, the deeper they dug in and the more havoc they could wreck on the regional railroads and supply lines. The politics of a transfer of the war back to Nashville from Atlanta was not favorable for the Lincoln administration. Grant complained to Sherman, "It has been very hard to get Thomas to attack Hood." Thomas later complained to a friend, "I thought, after what I had done in the war, that I ought to be trusted to decide when a battle should be fought." George Thomas refused to risk his men before he was ready, even if his career was in jeopardy. "A weaker man than Thomas would have yielded to importunity and attacked before he was ready," a prewar colleague wrote. Thomas was ready to move on December 10, but the cold and ice delayed any action until the 15th. During the wait for a thaw, Grant threatened to relieve Thomas. "You have been slow," Grant admonished him. Thomas wondered how he was supposed to take a patchwork army into battle during an ice storm and held firm. "As soon as we have a thaw, I will attack Hood."[17]

Grant would have none of it and sent Major General John A. Logan—the most aggressive general at hand despite being a volunteer officer—to Nashville on the 12th with instructions to assume command unless Thomas had begun his attack. Grant saw Logan as the perfect choice to replace Thomas, who was one of the West Pointers that kept Logan from commanding the Army of the Tennessee when McPherson was killed. The next day, when Grant realized that relieving Thomas would touch off an argument between Logan and Schofield over rank, he decided he needed to go to Nashville. But first Grant would need to stop in Washington and talk to Lincoln and Stanton.[18]

Back in Tennessee, the antagonists were forced to wait out the ice storm. Rain on the 13th, melted the ice. At 8 p.m. on December 14, all federal brigade commanders received orders to be ready to move at 8 a.m. The Yankee infantrymen knew, without being told, that an attack was imminent when they were issued three days of rations and 60 rounds of ammunition. Supply and ordnance wagons were loaded, and double teamed—as many as 12 mules per wagon—to better move the wagons along mud-clogged roads.[19]

With no re-enforcements and the cavalry and some infantry dispatched to Murfreesboro, Hood would find himself fighting with fewer men than he had when he left Franklin. On the morning of the 15th, he ordered that the detached redoubts be modified so that artillery could fire in any direction and the Confederate soldiers therein were ordered "not to surrender under any circumstances."[20]

General Wilson had 12,000 cavalrymen—three fourths mounted and armed with repeating rifles which magnified their numbers—were to constitute the rim of the grand wheel. Thomas gave the attack order to Wilson's cavalry and Smith's infantry at 8:30, but it was 10 a.m. before the dense fog cleared sufficiently to advance—visibility was critical to execute the wheeling movement. Smith's corps first encountered the enemy lines half mile south of the Hardin Pike and captured two small forts. Initially, the swinging gate squeaked, but by noon and with little opposition, it had reached the Hillsboro pike.[21]

Bugles roused the Fourth Corps at 4 a.m. December 15 to same cottony fog so dense it obscured the sun and gave soldiers moving through it a spectral quality. At corps' headquarters, Tom Wood—a brigadier general commanding a corps—nursed the hope that a stellar performance in the coming battle might land a second star on his shoulder. He led the largest federal corps—13,500 infantrymen available the morning of the 15th—arrayed in the center of the Union defenses. As a crucial part of the hinge for General Smith's wheeling movement, Wood had issued detailed instructions to his division commanders. Everyone was to be prepared to move by 6 a.m. Elliott's division held the corps' right flank and was to advance in concert with A. J. Smith's men. General Kimball—on Elliott's left—was to move out the Hillsboro Pike, form on Elliott's left and move when Elliott did. Finally, Beatty was to form on Kimball's left. Wood further specified that each division was to try to hold one brigade in reserve and have five wagons of ammunition, 10 ambulances and wagons with entrenching tools following as closely as possible. The Second division would have a battery of rifled guns, the other two divisions, smoothbore 12-pounders. All remaining wagons and artillery would wait within the defensive lines.[22]

Opdycke's brigade was on the Fourth Corps' right flank. Colonel Lane's brigade was on Opdycke's left and Conrad was in reserve. The First Brigade was positioned to the right of the Hillsboro Pike, facing southwest. The consolidated 74th and 88th Illinois and the 125th Ohio formed the brigade front and were a few paces to the left and 200 yards to the rear of A. J. Smith's corps' left flank. The 36th and the 73rd Illinois and 24th Wisconsin formed the second battle line 300 yards to the rear.[23]

Wood's men—having advanced about 600 yards to their jump off points—waited for Wilson and Smith's wheel to reach them. Wood's skirmishers and the rebels kept up a brisk fire. About 10 a.m. and the opposing artillery commenced firing. One Ohioan maintained that "the firing was so intense and ceaseless that not an individual gun could be distinguished." The Fourth Corps guarded a prominent salient in the federal line located on a hill between the Hillsboro and Granny White Pikes. Straight ahead of the salient—less than a mile—was Montgomery Hill which anchored the left of Hood's heavy, advanced skirmish line. Montgomery was a conical hill, 150 feet in height with wooded slopes and at 800 yards it was the closest point in Hood's line to Thomas' earthworks. At mid-day Smith's corps drew up even with the Fourth Corps and Wood ordered the advance. Thirty thousand Northerners descended on A. P. Stewart's beleaguered corps on Hood's left flank. Watching the advance from the rear, General Wood called the spectacle "magnificently grand and imposing" and believed it offered "the happy presage of the coming glorious victory." Union artillery opened fire on Montgomery Hill, and the Southern skirmishers hunkered down to resist the Union advance.[24]

When the first of Wood's two battle lines crested a ridge and Montgomery Hill came into full view, rebel artillery on the hill opened fire. To the federal officers glassing the crest, Montgomery Hill appeared heavily fortified with strong entrenchments and abatis. The ground between the Wood's men and their objective descended sharply before gently rising through an open wood as it approached the rebel trenches. Stone walls and felled trees provided obstacles to the bluecoats advance. About 1 p.m., Wood sent Colonel Phillip Post's brigade of his old Third Division forward to take the hill. Wood's front line shifted about 30 degrees to the right, advanced across a ravine and went half way up the hill. Post's men discovered that, except for a few skirmishers, the Confederates had departed.[25]

South of Montgomery Hill was a salient in Hood's line anchored by an earthen fort the Confederates simply named Redoubt No. 1. As Kimball and Elliott's divisions approached the enemy's position, Wood had it shelled. About 4 p.m. Elliott—west of the Hillsboro Pike—was ordered to take the unfinished redoubt. Following orders to maintain contact with Smith's corps on his right, Elliott dutifully waited for them to catch up. By 4:30, Elliott had not moved, dusk was at hand and an impatient Wood ordered Kimball's division—east of the pike—forward. Kimball's men slogged across 200 yards of sticky mud in an old cornfield straight at good breastworks held by three Confederate brigades. Two of Kimball's brigades, loaded down with their knapsacks, led the assault through the muck and up a slope. Seventy yards from the enemy, federal officers belatedly halted their men to drop their packs, after which the men plunged forward with renewed energy. By the time they reached the enemy line, the Johnnies were in retreat.[26]

Tardy, but eager, Elliott's division joined the attack led by the ever aggressive Opdycke with Lane's brigade on his left. The 36th Illinois was deployed as skirmishers. Some of the regiment had worked their way down a stone wall just west of the Hillsboro Pike to a point south of the fort that formed the angle of the Confederate line. Here, with one of A. J. Smith's brigades on their right and Kimball attacking from the north, the Illinois skirmishers, led by an audacious lieutenant, seized the initiative. "How many of you are ready to go in?" roared Lieutenant William Hall as he led his men across the turnpike. In moments, the skirmishers were over the fortifications at the rear of the fort and among the defenders where a brief hand to hand contest ensued. They were joined by Smith's men, while in their front, Kimball's division attacked. In 10 minutes, the last remaining stronghold of A. P. Stewart's corps was gone. The victors milled around squabbling over a battery of artillery, hundreds of prisoners, battle flags and countless swords and pistols. The Confederate retreat was in the words of one rebel soldier a "full stampede." Union casualties were light. Lieutenant Richard Hulse of the 125th, commanding a squad of skirmishers, captured an artillery piece and fired a couple of parting shots at the Johnnies.[27]

Schofield's corps had been in reserve until after the Fourth Corps attack, and went into action on the right of A. J. Smith's corps. Wilson's cavalry dismounted, put their seven shot carbines to good use and bulled their way across the Granny White Pike into Hood's rear, effectively flanking Hood on his left. The Confederates retreated eastward toward the Franklin Pike, the left half of their line having collapsed. General Lee's corps on the right was pressured by Steedman's bluecoats and retired south to Overton's Hill. By day's end, Hood's left had given way, his right was battered, but it was not a rout. Under cover of darkness, the rebels labored on a second line of trenches from Shy's Hill to Overton's Hill encompassing the Granny White and Franklin Pikes. "The whole enemy's left driven back, a grand success," wrote Major Joe Bruff reveling in his new position as commander of the 125th Ohio on a day it suffered no casualties.[28]

The very day Thomas launched his attack, Major General John Logan was in the final leg of his journey to Nashville. Grant had met with Lincoln, Stanton, and Halleck, all of whom tried to talk him out of sacking Thomas. The stubborn Grant was unmoved and ready to act when the telegraph brought word that the battle for Nashville had begun. Near Louisville, Logan heard the news and left Grant's order folded in his pocket. One veteran—referring to Logan's volunteer status—rhetorically asked, "Was there a regular officer in the union service that would have been that magnanimous?"[29]

Thomas' cobbled together army had been successful, but the various pieces were scattered at the end of the day. With darkness expected to descend by 6 p.m., Thomas wanted to press on after the retreating enemy, but only Tom Wood was given clear instructions to advance southeasterly toward the Franklin Pike—two and a half miles away—and form his corps across it, facing south. Wood didn't receive the order until sunset and it took half an hour to organize the move. Opdycke's brigade advanced just before dark, facing east, with the 24th Wisconsin as skirmishers. The Corps battle line crept forward, and after crossing the Granny White Pike, bumped into rebel skirmishers. Full darkness at 7 p.m., necessitated a halt for the night, three quarters of a mile short of the Franklin Pike. The Fourth Corps had suffered just 350 casualties and Wood saw no reason to add to that number from friendly fire in the darkness. Opdycke's brigade had moved from the right of the Second Division to the left in the new federal front that was at right angles to the old one. Wood's line rested in the old Confederate earthworks on the left and his right connected with Smith's corps.[30]

By day's end, Hood had retreated two miles, lost 16 cannon and over 2000 men. His new trench line faced north, and was midway between the Union defenses of Nashville and the town of Brentwood, four miles south. It was anchored on the left by what would be known as Shy's Hill. On the right was Overton's Hill, a wide rounded hill protected by a strong earthwork. Shy's was high, but less broad, and the poorly placed earthworks were less formidable. Between the elevations, the terrain was rolling. As the beleaguered butternuts prepared for a cold night, the Yankees were poised to hammer them from the north and west with strong infantry and threaten their escape route down the Franklin Pike with cavalry. Men on both sides were left to ponder what tomorrow would bring.[31]

Facing much of the federal army on his left, Hood repositioned Cheatham's corps from the right flank to the left. East of the Franklin Pike, Overton's Hill anchored the right of Lee's corps which sat across the turnpike. Stewart's corps was on Lee's left in the center with its left on the Granny White Pike. Shy's Hill on the left flank was held by Cheatham's corps. Both rebel flanks were refused back for half a mile. This new, compact line was about three and a half miles in length as it spread across the rolling terrain. Wilson's cavalry threatened Hood's flank southwest of Shy's. Schofield's infantry held the Union right flank opposite Shy's Hill with A. J. Smith's divisions on the left across the Granny Smith Pike. Tom Wood's corps was between the pikes and within striking distance of the Franklin Pike. Steedman's men on Thomas' far left confronted Overton's Hill, four miles from Brentwood.[32]

For once, Hood saw clearly his chances: outnumbered, outgunned and on the verge of being cut-off and surrounded. A gambler if nothing else, Hood decided to risk annihilation, roll the dice and fight. His strategy was modest: take strong positions and invite Thomas to attack. As historian Shelby Foote saw it, "What better way was there to go down, or out, than in a blaze of glory?" As a concession to the odds, Hood ordered his wagon trains south to the Harpeth River and gave his commanders directions for escape should disaster befall his small army. Hood's men worked feverishly during the night improving their new position. By dawn on December 16, many of Hood's men—long-suffering veterans who had marched three times a far as Schofield's men since leaving Alabama—had reached their breaking point.[33]

George Thomas was good spirits when the battle's first day closed. "Attacked enemy's left this morning; drove it from the river, below the city, very nearly to Franklin pike, distance about eight miles," Thomas informed Washington at 9 p.m. Nevertheless, General Grant urged quick, aggressive action: "Push the enemy now and give him no rest until he is entirely destroyed." Thomas was prepared to go forward in the morning depending on what Hood did during the night. To guard against a surprise Confederate assault, Thomas would hold Wilson's cavalry back until Hood's intentions were clear. General Wood received no orders, sought Thomas out after dark and was told to attack or pursue at dawn as the situation dictated.[34]

At sunrise on the 16th, Wood did just that, advancing Elliott's division at 6 a.m., in a light fog, toward the Franklin Pike. With the 24th Wisconsin on the skirmish line, the left of Opdycke's brigade hit the turnpike about 8 a.m. Opdycke ordered a change of front to face south with his left flank on the Franklin Pike and his right connecting with Lane's brigade. Opdycke could only deploy a two regiment front—the 36th and 44th Illinois—and the 125th Ohio was in the brigade's second of three battle lines. After moving forward two miles, Wood's corps encountered Southern skirmishers behind a barricade three fourths of a mile in front of Hood's main line. After a halt to realign, the Fourth Corps advanced and drove the skirmishers back into the main rebel entrenchments. In front of

Wood's men, the Southern earthworks passed around the north side of the 300 foot Overton's Hill and receded to the south for a short distance in Opdycke's front.[35]

Brigadier General Samuel Beatty—an unheralded, Ohio farmer and volunteer officer—advanced his division to attack the north approach to Overton's, while Opdycke's brigade bypassed Overton's Hill to the west to a point where the left of the brigade's first battle line was at a right angle to Hood's main line just 150 yards distant. In that position, enemy muskets and cannon could enfilade Opdycke's front line. Reacting, Opdycke sent his second and third battle lines into the gap between his front line's left and Beatty's division's right, facing them southeast. The entire brigade hastily constructed an adequate log barricade while under fire. During this movement, two privates from Company K were killed—Francis Willis and Henry Walker.[36]

Behind those well-fortified lines on Overton's Hill were six strong Confederate brigades. Thomas left the decision to attack the Hill to Wood's discretion. Colonel Philip Post—now commanding what had been Bill Hazen's old brigade—believed that he could take the hill with support from General Steedman's brigades on his left. With Wood's approval, Post attacked and got within 30 yards of the enemy's breastworks before being stopped by impenetrable abatis, heavy artillery and musketry. Colonel Post was severely wounded by a canister shot and his attack floundered as did Steedman's regiments. This failed attack on Overton's Hill by Post and Steedman resulted in 1000 casualties—the most costly single action by the Union forces during the battle. Opdycke had wanted his brigade to join the assault and Wood left the decision to him. Before he could move, however, General Elliott told Opdycke not to attack without his approval, and that approval was not forthcoming. Elliott must have believed as General Cox later wrote that attackers of a well-entrenched line were at a "terrible disadvantage." Captain Clark later remarked that "more of us are now living as a consequence of General Elliott's order, without doubt."[37]

In response to the attacks on Overton's, Hood sent infantry re-enforcements from Shy's Hill to Overton's leaving the position on Shy's thinly held. Shy's Hill was an impossible position to hold anyway with federal infantry poised north and west, and Wilson's cavalry pushing its way across the Granny White Pike to the south. Union musket balls and artillery shells occasionally passed over the Hill going in opposite directions. Cheatham's infantry on Shy's Hill suffered from both heavy artillery and sniping throughout the day. One Confederate general labeled the artillery unsurpassed "for heaviness, continuance and accuracy." The Northern cannon demolished a section of the rebel defenses—composed mostly of trees and logs—at an angle in the fortifications. Due to a misunderstanding, the First Division of Smith's Corps attacked the hill impetuously, without orders, at 4 p.m. General Thomas had his bugler sound the advance to make it official and the call was taken up by a hundred other bugles along the Union front. Smith's other divisions joined the attack as did Schofield's corps. With federals coming from three sides, Hood's men on Shy's Hill abandoned their fortifications and much of their artillery as they ran away or surrendered. When other Southerners along Hood's line saw the Stars and Stripes on Shy's Hill, the contagion of defeat took hold. In General Cox's words, the rebels "peeled away from the works in wild confusion." No one wanted to die in a lost cause. When the division on Smith's left flank went forward, the movement was emulated by the Fourth Corps divisions in succession from right to left as Cheatham's Corps collapsed, and dissolved into chaos. When the fleeing Confederates encountered Wilson's cavalry armed with repeating rifles, they became a stampede, throwing away muskets and kicking off mud-caked shoes to gain speed.[38]

When the Confederate rout reached Overton's Hill, Opdycke's brigade swung right, facing forward until the brigade was parallel to the rebel line, and then it charged with the 24th Wisconsin in front, followed by the 36th and 44th Illinois. The 125th Ohio was 300 yards back in the second battle line. As panicked Johnnies to their left streamed to the rear, the Confederates on Overton's began to withdraw. Survivors from Post's failed attack hiding in the abatis were the first over the deserted Southern earthworks capturing still hot cannon and battle flags. Captain Powers of the 125th—now part of Wood's staff—went over the works with Opdycke and personally captured a secessionist major and a number of privates. Opdycke's Tigers grappled for battle flags and rounded up prisoners. As the mob of demoralized Southerners fled down the Franklin Pike toward Brentwood, Opdycke deployed the 125th as skirmishers and sent them ahead of the brigade in pursuit.[39]

Hood's army was thoroughly routed. So sudden and complete was the collapse that Hood, awkwardly strapped to his horse, almost a mile away, was dumbfounded. "I beheld for the first and only time a Confederate army abandon the field in confusion," Hood wrote afterward. Many of the veterans from Tennessee and Kentucky "threw away their arms and accouterments and went to their homes, never to enter the service again," according to one Ohio soldier. Personally, Major General Frank Cheatham had difficulty stopping a single private, but General Stephen Lee managed to patch together a Southern rear guard in a wood a half mile south of the Overton farmstead on the Franklin Pike. This illusion of an organized resistance in the rain and gray of dusk was sufficient to inject some caution into the Fourth Corps pursuit.[40]

George Thomas rode up Overton's Hill in time to witness the spectacle of his boys swarming over the hill, waving flags and cheering. On the crest, he saw his men rounding up Confederate prisoners and marching them toward Nashville. The two day haul would prove to be 4500 prisoners, 53 cannon and a couple dozen battle flags. In terms of killed and wounded, Thomas lost about 3000, similar to Schofield's loss at Franklin. Hood lost half that number at Nashville to bullets, grape shot and shrapnel—far more became prisoners or just disappeared. Surveying the battlefield in the fading light, an unusually exuberant Thomas raised a salute. "Oh, what a grand army I have! God bless each member of it."[41]

On the 16th, the Fourth Corps captured 14 cannon, 980 prisoners and two battle flags. The Corps' losses were fewer than a thousand. Unable to resist bragging in his official report, Tom Wood boasted, "Military history scarcely affords a parallel of a more complete victory." Two soldiers from the 125th had been killed in the action and a handful wounded. "The 125th," Captain Clark proclaimed, "by fortune of war, was less conspicuous at Nashville than in any other general engagement. In performing the part assigned to it, the regiment was so fortunate in position as to suffer slight loss."[42]

General Thomas sent Wood's reliable Fourth Corps in pursuit down the Franklin Pike while General Wilson's cavalry was sent down the Granny White Pike and across country to intercept the fugitives further south on the Franklin Pike. Schofield and Smith's corps were halted to avoid accidently shooting each other in the increasing darkness. Most of the fleeing Confederates from Hood's left flank crossed the Brentwood Hills singly or in unorganized groups aiming for the Franklin Pike. According General Cox, "There was hardly the semblance of organization among them." A brigade from A. P. Stewart's corps had been directed to the Brentwood Hills, and they were able to slow the Union cavalry sufficiently in their ride for the Franklin Pike to prevent, in General Cox's opinion, "the larger part of Hood's army from capture." General Forrest spurred his cavalry across the country from Murfreesboro to the Franklin Pike to relieve Stewart's two brigades and act as rearguard.[43]

While Stewart's rearguard kept the Yankee cavalry at bay, General Lee gradually took his men south on the Franklin Pike until halting at midnight two miles south of Brentwood, six miles from the Harpeth River. Wood's corps—the 125th in the forefront of Opdycke's brigade—forged ahead until darkness and uncertainty of what lay ahead dictated a halt eight miles from Nashville and one mile north of the Brentwood Pass. At 10 p.m., a rain storm broke leaving the victorious, but weary Northerners, to seek dry shelter as best they could from the cold rain. In a letter home, Opdycke reported that General Hood' army was in "a demoralized state" and was retreating rapidly.[44]

As the telegraph chattered back in Washington, someone in the press labeled Thomas—once the Rock of Chickamauga—"the Sledgehammer of Nashville." Secretary of War Edwin Stanton woke President Lincoln at the White House and briefed him on the Nashville victory. The next morning Lincoln congratulated Thomas and his scratch army. Yet Lincoln, who had seen too many defeated secessionist armies escape to fight another day, admonished Thomas, "You have made a magnificent beginning; a grand consummation is within your easy reach. Do not let it slip."[45]

"The next ten days," historian Stanley Horn wrote 90 years later, "were a nightmare of nerve wracking hardship and struggle to both armies. Alternately marching and fighting, worn down by battle fatigue and sheer physical exhaustion, they somehow managed to carry on an almost continuous running battle from Nashville to the Tennessee River."[46]

Thomas' patchwork army was eager to finish the Confederate Army of the Tennessee. The Fourth Corps began its pursuit down the Franklin Pike on December 17 in the rain. The reliable and disciplined 125th started south at 7 a.m. as skirmishers on the east side of the Franklin Pike. After an exhausting trek of two or three miles through rough fields and thick woods, the Ohioans were replaced Wilson's cavalrymen—now leading the chase—six miles from Franklin. Remnants of Lee's corps performed yeoman's service for Hood by holding Thomas' cautious pursuit at bay until what remained of the rebel army crossed the Harpeth River at Franklin in the late morning and burned their bridge behind them. By early afternoon the Confederate rearguard took up a blocking position on Winstead Hill. General Wilson got one of his cavalry divisions across the Harpeth below Franklin and flanked Lee's soldiers out of the heights. That evening, the Confederates reached Spring Hill.[47]

With the bridges gone, the rain swollen Harpeth River blocked the way south for Thomas' foot soldiers. When evening came, Opdycke's brigade camped opposite Franklin on the north bank of the river. Opdycke wrote his wife that the great Nashville victory was "the result of Thomas's splendid Generalship." The First Brigade captured one battle flag, three cannon and 205 Confederates, while its losses amounted to just 50 men. It had been an easy battle for the First Brigade and Opdycke thought it deservedly so.[48]

By the morning of the 18th, Union pioneers had pieced together a temporary bridge in Franklin. At 8 a.m. Opdycke's brigade crossed the Harpeth River with the rest of the Fourth Corps. Franklin, the Yankees discovered, was a depressing place filled with melancholy, suffering and death. Wounded men lay in makeshift hospitals everywhere. Sixteen hundred wounded enemy soldiers and their 400 or 500 attendants surrendered. Two hundred seriously wounded bluecoats were repatriated. The Union army passed through the battlefield on its march down the Franklin Pike and saw Union corpses in shallow graves exposed after recent rains. The vast number of Southern graves on the plain south of town revealed the extent of the carnage on November 30. Colonel Opdycke thought the battlefield a scene of "awful desolation."[49]

Elliott's division continued through Spring Hill, and camped four miles south of the town. Further down the Franklin Pike on the morning of the 18th, the pursuing Yankees encountered Rutherford Creek running swift, deep and unfordable. A pontoon bridge was the only remedy. What remained of Cheatham's corps was re-organized in defensive positions on the south side. Hood hoped to be able to fall back behind the Duck River at Columbia and winter in its fertile valley as Braxton Bragg had done in 1862. Yet, he received conflicting advice from his generals about where he should hold the line. The Duck River line would leave some of Tennessee in Confederate hands—a symbolic victory compensating for all the lives Hood's sortie into Tennessee had cost the South. On the other hand, retreating to south of the Tennessee River was far safer, even if it was bad for morale. During the night of the 18th, the Confederates began crossing the Duck River in Columbia on a makeshift pontoon bridge. A weary and disgruntled General Forrest arrived in Columbia and bluntly told Hood that unless he could beyond doubt hold the Duck River line, the army should immediately retreat to below the Tennessee River. Hood acquiesced, and issued orders to retire below the Tennessee in Alabama because of "the condition of the army."[50]

The Yankees broke camp at 6:30 the 19th and moved toward Rutherford Creek where any crossing or bridge construction was sure to be contested. By day, rain, sleet, snow and heavy traffic turned the roads into quagmires and at night they froze into a rutted and impassable surface. General Thomas canceled maneuvers at 8:30 a.m. due to the weather, directing that the men should remain in their camps and be provisioned. For Tom Wood, the weather was the worst he had seen in almost 20 years of soldiering. The pontoon train had mistakenly been sent toward Chattanooga, and had to be recalled and redirected south on the nearly impassable roads. Forage had not arrived for the animals and units from the Fourth Corps were dispatched to secure whatever fodder they could. To replace rotting shoe leather, Wood sent a request for 15,000 pairs of shoes to Nashville. In the end, the Confederates gained a day in their race to the Tennessee River. In skirmishing across Rutherford Creek, Elliott's Second Division took some casualties, but not the 125th which was encamped out of range of the Southern guns. General Elliott sent Opdycke and three escorts on a personal reconnaissance with an eye toward bridging the Creek at night, but after creeping just 300 yards forward, the Colonel confirmed that a night crossing was impossible.[51]

By dawn on the 20th, the Southerners across Rutherford Creek were gone. The 125th joined the brigade's pioneers in constructing a bridge for the Franklin Pike. Finished by 2, Opdycke's brigade crossed the Creek, pressed forward five miles and camped one mile north of the Duck River, opposite Columbia. Falling temperatures were accompanied by sleet during the night. The following day, Wednesday the 21st, with the Confederates on the south bank of the Duck River, the 125th shivered on the north bank in bitter cold waiting for other units to secure a crossing, and erect the pontoon bridge. Major Bruff sent two or three men from each company out foraging for supplies for the pioneers and fodder for the animals. With temperatures hovering near 15 degrees, the pioneer corps, unskilled in bridge construction, cobbled together a rickety, poorly secured bridge over the Duck River by 7 p.m. Soldiers, artillery and supplies were pushed across during the night. Elliott's division was rotated to the rear of the Corps and consequently did not cross until 10 p.m. in what had become another bitter cold night. Once across, at 1 a.m., Elliott's division camped near Columbia, to the east of the road to Pulaski. Opdycke claimed 1000 of the demoralized enemy disserted the rebel cause in Columbia.[52]

There were those in Washington and at Grant's headquarters, safe from the harsh Tennessee weather, who criticized Thomas' pursuit of Hood. On December 22, Thomas informed the War Department that the weather was bad and the rivers and creeks swollen. Furthermore, Thomas complained that Sherman had taken a well-equipped army into Georgia—the healthiest men and the best draft animals—leaving Thomas "only two corps—partially stripped of their transportation ... to oppose the advance into Tennessee of that army which had resisted the advance" of Sherman in the Atlanta campaign, and now included Forrest's cavalry. Secretary Stanton sought to reassure George Thomas. "It is proper for me to assure you that this Department has the most unbounded confidence in your skill, vigor, and determination...," On Christmas Eve, Stanton, and Lincoln overrode Grant and nominated George Thomas for a major generalship in the regular U.S. Army. Privately, Thomas told an aide, "I earned this at Chickamauga."[53]

The afternoon of the 23rd, Wood's infantry moved just five miles south from Columbia before camping—the 125th in a barren wood. It was noon on the 24th before Elliott's division got on the road leading the corps. Opdycke's brigade led Elliott's division and the 125th Ohio was the second regiment in the column. Wilson's cavalry still led the chase, which was contested by General Forrest—a trail of dead Southern cavalrymen and their horses along the road as proof of his determination. Elliott's men covered a hard 15 miles that afternoon. The 125th Ohio camped four miles south of Lynnville, Tennessee.[54]

There was no rest on Christmas Sunday. The Second Division was now last in the Corps column, and the 125th did not march until late morning. After crossing Richland Creek on an unburned bridge, the roads deteriorated to what Opdycke described as "mud, mud, mud deep and almost impassable." Elliott's Second Division reached the familiar country around Pulaski at 2. The railroad terminated at Pulaski, and the Confederates had abandoned large amounts of equipment for lack of draft animals to move it south. Hood's foot soldiers broke into small units and took to the fields for the quickest route to the Tennessee River. The First Brigade counted 21 wagons, two caissons, several ambulances and 10 partially burned wagons of ammunition left by the road. According to one officer in the 125th, the enemy was "evidently retreating in disorder, throwing away many guns." Four miles from Pulaski and 16 miles from their last bivouac, the Brigade halted. To ease the burden on the dwindling supply of horses and mules, General Wood reduced the number of ammunition wagons and reduced their loads to just 10 boxes—10,000 rounds. Food and fodder supply wagons had not keep pace on the impossible roads, and the foraging was abysmal. According to Captain Hinman, "For more than a week we lived almost entirely upon parched corn, now and then greased by stray bit of fresh pork. Those were days of great privation, hardship and suffering." Opdycke and five staffers spent the night in the two room cabin of a Unionist family—eight civilians and two recuperating rebel soldiers. Before departing in the morning Opdycke gave the family a box of hardtack and $5. He echoed the sentiments of many Yankees chasing Hood's dwindling numbers when he wrote home on the 26th that he feared the enemy was too far ahead to catch and that his men deserved to go into winter quarters.[55]

Opdycke's brigade awoke hungry on the 26th and no supply wagons were in sight. Muddy, rutted roads and a shortage of draft animals—Wilson's cavalry having run 6000 horses into the ground since leaving Nashville—stranded the Fourth Corps in camp outside of Pulaski. Some of the Yankees could be seen scouring harvested fields for stray kernels of corn. When rations did arrive, each man drew three days with orders to make them last for five.[56]

What organization remained of Hood's army—one in five barefoot and surviving on parched corn—crossed the Tennessee River on a captured pontoon bridge on December 26 at Bainbridge, Alabama, a few miles upstream from Florence and undeterred by two Union gunboats. By the 27th, Hood and his army of less than 20,000—half what it was a month ago and with most of its artillery gone—was destined for winter quarters in Tupelo, Mississippi. Union cavalry crossed the river at Decatur, Alabama and captured much of what remained of Hood's wagon trains.[57]

At least two days behind Hood on December 27th, the Fourth Corps, trekked 10 miles, halted and gathered fence rails and ignited in huge bonfires for warmth. The next day Opdycke's brigade—the 125th was the tail of the brigade column—led the division. Fifteen miles southwest of Pulaski, near Lexington, Alabama, and 20 miles from Florence, Alabama, the Corps bivouacked for the night. One officer described the region as a wilderness marked by empty homes and roads littered with wrecked wagons and animal carcasses. To help ease the shortage of rations and animal fodder, the pioneers from each regiment went to work making the road to Pulaski passable for supply wagons. Foraging parties were dispatched into the surrounding countryside with their only restriction being "not to enter a house or pillage." Only a modest amount of corn was procured.[58]

George Thomas finally conceded that Hood's "disheartened and disorganized rabble of half-naked and barefoot men," had escaped his grasp. General Cox wrote that the Confederate army that limped into Tupelo "seemed almost to lose the character of a disciplined army." After 10 days and 100 miles, the pursuit was over. Thomas ordered Wood to concentrate his corps at Huntsville, Alabama. On the morning of the final day of 1864, the Yankees were told to build good fires to dry all tents and blankets before marching back to Lexington. A supply train provided the men with another three days of rations. The day ended with an eight mile march northeasterly toward Athens where the Northerners spent a very cold New Year's Eve in the open.[59]

Hood's invasion of central Tennessee had morphed into a stunning Union victory. As one of Thomas' biographers concluded, "one of the two great armies of the Confederacy was eliminated." Thomas ended the campaign with over 13,000 Confederate prisoners and 72 captured cannon. John Bell Hood asked Richmond to relieve him of command in January. "Thomas is a great general," a proud Emerson Opdycke proclaimed. "What has Sherman ever done that equals this?"[60]

The momentous year of 1864 had come to a close. Pre-eminent Civil War historian Bruce Catton 90 years later noted that "it had been a long year and a hard year" marked by two momentous events in the history of warfare—soldiers voting to continue the fight and civilians back home giving the national government a mandate to carry the war to conclusion. Now as the triumphant year closed, Catton wrote, "Grant remained in front of Richmond, Thomas held Tennessee, and Sherman was in Savannah. The Confederacy now consisted of the Carolinas and southern Virginia—no more than that. Spring was not far away, and spring would inevitably bring the end."[61]

20

FROM HUNTSVILLE TO COLUMBUS

New Year's Day was also the Sabbath, but there was no rest for the Fourth Corps. Instead its soldiers marched eight or nine miles to the Elk River in northern Alabama and waited for a bridge to be completed. Opdycke's brigade appropriated a gristmill and the flour and cornmeal produced was a welcome addition to meager rations. January 4 was marked by a marathon march of 22 and a half miles over terrible roads. Opdycke gave his men 10 minutes of rest every hour and avoided the straggling that plagued other brigades in the division. Opdycke's men finally concluded their journey on January 5 a mile west of Huntsville, Alabama.[1]

Although the weather was unpleasant on the 6th, the arrival of mail and construction of winter quarters cheered the men. Trees were felled and building materials were ripped from existing structures. One wag in the 125th noted, "Unless the guards do better work, Huntsville will be destroyed to furnish materials for the camp." This work continued until the 11th. The four-man log "houses" were nine by 10 feet. One Ohioan described the Fourth Corps winter camp as "shanties, huts and nondescript affairs of various kinds supplemented with tents." A corps-wide inspection found the Opdycke's First Brigade had constructed the best winter quarters. As reward, Opdycke relaxed the reins on foraging for a day. But two days later, when the sutlers arrived in camp—Lieutenant Rice's older brother was the 125th's sutler—Opdycke re-instituted a camp guard to limit foraging.[2]

An understanding Colonel Opdycke allowed his black servant to go home to visit his wife that winter. While the Yankees could be kind to former slaves, the local residents could be hostile. In a harbinger of things to come, racially motivated violence occasionally became an army problem. On January 17, James Clemens, a nephew of former secessionist Alabama senator Jeremiah Clemens, fatally shot an unarmed black man in a dispute over the sale of cotton. The nephew's defense was that he had a permit to carry a gun from General Gordon Granger. "I could not see that it anywhere allowed him to kill a fellow man," Opdycke wrote of the incident and sent an outraged Clemens to the provost marshal for trial in Nashville.[3]

The entire Fourth Corps settled into a winter routine. Drill and dress parades were initiated, soft bread was added to the diet and small libraries sprouted up. A renewed interest in religion blossomed with one soldier reporting that there was "a great revival of religion" in January 1865. Services became more frequent and better attended, and revivals became popular, twice a week affairs. John W. Lewis—a former circuit preacher—had been the 125th chaplain since November 1863, joining the regiment in February 1864 after recruiting duties. David Moore wrote Opdycke of the chaplaincy in October 1863,

"I propose making Lewis chaplain, if he does not succeed in securing a lieutenancy. He is a noble man, full of energy, faithful and consistent as a Christian, a persistent worker.... He is a very good preacher." On the other hand, Moore admitted Lewis was not a great orator or penman. However, "he will not intermeddle with business belonging to headquarters, as some Chaplains do." In the spring of 1864, Opdycke thought Lewis "a better pastor than preacher; but he is well liked ... and is doing good." However, conflicts with now Lieutenant Colonel Joe Bruff, led Lewis to resign on January 25, stating in his letter of resignation that he was "unwilling to remain in a position where I find myself unable to render that service which I think required by my Office." Bruff endorsed Lewis' resignation "approved. This officer is entirely worthless to the Regiment. He has neither the respect or confidence of officers or men and his influence is bad." As noted by historian Bell Wiley, "Spiritual efforts in many organizations were seriously hindered by the uncooperative attitude of tactical leaders." Lewis may have been seen by Bruff as Opdycke and Moore's man. The chaplain of the 24th Wisconsin was recognized for his superior ability, and many Ohio Tigers transferred to his services. Army chaplains in general got mixed reviews, and many came in for criticism. One critical observer in the Fourth Corps expressed his opinion of the army's chaplains in general in the *Cleveland Leader*, "It is a notorious fact that the majority of chaplains in our army are a disgrace to their holy calling." Nevertheless, Wiley concluded that "many chaplaincies throughout the war were held by good men impelled by lofty motives and thoroughly devoted to the cause of righteousness." The dedicated Lewis didn't leave the army. A month later he moved to the Fourth Corps First Division as chaplain of the 45th Ohio.[4]

Although there was no rebel army nearby to fear, Confederate cavalry was still active in northern Alabama. The region was also home to what one veteran described as "bushwackers, guerilas, and other roving bands of cowardly assassins," often indistinguishable from organized Southern cavalry and often outfitted with fragments of Union uniforms. On January 18, the Third Division lost a foraging party of 10 wagons and its guard to enemy cavalry. Two days later, a half dozen foragers from the 101st Ohio were captured as were four more Ohio soldiers guarding local Unionist families. The home guards were ordered back to camp and the foraging expeditions were more heavily armed.[5]

By the end of January, General Stanley returned to command of the Fourth Corps. When Opdycke saw Stanley, on the 30th, the General seemed to agree that Opdycke's actions during the Franklin battle were of singular importance. This naturally pleased Opdycke. According to General Wood, George Thomas expressed his desire after the Nashville battle to "do something" for Opdycke. Thomas, who understood army politics, wanted to act quickly—while all was "warm." Desiring a star, but being realistic, Opdycke sagely observed to his wife, "It is much better to have one's record exceed one's rank than to have the rank exceed one's record." Still he acknowledged his ambition by admitting that if he commanded a division he would want a corps. Opdycke was granted much deserved leave and left for Warren on February 3, stopping in Columbus briefly to lobby for Captain Bates' promotion to major. On February 7, Emerson Opdycke's often promised promotion to brigadier general arrived. He bought the trappings of a general officer: two pairs of general's stars for the "awful" price of $16.50, and a sword and belt for $35. Captain Bates was promoted, but he could not be mustered because, although he was on Opdycke's staff, the 125th was his regiment and its reduced numbers only authorized a lieutenant colonel.[6]

Returning from leave on March 4, Opdycke was stranded in Nashville as heavy rains washed out many of the bridges on the route to Huntsville. Tennessee's capital was full of Yankee soldiers and had terrible accommodations, even for general officers. Opdycke's mood was black when complained to Lucy about the dirty, uncomfortable, lice infested hotel where he lodged. He began to think about leaving the service and going back into business since he believed the fighting was over and the army could do without him. Opdycke and a handful of fellow officers made arrangements to travel overland to Murfreesboro and then south to Stevenson, Alabama where they arrived on Wednesday, March 8. A fast train to Huntsville and an escort of Ohio cavalry put Opdycke in camp by nightfall where he was serenaded by the 24th Wisconsin's band. He ordered a brigade review for the next day.[7]

By a vote of the regimental officers, the 125th's old, tattered battle flag was awarded to General Opdycke. Lieutenant Colonel Bruff wanted to have the flag given to the state so he could deliver it and make a presentation speech, but he lacked the votes. The presentation took place on the 13th as the entire regiment stood at attention in front of Opdycke's headquarters. Captain Ridgely Powers—whose post-war career would include a brief stint as carpetbagger governor of Mississippi—made the presentation. It was an emotional moment for Emerson Opdycke. Captain Powers left on leave a day or two later, and took Opdycke's colonel's sword, sash and the old flag with him to deliver to Mrs. Opdycke. The old flag eventually found its way to into Ohio state custody after Opdycke's death.[8]

On a rainy March 28, Stanley's corps boarded trains in Huntsville bound for Knoxville as part of a blocking force in case Confederate units in Virginia attempted to flee west. Opdycke's brigade traveled in five sections of 13 cars each, which meant some of the men had a very uncomfortable ride atop the cars. During the night the train passed through Stevenson and Bridgeport and reached Chattanooga at 5 a.m. on the 29th. Three hours later, the journey resumed only to be interrupted by a six car derailment three miles west of Cleveland, Tennessee. Five men were injured, and one—an Illinois quartermaster—was killed. The brigade reached Cleveland at 3 p.m. where the garrison was commanded by Colonel John Q. Lane, whose brigade had been devastated at Franklin. An altercation between two of Lane's staff officers and a member of the 125th, led to an exchange between Lane and Opdycke over the "ungentlemanly manner" in which Lane's men had acted. Opdycke's star put an end to any further discussion. The military train passed through Loudon at 5 a.m. and arrived at Knoxville at 3 p.m. March 31. Continuing east, the first stop Saturday morning, April 1, was at New Market and finally at Bull's

Brigadier General Emerson Opdycke. Library of Congress.

Gap, Tennessee, where at 8 a.m.—after journeying 275 miles by rail—the men left the cars. They camped on a ridge 50 miles northeast of Knoxville.[9]

News of the fall of Richmond reached the Fourth Corps on April 3, at 2 p.m., and was celebrated with a 100-gun salute. The Confederate capital may have fallen, but the Fourth Corps was ordered to send its excess baggage to Knoxville for storage and be prepared to march. To Opdycke that sounded like "campaigning in earnest," but in a visit later that day, General Wood told Opdycke he believed—correctly it turned out—the Corps would have no part in any coming hostilities.[10]

On the evening of Monday, April 10, after a day of repairing the railroad, a dispatch arrived announcing Lee's surrender at Appomattox. According to Captain Clark, "The boys went wild. Everybody turned out. Ammunition was wasted recklessly. It will not be needed any more." Captain Whitesides—who spent part of his days as Provost Marshal administering the oath of allegiance to former secessionists—witnessed a more sedate celebration at division headquarters marked by a serenade by the 24th Wisconsin band followed by a grand jubilee. Opdycke himself stayed at his headquarters and was amused by the many officers who went to division headquarters sober and afterward, required assistance to find their camps. The following morning the army began shifting to a peacetime mode as orders were issued to stop burning fence rails and prohibiting the destruction of field crops. On Saturday, April 15—at the end of a beautiful day in the mountains—news arrived of Lincoln's assassination. Opdycke wrote Lucy, "Was the sacrifice needful? God above us alone knows."[11]

With the war over in the minds of many soldiers, the Fourth Corps was ordered to Nashville on the 18th. Speculation was rampant on the future of the corps: would it be disbanded and the men sent home or would it move down the Mississippi River? On the 19th at 5 a.m., Opdycke's brigade began the long journey to Nashville. The bulk of the brigade went west by rail while the 125th rode the wagon train to guard against bushwackers. On the 23rd the Ohioans passed through Knoxville and camped near the railroad west of town. The 125th finally left Knoxville by rail at 7 p.m. on the 27th. The trip west passed through Chattanooga, northern Alabama, Tullahoma and Murfreesboro finally reaching Nashville at daylight on the 29th. A day later, the 125th was in Camp Harker three miles from the city where General Opdycke had appropriated the parlor of a brick mansion for his headquarters. He assured his wife that the "love lorn" widow who occupied the place was of no interest to him.[12]

The Nashville papers dated the 29th carried the news of the generous surrender terms General Sherman had offered General Joe Johnston's Confederate army in North Carolina. The Fourth Corps future remained a mystery. All that was known was that General Thomas was ordered to concentrate his forces near Nashville. On May 1, Captain Clark wrote, "The war is surely ended." To mark the occasion, a grand review of the Fourth Corps—the Twenty-Third Corps having been transferred to North Carolina during the winter—by General Thomas was scheduled for the 8th. This review would be a smaller, but no less meaningful than the Grand Review held in Washington for Grant and Sherman's men. The *Nashville Daily Union* on May 6 reported that the review, which would be held between the Franklin and Hardin Pikes, would be the largest ever seen west of the Alleghenies. The 19,000 men filling the mile long Fourth Corps column represented more than at any time since the corps was organized in 1863. Stanley, with disgust, noted that the increase in numbers was partly due to "unworthy men, skulkers, who hastened to join their ranks now that fighting was over" and large numbers of conscripted men. Captain Clark labeled it "a great show for the citizens of Nashville." The troops passed in review before General Thomas with each general officer taking his place near the commanding general when his men passed in review. When Thomas desired to see one last charge, Opdycke's First Brigade, "the Saviors of the army" at Franklin, was selected. It was done with the 125th Ohio in the first battle line, and in hindsight, Clark labeled it "our last charge." Afterward Thomas was heard to exclaim, "Ah! That was first rate, first rate." Everyone agreed it was a fine show, and once concluded, a reception for the brigade and divisional officers was held at Corps headquarters. Sandwiches were washed down with beer and champagne. The spirits flowed freely, but Opdycke drank nothing but water.[13]

Many soldiers saw the grand review as the logical end to their service, yet, drill resumed on the 13th. Captain Clark wrote, "Drills repeated. Some of the boys say we are preparing for the next war." Ten days later a local farmer complained of First Brigade soldiers stealing his fence rails for firewood. Ordered to make new rails, the project failed when the officers and men colluded to cut too many trees and split too few rails. The officers in charge were under suspicion in the affair, but protected by Opdycke.[14]

By late spring, Nashville was overrun with returning former Confederates. A rebel cavalry lieutenant pragmatically told a correspondent for the *Cleveland Leader* on May 22, "We have either got to live under the old flag or leave the country—Slavery, to preserve which I entered the army, is played out, and I am going home determined to earn an honest living and do my duty to the old government." When Confederates west of the Mississippi surrendered on May 26, Captain Clark was moved to write, "We are now confident that the Fourth Corps will be mustered out within a few days." The next day, Lieutenant Colonel Bruff sent a request to the War Department for the 125th to be mustered out en mass when Company A, the senior company, was released.[15]

Ohio would elect a governor in 1865. The Republican Union Party would hold its convention to select a candidate on June 21 and Jacob Cox—now a major general and military commander of the western district of North Carolina—was the leading candidate. Each Ohio regiment was entitled to send a delegate, and the politician/soldier Joseph Bruff was the 125th's. Unlike Bruff's request for leave that proved so contentious a year ago, his application for 20 days of leave to attend the convention was endorsed by Generals Opdycke and Elliott.[16]

The war was over and the volunteers were ready to go home, but no one knew how this would happen. A correspondent for the *Cleveland Leader* observed, "Everyman has a stock of facts on hand, selected for his own comfort to substantiate opinions founded on his wishes." On June 2, the long-awaited muster out protocol arrived from Washington, and brought disappointment to many. Only those men whose enlistments expired before September 1, 1865, were to be released, which meant only Company A of the 125th. In Opdycke's brigade, however, all but two of his regiments and nine companies of the 125th were going home. The 73rd, 74th, and 88th Illinois and the 24th Wisconsin were being discharged. Opdycke wrote, "God bless them all." On June 8, Company A was mustered out, and left for home three days later. Captain Whitesides was breveted major, and Dr. McHenry resigned. Because of its reduced numbers, the 125th would now only have only acting field officers. Brevet Brigadier General Emerson Opdycke would be retained, for now. There were rumors that Opdycke might be considered for a coveted regular army commission, but he downplayed this in letter to his wife. In reality, he lobbied for a colonelcy writing General Thomas on June 27, "I would like to have it, because I am desirous of continuing in the profession of arms." A regular army commission was never formally offered to him.[17]

After all the discharges, the Second Division of the Fourth Corps would have only two consolidated brigades, the First and Third. The First would now be composed of the 36th and 44th Illinois, the 125th Ohio and transfers from the Second Brigade: the 26th Ohio, 40th and 57th Indiana. Opdycke's only comment on his new regiments was that the 26th had a good band. A rumor that the Fourth Corps was going to Galveston, Texas, proved true. In mid–June, orders arrived sending the corps first to New Orleans, and eventually Texas. Since the winter of 1861, European adventurism in Mexico had been a concern for the Lincoln administration. Only the French remained in Mexico by 1864 and Austrian Archduke Maximilian had been installed as emperor in April. Opposing the French and Maximilian was a rag-tag Mexican Republican force lead by President Benito Juarez. For the most part, the French occupied the major cities while the Mexican Republicans controlled the countryside. The Lincoln administration refused to recognize Maximilian's legitimacy and supplied the Mexican rebels with arms. Although there were fears of French incursions into U.S. territory with the collapse of the Confederacy, such concerns were overblown. In Mexico, even the hint of an invasion by the United States in 1865 to assist Juarez was sufficient to cause many Maximilian loyalists to desert their emperor. In Texas, the Fourth Corps would be a deterrent to any cross border incursions by the French and be viewed as a possible invasion force by Maximilian. General Stanley's long-suffering Midwesterners were going to be pawns in a diplomatic chess game which none had enlisted for, and of which they were never fully apprised. Company B of the 125th was to remain in Nashville to muster out.[18]

To begin the journey south, the Second Division boarded trains on June 15 for Johnsonville, Tennessee, 60 miles due west of Nashville on the Tennessee River. The next day, the 125th boarded the 500-foot sidewheel steamer *Nicholas Longworth* in the forenoon, and 10 days' rations were distributed. Unseasonably low water would prevent sailing at night or in poor visibility. Overcrowding on the steamer meant many men faced an unpleasant journey on the open deck. But this was not the most serious problem. Insubordination, fueled by consternation over this deployment to Texas no one wanted, had infected the once steadfast Fourth Corps. Captain Wilbur Hinman of the 65th Ohio wrote that many soldiers "felt most keenly, that they were not treated with that fairness, justice and consideration to which they were entitled." Other men who had fought less and served less time were going home. Why not them? It was discovered at Johnsonville that several men from the Second Division had taken unauthorized leave in Nashville. Many others openly boasted that they would leave if they got the chance. Private Tom Brown of the 125th, walked away in Nashville, but reappeared when his original company, B, was mustered out in Cincinnati and simply followed them home. The veterans blamed the unrest on the new conscripts and substitutes, and they were the worst offenders.[19]

The journey south began on the 17th. On the night of the 18th, the *Longworth* anchored in heavy fog. A number of Third Brigade men went missing. According to Captain Clark, many of the men in the 125th were likewise "rebellious." Neither Opdycke, Bruff nor Bates were with the regiment, and the acting commander—the German-born Captain Anthony Vallendar—had spent much of his service on detached duty and was hardly known to the men. General Elliott and his staff were aboard, but were oblivious to the problem. In the end, the superior discipline in the 125th won out. Open mutiny occurred in General Conrad's Third Brigade, but a solution was negotiated. Other regiments in the corps were disarmed as a precaution. Eventually, the talk of mutiny in the Fourth Corps subsided. At last, late in the afternoon of June 22, New Orleans came into view. The following day, the *Longworth* offloaded the men onto the old battlefield where Andrew Jackson defeated the British in 1814, four miles below the city. The Mississippi delta was a new world for the Ohio boys. There were oranges on the trees, Magnolia blossoms, 10-foot alligators and snakes in the grass. Mosquitos were plentiful and aggressive. First Brigade headquarters was in a sugar refinery with a view of the Mississippi. The only water came from the river and was totally unfit for drinking except when boiled to make coffee.[20]

Division commander George Washington Elliott was transferred to the Department of Kansas, a military backwater, on the 24th. Elliott had been barely known to the men of the division he had commanded—less than half could recognize him by sight—and his departure was hardly noticed. The next day, General Opdycke was ordered to take temporary command of the Second Division. This promotion jumped Opdycke ahead of brigadiers in the Division and the Corps with more seniority. He wrote his wife that the new command was unexpected and the division needed his attention to return it to it former efficiency. Colonel John Russell of the 44th Illinois assumed command of the First Brigade.[21]

On the 27th, Major General Phil Sheridan, now commander of the Military Division of the Southwest, visited the Division he once commanded. While Opdycke bemoaned leaving General Thomas' command, he endorsed Phil Sheridan as his next choice. Opdycke's opinion of Thomas—one of six regular army major generals—was not shared in the War Department where "the Sledgehammer of Nashville" was not given command of one of the postwar geographic military divisions in the United States.[22]

The final muster rolls for June for the 125th showed 63 men mustered out and 33 no longer fit for service. One of the men mustered out with Company B was Apollos Morse. The real Morse took sick and left the regiment before it departed Ohio in 1862 and he paid a substitute to take his place rather than return. The substitute, Joel Carr, mustered out in Morse's place and name in 1865 having served honorably. Captain Ridgely Powers, now acting assistant adjutant general for the First Brigade, would be mustered out with his original company, B. Powers would leave the regiment with a recommendation for a brevet lieutenant colonelcy endorsed by generals Opdycke, Elliott, Stanley and Sheridan. Captain Charles Clark of the 125th took Powers place on the brigade staff.[23]

On July 5 as Wood's division began boarding the ships for the journey to Texas, General Sheridan gave Opdycke 30 days leave. Opdycke and Captain Powers hurriedly boarded a steamer bound for Washington. By the 13th, the two officers were in Fortress Monroe, Virginia, on their way to Warren, Ohio, via Washington and New York City.[24]

After a month in the unhealthy Mississippi delta, the Second division began boarding the steamer *Champion* on July 16 for the journey to Texas. The 125th joined three other regiments, brigade and division headquarters aboard. The steamer sailed early on the 17th, and by afternoon the Yankees were in the Gulf of Mexico and in the grip of an epidemic of seasickness. An estimated that 19 out of 20 men were seasick. Relief didn't arrive until the 19th when the steamer anchored at the entrance to Matagorda Bay on the Texas coast. Transferring from the steamer to lighters for the run into the Bay was time-consuming and it was July 23 before the 125th was offloaded. The small ramshackle village of Indianola on the Bay was destined to be the depot for the Fourth Corps once the wooden piers were replaced. Until then, the lighters ran 12 miles up the Bay to Port

Lavaca, bypassing Indianola with its brackish, dysentery-inducing water. Port Lavaca was a marginally more pleasant town. Aside from the watermelons blamed for cholera, and clouds of flies and mosquitoes—mosquito nets became standard issue—there was a nice little hotel with a pleasant, plump landlady.[25]

By July 24 most of the Second Division was on the road to Victoria, Texas—25 miles northwest—where General Stanley established his headquarters. The 125th arrived there after an unpleasant trek across a barren, dry plain under a boiling sun. "The country, as far as the eye can reach," recorded one unimpressed soldier, "is one vast sand plain, very productive of short grass, spotted cattle and villainous mosquitoes, and little else." These veterans of the Atlanta campaign found the march "beyond our previous experience." The officers turned a blind eye to straggling and it was long after dark when the last man reached camp.[26]

The Corps new posting had abundant, but stagnant water, from the Guadalupe River—tepid, nauseous and polluted by local herds of horses and cattle. The banks of the Guadalupe were lined with oak trees dripping with Spanish moss that was infested with insects and snakes. The oaks, however, were the only shade for miles. What the surgeons deemed malarial poisoning was a constant threat. Some of the men simply dropped dead from undiagnosed maladies. General Stanley felt the weather was "very warm and tiresome." The First Brigade was posted on the plain along the Lavaca River eight to 10 miles from Matagorda Bay on an old Mexican War post known in 1846 as Camp Irwin. The land was owned by a local rancher who was with the Mexican army opposing the French. Due to the heat, there would be no drill. The only camp guards oversaw the quartermaster and commissary stores as no sane soldier would hike 10 miles under a relentless sun to reach Port Lavaca. The brigade's horses had been left at New Orleans, so local ponies and mules were the only transport.[27]

This new duty in Texas caused unrest among the long suffering veterans. Captain Clark asked in the regiment's history, "What did the Fourth Corps do or leave undone in its long career that led to this banishment?" According to General Stanley, one corps of the Army of the Tennessee was destined for Texas also, but the soldiers refused and General Logan got the order rescinded. Colored troops from the 25th Corps were sent to act as stevedores at the ports to free white troops to fight. Stanley claimed that the superior discipline in the Fourth Corps was a major reason it was sent to Texas. Acknowledging that the Corps was there to deter French adventurism, Clark wrote, "We did not enlist for two wars, but ... would rather fight Maximilian's army than stay here." Stanley admitted that morale was poor and "discipline was none too good." With some sympathy, Stanley recalled, "In truth, our men felt so wronged in having been sent to Texas at all that it is a wonder we could hold them in hand."[28]

During the last six months of 1865, the closest French troops to Victoria were elements of the French Foreign Legion over 600 miles west at Chihuahua where the Legionnaires were rapidly alienating the resident Mexican aristocracy with a variety of depredations. The Legion didn't concern General Stanley who later wrote, "the rank and file of this nondescript corps of the French army was then made up of rapscallions and sweepings of the low quarters of Paris." The three Fourth Corps divisions were spread from San Antonio to the Gulf shore. The Second Division was arrayed along a derelict rail line that ran from Lavaca to Victoria, 12 miles. The primitive, strap rail, ungraded track had been destroyed during the war. The Division made a half-hearted effort to repair it and were successful enough to allow a couple wheezy engines and rickety cars to move supplies to the brigades. The Division headquarters was located in the camp of the Third Brigade, two miles downstream, from Victoria. With General Opdycke on leave, command of the division fell to the balding, Prussian-trained Brevet Brigadier General Joseph Conrad. It was boring duty and the Yankees sat around camp playing games and eating good quality beef from steers that were cheap at $5. At the end of July, the muster rolls of the 125th recorded the names 370 men of which 218 were actually present.[29]

By early August the unbearable heat had cost the lives of three men in the First Brigade and the rest were prohibited from wandering more than two miles from camp. Nevertheless, the prospect of heat stroke couldn't keep men in camp and roll calls were held five times a day. Some Yankees were shooting cattle on the prairie for sport and faced court-martial if caught. General Opdycke returned from leave and met with General Sheridan in New Orleans on August 21. General officers were being mustered out of the service and Opdycke, after seeing home, was willing to leave the army, adding, "I shall urge Gen. S. to muster out the 125th Ohio and I think I can persuade him to do it." Opdycke never returned to the Fourth Corps or his beloved 125th. A week later, he was on his way home to Ohio for good.[30]

By mid–August the mosquito-borne tropical fevers were on the increase, striking enlisted and officers equally. After a soldier in the 44th Illinois succumbed, Captain Clark was blunt in his assessment: "If he had been discharged at Nashville, he might have lived many years." The mosquitoes, multiplying to a peak in the fall, were an unconquerable foe held only partially at bay by netting and smudge fires. Tarantulas were an ever present danger, and the medicinal whiskey administered to counteract their stings led to many faked tarantula stings until the surgeons caught on and began lacing the whiskey with castor oil. The Yankees' diet was, at least, more varied than the Atlanta campaign with melons, fish, sweet potatoes, milk, oysters and poultry.[31]

A re-organization on September 1 abolished the storied Fourth Corps and the 125th became part of the Second Division, District of Texas. A correspondent to the *Cleveland Leader* reported on September 11 that the "troops are almost universally dissatisfied.... Despite the stringent measures on the part of commanding officers, it is a patent fact that the morale of the Corps is gone." Dissolution of the proud Fourth Corps, it was the correspondent's opinion, robbed the men of their corps identity and reduced them to "little better than a mob." A disgruntled soldier from Warren wrote a letter to the *Western Reserve Chronicle*. "I should endeavor to ask you why it is that we are kept in a country such as this with nothing to do but fight mosquitoes, drink filthy water and consume rations that were brought to this country in 1492."[32]

Perhaps General Opdycke had some influence with General Sheridan, because on the 8th, it was rumored that muster out orders for the 125th were at division headquarters. Some of the men of the 125th serving in the Veteran Reserve Corps—composed of men unfit for regular duty, but still able to serve—had already been mustered out. On the 18th at 8 a.m., blank muster out rolls arrived in the 125th's camp, and work began immediately. The paper forms were "as large as a barn door" and nearly 90 were required for a regiment. Men on detached duty were returned to camp to be mustered-out with their companies. The rolls were completed on the 22nd. Clark, in his regimental history, lists 310 men who signed the muster out roll with the regiment in Texas on September 23, 1865. He summed up the euphoria: "We are citizens." The chaplain from the 65th Ohio, Thomas Powell, conducted the regiment's final religious service. In his sermon, Powell chose an appropriate Bible passage around which to build his message. Powell quoted John XIX:30 to the former Tigers. "When he had received the drink, Jesus said, 'It is finished.' With that, he bowed his head and gave up his spirit." The last volunteer regiments remained in Texas until the end of the year.[33]

September 25, reveille was at 2 a.m. The 26th Ohio's band played a farewell and the almost civilians of the 125th marched away. At Port Lavaca the men boarded a small steamboat for transfer to the ship *Suwanee* which sailed eight miles down the bay and anchored to await out a gale before crossing the sand bar. It was the 29th before the steamship crossed the bar into a rough sea that reacquainted the men with seasickness. On the 30th, the *Suwanee* docked at Galveston and was resupplied before sailing the afternoon of October 1 for New Orleans. The next day, a chronically ill Private Michael Quirk died and was buried at sea. The 3rd, the ship entered the Mississippi River and on the 4th, the *Suwanee* docked at a wharf in the upper end of New Orleans. After a day spent waiting in an old cotton warehouse, the 125th marched on the 6th to the new steamboat, *Magnolia* and started up the Mississippi in the late afternoon. Indignation swept through the veterans, when the boat's officers refused to lease empty staterooms to soldiers at any price, even though two thirds of the staterooms were empty.[34]

On October 8, Private John Hall died of a chronic illness and his remains were sent to the Union hospital in Vicksburg. The next day a cylinder head blew out in the steamer's engine and one man from Company I was severely injured by steam and several others sustained lessor injuries. The *Magnolia* limped slowly north on one paddlewheel. Another man from Company I, Private August Weber, died of illness contracted in Texas—the last Tiger to die in uniform. After very slow sailing, the boat reached Cairo, Illinois, late in the evening of October 11. The men marched from the wharf to the Illinois Central Railroad where they boarded a train of freight cars. Of their accommodations Clark wrote, "We are still cattle, but will be men in a few days." The train left Cairo in rain and falling temperatures. At daylight, the train was transferred to Ohio and Mississippi Railroad tracks where heavy rail traffic caused delays. As Clark wrote, "We would prefer to march." Lieutenant Colonel Bruff—re-elected to the Ohio legislature, but back with the men—joked that the regiment was not shipped as fast freight.[35]

On the morning of October 15, the men of the 125th arrived at Cincinnati. They marched to the Little Miami depot and boarded a train for Columbus where they would be paid. At 4 p.m. the train arrived in Columbus and the men were marched out to Camp Chase and assigned barracks. Sleep was difficult that night as the men, who were not reacclimated to the colder Ohio fall weather. During the day, they huddled around campfires, waited on the paymaster and planned their futures. Finally, on October 18, the paymaster appeared. Each man was paid and received a discharge paper. Most left camp immediately for the city in omnibuses provided by local merchants. Two days later, complimentary promotions—the recipients would never be mustered at that rank—were awarded: Lieutenant Colonel Bruff to colonel; Major Bates to lieutenant colonel; Captain Stiuger to major; and Lieutenant Hulse to captain. The war over, the Union preserved, the 125th Ohio, like all the volunteer regiments, passed into history. In 1895, Captain Clark bade a final farewell to the regiment with these words. "The growl of the tiger will be heard no more. Good-bye 125th Ohio; good-bye." There would be reunions, beginning in 20 years, and monuments on fields of battle, but for most of the men nothing in their lives would be more memorable than their years as members of Opdycke's Tigers. They had given the country the best they had, in some cases their lives, and helped preserve the Union. What more could their country ask of them?[36]

Roster

This roster is adapted from the original in Charles Clark's 1895 history. It pertains only to each soldier's military service, 1862 to 1865, with a few notable exceptions. Clark's roster begins with soldiers present in January 1863. Inaccuracies no doubt exist, and for more specific details readers should consult the National Archives, Ohio History Connection and genealogy websites. Abbreviations are employed to save space: *=mustered out of service in 1865; DD=disability discharge, either combat or noncombat related; DS=died in service, usually noncombat related; VRC=veteran reserve corps.

Field and Staff Officers

Opdycke, Emerson, Lieutenant Colonel, Colonel, wounded at Resaca; command of 1st Brigade, 2nd Division, August 1864; Brigadier General, February 1865; command of 2nd Division, June 1865; Brevit Major General, July 1865*; post-war dry goods merchant in New York City; died of accidental gunshot wound, April 1884; buried in Warren, Ohio.

Banning, Henry, B., Lieutenant Colonel, transferred to 121st Ohio Infantry, April 1863

Moore, David H., Major, Lieutenant Colonel, resigned, September 1864; post-war minister in Methodist Episcopal church; chancellor of University of Denver and president of Colorado seminary, 1875; editor of *Western Christian Advocate,* 1889; named bishop in 1900; China missionary 1900–1904; appointed bishop in Cincinnati, 1914; died, November 1915, buried in Athens, Ohio.

Bruff, Joseph, Captain, Major, Lieutenant Colonel, Brevit Colonel: see Company A

Wood, George L., Major, resigned, April 1863

McHenry, Dr. Henry, Surgeon, resigned, June 1865*

Darby, Dr. John E., Assistant Surgeon, promoted to Surgeon of 42nd U.S. Colored Troops, May 1864

Yates, Dr. Porter, Assistant Surgeon, resigned, May 1863

Buchanan, Dr. James G., Assistant Surgeon, resigned, January 1865*

McKim, Dr. William E., appointed Assistant Surgeon, March 1865*

Carter, Abner B., Quartermaster, resigned June 1864

Crowell, William H., Quartermaster Sergeant, 1st Lieutenant, Quartermaster*

Lewis, the Rev. John W., Chaplain, resigned, January 1865*

Noncommissioned Staff

Smith, Seabury, Sergeant Major, see Company I

Collins, Freeman, Sergeant Major, see Company D

Bell, Henry, Sergeant Major, wounded at Resaca*

Hillis, Melvin E., Quartermaster Sergeant; DD, May 1863

Lord, Henry, Quartermaster Sergeant*

Steadman, Hezekiah N., Commissary Sergeant, see Company K

Trimble, Thomas, Commissary Sergeant*

Herring, Simon, Hospital Steward; DS, April 1863

Detrick, George, Hospital Steward*
Demme, Peter, Musician
Sidlinger, Samuel H., Musician*
Young, Benjamin F., Musician*
Hull, William, Servant for Major Bruff, joined, July 1864*
Davis, Francis R., Servant for Company A, joined, October 1864*

Company A

Bruff, Joseph, Captain, Major, Lieutenant Colonel, breveted Colonel, wounded at Missionary Ridge*, post-war farmer and served in Ohio legislature, committed suicide on his son's grave in Damascus, Ohio, November 1885.
Whitesides, Edward G., Captain, breveted Major, wounded at Kennesaw Mountain, served on brigade and division staffs*
Blystone, David K., 1st Lieutenant, wounded at Franklin*
Mahan, Thomas R., 1st Lieutenant*
Bush, Daniel K., breveted 2nd Lieutenant, Orderly Sergeant*
Morris, James B., 1st Sergeant, Orderly Sergeant, killed at Chickamauga
Townsend, William, Sergeant, wounded near Atlanta
Thomas, Nathan J., Sergeant*
Naylor, Joseph B., Sergeant; DD, April 1863
Woolford, Michael, Sergeant, wounded at Resaca; DD, March 1865*
King, Robert P., Sergeant, wounded at Resaca; DD, May 1865*
Calvin, Luther S., Corporal, wounded at Rocky Face Ridge*
Coy, Silas, Corporal*
Crouse, Joshua, Corporal, wounded at Kennesaw Mountain: DD, March 1865*
Dickson, James R., Corporal, color guard, wounded and captured at Chickamauga, paroled, wounded near Kennesaw Mountain, regimental postmaster, October 1864*
Dickson, James, Corporal*
Hoffman, George, Corporal; DD, February 1863
Hutton, William, Corporal, wounded at Franklin; DD, May. 1865*
Pollock, Alex D., Corporal, died in service, June 1863
Snyder, Ephraim, Corporal, killed at Resaca

Stamp, John H., Corporal, transferred to VRC, February 1864
Thoman, Irvin, Corporal*
Wagner, Charles, Corporal, wounded at Lovejoy Station*
Young, Dighton, Corporal, wounded at Chickamauga and Kennesaw Mountain*

Privates

Arbuckle, George, wounded at Rocky Face Ridge; DD, May 1865*
Baker, Sylvanus*
Barricks, Henry L.; DD, April 1863
Bates, George W., wounded at Chickamauga*
Baughman, Jacob, DD, May 1865*
Beerman, George*
Blim, Jacob S., transferred to VRC, August 1863
Blim, John*
Boner, John, DD, May 1865*
Bunnel, Horace, DS, June 1863
Bunnel, Ruebin, killed at Missionary Ridge
Callahan, Albert*
Callahan, Jeremiah, mortally wounded at Resaca
Callahan, Joshua, DD, July 1863
Callahan, Mathias C., wounded at Dandridge*
Calvin, George W., DS, May 1863
Calvin, Jacob B., DS, March 1863
Calvin, John P., DD, December 1862
Carr, Edward, deserted from hospital, July 1864
Color, Solomon, DD, March 1863
Coy, Simon S., DD, August 1863
Creps, Jacob, killed at Chickamauga
Creps, Jeremiah*
Danforth, John, killed at Resaca
Detchon, Cornelius, killed at Resaca
Dickson, William, mortally wounded at Resaca
Erb, David B.*
Flack, James, killed at Resaca
Fosnaught, Emory A., DD, April 1865*
Getz, John, DD, May 1865*
Goodman, Isaac, DD, May 1863
Harriff, Sylvester, mortally wounded at Chickamauga
Hartzell, Joseph*
Hilton, Henry*
Infildt, Cornelius, killed at Rocky Face Ridge
Kelly, Eli C., wounded at Missionary Ridge*

Lazarus, Orin L., DD, May 1865*
Lloyd, David, DS, November 1863
Meiger, Peter, wounded at Chickamauga*
Miller, Alexander, mortally wounded at Chickamauga
Miller, Samuel*
Morningstar, Samuel, wounded at Resaca; DS, January 1865
Naylor, John C., DS, February 1863
Osborn, William, DS, June 1863
Ramsey, James P., wounded at Franklin*
Richmond, Thomas, wounded at Resaca*
Ruppert, Jacob W., wounded at Nashville*
Schroy, Aaron, DD, December 1863
Shenafield, Jared*
Shoff, John, enlisted March 1864; deserted May 1864
Spickler, Thomas*
Steves, John, DD, February 1863
Sullivan, Humphrey, deserted in Cleveland, December 1862
Stone, Albert*
Tool, Francis, transferred to VRC, March 1864*
Webb, Lewis, mortally wounded at Chickamauga
Weikart, George W.*
Wining, Jonathan, wounded at Resaca, DD, May 1865*
Wining, Nicholas, wounded at Resaca*

Company B

Yeomans, Albert, Captain, wounded at Chickamauga, resigned, May 1864
Powers, Ridgely C., Captain, regimental and brigade adjutant*, breveted major for Missionary Ridge and Lieutenant Colonel for Franklin, Mississippi cotton planter, Mississippi governor 1871
Rice, Ralsa C., Captain, wounded at Kennesaw Mountain*, died November 1911 in Trumbull County, participated in every battle
Glenville, Henry, 1st Lieutenant, wounded at Chickamauga*
Harshman, Charles, 2nd Lieutenant, resigned, May 1863
Burnham, Thomas M., 2nd Lieutenant, mortally wounded at Kennesaw Mountain
Woods, Rufus E., 2nd Lieutenant, Ordnance Sergeant, wounded at Missionary Ridge*
Matthews, Albert, Sergeant*
Knight, Frederick H., Sergeant*
Fitch, William R., Sergeant*
Murdock, James M., Sergeant, killed at Franklin
Davis, George P., Sergeant*
Allen, Darwin F., Corporal, DD, May 1863
Harshman, Sylvester T., Corporal*
Root, Lyman, Corporal, division postmaster, March 1865*
Henry, Wallace J., Corporal, wounded at Missionary Ridge and Kennesaw Mountain*
Brown, Isaiah, Corporal*
Thompson, John, Corporal*
Johnson, William M., Corporal, killed at Chickamauga
Wasson, William, Corporal, wounded at Chickamauga*
Lee, William H. Corporal, wounded near Kennesaw Mountain, DD, April 1865*

Privates

Adkins, Dennis J., DD, July 1863
Allen, George, deserted, December 1862
Austin, Charles A., DD, July 1863
Brainard, Emerson, DD, April 1863
Briggs, Ethan C., mortally wounded at Chickamauga
Britton, Darius, wounded at Chickamauga*
Brown, Morgan, DD, June 1863
Brown, Oliver R.*
Brown, Thomas*
Brown, Walter*
Bundy, Orlando*
Burnett, James, transferred to VRC, May 1865*
Carr, Joel, substitute for A. P. Morse*
Carey, Jesse H., wounded at Chickamauga*
Cook, Gilbert L.*
Covert, William A., DS, March 1863
Cranston, James*
Dana, William A., mortally wounded at Rocky Face Ridge
Davis, William E., transferred to VRC, November 1864
Fenn, Samuel, wounded at Kennesaw Mountain, DD, May 1865*
Fishel, Warren H., wounded at New Hope Church*
Fishel, Wesley C., wounded near Kennesaw Mountain, DD, May 1865*
Fitch, Adrian, killed at Kennesaw Mountain

Fitch, C. Orasmus, wounded at Rocky Face Ridge*
Fitch, Perry, wounded and captured at Chickamauga, died in Andersonville
Fitch, William
Floody, James, wounded at Chickamauga, DD, November 1864
Fobes, Franklin J., wounded at Dandridge, transferred to VRC*
French, Caleb*
French, George, DD, April 1863
Gartner, John P., DD, May 1865*
Gates, Orin F., DS, May 1863
Giddings, Harvey*
Gildard, Henry B., DD, October 1863
Gillis, John*
Gilmore, Emory, wounded at Kennesaw Mountain*
Goff, Porter A., wounded at Chickamauga
Griffith, Hezekiah L., wounded at Chickamauga
Hager, Asa, mortally wounded at Kennesaw Mountain
Hatch, Nathan B., killed at Kennesaw Mountain
Heath, Thomas P., DS, August 1863
Henry, Charles W., DS, April 1863 in Columbus, Ohio
Jones, Washington, DD, October 1863
Kelly, Kenny, deserted, December 1862
King, John W., wounded at Kennesaw Mountain*
Loutzenhiser, Thomas, wounded at Chickamauga*
McMichael, Dudley, DD, April 1863
Meacham, Norris*
Moses, Seth F., DD, October 1863
Mossman, John C.*
Mossman, Rufus H., killed at Chickamauga
Murdock, George, wounded at Kennesaw Mountain and Franklin*
Paden, James, transferred to VRC, December 1863
Pauquette, Theophile, wounded at Resaca
Peck, Almond*
Peck, Ephraim E., transferred to VRC, March 1863
Perringer, Michael, DD, June 1863
Pigott, George*
Pollock, James M., wounded at Missionary Ridge*
Reynolds, Edwin M.*
Rice, Robert F., killed at Kennesaw Mountain
Robinson, Gideon*
Smith, William M., transferred to VRC, October 1863
Smith, William T., DD, June 1863
Splitstone, Levi, DS, April 1863
Sprague, Francis, wounded at Chickamauga, DD, June 1864
Stratton, George*
Stroble, George, DS, September 1863
Tidd, James M., DS, November 1863
Tracy, Henry N., wounded and captured at Chickamauga, paroled*
Turner, Harrison, DD, July 1863
Vesey, William, D., transferred to VRC, Captain in 177th Ohio, September 1864*
Warren, Jones K.*
Waters, Elmer H., DS, May 1863
Welch, Patrick, wounded and captured at Chickamauga, paroled*
Welch, John W., mortally wounded at Chickamauga
Williams, Joel N., DS, June 1863
Wood, David B., wounded at Chickamauga and Missionary Ridge, DD, May 1865*
Woodworth, Edwin C., wounded at Peach Tree Creek*

Company C

Bates, Edward P., Captain, breveted, but never mustered Major and Lieutenant Colonel, by 1865 the most senior captain in the Army of the Cumberland, brigade quartermaster*, postwar mining engineer, died Oakland, CA, August 1916
Harmon, Hemon R., 1st Lieutenant, resigned, April 1863
Hulse, Richard K., 1st Lieutenant, breveted, but never mustered Captain*
Dilley, Alson C., 1st Lieutenant, killed at Kennesaw Mountain
Keith, Mark, 1st Sergeant*
Jones, Silas N., Sergeant, transferred to VRC, March 1864
Canon, John A., Sergeant, wounded at Rocky Face Ridge, DD, June 1865*
Higgins, Sidney, Sergeant*
Phelps, Clinton, Sergeant, wounded at Rocky face Ridge*
Murphy, John, Sergeant, wounded at Kennesaw Mountain*
Morris, Zalmon F., Sergeant, wounded at New Hope Church*

Simpson, George W., Corporal, wounded at Chickamauga, mortally wounded at Resaca

Wilson, Joseph, Corporal, captured, July 1863 in TN, paroled, September 1863, deserted in Nashville, June 1865

Thorn, William S., Corporal, color guard wounded at Chickamauga*

Sanner, James, Corporal, wounded at Chickamauga and Resaca*

Parker, Robert, Corporal, wounded at Resaca*

Davis, Rees C., Corporal*

Van Wie, Clark, Corporal*

Hill, Archibald, Corporal*

Comerford, Thomas D., Corporal*

Tuttle, Chester, Corporal, wounded outside Atlanta, September 1864, DD, April 1865*

Privates

Abrams, Edwin Z., killed at Chickamauga

Andrews, Joseph, DS, March 1863

Andrews, Simon H., DD, June 1865*

Armstrong, Sanford, duty at division headquarters*

Arnold, William R.*

Baker, Henry, died in service, August 1863

Bascom, Howard, wounded at Kennesaw Mountain and Franklin, DD, June 1865*

Bell, John T.*

Borden, Trumen, transferred to VRC

Bouton, Jared*

Boyd, Enoch, wounded at Resaca*

Brainard, Erastus, DD, August 1863

Brainard, Chauncey, DD, September 1863

Brimer, Edward*

Brockett, Linus, DD, April 1863

Brown, Charles*

Burrow, Anthony, wounded and captured at Chickamauga, paroled

Campbell, John, DD, May 1865*

Carleton, Simeon, killed at Rocky Face Ridge

Case, Jason, transferred to VRC, December 1864

Charles, William, DD, March 1865*

Cheney, Walter, wounded at Dandridge, one of youngest men, born November 1848*

Clark, Christopher C., wounded at Chickamauga, DD, August 1864

Coats, Cassius, wounded at Kennesaw Mountain, DD, February 1865*

Comerford, Bernard*

Cook, Gilbert L.*

Corcoran, James, wounded at Franklin*

Cowdry, Leolin, DS in Cleveland, December 1862

Curtis, Leonard H., wounded at Rocky Face Ridge, DD, August 1865*

Custer, Joseph, DS, August 1864

Dilley, Jonathan, DS, March 1863

Fay, Thomas, wounded at Resaca*

Fenton, John, transferred to VRC, December 1863

Fuller, Leroy*

Moran, Gray, DD, July 1865*

Hall, Asahel B., DD, February 1863

Hall, Benjamin, wounded at Chickamauga, DD, May 1865*

Hall, John*

Hall, Levi H., DD, February 1865*

Handley, John*

Harrison, Kimmel K.*

Harwood, John Avery, wounded at Kennesaw Mountain*

Hayden, Chauncey B., transferred to VRC, December 1863

Hayford, Anson E., captured at Danville, died at Andersonville, June 1864

Higbee, Elbert R., DD, August 1863

Higgins, Hiel, killed at Franklin

Jack, David, DS, at Nashville, April 1863

Jestin, George, DD, July 1864

Keck, Frederick*

Keck, Nicholas, DS, April 1863

King, John, W.*

Lamb, Harvey, W., wounded at Kennesaw Mountain, DD, February 1865*

Latin, Quincy, wounded at Resaca and Spring Hill*

Leet, James W.*

Lerontie, Bates, captured July 1863 near Hillsboro, TN, DD, June 1865*

Luse, Jesse B., wounded at Nancy's Creek, DD, April 1865*

McKinley, William, wounded at Chickamauga and Rocky Face Ridge*

McNutt, Cornelius C., DD, February 1863

Mahan, John D., wounded at Dandridge*

Meacham, Samuel*

Miller, Joseph*

Morrison, Samuel T., DD, April 1863

Odell, Philander, captured at Cassville, GA, September 1864, imprisoned at Andersonville, DD, June 1865*

Orr, William*

Osborn, John C.*
Perkins, George, wounded at Chickamauga*
Pinks, Thomas R.*
Pigott, George*
Porter, Ralph, H.*
Powers, John W., DS, October 1863
Radcliff, Minos, wounded at Resaca*
Richardson, Gilbert, recruit, died enroute to regiment near Chattanooga, December 1863
Row, Lorenzo, DD, June 1865*
Sample, Jesse, mortally wounded at Rocky Face Ridge
Sawdry, Warren*
Seaborn, William, wounded at Missionary Ridge, DD, April 1865*
Shields, Mark, wounded at Muddy Creek, transferred to VRC, December 1864
St. John, Seneca, wounded at Resaca*
Stratton, George*
Swarts, Michael, wounded and captured at Chickamauga, paroled*
Swinehart, Eli, killed at Rocky Face Ridge
Swinehart, Jeremiah, wounded at Rocky Face Ridge, DD, March 1865*
Thompson, Thomas M., transferred to VRC, December 1863
Thompson, William*, died November 1865
Tod, William D., DD, June 1865*
Tyler, Festus G., DS, August 1864, near Atlanta
Vesey, Alexander*
Warden, Nathan C.*
Waterman, George, wounded at Kennesaw Mountain, discharged, September 1864*
Waterman, Sylvester, mortally wounded at Kennesaw Mountain
Watkins, William H., wounded at New Hope Church, DD, May 1865*
West, Wilmer J., DD, April 1863
Williams, John, transferred to VRC, December 1864
Williams, Lewis*
Zedaker, Cassius M., wounded at Chickamauga*
Rummage, George, colored under-cook*

Company D

Spaulding, Issac D., Captain, resigned, April 1863
Stewart, Robert B., Captain, killed at Franklin
Thoman, Freeman, Captain, wounded at Kennesaw Mountain, Adjutant*
Richards, Marshall M., 1st Lieutenant, resigned, June 1863
Evans, Ephraim P., 1st Lieutenant, mortally wounded at Kennesaw Mountain
Leimbach, Charles, 1st Lieutenant, wounded at Kennesaw Mountain*
Collins, Freeman, sergeant major, 2nd Lieutenant, killed at Noses Creek near Kennesaw Mountain
Fitch, Hudson, Ordnance Sergeant, 2nd Lieutenant, captured during siege of Atlanta while 1st Sergeant*
Whitaker, John H., 1st Sergeant, Ordnance Sergeant, DD, August 1865*
Giddings, Jonathan C., Sergeant*
Scripture, Edwin D., Sergeant, wounded at Chickamauga*
Williams, John S., Sergeant, wounded at Chickamauga*
Allen, Frederick L., Sergeant*
Lindsey, Darius C., Sergeant, died on furlough in Ohio
Edwards, Wallace D., Sergeant, wounded at Missionary Ridge, DD, October 1864
Evans, Thomas C., Corporal, transferred to VRC*
Gilbert, Edwin A., Corporal, DD, December 1863
Force, Sylvanus, Corporal*
Oharo, Henry E., Corporal*
Young, Henry, Corporal*
Gillen, Thomas, Corporal, DD, August 1863, re-enlisted January 1864*
Krider, David B., Corporal*
Hitching, Almond, Corporal*
Evans, Meredith F., Corporal, DS, April 1863

Privates

Allen, Hiram, wounded at Resaca*, died in military hospital, November 1865
Ames, Solomon, DD, June 1864
Baninger, Michael, absent without leave, November 1864
Baxter, David, DD, May 1863
Beggs, James, wounded at Franklin, DD, May 1865*
Black, Issac S.*
Bloomer, Daniel, wounded at Resaca, DD, May 1865*
Briner, William L., killed at Chickamauga
Clark, Marcus B., DD, August 1863

Corley, Timothy, killed at Resaca
Dawson, Henry E.*
Ducquet, Theophile, wounded at Resaca
Durant, William, wounded and captured at Chickamauga, paroled
Fagley, Israel, DD, May 1865*
Flack, John, wounded at Missionary Ridge*
Fuller, Mortimer J., enlisted April 1864, DD, June 1864
Gilbert, C. Lafayette*
Gilbert, John, wounded at Resaca, captured, died in prison, July 1864
Gilbert, Linus, S., DD, August 1865*
Gillen, Andrew J., wounded at Resaca*
Green, Henry, mortally wounded near Kennesaw Mountain
Hamilton, Alva, DD, February 1863
Harbaugh, Benjamin F., DD, February, 1863
Hathaway, James E., wounded at Resaca, DD, March 1865*
Hill, George S., DD, March 1865*
Hist, Henry*
Hollister, Edward B., mortally wounded at Resaca
Hollister, William, DD, June 1863
Hotchkiss, Harris B., DD, February 1863
Huntsberger, Amos, DS, May 1863
Jones, John, DD, August 1863
Jones, Thomas G., DS, July 1863
Keck, David, wounded at Franklin, DD, March 1865*
Kessler, Samuel, DS, April 1863
King, John*
Likens, Richard P., killed at Dandridge
McLane, Edward, wounded at Resaca, DD, June 1865*
Miller, Levi F., DD, March 1864
Moran, John, wounded at Resaca, DD, April 1865*
Morris, Evan G., transferred to VRC*
Morrison, James, wagoneer*
Mullaney, James*
Niner, Frank, DS at Louisville, KY, November 1863
Peyeatt, Robert, DS at Chattanooga, November 1863
Pfaff, George, transferred to VRC, December 1864
Putnam, John, wounded at Resaca*
Stump, George, DD, May 1865*
Thomas, John O., DS, April 1863
Todd, Calvin, DS, March 1864
Tuttle, Joseph, duty at National Cemetery in Chattanooga, DD, May 1865*
Van Order, Joseph, absent without leave from June 1865
Vine, John, DD, June 1865*
Walters, John*
Wetmore, Horace*
Winans, Jacob, transferred to VRC, February, 1864
Woffinden, James W., DD, June 1865*
Wright, Andrew J., transferred to U.S. Navy, March 1864

Company E

Baugh, Calton C., Captain, resigned, May 1863
Moses, Elmer, Captain, wounded at Kennesaw Mountain, resigned January 1865*
Williams, Waldren S., Captain, commanded pioneers*
French, Sharon, 1st Lieutenant*
Barnes, Albert, 2nd Lieutenant, mortally wounded at Chickamauga
Kime, John J., 1st Sergeant*
Fisher, Carlos W., Sergeant, DD, July 1863
Willour, Henry, Sergeant, mortally wounded at Missionary Ridge
Nickerson, William V., Sergeant*
Brown, Francis, Sergeant*
Needs, James A., Sergeant, wounded at Chickamauga*
Bell, John A., Sergeant*
Corwin, Samuel, Sergeant, DS, May 1863
Sharp, Thomas, Sergeant, DD*
Holloway, Bert, Corporal, transferred to VRC, August 1863*
Randolph, Clarkson F., Corporal*
Stahl, William S., Corporal, duty with hospital train, March 1865, DD, June 1865*
Hargraves, Duckworth, Corporal*
Booker, Carsner, Corporal*
Danley, Heil M., Corporal, wounded at Franklin*
McGachey, William, Corporal, wounded at Resaca*
Michael, Conrad, Corporal*
Phifer, E. Prindle, Corporal*
Carlin, James, Corporal, wounded at Missionary Ridge
Hawkins, Abraham W., Corporal, transferred to VRC, November 1863
Gibson, Norman, Corporal, killed at Kennesaw Mountain

Privates

Anthony, William*
Arnold, George L., wounded at Chickamauga, transferred to VRC*
Baldwin, Jesse, DS, May 1863
Beeman, Richard, wounded and captured at Chickamauga, paroled
Booker, Curtis F., killed at Chickamauga
Bradfield, Peter S., mortally wounded at Missionary Ridge
Brindley, Henry, mortally wounded, died July 1864
Campbell, James R.*
Case, Ira, transferred to VRC*
Chamberlain, William, wounded at Resaca
Charman, Henry, died in service at Chattanooga, October 1864
Countryman, Charles, H., wounded at Chickamauga, DD, June 1864
Darrow, Addison, wounded at Resaca
Dillion, Eli H., killed by lightning, March 1863
Dunn, Michael, DD, June 1863
Elder, Thomas, transferred to VRC*
Gassaway, Benton, DD, April 1863
Genster, Martin*
Guilford, Robert, DS, May 1863
Holden, Albert, mortally wounded at Resaca
Jacobs, Thomas, mortally wounded at Franklin
Johnson, Joseph, killed at Chickamauga
Johnson, Thomas, wounded at Resaca, DD, January 1865*
Kerr, David M., wounded at Chickamauga, DD, March 1864
McElhenny, Henry M., transferred to VRC, December 1863
McFarland, John, wounded at Chickamauga*
McMillian, Thomas, DD, June 1865*
McNamar, Richard, DD, March 1863
Mason, Tarlton*
Maxwell, Samuel, DD, March 1864
Merryhue, James H.*
Miller, William, real name David Barber, killed at Missionary Ridge
Okey, Benjamin*
Oldridge, Lewis, DS, April 1863
Randolph, Joseph F., wounded at Chickamauga, transferred to VRC*
Rhodes, Uldridge, DD, April 1865*
Rogers, Samuel, killed at Nancy's Creek
Scott, James B., wounded at Resaca*
Sell, Adam, wounded and captured at Chickamauga, died in Andersonville
Sheets, David W., DD, July 1865*
Shenard, William, DS at Chattanooga, September 1863
Sigler, James, DD, May 1863
Smith, James P., captured in Charleston, TN, December 27, 1864, died in prison
Snyder, Marion, transferred to VRC, April 1865*
Stahl, Thomas G., killed during siege of Atlanta, September 1864
Thompson, Charles*
Tippie, John M., wounded at Rocky Face Ridge*
Trube, John, DS, April 1863
Tucker, Granville, DS, August 1863
Tucker, Samuel, wounded and captured at Chickamauga, paroled, DD, April 1865*
Vallingdingham, George B., transferred to VRC, April 1865*
Vanhoof, John, killed at Muddy Creek
Walters, Lewis*
Watson, William, DS, April 1863
Willour, Lewis, mortally wounded at Chickamauga
Wyble, Jacob, mortally wounded at Kennesaw Mountain
Woodard, James, transferred to VRC*
Woodyard, Nathan*
Hardon, Jordan, colored under-cook, mustered March 1863, at Franklin

Company F

Parks, Steen B., Captain, wounded at Rocky Face Ridge, resigned, June 1864
Clark, Charles T., Captain, youngest officer, born January 17, 1845*
Humphreys, David, 1st Lieutenant, resigned, October 1863
Blackburn, Josiah H., 1st Lieutenant, adjutant*
Russell, Henry G., 2nd Lieutenant, wounded at Chickamauga*
Jewell, Jacob, Sergeant, wounded at Chickamauga and Nancy's Creek*
Stringer, Jeremiah S., Sergeant, wounded at Resaca*
Brown, James R., Sergeant, DD, March 1863
Warman, John, Sergeant, promoted to color sergeant, June 1864*

Clark, John R., Sergeant, wounded at Chickamauga*
Sims, Johnson, Corporal, wounded at Chickamauga, DD, November 1864
Beatty, John L., Corporal, wounded at Chickamauga, DD, May 1864
Reagh, William H., Corporal, mortally wounded at Chickamauga
Hall, Nathan R., Corporal*
Whitmer, Henry, Corporal, wounded at Missionary Ridge*
Willemin, James, Corporal, wounded at Franklin*
Getz, John, Corporal, wounded at Chickamauga*
Beckholt, William, Corporal*
Beeny, William H., Corporal, wounded at Chickamauga and Missionary Ridge*
Scott, William B., Corporal, wounded at Kennesaw Mountain*
Forney, Adam L., Corporal*
Porter, William, Corporal, wounded at Chickamauga, mortally wounded at Resaca

Privates

Broadbelt, Gershon, enlistment expired, mustered out, April 1864
Brower, Frederick, mortally wounded at Missionary Ridge
Cattrell, Leander, DD, June 1863
Chapman, George W.*
Clere, Claude, transferred to VRC, October 1864*
Cooper, Daniel C.*
Denny, James F., DD, December 1863
Duchman, Augustus, DD, July 1863
Dulybon, Matthew, transferred to VRC, August 1863*
Fawcett, Thompson J., DS in Nashville, March 1863
Fleming, James C.*
Foltz, Eli J., DS in Nashville, June 1863
Graham, Henry, wounded at Dandridge*
Grime, Joseph, wounded at Chickamauga
Harbye, Charles, DD, April 1863
Hall, Thomas J., killed at Chickamauga
Harris, Manoah P., wounded at Resaca, DD, July 1865*
Hess, David K., transferred to 1st Ohio Sharpshooters
Jennings, William T., killed at Chickamauga
Keys, Joseph H., wounded at Resaca*
Kime, Franklin, mortally wounded at Chickamauga
Kline, George, DD, May 1865*
Lawyer, Michael W., DD, May 1865*
Ling, Conrad, killed at Dandridge
Lowry, William*
McMerrill, John, transferred to VRC, March 1863
McNurland, John*
McNurland, William*
McNatt, Issac, DD, May 1865
Maloy, William, DS in Nashville, May 1863
Maxon, Alfred, wounded at Chickamauga and Rocky Face Ridge, transferred to VRC*
Meek, William A., mortally wounded at Chickamauga, left on field for five days
Melick, Jefferson, captured at Chickamauga, survived Andersonville*
Muck, Aaron, DD, April 1863
Murphy, Marion T., killed at Rocky Face Ridge
Newcomer, Christian, wounded at Missionary Ridge and Kennesaw Mountain, DD, June 1865*
North, John, wounded at Resaca, DD, August 1865*
Pfister, Mathias, DD, October 1863
Ransom, William H., wounded at Resaca
Reagh, John P.*
Ross, Elmos N.*
Sailor, Samuel, killed on picket during the siege of Atlanta
Sautter, Jacob, wounded at Chickamauga*
Schneider, Henry, discharged in January 1865*
Scott, James Foster*
Searwright, Clay C., brigade orderly*
Seignuer, George, DD, July 1863
Shoults, Orlando, wounded at Dandridge, DD, February 1865*
Sigler, Philip M.*
Sperry, Joseph H., DS in Chattanooga, September 1863
Stewart, John A., DS in Nashville, April 1863
Sullivan, Michael*
Thompson, James, DS in Louisville, KY, April 1863
Tipton, Elijah J.*
Tuttle, Amos, DS, March 1863
Tuttle, Carey, wounded at Chickamauga*
Vaughn, Benjamin, captured at Dandridge, died in Andersonville, August 1864

Wilcox, Edward, DS, May 1863
Williams, David, missing, November 1864, at Pulaski, TN
Williams, Joseph, detailed as teamster*
Woodruff, Marion, transferred to VRC*
Yoder, Alexander, wounded at Chickamauga*
Yoder, Eli*
Yoder, Jacob*

Company G

Bunts, William C., Captain, resigned for disability, March 1864
Stinger, Daniel, Captain, breveted Major, October 1865*
Barnes, Rollin D., 1st Lieutenant
Donaldson, Henry A., 1st Lieutenant, wounded at Kennesaw Mountain*
King, Martin V. B., 2nd Lieutenant, wounded at Chickamauga, resigned for disability, March 1864
Coats, Charles C., 1st Lieutenant, wounded at Kennesaw Mountain
Silliman, Justus M., 1st Sergeant, DD, April 1863
Pero, Joseph E., 1st Sergeant*
Thompson, Robert W., Color Sergeant, DD, July 1865 in Texas*
Logan, James, Sergeant*
Christy, Andrew J., Sergeant, DD, March 1864
Strealy, Senseny J., Sergeant*
Simpson, John, Sergeant, wounded at Franklin*
Reynolds, James M., Sergeant, wounded at Resaca*
Van Gorder, Alexander, Sergeant, wounded at Resaca*
McGittigan, William, Color Corporal, killed at Chickamauga
Irwin, John, Corporal, killed at Kennesaw Mountain
Hanna, Thomas R., Corporal, wounded at Franklin*
Strausbaugh, Michael, Corporal*
Shaffer, David, Corporal*
Hands, Richard J., Corporal*
Elliott, Richard M., Corporal, DS, December 1863
Heiner, John, Corporal, mortally wounded during siege of Atlanta

Privates

Adams, Henry H., captured September 1864, DD, March 1865*
Adams, John, DD, June 1865*
Badenborrough, John, DS, January 1863
Barbour, John, DD, May 1863
Bassett, Adam, DS in Franklin, June 1863
Benson, William*
Berry, Christopher*
Breece, Tobias, DD, June 1865*
Bryant, Joseph, killed at Franklin
Clodell, Charles*
Criss, William, detached for duty on military railroad as engineer
Daley, John, transferred to VRS, December 1865*
Donevan, John*
Ferguson, Dryden, mortally wounded at Kennesaw Mountain
Fitch, Harrison H.*
Foust, John, DS, May 1865
Garety, Joseph*
Griffin, Morris, DD, June 1863
Grime, Ferdinand, transferred to VRC, DD*
Hall, Traverse A.*
Hartman, William*
Hiltabiddle, Daniel W., DD, May 1865*
Hudson, Edwin*
Hunkler, John, transferred to VRC, August 1863
Jones, Thomas, DS in Louisville, June 1863
Kelley, James, DD, May 1865*
Knapp, Charles H., wounded at Resaca, transferred to VRC*
Krocker, Henry, captured at Chickamauga, died in prison
Lambody, Victor, DS, May 1863
Lyons, David*
Major, William O., wounded at Muddy Creek*
McGhee, Andrew J., missing from hospital in Nashville
Mead, Daniel*
Middleton, Henry, mortally wounded at Chickamauga
Miller, Frank, DS at Cumberland, MD, August 1863
Misler, Anton*
Nichols, Edward, DD, January 1865*
Osborn, Charles, detached duty at Camp Butler, Illinois
Randall, Alexander*

Randall, Charles B., wounded at Kennesaw Mountain
Richardson, George H.*
Robson, David*
Rotterdam, John, G., DD, December 1863
Schelhass, Henry, transferred to VRC, August 1863
Seiler, Alois, killed at Chickamauga
Shay, Daniel*
Shay, James, DD, May 1865*
Shenefield, George, mortally wounded during the siege of Atlanta
Smith, John*
Snyder, Peter, last report in hospital in Louisville, KY
Sommer, John, killed at Chickamauga
Spickler, Lewis*
Stephens, Issac S., DD, October 1863
Stoker, George S.*
Strealy, John C., mortally wounded at Chickamauga
Tannyhan, James*
Wade, James*
Walker, Joseph A., DD, May 1863
Withers, Joseph, DD, February 1864
Young, Calvin*

Company H

Vallendar, Anthony, Captain, wounded at Rocky Face Ridge, returned May 1865*
Merrill, Riley M., 1st Lieutenant, resigned April 1863.
Thoman, Freeman, 1st Lieutenant, wounded at Kennesaw Mountain, Captain Co. D*
Payne, Darius, 1st Lieutenant, wounded at Franklin*
Hendry, Francis, 1st Lieutenant, resigned March 1863.
Liembach, Charles, 2nd Lieutenant, wounded at Kennesaw Mountain, 1st Lieutenant, Co. D*
Glenville, Henry, 2nd Lieutenant, wounded at Chickamauga, 1st Lieutenant, Co. B*
Muller, Charles, 1st Sergeant, wounded at Franklin, DD, May 1865*
Ross, Henry, 1st Sergeant*
Webster, Roswell, Sergeant, DD, October 1863
Stoughton, William, Sergeant, transferred to VRC, October 1863
Thompson, Leroy, Sergeant*
Duffy, John, Sergeant*
Brandan, John, Sergeant*
Willey, Noah, Sergeant, wounded at Dandridge*
Morrow, John A., Sergeant, wounded at Missionary Ridge, DD, August 1864
Cunningham, George, Corporal, discharged December 1862 for typhoid fever
Brittain, Brookens H., Corporal, captured at Danville, died in Andersonville, August 1864
Joslin, Samuel, Corporal*
Darling, Fayette, Corporal*
Mason, William, Corporal*
Sillfleisch, Rhinehard, Corporal*
Meyer, Anslem, Corporal*
Henson, John, Corporal, wounded at Kennesaw Mountain, duty on military railroad in Texas*
Weir, John, Corporal, DD, May 1865*
Bedell, William R., Corporal, killed at Chickamauga
Large, Alpha, Corporal, killed at Franklin

Privates

Allardt, Theodore*
Ames, Oscar C., wounded at Resaca*
Anderson, Samuel W., DD, March 1863
Archer, James F., DD, June 1865*
Astle, William, transferred to VRC*
Barry, John, mortally wounded at Chickamauga
Beckwith, George R., killed at Dandridge
Berner, Jacob, DS, September, 1864
Bronson, Daniel, DD, March 1864
Bugby, Daniel D., DD, November 1863
Burr, John F., DD, October 1863
Caldwell, Warren M., DD, May 1865*
Collister, Jack, mortally wounded at Chickamauga
Coughlin, James, absent without leave, May 1865
Dahlem, John, DD, May 1865*
Dailey, William, wounded at Kennesaw Mountain, transferred to VRC*
Degraff, William, transferred to U.S. Navy, February 1864
Diamond, Patrick, left company May 1865
Dodge, James R., DS, May 1863
Dolan, William, absent without leave, July 1865
Eckerman, Charles*
Elliott, Michael, killed in battle
Esch, Franz, DS, January 1865

Fost, Henry, wounded at Chickamauga, captured and paroled
Glanzer, Jacob, missing at Nashville
Gleich, George, no record after May 9, 1864
Gleich, Valentine*
Goodwill, David B., killed at Kennesaw Mountain
Groebe, Ernst, no record after hospitalization in June 1864
Harvey, Charles, DD, May 1863
Howe, James, never returned from furlough, July 1864
Howell, William, killed at Chickamauga
Jackson, James H., captured at Franklin, paroled, DD, May 1865*
Jones, Herman F.*
King, Jacob, mortally wounded before Atlanta, August 1864
Knapp, Peter, wounded and captured at Chickamauga, released from Andersonville, June 1865*
Krum, Francis S., DS, November 1863
Laurence, Charles W., left company in May 1865
Lowman, James L., killed at Kennesaw Mountain
Meno, Frederick, DD, May 1863
Morris, William, wounded at Chickamauga, transferred to 23rd Ohio
Murphy, Patrick, DD, September 1864
Nauck, Frederick, wounded at Kennesaw Mountain*
Osburn, Thomas S., missing November 1864 at Athens, Tennessee
Pflenger, Valentine, DD, June 1865*
Phillips, Martin V., DD, February 1863
Pierson, James, captured at Dandridge, died in Andersonville, August 1864
Pietsch, August, wounded at Resaca*
Putnam, George, transferred to VRC*
Quirk, Michael, DS, October 1865, buried at sea
Rath, Albert, left in May 1865
Rawdon, William H.*
Reed, Charles, wounded at Chickamauga, DD, July 1864
Richter, Gottfried, left company, May 1865
Ritgart, Peter, missing after Resaca
Rood, Fayette C., DD, October 1863
Schelden, Lewis, DD, April 1864
Schener, Henry, DD, May 1865*
Schmitz, Nicholas, died in Andersonville, October 1864
Schultz, Gottlieb, killed at Kennesaw Mountain
Seyfert, George*
Shellhorn, Joseph, left company May 1865
Silverthorn, Alva, DD, June 1863
Smith, Merrick Q.*
Stewart, George, DD, May 1863
Stewart, Robert, left company, May 1865
Stolliker, Lester C.*
Summerby, William, DD, May 1865*
Thiele, Henry, DS at Nashville, August 1863
Thompson, Malcolm, disappeared near Triune, TN, June 1863
Wagner, Frederick, discharged from hospital, April 1865*
Waters, Lucius W., DD, May 1865*
Weedle, Conrad, DD, March 1865*
Weller, John, DS, February 1864
Wheeler, Seymour O., DD, May 1865*
Wilkinson, Thomas, DS at Nashville, November 1863
Williams, Charles, killed at Kennesaw Mountain
Williams, George, DS, December 1865*
Williams, John, mortally wounded at Chickamauga
Wilson, Thomas, DD, February 1863
Winright, William, missing November 7, 1864
Wolf, Frederick*
Zeller, Peter, discharged September 1865 in Missouri*

Company I

Coonrod, Aquila, Captain, resigned May 1864.
Cushing, William, Captain, duty as conductor on military railroad, resigned May 1865.
Chapman, Charles C., Captain*
Welch, Horace, 1st Lieutenant, resigned for disability March 1864.
Phillips, Nyrum, 1st Lieutenant, quartermaster, adjutant, July 1864*
Gardner, Benjamin F., 1st Lieutenant*
Smith, Seabury A., 2nd Lieutenant, acting adjutant, killed at Dandridge
Penfield, Henry N., 2nd Lieutenant, ordnance sergeant, wounded at Chickamauga
Blackburn, Josiah H., 2nd Lieutenant, acting adjutant, July 1865*
Payne, Darius W., 2nd Lieutenant, wounded at Franklin*

Hanson, James, 1st Sergeant, ordnance sergeant, captured at Dandridge sent to Andersonville*
Cassil, Francis, 1st Sergeant*
Stoner, John W., Sergeant*
Steele, Reubin M., Sergeant, wounded at Resaca*
Roessler, Richard, Sergeant*
Barrett, Thomas, Sergeant*
Edwards, Squire C., Sergeant, killed at Kennesaw Mountain
Weimer, William G., Sergeant, killed at Kennesaw Mountain
Bell, Isiah, Sergeant, Sergeant, DD, 1865*
Corbin, William, Corporal*
Primmer, Simon P., Corporal*
Rath, George, Corporal*
Wetz, George, Corporal
Phillips, Henry, Corporal*
Caughey, William, Corporal, wounded at Rocky Face Ridge*
Dunker, William, Corporal, wounded at Franklin*
Gerlock, Francis M., Corporal, killed at Rocky Face Ridge
Hair, James W., Corporal, wounded at New Hope Church*
Kessler, Elijah, Corporal, DD, 1865
Duncan, William, Corporal*

Privates

Alabaugh, Charles, DS, August 1864
Babcock, Thomas Z.*
Baker, John*
Ballinger, Jonathan*
Bently, Martin, DD, May 1865
Blair, Peter S., DS, March 1864
Bohn, John, wounded at Resaca, DD, June 1865
Brooks, Jacob, captured at Dandridge, died at Andersonville, June 1864.
Brown, George, DD, June 1865*
Brown, Joseph M.*
Butler, John, DS, April 1864.
Cassady, Thomas, mortally wounded at Rocky Face Ridge
Cay, David, DD, May 1865*
Close, John, DD, May 1865*
Couch, Andrew J., wounded at Franklin, detailed as teamster*
Cramer, George, mortally wounded at Kennesaw Mountain
Curtis, Aurelius*
Daley, Elden R., alias Eldon Porter, wounded at Resaca*
Davidson, William W.*
Davis, Charles F., DD, August 1865*
Davis, Thomas, wounded at Resaca
Donely, Hugh, DD, May 1865*
Donoghue, Patrick, wounded at Resaca, transferred to VRC
Edwards, John, DS in Chattanooga, November 1863
Edwards, Joseph, transferred to VRC, May 1865*
Figley, Simon, discharged June 1865*
Fisher, Albert W.*
Friend, Joseph*
Friend, William H., mortally wounded at Missionary Ridge
Gable, Michael, mortally wounded at Resaca
Gartner, Manlius, transferred to VRC, March 1864
Getz, Samuel, DD, August 1865
Gibson, Isaac, wounded at Franklin*
Gilpin, Alfred, alias Harrison Lee, captured at Franklin*
Gorrell, Daniel*
Green, Samuel, wounded at Rocky Face Ridge*
Gunter, David*
Hair, Daniel W., DS, March 1865
Haley, James S., wounded at Resaca*
Hamilton, Charles N., DD, May 1865*
Hardy, John J.*
Hatfield, Edward, wounded at Franklin*
Hill, Michael, wounded at Missionary Ridge*
Housweitt, Jacob, DS, Louisville, KY, October 1863
Hudson, John*
Jacoby, E. G., alias Augustus Jacobs
Justice, Samuel*
Kelly, John, transferred to VRC, December 1865
Kibble, John*
King, John H., missing, November 1864 at Stephenson, Alabama
Longsmith, Henry, wounded at Missionary Ridge, DD, August 1864
McHenry, William, DD, November 1864
Mikesell, Crowell*
Milburn, Edward E.*
Miller, George*
Miller, Ohio*
Miller, Charles, wounded at Missionary Ridge*

Musser, Jacob, wounded at Resaca, DD, May 1865*
Nason, Job*
Pepple, James*
Phillips, David S., wounded at Rocky Face Ridge, captured at Pulaski, discharged June 1865*
Pool, Frederick, DD, March 1864
Porter, Anthony, mortally wounded at Rocky Face Ridge
Prince, James F., DD, June 1865*
Radel, Albert*
Richardson, Daniel, wounded, New Hope Church, DD, June 1865*
Richardson, Oliver, mortally wounded at Missionary Ridge
Roberts, William C., wounded at Resaca
Rockafield, John C.*
Seydler, Gustave*
Shear, John P., DD, May 1865*
Sheets, William C., mortally wounded at Kennesaw Mountain
Spronce, Jerome, transferred to VRC, March 1864
Stull, George H., transferred to VRC, February 1864*
Swihart, William N.*
Tufford, William*
Weber, August, wounded at Resaca*
Wharton, George, DS, January 1864
Wise, Samuel, transferred to VRC, May 1864
Worth, Frank C., wounded at Resaca
Wretherford, William*
Wright, Martin L., DS at Chattanooga, January 1864
Young, John, missing at Franklin
Zeller, Peter*
Zufall, Elijah J.*

Company K

Manchester, Sterling, Captain, killed at Kennesaw Mountain
Dickson, Alexander, Captain, resigned June 1865*, participated in every battle
Steadman, Hezekiah, Commissary Sergeant, 1st Lieutenant, Captain*
Postlewait, Alexander H., 1st Lieutenant, wounded at Resaca*
Heikes, Samuel, 2nd Lieutenant
Maltby, Charles M., 2nd Lieutenant*
Jones, William, 1st Sergeant, died while on furlough, February 1865
Wetzel, James, Sergeant, killed at Kennesaw Mountain
Morgan, Josiah W., Sergeant, wounded at Franklin*
Porter, John, Sergeant*
Payne, Oren V., Sergeant, wounded at Resaca*
Rathbun, John R., Sergeant*
Sherer, John F., Sergeant*
Montezuma, St. John, Corporal*
Ferris, James A., Corporal, DD, May 1865
Mathews, Daniel W., Corporal*
Shaffer, David, Corporal*
Carter, James M., Corporal, wounded at Resaca*
Amidon, Chauncey W., Corporal*
Gibbons, Thomas, Corporal*
Crouch, John, Corporal*
Welling, Henry, Corporal, wounded at Resaca and Franklin
Carr, William R., Corporal*

Privates

Abbott, John, DD, May 1865*
Algoe, John S.*
Amidon, Nathaniel D., DD, May 1865*
Amy, Major P.*
Andre, Whitfield, wounded at Franklin, DD, May 1865*
Atwood, William H., DD, June 1865*
Barnes, David, DS, July 1864
Border, David, mortally wounded at Resaca
Brandenberry, John H., wounded New Hope Church, DD, June 1865*
Burley, Eli*
Chisom, Byron, DD, May 1865*
Cleveland, Alexander W., DS, March 1864
Coon, Perry, DS, March 1864
Curtis, Adelbert, DD, June 1865*
Dailey, Michael, DD, May 1865*
Davison, William*
Finsterwald, Charles*
Finsterwald, Jacob*
Fox, David*
France, William H., wounded at New Hope Church, DD, June 1865*
Fulton, Franklin, DD, July 1865*
Fulton, Robert L., wounded at Kennesaw Mountain*
Fulton, Zephaniah*
Furguson, Noah W.*
Hackett, Warren S.*
Hall, Hamlin, left June 1865

Halstead, Daniel S., wounded at Resaca*
Hardman, John, wounded at Kennesaw Mountain*
Harman, Benjamin*
Howells, Samuel D., DD, January 1865*
Jeffers, William*
Kilburn, Benjamin J., wounded at Kennesaw Mountain, DD, January 1865*
Knapp, David*
Knapp, Nicholas*
Kohler, Daniel, DD, August 1865*
Lamphear, George W., died in Andersonville prison, August 1864
Laurence, Abram, DS, September 1864
Lowry, Morris R.*
Lutz, Ernst, DS, March 1864
Lyman, George W.
Lyman, Henry, wounded at Resaca
Masters, G. Henry*
Masters, Joseph D.*
McCollum, George, killed at Rocky Face Ridge
Meeker, Charles*
Menen, Jacob*
Miller, William H., killed at New Hope Church
Moler, David, wounded at Resaca*
Moley, Joseph, missing at Nashville, 1864
Orr, Oscar*
Overmyer, George*
Robinson, Lewis A., DD, September 1865*
Sanders, Michael*
Sikes, Herbert V., DD, April 1865*
Sleinel, William, killed at Rocky Face Ridge
Smith, William, DD, May 1865*
Swett, Edmond, wounded at New Hope Church, DD, June 1865*
Swett, John, mortally wounded at New Hope Church
Swift, Horace F.*
Walch, Joseph, DD, May 1865*
Walker, Henry A., mortally wounded at Nashville
Warner, John*
Welling, William, wounded at Franklin*
Warren, Henry*
Willis, Francis, killed at Nashville
Wooley, Ira*
Wolcott, Ferris, DD, August 1864
Young, William*

Chapter Notes

Preface

1. Lewis, 11; Day, v.; Hannaford, 17.
2. Cozzens, *This Terrible Sound*, 534–535.
3. Clark, 126; *Official Records*, vol. 30, part 1, 640.
4. Clark, 126, 442.
5. Clark, 335–336; Reid, vol. 2, 646.
6. Dyer, 30, 44.

Introduction

1. Opdycke, 2.
2. Opdycke, xx–xxv.
3. Opdycke, xxiii.
4. Opdycke, xxxii; Schmiel, 9–10, 14–16.
5. Opdycke, xxiv–xxv; Kimberly and Holloway, 142–144.
6. Opdycke, 8, Kimberly and Holloway, 9–10; Reid, vol. 1, 765.
7. Opdycke, 8.
8. Reid, vol. 2, 261; Opdycke, 21; Kimberly and Holloway, 8–17; Hinman, 805.
9. Opdycke, 12; Kimberly and Holloway, 19.
10. Opdycke, 27–28, 50, 137; Emerson Opdycke letter to Albert Opdycke, May 25th, 1862, Emerson Opdycke File, Ohio History Connection, Columbus, Ohio; Kimberly and Holloway, 23–24.
11. Kimberly and Holloway, 20; Opdycke, 30, 33.
12. Kimberly and Holloway, 29; Opdycke, 42–45.
13. Opdycke, 127.
14. Opdycke, 43–45.
15. Reid, vol. 1, 64–82; http://ww2.ohiohistory.org/onlinedoc/ohgovernment/governors/tod.html.
16. Opdycke, 42–45; Reid, vol. 2, 641; *Western Reserve Chronicle*, Aug. 27, 1862; Schmeil, 14; *Yankee Tigers II*, 13–15; *Warren Tribune*, Aug. 20, 1862.

Chapter 1

1. Gallman, 139–141, 155, 166; Moffat, William C., "Soldier's Pay," a Cincinnati Civil War Roundtable presentation, January 1965, accessed at www.cincinnaticwrt.org/data/ccwrt_history/talks_text/moffat_soldierspay...; Reid, vol. 2, 5.
2. Clark, 5; *Yankee Tigers II*, 14–16; Reid, vol. 1, 64–82, vol. 2, 4–5; Moffat, "Soldiers Pay."
3. Clark, 3, *Yankee Tigers II*, 15–16; *Western Reserve Chronicle*, Aug. 31, 1859; *Daily Ohio Statesman*, Feb. 5, 1861, Apr. 4, 1861.
4. Clark, 1–7; Opdycke, 47; Rice, 24; Woodworth, Edwin C., *Woodworth Papers*, November, 1862.
5. Woodworth, Edwin C., *Woodworth Papers*, December, 1862.
6. Rice, 21; Clark, 2–3.
7. Rice, 21, 26.
8. Clark, 5–6.
9. Rice, 21.
10. Clark, 6–8; *Yankee Tigers II*, 27–28; Military Service Record of R. C. Powers, National Archives and Records Administration, Washington, DC; Pension Record of E. P. Bates, National Archives and Records Administration, Washington, DC.
11. Clark, 7, 12–14; *Yankee Tigers II*, 8, 10–11, 48; Pension Record of R. C. Rice, National Archives and Records Administration, Washington, DC.
12. Opdycke, 75–76; *Yankee Tigers II*, 17; *Revised Regulations. U.S. Army Regulations of 1861*, accessed at www.archive.org/stream/revisedunitedsta00unittrich/166.
13. Reid, vol. 2, 485–491; Clark, 12–13.
14. Hunt and Brown, 30; Clark, 12–13; *Yankee Tigers*, 18; Reid, vol. 1, 55–60.
15. Opdycke, 55; Clark, 13–14; Rice, 205; Reid, vol. 2, 245.
16. Clark, 12–15; Opdycke, 47–48, 62.
17. Clark, 12–15; Opdycke, 47–48; Lewis, 15.
18. Clark, 14–15.
19. Clark, 17; Opdycke, 47.
20. Davis, 49–59; Lord, 242, 251.
21. Clark, 17–20; Lewis, 14, 19.
22. Davis, 51–56; Tourgee, 121.
23. Davis, 202–203; *Yankee Tigers II*, 34.
24. Sifakis, *Who Was Who in the Union*, 341–342; Clark, 18–19.
25. Opdycke, 48.
26. Rice, 22; Clark, 15–16, 25–26.
27. Rice, 26; *Yankee Tigers II*, 39; Clark, 20–21; Opdycke, 49, 56.
28. Warner, *Generals in Blue*, 173–174.
29. Clark, 21–26; Opdycke, 51–52; *Yankee Tigers II*, 39–41; Rice, 38.

30. *Ibid.*
31. Adams, *Doctor's in Blue*, 15; Clark, 21–26; Opdycke, 52–53; *Yankee Tigers II*, 45.
32. *Yankee Tigers II*, 47.

Chapter 2

1. Rice, 42.
2. Clark, 36; Rice, 42–45; Opdycke, 55.
3. Clark, 36; Rice 45; Opdycke, 54–55.
4. Clark, 37–39; Rice, 46.
5. Clark, 37–40; Rice, 46–48.
6. *Yankee Tigers II*, 49–51; Rice, 42; Clark, 37–40; Opdycke, 55.
7. Clark, 36–40, 55–63; *Yankee Tigers II*, 49–51; Rice, 48.
8. Lewis, 23; Rice, 48; Opdycke, 60.
9. Opdycke, 54–59; Rice 48.
10. Opdycke, 55–56.
11. Opdycke, 53, 59, 62.
12. Lewis, 26; Opdycke, 60–61, 74; Reid, vol. 2, 873; Rice, 49.
13. Opdycke, 62; Warner, *Generals in Blue*, 181; Clark, 46–47.
14. Opdycke, 65–66; Linderman, 117; Clark, 50–51.
15. Clark, 48; Lord, 279.
16. Opdycke, 70; Clark, 48.
17. Opdycke, 62–65; Clark, 59.
18. Opdycke, 62–65; Dyer, 589; *Yankee Tigers II*, 59.
19. Opdycke, 67–68; Clark, 52–56; Rice, 49; *Yankee Tigers II*, 62–63; Dyer, 586–591; *Official Records*, vol. 23, part 1, 225–227.
20. Opdycke, 68–69; Dyer, 589; Clark, 54–55; *Yankee Tigers II*, 62–63; *Official Records*, vol. 23, part 1, 225–227; Warner, *Generals in Blue*, 470.
21. Clark, 54–55; Opdycke, 69.
22. *Yankee Tigers II*, 70; Clark 57.
23. Opdycke, 71–72.
24. Opdycke, 74–79; Clark, 57; *Yankee Tigers II*, 231–234.
25. *Yankee Tigers II*, 231–234.
26. *Yankee Tigers II*, 21–22; Wiley, 42–43; Gallman, 238.
27. Reid, vol. 1, 64–81, 99–130; Gallman, 126–131; Foote, vol. 2, 107–108.
28. Clark, 56–58; *Yankee Tigers II*, 64.
29. Clark, 396; Gallman, 255; Moffat, William C., "Soldier's Pay" a Cincinnati Civil War Roundtable presentation January 1965, accessed at http://cincinnaticwrt.org.
30. *Yankee Tigers II*, 232, 235; *Lancaster* (Ohio) *Gazette*, June 25, 1863; *Holmes County* (Ohio) *Farmer*, June 25, 1863; Clark, 396; Opdycke, 58.
31. *Yankee Tigers II*, 76; Rice, 55.
32. Clark, 55–63; Opdycke, 77, 80; Warner, *Generals in Blue*, 166–167.
33. *Yankee Tigers II*, 77; Opdycke, 79; Hinman, 43; Warner *Generals in Blue*, 207.
34. Opdycke, 83, 85; Tucker, *Chickamauga...*, 251; Sifakis, *Who Was Who in the Union*, 463; Warner *Generals in Blue*, 569–70.
35. Opdycke, 80; Warner, *Generals in Blue*, 100; Tucker *Chickamauga...*, 103–104; Cozzens, *This Terrible Sound*, 10.
36. McDonough, 40; Longacre, Edward G. "A Vanquished General in the West" in *Civil War Times Illustrated*, October 1985, 16–19; Warner, *Generals in Blue*, 410–411.
37. Reid, vol. 1, 311–340; Cozzens *This Terrible Sound*, 8; Longacre, "A Vanquished General...," 16–19; McPherson, 137–138.
38. Foote, vol. 2, 85–103; Reid, vol. 1, 333–334; McDonough, 231; Warner, *Generals in Blue*, 410–411; *Yankee Tigers II*, 66; Opdycke, Emerson, letter to John Opdycke, June 23, 1863, Emerson Opdycke Papers, Ohio History Connection, Columbus.
39. Moore, David H. letter to Emerson Opdycke June 27, 1863, Emerson Opdycke Papers, Ohio History Connection, Columbus, Ohio; Moore, David H., *An Escape That Did Not Set Me Free: A By-product of Morgan's Raid. A Paper Read Before the Ohio Commandery of the Loyal Legion April 7, 1915*; *Yankee Tigers II*, 237–240.
40. Horwitz, 47, 106; Thomas, 74; *Yankee Tigers II*, 240–6.
41. Horwitz, 198–199; *Yankee Tigers II*, 241–6.
42. *Yankee Tigers II*, 232, 241–246; Horwitz, 244–246.

Chapter 3

1. Foote, vol. 2 663–665; Reid, vol. 1, 336.
2. Foote, vol. 2, 663–665; Reid, vol. 1, 335–337.
3. Clark, 55–63; Opdycke, 77–80; Warner, *Generals in Blue*, 166–167; Opdycke, Emerson letter to John Opdycke in Emerson Opdycke Papers, Ohio History Connection, Columbus, Ohio.
4. Clark, 65–67; Robertson, 1–7.
5. *Ibid.*
6. Clark, 68–70; Opdycke, 81.
7. Foote, vol. 2, 667; Opdycke, 82; Clark, 70; Tourgee, 203; *Yankee Tigers II*, 77; Rice, 57.
8. Clark, 67–71.
9. Clark, 67–71, 75; Opdycke, 82; Reid, vol. 1, 338; *Yankee Tigers II*, 78.
10. Warner, *Generals in Blue*, 410–411; Opdycke, 85; Reid, vol. 1, 338; Cozzens, *This Terrible Sound*, 21.
11. Opdycke, 79–85; Clark, 74–75; Rice, 60; Hinman, 398–399; *Yankee Tigers II*, 43, 78, 86; Rice, 60; Warner, *Generals in Blue*, 207.
12. *Yankee Tigers II*, 79, 83; Clark, 73–75.
13. Moffat, William C., "Soldiers' Pay" a Cincinnati Civil War Roundtable presentation, January 1965, http://www.cincinnaticwrt.org.; Hinman, 401
14. Clark, 73–74; *Yankee Tigers II*, 79, 275; Opdycke, 80.
15. *Yankee Tigers II*, 232, 258–260; Moffat, "Soldiers' Pay"; Reid, vol. 1, 296; Opdycke, 109.
16. Tod, David, Letter to Emerson Opdycke, June

28, 1863 in Emerson Opdycke Papers. Ohio History Connection, Columbus, Ohio; Opdycke, 85; Reid, vol. 1, 169, 179, 221.
17. Clark, 76.
18. *Yankee Tigers II*, 75; Lord, 112–113.
19. Opdycke, 86–88; Clark, 81–82; *Yankee Tigers II*, 86; Burdoin, Franklin, "Notes From An Army Blacksmith," in *Personal Reminiscences and Experiences by Members of the One Hundred Third Ohio Volunteer Infantry*, 271.
20. Opdycke, 88; Rice, 61–62; *Yankee Tigers II*, 88.
21. Opdycke, 89.
22. *Official Records*, vol. 30, part 1, 688; Clark, 78–79; Opdycke, 90.
23. *Official Records*, vol. 30, part 1, 628, 681, 688.
24. Opdycke, 92; *Official Records*, vol. 30, part 1, 628, 681–682, 688.
25. Hinman, 412; *Official Records*, vol. 30, part 1, 688–689.
26. Catton, 274; McPherson, 193.
27. Grant, 405.
28. McWhiney, vol. 1, 190; Warner, *Generals in Gray*, 31; Tucker, *Chickamauga...*, 63.
29. McWhiney, vol. 1, 190.
30. Kimberly and Holloway, 48; Tucker, *Chickamauga...*, 63.
31. Clark, 80; *Official Records*, vol. 30, part 1, 629, 688–9.
32. *Official Records*, vol. 30, part 1, 630, 685–687.
33. *Official Records*, vol. 30, part 1, 630, 685–687, 690; Hinman, 415; Tucker, *Chickamauga...*, 17–18; Opdycke, 94–95.
34. *Official Records*, vol. 30, part 1, 630, 685–687.
35. *Official Records*, vol. 30, part 1, 685–687; Opdycke, 94.
36. *Official Records*, vol. 30, part 1, 690; Hinman, 415; Opdycke, 94.
37. Clark, 86; *Official Records*, vol. 30, part 1, 690, 706–707; Hinman, 415; Opdycke, 94–95.
38. Clark, 83–86; Rice, 63.
39. *Official Records*, vol. 30, part 1, 690; Hinman, 415–416.
40. Tucker, *Chickamauga...*, 122–123; *Official Records*, vol. 30, part 1, 249; Kimberly and Holloway, 4, 48; Cozzens, *This Terrible Sound*, 90–91.

Chapter 4

1. Clark 83; Hill, D. H. "Chickamauga—The Great Battle of the West" in *Battles and Leaders of the Civil War*, vol. 3, 646–647; Cozzens, *This Terrible Sound*, 98–99.
2. Hill, "Chickamauga...," 645–649.
3. Clark, 88–89.
4. *Ibid.*
5. Clark, 90–91; Cozzens, *This Terrible Sound*, 123.
6. Tucker, *Chickamauga*, 118–125; Hinman, 418–419.
7. Clark, 91.
8. Hinman, 418; *Official Records*, vol. 30, part 1, 634, 690–691.
9. Cozzens, *This Terrible Sound*, 201–202; *Official Records*, vol. 30, part 1, 634, 690–691; Hinman, 418.
10. Cozzens, *This Terrible Sound*, 208–212; *Official Records*, vol. 30, part 1, 630–632.
11. *Official Records*, vol. 30, part 1, 691.
12. *Yankee Tigers II*, 29, 91.
13. Cozzens, *This Terrible Sound*, 166, 214; *Official Records*, vol. 30, part 1, 632, 691; Manville, Craig J., "The Limits of Obedience: Brigadier General Thomas J. Wood's Performance During the Battle of Chickamauga," Master's Thesis, Fort Leavenworth, KS, 2005, 35.
14. Cozzens, *This Terrible Sound*, 166, 214; *Official Records*, vol. 30, part 1, 691.
15. Clark, 94; Cozzens, *This Terrible Sound*, 259; *Official Records*, vol. 30, part 1, 707.
16. Tucker, *Chickamauga...*, 171–175; Clark, 94–95.
17. Clark, 94–95; *Official Records*, vol. 30, part 1, 692, 707; Cozzens, *This Terrible Sound*, 214, 256–260; *Yankee Tigers II*, 91; Whitesides, *Diary*, Sept. 19 and 20, 1863.
18. Clark, 100.
19. *Official Records*, vol. 30, part 1, 692, 700; Cozzens, *This Terrible Sound*, 260.
20. *Official Records*, vol. 30, part 3, 481; Cozzens, *This Terrible Sound*, 261.
21. Cozzens, *This Terrible Sound*, 261–262; Clark 98–100.
22. *Official Records*, vol. 30, part 1, 691–693; Cozzens, *This Terrible Sound*, 212–213, 259–262; Clark, 94–101; Hinman, 420–422; *Yankee Tigers II*, 90–91.
23. Cozzens, *This Terrible Sound*, 262; Hinman, 423; Tucker, *Chickamauga...*, 172.
24. *Official Records*, vol. 30, part 1, 455–456.
25. *Official Records*, vol. 30, part 1, 633–634, 649–650, 692–693; Hinman, 424; Manville, "The Limits of Obedience...," 43–52.
26. Tucker, *Chickamauga...*, 172, 175.
27. *Yankee Tigers II*, 93; *Official Records*, vol. 30, part 1, 192; Cozzens, *This Terrible Sound*, 305.
28. Clark, 93.
29. Foote, vol. 2, 763, 725.
30. Cozzens, *This Terrible Sound*, 295–300; *Official Records*, vol. 30, part 1, 192.
31. Cozzens, *This Terrible Sound*, 295–300.
32. Tucker, *Chickamauga...*, 197–201; *Official Records*, vol. 30, part 1, 57; Cozzens, *This Terrible Sound*, 297.
33. Hinman, 440–441; *Official Records*, vol. 30, part 1, 224–225.
34. Cozzens, *This Terrible Sound*, 147; Tucker, *Chickamauga...*, 134; Hinman, 426.

Chapter 5

1. Clark, 101–102; *Official Records*, vol. 30, part 1, 634; Cozzens, *This Terrible Sound*, 288–90.
2. Tucker, *Chickamauga...*, 203; Cozzens, *This Terrible Sound*, 312–313.
3. Hill, Daniel H., "Chickamauga—The Great Battle

of the West," in *Battles and Leaders*, vol. 3, 649–653; Clark 86–94; Echenrode and Conrad, 227–229, 234.

4. Foote, vol. 2, 718; Cozzens, *This Terrible Sound*, 310–312; Robertson, 24; Tucker, *Chickamauga...*, 40.

5. Clark, 102–104; Cozzens, *This Terrible Sound*, 305.

6. Clark, 102–104, 125; Cozzens, *This Terrible Sound*, 312–5; Hannaford, 465; Manville, Craig J., "The Limits of Obedience: Brigadier General Thomas J. Wood's Performance During the Battle of Chickamauga," Master Thesis, Fort Leavenworth, Kansas, 2005, 61–62.

7. Cozzens, *This Terrible Sound*, 314–315.

8. Manville, "The Limits of Obedience...," 10; Cozzens, *This Terrible Sound*, 356–362.

9. Scott, *Philander P. Lane*, 237; Cozzens, *This Terrible Sound*, 356, 361–362; *Official Records*, vol.30, part 1, 580; Manville, "The Limits of Obedience...," 73.

10. Cozzens, *This Terrible Sound*, 362; Shanks 475, Manville, "The Limits of Obedience," 60–70.

11. Shanks, 475; Cozzens, *This Terrible Sound*, 363; Manville, "The Limits of Obedience...," 69–70; Hinman 426–427.

12. Cozzens, *This Terrible Sound*, 363–367; Hunt and Brown, 88; Clark, 123.

13. Hill, "Chickamauga—The Great Battle in the West," 658; Opdycke, Emerson, "Notes on the Chickamauga Campaign," in *Battles and Leaders*, vol. 3, 670; Cozzens, *This Terrible Sound*, 367–368.

14. Cozzens, *This Terrible Sound*, 370–373.

15. Robertson, 41–43.

16. Cozzens, *This Terrible Sound*, 375; Robertson, 41–43.

17. Cozzens, *This Terrible Sound*, 372; Hinman, 427; Bobrick, 183; *Official Records*, vol. 30, part 1, 60.

18. Clark, 133–134.

19. *Official Records*, vol. 30, part 1, 224–225.

20. Hinman 441; Adams, 94–95.

21. *Official Records*, vol. 30, part 1, 635–636.

22. Cozzens, *This Terrible Sound*, 400–402.

23.. *Official Records*, vol. 30, part 1, 635–636, 708; Clark, 123; Cozzens, *This Terrible Sound*, 407; Clark, 106, 127–128; Opdycke, 99–102; Robertson, 41–43.

24. Clark, 106.

25. Clark 106, 127–128; *Official Records*, vol. 30, part 1, 708; Cozzens, *This Terrible Sound*, 399–409.

26. Foote, vol. 2, 738; Robertson, 41–43; Tourgee, 224–225; Cozzens, *This Terrible Sound*, 410–412.

27. Wiley, 88; Lindeman, 23, 31, 95; Opdycke, 100, 126; Clark, 106–107, 117–118, 123; Adams, 138; Rice, 70, 213; *Official Records*, vol. 30, part 1, 636–637; Lewis, 59.

28. Clark, 13, 123; Opdycke, 97; Rice, 70.

29. Cozzens, *This Terrible Sound*, 409–10.

30. Rice, 70; Clark, 107; Cozzens, *This Terrible Sound*, 413; *Official Records*, vol. 30, part 1, 637.

31. Clark, 107; *Official Records*, vol. 30, part 1, 252.

32. Wiley, 93; *Official Records*, vol. 30, part 1, 694–695.

33. Cozzens, *This Terrible Sound*, 413, *Official Records*, vol. 30, part 1, 708; Opdycke, 100; Clark, 108–109, 129; Rice, 68.

34. Clark, 133–134; Cozzens, *This Terrible Sound*, 415–416.

35. Clark, 133–134; Cozzens, *This Terrible Sound*, 415–416; Opdycke, 100; Hight, 192–193.

36. Cozzens, *This Terrible Sound*, 413–416.

37. *Official Records*, vol. 30, part 1, 708; Rice, 68, 212; Opdycke, 100; Clark, 108–109, 127, 129.

38. *Official Records*, vol. 30, part 1, 695; Opdycke, 100; Clark, 110, 127–130.

39. Clark, 106–109.

40. Clark, 128, 394.

41. Cozzens, *This Terrible Sound*, 410.

Chapter 6

1. Cozzens, *This Terrible Sound*, 172–173, 417; Tucker, *Chickamauga...*, 330; *Official Records*, vol. 30, part 1, 637.

2. Clark, 111; Robertson, 46; Opdycke, 99.

3. Cozzens, *This Terrible Sound*, 421–422; Tucker, *Chickamauga...*, 330; Clark, 111–113.

4. Opdycke, 101–102; *Official Records*, vol. 30, part 1, 636, 695; Cozzens, *This Terrible Sound*, 421–422; Rice, 68; Foote, vol. 2, 748; Clark 117.

5. Cozzens, *This Terrible Sound*, 429–431; Clark 113–115.

6. Clark, 113–115; Foote, vol. 2, 749; Cozzens, *This Terrible Sound*, 429–431.

7. Cozzens, *This Terrible Sound*, 426–431; Clark 113–115.

8. Clark, 113.

9. Clark, 113; Opdycke, 97, 101–104; Whitesides, *Diary*, Sunday, Sept. 20, 1863; Cozzens, *This Terrible Sound*, 431; Rice, 74–75.

10. Hinman, 430; Linderman, 22.

11. Cozzens, *This Terrible Sound*, 440; Foote, vol. 2, 750–751; Tucker, *Chickamauga...*, 341; Warner, *Generals in Blue*, 473.

12. Cozzens, *This Terrible Sound*, 442–443; Shanks, W. F. "Recollections of Thomas" in *Harper's New Monthly Magazine*, vol. 30, issue 180 (May 1865) 755.

13. Cozzens, *This Terrible Sound*, 432–461, 471; Tucker, *Chickamauga...*, 340–346.

14. Cozzens, *This Terrible Sound*, 432–453, 457–461, 471; Tucker, *Chickamauga...*, 340–346; Hight, 193; Reid, vol. 2, 621; Scott, 251.

15. Cummings, 263; *Official Records*, vol. 30, part 1, 62; Cozzens, *This Terrible Sound*, 453; Foote, vol. 2, 752.

16. Cozzens, *This Terrible Sound*, 404–405; Tucker, *Chickamauga...*, 313; Warner, *Generals in Blue*, 166–167; *Official Records*, vol. 30, part 1, 60.

17. *Official Records*, vol. 30, part 1, 141; Cozzens, *This Terrible Sound*, 470–471.

18. Cozzens, *This Terrible Sound*, 478–479; *Official Records*, vol. 30, part 1, 192–193.

19. Lewis, 69; Wiley, 64; Kimberly and Holloway, 50–51; Hinman, 430.

20. Cozzens, *This Terrible Sound*, 471–474; Piston, 71.
21. Opdycke, 101, 118; Reid, vol. 2, 872–875; Clark, 113–114; Tuttle, 146; *Official Records*, vol. 30, part 1, 235, 708; McElroy, 131.
22. Cozzens, *This Terrible Sound*, 472–480; *Official Records*, vol. 30, part 1, 764, 769, 774; Hazen, 137.
23. *Ibid*.
24. Clark, 115–116; Cozzens, *This Terrible Sound*, 426; Piston, 71.
25. *Official Records*, vol.30, part 1, 140; Opdycke, 117.
26. Cozzens, *This Terrible Sound*, 467–477, 513; Tuttle, 146; Hazen, 137; Clark, 118.
27. Kimberly and Holloway, 54; Scott, 259.
28. Kimberly and Holloway, 54; Catton, 286.
29. Opdycke, 104, 115; Clark, 128–129, 216; *Official Records*, vol. 30, part 1, 62, King, M. V. letter to Emerson Opdycke Nov. 19, 1863 in Emerson Opdycke File, Ohio History Connection, Columbus, Ohio.
30. Foote, vol. 2, 748; Bobrick, 186; *Official Records*, vol. 30, part 1, 194–195.
31. Clark, 117–118, 124–125, 131; *Yankee Tigers II*, 98.
32. Clark, 131; *Yankee Tigers II*, 98–100.
33. Foote, vol. 2, 758; Cozzens, *This Terrible Sound*, 534; Eckenrode and Conrad, 283; Piston, 71.
34. Cozzens, *This Terrible Sound*, 514; Tucker, *Chickamauga*..., 377, 392; Eckenrode and Conrad, 237.
35. Cozzens, *This Terrible Sound*, 515; Lewis, 52; Hannaford, 455; Catton, 277.

Chapter 7

1. Clark, 118–121; Day, 176–177; Whitesides, *Diary*, 09/21/1863.
2. Clark, 132–133; Davis, *Fighting Men*, 58; Duncan, 302.
3. *Official Records*, vol. 30, part 1, 197; vol. 30, part 3, 791; Donald, 457; Opdycke, 101; Rice, 72.
4. Tourgee, 231-2; Cozzens, *This Terrible Sound*, 534; Opdycke, Emerson, "Notes on the Chickamauga Campaign" in *Battles and Leaders*, vol. 3, 670.
5. Cozzens, *Shipwreck*..., 15–16; Grant, U.S. "Chattanooga" in *Battles and Leaders*, vol. 3, 685; Foote, vol. 2, 804.
6. Foote, vol. 2, 804; Cozzens, *Shipwreck*, 15–16; Davis, *Atlas*..., plate 50.
7. Rice, 72.
8. Day, 176–177; Kimberly and Holloway, 56; *Official Records*, vol. 30, part 3, 765.
9. Opdycke, 98; Whitesides, *Diary*, 09/23/1863; Tourgee, 249.
10. Opdycke, 99; Cozzens, *This Terrible Sound*, 522–528.
11. Opdycke, 97, 104, 110, 118, 133; Day, 186–187; Clark, 147, 396, 456; *Official Records*, vol. 30, part 1, 225–227; Rice, 70–71; *Overland Monthly*, "Defenders of the Union," 67.
12. Clark, 135–138; Opdycke, 108; Cozzens, *Shipwreck*, 34; Hinman, 447. Opdycke 104, *Official Records* Part I, 225–227; Day 136–137.
13. Clark, 137; Hunt and Brown, 81–84; Cozzens, *Shipwreck*, 17–18, 34; Whitesides, *Diary*, 09/23/1863, 10/03/1863; Hinman, 447; Clark, 135–138; Opdycke, 108; Day, 184.
14. Clark, 138–139; Hurst, 81–84; Griess, 131; Cozzens, *Shipwreck*, 43–44; Kimberly and Holloway, 64.
15. Opdycke, 106–107, 116; Clark, 126–128; Whitesides, *Diary* 10/08/1863.
16. Cozzens, 525–526; Opdycke, 109, 116; Warner, *Generals in Blue*, 342, 522.
17. Opdycke, 122, 127; Warner, *Generals in Blue*, 437–438.
18. Opdycke, 110, 127; Hinman, 447–448; Warner, *Generals in Blue*..., 41.
19. Cozzens, *Shipwreck*, 17–20; Clark, 136–138; Hinman, 443–445.
20. Opdycke,107; *Yankee Tigers II*, 232–235, 260–262.
21. Cozzens *Shipwreck*, 11; Donald, 457; Lewis, 78.
22. Clark, 135–140; Cozzens *Shipwreck*, 19; Lewis, 83.
23. Opdycke, 108–111; *Official Records*, vol. 30, part 1, 640.
24. Opdycke, 112; Clark 142; Reid, vol.1, 176–177; Thomas, 421; Previts, Fred, "Battlefield Ballots. The 1864 Preaidential Election" in *Timeline*. October-December 2009, 39–54.
25. Opdycke, 119; Cozzens, *Shipwreck*, 3–7; Tourgee, 267–269; Grant, 410–411; Bobrick, 114.
26. Opdycke, 116; Hinman, 448; Lewis, 78.
27. Opdycke, 119; Sherman, *Quest for a Star*..., 76; Hinman, 448.
28. Cozzens, *Shipwreck*, 9, 21–22; Sherman, *Quest for a Star*..., 69; Opdycke, 117–119; Lewis, 84–85.
29. Opdycke, 124; Tourgee, 262.
30. Porter, 2–6, 14–15; Grant, 411–412; Foote, vol. 2, 803; Rice, 75.
31. Clark, 145–147; Reid, vol. 1, 393; Cozzens, *Shipwreck*, 21, 73, 100, 105; Grant, 413–418.
32. Cozzens, 108–111.
33. *Ibid*.
34. Opdycke, 109, 126; Clark, 147; Hinman, 451; *Yankee Tigers II*, 106.
35. Cozzens, *Shipwreck*, 104–105.

Chapter 8

1. Davis, *Official Atlas*, plates 48,49; Grant, 427–428.
2. *Ibid*.
3. Grant, 427–428; Catton, 295–298; Sherman, *Memoirs*, 276.
4. *Official Records*, vol. 31, part 2, 30.
5. *Official Records*, vol. 31, part 2, 128–129; Cozens, *Shipwreck*..., 114–116; Clark, 150, Hinman, 452; Foote, vol. 2, 838–841.
6. Cozzens, *Shipwreck*..., 127–128; *Official Records*, vol. 31, part 2, 40, 188, 253, 229, 255; Grant, Ulysses S., "Chattanooga," in *Battles and Leaders*, vol. 3, 698.
7. *Official Records*, vol. 31, part 2, 128–129, 254; Cozzens, *Shipwreck*..., 128.

8. *Official Records*, vol. 31, part 2, 188; Clark, 152; Shellenberger, John K., "With Sheridan's Division at Missionary Ridge," in *Sketches of the War History 1861–1865. Papers Prepared for the Ohio Commandary of the MOLLUS 1890–1896*, vol. 4 (Cincinnati: Robert Clarke Co. 1896) 51–53.

9. Cozzens, 129–130; *Official Records*, vol. 31, part 2, 65, 188, 254; Opdycke, 134.

10. *Official Records*, vol. 31, part 2, 281, 295; Cozzens, *Shipwreck...*, 130–132; Opdycke, 133; Grant, 434.

11. *Official Records*, vol. 31, part 2, 228.

12. *Official Records*, vol. 31, part 2, 229, 233, 241–243; Davis, *Official Atlas*, plate 50; Clark 154; Opdycke 133.

13. Cozzens, *Shipwreck...*, 129, 133; *Official Records*, vol. 31, part 2, 104, 188–189, 229, 243–244; Grant, 434; Clark, 155; Opdycke 134.

14. Cozzens, *Shipwreck...*, 135, 143; *Official Records*, vol. 31, part 2, 24.

15. Clark, 151–156; *Official Records*, vol. 31, part 2, 229.

16. Cozzens, *Shipwreck...*, 137–142.

17. Grant, U.S., "Chattanooga" in *Battles and Leaders*, vol. 3, 691, 693, 696.

18. Cozzens, *Shipwreck...*, 144.

19. Cozzens *Shipwreck...*, 145–149, 153–155; Grant "Chattanooga," 695; Catton, 296.

20. Opdycke, 134.

21. Cozzens, *Shipwreck...*, 180–195, 199–200; Catton, 296; Opdycke, 134–135; Clark, 156–160; *Official Records*, vol. 31, part 2, 233.

22. Cozzens, *Shipwreck...*, 197–198; Opdycke, 135; Grant, "Chattanooga," 710.

23. Cozzens, *Shipwreck...*, 200–210; Grant, "Chattanooga," 704.

24. Cozzens, *Shipwreck...*, 203; Sherman, *Memoirs*, 276.

25. Catton, 297; Cozzens, *Shipwreck...*, 210, 234–243; Clark, 160–162; Sherman, *Memoirs*, 288–289.

26. Cozzens, *Shipwreck...*, 244–248, 258–259; Grant, "Chattanooga," 705–707; Sherman, *Memoirs*, 289; Clark, 167–170; Catton, 297.

27. Warner, *Generals in Blue*, 15, 253; Clark, 167–170; Opdycke, 148; *Official Records*, vol. 31, part 2, 228, Shellenberger, "With Sheridan's Division...," 56–59; Sherman, *Quest for a Star*, 84.

28. *Official Records*, vol. 31, part 2, 242.

29. *Official Records*, vol. 31, part 2, 230–233, 241.

30. Cozzens, *Shipwreck...*, 251–255.

31. Lewis, 99; Cozzens, *Shipwreck...*, 259–261; Grant, "Chattanooga," 689; Woodworth, Edwin C., *Woodworth Papers*, November 12, 1863.

32. Cozzens, *Shipwreck...*, 261–262.

33. *Official Records*, vol. 31, part 2, 242; Clark, 176–178.

34. Clark, 180–181; Cozzens, *Shipwreck...*, 303–305.

35. Kimberly and Holloway, 68; Clark, 164; Shellenberger, "With Sheridan's Division...," 51–55, 59; *Official Records*, vol. 31, part 2, 8, 230, 234; Opdycke, 135.

36. Cozzens, *Shipwreck...*, 264–265; Opdycke, 135; *Official Records*, vol. 31, part 2, 230–234; Grant, "Chattanooga," 707; "From the 125th O.V.I." in *Western Reserve Chronicle*, Dec. 16, 1863, 1; Bierce, Ambrose, "What I Saw at Shiloh" in *Civil War Stories*, 9.

37. Clark, 163–170; Kimberly and Holloway, 70–72; *Official Records*, vol. 31, part 2, 236, 242.

38. Clark, 163–170; Shellenberger, "With Sheridan's Division...," 59–60; *Official Records*, vol. 31, part 2, 236, 242; Cozzens, *Shipwreck...*, 268.

39. Cozzens, *Shipwreck...*, 270, 276; Shellenberger, "With Sheridan's Division...," 61–62; *Official Records*, vol. 3, part 2, 234, 238; Grant, "Chattanooga," 707.

40. Cozzens, *Shipwreck...*, 270–273; Clark, 169; *Official Records*, vol. 31, part 2, 236.

41. Cozzens, *Shipwreck...*, 276, 283.

42. Cozzens, *Shipwreck...*, 282–284; Opdycke, 204.

43. Cozzens, *Shipwreck...*, 273, 283–285; *Official Records*, vol. 31, part 2, 234, 244, Shellenberger, "With Sheridan's Division...," 63; Sherman, *Quest for a Star*, 84–85.

44. Cozzens, *Shipwreck...*, 278–279, 285–286; Hinman, 456; Clark, 169–70; Opdycke, 135.

45. Clark, 176–178; *Official Records*, vol. 31, part 2, 244; "From the 125th O.V.I." in *Western Reserve Chronicle*, 1.

46. Opdycke, 135; *Official Records*, vol. 31, part 2, 234.

47. Cozzens, *Shipwreck...*, 286–288; Grant, "Chattanooga," 707; Clark, 170–171; Sherman, *Quest for a Star*, 86; "From the 125th O.V.I." in *Western Reserve Chronicle*, 1.

48. Cozzens, *Shipwreck...*, 289–291, 297–298, 303; Clark, 166–167; Hinman, 456; Sherman, *Quest for a Star*, 86; Kimberly and Holloway, 71.

49. Clark, 170–171; *Official Records*, vol. 31, part 2, 231, 238, 242.

50. Cozzens, *Shipwreck...*, 304–306; Opdycke, 137.

51. Opdycke, 135; Clark, 174–175; "From the 125th O.V.I.," in *Western Reserve Chronicle*, 1; Grant, "Chattanooga," 717.

52. Sherman, *Quest for a Star...*, 87; Opdycke, 137; Shellenberger, "With Sheridan's Division...," 65; *Official Records*, vol. 31, part 2, 234–236; Cozzens, *Shipwreck...*, 305–306.

53. Clark, 176–180; Opdycke, 135; "From the 125th O.V.I.," in *Western Reserve Chronicle*, 1; *Official Records*, vol. 31, part 2, 245.

54. Cozzens, *Shipwreck...*, 298–299, 306–307; Catton, 300; *Western Reserve Chronicle*, Jan. 6, 1864, 1.

55. Lewis, 104; Clark, 171.

56. Cozzens, *Shipwreck...*, 336–337.

57. *Official Records*, vol. 31, part 2, 231, 234.

58. *Official Records*, vol. 31, part 2, 231; Warner, *Generals in Blue*, 533.

59. Opdycke, 136; *Official Records*, 231, 234; *Western Reserve Chronicle*, Jan. 6, 1864, 1.

60. Cozzens, *Shipwreck...*, 342, 349–351; *Official Records*, vol. 31, part 2, 231, 234; Grant, "Chattanooga," 708; Foote, vol. 2, 857.

61. Cozzens, *Shipwreck...*, 352, 343–349; Opdycke, 136; Clark, 170–178; *Official Records*, vol. 31, part 2, 235.

Chapter 9

1. Rentfro, Jack, "Remnants of Civil War Knoxville" in *Civil War Times Illustrated.* M/J 1994, 50–60; Davis, *Official Atlas*, plates 24, 48; Smith, *Campaign to Nowhere*, 2–3; Poe, Orlando M., "The Defense of Knoxville" in *Battles and Leaders*, vol. 3, 731.
2. Foote, vol. 2, 862; Cozzens, *Shipwreck...*, 354; Smith, *Campaign to Nowhere*, 10.
3. Grant, 454–6; McFeely, 148–150; Cozzens, *Shipwreck...*, 370–384.
4. Cozzens, *Shipwreck...*, 387; Hinman, 464.
5. Cozzens, *Shipwreck...*, 386; Grant, 454; Sherman, *Memoirs*, 279; Foote, vol. 2, 861; Hinman, 464.
6. Clark, 185; Opdycke, 137–141; Cozzens, 353, 386–387; Grant 452.
7. Opdycke,139; Clark, 186; Hinman, 464; Cozzens, *Shipwreck...*, 386–387; Kimberly and Holloway, 75–75.
8. Clark, 186–187; Hinman, 464–465; Kimberly and Holloway, 75–76; Lewis, 112.
9. Cozzens, 387; Opdycke, 140–141; Hinman, 465–466; Lewis, 112; Clark, 187.
10. Sherman, *Memoirs*, 280; Hinman, 465.
11. Opdycke, 143–144; *Yankee Tigers II*, 117–119.
12. Opdycke, 142–143; Warner, *General in Blue*, 359.
13. Clark, 188–189.
14. Opdycke, 145–147; Hinman, 465–466; Kimberly and Holloway, 76.
15. Clark, 182–191; Smith, *Campaign to Nowhere*, 26; Sherman, *Memoirs*, 95–96.
16. Smith, *Campaign to Nowhere*, 28; Woodworth, Edwin C., *Woodworth Papers*, December 25, 1864.
17. Clark, 198–200; *Yankee Tigers II*, 273.
18. Clark, 198–200; Starr, vol. 3, 351; Opdycke, 151–152.
19. Clark, 190–193; Grant, 459; Smith, *Campaign to Nowhere*, 83–86; Clark, 190–193.
20. Clark, 196–198.
21. Clark, 200–201.
22. Opdycke, 153; *Yankee Tigers II*, 126; Woodworth, Edwin C., *Woodworth Papers*, February 2, 1864.
23. Opdycke, 154; Clark, 194.
24. Clark, 191–195.
25. Clark, 197; Opdycke, "Field Diary," Jan. 15, 1864; Hayes, P.C., "March to Dandridge and Back" in *Personal Reminiscences and Experiences by Members of the One Hundred and Third Volunteer Infantry* (Oberlin: News Printing Co. n.d.) 14.
26. Clark, 201; Smith, *Campaign to Nowhere*, 100; *Yankee Tigers II*, 127.
27. Smith, *Campaign to Nowhere*, 103–110.
28. Smith, *Campaign to Nowhere*, 112–114.
29. Davis, *Official Atlas*, plates 24, 142; Clark 207–209; Smith, *Campaign to Nowhere*, 120; *Yankee Tigers II*, 127–137.
30. Smith, *Campaign to Nowhere*, 120–123; Clark 201–210.
31. *Ibid.*
32. Smith, *Campaign to Nowhere*, 120–122.
33. Smith, *Campaign to Nowhere*, 122–124; Clark, 208.
34. *Yankee Tigers II*, 127,137; Clark, 207–209.
35. Clark, 207–209; Reid, vol. 2, 518,604, 803.
36. Clark, 201–211; *Yankee Tigers II*, 132–133; Smith, *Campaign to Nowhere*, 126.
37. Rice, 83; Clark, 213; Smith, *Campaign to Nowhere*, 126.
38. *Yankee Tigers II*, 127–137.
39. Clark, 207–209, 212; Reid, vol. 2, 644; *Yankee Tigers II*, 128–129.
40. Clark, 201–213; Smith, *Campaign to Nowhere*, 128; Demoret, 38–39.
41. Opdycke, 155.
42. Clark, 208–211; Reid, vol. 2, 796–802.
43. Clark, 208–209, Reid, vol. 2, 518, 644, 664, 802; Rice, 84; Smith, *Campaign to Nowhere*, 128–130; Hinman, 488; Woodworth, Edwin C., *Woodworth Papers*, February, 29, 1864.
44. Opdycke, 155–156; *Yankee Tigers II*, 211–213, 135–137; Smith, *Campaign to Nowhere*, 130.
45. Hinman, 488; Rice, 84; Hayes, "March to Dandridge and Back," 15.
46. Clark, 202–211; Rice, 83–84; Opdycke, 155–156; Starr, vol. 3, 351; *Yankee Tigers II*, 132–133, 266; Smith, *Campaign to Nowhere*, 132.
47. Opdycke, 155–157; Hayes, "March to Dandridge and Back," 15.
48. Opdycke, 139, 156–157; Clark, 213–214; Moore, David H. Letter to Emerson Opdycke, Feb. 23, 1864, Emerson Opdycke file, Ohio History Connection, Columbus.
49. Company Descriptive Book, Military Record of Joseph Bruff, NARA, Washington, D.C.; 1860 U.S. Census for Mahoning County, Ohio, Ancestry.com/LibraryEdition; Pension Record for Edward P. Bates, NARA, Washington, D.C.
50. *Yankee Tigers II*, 255; Opdycke "Field Diary" Feb. 4, 1864; Military Record for Edward P. Bates, NARA.
51. Opdycke, 290; Reid, vol. 1, 222; Moore, David H., letter to Emerson Opdycke, Feb. 29, 1864, Emerson Opdycke file, Ohio History Connection.
52. Moore, David H., letters to Emerson Opdycke, Feb. 14, Feb. 24, Feb. 27, Feb. 29, Mar. 6, Mar. 9, 1864, Emerson Opdycke File, Ohio History Connection, Columbus.
53. Opdycke, 166; Moore, David H., letter to Emerson Opdycke, Feb. 14, 1864, Emerson Opdycke file, Ohio History Connection, Columbus.
54. Clark, 214; Opdycke, 124; Moore, David H., letter to Emerson Opdycke, Feb. 14, Feb. 27, Mar. 6, 1864, Emerson Opdycke file, Ohio History Connection, Columbus.
55. Opdycke, 160–164; Grant, 480.
56. Opdycke, 162–164; Clark, 216.

(Chapter 8 continued:)
62. Clark, 178–179; Rice, 77; Hinman, 458; *Official Records*, vol. 31, part 2, 231, 235; Opdycke, 136–137.
63. Foote, vol. 2, 858–859; Dyer, 866; Grant, "Chattanooga," 711.

Chapter 10

1. Grant, 469–472; Sherman, William T. "The Grand Strategy of the Last Year of the War," in *Battles and Leaders of the Civil War*, vol. 4, 247; McFeely, 155–157.
2. Sherman, *Memoirs...*, 240; Woodworth, 106–108; Luvaas and Nelson, 341–348.
3. Clark, 215–216; Hinman, 510; Schmiel, 122.
4. Opdycke, 163; Warner, *Generals in Blue*, 237–238.
5. Warner, *Generals in Blue*, 344–345; Opdycke, 165; Hinman, 505.
6. Opdycke, 166–167; Cox, *Atlanta*, 25; Whitesides, *Diary*, May 3, 1864.
7. Sherman, *Memoirs*, 241–250; Woodworth, 106.
8. Sherman, *Memoirs*, 240–250; Cox *Atlanta*, 59–60; Hinman, 493, 502–504.
9. Sherman, *Memoirs*, 240–244.
10. Cox *Atlanta*, 30–31.
11. Clark, 222; Opdycke, 169; Cox, *Atlanta*, 30–31.
12. Clark, 222–223; Sherman, *Memoirs*, 239–241.
13. Opdycke, 169–170; Howard, Oliver O. "The Struggle for Atlanta" in *Battles and Leaders of the Civil War*, vol. 4, 296; Whitesides, *Diary*, May 3, 1864.
14. Tuttle, 177; Hinman, 513; Lewis, 139; Kimberly and Holloway, 80; Clark, 224; Howard, "The Struggle for Atlanta," 296; Opdycke, 224.
15. Foote, vol. 3, 324; Clark, 171.
16. *Official Records*, vol. 38, part 1, 367–368.
17. Hinman, 514; Clark, 222; *Official Records*, vol. 38, part 1, 367–368.
18. Hinman, 514; Opdycke, 171; Tuttle, 178; Howard, "The Struggle for Atlanta," 297; Moore, David H., "Freaks of a Bullet" in *Confederate Veteran*, vol. 26, 1–3, http://www.civilwar.org/battlefields/rocky-face-ridge/rfr-history/freaks.
19. Clark, 226; Opdycke, 171; *Official Records*, vol. 38, part 1, 367–368.
20. Tuttle, 178; Clark, 225–226; *Official Records*, vol. 38, part 1, 368; Rice, 90–95; Hinman, 513–514; Reid, vol. 1, 158–160.
21. Clark, 227–228.
22. Opdycke, 171; Tuttle, 178; *Yankee Tigers II*, 224–226.
23. Clark, 254–255; Cox, *Atlanta*, 37; Castel, 122, 567–568; Johnston, Joseph E., "Opposing Sherman's Advance to Atlanta" in *Battles and Leaders*, vol. 4, 266.
24. Clark, 228–229; *Official Records*, vol. 38, part 1, 368.
25. Bierce, 64.
26. Cox *Atlanta*, 38; Opdycke, 127; Clark, 229; *Official Records*, vol. 38, part 1, 368; Hinman, 519; Chamberlain, Robert, S. "Go back! Hospital right back there!" in *Echoes of Battle*, 73.
27. Clark, 225–234.
28. Hinman, 522; Clark, 228–231; *Official Records*, vol. 38, part 1, 368; Moore, "Freaks of a Bullet," 2.
29. Opdycke, 171–172; Tuttle, 179–180; Clark, 228–231; Rice, 91; Cox, *Atlanta*, 38.
30. Cox, *Atlanta*, 38; Hinman, 524.
31. Clark, 232; Hinman, 523.
32. *Official Records*, vol. 38, part 1, 368; Hinman, 524; Clark, 232–233; Opdycke, 172–173.
33. Cox, *Atlanta*, 41.
34. Rice, 91.
35. Rice, 91; Clark, 232; Hinman, 526; Lewis, 142; *Official Records*, vol. 38, part 1, 367–368.
36. Cox, *Atlanta*, 44, 63; Secrist, 5–16; Castel, 122.

Chapter 11

1. Clark, 234; Dyer, John Will, "Run, Johnny, Run!" in *Echoes of Battle*, 82.
2. Clark, 234–235; Opdycke, 173; Rice, Ralsa C. "When Greek meets Greek, then comes the tug of war." in *Echoes of Battle...*, 40.
3. Cox, *Atlanta*, 44, 63; Clark, 234; Castel, Albert, "The Battle That Should Not Have Been," in *Civil War Times Illustrated*. Nov/Dec 1992, 44–45.
4. Castel, "The Battle That Should Not Have Been," 44.
5. Castel, "The Battle That Should Not Have Been," 44–45; Cox *Atlanta*, 44–45; Scofield, Levi T., "The Color-Guard of the One Hundred and Third at Resaca," in *Personal Reminiscences and Experiences by Members of the One Hundred Third Ohio Volunteer Infantry*, 34–35.
6. Opdycke, 173; Clark, 237–239; Rice, "When Greek meets Greek...," 40.
7. *Yankee Tigers II*, 150.
8. Rice, "When Greek meets Greek," 41; Opdycke, 175; Reid, vol. 2, 559; Hinman, 527.
9. Clark, 238; Rice, "When Greek meets Greek...," 41.
10. Clark 242; *Yankee Tigers II*, 150; Rice, "When Greek meets Greek...," 41.
11. Tuttle, 183.
12. Opdycke, 173; *Yankee Tigers II*, 159.
13. Castel, "The Battle that Should Not Have Been," 45.
14. Cox, *Atlanta*, 44–45; Secrist, 33–38; Castel, "The Battle that Should Not Have Been," 68.
15. Cox, *Atlanta*, 46–48; Castel, "The Battle that Should Not Have Been," 74.
16. *Yankee Tigers II*, 152; Woodworth, Edwin C., *Woodworth Papers*, May 21, 1864.
17. Opdycke, 173; *Yankee Tigers II*, 152; Woodworth, Edwin C., *Woodworth Papers*, May 21, 1864.
18. Secrist, 47–57; Day, 208; Castel, "The Battle that Should Not Have Been," 78–83.
19. Clark 240–241; Cox, *Atlanta*, 47; Rice, "When Greek Meets Greek," 41.
20. Clark, 237, 243; *Official Records*, vol. 38, part 1, 369; Tuttle, 183; Opdycke, 173–175; Sherman, *Memoirs*, 256; Griswold, L. D., "The One Hundred and Third at Resaca," in *Personal Reminiscences and Experiences by Members of the One Hundred and Third Ohio Volunteer Infantry*, 347–350.
21. Secrist, 57; Cox, 63; Hurst, 120; Sherman, *Memoirs*, 256.

22. Cox, *Atlanta*, 49, 63; Castel, 187; Blount, 37.
23. Clark, 243–244; Opdycke, 173; Cox, *Atlanta*, 52; Rice, "When Greek Meets Greek," 41; Castel, 190; *Yankee Tigers II*, 154.
24. Vermilya, 39–40; Cox, *Atlanta*, 54–57.
25. Cox, *Atlanta*, 56; Vermilya, 40.
26. Castel, 193; Clark, 246; Sherman, F.T. *Quest for a Star*, 114; *Yankee Tigers II*, 149–150.
27. Opdycke, 174; Tuttle, 185; Clark, 246–247; Castel, 194–198.
28. Lewis, 144; *Yankee Tigers II*, 149–150.
29. Castel, 198–200.
30. Clark, 248–249; Castel, 200–202; Johnston, Joseph E., "Opposing Sherman's Advance to Atlanta," in *Battles and Leaders*, vol. 4, 268.
31. Clark, 249; Cox, *Atlanta*, 52–56; Castel, 202–207.
32. Castel, 207–208; Clark, 245–250; Opdycke, 174–175.
33. Castel, 213; Sherman, *Memoirs*, 260; Cox, *Atlanta*, 64–65; Castel, 213, 221.

Chapter 12

1. Foote, vol. 3, 347; Opdycke, 175; Cox, *Atlanta*, 66–67; Castel, 208.
2. Warner, *Generals in Blue*, 267; Sherman, *Quest for a Star...*, 115.
3. Clark, 245–250; Cox, *Atlanta*, 54–56; Opdycke, 174; *Yankee Tigers II*, 149–150.
4. Clark, 252; Tuttle, 186.
5. Clark, 251–252; Lewis, 146; Opdycke, 114; *Yankee Tigers II*, 156.
6. Cox, *Atlanta*, 67–69.
7. Blount, 41–45, 55; Morgan, 6.
8. Blount, 45–50.
9. Clark, 253; Cox, *Atlanta*, 70–73; Blount, 55–62; Foote, vol. 3, 348.
10. Clark, 253; Cox, *Atlanta*, 71–73; Tuttle, 187.
11. Clark, 253; Cox, *Atlanta*, 72–75.
12. Clark, 254, Tuttle, 187; Foote, vol., 348.
13. Cox, *Atlanta*, 82; Dwight, Henry O. "How We Fight At Atlanta" in *Harper's New Monthly Magazine*, October 1864, 664.
14. Opdycke, 176; Cox, *Atlanta*, 73–76; Clark, 254–255.
15. Rice, 100.
16. Rice, 101–104.
17. Hinman, 530–534; *Yankee Tigers II*, 156; Sherman, *Memoirs*, 262.
18. Luvaas and Nelson, 215; Blount, 82; Cox, *Atlanta*, 77.
19. Blount, 81–83.
20. Luvaas and Nelson, 216; Blount, 97–109; Lewis, 149.
21. Opdycke, 177; Clark, 257; Lewis, 155; Kimberly and Holloway, 87; Cox, *Atlanta*, 80; Luvaas and Nelson, 227–230.
22. Rice, 104–5; Clark, 257.
23. Tuttle, 188; Cox, *Atlanta*, 86–87; Blount, 130–143.

24. Opdycke, 177–178; Tuttle, 188.
25. Tuttle, 189; Opdycke, 178; Woodworth, Edwin C., *Woodworth Papers*, May 31, 1864.
26. Castel, 255; Sherman, *Memoirs*, 262; Opdycke, 178; Tuttle, 189.
27. Catton, 341; Kimberly and Holloway, 89; Castel, 255; Gillett, 245.
28. Opdycke, 179.
29. Cox, *Atlanta*, 93; Castel, 258–260.
30. Castel, 261.
31. Opdycke, 180–182; Howard, Oliver O., "The Struggle for Atlanta," in *Battles and Leaders*, vol. 4, 307.
32. Clark, 258–260; Opdycke, 177–179; *Yankee Tigers II*, 155–157.
33. Opdycke, 180–184; Vermilya, 52; Tuttle, 191; Hinman, 535; Clark, 263–264.
34. Vermilya, 55.
35. Vermilya, 50–51; Luvaas and Nelson, 24
36. Sherman, *Memoirs*, 263–264; Cox, *Atlanta*, 88–94; Clark, 258.
37. Vermilya, 50–51.
38. Castel, 264.
39. Cox, *Atlanta*, 94; Vermilya, 52–53; Howard, "The Struggle for Atlanta," 309.
40. Vermilya, 114.

Chapter 13

1. Clark, 264; Opdycke, 183; Tuttle, 191; Cox, *Atlanta*, 95–98; Vermilya, 56.
2. Opdycke, 184; Warner, *Generals in Blue*, 36.
3. Castel, 270–274; Sherman, *Memoirs*, 266; Hinman, 540; Tuttle, 192.
4. Castel, 276; Clark, 265–267; Hess, 9–10; Opdycke, 184.
5. Clark, 265–267; Castel, 279–280; Clark, 265–266; Cox, *Atlanta*. 97–98; Opdycke, 184.
6. Hess, 11–13; Castel, 281; Opdycke, 185; Cox, *Atlanta*, 100.
7. Hess, 14; Castel, 284.
8. Opdycke, 181–191; Hess, 13–14; Clark, 167; Cox, *Atlanta*, 100.
9. Hess, 15; Opdycke, 185; Clark, 267–268; Rice, 108; Tuttle, 195; Hinman, 541.
10. Vermilya, 60; Castel, 269; Hess, 13; Clark, 268.
11. Opdycke, 185; Clark, 269; Rice, 108; Howard, Oliver O., "The Struggle for Atlanta," in *Battles and Leaders*, vol. 4, 310.
12. Hinman, 540; Clark, 269; Opdycke, 185; Rice, 106.
13. Opdycke, 186; Clark, 270; Hess, 18.
14. Opdycke, 186; Rice, 108–109; Clark, 270.
15. Hess, 18, 25–27; Castel, 210; Vermilya, 70–71.
16. Opdycke, 187; Clark, 270–271.
17. Hess, 28; Castel, 290–291.
18. Castel, 292–295; Hess, 33–37; Cox, *Atlanta*, 112.
19. Hess, 44–47; Vermilya, 77; Castel, 297–298; Sherman, *Memoirs*, 271; Cox, *Atlanta*, 112.
20. Clark, 267–272; Opdycke, 187; *Official Records*, vol. 38, part 1, 334–336; Reid, vol. 2, 537.

21. Bierce, 53–54.
22. Rice, 109–110; *Official Records*, vol. 38, part 1, 334.
23. Fielder, 160; Foote, vol. 3, 394.
24. Clark, 272; *Official Records*, vol. 38, part 1, 334, 345.
25. Rice, 109–110; *Cleveland Herald*, July 25, 1864, 1.
26. *Official Records*, vol. 38, part 1, 334–335, 370; Fielder, 160; Opdycke, 187–188; Rice, 109–110.
27. *Yankee Tigers II*, 162–165, 181; Opdycke, 187; Clark, 272–273; Hinman, 546–547; Rice, 110.
28. Vermilya, 77–79; Castel, 300–301; Cox, *Atlanta*, 117–118; Luvaas and Nelson, 254–256; Sherman, *Memoirs*, 271.
29. Castel, 304–305; Vermilya, 107.
30. Vermilya, 79; Luvaas and Nelson, 256; Castel, 300.
31. Opdycke, 187–188; Clark, 272–273; Rice, 110.
32. Vermilya, 80–81; Cox, *Atlanta*, 120; Castel, 301; Hess, 68; Stanley, 173.
33. Castel, 302; Royster, 297–299.
34. Vermilya, 80–83, 182; Clark, 273; Cox, *Atlanta*, 121; Royster, 304.
35. Luvaas and Nelson, 296–297; Vermilya, 108–115; Castel, 307; Cox, *Atlanta*, 129; Royster, 305.
36. Griffith, 137, 143, 152; Castel, 307; Royster, 306; *The Jeffersonian Democrat*, October 21, 1864, 1.
37. Vermilya, 88–89; Sherman, *Memoirs*, 271.
38. Vermilya, 88–89; Castel, 305–306; Tuttle, 198; Clark, 272–273; Rice,110.
39. Clark, 276; Rice, 112; Rice, Ralsa, "Letter," in *National Tribune*, October 9, 1890, 3.
40. Rice, 187–189; Hess, 68; Castel, 311.
41. Vermilya, 123; Royster, 304.
42. Castel, 307–309; Royster, 306.
43. Clark, 275; Whitesides, *Diary*, June 27, 1864; Vermilya, 108–115; Luvaas and Nelson, 296–297.
44. Hess, 97; Clark, 273–281; Opdycke, 189; Kerwood, 262–264; Rice, 220.
45. Rice, 112–113.
46. Hess, 96–99.
47. Tuttle, 198–200; Clark, 277; Hinman, 547; Hess, 98; Griffith, 117–136; Castel, 315.
48. Clark, 282; Opdycke, 189–190, 285; Castel, 311; *Official Records*, vol. 38, part 1, 346–347.
49. Clark, 278; Opdycke 189–190; Cox, *Atlanta*, 125; *Official Records*, vol. 38, part 1, 370–371, Rice, 114.
50. Clark, 279–280; Luvaas and Nelson, 297; Vermilya, 111; Kerwood, 262–264.
51. Hess, 100–103.
52. Tuttle, 200; Clark, 279–280; Royster, 310.
53. Vermilya, 116; Castel, 115; Royster, 311; Rice, 116; *Official Records*, vol. 38, part 1, 371.
54. Rice, 115–116.
55. Rice, 116; Reid, vol. 2, 646; Opdycke, 189; Hess, 101–102; Vermilya, 116.
56. Hinman, 547–551; Clark, 283; Opdycke, 189; Rice,116; *Yankee Tigers II*, 172–173.
57. Clark, 280–284; Opdycke, 189; Woodworth, Edwin C., *Woodworth Papers*, June 28, 1864.
58. Clark, 281; Whitesides, *Diary*, June 27–30, 1864.
59. Tuttle, 200; Warner, *General in Blue*, 41.
60. Clark, 278–281; Vermilya, 113; Opdycke, 189; Howard, "The Struggle for Atlanta," 310; *Yankee Tigers II*, 168.
61. Tuttle, 199–200; Kerwood, 262–264; Hinman, 552; Royster, 311; *Official Records*, vol. 38, part 1, 371.
62. Tuttle, 200; *Official Records*, vol. 38, part 1, 304, 361.
63. Tuttle, 200.
64. *Official Records*, vol. 38, part 4, 608–609.
65. Rice, 117; Hinman 548; Opdycke, 190; Luvaas and Nelson, 285; *Official Records*, vol. 38, part 1, 370–371.
66. Hess, 113–127; Castel, 314–319; Clark, 274–275; Vermilya, 124–128; *Official Records*, vol. 38, part 1, 703–704.
67. Luvaas and Nelson, 288.
68. Hinman, 549–550; Reid, vol. 1, 918; Rice, 187–188; *Official Records*, vol. 38, part 1, 295–296.
69. Tuttle, 199; Clark, 283–284; Howard, "The Struggle for Atlanta," 310; *Yankee Tigers II*, 160, 175; Opdycke, 189–190; Kerwood, 262–264.
70. Vermilya, 90–101.
71. Castel, 317; Royster, 316–317; Cox, *Atlanta*, 129; Opdycke, 190.
72. Cox, *Atlanta*, 124.
73. Castel, 318.
74. Royster, 317; Vermilya, 158; Cox, *Atlanta*, 130.
75. Opdycke, 190; Vermilya, 148; Whitesides, *Diary*, June 28–30, 1864.
76. *Official Records*, vol. 38, part 1, 296; Opdycke, 190, 201; *Yankee Tigers II*, 169.
77. Cox, *Atlanta*, 130–132.
78. Clark, 279, 283–284; Woodworth, Edwin C., *Woodworth Papers*, June 28, 1864.
79. Opdycke, 191; Clark, 279; Hinman, 549, 552.
80. Cox, *Atlanta*, 132; Opdycke, 191; *Official Records*, vol. 38, part 1, 151.

Chapter 14

1. Hess, 188–191.
2. Cox, *Atlanta*, 136; Sherman, *Memoirs*, 273.
3. Hess, 180, 196; Tuttle, 201.
4. Hess, 195–202; Kimberly and Holloway, 91; Tuttle, 201.
5. *Ibid*.
6. Hess, 204–205.
7. Rice, 120; Clark, 284; Opdycke, 193.
8. Opdycke, 193; Tuttle, 202; Hess, 207.
9. Clark, 284; Hinman, 569; Tuttle, 202; Hess, 208–211.
10. Hess, 211–213; Clark, 285; Royster, 319–320.
11. Foote, vol. 3, 403; Cox, *Atlanta*, 135.
12. Clark, 285.
13. Cox, *Atlanta*, 135.
14. Cox, *Atlanta*, 137–140; Spencer, Albert H. in "Crossing of the Chattahoochee," in *Personal Reminiscences and Experiences by Members of the One Hundred and Third Ohio Volunteer Infantry*, 44-49.

15. Opdycke, 194–195; Cox, *Atlanta*, 141; Clark, 286; Rice, 123.
16. Opdycke, 194–195; Hinman, 571; Rice, 123.
17. Castel, 341; Foote, vol. 3, 406–407.
18. Clark, 286; Opdycke, 176.
19. Castel, 348–352.
20. Opdycke, 198; Sifakis, *Who Was Who in the Union*, 74–75.
21. Cox, *Atlanta*, 148–9; Catton, 342; Sherman, *Memoirs*, 278; Sifakis, *Who Was Who in the Union*, 134; Hinman, 575.
22. Clark, 286–287; McCarley, 15; Cox, *Atlanta*, 142–146; Sherman, *Memoirs*, 278.
23. Opdycke, 189, 193.
24. Opdycke, 199; Tuttle, 205–206; Clark, 288; Rice, 123–124.
25. Hinman, 372; Opdycke, 200; Clark, 287.
26. Opdycke, 200.
27. Hinman, 577; Tuttle, 206; *Official Records*, vol. 38, part 1, 297.
28. Castel, 365, 369, Kimberly and Holloway, 92, Clark, 288–289.
29. Clark, 290; Cox, 146–147, 153; Castel, 367–369.
30. Clark, 288–289; Castel, 370; *Official Records*, vol. 38, part 1, 297.
31. Kimberly and Holloway, 92; *Official Records*, vol. 38, part 1, 337–338, 355, 364.
32. Rice, 127; Clark, 288–289; Castel, 369; Cox, *Atlanta*, 155; *Official Records*, vol. 38, part 1, 297, 355.
33. Castel, 371; *Official Records*, vol. 38, part 1, 297, 326–327.
34. Castel, 372–374; Fielder, 188–189.
35. *Official Records*, vol. 38, part 1, 297, 326–327.
36. Castel, 375; Catton, 343; Thompson, 261; *Official Records*, vol. 38, part 1, 348–349.
37. *Official Records*, vol. 38, part 1, 297–298; Castel, 376; Opdycke, 201; Hinman, 579; Rice, 127.
38. Cox, *Atlanta*, 155.
39. Clark, 291; Hinman, 570, 579; Tuttle, 207; *Official Records*, vol. 38, part 1, 298, 361–365, 356; Opdycke, 201; Rice, 201.
40. Castel, 376.
41. Rice 128; Howard, Oliver O. "The Struggle for Atlanta" in *Battle and Leaders of the Civil War*, vol. 4, 314.
42. Clark, 292; Hinman, 579–580; Tuttle, 207; Fielder, 188–189; Castel, 201, 376.
43. Rice, 128; Cox, *Atlanta*, 156; Castel, 377; *Official Records*, vol. 38, part 1, 298.
44. Castel, 378; Cox, *Atlanta*, 160.
45. Castel, 378–340; Cox, *Atlanta*, 161–162; Howard, "The Struggle for Atlanta," 314.
46. Rice, 129–130; Hinman, 580; Cox, *Atlanta*, 160–162.
47. Clark, 291–293; Tuttle, 208; Opdycke, 201–202; Cox, *Atlanta*, 160–162.
48. Opdycke, 203–204; *Official Records*, vol. 38, part 1, 156.
49. Castel, 380; Sherman, *Memoirs*, 279.
50. Castel, 384–386; Cox, *Atlanta*, 163–166.
51. Castel, 387; Clark, 293; Foote, vol. 3, 476.
52. Castel, 387–389; Foote, vol. 3, 475.

Chapter 15

1. Rice, 130.
2. Cox, *Atlanta*, 166–167; Castel, 389.
3. Clark, 293–295; Hinman, 580.
4. Castel, 393–395; Clark, 294; Foote, vol. 3, 478.
5. Castel, 393–395; Clark, 294–295; Cox, *Atlanta*, 168–169; Warner, *Generals in Blue*, 281–282; 306–308.
6. Cox, 169–175; Sherman, *Memoirs*, 285; Castel, 414.
7. Clark, 295.
8. Cox, *Atlanta*, 170–174; Foote, vol. 3, 480; Opdycke, 202; Howard, Oliver O. "The Struggle for Atlanta" in *Battles and Leaders of the Civil War*, vol. 4, 319.
9. Rice, 132–133.
10. Rice, 132–133; Clark, 293–295; Hinman, 580.
11. Foote, vol. 3, 485; Sherman, *Memoirs*, 288; Cox, *Atlanta*, 178; Castel, 418–422.
12. Foote, vol. 3, 485; Cox, *Atlanta*, 178; Castel, 422; Opdycke, 204.
13. Opdycke, 203–204; Hinman, 591; Sherman, *Memoirs*, 294.
14. Opdycke, 202.
15. *Ibid*.
16. Tuttle, 209; Opdycke, 203; Hinman, 582.
17. Cox, 181–183; Foote, vol. 3, 486.
18. Clark, 297–298; Tuttle, 210; Cox, *Atlanta*, 184; Howard, "The Struggle for Atlanta," 319.
19. Castel, 434; Clark, 298; Sherman, *Memoirs*, 292; Howard, "The Struggle for Atlanta," 319.
20. Foote, vol. 3, 490; Cox, 185–187; Castel, 436; McCarley, 70.
21. Opdycke, 204–206; Clark, 301; Castel, 433; Foote, vol. 3, 491.
22. Clark, 299, 302; Tuttle, 210.
23. Clark, 299–300.
24. Tuttle, 210–211; Rice, 133; Opdycke, 207.
25. Tuttle, 211; Hinman, 585.
26. Tuttle, 212; Castel, 454–465; Cox, *Atlanta*, 194.
27. Opdycke, 210.
28. Opdycke, 210–215; Clark, 302.
29. Davis, Stephen, "Atlanta Campaign: Hood Fights Desperately. The Battles for Atlanta. Actions from July 10 to September 2, 1864" in *Blue & Gray Magazine*, vol. 6, Issue 6, August 1989, 46; Clark 300; Rice, 135, 223; Opdycke, 211; Tuttle, 212.
30. Foote, vol. 3, 519–520; Castel, 466–470.
31. Donald, 229, 518; Opdycke, 217; Castel, 454, 468, 479–482.
32. Cox, *Atlanta*, 196–200; Castel, 468.
33. Castel, 479–484.
34. Clark, 302; Rice, 133; Opdycke, 214–216.
35. Opdycke, 214–215; Clark, 302; Tuttle, 214.
36. Clark, 302–303; Castel, 470; Tuttle, 214; Sherman, *Memoirs*, 296.
37. Opdycke, 217.
38. Tuttle, 213; Hinman, 586–588; Castel, 480–482.

39. *Official Records*, vol. 38, part 1, 356; Tuttle, 215; Cox, *Atlanta*, 196; Castel, 474–475; Foote, vol. 3, 521.
40. *Official Records*, vol. 38, part 1, 356.
41. Hinman, 594; Clark, 303–304.
42. Clark, 303–304; Hinman, 595; Cox *Atlanta*, 196; Opdycke, 218; *Official Records*, vol. 38, part 1, 356; Castel, 485–488.
43. Cox, *Atlanta*, 198; Castel, 486; Foote, vol. 3, 521.
44. Clark, 304; Castel, 488–492; Opdycke, 219; *Official Records*, vol. 38, part 1, 356.
45. Clark 305; Castel, 492.
46. Castel, 494–495; Tuttle, 217; *Official Records*, vol. 38, part 1, 356.
47. Cox, *Atlanta*, 199; Castel, 495–496; Foote, vol. 3, 526.
48. Tuttle, 217; Castel, 505.
49. Castel, 497, 500–504; Cox, *Atlanta*, 201; Davis, "Atlanta Campaign…," 52, 59; Clark, 305.
50. Castel, 507–508.
51. Hinman, 596; *Official Records*, vol. 38, part 1, 372.
52. Clark, 304–305; Foote, vol. 3, 527; Sherman, *Memoirs*, 302.
53. Sherman, *Memoirs*, 302; Clark, 305–306; Foote, vol. 3, 528.
54. *Yankee Tigers II*, 180–183; *Official Records*, vol. 38, part 1, 299, 356, 372; Opdycke, 221–225; Rice, 137–139.
55. Clark, 305–306; Sherman, *Memoirs*, 303; Foote, vol. 3, 529.
56. Clark, 306; Opdycke, 221.
57. Foote, vol. 3, 530; Davis, "Atlanta Campaign…," 61; McClarey, 84.
58. Sherman, *Memoirs*, 304, 307; Foote, vol. 3, 530.
59. Opdycke, 221; Clark, 306; Rice, 139, 224.
60. Clark, 305–307, 309; Opdycke, 222–223; *Yankee Tigers II*, 180–183.
61. Clark, 307; Opdycke, 223.
62. Clark, 307.

Chapter 16

1. Grant, 634; Sherman, *Memoirs*, 327; Clark, 309, Marszalek, John F., "Fighting Peacemaker" in *Timeline*, Dec. 1988, 13.
2. Opdycke, 225–226, 233–234; Rice, 142.
3. Opdycke, 223, 227.
4. Opdycke, 227; Clark, 309.
5. Opdycke, 225–228.
6. Clark, 309; Opdycke, 228.
7. Sherman, *Memoirs*, 324.
8. Clark, 309–310, 359; Sherman, *Memoirs*, 328, 332; Cox, *March to the Sea*, 11–12.
9. Sherman, *Memoirs*, 324; Opdycke, 228, 230–231.
10. Clark, 310; Opdycke, 231.
11. Opdycke, 230–231.
12. Opdycke, 231, 233; Warner, *Generals in Blue*, 533–534; Whitesides, *Diary*, October 7, 1864.
13. Sherman, *Memoirs*, 332–337; Clark, 311–312.
14. Opdycke, 233–234; Rice, 142.
15. Sherman, *Memoirs*, 337.
16. Clark, 313–314; Sherman, *Memoirs*, 337, 345; Opdycke, 239; Scofield, 7; Whitesides, *Diary*, October 20–26, 1864.
17. Opdycke, 224, 235; Previts, Fred, "Battlefield Ballots. The 1864 Presidential Election" in *Timeline*. October-December, 2009, 39–54.
18. Clark, 313–314; Opdycke, 239; Whitesides, *Diary*, Oct. 19–20, 1864.
19. Opdycke, 240; Whitesides, *Diary*, Oct. 27–30, 1864.
20. Grant, 639–641; Cox, *March to the Sea*,5.
21. Cox, *March to the Sea*, 18; Sherman, *Memoirs*, 345.
22. Opdycke, 243–245; Whitesides, *Diary*, Oct. 31–Nov. 2, 1864.
23. Opdycke, 243–245; Hinman, 628; Whitesides, *Diary*, October 30–November 3, 1864.
24. *Ibid*.
25. Rice, 143–145; Wiley, 259.
26. Rice, 143–145.
27. Whitesides, *Diary*, November 8, 1864; Opdycke, 245; Previts, "Battlefield Ballots…," 39–54.
28. *Proceedings of a Board of Examiners Convened at Pulaski, Tennessee on Thursday the Tenth Day of November, AD 1864* in Military Service Record of Joseph Bruff, NARA, Washington, D.C., November 10, 11, 12, 14, 1864.
29. *Ibid*.
30. *Ibid*.
31. *Ibid*.
32. Moore, David H., letters to Emerson Opdycke, February 24, and February 27, 1864, in Emerson Opdycke File, Ohio History Connection, Columbus, Ohio; *Proceedings of a Board of Examiners…*, November 11, 1864.
33. *Proceedings of a Board of Examiners…*, November 11, 1864; Opdycke, 247.
34. Scofield, 8; Clark, 314–318; Cox, 62–65; Davis, *Sherman's March…*, 3–7; Sherman, *Memoirs*, 351.

Chapter 17

1. Cox, *March to the Sea*, 64–66; Scofield, 9; Horn, 17; Clark, 318–319.
2. Cox, *March to the Sea*, 64; Opdycke, 241; Warner, *Generals in Gray*, 92.
3. Cox, *March to the Sea*, 64–65; Clark, 318–322.
4. Cox, *March to the Sea*, 78–79; Clark, 318–322; *Overland Monthly*, "Defenders of the Union," 67.
5. Smith, D.W., "Hood's Last Campaign" in *National Tribune*, Nov. 20, 1890, 4; Monlux, George, "A Cavalryman's View" in *National Tribune* Mar. 30, 1911, 3; Opdycke, 247–248; Cox, *March to the Sea*, 66–73; Clark, 320–323.
6. Smith, "Hood's Last Campaign," 3.
7. Clark, 323; Rice, 153.
8. Sherick, John W., "With Opdycke at Franklin" in *National Tribune* Mar. 30, 1911, 3; Smith, "Hood's Last Campaign" 3.
9. Rice, 153; Clark, 323–324; Rice, R.C., "Opdycke at Franklin" in *National Tribune*, Mar. 30, 1911, 3.
10. Hinman, 666; Clark, 323–324.
11. Rice, 153; Clark, 323–324; Cox, *March to the Sea*, 75.

12. Hinman, 638; Cox, *March to the Sea*, 75.
13. Hinman, 640.
14. Hinman, 641; Opdycke, 248–249; Clark, 324–327; Warner, *Generals in Blue*, 41; Jacobson and Rupp, 194.
15. Rice, 155; Rice, "Opdycke at Franklin," 3; Opdycke, 249.
16. Jacobson and Rupp,151; Cox, *March to the Sea;* 74–77; Scofield, 14, 17; Rice, 155; Opdycke, 248.
17. Cox, *March to the Sea*, 77–78; Scofield, 17; Rice, 155; Rice, "Opdycke at Franklin," 3.
18. Jacobson and Rupp, 164–166.
19. Opdycke, 249; Hinman, 668; Jacobson and Rupp, 163–164; Kimberly and Holloway, 100.
20. Clark, 324–327; Cox, *March to the Sea*, 77–79; Jacobson and Rupp, 176–177; Scofield, 21.
21. Opdycke, 249; Jacobson and Rupp, 177.
22. Rice, 155; Cox, *March to the Sea*, 86; Opdycke, 249; Jacobson and Rupp, 235–236.
23. Hunt and Brown, 566; Clark, 332; Rice, 155–157; Rice, "Opdycke at Franklin," 3.
24. Cox, *March to the Sea*, 80; Sword, Wiley, *The Confederacy's...*, 152–153.

Chapter 18

1. Opdycke, 55–56; Rice, 48; Schmiel, 149–150.
2. Cox, *March to the Sea*, 82-3, 237.
3. Cox, *March to the Sea*, 82–83; Opdycke, 249; Jacobson and Rupp, 209.
4. Schmiel, 153; Cox, *March to the Sea*, 84–86; Cunningham, S.A., "Battle of Franklin" in *Confederate Veteran*, vol. 1, 101.
5. Opdycke, 55–56; Jacobson and Rupp, 266.
6. Jacobson and Rupp, 228–229; Cox, *March to the Sea*, 82–85; Scofield, 26; Rice, R.C. "Opdycke at Franklin" in *National Tribune*, Mar. 30, 1911, 3.
7. Jacobson and Rupp, 230–231; Clark, 329–330.
8. *Ibid*.
9. Sword, 170.
10. Rice, 155; Hinman, 654; McDonough and Connelly, 90.
11. Opdycke, 248–250; Sword, 172.
12. Jacobson and Rupp, 238; Cox, *March to the Sea*, 86; Clark, 331–332; Foote, vol. 3, 663.
13. Foote, vol. 3, 665; *Official Records*, vol. 45, part 1, 255.
14. Clark, 330; Jacobson and Rupp, 240–241; Sword, *The Confederacy's...*, 173; *Official Records*, vol. 45, part 1, 255.
15. Jacobson and Rupp, 242; McDonough and Connelly, 90; Hinman, 654; Clark, 330.
16. Sword, *The Confederacy's...*, 174.
17. Opdycke, 249; Sword, *The Confederacy's...*, 174; Jacobson and Rupp, 244–245; Rice, "Opdycke at Franklin," 3.
18. Clark, 330–331; Opdycke, 249; Rice, 155–157; Jacobson and Rupp, 244–245; Sword, *The Confederacy's...*, 174; Hinman, 653.
19. Rice, 157; Opdycke, 249.
20. Figuers, Hardin P., "A Boy's Impression of the Battle of Franklin" in *Confederate Veteran* vol. 23, 4–7; Jacobson and Rupp, 252; Sword, *The Confederacy's...*, 178.
21. Jacobson and Rupp, 252–253; Foote, vol. 3, 666; Losson, 218; Stiles, 163.
22. Scofield, 24; Cox, *March to the Sea*, 237–238; Bobrick, 271.
23. Sword, *The Confederacy's...*, 180–184; Figuers, "A Boy's Impression...," 4–7.
24. Clark, 330; Hunt and Brown, 345; Jacobson and Rupp, 244–245; Shellenberger, John K., "The Battle of Franklin" in *MOLLUS*, Minnesota, vol. 5, 495–521.
25. Shellenberger "The Battle of Franklin," 495–521; Jacobson and Rupp, 245–246; Schmiel, 154.
26. Cox, *March to the Sea*, 88.
27. Jacobson and Rupp, 384; Sword, *The Confederacy's...*, 209–211.
28. Scofield, 34–35; McDonough and Connelly, 152.
29. Figuers, "A Boy's Impression...," 4–7.
30. Shellenberger, "The Battle of Franklin," 495–521; Jacobson and Rupp, 266; Scofield, 33; Sword, *The Confederacy's...*, 189.
31. Jacobson and Rupp, 261, 271–276; Scofield, 34; Sword, *The Confederacy's...*, 188.
32. Sword, *The Confederacy's...*, 197.
33. Clark, 336; Stanley, 206.
34. Jacobson and Rupp, 271–273, 285; Clark, 349; Opdycke, 249; Shellenberger, "The Battle of Franklin," 495–521.
35. Scofield, 34; Stiles, 139.
36. Cox, *March to the Sea*, 88–89; Hinman, 655.
37. Scofield, 35; Opdycke, 249–256; *Official Records*, vol. 45, part 1, 271, 256; Clark, 334–335; Cox, *March to the Sea*, 88–89; Jacobson and Rupp, 294–295.
38. Rice,157; Opdycke, 247–250; Clark, 336-7; Rice, R.C. "Battle of Franklin: A Defense of the Conduct of Gen. Schofield" in *National Tribune*, May 1, 1902, 3; Young, B.F. Letter in *National Tribune*, April 7, 1892, 4.
39. Jacobson and Rupp, 327; *Military History of Ohio*, 255; Sword, *The Confederacy's...*, 193.
40. Sword, *The Confederacy's...*, 195; Jacobson and Rupp, 332–336, 384; Reid, vol. 2, 592, 725.
41. Clark, 344–345; Reid, vol. 2, 563; *Official Records*, vol. 45, part 1, 326, 419; Jacobson and Rupp, 333, 297, 349; Opdycke, 256; Sword, *The Confederacy's...*, 193.
42. Jacobson and Rupp, 327; Rice, R.C., "Battle of Franklin," 3; Shellenberger, "The Battle of Franklin," 13; Cox, *March...*, 89.
43. Sword, *The Confederacy's...*, 193; Cox, *March to the Sea*, 90; Scofield, 37–38; *Official Records*, vol. 45, part 1, 326, 330; Reid, vol. 2, 878–879; Opdycke, 250–251; Jacobson and Rupp, 226, 342.
44. Scofield, 37; Jacobson and Rupp, 420.
45. Jacobson and Rupp, 347.
46. Scofield, 37; Jacobson and Rupp, 347–349; Reid, vol. 2, 710; Dyer, 1646; Williams, T.W. in "Checking a Pursuing Foe" *National Tribune*, May 31, 1900, 3.
47. Clark, 336–337; Cox, *March to the Sea*, 88–89; Opdycke, 248–258; *Official Records*, vol. 45, part 1, 251.
48. Cox, *March to the Sea*, 89.

49. Jacobson and Rupp, 338, 344; *Official Records*, vol. 45, part 1, 248; Cox, *March to the Sea*, 89; Opdycke, 256; Sword, *The Confederacy's...*, 201–204.
50. Rice, 157; *Official Records*, vol. 45, part 1, 251; Clark, 337; Sword, *The Confederacy's...*, 201; Opdycke, 256–257.
51. Jacobson and Rupp, 338–344.
52. Sword, *The Confederacy's...*, 201–204; Jacobson and Rupp, 344.
53. Sword, *The Confederacy's...*, 202.
54. Sword, *The Confederacy's...*, 202; Rice, 158, 161–165; Clark, 337; *Official Records*, vol. 45, part 1, 251.
55. Rice, 161–165, 194; Clark, 337; Sword, *The Confederacy's...*, 203–205; Williams, "Checking a Pursuing Foe," 3.
56. Clark, 339–343; *Official Records*, vol. 45, part 1, 253.
57. Sword, *The Confederacy's...*, 198–199; Clark, 335–336; Opdycke, 250.
58. Clark, 336; Opdycke, 256–257.
59. Clark, 344–346; Reid, vol. 2, 563.
60. Clark, 341–348; Schmiel, 159; Rice, 161; *Official Records*, vol. 45, part 1, 352–354.
61. Opdycke, 248–252, 257; Scofield, 38–39; Clark, 343; Schmiel, 159.
62. Rice, 164; Lord, 13.
63. Scofield, 39; Opdycke, 248–254; Rice, R. C., "Battle of Franklin," 3.
64. Shellenberger, "The Battle of Franklin," 495–521; Opdycke, 250–251; Rice, 157–158; Clark, 339, 343, 353.
65. Rice, 160–164, 228; *Official Records*, vol. 45, part 1, 353; Cox, *March to the Sea*, 90; Opdycke, 248–252.
66. Opdycke, 48–50; Scofield, 41–46; Williams, "Checking a Pursuing Foe," 3.
67. Rice, 228; Cunningham, "Battle of Franklin," 101.
68. Scofield, 41; Jacobson and Rupp, 314; Hinman, 671–672; Shellenberger, "The Battle of Franklin," 495–521; Banks, 69–70.
69. Sword, *The Confederacy's...*, 245–248; Jacobson and Rupp, 403–405.
70. *Ibid.*
71. Rice, 164; Cox, *March to the Sea*, 238; Stanley, 209.
72. Schmiel, 160–161; *Official Records*, vol. 45, part 1, 343; Grant, *Memoirs*, 655.
73. Scofield, 53; Clark, 354.
74. Clark, 354–356; Opdycke, 257; McDonough and Connelly, 156–157.
75. Rice, 165–167; Hinman, 660.
76. Rice, 167; Hinman, 660; Clark, 354–355; Catton, 365.
77. Opdycke, 253.
78. Shellenberger, "The Battle of Franklin," 495–521; Figuers, "A Boy's Impressions of...," 4–7; Sword, *The Confederacy's...*, 259; Jacobson and Rupp, 438.
79. Jacobson and Rupp, 431; Opdycke, 252.
80. Jacobson and Rupp, 268.
81. Jacobson and Rupp, 439, 441; McDonough and Connelly, 3.
82. Cox, *March*, 97–98; Hinman, 657.
83. Opdycke, 248–252; Clark, 338, 352–354; Reid, vol. 2, 640; *Official Records*, vol. 45, part 1, 233–234, 353.
84. Jacobson and Rupp, 438; Stanley, 209.

Chapter 19

1. Hinman, 675; Rice, 167.
2. Opdycke, 250; Clark, 352, 356.
3. *Cleveland Morning Leader*, Dec. 20, 1864, 2; *New York Daily Tribune*, Dec. 5, 1864, 1; Opdycke, 250–257; *Official Records*, vol. 45, part 1, 232, 342; Opdycke, 250–256; Clark, 352.
4. Clark, 356; Opdycke, 253; Sifakis, *Who Was Who in the Union*, 432.
5. Clark, 356, 370; Opdycke, 245–246, 266; *Proceedings of a Board of Examiners...*, Nov. 10, 1864.
6. Opdycke, 253; Clark, 356; Warner, *Generals in Blue*, 141–142.
7. Clark, 356; Horn, 31–34.
8. Cox, *March to the Sea*, 101; Horn, 23.
9. Clark, 357; Opdycke, 253; Horn, 38.
10. Clark, 361; Horn, 43; Foote, vol. 3, 675–679, 689.
11. Clark, 357–359; Opdycke, 255.
12. Clark, 357–359; Cox, *March to the Sea*, 136; Horn, 1; Warner, *Generals in Blue*, 454.
13. Foote, vol. 3, 682; Cox, *March to the Sea*, 135–136; Sword, *The Confederacy's...*, 290.
14. *Official Records*, vol. 45, part 1, 131; Clark, 360; Horn, 47; Foote, vol. 3, 676.
15. Clark, 360–361; Cox, *March...*, 110; Horn, 1, Foote, vol. 3, 677, 688–689.
16. Foote, vol. 3, 680–681, 685–686; Cox, *March to the Sea*, 108; Horn, 63–64.
17. Clark, 360; Bobrick, 287; Grant, 659; Sherman, *Memoirs*, 391; Horn, 45, 58.
18. Clark, 360; Sifakis, *Who Was Who in the Union*, 240; Bobrick, 289; Lewis, 206.
19. Foote, vol. 3, 687; Horn, 59; *Official Records*, vol. 45, part 1, 242.
20. Horn, 69, 72.
21. Clark, 362; Foote, vol. 3, 691; Bobrick, 292; Horn, 77.
22. Horn, 86–87; *Official Records*, vol. 45, part 1, 129.
23. *Official Records*, vol. 45, part 1, 242; Clark, 361–362; Sword, *The Confederacy's...*, 333; Horn, 73.
24. Clark, 362; Lewis, 207; Horn, 87–88; *Official Records*, vol. 45, part 1, 129; Foote, vol. 3, 690–691.
25. Horn, 88–89; *Official Records*, vol. 45, part 1, 243.
26. Sword, *The Confederacy's...*, 341; Horn, 102.
27. Clark, 363–369; Foote, vol. 695; Sword, *The Confederacy's...*, 341–342; *Official Records*, vol. 45, part 1, 243.
28. Clark, 363; Sword, *The Confederacy's...*, 341–343; Bobrick, 293; Cox, *March to the Sea*, 113–114.
29. Clark 360; Warner, *Generals in Blue*, 282; Bobrick, 289; Lewis, 206.
30. *Official Records*, vol. 45, part 1, 130, 243; Horn,

105; Clark, 363; Sword, *The Confederacy's...*, 363.
31. Cox, *March to the Sea*, 113–116; Sword, *The Confederacy's...*, 343–344.
32. Clark, 363; Cox, *March to the Sea*, 114–115; Sword, *The Confederacy's...*, 347–348; Horn, 108–112.
33. Clark, 363; Cox, *March to the Sea*, 114–115; Sword, *The Confederacy's...*, 347–348; Horn, 108–112.
34. Grant, 660; Foote, vol. 3, 695–697; Bobrick, 294–295; Cox, *March to the Sea*, 117; Horn, 107, 114.
35. Clark, 364.
36. Clark, 364–365; Horn, 116; *Official Records*, vol. 45, part 1, 130, 243–244.
37. Clark, 366; Horn, 108, 116; Sword, *The Confederacy's...*, 360–363; Kimberly and Holloway, 104–105.
38. Foote, vol. 700–702; Hinman, 680; Cox, *March to the Sea*, 120–123; Clark, 367; Horn, 124; Losson, 238.
39. *Official Records*, vol. 45, part 1, 234–244; Clark, 367–368; Horn, 117–120; Kimberly and Holloway, 105–107.
40. Clark, 367–368; Horn, 146–150; Lewis, 211; Losson, 238.
41. Clark, 368; Bobrick, 297; Foote, vol. 3, 704.
42. *Official Records*, vol. 45, part 1, 134; Clark, 368; Cox, *March to the Sea*, 127.
43. Cox, *March to the Sea*, 124.
44. Hinman, 681; Sword, *The Confederacy's...*, 388–391; *Official Records*, vol. 45, part 1, 134; Opdycke, 260.
45. Bobrick, 299.
46. Horn, 154.
47. Sword, *The Confederacy's...*, 400–401; Horn, 160; Foote, vol. 3, 707.
48. Clark, 369; Opdycke, 260.
49. Clark, 370; Sword, *The Confederacy's...*, 396, 430; Opdycke, 261.
50. Sword, *The Confederacy's...*, 405–406; *Official Records*, vol. 45, part 1, 135; Foote, vol. 3, 707.
51. Clark, 370; Opdycke, 261; Sword, *The Confederacy's...*, 410–411; Grant, 661; Horn, 154.
52. Clark, 370; Opdycke, 263; Sword, *The Confederacy's...*, 413.
53. Bobrick, 300–303.
54. Clark, 370–371; Opdycke, 263; *Official Records*, vol. 45, part 1, 137.
55. Opdycke, 263–264; Hinman, 684; Clark, 371; *Official Records*, vol. 45, part 1, 137.
56. Clark, 371; Opdycke, 264; Sword, *The Confederacy's...*, 419–420.
57. Bobrick, 300; Hinman, 685; Cox, *March to the Sea*, 126; Horn, 163.
58. Clark, 371; Opdycke, 264–265; Cox, *March to the Sea*, 129; *Official Records*, vol. 45, part 1, 137.
59. Clark, 371; Opdycke, 266; Bobrick, 300; Cox, *March to the Sea*, 127.
60. Opdycke, 265; Clark, 371; Horn, 166; Foote, vol. 3, 709–710.
61. Catton, 369.

Chapter 20

1. Clark, 373; Opdycke, 266–267.
2. Day, 320–322; Opdycke, 271–272; Clark, 374–375.
3. Opdycke, 273–274; Whitesides, *Diary*, 17 Jan. 1865.
4. Clark, 375–376; Wiley, 264–274; *Yankee Tigers II*, 181, 262, 270; Opdycke, 162.
5. Clark, 376; Opdycke, 274; Day, 318–320.
6. Clark, 377–379; Opdycke, 271–272, 276–280.
7. Opdycke, 278–283; Clark, 380–382.
8. Opdycke, 279–280; Clark, 380–382.
9. Whitesides, *Diary*, March 28–April 15, 1865; Clark, 380–383; Opdycke, 280–283.
10. Clark, 382; Opdycke, 283; Whitesides, *Diary*, April 10, 1865.
11. Clark, 383; Opdycke, 284–285; Whitesides, *Diary*, April 15, 1865.
12. Clark, 384–385; Opdycke, 285–287.
13. Clark, 386; Opdycke, 287–291; Stanley, 226.
14. Clark, 387.
15. Clark, 388; Opdycke, 292–293.
16. Bruff, Joseph, Certificate of Election, May 20, 1865, and letter to General Whipple, May 25, 1865, in Service Records of Joseph Bruff, National Archives and Records Administration, Washington, D.C.; Opdycke, 286–288; Schmiel, 171, 182.
17. Clark, 389–390; Opdycke, 294–295; *Cleveland Leader*, Morning Edition, June 9, 1865; Opdycke, Emerson, letter to Major General George H. Thomas, June 27, 1865, in Service Records of Emerson Opdycke, National Archives and Records Administration, Washington.
18. Clark, 390–392; Opdycke, 194, 294–295; Sifakis, *Who Was Who in the Union*, 265; *Cleveland Leader*, Morning Edition, June 24 and Aug. 3, 1865.
19. Rice, 184; *Cleveland Leader*, Morning Edition, June 24, 1865; Clark, 393; Hinman, 730–731; Stanley, 227.
20. Clark, 393; Opdycke, 289, 299–300; Hinman, 734–735.
21. Clark, 392; Opdycke, 300–302.
22. Opdycke, 300–302; Bobrick, 317.
23. Opdycke, 300–304; Clark, 394–396.
24. *Ibid.*
25. Clark, 397–398; Hinman, 741, 746; Stanley, 229; *New York Herald*, Aug. 3, 1865; *Cleveland Leader*, Morning Edition, Aug. 14, 1865.
26. Clark, 398–400; *New York Herald*, Aug. 3, 1865.
27. Stanley, 229; Clark, 400; Hinman, 747.
28. Clark, 400; Stanley, 231; *Cleveland Leader*, Morning Edition, August 26, 1865.
29. Stanley, 235; Hinman, 748–749, 756, 776; Clark, 401; Hunt and Brown, 127.
30. Clark, 395, 402–403; Hinman, 759–760; Opdycke, 302–304.
31. Clark, 405–406; Hinman, 750–753.
32. *Cleveland Leader*, Morning Edition, Sept. 11, 1865; *Western Reserve Chronicle*, Oct. 18, 1865.
33. Clark, 410, 414; Hinman, 775, 1005.
34. Clark, 416–418.
35. Clark, 420.
36. Clark, 416–423, *Daily Ohio Statesman*, Oct. 20,

Bibliography

Articles

Andrews, Peter. "The Rock of Chickamauga." *American Heritage* March 1990.

Bilby, Joseph. "The Story of Buck and Ball." *American Rifleman*. May 1993.

Castel, Albert. "The Battle That Should Not Have Been." *Civil War Times Illustrated*. November/December 1992.

Cunningham, S. A. "Battle of Franklin." *Confederate Veteran*. Volume 1.

Davis, Stephen. "Hood Fights Desperately. The Battles for Atlanta." *Blue and Gray Magazine*. August 1989.

Dwight, Henry O. "How We Fight at Atlanta." *Harper's New Monthly Magazine*. October 1864.

"Emerson Opdycke's Civil War." Ohio Historical Society Album, *Timeline*. July–September 2012.

Evans, David. "The Atlanta Campaign." *Civil War Times Illustrated*. Summer 1989.

Figeurs, Hardin O. "A Boy's Impression of the Battle of Franklin." *Confederate Veteran*. Volume 23.

Kelly, Dennis. "Mountains to Pass, a River to Cross." *Blue and Gray Magazine*. June 1989.

Klinger, Michael J. "Gallant Charge Repulsed." *America's Civil War*. January 1989.

Longacre, Edward G.. "A Vanquished General in the West." *Civil War Times Illustrated*. October 1985.

Marszalek, John F. "Fighting Peacemaker. William T. Sherman." *Timeline*. December 1988/January 1989.

McMurray, Richard M. "Rocky Face to the Dallas Line. The Battles of May 1864." *Blue and Gray Magazine*. April 1989.

Monlux, George. "A Cavalryman's View." *National Tribune*. March 30, 1911.

Moore, David H. "Freaks of a Bullet." *Confederate Veteran*. Volume 26.

Previts, Fred. "Battlefield Ballots. The 1864 Presidential Election." *Timeline*. October/December 2009.

Rentfro, Jack. "Remnants of Civil War Knoxville." *Civil War Times Illustrated*. May/June 1994.

Rice, R.C. "Battle of Franklin: A Defense of the Conduct of General Schofield." *National Tribune*. May 1, 1902.

Rice, R.C. "Opdycke at Franklin." *National Tribune*. March 30, 1911.

Shanks, W.F. "Recollections of Thomas." *Harper's New Monthly Magazine*. May 1865.

Shellenberger, John K. "The Battle of Franklin." *MOLLUS*, Minnesota, Volume 5.

Shellenberger, John K. "Schofield at Franklin." *National Tribune*. September 12, 1901.

Shellenberger, John K. "With Sheridan's Division at Missionary Ridge." *Sketches of the War History, 1861–1865. Papers Prepared for the Ohio Commandery of the Loyal Legion of the United States, 1890–1896, Volume 4*. Cincinnati: Robert Clarke, 1896.

Smith, D.W. "Hood's Last Campaign." *National Tribune*. November 20, 1890.

Tucker, Glenn. "The Battle of Chickamauga." *Civil War Times Illustrated*. May 1969.

Williams, T.W. "Checking a Pursuing Foe." *National Tribune*. May 3, 1900.

Books

Adams, George Worthington. *Doctors in Blue: The Medical History of the Union Army in the Civil War*. Dayton: Morningside, 1985.

Banks, R.W. *The Battle of Franklin*. Dayton: Morningside, 1988.

Battles and Leaders of the Civil War. Popular edition, 3 volumes. New York: Thomas Yoseloff, 1956.

Bierce, Ambrose. *Civil War Stories*. New York: Dover, 1994.

Brobrick, Benson. *Master of War: The Life of General George H. Thomas*. New York: Simon & Schuster, 2009.

Castel, Albert. *Decision in the West: The Atlanta Campaign of 1864*. Lawrence: University of Kansas Press, 1992.

Catton, Bruce. *This Hallowed Ground: The Story of*

the Union Side of the Civil War. Garden City, NY: Doubleday, 1956.

Cist, Henry M. *The Army of the Cumberland*. New York: Charles Scribner's Sons, 1882.

Clark, Charles T. *Opdycke Tigers: A History of the Regiment and of the Campaigns and Battles of the Army of the Cumberland*. Columbus: Spahr and Glenn, 1895.

Cox, Jacob D. *Atlanta*. New York: Charles Scribner's Sons, 1882.

Cox, Jacob D. *The March to the Sea—Franklin and Nashville*. New York: Charles Scribner's Sons, 1882.

Cozzens, Peter. *The Battles for Chattanooga*. Eastern National Park and Monuments Association, 1996.

Cozzens, Peter. *The Shipwreck of Their Hopes. The Battles for Chattanooga*. Urbana: University of Illinois Press, 1994.

Cozzens, Peter. *This Terrible Sound. The Battle of Chickamauga*. Urbana: University of Illinois Press, 1992.

Cummings, Charles M. *Yankee Quaker Confederate General: The Curious Career of Bushrod Rust Johnson*. Columbus: The General's Books, 1993.

Davis, Burke. *Sherman's March*. New York: Vintage, 1988.

Davis, George B., Leslie J. Perry, and Joseph W. Kirkley. *The Official Military Atlas of the Civil War*. Calvin Cowles, compiler. New York: Fairfax Press, 1983.

Davis, William C. *The Fighting Men of the Civil War*. Norman: University of Oklahoma Press, 1989.

Day, L.W. *Story of the One Hundred and First Ohio Infantry*. Cleveland: W. M. Bayne Printing Co., 1894.

Demoret, A. *A Brief History of the 93rd Regiment, Ohio Volunteer Infantry. Recollections of a Private*. Privately published, 1898.

Donald, David Herbert. *Lincoln*. London: Jonathan Cape, 1995.

Duncan, Louis C. *The Medical Department of the United States Army in the Civil War*. Gaithersburg, MD: Butternut Press, 1985.

Dyer, Frederick H. *A Compendium of the War of the Rebellion*. Dayton: Morningside, 1978.

Echoes of Battle. The Atlanta Campaign. Larry M. Strayer and Richard A. Baumgartner, editors. Huntington: Blue Acorn Press, 1991.

Eckenrode, H.J., and Bryan Conrad. *James Longstreet: Lee's War Horse*. Chapel Hill: University of North Carolina Press, 1999.

Fielder, Alfred Tyler. *The Civil War Diaries of Captain Alfred Fielder: 12th Tennessee Regiment of Infantry*. Ann York Franklin, compiler. Louisville: privately printed, 1996.

Foote, Shelby. *The Civil War. A Narrative*. 3 volumes. New York: Vintage, 1963.

Gallman, J. Matthew. *Defining Duty in the Civil War: Personal Choice, Popular Culture and the Union Home Front*. Chapel Hill: University of North Carolina Press, 2015.

Gillett, Mary C. *The Army Medical Department, 1818–1865*. Washington: United States Army Center of Military History, 1987.

Grant, Ulysses S. *Memoirs and Selected Letters*. New York: Literary Classics of the United States, 1990.

Griffith, Paddy. *Battle Tactics of the Civil War*. New Haven: Yale University Press, 2001.

Guide to the Atlanta Campaign: Rocky Face Ridge to Kennesaw Mountain. Jay Luvaas and Harold W. Nelson, editors. Lawrence: University Press of Kansas, 2008.

Hannaford, E. *The Story of a Regiment: A History of the Campaigns and Associations of the Sixth Regiment Ohio Volunteer Infantry*. Cincinnati: privately published, 1868.

Hazen, William B. *A Narrative of Military Service*. Boston: Ticknor and Company, 1885.

Hess, Earl J. *Kennesaw Mountain. Sherman, Johnston and the Atlanta Campaign*. Chapel Hill: University of North Carolina Press, 2013.

Hight, John J. *History of the 58th Regiment of Indiana Volunteer Infantry*. Clarion: Clarion, 1895.

Hinman, Wilbur F. *The Story of the Sherman Brigade*. Alliance, OH: Daily Review, 1897.

Horn, Stanley F. *The Decisive Battle of Nashville*. Knoxville: University of Tennessee Press, 1986.

Horwitz, Lester V. *The Longest Raid of the Civil War*. Cincinnati: Farmcourt, 2001.

Hunt, Roger D., and Jack R. Brown. *Brevet Brigadier Generals in Blue*. Gaithersburg, MD: Olde Soldier Books, 1990.

Hurst, Samuel H. *The Journal History of the Seventy-Third Ohio Volunteer Infantry*. Chillicothe: privately published, 1866.

Jacobson, Eric A., and Richard A. Rupp. *For Cause and for Country: A Study of the Affair at Spring Hill and the Battle of Franklin*. Franklin, TN: O'More Publishing, 2006.

Kerwood, Ashbury L. *Annuals of the 57th Regiment Indiana Volunteers: Marches, Battles and Incidents of Army Life*. Dayton: O.W.J. Shuey, 1868.

Kimberly, Robert L., and Ephraim S. Holloway. *The Forty-First Ohio Veteran Volunteer Infantry in the War of the Rebellion*. Cleveland: W. R. Smellie, 1897.

Lewis, G. W. *The Campaigns of the 124th Regiment, Ohio Volunteer Infantry*. Akron: The Werner Company, 1894.

Linderman, Gerald F. *Embattled Courage: The Experience of Combat in the American Civil War*. New York: The Free Press, 1987.

Longacre, Edward G. *Ulysses S. Grant: The Soldier and the Man*. Cambridge: Da Capo Press, 2006.

Lord, Francis A. *Civil War Collectors Encyclopedia.* Secaucus, NJ: Castle, 1963.

McCarley, J. Britt. *The Atlanta Campaign. A Civil War Driving Tour of Atlanta Area Battlefields.* Atlanta: Cherokee Publishing Co., 1989.

McDonough, James Lee, and Thomas L. Connelly. *Five Tragic Hours: The Battle of Franklin.* Knoxville: University of Tennessee Press, 1987.

McFeely, William S. *Grant: A Biography.* New York: W.W. Norton, 1981.

McPherson, James M. *Tried by War: Abraham Lincoln as Commander in Chief.* New York: Penguin Press, 2008.

McWhiney, Grady. *Braxton Bragg and Confederate Defeat.* Volume 2. New York: Columbia University Press, 1969.

The Military History of Ohio, Illustrated. Trumbull County edition. New York: H.H. Hardesty, 1888.

Morgan, John. *Army Life of John Morgan.* Robert M. Bricker, editor. Akron: The Bookseller, 2001.

Opdycke, Emerson. *The Battle for God and the Right: The Civil War Letterbooks of Emerson Opdycke.* Glenn V. Longacre and John E. Haas, editors. Urbana: University of Illinois Press, 2003.

Personal Reminiscences and Experiences by the Members of the One Hundred and Third Ohio Volunteer Infantry. Oberlin: News Printing Co., 1900.

Piston, William Garrett. *Lee's Tarnished Lieutenant: James Longstreet and His Place in Southern History.* Athens: University of Georgia Press, 1987.

Porter, Horace. *Campaigning with Grant.* Alexandria: Time-Life Books, 1981.

Reid, Whitelaw. *Ohio in the War: Her Statesmen, Her Generals and Soldiers.* 2 volumes. Cincinnati: Moore, Wilstach & Baldwin, 1868.

Rice, Ralsa. *Yankee Tigers: Through the Civil War with the 125th Ohio.* Richard A. Baumgartner and Larry M. Strayer, editors. Huntington, WV: Blue Acorn Press, 1992.

Robertson, William G. *The Battle of Chickamauga.* Civil War Series. Eastern National Park and Monument Association: 1995.

Royster, Charles. *The Destructive War.* New York: Vintage, 1993.

Schmiel, Eugene D. *Citizen General: Jacob Dolson Cox and the Civil War Era.* Athens: Ohio University Press, 2014.

Scofield, Levi T. *The Retreat from Pulaski to Nashville, Tennessee. Battle of Franklin, Tennessee, November 30, 1864.* Cleveland: Press of the Caxton Co., 1909.

Scott, William F. *Philander P. Lane: Colonel of Volunteers in the Civil War. Eleventh Infantry.* Privately printed, 1920.

Secrist, Philip L. *The Battle of Resaca.* Macon: Mercer University Press, 2010.

Shanks, William F.G. *Personal Recollections of Distinguished Generals.* New York: Harper and Brothers, 1866. Accessed at http://archive.org/stream/personalrecollec...

Sherman, Francis T. *Quest for a Star. The Civil War Letters and Diaries of Colonel Francis T. Sherman of the 88th Illinois.* C. Knight Aldrich, editor. Knoxville: University of Tennessee Press, 1999.

Sherman, William T. *The Memoirs of General W.T. Sherman.* Middlesex: The Echo Library, 2006.

Sifakis, Stewart. *Who Was Who in the Union.* Volume 1 of Who Was Who in the Civil War. New York: Facts on File, 1988.

Smith, David C. *Campaign to Nowhere: The Results of General Longstreet's Move into Upper East Tennessee.* Dandridge, TN: Jefferson County Historical Society, 2013.

Stanley, David S. *Personal Memoirs of Major General D.S. Stanley, USA.* Cambridge: Harvard University Press, 1917.

Starr, Stephen Z. *The Union Cavalry in the Civil War. The War in the West. 1861–1865.* Volume 3. Baton Rouge: Louisiana State University Press, 1985.

Stiles, T. J. *Custer's Trials. A Life on the Frontier of a New America.* New York: Alfred Knopf, 2015.

Sword, Wiley. *The Confederacy's Last Hurrah: Spring Hill, Franklin and Nashville.* Lawrence: University of Kansas Press, 1992.

Sword, Wiley. *Shiloh: Bloody April.* Dayton: Morningside, 1983.

Their Patriotic Duty: The Civil War Letters of the Evans Family of Brown County, Ohio. Robert F. Engs and Corey M. Brooks, editors. New York: Fordham University Press, 2007.

Thomas, Benjamin P. *Abraham Lincoln.* New York: Book-of-the-Month Club, 1980.

Thomas, Edison H. *John Hunt Morgan and His Raiders.* Lexington: University of Kentucky, 1985.

Thompson, Lewis N. *History of the Orphan Brigade.* Louisville: Ed Porter Thompson, 1898.

Tourgee, Albion W. *The Story of a Thousand: Being a History of the Service of the 105th Ohio Volunteer Infantry.* Buffalo: S. McGerald & Son, 1896.

Trask, William L. *Civil War Journal of William L. Trask.* Kenneth A. Hafendorfer, editor. Louisville: Kentucky History Press, 2003.

Tucker, Glenn. *Chickamauga: Bloody Battle in the West.* Dayton: Morningside, 1984.

Tuttle, John W. *The Union, The Civil War and John W. Tuttle: A Kentucky Captain's Account.* Tapp Hambleton and James C. Klotter, editors. Frankfort: The Kentucky Historical Society, 1980.

Van Horne, Thomas. *History of the Army of the Cumberland.* Cincinnati: R. Clarke & Co., 1895.

Vermilya, Daniel J. *The Battles of Kennesaw Mountain.* Charleston: The History Press, 2014.

The War of the Rebellion: A Compilation of the Official Records of the Union and Confederate Armies. Series I. Washington, D.C.: U.S. Government Printing Office, 1880.

Warner, Ezra J. *Generals in Blue: Lives of the Union Commanders*. Baton Rouge: Louisiana State University Press, 1986.

Warner, Ezra J. *Generals in Gray: Lives of the Confederate Commanders*. Baton Rouge: Louisiana State University Press, 1988.

Wiley, Bell Irvin. *The Life of Billy Yank: The Common Soldier of the Union*. Garden City, NY: Doubleday, 1971.

Wood, George L. *The Seventh Regiment: A Record*. New York: James Miller, 1865.

Woodworth, Steven E. *Sherman*. New York: Palgrave MacMillan, 2009.

Yankee Tigers II: Civil War Field Correspondence from the Tiger Regiment of Ohio. Richard A. Baumgartner, editor. Huntington, WV: Blue Acorn Press, 2004.

Newspapers

The Cleveland Herald
The Cleveland Leader
Daily Ohio Statesman
The Holmes County Farmer (Ohio)
The Jeffersonian Democrat (Ohio)
Lancaster Gazette (Ohio)
The National Tribune
New York Daily Tribune
New York Times
The Ohio Democrat
Warren Constitution (Ohio)
The Warren Tribune (Ohio)
Western Reserve Chronicle (Ohio)

Other Sources

Bruff, Joseph. *Roster for Company A*. Bruff Family Records, Volume 1380, Ohio History Connection, Columbus, Ohio.

Coleman, W.S. *Diary of W.S. Coleman. November 6, 1861–December 28, 1863*. Mississippi State Department of Archives and History, Jackson, Mississippi.

Emerson Opdycke Papers, Ohio History Connection, Columbus, Ohio.

Manville, Craig J. *The Limits of Obedience: Brigadier General Thomas J. Wood's Performance During the Battle of Chickamauga*. Master's Thesis. Fort Leavenworth, KS, 2005. www.dtic.mil/dtic/tr/fulltext/u2/a437039.pdf.

Moffat, William C., Jr. "Soldier's Pay." Cincinnati Civil War Roundtable Presentation, January 1865. http://www.cincinnaticwrt.org.

Overland Monthly. "Defenders of the Union." Ronusevelle Wildman, editor. Volume 28, second series, San Francisco: Overland Monthly Publishing Co., 1896.

Proceedings of a Board of Examiners Convened at Pulaski, Tennessee, on Thursday, the Tenth Day of November, AD 1864. Military Service Record of Joseph Bruff. National Archives and Record Administration, Washington, D.C.

Whitesides, E.G. *Diary. E. G. Whitesides, Adjutant 125th Ohio Vol. Infantry, September 19, 1863 to April 30, 1865*. Department of the Army, U.S. Army Heritage and Education Center, U.S. Army Military History Institute, Carlisle, PA.

Woodworth, Edwin C. *Edwin Woodworth Papers*. Ohio History Connection, Columbus, Ohio.

INDEX

Numbers in *bold italics* indicate pages with illustrations

Acworth, Georgia 134, 138, 140, 200
Adairsville, Georgia 130-131
Adams, Henry 198, 235
Alabama 188, 200-201
Allatoona Hills 130, 133, 138, 141, 200
Allegheny Mountains 113, 116
Alpine, Georgia 201
Andersonville Prison 109
Army of the Cumberland 16, 26, 28, 30-32, 41, 48, 84-85, 94, 117-118, 125, 132-134, 137, 143-145, 147, 166-175, 178-182, 184, 186, 198; reorganization 113
Army of the Ohio 113, 130, 137, 140, 171, 180-182, 186, 190
Army of the Tennessee (CSA) 30, 38, 98, 113, 120, 144, 157, 171, 188, 196, 231
Army of the Tennessee (USA) 79, 113, 117, 181-185, 191-193, 238, 244, 255
Athens, Alabama 201-202, 247
Athens, Georgia 198
Athens, Ohio 28-29
Atlanta and Montgomery Railroad 171
Atlanta and West Point Railroad 184
Atlanta, Battle of 180-183
Atlanta Campaign **114**, ***167***
Atlanta Constitution 139
Atlanta, Georgia 117, 124-125, 129, 132, 133-135, 138, 141-144, 147, 154, 164-166, 169-177, 179-***181***, 184-196, 198-201, 204, 233, 237, 246

Badenborrough, John 18
Bainbridge, Alabama 247
Bald Hill 179, 182
Banning, Henry 13, 24, 120, 163
Barnes, Albert 55, 72
Barnes, Rollin 19, 55
Barnes, Sidney 49, 51
Barney 13, 24, 35, 55, 62, 92, 99, 126-127, 172

Bartleson, Frederick 49, 148-149
Bate, William 175-176, 219, 228, 231
Bates, Edward 36, 62, 104-111, 119, 184, 195, 199-200, 203, 208, 233, 249, 253, 257; biographical sketch ***12***, 24; Franklin 217, 224-226, 230; Missionary Ridge 84, 89, 92, 96
Bean's Station, Tennessee 103
Beatty, Samuel 233, 238, 242
Beauregard, P.G.T. 233
Bell, Henry 127
Ben 216
Bickham, William 48-49
Bierce, Ambrose 90, 121, 138, 148
Big Shanty, Georgia 141, 143, 147, 164, 200
Blaine's Crossroads, Tennessee 100-104
Blair, Francis 141, 143
Blake, John 174, 176, 177
Blanch, Will 156
Blystone, David K. 229
Bradley, Luther 74, 126, 129, 153, 156, 162, 165, 168-174, 176-180, 182-186, 189-195, 199, 203, 208-211, 217, 219; biographical sketch 161; wounded 209
Bragg, Braxton 30-31, 34, 36, 41, 48, 51, 65, 78-79, 83-86, 89, 93-94, 96-97, 113, 117, 141, 245
Branch, Willis 175
Brannon, John 51, 60
Breezy Hill, 215, 216
Brentwood, Tennessee 218, 229, 230, 236-237, 246, 243-244
Bridgeport, Alabama 34-35, 73, 199-201, 250
Briggs, Ethan 72
Brotherton Farm 48-49
Brough, John 76, 110-111, 184, 204
Brown, Isaac 158
Brown, John 219, 221, 225, 228, 231
Brown, Samuel 56
Brown, Tom 253
Bruff, Joseph 2, 24, 57, 89, 92, 110-111, 119, 121, 136-137, 140, 146, 149, 162, 168-169, 184, 187, 195, 197, 199, 203-204, 208, 233, 245, 249-253, 257; arrested 198; biographical sketch ***10***; hearing 205; Nashville 240
Brush Mountain, Georgia 142-143
Brushy Knob 84
Buchanan, James 198
Buckhead, Georgia 171-172
Buckner, Allen 88, 91, 121, 219
Buell, Don Carlos 6, 7, 28
Buell, George 36, 38, 45-46, 51
Bullitt, William 121
Bull's Gap, Tennessee 102, 250
Bunnell, Rueben 96
Burnham, Thomas 160
Burnside, Ambrose 36, 79-80, 82, 85, 97, 99-100
Burnt Hickory, Georgia 133-134, 153
Bushnell, Seth 6
Buzzard's Roost Gap 117, 120

Cairo, Illinois 257
Calhoun, Georgia 129-131, 200
Callahan, Mathias 109
Calvin, Luther 122
Camp Chase 257
Camp Cleveland 10
Camp Creek 125-127, 190-191
Camp Harker 251
Carlton, Simeon 120
Carr, Joel 25, 254
Carter, Abner 92
Carter cotton gin 212, 218, 222-223, 227
Carter Creek Pike 212, 215
Carter House 20, 211-***213***, 216, 217, 219-231
Cassidy, Thomas 122
Cassville, Georgia 130, 132
Castel, Albert 141, 189
Catton, Bruce 67, 247
Champion 254
Chase, Salmon 6
Chattanooga Creek 87
Chattahoochee River 116, 132, 141-

293

Index

147, 164–165, 168–170, 173, 185, 188, 190–192, 194, 198, 200
Chattanooga, Tennessee 31–36, 70–71, **82**, 96–97, 100, 113, 116, 141, 165, 184, 188, 190, 198–201, 235–236, 245, 250–251; description 72
Cheatham, Benjamin Franklin 153–155, 163, 168, 171, 173, 175–179, 182, 184, 208–209, 211, 216, 218–219, 230, 236, 242–243, 245
Cheatham Hill 156, 165
Cheney, Walter 108
Cheshire, Ohio 29
Chickamauga, Battle of 41–69, **60**, 200
Chickamauga Creek 36–39, 86, 96, 117
Chickamauga Station 95–96
Chihuahua, Mexico 255
Chucky Bend Road 104
Cincinnati, Ohio 15, 253, 257
Clark, Charles 2, 15, 17–21, 33–34, 41–42, 44, 46, 55, 57, 61, 66, 74, 76, 83, 91, 94–95, 101–103, 107, 129, 139, 177, 182, 186, 200, 233, 242–243, 245; biographical sketch **16**; Dyer field 58; Franklin 225, 230; Kennesaw 156, 161
Clark, Merwin 222
Clear Creek, Georgia 180
Cleburne, Patrick 94–95, 137–138, 153–154, 157–159, 162–163, 168, 178, 209–210, 218–219, 221, 225, 231
Clemens, James 248
Clemens, Jeremiah 248
Cleveland Herald 15, 22, 28, 33
Cleveland Morning Leader 94, 232, 249, 252, 256
Cleveland, Ohio 6
Cleveland, Tennessee 111, 117, 200, 250
Cliffe, Daniel 20–23, 213, 217, 220–221
Clinch Mountain 100
Cobb's Kentucky Battery (CSA) 92–93
Coburn, John 21
Coleman, Cicero 29
Collier's Bridge 173–174
Collins, Freeman 13, 146
Columbia Pike 208–209, 212–213, 216, 219, 222–227
Columbia, Tennessee 206–207, 209, 211, 216, 245–246
Columbus, Ohio 249, 257
Conley, Ira 222
Connasauga River 125
Connelly, Thomas L. 231
Conrad, Joseph **175**, 203, 209, 211, 215–223, 231–232, 239, 253, 256
contraband 22
Coolville, Ohio 29
Coonrod, Aquila 33–34, 79, 84, 111
Coosa River 130, 200
copperheads 25
Corinth, Mississippi 7

Cox, Jacob 6, 8, 26, 117, **119**, 120, 122–127, 129, 131, 134–136, 141, 147, 164–165, 169–171, 180, 182, 184–185, 187, 192–193, 206, 209–211, 232, 235, 242–244, 247, 252; biographical sketch 118; Franklin 212–229
Cozzens, Peter 58
cracker line 78
Crawfish Springs, Georgia 52
Crittenden, Thomas 27, 31, 50–51, 53, 72
Crooked Creek 192
Crow Valley 117–120, 123
Cumberland Gap 97
Cumberland Mountains 30, 34
Cumberland River 233, 236
Cushing, William 23

Dallas, Georgia 132–135, 138
Dalton, Georgia 96–97, **98**, 117–118, 120, 123, 200
Dana, Charles 47, 52, 64, 67, 71–75
Dana, William 122
Dandridge, Battle of 101, 103–105, **107**, 108–109
Darby, John 14
Davis, Pres. Jefferson 131, 141, 153, 185, 206, 233
Davis, Jefferson C. 43, 51, 153–154, 157, 160, 162–163
Davis, William 16
Decatur, Alabama 113, 201, 247
Decatur, Georgia 171–175, 179–182
Democrat Party 188, 193
Dennison, William 6
deserters 17
Diamond 15
Dickson, Alex 195
Dickson, James 56
Dilley, Alson 24, 131, **160**, 165
Dodge, Glenville 181
Donaldson, Henry 150
Dry Valley Road 52, 54, 61
Duck River 30, 206–207, 245
Duequet, Theophile 225
Dug Gap 120
Dunlap, Henry 44, 57, 91–92, 127, 161
Dyer Field 48, 51–57

Early's Creek 173–174, 177
East Point, Georgia 184, 190–192
East Tennessee 97
East Tennessee and Georgia Railroad 117–118
East Tennessee and Virginia Railroad 97, 100
Eckenrobe, H. J. 68
Eighteenth Corps 141
18th Ohio Independent Battery 65
8th Tennessee Infantry (USA) 223
88th Illinois Infantry 187, 195, 203, 207, 211, 221, 224, 227, 230, 239, 252
85th Ohio Infantry 13
87th Ohio Infantry 13
Election of 1862 25

Election of 1863 75
Election of 1864 201, 203
Eleventh Corps 113
Elk River 201–202, 206, 248
Elliott, George Washington 233, 238–242, 245–246, 252–254
Emancipation Proclamation 25
Enfield rifle 137
enlistment bounty 17, 33, 75
Etowah River 116, 130, 132–134, 144, 169, 188
Euharlee Creek 133
Evans, Ephraim 157, **160**
Ezra Church, Battle of 184–187

Fairburn, Georgia 191
Federal Enrollment Act of 1863 33
Fielder, Alfred 177
Fifteenth Corps 99, 181
15th Indiana Infantry 199
15th Missouri Infantry 175, 187, 195, 203, 209, 216
15th South Carolina Infantry 61
50th Ohio Infantry 222, 227
58th Indiana Infantry 51, 55–56
51st Illinois Infantry 74, 88–89, 115, 126, 156, 159, 165
57th Indiana Infantry 148–150, 156, 158, 162, 174, 253
1st Illinois Artillery 115, 176, 178
1st Kentucky Light Artillery (USA) 223, 226
1st Michigan Artillery 177
1st Ohio Artillery 115, 174–176, 215, 219, 226
1st Tennessee Infantry (CSA) 155, 231
1st Wisconsin Cavalry 105
1st Wisconsin Infantry 119
Fishel, Warren 138
Fishel, Wesley 146
Fitch, Hudson 191
Fitch, Perry 68
Fitch, William 136
Flint River 192
Floody, James 55
Florence, Alabama 201, 206, 247
Floyd, Watt 45
Foote, Shelby 67, 185, 241
Forrest, Nathan Bedford 22, 38, 198, 206–208, 210–211, 215, 218, 230, 235–236, 244–246
Fort Donelson, 17–18
Fort Granger 22, 212, 228
Fort Negley 230
Fort Opdycke 186
Fort Wood 70, 73, 82, 199
40th Indiana Infantry 158, 174, 253
40th Ohio Infantry 23
Fortress Monroe 254
45th Ohio Infantry 249
41st Ohio Infantry 6, 7, 65–66, 83, 90, 210
41st Tennessee Infantry (CSA) 228
44th Illinois Infantry 174, 187, 195, 209, 226–227, 241, 243, 253–256
44th Missouri Infantry 219, 222, 227

Index

42nd Illinois Infantry 74, 88, 90, 115, 130, 156, 159
Foster, John G. 100–104
Fourteenth Corps 98–99, 113, 125, 135, 143, 146, 151, 174, 191, 193
Fourth Corps 2, 74, 87, 97–102, 104–105, 108, 111, 113, 115, 117–119, 123–127, 130–131, 133–137, 143–148, 150, 153, 156, 168–174, 177–180, 183–186, 189–196, 198, 200–201, 203, 206–208, 215, 226–230, 248–256, 232–247
4th U.S. Artillery 211, 215
Franklin, 1864 Battle of 23, *214*, 215–230
Franklin Pike 210, 233, 236, 240–241, 243–245, 251
Franklin, Tennessee 2, 19, 203, 210–211, 212–219, 221, 223, 226–232, 238, 243–244, 249–252,
French, Caleb **127**
French, George 21
French, Sharon 123, 227–228
French Broad River 97, 102, 104
French Foreign Legion 255
Fulton, Georgia 166

Gadsden, Alabama 200
Galveston, Texas 253, 256
Garfield, James 6, 26, 30, 47, 50, 64, 66, 72, 115, 117
Garrard, Israel 104–105, 108
Gartner, John 187
Georgia Military Institute 168
Georgia Railroad 171, 173, 177, 179–182, 187–188
Gilbert, C.C. 17, 19–22
Gilgal Church, Georgia 143–144, 146
Gilley's Bridge, Georgia 133
Gilmore, Emory 150
Glenville, Henry 18, 23, 28, 54, **55**, 72, 207
Goetz, John 68
Goodspeed, Wilbur 174, 176
Gorlock, Francis 122
Gracie, Archibald 65
Granger, Gordon 21, 23, 31, 32, 62, 63, 74, 86–88, 91, 96–103, 105, 109, 115, 248
Granny White Pike 236, 239–243
Grant, Ulysses S. 7, 16, 28, 36, 77–80, 97–98, 100, 102, 113, 117, 141, 164, 182, 188, 195, 197, 200–202, 229, 237–241, 246–247; Chattanooga 78–80; Missionary Ridge 80–96
Green, Henry 145
Guadalupe River 255
Gulf of Mexico 254–255

Hall, John 257
Hall, Thomas 57
Hall, William 240
Halleck, Henry 28, 240
Hardee, William 134, 140, 142, 146–151, 153, 171–182, 185, 192–195
Hardin, Jordan 22

Hardin, Pike 232, 238, 251
Harker, Charles G. **27**, 30–38, 42–47, 51, 53, 56–57, 68, 74, 76, 133, 135–136, 138–142, 184, 189; biographical sketch 26; Kennesaw Mountain 143–148, 153–159, 162–164; killed 160–161
Harpeth River 19, 212, 215–220, 223, 228–230, 233, 241, 244
Hatch, Nathan 136, 150
Hayes, Edwin 226
Hazen, William 6–7, 39, 65–66, 137–138, 142, 174, 242
Hight, John 63
Hillis, Merwin 23
Hillsboro Pike 232, 236, 238–240
Hillsboro, Tennessee 32
Hindman, Thomas 63
Hinman, Wilbur 51, 62, 75, 77, 146, 160, 163, 171, 176, 193, 217, 221, 232, 246, 253
Holmes County, Ohio 26
Hood, John Bell 2, 53–54, 134, 137–138, 142, 147, 151, 173, 175–182, 184–186, 188–201, 204, 206–207, 209–212, 216–217, 219–222, 225, 228–231, 233, 235; replaces General Johnston 171
Hooker, Joseph 73, 78, 90, 134–137, 142–146, 148, 171, 173–174, 177, 180, 183
Horn, Stanley 244
horses and mules 75–76, 235–236, 246–247
Horseshoe Ridge 60–65
hospitals 53–54, 70, 74, 244
Howard, Oliver O. 73, 135, 137–138, 140, 143–147, 153–154, 160, 163, 168–173, 178–179, 182–186, 191–194; biographical sketch **115**; promoted 184
Howard, Thomas 180
Howell's Mill 173
Huey's Mill, Tennessee 207
Hull, William 168
Hulse, Richard 240, 257
Humphreys, Benjamin 62
Huntsville, Alabama 247, 249–250

Illinois Central Railroad 257
Indianola, Texas 254
Infildt, Cornelius 120

Jeffersonian Democrat 133, 137
Jenkins, Micah 104
Jennings, William 57
Jewell, Jacob 68, **69**, 172
John Ward Creek 156
Johnson, Bushrod 42, 45, 51, 53–54, 63, 104, 106
Johnson, Edward 229
Johnson, Richard 65
Johnston, Joseph 113, 117, 120, 123, 125, 128–132, 134, 137–141, 144–148, 150, 153, 164–166, 168–171, 173, 184–185, 251
Jonesboro, Battle of 188–195
Juarez, Benito 253
Judah, Henry 125

Kennesaw Mountain 132, 141, 143–146, *151*–154, 163, 166, 168, 184, 200; Battle of *152*, 155–163
Kentucky Orphan Brigade 175
Kershaw, Joseph 56–57, 61–62, 65
Kilpatrick, Judson 189
Kimball, Nathan 133, 156, 161–165, 173–177, 180, 187, 192–194, 206, 209–210, 214, 230, 238–240
Kimberly, Robert 64, 66, 90, 139, 210
King, M.V.B. 56, 67, **68**, 72
Kingston, Georgia 130–133
Kinsman, Ohio 184
Knapp, Peter 57
Knight, Fred 183
Knoxville, Tennessee 36, 79, 82, 85, 97, 99–100, 102, 110, 117, 188, 250
Kolb Farm, Battle of 147

La Fayette, Georgia 201
La Fayette Road 37–38, 41–46, 51, 63
LaGrange, Oscar 104
Laiboldt, Bernard 102–103
Lane, John Quincy 176, 208–209, 215–216, 219–223, 231, 233, 239, 241, 250
Lawrenceburg, Tennessee 206
Lee, Stephen D. 185, 192–193, 213, 236, 240–244
Lee, William 147
Lee and Gordon's Mill **37**–38, 41, 200
Lewis, George W. 77, 95, 138, 248
Lewis, J.W. 150
Lewisburg Pike 216
Lexington, Alabama 247
Lickskillet Road 186
Lincoln, Abraham 6, 28, 46, 70, 73–76, 97, 171, 184, 188, 195, 201–202, 237–238, 240, 244, 246, 251, 253
Linderman, Gerald 22, 62
Logan, John 181–183, 185, 238, 240
Longstreet, James 48, 51, 62–66, 79, 82, 97, 99–104, 109–110
Lookout Mountain 35, 71, 80, 85, 201
Lost Mountain 140–143
Loudon, Tennessee 99, 103, 110, 250
Louisville, Kentucky 6, 17, 195
Loutzenhiser, Thomas 68
Lovejoy Station, Georgia 192, 194–195
Lunette Opdycke 202
Luse, Jesse 172
Lynneville, Tennessee 206, 246

Macon and Western Railroad 184, 188–192, 194
Macon, Georgia 187
Magnolia 257
Mahoning County, Ohio 8
Manchester, Sterling 14, 29, 75, 102–103, 149–**150**
Manchester, Tennessee 31–32

Maney, George 177
Marietta, Georgia 132–134, 140–147, 164, 166, 168–169, 188, 200
Martin, Will H. 162
Matagorda Bay, Texas 254
Matthews, Albert 225
Maximilian, Emperor 253–256
McArthur, Arthur 224
McClellan, George 193, 203
McCollum, George 122
McCook, Alexander 31, 50, 72
McCook, Dan 163–164
McCook, E.M. 104
McCoy, Daniel 224
McCreery, James 7
McDonough, James Lee 231
McFarland's Gap 52, 60
McGittigan, William 52
McHenry, Henry 14, 18, 33, 98, 140, 164, 197, 252
McIlvain, Alexander 44, 121
McLemore's Cove 37
McPherson, James B. 113,120, 125, 129–130, 132, 135–139, 143, 146, 150–154, 163–164, 166, 168–171, 173, 175, 177, 179, 180, 238; killed 181–183
Medal of Honor 231
Meek, William 44
Merrill, Riley 22
Military Division of the Southwest 254
Militia Draft Act 9, 25–26
Mill Creek Gap 117–118, 120
Miller, William 96, 138
Missionary Ridge 48, 70–71, 80, 83–91; Battle of **81**–96
Mississippi River 252, 254, 256
Mobile, Alabama 184
Moccasin Point 71
Montgomery Hill 236, 239
Moore, David H. 2, 14, 25–26, 33, 75, 102–104, 110–111, 119, 121, 127–128, 139–140, 147–150, 169, 176, 184, 187, 189, 195, 197–198, 203–204, 249; biographical sketch **24**; chasing Morgan 29; Dandridge 105–109; Kennesaw 156, 158–159, 162; Rocky Face Ridge 122
Morgan, John Hunt 29
Morris, James 44
Morris, Zalmon 123
Morrison, James 52
Morse, Appollos 25–26, 254
Moses, Elmer 12, 19, 95, **155**–156, 158, 184
Mossy Creek 101–102, 104
Motherspaw, Thomas 175, 224
Mount Gilead Church, Georgia 191
Mount Pleasant, Tennessee 206
Mud Creek 144–145
Murdock, George 107
Murdock, James 194, 225
Murfreesboro, Tennessee 30, 235, 238, 243, 250–251
Murphy, Marion 120
Mygatt, George 6

Nancy Creek 171
Napoleon Bonaparte 233
Nashville, Battle of 238–244
Nashville and Chattanooga Railroad 236
Nashville and Decatur Railroad 209
Nashville Daily Union 251
Nashville, Tennessee 7, 18, 113, 116, 164–165, 188, 198, 200–204, 206, 208–209, 213–217, 220, 229–**234**, 235–**237**, 238–253, 256
Needs, James 68
Negley, James 60
Nelson, William 6
New Hope Church, Battle of 134–142
New Market, Tennessee 102, 109, 250
New Orleans, Louisiana 253. 257
New York Daily Tribune 232
New York Herald 50
Newton, John 113, 118, 120, 122–126, 129–131, 133, 135, 143–148, 150, 153–157, 160–162, 165–166, 180, 183, 185–187, 190–194, 199; biographical sketch 115; drinking 184; Peachtree Creek 168–179
Nicholas Longworth 253–254
19th Ohio Infantry 8
97th Ohio Infantry 176
93th Ohio Infantry 105–106, 108–109
Ninth Corps 100–102
9th Indiana Infantry 65
Nolensville Pike 236
North, John 70
Noses Creek 146

Oberlin College 6
Ohio Adjutant General's Office General Orders No. 5 110
Ohio River 206
Olley's Creek 164
Olson, Porter 224–225
183rd Ohio Infantry 219, 222
111th Ohio Infantry 222
105th Ohio Infantry 8, 14, 54
101st Ohio Infantry 249
104th Ohio Infantry 222–223, 226
175th Ohio Infantry 223–224, 228
103rd Ohio Infantry 103, 126, 170
113th Ohio Infantry 23, 164
121st Ohio Infantry 24, 120, 163
124th Ohio Infantry 20–21, 138
100th Illinois Infantry 148–149, 158, 174
100th Ohio Infantry 222–223, 226
Oostanaula River 116, 124–125, 128–131
Opdycke, Emerson 1–2, 11, 13–17, 19–23, 25, 31–34, 38–39, 43–45, 49, 53–57, 60–62, 65, 71–77, 98–100, 103, 108–112, 115, 117–123, 133–136, 138–141, 180, 182–184, 186–187, 189, 191, 194–196, 197–204, 206–211, 213, 231–235, 239–248, **250**–256; appointed colonel 8; early life **5**–6; 41st Ohio Infantry 6–8; Franklin 215–230; Kennesaw Mountain 144–146, 150, 153, 156–158, 161–165; Missionary Ridge 84, 86–96; Nancy Creek 171–172; Peach Tree Creek 174–178; promoted to general 249; wounded 125–126, 128–132
Opdycke, Leonard E. 6
Opdycke, Lucy S. 6, 118, 140, 146–147, 230, 232, 250
Opdycke's Tigers 61
Orchard Knob 82–83, 88
Overton Hill 236, 240–243
Overton Mansion 233, 243

Pace's Ferry 169, 200
Palmer, John 31, 39, 65, 143–144, 151, 153, 171, 173
Palmetto, Georgia 198
Park, John G. 100, 105, 109, 110
Parks, Steen 14, 33, 91, 95, 120
Patch, Oliver 5, 6
Payne, Darius 225
Pea Vine Creek 173–174
Peach Tree Creek, Battle of 170–180, 186
Penfield, Henry 68
Perrin, Glover 72
Philadelphia, Tennessee 99
Philbrook, Alva 224
Picket's Mill, Georgia 137–138, 141–142
Pigeon Hill 145, 153, 163
Pine Mountain 143–144
Polk, Leonidas 48–49, 129–132, 134, 142, 144
Pollock, James 187
Port Lacava, Texas 255, 257
Porter, Antony 122
Porter, Benjamin 160
Porter, William 68
Post, Philip Sidney 239, 242–243
Postlewait, Alexander 127
Powder Sprigs Road 147–148, 153
Powell, Thomas 256
Powers, Ridgely **12**, 18, 22, 32–33, 95, 100, 115, 123, 163, 172, 184, 187, 194, 197, 231, 243, 250–254
Power's Ferry 170–171
Preston, William 65
Privet Knob 216, 219
Proctor's Creek 190–191
Pulaski Pike 206–207
Pulaski, Tennessee 201–203, 206, 218, 246–247
Pumpkin Vine Creek 132–137

Quirk, Michael 257

Ramsey, James 52
rations 190
Rawdon, William 164
Red Oak 191
Redoubt No. 1 239
Reed, Charles 57
regimental flag 15
Reid, Whitelaw 9, 28, 30, 32
Reilly, James 223–224

Index

Renfroe Place, Georgia 192
Republican Party 188, 196
Republican-Union Party 252
Resaca, Battle of 126–*128*, 129–130
Resaca, Georgia 117, 120, 123–125, 128–131, 200–201
Rice, Ralsa 11, *13*, 17–18, 23, 39, 62, 71, 107–108, 123, 126, 136, 146, 180–184, 187, 189, 194; 202–203, 209–212, 232, 248; biographical sketch 12; Franklin 215, 217, 221, 225–230; Kennesaw Mountain 149–150, 154–159, 162, 168, 170, 172, 178
Rice, Robert *149*–150
Richards, Henry 22
Richland Creek 246
Ringgold, Georgia 41, 96, 118, 200
Roberts, William C. 225
Rocky Face Ridge, Battle of 117–123, 130, 200
Rogers, Samuel 172
Rome, Georgia 130, 199–200
Root, Lyman 155
Rosecrans, William S. 16, 19, 22, 26, 28, 30–32, 34, 36, 41, 46–50, 52, 64–67, 71–72
Ross, Henry 228
Rosseau, Lawrence 223
Rossville, Georgia 38, 51, 64, 68, 70, 85, 87, 201
Roswell, Georgia 169–171
Rough and Ready, Georgia 191–193, 195
Ruger, Thomas 223
Rummage, George 22
Russell, Henry 70
Russell, John 226, 254
Russellville, Tennessee 101
Rutherford Creek 21, 209, 245
Rutland, Ohio 29

Sailor, Samuel 185
Sample, Jesse 122
San Antonio, Texas 255
Sandtown Road 143, 168, 186, 191
Savannah, Georgia 184
Schofield, John M. 2, 113, 117, 125, 127, 131–132, 135, 140, 143, 166, 169–177, 179–182, 185–186, 191–192, 194, 200, 205–207, 209–213, 215–220, 230–232, 236, 238, 240–243; Franklin 215–220; Kennesaw Mountain 144–147, 151–154, 164
Scofield, Levi 219, 221, 223–224, 227–228
Scott, James 89
Scoville, Charles 219, 223
Searight, Clay 235
2nd Illinois Artillery 189
Sequatchie Valley 75
Seventeenth Corps 143, 199
75th Ohio Infantry 232
74th Illinois Infantry 187, 195, 207, 211, 221, 224, 227, 239, 252
79th Illinois Infantry 74, 84, 88, 90–94, 115, 121, 153, 156, 174, 219
72nd Illinois Infantry 222

77th Article of War 203
73rd Illinois Infantry 175, 187, 195, 207, 211, 224, 227, 239, 252
Shanks, William 50
Sharp, Thomas 221
Sheets, William 148
Shelbyville, Tennessee 30–31
Shellenberger, John 89–91, 95, 220–222
Shenefield, George 185
shelter tents 22
Sheridan, Philip 51, 55, 74, 82–84, 87–96, 98–100, 103–105, 108–109, 111, 254–256
Sherman, Ellen 141
Sherman, Francis T. 77, 83–84, 88–89, 92, 94, 115, 123, 127, 129, 131, 133
Sherman, William T. 26, 76–80, 84–85, 87, 98–100, 113–118, 120, 122–125, 128–135, 137–141, 166–171, 173, 178–179, 197–202, 204, 206, 237, 246–247, 251; Kennesaw Mountain 143–154, 162–164; Peach Tree Creek 180–184, 187, 189, 191–195
Shields, Mark 145
Shiloh, Battle of 7
Shy's Hill 240–242
Simpson, John 94, 106, 108
Sixteenth Corps 170, 236
16th Kentucky Infantry (USA) 223
6th Ohio Artillery 38–39, 42, 46, 73, 184, 210
65th Ohio Infantry 26, 43–45, 55–57, 60, 84, 87–90, 94, 96, 115, 119, 122, 136, 145–146, 156, 162–163, 171–172, 176, 180, 186, 193, 216–217, 253, 256
64th Ohio Infantry 26, 38–39, 43–44, 55–57, 61, 88–90, 93, 115, 119, 121, 123, 130, 138, 156, 160, 162–163, 171–172, 176, 208–209, 216, 220
Sleinel, William 122
Slocum, Henry W. 73, 194
Smith, A.J. 218, 229, 235–243
Smith, George 203, 224–225
Smith, Seabury 33, *106*, 109
Smyrna, Georgia 164–165, 168–169, 200
Snake Creek Gap 117, 120, 128
Snodgrass Hill 56, 60, 64–66
Soap Creek 169–170
soldier's pay 9
Sperry, Joseph 73
Spencer rifles 235
Spring Hill, Battle of 208–209
Spring Hill, Tennessee 21, 23, 207–209, 211, 215–216, 222, 244–245
Springfield musket 15–16
Stahl, Thomas 195
Stanley, David S. 2, 23, 118, 131, 143, 146–150, 153–156, 159–162, 168, 170, 173, 201–202, 206–208, 210–211, 231–232, 248–255; biographical sketch *183*; Franklin 215–217, 220, 226–230; Kenne-

saw Mountain 180, 185–187, 192–194
Stanton, Edwin 28, 73, 238, 240, 244, 246
Starling, Lyne 43, 50
Statler, Henry 22
Steadman, Henry 133–134, 137
Steadman, Hezekiah 68, 197, 202
Steedman, James 63, 235–236, 240–242
Steele, Reuben 127
Stephenson, Alabama 250
Stewart, A.P. 171, 173, 175, 179, 185, 209–210, 216, 218–219, 228, 236, 239–243
Stewart, Robert 10, 225
Stiles, T.J. 218
Stinger, Daniel 257
Stinger, Jeremiah 91
Stone Mountain, Georgia 171–173
Stone's River, Battle of 16
Strawberry Plains, Tennessee 100–*101*, 104, 109, 110
Strealy, John 66
Sturgis, Samuel 104
Suman, Issac 65
Suwanee 256
Swinehart, Eli 120
Sword, Wiley 211

Taylor, Ezra B. 13
Tempest 13, 146, 172
Tennessee River 7, 30–34, 71, 73, 83, 85, 98, 103, 110, 188, 199, 201, 244–247, 253
3rd Kentucky Infantry (USA) 26, 39, 43–45, 55, 57, 60, 63, 88, 90, 93, 115, 120, 124–125, 130, 135, 139, 143–145, 171–172, 176, 178, 184, 186, 189, 191; Kennesaw Mountain 154–156, 160–162, 165
36th Georgia Infantry (CSA) 123
36th Illinois Infantry 187, 195, 209, 224, 227, 239–241, 243, 253
Thomas, Freeman 92
Thomas, George 31–32, 40, 47–51, 53–56, 61–63, 66–67, 77–78, 86–87, 91, 93, 95–96, 102, 113, 116–117, 120, 125, 127, 130–132, 197–201, 204–205, 206, 209–210, 212, 218–219, 229, 232–247, 249–252, 254
Thompson, Malcolm 23
Thompson, William 184
Thompson's Station, Tennessee 21, 203, 208–211
Thorn, William 56, *58*, 93
Tilton, Georgia 125
Tod, David 8, 15, 24, 34, 110
Todd, John M. 127
Tourgee, Albion 71, 77–78
Truett, Alpheus 220
Trumbull County, Ohio 9
Tucker, Glenn 47
Tullahoma, Tennessee 30, 251
Tunnel Hill 85–86
Tupelo, Mississippi 247
Turner's Ferry, Georgia 169
Tuttle, Chester 100, 195

Tuttle, John 135, 143, 154, 157, 159, 161–162, 172, 178, 184, 186, 190–191
Twelfth Corps 113
12th Kentucky Cavalry (USA) 113, 120
12th Kentucky Infantry 223
12th Tennessee Infantry (CSA) 150, 177
Twentieth Corps 134–135, 143, 146, 174, 188, 190, 194, 200
20th Ohio Artillery 219
Twenty-fifth Corps 255
24th Wisconsin Infantry 187–195, 208, 224–225, 227, 239–243, 248, 250–252
29th Tennessee Infantry (CSA) 160
22nd Illinois Infantry 74, 88–89, 115, 153
27th Illinois Infantry 74, 88, 126, 156–160, 172
26th Ohio Infantry 148, 150, 160, 253, 257
Twenty-third Corps 100, 102, 104, 125, 135, 137, 151, 201, 207, 212, 215, 222–223, 227, 235–236, 251

Union Party 8
Utoy Creek 186, 191

Vallandingham, Clement 25, 76
Vallendar, Anthony 14, 33, 122, 253
Van Cleve, Horatio 31, 51
Van Dorn, Earl 21, 23
Vanhoof, John 145

Vesey, Alexander 68
Veteran Reserve Corps 256
Victoria, Texas 255–256
Vining Station, Georgia 169

Wagner, George 37, 83–84, 88, 90–91, 93, 95, 115, 120–121, 133, 145, 148, 156, 158. 161–163, 174, 180, 194, *200*–202, 206–209, 211, 231–233; biographical sketch 199; Franklin 215–223, 227, 229
Walker, Henry 242
Walker, William 176, 178
Walton, Clairborne 164
Walworth, Nathan 84, 87, 95
Ward, William T. 174–177
Warman, John 57, 93
Warren, Ohio 5–6, 8, 249, 254, 256
Warren Tribune 8
Watkins, Sam 68–69, 155, 230–231
Weber, August 257
Welch, Patrick 72
Western and Atlantic Railroad 80, 113, 116–118, 124–125, 130–132, 137, 143, 145, 164, 168–170, 173, 188, 190
Western Reserve Chronicle 8, 18, 25, 33, 94, 100, 131, 163, 256
Wetzel, James 145
Wheeler, Joe 130–131, 171–172, 178–179, 188, 198
Whitbeck, Horatio 45, 160
Whitesides, Edward *15*, 44, 62, 74, 115, 121, 136, 155–156, 160, 165, 187, 202, 219, 233–246, 251–252;
biographical sketch 13–14; provost marshal 200; wounded 161, 164
Whitworth rifle 137, 166
Wiley, Aquila 7, 83, 90
Wiley, Bell Irvin 56, 249
Wiley, Noah 106
Willemin, James 161, 172
Williams, John 68, 74
Williams, Nahum 160
Williams, Waldren 189
Willich, Augusta 126
Willis, Francis 242
Wilson, James 235
Wilson, Joseph 226
Wing, Conrad 106
Winstead Hills 211, 215–217
Wolford, Frank 104–105
Wood, George 13, 17–18, 21
Wood, Thomas 2, 26, 31–38, 74, 76, 82–83, 87–91, 99–100, 105, 109, 118, 131, 135–138, 143–147, 168–170, 173–174, 179–180, 190–191, 193–194, 201, 206–207, 209–210, 215, 229, 230, 233–236, 238–247, 249, 251, 254; biographical sketch *27*; Chickamauga 42–43, 46–47, 49–55, 57, 60–64, 68
Woods, Rufus 170, 180
Woodworth, Edwin 10, *11*, 139, 161, 165

Yates, Porter 14
Yeomans, Albert 12, 19, 35, 55

Zollicoffer Barracks 203

www.ingramcontent.com/pod-product-compliance
Lightning Source LLC
Chambersburg PA
CBHW081541300426
44116CB00015B/2709